CULTURE, COMMUNICATION AND CONFLICT

READINGS IN INTERCULTURAL RELATIONS

EDITED BY

GARY R. WEAVER

SIMON & SCHUSTER PUBLISHING

ISBN 0–536–00373–4
BA 97254

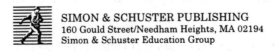

SIMON & SCHUSTER PUBLISHING
160 Gould Street/Needham Heights, MA 02194
Simon & Schuster Education Group

COPYRIGHT
ACKNOWLEDGMENTS

CONTENTS

Section Two
Managing Diversity 89

Section Three
Cross-Cultural Adaptation 173

Section Four
Education and Counseling   267

Section Five
The Mass Media,
Conflict, and National Images   397

Section Six
Intercultural Aspects of
Conflict and Negotiation   465

PREFACE

In the past three decades the field of cross-cultural and intercultural communication studies has grown from a handful of books to well over 500 texts and several major journals. Professional associations have emerged and grown with memberships numbering in the thousands. Today, almost every college and university offers courses in this area of study.

Domestic and international issues and concerns increasingly mix together. It is difficult to separate the local from the global when it comes to living in today's shrinking world. The workplace and the community require that we become more than simply "global citizens" who are informed and involved in multicultural and international affairs. We also need to become more adept at interacting with those who are different. Cross-cultural communication barriers must be overcome in the world we face at the turn of the millennium.

No longer can we remain encapsulated in a world of our "own kind." Whether it is interacting with neighbors or conducting business overseas, knowledge of inter-cultural relations and the ability to interact with people of other cultures is as vital for our success in the modern world as understanding and using computers and modern telecommunications.

Gaining knowledge of other cultures and the dynamics of cross-cultural com-munication so we can more easily communicate with people from other cultures will allow us to do our jobs better and to raise our children to prosper in this culturally diverse, interdependent world. At the very least, this knowledge and these skills will allow us to minimize the misunderstandings and conflict that are a result of cultural differences. We may also be better prepared to prevent war, or negotiate peace.

Cross-Cultural Training

Most corporations or government agencies provide cross-cultural briefings and orientation for their employees going abroad. These programs usually include information about specific cultures and the broad areas of cross-cultural communi-cation, negotiation, conflict and adjustment. In addition, many help participants improve their cross-cultural communication and analytical skills.

Student exchange and study abroad programs routinely give participants cross-cultural predeparture, arrival and reentry orientation. Furthermore, colleges and universities feature special orientation programs for their international students that help them better adjust to new campuses and cultures.

These training programs provide very practical information and skills. The more we know about the dynamics of cross-cultural communication, adjustment and conflict, the more effective we will be while living, working or studying in another culture. And, the severity and duration of the stress of adjusting to that culture

(culture shock) and readjusting to our home culture (reverse culture shock) might also be lessened with this knowledge.

Cultural Diversity in the Workplace

Most private and public sector jobs require employees who can work effectively in various cultures, both at home and abroad. Companies cannot afford to continually bring people home who have difficulty adjusting to another culture. The costs of hiring and training new people and the business opportunities which are lost because of cultural insensitivity are simply unnecessary.

This is not just a matter of a shrinking globe. Most countries are becoming more diverse. In the U.S. alone, between 1988 and the year 2000, 43 million people will have entered the American labor force, 68 percent of them women and minorities.[1] Cross-cultural awareness and intercultural communication skills are essential regardless of one's occupation.

As the society and workplace become more ethnically, racially and culturally diverse, it is more difficult to conduct meetings or manage employees. How do you recruit and retain a diverse work force? What criteria are used to determine advancement? How much room is there in the organization for diversity, and how much does the individual have to adjust to the organization? All of these issues are addressed in "diversity training," which is now fairly common for most organizations.

Many of the concepts and methodologies used to prepare people for going abroad have been modified for diversity training. The concept of "culture" has been broadened to include such differences as gender, sexual orientation, religion, age, disability, and so forth.

Whether you are a student, diplomat, manager, teacher, counselor, child care worker, law enforcement officer or negotiator, knowledge of intercultural relations and the ability to interact effectively with those who are culturally different are vital to your success.

The demands of an interdependent world and demographic changes will surely increase in the future. Everyone will need an understanding of intercultural communication, negotiation and conflict. The ability to work effectively and efficiently with those who are different may be a factor determining advancement to a managerial position. Intercultural knowledge and competence will become prerequisites in almost every occupation.

Careers in the Area of Intercultural Relations

The cultural diversity manager is now a fixture in most American company hierarchies. This job requires developing policies and programs to make all employees sensitive to differences and to allow minority workers equal access to upper-level positions. The manager might organize seminars on ethnic values, review promotions, or lack of them, and set up discussion groups among employees about cultural issues.

The diversity manager is often found in the human resource development or personnel office. Some are vice presidents in the CEO's office. As of 1991, the average salary for such a position was $65,000 to $79,000.[2] There are also consultants who train people for working in a diverse workplace. In 1993, one consultant estimated that diversity training was a $200 million-per-year industry and that incomes of $300,000 per year were not uncommon.[3]

Career opportunities for specialists and consultants in cross-cultural training, negotiation, counseling and conflict resolution are likely to greatly expand. As the field of intercultural relations grows, there is also a greater need to professionalize this field, without distracting from its interdisciplinary, applied and creative aspects.

Intercultural Relations: a Profession and Field of Study

Many intercultural scholars and practitioners agree that experience is necessary for all intercultural relations experts. As with the profession of counseling—one cannot simply read books in the field. It is necessary to actually counsel others. There are people claiming to be intercultural or diversity experts with very limited depth and breadth of practical, hands on experience. Eventually, they will be found out. Until then, they discredit the field.

On the other hand, experience alone is not enough if the field is to grow both academically and professionally. Practitioners must be able to provide evidence for the efficacy of their work and relate their training to theoretical and conceptual models developed by researchers. A great deal of valuable research has been conducted in the past few decades, and universities are developing rigorous courses in intercultural, cross-cultural, and international communication. This body of knowledge will allow the field to grow into an area of study.

Intercultural relations, as a profession and field of study, requires both practice and research. One is literally contexted in the other. Much of our research comes from formative and summative evaluation of training programs, various case studies, and longitudinal data gathered from sojourners and immigrants.

Research in intercultural relations may be applied to the individual within a particular culture or to nation-states within the international system. The range of application is enormous and growing daily. Educators, counselors, negotiators, managers and diplomats can freely extrapolate from intercultural research and experience in each other's work.

Interpersonal and international conflict and misunderstanding may decrease with the growth of intercultural relations studies and competencies. As we learn to more effectively interact with those who are culturally different, we also learn more about them and their cultures. We will discover new ways of perceiving reality and solving problems. Perhaps more importantly, we will also learn more about ourselves and our own culture.

ORGANIZATION AND APPROACH

Readings in this anthology are divided into six sections and are sequenced to move from domestic to international issues, although there is no firm dividing line between these areas of concern. Each section includes both theoretical and applied articles and is preceded by a short introduction which explains the importance of the topic and the reason each article was selected.

While each section is self-contained and serves as a short collection on a particular topic, the sections are sequenced to allow for the progressive development of concepts which are woven into many of the articles. For example, the difference between the process of assimilation and acculturation, the importance of internal culture, how perception is influenced by culture and the dynamics of cross-cultural conflict are topics that are discussed and emphasized in many different articles in many different ways.

The scope of this anthology is very wide. We consider the impact of cultural diversity in the workplace and community at home as well as in the international arena. The dynamics of intercultural interaction are discussed in terms of interpersonal and international communication. Furthermore, the approach is completely interdisciplinary and multidisciplinary, ranging from education, psychology, sociology, and anthropology to communications, politics, economics and international relations.

With the end of the Cold War and the increase in international commerce, we are faced with new challenges. Modern telecommunications may bring us closer together, but it also allows for images and messages to be communicated simultaneously almost anywhere on the globe. The mass media can bring ethnic conflicts into living rooms in Iowa as well as Spain. And popular entertainment media can determine whether we see peacemakers or terrorists.

Rather than fighting wars between nations over political ideologies, conflicts between ethnic and religious groups—perhaps even cultures and civilizations—are becoming more common. Understanding long-standing animosities between groups and the stereotypes that have perpetuated and inflamed these conflicts will be essential to bring about peace in the next century. There are no quick fixes in this complex, interdependent world. But, understanding intercultural relations may provide some tools for preventing and resolving conflict in the post-Cold War era.

CONTRIBUTORS

There has been no attempt to be comprehensive or represent all cultures or issues. However, each section does include authors who have made major contributions to the field of intercultural relations.

In this second edition, about one-third of the articles are new. Many were written expressly for this edition. All of the introductory segments have been rewritten to consider new issues, new data and research, and new authors to this edition. And some sections were expanded to reflect changing concerns in the area of intercultural relations. For example, authors such as Huntington and Schwarz are included to discuss the impact of culture on international relations in the post-Cold War world.

Articles were selected from professional journals, texts, magazines and newspapers because they are conceptually and intellectually sound, well-written and interesting. They vary in terms of style and length, yet each is a vital part of the mosaic of this anthology.

Authors include both researchers and practitioners. Many are both. Some articles were selected because they are seminal pieces, others because they are controversial, provocative or unusual. All provide a depth and breadth of conceptual understanding not provided in most books on intercultural relations.

THANKS

I am greatly indebted to all of the contributors, many of whom have written pieces for this edition. Their cooperation and patience with the process of preparing this anthology is greatly appreciated.

Many people helped prepare this collection by suggesting articles or editing manuscripts. They include students and/or teaching and research assistants such as Jadijhe Schabib, Christine Mataya, Shawn Bates, Cynthia Dowdell, David Gammel, Barbara Belzer, Elizabeth Kanter, Pema Geller, and Tammy Barnhouse. Faculty members, such as Dr. Christine Chin and Dr. Gary Wright, provided enthusiastic encouragement to consider new sources and issues in the fast-changing field of intercultural relations.

I am especially grateful to Mary Finch who not only devoted endless months searching for the very best pieces on particular topics but also offered her critical observations on my own writings. More importantly she gently, but persuasively, pushed the preparation of this new edition along until it was finally completed.

I am certain that I inadvertently omitted the names of others who have given their time, energy, expertise and enthusiasm in preparing this anthology. Many, many thanks to everyone.

Gary R. Weaver

ENDNOTES

[1]Sources: Society for Human Resource Management, William M. Mercer Inc., cited in article "Hot Tracks in 20 Professions," *U.S. News & World Report,* 11 November 1991, 100.

[2]*Ibid.*

[3]Amy Bernstein, "Outlook: Eye on the '90s," *U.S. News & World Report,* 8 February 1993, 24.

I

Culture and Communication

THE CONCEPT OF CULTURE

The word "culture" was seldom heard in casual conversation less than two decades ago, and it had various confusing meanings. Some thought of culture as "good taste," for others it was art or music, and for many it was something that people in exotic foreign lands had.

Today everyone seems to be talking about culture, and most of us would agree that it is simply the way of life of a group of people passed down from one generation to the next through learning. Culture is not inherited but instead acquired unconsciously during childhood simply by participating in human interactions with others. This process of learning or acquiring our native culture is termed *enculturation*. Learning or adapting to another culture is referred to as *acculturation*.

Because we informally or tacitly acquire a culture well before adolescence, we usually take our own culture for granted until we are surrounded by people who are different. At that time, we contrast and compare our own culture with theirs and become more consciously aware of our own.

People who go to other countries to work or live do not lose their culture by adapting to another culture. Instead, most return home more consciously aware of their own culture. The irony is that the way to find your culture is to leave it and enter another culture.[1]

Throughout this text you will find many different ways authors describe or explain culture. We can discuss culture in terms of typical ways in which people in a society, group or organization behave, communicate, think, or perceive reality. And, we can explain culture as a system of values and beliefs which we share with others, all of which give us a sense of belonging or identity.

The reason for this variation in definition is because *culture is an abstraction or a concept rather than something tangible or concrete.* Art, music, and literature are the artifacts, relics or results of culture. We might examine these external aspects of culture to infer that people from a particular society have roughly the same system of values, beliefs, thought patterns and perceptions. However, culture is not what people produce. It is mostly internal or inside our heads. Just as we cannot understand individual human behavior without understanding the concept of "personality," it is virtually impossible to discuss the behavior of people in a particular society without understanding the concept of "culture."

Culture is also a generalization. There are many individual differences between people within the same group or society. Nevertheless, culture is a very useful framework for explaining and predicting the characteristic behavior of a group of people as long as we realize that our descriptions are generalizations—*they can never apply to everyone in every situation.* It is true that every tree in the forest is unique, but

1

we can discuss categories of trees such as maples, oaks and pines. A cultural generalization offers a good "first guess" as to why a person may behave as he or she does. It allows us to simplify and focus our search for explanations for behavior. When it is obviously inaccurate or untrue for most people within a group, it is no longer useful and must be discarded.

Cultural stereotypes are also generalizations, but they do not allow for exceptions or individual variation—we force everyone to fit our category. Furthermore, both positive and negative cultural stereotypes are almost always false or misleading and thus are not useful for understanding others.

Individuals belong not just to one culture, but instead to a hierarchy of cultures. The ranking or importance of cultural identities may change throughout your life, but your primary culture remains the one that you were born into. You might grow up in rural Kenya but later you study at a large university in Philadelphia. Added to your basic culture is the university student culture and perhaps an urban, American culture. However, the values, beliefs, and ways of thinking that you learned in Kenya tend to stay with you the rest of your life.

We tend to perceive the world in a similar way with others in our culture and that culture gives us a sense of identity and belonging. We may even explain our viewpoint or perception of reality by uttering the phrase, "as a young, middle-class European Catholic male" or "as an older Muslim in the business world."

PATTERNS OF COMMUNICATION

What we communicate and how we communicate are largely determined by our culture. People who come from the same background tend to pay attention to similar messages and share meanings attributed to those messages.

There are many ways we might discuss communication. It can range from a gesture, which has specific meaning only to two people in love, to war between many nations. It involves the sending of messages between people of the same culture (intracultural communication), messages sent between people of different cultures (intercultural communication), to messages sent around the world by nation-states, their institutions and organizations or representatives (international communication). And, it might be face-to-face (interpersonal) or via telecommunications (mass communication).

We send messages, but not meanings. People who have had similar experiences give similar meanings to the same message. For example, those who adapt to another culture go through a stressful period of adjustment called *culture shock* during which they may be disoriented, homesick, sad, or angry. They know what the words "culture shock" mean because they have experienced it. For those who have never adapted to another culture, this phrase may mean something entirely different or it may have no meaning whatsoever.

Language is obviously a key component of communication in any culture. It reflects, and perhaps shapes, the values and perceptions of a group of people. However, the most basic way we communicate feelings is primarily through the use of *nonverbal* communication—facial expressions, vocal patterns, posture, social distance, and the use of time. The study of these ways of communicating includes all of the "ics" in cross-cultural communication—kinesics, proxemics, chronemics, and so forth.[2]

We learn the meanings to these nonverbal messages tacitly simply by participating in a given culture. Thus, these meanings are mostly internalized and unconscious, especially in cultures such as the mainstream American culture where great emphasis is placed upon verbal, and even written, communication.

OVERVIEW OF ARTICLES

This section begins with the writings of Edward Hall ("How Cultures Collide" and "Learning the Arabs' Silent Language"). Hall is certainly one of the most significant theorists in the field of cross-cultural communication with his discussion of high- and low-context cultures, polychronic and monochromic time and organizations, and nonverbal communication.

Hall offers a fascinating blend of academic approaches to explain cross-cultural communication and conflict. He is an anthropologist who has been greatly influenced by psychoanalytic and linguistic theory and methodology. This allows him a depth and breadth of analysis and interpretation which cannot be achieved with any one of these approaches.

Albert Mehrabian's seminal piece, "Communication Without Words," provides evidence that nonverbal communication is the most vital aspect of all face-to-face interactions. His examples come from the United States, where he demonstrates how the importance and conscious use of nonverbal communication may vary with ethnicity and social class.

Marshall R. Singer's "The Role of Culture and Perception in Communication" explains how perception is shaped by our culture which, in turn, affects how we communicate. We tend to perceive reality in ways similar to others in our group. When we share perceptions with others, we also share the meanings given to that which we perceive—messages, words, nonverbal cues, events, and so forth. And we identify with members of those groups who share our perceptions and meanings.

Singer believes that every identity group has a culture of its own and we can belong to hundreds of different identity groups simultaneously. Furthermore, because no one belongs to exactly the same groups as another person, each of us must be considered culturally unique.

We can learn and adapt to another culture (acculturate) and yet still not be admitted into that culture as an equal participant (assimilate). Acceptance into the mainstream of society is often controlled by those in the dominant culture. The more one physically resembles and behaves as those in power, the easier it is to become part of the society.

This power relationship is vividly illustrated in post-colonial cultures, especially when there are racial differences. Indeed, the process of *acculturation* and *assimilation* are often confused. In everyday language, the two terms are sometimes used interchangeably and yet they are very different. Andrea Rich and Dennis Ogawa explore the differences between these two processes in their article "Intercultural and Interracial Communication: An Analytic Approach."

"American Identity Movements" provides a case study of cross-cultural conflict in America during the late 1960s and early 1970s, with the rise of cultural identity groups that challenged assumptions of the dominant culture. Both the youth and the civil rights movements are examined as cultural rather than simply sociological or political phenomena.

The youth rebellion and black identity movements of the 1960s were not only countercultural but also contrast-cultural movements. They often opposed the conventional values, attitudes and behaviors of the dominant culture. Rather than trying to assimilate or fit into the mainstream society by giving up their cultural differences, they asserted their differences.

The 1960s youth and black movements were the forerunners of the Chicano, feminist, gay liberation and dozens of other identity movements in the 1970s. The pendulum moved back to the dominant culture for college students of the 1980s. This was the generation of the "me decade," and "the age of narcissism."[3] The 18–24 year-old age group voted for President Reagan in greater percentages than any other age group in the population. Young people were more like those of the 1950s on college campuses. They often joined groups not to oppose or change the social system, but rather to get into the dominant society.[4] This was no longer the countercultural generation, but rather a generation of those who wanted to advance professionally, economically and socially based upon their assimilation into the mainstream or dominant culture.

While the pendulum may have swung back to the values and beliefs of the 1950s for many young people, the conflicts of the 1960s still continue to erupt in communities in the United States. To become an equal participant in the mainstream society, do Americans have to give up their ethnic, racial, gender or sexual orientation differences? Is the American culture a "melting pot" or a "cookie cutter"? Should it be a "salad bowl," "tapestry," "mosaic" or "patchwork quilt"? The metaphor is important because it shapes or frames our identity—how we see ourselves in our society.

The contrasts and comparisons between cultures discussed in "American Identity Movements" as well as the dynamics of a multicultural society, cross-cultural conflict, and cultural identity will be expanded upon and further developed by numerous authors throughout this text.

The forerunner of all models which contrast cultures is surely sociologist Ferdinand Tönnies' "*Gemeinschaft* and *Gesellschaft*." While he contrasts the homogeneous, rural community (*Gemeinschaft*) with the more heterogeneous, urban society (*Gesellschaft*), his description of social organizations easily applies to so-called modern and traditional, Western and non-Western, or even Northern and Southern cultures around the world.

Most cultures fall somewhere along the continuum between a *Gesellschaft* and a *Gemeinschaft*—it is all a matter of degree. Urbanized northern European cultures tend to be typical of *Gesellschafts* while rural, African cultures tend to be more typical of *Gemeinschafts*.

Along this continuum we can place other contrasts such as Edward Hall's low- to high-context cultures or David McClelland's need for achievement and need for affiliation. "Contrasting and Comparing Cultures" is a compilation of various cultural contrast models commonly found in cross-cultural and intercultural communication studies. It is not exhaustive, yet it includes most of the contrasts developed by authors in this anthology.

Although the terms cross-cultural communication and intercultural communication are often used interchangeably in everyday discourse and by some of our authors, many scholars in this field would distinguish cross-cultural and intercultural communication in terms of how culture is studied. *Cross-cultural* communication involves comparing and contrasting cultures while *intercultural* communication includes the actual interaction of people from various cultures. Comparing Russian and American values and ways of communication is cross-cultural communication. Analyzing and interpreting what occurs when a Russian diplomat negotiates with an American diplomat is intercultural communication.

Both fields of study include areas of inquiry and research in disciplines such as anthropology, communications, social psychology, and even education or counseling. However, in Japanese and many American universities cross-cultural communication and intercultural communication studies are considered to be part of international relations or international communication.

We usually begin to understand the dynamics of communication with people of other cultures by first understanding aspects of our own culture. We then try to understand their culture, using our own culture to contrast and compare. This is why cross-cultural studies generally preceed intercultural studies. The encompassing area of knowledge and the understanding of the theory, practice and research in intergroup relations can be broadly considered as *intercultural relations*.[5]

Lastly, why should we study intercultural communication? Many educators and trainers give three principal reasons: interpersonal adjustment, job skills, and cosmopolitanism. However, as early as 1982, Alfred G. Smith challenged the field to change its content from what he considered its somewhat trivial concerns to more urgent and consequential issues. He envisioned the field becoming more of an international policy science than the study of interpersonal psychodynamics.

In "Content Decisions in Intercultural Communication," Smith agrees that "the world needs better human relations, but that depends on alleviating poverty, ignorance, injustice and war, and that cannot be done on the interpersonal level. It takes better economic conditions, a job for everyone, freedom, and peace."[6] These more important root problems cannot be solved at an interpersonal level. They can only be seriously considered if intercultural communication studies have a broader scope of inquiry at the international level.

Many of the job skills taught in intercultural communication courses are far too general and non-technical to deal with the causes of major problems of intercultural communication. They often are simply intercultural versions of sensitivity training.

However, Smith asserts that that main job of intercultural communication should be to broaden intercultural skills to tackle such problems as negotiation and war or considering transborder data flows around the globe. These more technical skills may best be learned through a case method as used in business and law schools.

While personal cosmopolitanism may be a goal in intercultural communication studies, Smith urges us to make it more of a "global view for assessing international conditions and for making world decisions."[7]

Paul E. Rohrlich claims that "by severing the connections between the interpersonal and the global, Smith weakens the field rather than strengthens it."[8] In his article, "Why Do We Study Intercultural Communication?" he explains how the study of intercultural communication actually does address global problems. For example, interstate relations always become interpersonal at some stage in the communication process. It may involve diplomats or heads of state in face-to-face, interpersonal communication. The effectiveness of this communication can only increase understanding while poor communication can lead to misunderstanding.

> Why do we study intercultural communication? Because like a science it helps us understand the world around us, and like the humanities it helps us understand ourselves. It can help us with business, government, education, and language skills, all fields which ultimately depend upon interpersonal contact. As the crucial link between the individual and the larger world, intercultural communication as a field appeals to people precisely because it is interpersonal in how it addresses the "real issues."[9]

ENDNOTES

[1]One of the earliest studies of this phenomenon is by Ithiel de Sola Pool, Suzanne Keller, and Raymond A. Bauer, "The Influence of Foreign Travel on Political Attitudes of American Businessmen," *The Public Opinion Quarterly* 20 (Spring 1956): 147–161.

[2]Kinesics is the study of human movement or body motions such as facial expressions, gestures, or posture. Proxemics involves how people use space. The distance people maintain between themselves when conversing and even how furniture is arranged are all examples of proxemics. Chronemics is the study of how time is used in different cultures. It ranges from the rhythm or tempo of conversation to the socially acceptable time for arriving late for a party or meeting.

See Raymond Birdwhistell, *Introduction to Kinesics* (Louisville, KY: University of Louisville Press, 1952, 1974), Edward T. Hall, *The Silent Language* (Garden City, NY: Doubleday & Company, 1966), and Edward T. Hall, *The Dance of Life: The Other Dimension of Time* (Garden City, NY: Anchor Press/Doubleday, 1983).

[3]See Christopher Lasch, *The Culture of Narcissism: American Life in an Age of Diminishing Expectations* (New York: Norton, 1979).

[4]Gary R. Weaver "This Cutthroat College Generation," *The Washington Star*, 2 February 1981, 11 (A).

[5]The second page of the *International Journal of Intercultural Relations* contains a statement of its "Aims and Scope" with the following explanation of its area of inquiry: "The

International Journal of Intercultural Relations is dedicated to advancing knowledge and understanding of theory, practice, and research in intergroup relations."

[6]Alfred G. Smith, "Content Decisions in Intercultural Communication," *The Southern Speech Communication Journal* 57, no. 3 (Spring 1982): 254. Also in this section, 79.

[7]Ibid. 262. Also in this section, 83.

[8]Paul E. Rorhlich, "Why Do We Study Intercultural Communication?" *International Journal of Intercultural Relations* 11 (1987): 122. Also in this section, 84.

[9]Ibid. 127–8. Also in this section, 87.

1

How Cultures Collide

Edward T. Hall and Elizabeth Hall

Elizabeth Hall (for *Psychology Today*): For years, you've been saying that our ignorance of non-verbal communication threatens international relations, trade, and even world peace. Your new book, *Beyond Culture,* makes your warnings stronger and more specific. Just how, for example, does our ignorance of the silent language of behavior affect our relations with the People's Republic of China?

Edward T. Hall: All human beings are captives of their culture. When dealing with the Chinese, we are apt to try to read their true intentions from what they do rather than what they say. But in so doing, and by assuming that behavior means pretty much the same around the world, we anticipate their actions as if they were Americans—whereas they read our behavior with strong Chinese overtones. That could lead to serious misunderstandings.

One difference between us and the Chinese is in the way action chains are handled. An action chain is a set of events that resembles a dance, except that it is a dance with a goal. If any of the basic steps of the dance are omitted or distorted, the chain is broken and the action must begin all over again. The goal may be sex, marriage, corporate mergers, peace treaties—or something as simple as shaking hands or buying a gallon of paint. I doubt if any human social action exists that does not involve action chains.

In this culture, chains have clearly defined steps and stages; in China, the steps are not as clear to us. Faced with a troublesome

Reprinted from *Psychology Today,* 10, no. 7, (July 1976): 66, 69, 71–74, 97. Copyright © 1976, Sussex Publishers, Inc.

situation, the Chinese will often act as though nothing has happened. They believe that once one acknowledges an event, then one must take action and action may be very, very serious. This is why the Chinese may seem to ignore our actions in one instance and be hypersensitive in another. We misread their intentions both in Korea and in Vietnam.

pt: And we misread them because we couldn't decipher the steps in their action chains?

Hall: In part, yes. In Vietnam we misread Chinese intentions by thinking they were motivated the way we were and took them too seriously; in Korea we didn't take them seriously enough. They told us where the line was, but we didn't believe them. In the same way, the Chinese may fail to see when we are very serious, and they misread the signs in our action chains. Whenever the members of one culture believe that another possesses no subtlety, as some Chinese apparently believe of us, it is a clear sign that the first culture has grossly misunderstood the second; I know of no culture without subtlety.

pt: We were warned that allowing the North Vietnamese to win would topple the first in a chain of dominoes, that Vietnam would lead to a solidly Communist Asia, just as Munich led toward a Nazi Europe.

Hall: When we went into Asia, we tried to fit events into a pattern that we have seen work in Europe. We confused Vietnam with Munich. The parallels were nonexistent. For we shared a history as well as political and social institutions with the Czechs; we shared none of these with the South Vietnamese. When Hitler marched on Czechoslovakia, it was an authoritarian government opposing a democratic regime; in Vietnam there were two authoritarian regimes.

pt: Do you think that with a better knowledge of the Chinese culture we would have known that some of the actions we took with trepidation would not provoke the Chinese into sending troops?

Hall: Possibly. But with a better knowledge of other peoples, we might not have fallen for our own propaganda. And might have avoided Vietnam in the first place. Clearly we had no idea of what we were getting into.

pt: And if you have a Secretary of State who meets every international situation as if it were an episode in nineteenth century European politics. . . .

Hall: You have a problem. But it runs deeper than that, for we avoid knowing. Our Department of State rotates its overseas employees every two years. According to one undersecretary in charge of personnel, our policy assumes that when a U.S. citizen knows a country too well, he begins to represent them, not us. This is, of course, a head-in-the-sand attitude.

As far as China goes, we eliminated the old China hands in Joe McCarthy's heyday. When men like John Stewart Service and John Carter Vincent told us what was happening in China, that Mao's Communists were winning, they were drummed out of the State Department as disloyal.

But to return to action chains. Americans, if they are sophisticated, watch other people's behavior to anticipate events. The Chinese do not ignore behavior entirely, but they are apt to pay more attention to where the other person is placed in a social system. They believe that the system will ultimately dictate behavior. This is because China is a high-context culture and we're a low-context culture.

pt: Just what do you mean by high- and low-context cultures?

Hall: Context and communication are intimately interrelated. In some cultures, messages are explicit; the words carry most of the information. In other cultures, such as China or Japan or the Arab cultures, less information is contained in the verbal part of a message, since more is in the context. That's why American businessmen often complain that their Japanese counterparts never get to the point. The Japanese wouldn't dream of spelling the whole thing out. To do so is a put-down; it's like doing your thinking for you.

pt: Like talking down to someone, or explaining something to a child.

Hall: Exactly. This sort of misunderstanding is so common that a few Americans picked up one reliable cue that shows when Japanese diplomats, having tried to get across an important point, realize they've failed. When this happens, they start slugging down Scotch. Remember, however, that in situations such as these, expectations may have significant unconscious overtones. Since much of culture operates outside our awareness, frequently we don't even know that we know. We pick them up in the cradle. We unconsciously learn what to notice and what not to notice, how to divide time and space, how to walk and talk and use our bodies, how to behave as men or women, how to relate to other people, how to handle responsibility, whether experience is seen as whole or fragmented. This applies to all peoples. The Chinese or the Japanese or the Arabs are as unaware of their assumptions as we are of our own. We each assume that they're part of human nature. What we think of as "mind" is really internalized culture.

pt: Let's explore some of the differences between high- and low-context. How does a high-context culture handle personal responsibility?

Hall: The difference is built in, shared, preprogrammed information as it relates to the transmitted, public part of the message. In general, high-context cultures can get by with less of the legal paperwork that is deemed essential in America. A man's word is his bond and you need not spell out the details to make him behave. One depends more on the power and influence of established networks of friends and relatives. Even in rather mundane matters, the two systems can be seen in contrast. For instance, several years ago I was traveling in Crete and wanted to visit the ruins at Knossos. My traveling companion, who was from low-context, fast-moving New York, took charge of the arrangements. He bargained with a taxi driver, agreed on a price, and a deal was made. We would take his taxi. Without warning, just as we were entering the cab, he stopped, got out and asked another driver if he would take us for less money. Since the second driver was willing, my friend said, "Let's go." The first taxi driver felt he had been cheated. We had made a verbal agreement and it had been violated. But my friend, coming from a low-context opportunistic culture, felt no moral obligation at all. He had saved the equivalent of 75¢. I can still see the shocked and horrified look on the face of the first taxi driver.

pt: Your friend was accustomed to getting three bids for a job.

Hall: Yes, and insisting on competitive bidding can also cause complications overseas. In a high-context culture, the job is given to the man who will do the best work and whom you can control. In a low-context culture, we try to make the specifications so precise that a builder has trouble doing a bad job. A builder in Japan is likely to say, "What has that piece of paper got to do with the situation? If we can't trust each other enough to go ahead without it, why bother?"

There are further implications of this pattern. A friend of mine in the Middle East was out one evening with a large group of Lebanese men. He happened to mention casually that if he only had some money, he could make a bundle. Much later as the group was breaking up, one of the men whom he didn't know gave him his card and asked him to drop by the next day. When my friend called, the man asked him how much money he needed and for how long, stating that he had some extra money. Upon hearing the amount, he proceeded to write out a check. The Lebanese businessman did not know my friend personally, but knew that he was part of a particular group, and therefore trustworthy.

pt: In other words, he didn't have to run a credit check.

Hall: No. Our low-context approach frequently ties the hands of American bankers in the Middle East. Several years ago, before things deteriorated out there, I interviewed a number of bankers. I was told they just couldn't compete with the local banks. For every loan over a certain amount, the Americans had to send a profit-and-loss statement to New York for an OK. By the time New York passed on the loan, the customer had gone elsewhere.

pt: That would mean that only high-risk loans would be left for American banks. Members of a high-context culture would know by a man's group whether he was a good risk.

Hall: Precisely.

pt: A number of corporations have gotten into hot water by paying bribes to foreign officials.

Hall: Bribery, as far as I know, is not condoned anywhere in the world, even in countries where it is a general practice. For a long time, civil servants in many countries simply did not earn enough to live on. They made a living wage by accepting a little extra to do their official tasks. But it's a long way from tipping an agent for stamping your visa to passing out a million dollars for an aircraft contract.

pt: From what you have been saying, the high-context culture functions on the basis of whom you know, while the American culture functions according to rules of procedure. Maybe American companies who pay off so-called agents are merely trying to buy the friendship network.

Hall: You are so right. However, any American could establish the same network that he tries to buy, but it would take him longer to do it. Most companies are not willing to invest that much time. Instead of building a solid foundation of relationships against the time when we will need them, we take a short cut and use money instead.

pt: How would a high-context culture like Japan have handled Watergate?

Hall: Again there are some interesting differences. In Japan, the man at the top is responsible. Nixon would have committed suicide. In the case of the Mai Lai massacre, Westmoreland would have taken the rap. In low-context systems, responsibility is kicked as far down the system as possible. In a high-context culture, the top man shoulders the blame.

pt: So the sign on Harry Truman's desk, "The Buck Stops Here," was really a high-context sign. He did take responsibility; he always said that dropping the bomb was purely his own decision.

Hall: Truman had a deep moral sense, a sense of continuity, and was deeply conversant with the presidency as an institution. He came out of a past age. In the days of the Old West, a man's word was his bond in this country, in part because everyone really did know everyone else. Truman belonged to this tradition. Recently our culture has been becoming noticeably more low-context.

pt: I can't disagree. We've had the rise of experts who tell us how to do everything from having sex to rearing children to being assertive—things one would assume people did as a part of being human. And the new marriage contracts specify everything about the bond from who washes dishes to how many nights a week out each partner has.

Hall: One of the complications of a low-context culture is the fragmenting of experience. The plethora of experts testifies that. The marriage contracts may mean that our commitment to each other is diminishing. Commitment is greater in a high-context culture because the mass of the system is so great that you literally cannot escape, and it's almost impossible to change the rules.

pt: Nearly everything we have said shows up the advantages of a high-context culture. What are its disadvantages?

Hall: We've just said that they're very hard to move. Reforms come slowly. They're also likely to have rigid class structures and a family structure that holds people in a vise. You can't escape. The only way for a Japanese woman to get back at her mother-in-law is to wait until her own son marries. There's less mobility. Your occupation may be determined by what your father did. Or you may sign up with an employer for life as they do in Japan. High-context cultures are more group-oriented, and they sacrifice individualism. Individuals outside the group are apt to be helpless.

pt: Can you lay out some of the major cultures in terms of their context?

Hall: I would begin with the German-Swiss. They are low-context, falling somewhere near the bottom of the scale. Next the Germans, then the Scandinavians, as we move up. These cultures are all lower in context than the U.S. Above Americans come the French, the English, the Italians, the Spanish, the Greeks and the Arabs. In other words, as you move from northern to southern Europe, you will find that people move toward more involvement with each other. Look at the difference between a Swedish and an Italian movie.

pt: Sometimes people will discuss a Bergman movie and each will have a completely different motivation for the characters.

Hall: The first thing to remember about a Bergman movie is that no matter what it means to you, it means something else to a Swede. We can't possibly interpret all that's going on there.

pt: We're all becoming aware that the body does communicate. Books on body language have become popular. You can buy books that tell you how to succeed in business, be a smashing success at a cocktail party, or become popular with the opposite sex, all by reading body cues. Are these books generally helpful?

Hall: I think they are dreadful. Unfortunately, a few writers have exploited things that some of us have discovered about human behavior, and have managed to give the field a bad name. When a popularizer writes that sitting with your legs crossed has a certain specific meaning, he's just complicating life for everyone. In the final analysis, human beings have to deal with each other on a real-life basis.

pt: Are you implying that people who read these books will try to change their behavior?

Hall: That's the idea. It's manipulative, and I think it's not good for people to manipulate each other. Women don't like to be regarded as sex objects, because it involves manipulation.

pt: Besides the ethical objections, what about the practicality of such advice?

Hall: It's grotesque, and besides it just doesn't work. People are being taken advantage of, and they should feel quite angry when they find out.

pt: Does the problem lie in the fact that these books take the meaning of body language out of context?

Hall: You've put your finger on the crux of the matter. When body signals are not seen in context, their meaning can only be distorted. The popularizers of body language take a low-context, manipulative, exploitative view of high-context situations. When I speak of silent language, I mean more than body language. I refer to the totality of behavior as well as the products of behavior—time, space, materials, everything.

pt: One of the major differences in behavior you've found comes from a culture's way of handling time. How does time affect the shape of a culture or a person's view of the world?

Hall: Time, like space, communicates. It is not merely a convention, it's an organizing system. Our culture happens to organize most activities on a time base. We talk about time as if it were money; we spend it, save it or waste it. Time patterns are so deeply embedded in our central nervous system that we can't imagine getting along without them. The Western world couldn't function without its linear, one-thing-at-a-time system. Technology requires a monochronic approach. Railroads and airlines couldn't be integrated or run without schedules.

Of course, in the U.S. we don't begin to approach the Swiss in their slavery to time. Wherever a Swiss railroad stops, no matter how far into the mountains, passengers can look out the window at the nearest telegraph pole. On the pole will be a small white sign with a line down the middle and an arrow pointing in each direction, telling how many minutes—not kilometers—it is from the last station and how many it is to the next.

pt: It's apparently no accident that the Swiss are great watchmakers. But what is another way of handling time?

Hall: The Hopi Indians provide us with an excellent contrast because they don't have a single system that integrates everything. They believe that every living thing has its own inherent system and that you must deal with each plant or animal in terms of its own time. Their system is what I call polychronic, which hasn't always worked to their advantage. For example, if the Hopi had a slow-maturing variety of corn that would barely produce edible ears by the end of the growing season, they were apt to accept it. White Americans would be more apt to develop new strains that matured sooner; the old-time Hopi wouldn't think of altering a living time system.

pt: A bit of that polychronic time would help American mothers who become nervous if their children don't walk or talk at a certain age. They've been told each child has its own rate of maturation, but they don't believe it.

Hall: That's because we are wedded to some distant standard against which everything is measured. Even so, housewives have more experience with polychronic time than the rest of us. They must get husbands off to work, children to school, babies bathed and fed, meals ready, and clothes washed and dried. Each of those has its own time system, and it's one reason women have reacted so strongly to their

life. A polychronic system tends to minimize individuality at the expense of group needs while a monochronic system can restore feelings of identity sometimes to the extent of narcissism. But if your identity comes from the group, as a Pueblo Indian's does, a monochronic system can be quite destructive because it interferes with group cohesiveness.

pt: Does this difference in time systems contribute to cross-cultural conflicts?

Hall: Of course. It can and has generated all sorts of tension between peoples. For example, 40 years ago when I worked with the Hopi, they were building dams paid for by the taxpayers. The government knew how long it takes to build dams and expected them to be finished in a set period of time. The Hopi felt that a dam had no built-in schedule, and they would not be hurried. Now, if it had been possible to convince the Hopi that inherent in the dam's structure was the fact that it was supposed to be completed in 90 days, for example, the problem would have been solved. But we didn't know enough then.

pt: Do all Western countries run on monochronic time?

Hall: Not entirely. Latin American and Mediterranean countries tend to be polychronic. It goes with high-context cultures. This has caused American businessmen and diplomats some trouble. Both have made appointments with Latin Americans and been kept waiting. Typically the Latin American, left to his own way of doing things, would have an office full of people, each there for a different purpose, showing no favoritism. He fails to devote himself to the North Americans who happen to be there to see him. The North American, running on a monochronic system, almost inevitably believes that the Latin American is telling him that he is not important. The Latin interprets the American's resentment as narcissism.

pt: How does this affect the manufacturing plants that American companies opened in Latin America?

Hall: For years I worked with an American company that tried to run a plant in Mexico. They finally gave up. They had a high-quality product and just couldn't get the Mexicans to produce to their standards. You should understand that the problem was not just time. It was a case of not developing a system that the local people could understand in terms of their own culture.

There's always a solution. Unfortunately Americans frequently fail to find it. Aramco, for example, was losing money on one of their trucking operations in Saudi Arabia. Finally, an Arab was able to buy the franchise and set up his own system. Knowing his own people, he worked out a series of complex reinforcement schedules for each truck and driver. He even penalized them for every valve cap that was missing and rewarded drivers when nothing that was supposed to be there was missing. Oil levels in the crankcase, maintenance schedules, time schedules, everything was examined and recorded.

The cost per ton-mile dropped to a third of what it had been under American management.

pt: Sounds as if he simply imposed a behavior-shaping schedule on the drivers.

Hall: Yes, but he also organized a way of getting quality that the people understood and would accept. You couldn't set up such an arrangement with American drivers. It would be infringing on their territory to tell them how to take care of their trucks. We think of ourselves as successful managers, but the only people we can manage are other Americans, and we frequently don't do too well at that.

pt: How does all this affect our foreign relations in the Middle East?

Hall: Monochronic people tend to get their information from one or two sources, whereas polychronic people gather information from all over. The Arabs read several New York newspapers, *The Washington Post, Foreign Affairs,* everything they can get their hands on, and put the whole thing together. They come up with what they believe is the policy of the U.S. Once when I was in the Middle East during a crisis, I tried to tell Arabs that they had been reading the expression of several special-interest groups, which bore little or no resemblance to the policy of the U.S., but I didn't get very far. Instead of reacting to the policy of the State Department or Kissinger or Ford, they're reacting to some curious amalgam of the views of Kissinger, James Reston, various U.S. senators, the oil companies, the

Anti-Defamation League, and goodness knows what else.

Another difference between Europeans and Arabs concerns disputes and how they are handled. Arabs depend on outsiders to intervene in disputes. In Arab societies, if two people are arguing and one of them gets hurt, the bystander who failed to stop the fight is the guilty party.

pt: Is that why Egypt is open to Kissinger's diplomacy?

Hall: Kissinger has a healthy male ego. Not only is there a meshing of personalities, but Arabs understand personal diplomacy. Remember that the first Arab-Israeli accord came about when Ralph Bunche got both parties isolated on an island and put each on a separate floor of a hotel. He carried messages back and forth between the floors until, finally, things began to work. He was very persuasive. Kissinger has done something similar, but I am under the impression that he didn't design it that way.

pt: Do the different cultural backgrounds of the Arabs and the Israelis complicate the situation?

Hall: Naturally. The Middle East is a village culture, and village land is sacred in a way that is impossible to describe in the U.S. For example, about 25 years ago, a friend of mine conducted a census of a Lebanese village. The villagers claimed several times as many people as actually inhabited the village. People who had emigrated to Mexico and New York and Brazil and who hadn't been back for generations were counted and were still considered members of the village.

Europeans and Americans think in terms of nation states. Israel is a nation-state in the midst of a village-culture complex. We're not talking about mere convention. The Palestinian Arabs who were displaced from their land have not forgotten, and they will never forget. They still consider as their sacred home that village their fathers were driven out of 30 years ago.

On top of that, Zionism is a European thing. Israel has some of the same problems with her Yemenite Jews that she has with the Arabs. Indigenous Jews, as you know, have to be enculturated into a new European tradition.

pt: So before you even begin to talk about religion, you begin with two incompatible traditions.

Hall: It took the Arabs 20 years to discover that. They finally woke up and discovered that they were not fighting Jews, because they had gotten along with Jewish villages for centuries. They were fighting Europeans.

pt: In *The Hidden Dimension,* you have a photograph of a house built by an Arab to punish a neighbor. Do Arab spite patterns affect the conflict between Israel and the Arab States?

Hall: They haven't yet, but they could. That house looks like a big wall, four stories high. The man who built it owned a narrow strip of land along the road, and the man behind him pushed too hard in trying to buy the land, and told the owner his land wasn't worth anything because no one could build a house on it. The owner of the land said, "I'll show you," and he built this house about six-feet thick—and furthermore built it high enough to cut off his neighbor's view of the Mediterranean.

If the Arabs are pushed too far and a Holy War is declared, there will be a disaster. I don't even like to think about it because once an Arab is in the spite response, he's apt to do anything—wreck his life—the lives of his children—he's past caring. No warning is given and, once the spite pattern takes over, nobody can intervene successfully until it runs its course.

pt: Do the cultural differences between blacks and whites in this country cause misunderstandings?

Hall: The data we have show that they do. The black culture is considerably higher in context than the white culture. I'm not talking about middle-class blacks; they're likely to be as low-contexted, compulsive and obsessional as whites.

But take the matter of the way we listen or show that we are paying attention when someone is talking. I once got a young black draftsman a job with an architectural firm, where he almost got fired. He did his work well but his employer complained about his attitude. This mystified me until once when I was talking to him and noticed I wasn't getting any feedback.

He just sat there, quietly drawing. Finally I said, "Are you listening?" He said, "Man, if you're in the room, I'm listening. You listen with your ears." In their own mode, interacting with each other, ethnic blacks who know each other don't feel they have to look at each other while talking. They don't nod their heads or make little noises to show that they're listening the way whites do.

Old-time Pullman porters used to do a lot of head-bobbing and foot-shuffling and yessing, which was a response to their being hassled by whites. In those days, not knowing the nature of the white listening system, they didn't want to take chances and so they produced an exaggerated version of what whites expected, to show their customers that they were paying attention.

pt: What about the feeling many blacks have that they're invisible men?

Hall: That's another cultural difference. Depending upon the part of the country he's from, a white on the street looks at a person until he's about 12 to 16 feet away. Then, unless they know each other, whites automatically look away to avoid eye contact. This automatic avoidance on our part seems to give blacks the feeling of invisibility, because they use their eyes very differently than whites. As high-context people, they're more involved with each other visually and in every other way.

pt: Do blacks and whites handle time differently?

Hall: Their time is apt to be more polychronic than ours, which caused problems in Detroit when they first began to work on assembly lines and wouldn't show up. At times blacks jokingly refer to CPT or colored people's time when dealing with whites. Their system seems to run much closer to the way the body operates as well as being more situational in character.

Blacks also pay more attention than we do to nonverbal behavior. I once ran an experiment in which one black filmed another in a job interview. Each time something significant happened, the watching black started the camera. When I looked at those films, I couldn't believe my eyes. Nothing was happening! Or so I thought. It turned out that my cameraoperator was catching—and identifying—body signals as minor as the movement of a thumb, which foreshadowed an intention to speak. Whites aren't so finely tuned.

pt: Since many of our ethnic groups come from high-context cultures, I suppose that our low-context approach has caused problems for them as well.

Hall: There are many such problems, but particularly when urban renewal enters the picture. Planners and politicians are apt to mark ethnic neighborhoods as slums, and classify them for renewal because they do not see the order behind what appears to be disorder. Live, vital, cohesive ethnic communities are destroyed. To make way for a university in Chicago, planners wiped out a Greek and Italian neighborhood, over strong protests. The scars haven't healed yet. It is important to stress that when you scatter such a community, you're doing more than tearing down buildings; you're destroying most of what gives life meaning, particularly for people who are deeply involved with each other. The displaced people grieve for their homes as if they had lost children and parents. To low-context whites, one neighborhood is much like the next. To high-context people, it is something else again.

pt: You once said that urban renewal programs were as destructive as enemy bombing.

Hall: That was no mere metaphor. Take a good look at any neighborhood that's been hit by urban renewal. It's like a European city after a bombing raid. Furthermore, wasting communities is the first step in a chain of events that ends in destroying our cities. As a last resort and if absolutely necessary, neighborhoods should be relocated en masse. The whole community should be moved together—local policemen, streetcleaners, shopkeepers, and even postal clerks should be moved as a unit. Of course it will never happen. It would make too much sense.

pt: If I had to sum up our talk, I'd say that your work is a plea for sensing context.

Hall: If I have only one point to make, it is that nothing is independent of anything else. Yet in the U.S. we use a special-interest approach for solving political, economic and environmental problems, which disregards the interconnectedness of events. Unfortunately, our schools are no help because they consistently teach us *not* to make connections. I feel strongly that there should be a few people at least whose task is synthesis—pulling things together. And that is impossible without a deep sense of context.

2

Learning the Arabs' Silent Language

Edward T. Hall
interviewed by
Kenneth Friedman

In bargaining with the Arabs, we Americans too often speak the language of power and profit. The Arabs reply in kind. But they are also looking for a thousand-and-one body clues to the human relationship. For an informed opinion on how to get along with the Arabs, *Psychology Today* went back to Edward T. Hall, probably the best-known authority in the country on face-to-face contact between peoples of different cultures. Hall, who now lives in Santa Fe, New Mexico, has served as a consultant to government and business for more than 40 years; at one time, he helped train our diplomats in the cultures of their assigned countries. Hall, whose books *The Silent Language, Beyond Culture,* and *The Hidden Dimension* stress the importance of nonverbal language in cross-cultural communication—for instance, touching, distance between speakers, concepts of time—was interviewed by *Psychology Today* in July of 1976 on his general theories. Recently, we asked anthropologist Kenneth Friedman to visit Hall and talk in more detail about our relations with the Arabs. Although "Arab" peoples differ in a number of respects from country to country, region to region, and sect to sect, Hall talked about a few things that are common to the Arab culture and important for Americans to know. Here are excerpts.

Kenneth Friedman: Do we Americans understand the Arabs, or do we tend to caricature or stereotype them?

Reprinted from *Psychology Today* 13, no. 3, (August 1979): 45–54. Copyright © 1979, Sussex Publishers, Inc.

Edward T. Hall: I don't think we understand them. We tend to think of Arabs as underdeveloped Americans—Americans with sheets on. We look at them as undereducated and rather poor at anything technological. All we have to do is to make believers out of them, get them the proper education, teach them English, and they will turn into Americans.

To Americans, everyone is "like us" underneath. It just isn't true. Anwar Sadat, for instance, wears Western clothes, but he's not a Westerner. When he's sitting and talking with someone, he often has a hand on the other person's knee. This touching is very Egyptian and it's an important part of communication in Arab culture.

The problem is that most Americans don't really believe in the cultural dimension. A friend of mine, a political scientist who is an extraordinarily successful scholar in international relations and has done a lot of work throughout Asia, said to me, "You anthropologists, you just made up all that culture stuff." Whatever it is I am seeing, many other people are just not seeing.

Friedman: How do you explain this denial of cultural factors?

Hall: Well, I've developed a model of what motivates people to do almost anything. There seem to be economic, political, and ideological considerations, all of which exist on the level of awareness. Then, there are habitual illusional, and cultural factors that exist mostly behind awareness. Economic, political, and ideological aspects get most of the attention because they have a clear impact on people. Communication is the cultural part, and it tends to function automatically. People know as much about it as they do about the inner workings of their automobile, which isn't very much. So we're working at a level, an analytical level, that is not commonly recognized. But once you talk about communication in other cultures with people who have had actual experiences with it, the lights begin to go on. This whole thing is very personal and what you're doing is telling people some of the rules governing behavior that they have already experienced.

One time, a colleague and I were in a nightclub in Beirut—when there were night-clubs in Beirut—watching the show. There was an American black woman in the show, a singer who was quite good, so afterward, we asked her over for a drink. She made a remark that was sort of telling. "You know, I used to be married to a Lebanese in the U.S. and he was strange," she said. "I thought it was just him, but over here, they're all that way!"

This is a person who has experienced cultural difference and understands the depth of it. In contrast, Dean Rusk once told a friend of mine that he had made a big discovery: people have different conversational distances. This was almost 20 years after I wrote a book about it [*The Silent Language*].

Friedman: How are Arabs different from North Americans?

Hall: The basic difference is that Arabs are highly "contexted." They examine the entire circumstance in which events are happening in order to understand them. Everyone is aware there is a relationship between the context of a statement and its meaning. If a man says, "I love you" to a woman on the first date, she knows it doesn't mean the same thing that it might a year later.

The cultures of the world can be placed on a continuum, based on the amount of communication contained in the nonverbal context compared with the amount in the verbal message. A legal contract, for instance, is supposed to be context-free—all the meaning is in the words of the contract. Some cultures, like our own, are low context; they tend to put more emphasis on the verbal message and less on the context. In a low-context culture, you get down to business very quickly. The high-context culture takes considerably longer, and that's simply because the people have developed a need to know more about you before a relationship can develop. You might say that they simply don't know how to handle a low-context relationship with other people.

Friedman: What's the best way to approach an Arab in a business deal?

Hall: In the Middle East, if you aren't willing to take time to sit down and have coffee with people, you have a problem. You must learn to wait and not be too eager to talk business. You can ask about the family or ask, "How are you feeling?" But avoid too many personal questions about wives, because people are apt to get suspicious. Learn to make what we call chit-chat. If you don't, you can't go to the next step. It's a little bit like a courtship, and without all the preliminaries, sex becomes just like rape.

Friedman: You seem to be saying that there is a much stronger emphasis on personal contact and much less on procedures.

Hall: Yes, and we're not willing to accept this about Middle Eastern culture. Once I was interviewing American bankers working in the Middle East who said that they couldn't make loans above a certain amount unless they sent a profit-and-loss statement to New York. Being masters of financial manipulation, Arab businessmen were willing to provide any kind of profit-and-loss statement that they wanted. But by the time they get around to filling out such statements, they may not need the money anymore—and the American bankers will lose the deal. Americans were using criteria for insuring loans that were applicable in the United States, whereas in the Middle East, if you know the man and you know his business and he knows you and you're part of the same social group, he cannot afford not to pay back that loan.

Friedman: How really different is that from the U.S.? In American business, the people at the top do know each other. There is a pressure to socialize and major business deals take shape in face-to-face negotiations, not over the telephone.

Hall: In general, Arabs know more about each other than we do. The group is smaller and more intimate, and there are differences in what people take for granted in negotiating. Having had experience working with American business in negotiations, I find that usually things are not hammered out at the negotiating table. This is because people need to discover what kind of cards the other fellow is holding. It is essential to ascertain the rock-bottom dollar that the other fellow is going to take. Or what the minimal conditions for a deal are—I use the word "dollar" symbolically. Then, you must decide whether there's an overlap between what each side wants. If there isn't, you can't get together. The overlap is where the "give" in the system is. When there's a big overlap, both sides have a greater likelihood of coming out with the feeling that they have made a good deal. The bargaining table for us is a place for ratifying a decision that's been made informally outside the room. And usually it's the lower- or middle-echelon people who do the negotiating. The top people do not participate in the lengthy process of face-to-face haggling.

The whole thing [in the U.S.] is based on how much you can find out about the other fellow's position, to assess his strength. How bad he is hurting? If he's hurting badly enough, you're going to drive a harder bargain.

Essentially, the American strategy is to find out what percentage of the asking price to offer at the start of negotiations. But Arabs have many asking prices. They have what they consider the "insult price," the "go-away price," the "don't-bother-me price," the "I-don't-want-to-sell price." They also may indicate: "I'm willing to sell, but I'm not very enthusiastic." Or: "I would like to sell; I'm very anxious to sell; you're a very close friend of mine." There are all those different asking prices and you must know which one you're working with before you even start bargaining.

Friedman: How does an Arab tell an "insult price" from a genuine one?

Hall: Suppose you have a Rolex watch to sell that costs around $1,000. You're with two Arabs and one of them says, "That's a nice watch. Would you like to sell it?" The seller says, "Well, I don't know," and the Arab replies, "How much would you take for it?" If the Arab knows the market price of a new watch and the seller says $1,500, that's an insult—because that's 50 percent more than he would have to pay in a store. The seller might say, "I've had it for years, and you're a very close friend of mine. I'll sell it to you for $900." That's a decent price, because the Arab buyer will know that he's taking $100 away from you.

Friedman: It's one thing to sell a watch, but it's quite a different matter to sell 10 jet planes.

Hall: I've never sold 10 jet planes to an Arab. That certainly complicates the negotiations. There is a market price for those jet planes, and the Arabs know what it is. But different countries are competing with different kinds of planes, it gets a little more complex, and you get into the whole matter of influence peddling.

Our answer in the U.S. has been simply to pay such tremendous bribes that people cannot afford not to do business with us. If I read Arab people correctly, and if my own experience means anything, in many instances we could have sold the 10 planes for much closer to the market price, without paying exorbitant bribes—if we had taken the time to form proper relationships with the people. We think that price is everything. In this sense, we're kind of naive. Profit isn't as important to these people as a human relationship.

Friedman: Why haven't we developed these personal ties with Middle Easterners?

Hall: Let's go back to the ways of motivating people—the economic, political, and ideological ways. In the past, our attitude has been that if you have the power, why bother with all these things? The trouble with this approach is that by insisting on having things your own way, eventually other people learn your strategies and will use them against you.

This is precisely what the Arabs have done. They didn't invent the cartel. The cartel is a European invention. The question is: have we gone too far? Can we recoup our losses?

The Arabs seem to have learned that power is the only language Americans speak, and it's very difficult to argue with men of power. I've tried. Power is simple-minded; it's easy, but it takes a long time to build relationships in many parts of the world.

Friedman: How should the U.S. go about building those relationships?

Hall: We could start by being less paranoid. American bureaucrats and businessmen have a feeling that if we leave an American overseas too long, if he learns a foreign culture and he establishes relationships with the people, he's then going to be on their side. He will cease to represent the U.S. We'd much rather rotate people and not allow them to develop relationships. This is kind of nutty when you think about it: we can't trust our own citizens to learn a language, learn a culture, make friends, and still represent our government.

We're getting better, of course, particularly in the State Department, whose personnel are frequently required to learn the language. Unfortunately, they are not evaluated on either their mastery of the culture or the behavior matrix in which all languages are set.

Friedman: Do the oil companies or other firms doing business in the Middle East follow the same policy as the State Department? Or do they value the personal relationship?

Hall: Companies vary considerably. But look at what happened in Iran as a case history. There was very little general understanding of how the country really works, and how Americans could adapt to it. What you had were enclaves of Americans.

In general, the big companies tend to do better in business operations than do small ones. The big ones are clued in at the higher levels of government. In some cases, they've just fallen into it, simply because the attorneys or bankers they hired have the proper connections in the country. But this doesn't take care of people who can't afford such high-class connections.

Friedman: Have you trained people to work in the Middle East?

Hall: I trained a lot of people who were part of the Point IV [Truman's technical assistance] program. We didn't have time to teach people what to do or even to teach them the language. But we did have enough time to get them started on the right foot and to develop some effective shortcuts. We went to a lot of trouble to get them together with someone from the local culture. Their assignment was to find out how many times they had to meet with a person in the country they were going to before they could really get down to business. We had learned that Americans were getting down to business much too fast in the Middle East. They were skipping important steps in the action chain—we didn't have the action-chain model then because it hadn't been discovered yet, but we knew what an action chain was.

Friedman: Can you explain what you mean by an "action chain"?

Hall: An action chain is a behavioral sequence with two or more participating organisms, in which there are standard steps for reaching a goal. If you leave out one of those steps, the chain gets broken, and you have to start all over again. For example, a greeting has several parts. If you leave out a part, such as the proper body motions, people are confused and have trouble completing the chain. So we thought that maybe it would be possible to have our trainees discover the beginning segments of an action chain for getting down to business.

But this strategy was a mistake. The experience of a Ph.D. in agronomy who was going to Cuba—those were the days before Fidel Castro—illustrates how important it is to stick to basics. He was very ingenious at getting some notion of the soils from the Cuban we had found for him. When he reported on his three-day conference, he said: "You know, I couldn't get the answer to your question, because it wasn't until we had met three times that we got to know each other and could start talking about these things."

That in itself was an important lesson, however. In training people to work in another culture, the real job is to put them in a situation in which they continue to learn on their own.

Friedman: What advice can you give someone who is going to live in another culture? Lacking training in that culture, how can one begin to feel oriented?

Hall: Once you are in a country, and you have personal ties, it's possible to find a sort of cultural adviser, a friend who knows the place. For instance, Americans were paying two to three times as much rent as they should have in Syria. So I asked an Arab-Syrian friend, "If I were a Syrian going to go to Damascus and wanted to rent a house, how would I go about it?" He said: "First, you would not let anybody know that you were interested in a house, but you would drive around and decide where you wanted to live, and once you picked a neighborhood, you would get hold of an intermediary you could trust and ask him to find you a place in that neighborhood. Then, the intermediary would find somebody who is anxious to rent a place, but he wouldn't tell them that he has a client. He then returns to the client and says, 'I've got a place. What I want you to do now is to walk down such-

and-such street, but don't look at houses. Just walk down the street. Do this a couple of times. Then, the intermediary goes to the man who has the house to rent and says, 'You know this foreigner who has been through this neighborhood? Maybe we could interest him in your house.'" And it goes on like that, step by step. Eventually, if matters go well, the house is yours for about a third of what the average American is paying. It's a different action chain. The trouble is it's hard to get an American to take each step seriously and to be coached. Most Americans are too eager to buy and reluctant to take coaching. Only actors and athletes are accustomed to being coached. Doctors and industrialists and lawyers are the most difficult to coach. Even when you try to teach them to ski or fly an airplane, a lot of instructors tell me, they don't take directions very well.

Friedman: In the negotiations with Israel and Egypt, did Carter successfully bridge American and Middle Eastern cultures?

Hall: I think his approach was well adapted to the Middle East. The personalized part was important, as it was with Kissinger. We know this because Sadat kept asking about Kissinger. On several occasions, he was reported as saying, "I want to see Henry," because he felt that he had a personal relationship with Kissinger. The more the President can establish a personal relationship with these people in situations of this sort, the better his chances for success. This is an expensive way in terms of time, but it's probably worth it.

Even more so because the Middle East is a top-man culture. Americans have intermediaries between the top and the bottom of an organization, but in Islamic society there are no intermediaries between man and God, and really no intermediaries, in the bureaucratic sense, between the sheik and the peasants. They're used to the fact that the top man makes the decisions. In this instance, Carter's willingness to take the time was probably a very good thing.

Also, Arabs tend to depend upon outsiders to intervene in disputes, and we haven't always understood this. This is one case that Carter, and before him, Kissinger, did understand. The Arabs were depending on the U.S.

to play the role of a strong interventionist in a dispute.

Friedman: You mean something closer to a mediator…?

Hall: I mean intervention. For instance, the law in the Middle East is: if there's a fight and somebody is injured, the crowd is guilty because the crowd didn't stop it. This means disinterested third parties who watch disputes going on share the blame for the disputes. When you grow up in an atmosphere of this type, you can tell people all kinds of things in public because you know there are others there who will stop you from hurting someone or getting hurt. It makes for a very different kind of communication—more volatile but less risky.

Friedman: When you are talking about the people of the Middle East, the mass of the population, the cultural differences seem strong. But when you get to the government and business elites, aren't they all educated in France and the U.S.? Isn't there homogenization of the leaders?

Hall: Leaders these days come from the middle levels of society more and more. It is rare for such people to be bicultural. Children growing up in two cultures can be bicultural, but adults seldom are. Learning another culture is a bit like learning another language. People can learn how to deal with Americans, how to live with Americans. But as soon as they get back on their own home turf, they become what they were in the beginning. Learning another culture simply adds another layer onto the person. But that new culture doesn't change them that much. It doesn't eliminate what's underneath.

When Europeans come to this country, the thing that they appreciate most is what they call "freedom." They feel as though a 10-ton weight had been lifted off their backs. But when you look into what "freedom" is all about to them, it turns out to be a freedom from European bureaucracies and from social pressures to conform. In Switzerland, if you don't sweep your sidewalks every day, your neighbors will get on you. And, also in Switzerland, you can only wash your dishes until a certain time at night because the noise might disturb the neighbors. You can't even flush the john after certain times because that will disturb the neighbors. Freedom from the coercive cloak of your neighbors, the police, and the tax collectors is what American freedom means to many Europeans. So they have adapted to American culture, but in terms of the European culture they experienced first.

Friedman: Most people only experience foreign cultures as tourists. Is there anything tourists could do that would give them perspective on the depth of cultural differences?

Hall: Anything that brings them into much closer contact with the local population, like staying with a family, would help; but they move through so quickly that most people remain isolated. What they can do is train themselves to pay attention, rather close attention, to what they are feeling when things are happening—keeping their own emotional pulse. Keep diaries of what is about different situations that makes people feel happy, sad, hostile, or anxious. Is it because of voice loudness or because those people are too far away and you can't get close to them? Is it the intensity of the transaction or the abruptness of it? What are the details that set transactions apart from what one is used to? It's these little things that make up the entire culture and it's the little things we should pay attention to. When you're walking down the street and some Frenchman talking to a friend steps backward without looking, throws up his arms, and hits you in the face, you get used to watching out for people who are talking and gesticulating. You also give them a lot of room.

Friedman: You seem to have a bias toward cultures with more elaborate systems of nonverbal communication, toward cultures that stress human relationships. Would you prefer to live in a high-context culture?

Hall: Of course, there is no real choice involved. As an American, I know my own culture better than any other in the world and what I know of other cultures, inevitably, is relatively superficial. I can analyze behavior and tell people about things they don't know about themselves. But I also know that the only culture that I'm deeply contexted in is my own, so that regardless of what I know about another culture, I will never really know what is going on.

I want to stress that there is tremendous strength and vitality in this country. We have our problems, as every country has, and we've had more than our share in the last few years. But this is still a very vital, dynamic country. Like all countries, though, we could do some things better and we could be more effective.

In terms of high- and low-context, the U.S. is toward the middle of the scale. The low-context Swiss around Zurich don't even know their neighbors, and colleagues don't know one another. When I was on a cruise some time ago, attending a conference, I was walking with a famous Swiss geographer friend and said, "I suppose you know our friend and colleague, Professor-Doctor Heine Hediger [who was a professor of animal psychology at the University of Zurich]?" This man laughed and said, "You Americans don't understand us Swiss. One of the functions you perform for us is to get us together. We don't know each other!" So they are much more isolated, much more particular.

Friedman: Are we all trapped in our own culture?

Hall: You can't be a person without having a culture and you can't have a body without genes. Culture is the underlying pattern, but how you develop is up to you. Like a body, culture is the end product of multiple evolutionary changes. Whether people are trapped or not depends on the degree to which they allow themselves to perceive and believe in the reality that we call culture. Awareness is our key to freedom.

3

Communication Without Words

Albert Mehrabian

Suppose you are sitting in my office listening to me describe some research I have done on communication. I tell you that feelings are communicated less by the words a person uses than by certain nonverbal means—that, for example, the verbal part of a spoken message has considerably less effect on whether a listener feels liked or disliked than a speaker's facial expression or tone of voice.

So far so good. But suppose I add, "In fact, we've worked out a formula that shows exactly how much each of these components contributes to the effect of the message as a whole. It goes like this: Total Impact=.07 verbal+.38 vocal+.55 facial."

What would you say to *that?* Perhaps you would smile good-naturedly and say, with some feeling, "Baloney!" Or perhaps you would frown and remark acidly, "Isn't science grand." My own response to the first answer would probably be to smile back: the facial part of your message, at least, was positive (55 per cent of the total). The second answer might make me uncomfortable: only the verbal part was positive (seven per cent).

The point here is not only that my reactions would lend credence to the formula but that most listeners would have mixed feelings about my statement. People like to see science march on, but they tend to resent its intrusion into an "art" like the communication of feelings, just as they find analytical and quantitative approaches to the study of personality cold, mechanistic and unacceptable.

Reprinted from *Psychology Today* 2, (September 1968): 145–153. Copyright © 1968, Sussex Publishers, Inc.

The psychologist himself is sometimes plagued by the feeling that he is trying to put a rainbow into a bottle. Fascinated by a complicated and emotionally rich human situation, he begins to study it, only to find in the course of his research that he has destroyed part of the mystique that originally intrigued and involved him. But despite a certain nostalgia for earlier, more intuitive approaches, one must acknowledge that concrete experimental data have added a great deal to our understanding of how feelings are communicated. In fact, as I hope to show, analytical and intuitive findings do not so much conflict as complement each other.

It is indeed difficult to know what another person really feels. He says one thing and does another; he seems to mean something but we have an uneasy feeling it isn't true. The early psychoanalysts, facing this problem of inconsistencies and ambiguities in a person's communications, attempted to resolve it through the concepts of the conscious and the unconscious. They assumed that contradictory messages meant a conflict between superficial, deceitful, or erroneous feelings on the one hand and true attitudes and feelings on the other. Their role, then, was to help the client separate the wheat from the chaff.

The question was, how could this be done? Some analysts insisted that inferring the client's unconscious wishes was a completely intuitive process. Others thought that some nonverbal behavior, such as posture, position and movement, could be used in a more objective way to discover the client's feelings. A favorite technique of Frieda Fromm-Reichmann, for example, was to imitate a client's posture herself in order to obtain some feeling for what he was experiencing.

Thus began the gradual shift away from the idea that communication is primarily verbal, and that the verbal message includes distortions or ambiguities due to unobservable motives that only experts can discover.

Language, though, can be used to communicate almost anything. By comparison, nonverbal behavior is very limited in range. Usually, it is used to communicate feelings, likings and preferences, and it customarily reinforces or contradicts the feelings that are communicated verbally. Less often, it adds a new dimension of sorts to a verbal message, as when a salesman describes his product to a client and simultaneously conveys, non-verbally, the impression that he likes the client.

A great many forms of nonverbal behavior can communicate feelings: touching, facial expression, tone of voice, spatial distance from the addressee, relaxation of posture, rate of speech, number of errors in speech. Some of these are generally recognized as informative. Untrained adults and children easily infer that they are liked or disliked from certain facial expressions, from whether (and how) someone touches them, and from a speaker's tone of voice. Other behavior, such as posture, has a more subtle effect. A listener may sense how someone feels about him from the way the person sits while talking to him, but he may have trouble identifying precisely what his impression comes from.

Correct intuitive judgments of the feelings or attitudes of others are especially difficult when different degrees of feeling, or contradictory kinds of feeling, are expressed simultaneously through different forms of behavior. As I have pointed out, there is a distinction between verbal and vocal information (vocal information being what is lost when speech is written down—intonation, tone, stress, length and frequency of pauses, and so on), and the two kinds of information do not always communicate the same feeling. This distinction, which has been recognized for some time, has shed new light on certain types of communication. Sarcasm, for example, can be defined as a message in which the information transmitted vocally contradicts the information transmitted verbally. Usually the verbal information is positive and the vocal is negative, as in "Isn't science grand."

Through the use of an electronic filter, it is possible to measure the degree of liking communicated vocally. What the filter does is eliminate the higher frequencies of recorded speech, so that words are unintelligible but most vocal qualities remain. (For women's speech, we eliminate frequencies higher than about 200 cycles per second; for men, frequencies over about 100 cycles per second.) When people are asked to judge the degree of

liking conveyed by the filtered speech, they perform the task rather easily and with a significant amount of agreement.

This method allows us to find out, in a given message, just how inconsistent the information communicated in words and the information communicated vocally really are. We ask one group to judge the amount of liking conveyed by a transcription of what was said, the verbal part of the message. A second group judges the vocal component, and a third group judges the impact of the complete recorded message. In one study of this sort we found that, when the verbal and vocal components of a message agree (both positive or both negative), the message as a whole is judged a little more positive or a little more negative than either component by itself. But when vocal information contradicts verbal, vocal wins out. If someone calls you "honey" in a nasty tone of voice, you are likely to feel disliked; it is also possible to say "I hate you" in a way that conveys exactly the opposite feeling.

Besides the verbal and vocal characteristics of speech, there are other, more subtle, signals of meaning in a spoken message. For example, everyone makes mistakes when he talks—unnecessary repetitions, stutterings, the omission of parts of words, incomplete sentences, "ums" and "ahs." In a number of studies of speech errors, George Mahl of Yale University has found that errors become more frequent as the speaker's discomfort or anxiety increases. It might be interesting to apply this index in an attempt to detect deceit (though on some occasions it might be risky: confidence men are notoriously smooth talkers).

Timing is also highly informative. How long does a speaker allow silent periods to last, and how long does he wait before he answers his partner? How long do his utterances tend to be? How often does he interrupt his partner, or wait an inappropriately long time before speaking? Joseph Matarazzo and his colleagues at the University of Oregon have found that each of these speech habits is stable from person to person, and each tells something about the speaker's personality and about his feelings toward and status in relation to his partner.

Utterance duration, for example, is a very stable quality in a person's speech; about 30 seconds long on the average. But when someone talks to a partner whose status is higher than his own, the more the high-status person nods his head the longer the speaker's utterances become. If the high-status person changes his own customary speech pattern toward longer or shorter utterances, the lower-status person will change his own speech in the same direction. If the high-status person often interrupts the speaker, or creates long silences, the speaker is likely to become quite uncomfortable. These are things that can be observed outside the laboratory as well as under experimental conditions. If you have an employee who makes you uneasy and seems not to respect you, watch him the next time you talk to him—perhaps he is failing to follow the customary low-status pattern.

Immediacy or directness is another good source of information about feelings. We use more distant forms of communication when the act of communicating is undesirable or uncomfortable. For example, some people would rather transmit discontent with an employee's work through a third party than do it themselves, and some find it easier to communicate negative feelings in writing than by telephone or face to face.

Distance can show a negative attitude toward the message itself, as well as toward the act of delivering it. Certain forms of speech are more distant than others, and they show fewer positive feelings for the subject referred to. A speaker might say "Those people need help," which is more distant than "These people need help," which is in turn even more distant than "These people need our help." Or he might say "Sam and I have been having dinner," which has less immediacy than "Sam and I are having dinner."

Facial expression, touching, gestures, self-manipulation (such as scratching), changes in body position, and head movements—all these express a person's positive and negative attitudes, both at the moment and in general, and many reflect status relationships as well. Movements of the limbs and head, for example, not only indicate one's attitude toward a specific set of circumstances but relate to how dominant, and how anxious, one generally tends to be in social situations. Gross changes in body position, such as shifting in the chair, may show negative feelings toward the person one is talking to. They may also be cues: "It's your turn to talk," or "I'm about to get out of here, so finish what you're saying."

Posture is used to indicate both liking and status. The more a person leans toward his addressee, the more positively he feels about him. Relaxation of posture is a good indicator of both attitude and status, and one that we have been able to measure quite precisely. Three categories have been established for relaxation in a seated position: least relaxation is indicated by muscular tension in the hands and rigidity of posture; moderate relaxation is indicated by a forward lean of about 20 degrees and a sideways lean of less than 10 degrees, a curved back, and, for women, an open arm position; and extreme relaxation is indicated by a reclining angle greater than 20 degrees and a sideways lean greater than 10 degrees.

Our findings suggest that a speaker relaxes either very little or a great deal when he dislikes the person he is talking to, and to a moderate degree when he likes his companion. It seems that extreme tension occurs with threatening addressees, and extreme relaxation with nonthreatening, disliked addressees. In particular, men tend to become tense when talking to other men whom they dislike; on the other hand, women talking to men *or* women and men talking to women show dislike through extreme relaxation. As for status, people relax most with a low-status addressee, second most with a peer, and least with someone of higher status than their own. Body orientation also shows status: in both sexes, it is least direct toward women with low status and most direct toward disliked men of high status. In part, body orientation seems to be determined by whether one regards one's partner as threatening.

The more you like a person, the more time you are likely to spend looking into his eyes as you talk to him. Standing close to your partner and facing him directly (which makes eye contact easier) also indicate positive feelings. And you are likely to stand or sit closer to your peers than you do to addressees whose status is either lower or higher than yours.

What I have said so far has been based on research studies performed, for the most part, with college students from the middle and upper-middle classes. One interesting question about communication, however, concerns young children from lower socioeconomic levels. Are these children, as some have suggested, more responsive to implicit channels of communication than middle and upper-class children are?

Morton Wiener and his colleagues at Clark University had a group of middle- and lower-class children play learning games in which the reward for learning was praise. The child's responsiveness to the verbal and vocal parts of the praise-reward was measured by how much he learned. Praise came in two forms: the objective words "right" and "correct," and the more affective or evaluative words, "good" and "fine." All four words were spoken sometimes in a positive tone of voice and sometimes neutrally.

Positive intonation proved to have a dramatic effect on the learning rate of the lower-class group. They learned much faster when the vocal part of the message was positive than when it was neutral. Positive intonation affected the middle-class group as well, but not nearly as much.

If children of lower socioeconomic groups are more responsive to facial expression, posture and touch as well as to vocal communication, that fact could have interesting applications to elementary education. For example, teachers could be explicitly trained to be aware of, and to use, the forms of praise (nonverbal or verbal) that would be likely to have the greatest effect on their particular students.

Another application of experimental data on communication is to the interpretation and treatment of schizophrenia. The literature on schizophrenia has for some time emphasized that parents of schizophrenic children give off contradictory signals simultaneously. Perhaps the parent tells the child in words that he loves him, but his posture conveys a negative attitude. According to the "double-bind" theory of schizophrenia, the child who perceives simultaneous contradictory feelings in his par-

ent does not know how to react: should he respond to the positive part of the message, or to the negative? If he is frequently placed in this paralyzing situation, he may learn to respond with contradictory communications of his own. The boy who sends a birthday card to his mother and signs it "Napoleon" says that he likes his mother and yet denies that he is the one who likes her.

In an attempt to determine whether parents of disturbed children really do emit more inconsistent messages about their feelings than other parents do, my colleagues and I have compared what these parents communicate verbally and vocally with what they show through posture. We interviewed parents of moderately and quite severely disturbed children, in the presence of the child, about the child's problem. The interview was video-recorded without the parents' knowledge, so that we could analyze their behavior later on. Our measurements supplied both the amount of inconsistency between the parents' verbal-vocal and postural communications, and the total amount of liking that the parents communicated.

According to the double-bind theory, the parents of the more disturbed children should have behaved more inconsistently than the parents of the less disturbed children. This was not confirmed: there was no significant difference between the two groups. However, the *total amount* of positive feeling communicated by parents of the more disturbed children was less than that communicated by the other group.

This suggests that (1) negative communications toward disturbed children occur because the child is a problem and therefore elicits them, or (2) the negative attitude precedes the child's disturbance. It may also be that both factors operate together, in a vicious circle.

If so, one way to break the cycle is for the therapist to create situations in which the parent can have better feelings toward the child. A more positive attitude from the parent may make the child more responsive to his directives, and the spiral may begin to move up instead of down. In our own work with disturbed children, this kind of procedure has been used to good effect.

If one puts one's mind to it, one can think of a great many other applications for the findings I have described, though not all of them concern serious problems. Politicians, for example, are careful to maintain eye contact with the television camera when they speak, but they are not always careful about how they sit when they debate another candidate of, presumably, equal status.

Public relations men might find a use for some of the subtler signals of feeling. So might Don Juans. And so might ordinary people, who could try watching other people's signals and changing their own, for fun at a party or in a spirit of experimentation at home. I trust that does not strike you as a cold, manipulative suggestion, indicating dislike for the human race. I assure you that, if you had more than a transcription of words to judge from (seven per cent of total message), it would not.

REFERENCES

Davitz, Joel, ed. *The Communication of Emotional Meaning*, New York: McGraw-Hill, 1964.

Hall, Edward. *The Silent Language*, Garden City, NY: Doubleday, 1959; paperback, New York: Fawcett, 1961.

Knapp, Peter, ed. *Expression of the Emotions in Man*, New York: International University Press, 1963.

Wiener, Morton and Albert Mehrabian. *Language Within Language: Immediacy, A Channel in Verbal Communication*, New York: Appleton-Century-Crofts, 1968.

4

The Role of Culture and Perception in Communication

Marshall R. Singer

Back in the 1960s I argued that every identity group has a culture of its own.[1] I also argued then that every individual is a part of perhaps hundreds of different identity groups simultaneously and that one learns, and becomes a part of, all of the cultures with which one identifies. I will make those same arguments in the pages that follow.

At the time I wrote that article some anthropologists said that I was destroying the concept of culture. If it was to have any meaning it had to be applied only to very large groups like total societies or large language or ethnic groupings. As I saw it, the way the anthropologists viewed the problem forced them to describe the large degree of cultural variation that exists *within* every society as being "subcultural." For me that didn't seem to be a logical or useful way to deal with the problem—particularly when I realized that I was in some ways much closer to some "subcultures" in other societies than I was to many within my own. It seemed to me then—and still does today—much more logical and useful to talk about the culture of each group and then to examine—for each total society—the groups that comprise it. Each society is cer-

tainly different from every other society, but that is because no two societies contain all of the same groups and only those groups. I suppose it's a little like looking at two different kinds of cake. A chocolate cake is certainly quite different from, let's say, a fruitcake, yet they are both still cakes and as such have more in common with each other than either does to, let's say, a chocolate candy bar. But that does not distract from the fact that the chocolate in the cake and the chocolate in the candy bar are much more similar to each other than they are to any of the other ingredients of either the cake or candy bar.

Culinary analogies notwithstanding, over the course of the decades anthropologists themselves have now independently come to take a position very similar to the position I took then. Certainly they have not done so because of me but rather because of the compelling logic of the argument. In any event, in the pages that follow I hope to show the reader how the individual interacts with the groups of which she or he forms a part and how both the individual and the groups affect each other.

Now with this work, I am about to anger some anthropologists again, because I am pushing the concept still further. I am now going to argue that because no person is a part of all, and only, the same groups as anyone else and because each person ranks the attitudes, values, and beliefs of the groups to which he or she belongs differently, *each individual must be considered to be culturally unique*. Notice that I am *not* arguing that every person is a culture unto herself or himself. Culture is, after all, a group-related phenomenon. What I will argue is that each individual in this world is a member of a unique collection of groups. No two humans share only and exactly the same group memberships, or exactly the same ranking of the importance, to themselves, of the group membership they do share. Thus each person must be culturally unique.

If I am correct in this assertion—and I hope to be able to convince the reader in the pages that follow that I am—this means that every interpersonal communication must, to some degree, also be an intercultural communication. The implications of this conclusion, if true, are rather enormous. Some may have

Dr. Singer is Professor of International and Intercultural Affairs in the Graduate School of Public and International Affairs at the University of Pittsburgh. This is a revision of the first chapter of his book *Intercultural Communication: A Perceptual Approach* first published in 1987. A new version of his book is soon to be published by Intercultural Press, Yarmouth, Maine.

difficulty in accepting it. I hope the argument I make is sufficiently convincing that over the course of the next decades most scholars—regardless of discipline—will come to accept this way of viewing interpersonal and intergroup interactions.

There is another important concept I will introduce here. I will argue that every communication relationship has a power component attached to it, and we might as well deal with it openly and consciously. Until now very few communication specialists have been prepared to deal with the power aspect of the communication process. On the other hand, most political scientists until now have failed to recognize the importance of cultural differences in the situations they study. It is one of my most deeply held convictions that the study of intercultural communication informs the study of political behavior. It is also my contention that any study of communication relationships that ignores the power aspect of those relationships is one that misses a very important element of all communications.

One additional point that must be made: I do not believe that "better communication" is a panacea. Conflict at every level of analysis has always persisted and probably always will. I am convinced that to the degree that interpersonal, intergroup, or international communication can be facilitated (a) there is likely to be less misperception and fear of other actors, and (b) at least the actors can be certain, if they are in conflict, that they both agree on what the conflict actually is about.

In many ways the world is shrinking at an incredible rate. Strange and often frightening groups are coming into contact with each other at ever accelerating rates. Isolation is unthinkable. More people are living and working and studying among people of differing cultures today than at any previous time in history. That experience can be made easier, more productive, and more satisfying if we better understand the processes at work. And while intercultural communication may be a difficult task, it is not impossible.

CULTURE: WHAT IS IT?

Of all the animals known to exist, the human animal is perhaps the most social. Particularly in our earliest years, but throughout our entire lives as well, people exist—and must exist—in relationships with other human beings. Each of the humans with whom one comes into contact brings to that relationship his or her own view of the universe. More important, perhaps, each of the groups in which one has been raised or in which one has spent a good deal of time will have conditioned the individual to view the world from its perspective.

As animals, all of us must eat, drink, sleep, find shelter, give and receive affection, and meet all of the other biologic requirements "that flesh is heir to." But what we eat, when we eat, and how we eat are all behaviors we have learned from the groups in which we have grown up. Not only the language I speak and the way I think but even *what* I see, hear, taste, touch, and smell are conditioned by the cultures in which I have been raised.

Benjamin Lee Whorf, the noted linguist, has written:

> We are thus introduced to a new principle of relativity, which holds that all observers are not led by the same physical evidence to the same picture of the universe, unless their linguistic backgrounds are similar, or can in some way be calibrated.[2]

I would go a step further and substitute the word *cultural* for the word *linguistic*.

Every culture has its own language[3] or code, to be sure, but language is the manifestation—verbal or otherwise—of the perceptions, attitudes, values, beliefs, and disbelief systems that the group holds. Language, once established, further constrains the individual to perceive in certain ways, but I would argue that language is merely one of the ways in which groups maintain and reinforce similarity of perception.

Genetically, we inherit from our parents those physical characteristics that distinguish us as their offspring. Admittedly there is a good deal of individual variation physically and experientially, but there is a good deal of similarity. Given two white parents the overwhelming probability is that the offspring will be white. Given two English-speaking parents the overwhelming probability is that the offspring will speak English. The difference is that physical identity is—within a given range of probability—fixed, while cultural identity is not. The son of two white parents will always remain white no matter what happens to him after birth, but the son of two English-speaking parents may never speak English if immediately after birth he is raised by a totally non-English-speaking group. Thus while physical inheritance is relatively immutable, cultural inheritance is ever changing. The fascinating aspect of cultural conditioning, however, is that while there is theoretically an almost infinite number of possibilities, in fact, the number of group-learned experiences to which most individuals are exposed is amazingly limited. Thus for example, while there may be a whole world to explore, if not an entire universe, the incredibly overwhelming majority of individuals who inhabit this planet never stray more than a few miles from their place of birth. They will, in all probability, speak the language that their parents spoke; practice the religion that their parents practiced; support the political parties that their parents supported; and in broad outline accept most of the cultural perceptions that their parents accepted. In sum, they will perceive the world in a manner strikingly similar to the way their parents perceived the world. That is precisely what makes them a part of the same broad cultural groups of which their parents formed a part. All will deviate from the perceptions of their parents, of course (some only mildly, others more radically), but that is inevitable because every individual is unique. So too are the experiences that every person has. While most of those experiences will be learned from other groups into which the individual will be socialized in the course of his or her life, some of those experiences will not have been group related.

What is more, cultures themselves are constantly changing (in part because the environments in which people live are constantly changing), and thus people's perceptions of the world around them are also constantly changing. Further, some people—particularly in Western societies—rebel against the attitudes and values of their parents and adopt different group values for themselves. Though most people in the West go through a period

of rebellion while in their teens, by the time they are adults the vast majority seem to have returned to the cultures of their parents. Each of us is a member of a finite number of different identity groups, but it is a comparatively small number compared to the incredibly large number that exist in the world. A very large number of the most important groups to which we belong are the same groups to which our parents belonged.

It is a most basic premise of this work that *a pattern of learned, group-related perceptions— including both verbal and nonverbal language, attitudes, values, belief systems, disbelief systems, and behaviors—that is accepted and expected by an identity group is called a culture. Since, by definition, each identity group has its own pattern of perceptions and behavioral norms and its own language or code (understood most clearly by members of that group), each group may be said to have its own culture.*

Years ago Ruth Benedict said:

> The life history of the individual is first and foremost an accommodation to the patterns and standards traditionally handed down in his community. From the moment of his birth the customs into which he is born shape his experience and behavior. By the time he can talk, he is a little creature of his culture, and by the time he is grown and able to take part in its activities, its habits are his habits, its beliefs his beliefs, its impossibilities his impossibilities. Every child that is born into his group will share them with him. . . .[4]

And while she was referring there to total societal groups, everything she said then still holds with reference to all identity groups.

The early cultural anthropologists wanted to collect data on how different groups met their biological needs and related to their environments. In order to do that they felt that they had to find remote, isolated, "primitive" groups that had not been "contaminated" by contact with Western societies. Thus they went to the South Pacific, to isolated American Indian reservations, to the Latin American mountains and remote jungles, and to the Asian subcontinent looking for people who were presumed to have been so isolated that they would have been living and doing things the same ways for millenia. In the process they created the impression that it was only those "quaint" and "primitive" peoples who had cultures that were clearly differentiated from one another. Later anthropologists corrected that misconception by rightly demonstrating that all peoples have unique histories, belief systems, attitudes, values, traditions, languages, and accepted and expected patterns of behavior, and that these ensembles constitute culture. But even there the notion persisted that one had to look at a total society in order to understand its culture. Thanks most, perhaps, to the work of Benjamin Lee Whorf and Edward Sapir, the tremendously important role of language in shaping patterns of thinking—and thus the relationship between language and culture—was established. But in so doing they also created the impression that only peoples who spoke distinctly different languages—not dialects—had distinctive cultural patterns. Only in very recent times have scholars come to accept the notion that *every group* that shares a similar pattern of perceptions—with all that implies—constitutes a culture. Since every identity group has somewhat different learned cultural ensembles, in greater or lesser degree, then every identity group may be said to have its own culture.

C. T. Patrick Diamond paraphrases as follows a statement of P. Kay published in *Current Directions in Anthropology*:

> The worlds of café society, ethnic and sexual minorities, the social elite, professional or occupational groups and age cohorts each represent a shared but distinctive perspective that orders the respective field of experience to provide identification and solidarity for its members. Such groups possess sets of implicit assumptions or bases for discrimination. These conventional understandings provide their culture or their tacit theory of the world.[5]

Thus at least some modern anthropologists also share the view that every group has a culture of its own.

Why the importance of making this distinction? Because looking at it this way enables us to apply the tools and techniques of intercultural analysis and communication to all interpersonal, intergroup, and international interactions. Further, it enables us to look at any totality—a small informal group, a large organization, a city, or a tribe or nation—and ask, What are the identity groups present in that unit of analysis? To what degree are there linkages among the groupings? To what degree are the unit identities stronger than the group identities that comprise it? To what degree are the group identities stronger? How can communication between groups be encouraged? These and dozens of similar questions must be answered if the effectiveness of personal, group, or national communication is to be increased. And the effectiveness of those communications will be increased if we constantly keep in mind the cultural differences that must be dealt with.

Henry Hoijer has said:

> . . . to the extent that languages differ markedly from each other, so should we expect to find significant and formidable barriers to cross-cultural communication and understanding. . . .
>
> It is, however, easy to exaggerate . . . the . . . barriers to intercultural understanding. No culture is wholly isolated, self-contained, and unique. There are important resemblances between all known cultures—resemblances that stem in part from diffusion (itself an evidence of successful intercultural communication) and in part from the fact that all cultures are built around biological, psychological, and social characteristics common to all mankind. . . . Intercultural communication, however wide the differences between cultures may be, is not impossible. It is simply more or less difficult, depending on the degree of difference between the cultures concerned.[6]

To this Diamond adds the following, this time paraphrasing the psychologist G. A. Kelly:

> People belong to the same cultural group not merely because they behave alike nor because they expect the same things of others but especially because they construe their experiences in similar ways. However, people are not help-

lessly suspended in their culture. The task is to generate the imagination needed to envision the infinity of possibilities still open to people of any group; that is to construe their way out of cultural controls.[7]

PERCEPTIONS AND HUMAN BEHAVIOR

My first conscious awareness of the importance of perceptions to human behavior began with an incident when I was still a graduate student. At that time esoteric foods like chocolate-covered ants, fried grasshoppers, smoked rattlesnake meat, and sweet-and-sour mouse tails, were the culinary fad. Upon moving into a new apartment, I received from a friend (as a housewarming gift) a whole carton of these canned delicacies. Having at that time rather prosaic food habits, I did not proceed to consume the entire carton. Indeed, it sat untouched for the better part of a year while I alternately toyed with the idea of trying one of those less-than-tempting "goodies" myself or throwing the entire carton in the garbage. One evening while putting out a whole array of cheeses and other edibles in preparation for a cocktail party I was about to hold, it occurred to me that my opportunity had arrived. Without saying anything to anyone about what I planned, I opened a can of fried caterpillars into a little white dish and set them out on the table along with the other foods. Then I waited to see what would happen. Halfway through the evening one of the unsuspecting young ladies I had invited to the party came up to me and said, "Marshall, those fried shrimp you put out were delicious." "Fried shrimp?" I asked as innocently as I could. "I didn't serve any fried shrimp." "Yes you did," she insisted. "They were in a little white plate on the table. In fact, they were so good I ate most of them myself." "Oh," I said, pausing for maximum effect, "those weren't fried shrimp, they were fried caterpillars."

Virtually the moment I said that the smile disappeared from her face, her complexion turned markedly green, and she proceeded to become terribly sick all over my living room floor. I realized immediately—as I was cleaning up the floor—that what I had done was a terrible trick to play on anyone, and I have never done it again. But as I reflected on that incident, it amazed me that a food that could have been thought to be so delicious one moment—when it was *perceived* to be fried shrimp—could be so repugnant the next, when it was *perceived* to be something else. Suppose they really had been fried shrimp, and I had merely been pulling her leg? Would that have changed her physical reaction? I doubt it. In this case, as in most cases involving human behavior, reality was less important than one's perception of reality.

It is not the stimulus itself that produces specific human reactions and/or actions but rather how the stimulus is perceived by the individual that matters most for human behavior. It is perhaps the most basic law of human behavior that people act or react on the basis of the way in which they perceive the external world.

PERCEPTIONS: WHAT ARE THEY?

By *perception,* I mean the process—and it is a process—by which an individual selects, evaluates, and organizes stimuli from the external environment. Perceptions are the ways in which a person experiences the world. They also determine the ways in which we behave toward it. That "world" includes symbols, things, people, groups of people, ideas, events, ideologies, and even faith. In sum, we experience *everything* in the world not "as it is"—because there is no way that we can know the world "as it is"—but only as the world comes to us through our sensory receptors. From there these stimuli go instantly into the "data-storage banks" of our brains, where they have to pass through the filters of our censor screens, our decoding mechanisms, and the collectivity of everything we have learned from the day we were born. All of the information stored in the brain—including the "program" we have learned that teaches us how to learn about new data—in turn affects (if not determines) not only what relatively few bits of data we will attend to (from the literally millions available) but also how we will interpret each bit that we do select.

Perceptions, attitudes, values, and belief systems are not all the same thing (although throughout this work I will sometimes refer to *perceptions* as a shorthand way of referring to them all), but they all affect each other and they all constantly interact.

Technically speaking, group-related, learned perceptions (including verbal and non-verbal codes), attitudes, values, and belief and disbelief systems plus accepted and expected codes of behavior, taught by the groups with which we identify, are what constitutes culture. Perceptions that are not group taught (such as individual physical differences in sensory receptors, body chemistry, or individual unique experiences) should not be considered part of cultural perceptions. Neither should physical or environmental factors that affect perceptions. The trouble is that the distinction between these types of perception is extremely blurred.

They are all closely interrelated. G. A. Kelly has argued:

> Meaning is not extracted from Nature but projected by people upon it. People's behavior can be understood only in terms of their own constructs; that is, from their own internal frames of reference.
>
> Even people's most familiar constructs are not objective observations of what is really there; they are instead inventions of personal and group culture.[8]

Hence, virtually every message to which we attend will be *at least indirectly* affected by our cultural conditioning. Further, when we have finished discussing all of the factors that affect perceptions the reader will see more clearly, I think, what a profound effect our cultures do have on the way we perceive and what a minor effect (by comparison) other factors have in most cases. Thus if I am somewhat imprecise in the way I sometimes use the terms *culture* and *perceptions* synonymously, I ask the reader to forgive me. It should be understood, however, whenever I do use them synonymously that I am referring to *group-related, learned* perceptions only. I suspect that it will be easier for most readers to forgive some imprecision than it would be for them to forgive having constantly to wade through the phrase "the totality of all of the attitudes, values, beliefs. . . ."

Take any stimulus, whatever that stimulus may be—a person, an event, an idea—it doesn't matter. On the basis of all the previous stimuli that have gone into our data-storage banks and the way we have organized those stimuli, we make judgments about the new stimulus. Those judgments are called attitudes. Something is good or bad, right or wrong, useful or dangerous, beautiful or ugly. Each of the groups into which we have been socialized (and as we shall see shortly, we are socialized into a great many) teaches us *its* attitudes toward those stimuli. Many of the groups with which we identify will teach us conflicting judgments about the same stimuli. In some cases even the same group will, on specific issues, teach conflicting attitudes. Conflicting or not, what is important to note here is that *every* group teaches its members what *its* preferred attitudes are.

A value on the other hand is a desired event or situation—something we would like to see happen. After twenty-five years of research on human behavior Milton Rokeach says of values:

> A *value* is an enduring belief that a specific mode of conduct or end-state of existence is personally or socially preferable to an opposite or converse mode of conduct or end-state of existence. A *value system* is an enduring organization of beliefs concerning preferable modes of conduct or end-states of existence along a continuum of relative importance.[9]

He goes on to argue that values can be broken down into two categories: *institutional values,* which concern "desirable modes of conduct," and *terminal values,* which concern "desirable end-states of existence."[10]

Obviously, values are closely intertwined with attitudes. We desire certain events or situations above others because we have learned that they are good, right, and/or useful. Which attitudes and values the individual will adopt as his own will depend in very large part on the ranking he makes of the various group identities he holds at any given time. Yet the complexity of the process is such that those attitudes and values, in turn, will affect our identity, which in turn, will affect how we perceive any new stimulus. *The totality of all of the perceptions, attitudes, values, and identities that we hold—and the way we rank them at any moment in time—is referred to as a belief system.* Holding a particular belief system implies, however, that there are a host of other belief systems that we do not hold. Those are labeled disbelief systems. If, for example, I believe that people are basically hostile and "out to get me," then I do not believe that people are basically friendly and helpful. If I am a Buddhist believer, I am not a Buddhist nonbeliever. Nor will I likely be a Christian, Muslim, Jewish, Hindu, or any other kind of believer.

The totality of all of our group-related, learned perceptions, attitudes, values, and belief and disbelief systems *plus the ranking we make in any specific context* of all the groups with which we identify (our identities), plus the behaviors we normally exhibit, constitute what I call our personal culture. Some—indeed, even many—of those perceptions, attitudes, values, and identities we hold may be totally (more often partially) contradictory. Despite that, we somehow manage to hold them all and to apply different ones to our behavior in different situations. Further, there are times when our own behavior can alter those very perceptions, attitudes, values, identities, and beliefs we hold. Thus what I am suggesting is a circle of causality. Each affects the other and is in turn affected by them. (See Figure 1.[11])

Virtually all of these processes, of course, occur completely below our level of consciousness, and they occur continuously from the moment of our birth. We are hardly ever aware on a conscious level that they are occurring at all. They are almost totally involuntary processes despite the fact that they are very largely learned. But learned they are. Particularly in those early, formative years our most basic belief systems and our corresponding disbelief systems are being formed. And once formed, they change only very slowly—or when we are confronted by some event that is so dramatic and/or so discordant with an attitude, value, identity, or belief that we have held dear that we are forced to reevaluate. Most often we are forced to reevaluate when we interact with people who have different attitudes, values, or belief systems. While the ranking of our identities change from context to context, it is probably true that once hardened, attitudes and values change much more slowly than do other perceptions. Our most basic "central beliefs" (almost always held subconsciously) probably never change at all.

FACTORS THAT AFFECT PERCEPTION

There are a great variety of factors that affect perception. There is no question that the learned factors are by far the most important. But before we discuss them, there are some other factors that are not unimportant, and we will discuss those first.

Physical Determinants of Perception

The only way we can know about the world outside our own bodies is by the impressions of that outside world picked up by our sensory receptors. While most of us have all of these same sensory receptors, we know that no two

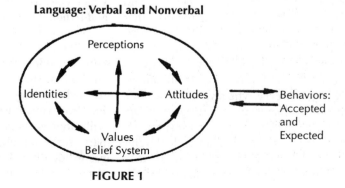

Language: Verbal and Nonverbal

FIGURE 1

individuals are identical physically. For example, empirical evidence has proven that the swirls on the tips of every human's fingers are ever so slightly different from anyone else's. It must then follow that each person's sense of touch must also be ever so slightly different. Yet far more important for the way people view the universe may be the still unanswered questions of physical variations in other sensory receptors. What about the configuration of cones and rods in the retina of the eye, or taste buds on the tongue, or fibers in the ear, or any of the other physical receptors of external stimuli? *If no two individuals have identical physical receptors of stimuli, then it must follow, on the basis of physical evidence alone, that no two individuals can perceive the external world identically.*

Yet physical differences in sensory receptors, while important, may be the least of the factors contributing to differences in perception. Consider for a moment that peculiar combination of physical and psychological factors called personality or temperament that makes each of us unique. Some scholars would argue that temperament is one of the key factors determining how we perceive the external world.[12] While I'm not certain that I would place it in as central a position with regard to perceptions, there is no doubt that it is a contributing factor.

Which of the factors that go into making up temperament are physical, and which are learned—and to what degree they are learned—it is impossible to say at this point in our knowledge. We know that some children are born with incredibly placid personalities, while others are born hyperactive. Certainly that is not learned. What are probably learned, however, are acceptable and unacceptable ways of coping with those physical characteristics. What is learned is that other people react to us in certain ways if we follow one behavior pattern and differently if we follow another.

Before I leave the subject of physical determinants of perception, there are a whole range of other physical differences that make us unique and deserve to be mentioned here because of the ways in which they affect our perceptions. I'm thinking here of the vast array of physical characteristics we inherit at birth. Height, weight, gender, skin color, hair texture, physical handicaps of one sort or another all have an impact on how we will perceive the world. It is not the physical characteristics themselves that necessarily determine our perceptions but rather other people's reactions to these physical characteristics that are so important in shaping our view of ourselves and of the world.

In summary, while I do not believe that physical factors are the most important determinant as to how individuals perceive the world, what I have attempted to show is that physical differences *alone* make it impossible that any two humans could perceive the world identically. That fact by itself would make it impossible for any two humans to communicate with 100 percent accuracy. As we shall see as we proceed, other factors individually and collectively make the probability of accurate communication even more remote and difficult to achieve.

Environmental Determinants of Perception

No matter how good, bad, or different people's visual sensory receptors are, in the absence of sufficient light no color can be perceived; in the absence of all light no visual images whatever can be received. Similarly if a sound is made above or below the threshold at which the human ear is capable of sensing it, no sound will be heard. (It is important for us to make the distinction, as we will later in greater detail, between stimuli that are received on the conscious level and those that are received below the level of consciousness. What I am discussing here are the factors that affect the perception of the stimuli, whether at the conscious or subconscious level.)

Physical environment also affects the way we perceive things. There is increasing evidence that people who live in tropical areas of the world may see reds and oranges very differently from the way people living in the Arctic see those colors. People living in a desert environment or a rain forest will certainly have very different perceptions of water. It is not an accident that Eskimos have twenty-seven different words for snow. And indeed

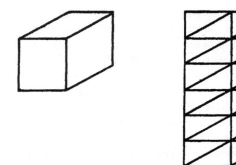

E   F

FIGURE 2 From Willis D. Ellis, *A Source Book of Gestalt Psychology* (New York: Humanities Press, 1967). Reprinted by permission of Humanities Press and Routledge & Kegal Paul Ltd.

people who grew up in a big city probably perceive a great many things very differently than do people who grew up on a farm in the country.

Relationship of stimulus to surroundings. Bernard Berelson and Gary Steiner say: "Even the simplest experiences are organized by the perceiver; and the perceived characteristics of any part are a function of the whole to which it appears to belong."[13] Observe Figure 2. The figure E is present in F, but it is very difficult to perceive it there consciously because of the surrounding elements in F.

What has been said thus far also applies to size. Look at Figures 3 and 4. Correct! The inner circles in both drawings in Figure 3 are the same size, as are the lines in Figure 4. Once again the surrounding elements (circles in Fig-

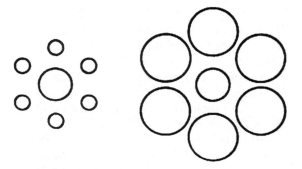

FIGURE 3 From Bernard Berelson and Gary A. Steiner, *Human Behavior: An Inventory of Scientific Findings* (Harcourt Brace Jovanovich, Inc., 1964). Reprinted by permission of the publisher.

ure 3, lines in Figure 4) distort and determine what we see. Subconsciously we may be able to see the similarity in these figures, but on a conscious level we would "swear" that they were different. Everything—including perceptions of "reality"—is relative and contextual.

All of these figures are presented here merely to demonstrate that we can't always trust our perceptions—even when they are culturally neutral. What we see may very well depend on what surrounds it, or what it is near. But many of the most important of our perceptions—like our attitudes, values, and beliefs—are not culturally neutral. Rather they have been taught by the groups that are most important to us. Further, everything that has been shown here about visual perception could be replicated for all of the other senses as well. It is just easier to reproduce pictures than it is to reproduce sounds, tastes, or smells.

What is more, different cultures will not even see the same things we do. Go back to Figure 4. Research has indicated that some cultures have no difficulty in seeing that the horizontal lines are of equal length.[14] It is precisely these kinds of differences in perception that are so very difficult to deal with. How do I communicate accurately with someone who perceives differently than I do when it would never occur to me that that person could possibly perceive differently?

Learned Determinants of Perception

Far more important than either physical or environmental differences in determining an individual's perceptions of the external world are the *learned* factors involved in the reception, organization, and processing of sensory data.

Even identical twins born into and raised by the same family (and thus presumed to have the same physical and learned inheritance) will not have identical perceptions of the world. If one could accurately measure perceptions, there is no doubt that the degree to which twins share similarity of perceptions would be considerably higher than for most other individuals, but those perceptions would be far from identical. Certainly the younger

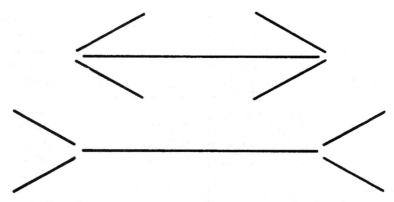

FIGURE 4 The Muller-Lyer illusion. From D. Price-Williams, "Cross-Cultural Studies," *New Horizons in Psychology*, ed. Brian M. Foss (Pelican Books, 1966), 398. Copyright © Penguin Books.

the identical twins were at the time the test was given the more similar their perceptions would likely be, but even so, anyone who lives with twins knows how different they can be, from the earliest age. Looking in from the outside, someone who is not a part of the family may not notice those differences. Indeed, the outsider is much more likely to be struck by the similarity of the children than by the differences. But a parent or siblings, from the first weeks, have no difficulty telling them apart physically, and by the end of a few months are amazed at the personality differences. Why this is so, is difficult to explain. It's relatively easy to understand that as twins get older their experiences are increasingly dissimilar, but it is startling to see how what appear to be minuscule variations in their exposure to the outside world can produce such profound differences in even the youngest children. Perhaps one caught a cold and the other did not. Perhaps while the twins were resting outdoors a bird flew close to one and startled it but was unnoticed by the other. Perhaps a dog "nipped" one and not the other. Whatever the specifics there is no question that while their experiences may indeed be far more similar than for most people, they are never identical. And because those experiences are not identical, they simply will not view the world identically.

It would push the concept of "personal culture" beyond credibility to argue that two very young identical twins would have different personal cultures since presumably each would have been exposed to all and only the same group-related perceptions. However, it would not violate the concept to argue that as the twins got older and did things separately their personal cultures would diverge. After all, *all* children are slowly, gradually, but inevitably, socialized into the multitude of cultures of which they ultimately become a part. On the other hand, it would not be incorrect to argue that even at a very early age identical twins do not have identical perceptions.

If for physical and experiential reasons it is not possible for any two individuals to perceive the universe in an identical manner, neither is it possible for them to have absolutely no similarities of perception. In a sense there is a continuum of similarity of perception among individuals. One extreme approaches—but never reaches—zero; the other approaches—but never reaches—100 percent. Actually, degree of similarity of perception can probably best be expressed not as a point on a continuum but as a range of points. For example: A Catholic from a wealthy third-generation Boston family and one from an illiterate and impoverished village in Zaire may share not more than perhaps a 10–15 percent similarity of perception, *as Catholics,* but to that degree they are a part of the broad identity called Catholics. Teachers, considered as a broad group, may have a 15–20 percent similarity of perception. If we narrow the group to include only college teachers, the range of similarity of perception may increase to 20–25 percent. If we further specify that the group consists only of Irish-Catholic, American, middle-class, urban, white, male, heterosexual, college teachers of quantum physics, with Ph.D.'s from the Massachusetts Institute of Technology, between the ages of 35 and 40, the range of similarity of perception might well increase to 75–80 percent.[15] Notice that while we have decreased the number of people who can be included in our group, we have increased the number of group identities the members share. By so doing, we have greatly increased the likelihood of easy communication among them and thus the likelihood of their sharing still greater similarities of perception in the future. It is no wonder that the smaller the group, the greater its cohesion is likely to be.

In order to illustrate how very different differences in perception of the same stimuli can be, a number of years ago I devised an exercise, which I have since run hundreds of times in many different societies. Allow me to describe it here in some detail to illustrate the enormous differences in perceptions of symbols that actually exist.

In this exercise I put four symbols on the board, one at a time, and ask the seminar or class participants to write on a piece of paper all of the meanings that come to their minds when they see the symbols. When they are done writing, I ask everyone in the room to tell me the meanings they attributed to the symbols. (See Figure 5.)

The answers I get vary enormously, depending upon the participants. There is strong

FIGURE 5

indication that they would vary even more if I could do the exercise in remote villages with unschooled individuals in their own languages. As it is, except on three or four occasions when simultaneous translators were present, I have always done the exercise in English, usually with highly educated participants. This has automatically skewed the sample in the direction of *more* similarity of perception because all of the participants shared a certain similarity of perception as speakers of English and usually as highly educated professionals. (Normally the participants are graduate students in public and international affairs or midcareer civil servants.)

The two most common answers I get for the first symbol are "cross"—in the religious sense—and "plus"—in the mathematical sense. Now, since more than half of the participants I get are educated Christians, that is not really a surprising result. Also, since most come from the more developed parts of developing countries, the third most frequent response—"crossroads"—is also not surprising. The surprises, for me at least, usually come because of my own perceptual limitations. I am not really surprised by answers like "the letter T," "quadrants on a map," "the hands of a compass," "check mark" as in *correct,* or "a check mark" as in *incorrect,* the word *yes,* the word *no,* "Red Cross," and "the sign for Switzerland," although they are not answers I would have thought of myself. The first real surprises came for me when I did this exercise at a United Nations school in Costa Rica with a group of senior Central American civil servants from all six Central American Republics and a Spanish interpreter. Virtually every answer I got for that symbol suggested Latin Catholic romantic symbolism: "death and transfiguration," "life after death," "love," "sacrifice," "eternal life," "suffering," "God's son," "redemption," "crucifixion," "resurrection." These were just some of the meanings that were suggested to those people by that symbol. Not having been raised in a Latin Catholic culture, there was no way I could see those meanings in that symbol. From a communication point of view it doesn't matter how *I* was raised. What is important is that *they* were raised in that culture, and those were the meanings that symbol held for *them*.

The second real surprise for me with that symbol came when I did the exercise at the University of Malaya in Kuala Lumpur, Malaysia, with a group of second-year university students. Virtually every Malaysian of Chinese extraction (about half the students were of Chinese extraction) saw the symbol as the Chinese number ten because—as I discovered that day—that indeed is the way the Chinese write the number ten. Not having studied Chinese myself, there simply is no way I could possibly have seen the number ten in that symbol. On the other hand, there is almost no way in which a person born of Chinese parents, who has been taught to read and write Chinese as her first language, could *not* see the number ten in that symbol.[16]

This is just another example of why communication across cultural barriers is so very difficult. If the way in which *you* perceive a stimulus is completely outside *my* perceptual ken, how can I possibly begin to communicate with you?

At the point where all the participants have told me the meanings they saw in the first symbol, I usually ask them which one is correct. Obviously the answer is that all of them are correct—for them. *Symbols have no intrinsic meaning. Meaning resides not in the symbol but in our minds.* If you see this + as the number ten or as a symbol of resurrection or as a red cross, who am I to say that you are wrong? What I can say is that it is not the meaning I had in my mind when I devised the exercise. When I decided to use that symbol I saw it as one horizontal line and one vertical line crossing more or less at the midpoint. But that is only what was in *my* head at the time. It is no more correct or incorrect than any other meaning that people ascribe to it. Yet if two people are to communicate effectively, each has to know with some degree of accuracy what the symbols they use mean to the other. All language, after all, is symbolic. If I attribute different meanings to your words than you do (and most often I probably do), then there is no way we can communicate accurately. But that is precisely the point being made here. *No two humans can communicate 100 percent effec-* *tively because no two humans have learned to perceive identically.*

For the second symbol I have gotten responses that in some ways were even more revealing to me. In one group of participants there was a man from Egypt. When I drew this symbol on the board, he violently threw down his pencil on the desk and in an angry voice said, "I will not draw that symbol! I give my life to oppose it! I will not play games with that symbol!"

"But it is only two triangles superimposed upon each other; one pointing down, the other pointing up," I said, surprised not at his perception of the symbol as something representing the State of Israel but by the violence of his reaction.

"No," he said, even more angrily than before, "it stands for everything evil in this world! Death! Destruction! Murder! Torture! Violence! Hate! I will not play games with such a symbol!" Whereupon he rolled back one shirt sleeve and asked, "Do you see that scar?" Pointing to a long, red scar about three inches above his right wrist. "I got that fighting murderous Zionism in Sinai in 1956." Then putting his wrist on his head he said, "I wear it like my halo of thorns! I will not play games with evil."

Now who am I to argue with his perception of that symbol? Obviously for him it really did mean all of those awful things, and nothing that I was going to say could change that perception. I recognized then, for the first time perhaps, at an emotional gut level, why it would be so difficult ever to resolve the Middle East situation.

The more I have thought about that Egyptian's reaction to that symbol, and compared it to other reactions I have gotten from different people with different life experiences, the more amazed I am that any communication at all ever takes place. When I have done this exercise with a group of predominantly Jewish, middle-class, American students from New York City I have gotten answers like "Manischewitz wine," "Mogen David products," "Jewish star," "star of David," "peace," "chicken soup," "high holy days," and many other meanings that only an American Jew could associate with that symbol. Now being a

New Yorker myself, none of these meanings really surprised me—not even the chicken soup—though I hadn't thought of them when I designed the exercise. Sharing some degree of similarity of perception with that group, I could certainly understand why they would associate those meanings with that symbol.

The third symbol, I have always drawn carefully the way it appears here. While there is usually some diversity among the answers—depending upon the audience—anywhere from 60 to 100 percent will see it as somehow associated with Hitler, fascism, or Nazi Germany. The fact is that the symbol I put on the board is *not* a Nazi swastika. Hitler's swastika always points to the right, no matter how it is turned, and it is usually turned like this:

But as the saying goes, "Don't confuse me with facts. My mind is made up." It is stylized enough and reminiscent enough of the German swastika to elicit exactly the same depth of emotion—particularly from older Jews who lost relatives during the Nazi period—that a Nazi swastika would. The fact that it is really an ancient Aryan (Indian) symbol in no way changes the depth of one's perception of it as a Nazi swastika.

The fourth symbol is much more ambiguous than the first three and is open to more interpretation. Still, a great many people see it as a "squiggle" or a "signature" or a "corkscrew." More people from developing countries see it as a "river," a "snake," or a "puff of smoke" than do people from developed countries. I once did this exercise at a graduate school of nursing, and more than 60 percent of the participants in that group saw it specifically as an "interuterine device (IUD)" or simply as a "coil" or a "birth-control device." But if you've never seen an IUD, there just is no way you can know what you don't know.

The last part of that last sentence really is at the heart of this exercise and my lengthy discussion of it here. It is so important and so obvious that it is often overlooked. *We know what we perceive; we don't know what we don't perceive. Since there is no way that we can know what we don't perceive, we assume that we perceive "correctly"—even if we don't.* We tend to assume that almost everyone perceives what we perceive, and that we perceive everything (or almost everything) that everybody else perceives. Thus we engage people in discussion on a very wide range of topics assuming that the people with whom we are attempting to communicate share the same perceptions that we do. The two exceptions to this rule usually are people who look terribly foreign (or don't speak our language) and people who are specialists in fields about which we know nothing.

Beyond those exceptions, however, most of us assume that we know what the other person meant when he said something until we discover, by whatever circumstances or accident, that we do not. I automatically assume that someone else perceives what I perceive until proven otherwise. If I didn't do that even the simplest communication would be exhausting.

The more specific the symbol, the more agreement about its meaning we are likely to find. The more abstract the symbol, the greater the variety of meanings we are likely to find associated with it. A word like *table,* for example, is a symbol. But because it is specific the range of perceptions associated with it are likely to be fairly limited. One may see a wooden table or a Formica table, a round one or a rectangular one. One might see a mathematical table, a statistical table, a water table, or a table of contents. But the range of choices is fairly limited. On the other hand, the range of choices one might—and does—associate with abstract concepts like "God," "justice," or "democracy" are truly mind boggling. There probably are as many different meanings associated with those abstract concepts as there are groups in the world.

Attitudes and Values

Attitudes

Daryl J. Bem says of attitudes:

> Attitudes are likes and dislikes. They are our affinities for and our aversions to situations, objects, persons, groups, or any other identifiable aspect of our environment, including abstract ideas and social policies . . . our likes and dislikes have roots in our emotions, in our behavior, and in the social influences upon us.[17]

Not only does each of the groups into which we have been socialized teach us *its* judgment toward specific stimuli (this one is good, that one is bad; this one is beautiful, that one is ugly), even more important, it teaches us an *attitudinal framework* through which we can evaluate all *new* stimuli that reach our sensory receptors. These attitudinal frameworks become an integral part of both our censor screens and our decoding mechanism. Many of the groups of which we consider ourselves to be a part may teach conflicting attitudinal frames. Which we will adopt as our own will depend in large part on the way we rank the various group identities we hold. Often these conflicting frameworks cause no difficulty, however, because the context of each is usually different. For example, our religious identity may teach us that life is precious, and that all killing—even of an unborn fetus—is wrong. Yet in a different context, our national identity may teach us that we have to defend our country, right or wrong, and that to kill our country's enemies in time of war is one of the most noble deeds we can perform. Ironically, it is often the very same people who are most devout in their religious beliefs who are also the most fervent in their nationalist ardor.

The variety of judgments about the same stimuli is truly astounding. In the same city in India one might find men who, as a sign of deference to God, never cut their hair (Sikhs), while a few blocks away at a Buddhist monastery one can find men who shave their heads and faces completely—as their sign of deference to God. In some places one finds it perfectly acceptable for a man to publicly walk down the street holding hands with a male friend, while he might be arrested (or at least disparaged) for walking down the same street holding hands with a female. In some places a woman could be killed for sleeping with the brother of her husband. In others she may be married to all the brothers in a family simultaneously. In some places if a man were to sexually molest a prepubescent boy he could be jailed and very possibly killed by the other inmates, while in other places it is not even considered immoral *provided* the boy is prepubescent. The contrasts and differences are almost endless. Which set of attitudes we adopt and how we rank them will depend very heavily on the degree to which we identify with each of the groups to which we belong.

It occasionally happens that we are confronted with a stimulus (it could be a thing, an event, or an idea) to which we simply do not know how to react. At those times we will sometimes check with "significant" other people from the groups with which we identify to see how they evaluate that stimulus. Their response then gives us our clues as to how we should react.

Sometimes we form an attitude about a stimulus based on the framework that is already in place and then check our judgment of that stimulus with significant others from the groups that matter most to us (people whom we know and trust and whose judgments we respect—meaning that generally their attitudes toward stimuli either conform to our own or are such that we have no difficulty accepting them as our own) just to reinforce our original assessment of the stimulus. But most of the time we don't need to check. Most of the time the attitudinal frame our groups have supplied are sufficient so that we can make judgments about a whole range of issues or events with which we may never before have been confronted.

Values

Recall that *values* are used in this work to mean the desired events or situations we would like to see happen. These refer to our desires, wants, needs, or goals. Those terms are all very close in meaning, although there are shades of differences. *Needs,* for example, connotes a desire having a physiological base.

One "needs" something in order to survive as opposed to just wanting it. I'll say more about that in a moment. Normally one speaks of people having needs, of groups or organizations having goals, and of very large groups like societies or countries having values. The reason that it may often be overlooked is, just as with individuals, groups and countries also have certain needs that must be met in order for those entities to survive. Be that as it may, every individual, group, or nation holds a number of values simultaneously. Just as with attitudes, some of the values an individual or group holds may be compatible but some may conflict with each other. Or an individual's values may conflict with the values of one or more of the groups to which he or she belongs. In fact, it is almost inevitable that they will. It may not be so much that the values themselves conflict—although that is certainly possible—but rather that the importance we attach to certain values may be different from the importance other individuals or groups attach to those same values. That is, each individual and group ranks the importance of those values (to themselves) differently. Each of the groups of which we are a part teaches us *their* ranking of values. Which ranking we accept, which we change, and which we reject outright is, I submit, a function of the degree to which we identify with each of those groups. That is why I argue that every individual is culturally unique.

Let us suppose that membership in group I implies acceptance of the hypothetical values listed in Figure 6. That does not mean that every member of group I will accept all of these values or will rank them in exactly that order. Indeed they will not. Membership in a group does imply acceptance of some of the

basic group values, but it is clear that each member of the group will accept some of the group's values and reject others. Even among those group values that are accepted by all, each individual will rank the importance of those group values somewhat differently. Indeed some members of group I, because of overlapping membership in some other groups, will inevitably hold some values that are completely alien to other members of group I.

While person 1 of group I (let's call her Mary) might have ranked the predominant group values as shown, persons 2 and 3 of the same group (let's call them Margaret and Mildred) might have ranked them as shown in Figure 7. Each individual is still holding all of the same group values but ranking them differently. The combinations possible—even for people holding all and only the same group values—are virtually endless.

Let's take some real-world examples. Being American implies acceptance of the value of American-style democracy, acceptance of the values of free speech and freedom of religion, toleration for groups other than our own, and acceptance of the essentially free-enterprise economic system, to mention just several of the predominant American values. Now, any American reading this might instantly take issue with the values I have chosen to list. Being just as American as I, they might rightly ask, "Why didn't you include the right to bear arms, the Judeo-Christian ethic, the right to life, love of country, willingness to fight to preserve what we have, or any of a number of other values that other Americans hold?" The answer is simply that I don't rank those values as highly as I do the values I listed. That doesn't make others, or me, any less American. It just makes us different.

Group I
(Mary)

A₁
B₆
C₃
D₄
E₁₇
F₂

FIGURE 6

Group I
Person 2
(Margaret)

A₁
B₆
C₃
D₄
F₂
E₁₇

Group I
Person 3
(Mildred)

F₂
E₁₇
D₄
C₃
B₆
A₁

FIGURE 7

But now complicate the picture still further by recognizing that no two humans are members of all and only the same groups. Thus, assuming membership in only twelve different identity groups (which is a vast underestimation of the number of groups of which all of us are simultaneously members), Mary's value structure might look something like Figure 8. Mary would be at the confluence of these twelve specific identity groups (remember that each group has a culture of its own) and presumably would rank the values of each of these groups in her own unique way. Another individual belonging to all and only the same groups as Mary—even if that were possible; and we have seen that it is not possible—would still be culturally different from Mary because of the probability that she—this other individual—would rank the values of each of those groups somewhat differently from the way Mary ranks them.

Margaret's value structure (also assuming membership in only twelve identity groups), even sharing membership in six of the same cultures as Mary, might look something like Figure 9.

I don't think the point has to be labored further. Of course every person is culturally unique. That is why every interpersonal communication is also an intercultural communication. Knowing that should allow us to recognize the differences for what they are and strive to find the cultural similarities—which just as certainly are going to be there, since each of us shares some similar group identities merely by virtue of being human—and start by building upon those. The more we explore another individual's value structure, the more we are likely to find that we share. From these we can learn how to learn about those other values we do not share.

Let's return to our discussion of values as such. Whatever we call them—needs, values, goals—the fact is that every individual and group has them. Some individuals and groups may have different values from other individuals and groups or they may have them in different proportions and/or they may rank them differently, but every human has values.

Some have argued that precisely because the human animal is, after all, just that—an animal—we must fulfill our most basic animal needs first. They would argue that either we eat, drink, sleep, and find shelter or we die. We either procreate or the species dies. Those are the basic animal needs to which we

Mary's Value Structure

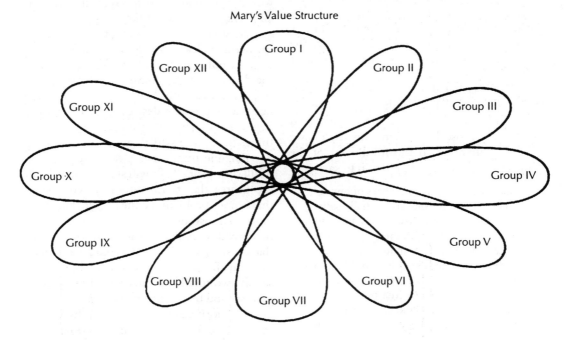

FIGURE 8

Margaret's Value Structure

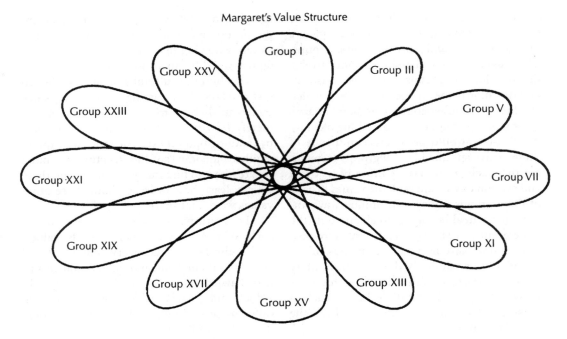

FIGURE 9

must first attend. But as a complex social animal, there are other needs to which we must also attend. Psychologists would argue that we *need* to feel safe and provide for the safety of those whom we care about; we *need* to give and receive affection; we *need* to have a feeling of self-esteem; and ultimately, if there is time and energy left over, and we have the chance to think about it, we have a *need* for self-actualization.

A. H. Maslow describes these as the hierarchy of needs.[18] That is, he argues that we must fulfill our most basic needs *first*, and only when those have been satisfied do we turn our attention to the fulfillment of the "higher order" needs. He goes on to say:

> In actual fact, most members of our society who are normal are partially satisfied in all of their basic needs and partially unsatisfied in all their basic needs at the same time. A more realistic description of the hierarchy would be in terms of decreasing percentages of satisfaction as we go up the hierarchy of prepotency. For instance, . . . it is as if the average citizen is satisfied perhaps 85% in his physiological needs, 70% in his safety needs, 60% in his love needs, 40% in his self-esteem needs and 10% in his self-actualization needs.[19]

Regardless of the percentages involved, Maslow would argue that we are always trying to fulfill all of those needs all of the time.

Now whether they are actually physiological needs or learned values does not have to overly trouble us here. I would argue that to the degree that they have a physical imperative associated with them they may indeed be needs as opposed to desires or wants or goals. Regardless of which they are, however, several things have to be said about them.

For one thing, it is clear that we try to fulfill several or all of them simultaneously. To the degree that those values are compatible that is not a problem. To the degree that one or more of those needs conflict, however, particularly if we rank them as equally important, that could be a problem. We could—and many of us do all the time—find ourselves trying to satisfy two totally conflicting values simultaneously and thus achieve neither. It is important to prioritize our needs, goals, and values in order to be able to direct our behavior toward meeting them all. But there is no way we can meet all of them simultaneously even if they don't directly conflict.

Second, except in those extreme cases where the deprivation is all consuming, many—indeed most—of these needs or values are perceived only on a subconscious level. Consciously we may deny vehemently—even to ourselves—that we are lonely, yet our actions can indicate loudly to the trained observer that much of our behavior revolves around trying to assuage that loneliness. Most often we are simply unaware consciously of what our needs are or how pressing some of them are at different times. Yet we try communicating with others (who may be no more conscious of *their* value ranking than we are) and oftentimes come away not knowing why we found the exchange so unsatisfying.

Third, to some degree fulfilling one need can partially—but only partially—substitute for another. Filling up on water is not really a substitute for food, but it does stave off hunger to at least some degree. People who eat compulsively don't do so because they are perpetually hungry. They may do so because eating provides instant gratification and substitutes for other needs that are not being gratified. Meeting self-esteem needs may not substitute for love needs, but may be perceived by the individual as a means to an end.

Fourth, and probably most relevant to this discussion, whatever our needs or values, or how we rank them, what they are and how they are ranked are learned from the groups with which we identify. We are taught which values we *ought* to hold by each of our groups. What is more, we are also taught in what ways it is acceptable to go about satisfying those desires and in what ways it is not. Milton Rokeach says of this:

> Values are the cognitive representation not only of individual needs but also of societal and institutional demands. They are the joint results of sociological as well as psychological forces acting upon the individual. . . .[20]

But that is just the point. Each group teaches *its* "societal and institutional demands," and each group—i.e., each culture—makes different demands. That is precisely what makes intercultural communication so difficult. If we fervently value "the greatest good for the greatest number" of our fellow humans, how do we possibly communicate effectively with those who just as fervently value getting all they can for themselves and their families? If we value peace and nonviolence above all else, how do we communicate effectively with someone who believes that one has to take what one wants by whatever means? All of us believe that our values are the best ones to hold. If we didn't we would hold other values. Because no two groups value exactly the same things or rank their values with the same intensity it is inevitable that there will be basic value conflict between individuals from different groups. Yet somehow, if communication among individuals from different groups is ever to be effective, we must not only recognize which values we rank most highly but we must also recognize that "they" are likely to rank perhaps totally different values just as highly. The first step to effective intercultural communication, it seems to me, is to recognize just what those value differences are. We may not like the values "they" hold, but we must recognize that their values are as important to them as ours are to us. The second step—and it is perhaps the most difficult one in the intercultural-communication process—is to find some way to reach an accommodation between those conflicting values.

One final point before we leave the discussion of values. The reason I have taken up so much space discussing values is that *so much of human behavior is geared toward satisfying those needs, goals, and/or desires.* Thus we interpret situations and relations with other people and groups in terms of trying to satisfy those needs and values. Having needs and desires, we try to fulfill them. I define *political behavior* as the attempt that all humans engage in to manipulate and/or structure their environment, people, and groups in order to achieve their own needs, goals, and/or values. The fact that most of those efforts are subconscious does not deny the fact that they motivate just about all of our behavior. They are crucial for understanding human behavior.

Virtually all of the values or needs scholars speak about are themselves components of power—i.e., the things that give the people or groups who have those values or needs the capability of influencing other people or groups who do not. That being true, it may well be that people seek these values not only for the "good" they do for the possessor of them (in and of themselves) but also because we may all instinctively know that they give us influence (power) over other people. If that assertion is correct, then those political scientists who have been arguing for years that the drive for power is the basic force motivating human behavior may well be correct. That is, it does not matter how we rank these values or whether we all have them all or only some of them. As long as we have any of them—and all of us, regardless of culture or personality have some—then to the degree that our behavior is geared toward trying to bring about some desired state or situation, we are engaged in political behavior—i.e., we are trying to exercise influence over either our environment or other people and groups. That is precisely why I argue that aside from being to some degree intercultural, all interpersonal, intergroup, and international relations are also to some degree "political." The study of political behavior very much enhances our understanding of the intercultural communication process. But what most political scientists seem to have overlooked until now is that the study of political behavior is very much informed by the study of intercultural communication.

Belief Systems

Earlier I argued that a belief system is the totality of perceptions, attitudes, values, and identities. I believe that something more should be said about them before we move on.

In an earlier work on belief and disbelief systems, Milton Rokeach wrote:

> The *belief system* is conceived to represent all the beliefs, sets, expectancies, or hypotheses, conscious and unconscious, that a person at a given time accepts as true of the world he lives in. The *disbelief system* is composed of a series of subsystems rather than merely a single one, and contains all the disbeliefs, sets, expectancies, conscious and

unconscious, that, to one degree or another, a person at a given time rejects as false.[21]

Not only is his concept of one belief system (and several contrary disbelief systems) held by all individuals important for this work, but what else he said in that book is also crucial to this work. For one thing, he differentiated between different kinds of beliefs: those that are most "central" to a person, those that are "intermediate," and those that are only "peripheral."

He says of beliefs in the "central region":

> Every person may be assumed to have formed early in life some set of beliefs about the world he lives in, the validity of which he does not question and, in the ordinary course of events, is not prepared to question. Such beliefs are unstated but basic.[22]

According to Rokeach these "primitive beliefs" have to do with the definition of a person's physical world, his or her social world, and feelings about self. These are the beliefs that are so basic that the individual believes that every other human also holds them. And precisely because these beliefs are so basic, they are probably least susceptible to change. This is the range of beliefs, of course, that make intercultural communication so very difficult. We take them so very much for granted that they are only rarely, if ever, consciously considered. Thus on a conscious level, at least, we are unaware that anyone could possibly have very different basic beliefs. If we are consciously made aware that other people hold different basic beliefs, we reject those beliefs as unworthy of serious consideration.

The importance of learning about their group culture—including their verbal and nonverbal languages—probably cannot be overstressed. One of the most common problems encountered by people from one group trying to deal with someone from a different group is that "they just don't think the way we do." That is quite correct. It shouldn't be surprising. What would be surprising is if they did. Thought patterns are buried so deep in what Rokeach has called the central regions of our belief system that it simply never occurred to us that anyone would think differently—nor is it at all easy to try to understand different thought patterns. Yet we must if we are to communicate effectively.

In an interesting article on the thought processes of different linguistic groups, Robert B. Kaplan has observed that while English writing—and thinking—is linear (a statement on which there is virtually unanimous agreement among logicians, linguists, anthropologists, and other scholars), those who speak and write Semitic languages (Arabic and Hebrew) seem to use various kinds of parallels in their thinking, and the writing and thinking of Chinese and Koreans (whom he lumps together as Orientals in his study) is marked by indirection. That is, a "turning and turning in a widening gyre." Kaplan has graphically represented the major groups he studies. (See Figure 10.) Now, while one must be careful not to fall into the trap of believing that *all* Chinese and Koreans think by a process of indirection, that *all* English-speaking people think in a linear manner all of the time, and so on, the fact is that most probably do, most of the time.

Similarly, the more different from us they are, the more likely we are to find that their belief system is, in fact, one of our disbelief systems. How then are we to cope with the differences? I submit that there is only one way, and that is by trying to understand rather than to judge. That's very difficult precisely because, as I noted earlier, it's virtually impossible to separate attitudes and values. Yet we must if we are to communicate effectively with someone from a group quite different from our own. We don't have to like another group's

values or way of thinking to communicate effectively with them, but we certainly do have to understand them.

According to Rokeach, beliefs of the "intermediate region" are predicated on reference to some authority (authority being defined as "any source to whom we look for information about the universe, or to check information we already possess"[23]).

Rokeach feels that this range of beliefs is important because "it spotlights a possible intimate connection between the way we accept and reject people and the way we accept and reject ideas stemming from authority."[24] More will be said about this in a moment. First let us go on to describe his "peripheral region" of beliefs.

Peripheral beliefs—or more specific beliefs—are derived from intermediate beliefs. For example, beliefs about such things as birth control, the New Deal, and the theory of repression Rokeach would consider peripheral beliefs because they are derived from one's beliefs about the Catholic church, Franklin D. Roosevelt, and Sigmund Freud,[25] respectively. All of the beliefs that are neither primitive nor held because of identification with some authority but rather are derived from that identification are in the peripheral region. And, of course, these are the ones most subject to change.

Let us return to that notion of the degree to which authority is accepted, which Rokeach discussed in his intermediate region. According to him—and his and other people's empirical research seems to bear it out—the way one views authority determines in very large measure how one will view the world. That is, the

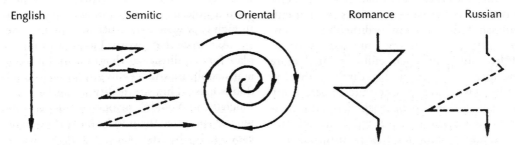

English   Semitic   Oriental   Romance   Russian

FIGURE 10 Thought processes of different linguistic groups. From Robert B. Kaplan, "Cultural Thought Patterns in Intercultural Education," in *Language Learning* 14, nos. 1 and 2 (1966): 15.

more one interprets information coming from the outside world, independent of the authority of the source of that information, the more "open" Rokeach considers that person to be. The more one relies on authority to determine his or her attitude toward information, the more "closed" he or she is considered.

While Rokeach would argue that all people are driven to some degree by both "open" and "closed" perceptions, his empirical research indicates strongly that most people tend to fall more strongly into one category or the other. And his research shows that an individual's way of looking at the external world ("open" or "closed") very much determines not only what he will see but also what he will not.

If Rokeach is correct in his assertion— and his empirical evidence is certainly very convincing, despite the fact that his conclusions are virtually all from research in the United States—then that finding is extremely important for intercultural communication at all levels of analysis. What it implies is that an individual or group with a more "open-minded" belief system will be much more likely to try to understand another individual or group with a different belief system—and thus will be much better able to communicate with "them"—than would an individual or a group with a different belief system. In other words, projecting his theory into the intercultural-communication field, individuals from cultures that rely heavily on unquestioning acceptance of authority would be much less likely to be open to different ideas, attitudes, values, and belief systems than would individuals from more "open" cultures. If that is so, then what it implies is that communication between individuals from different "closed-minded" cultures (or between individuals who are themselves more "closed" than others in their culture) should be much more difficult than communication between "open-minded" individuals from different "open" cultures. Much more specifically, intercultural research on this hypothesis will have to be conducted before any firm conclusions can be reached, but the prospects are intriguing that it will help to better understand (and facilitate) intercultural communication.

REALITY, PERCEPTION, AND MISPERCEPTION

Earlier we argued that objective reality may exist but that humans can never "know" reality: rather, they have perceptions of reality. That is an important enough assertion to warrant further discussion.

Whether in philosophy, politics, religion, or history, one always comes across assertions that there is a knowable reality and that honest people just have to be willing to look at all the facts to know that reality. I'm afraid that I must challenge that notion directly. If the people who study the way we learn about the world are correct—and everything I will say in this work assumes that they are—then we learn about the world through our sensory receptors. Further, I believe I have demonstrated here that each individual perceives "reality" differently. Now this raises some serious problems. If people's perceptions are valid for them, then how can any accurate communication occur between individuals? Can't individuals be wrong about something? Clearly they can. How then do we get out of the intellectual corner we seem to have painted ourselves into?

First, let me deal with reality. I am not arguing here that reality does not exist. Indeed, I'm certain it does. There are mountains and people and wars and even ideas. Rather, I have been arguing that reality may be less important, in both determining and understanding human behavior, than are perceptions of reality. Since I cannot know reality directly but only through my sensory receptors, I tend to treat my perceptions of reality *as though they were reality*. That is, through a long series of trial-and-error tests I behave toward objects, people, events, and ideas as though they were what I perceive them to be.

As I write those words I pause to contemplate how to illustrate what I mean. I look up at my bookcase and see row after row of books. Books exist. They are reality. I can hold and touch them. Wouldn't anyone—no matter from where—perceive them to be books? Not necessarily. In the first place, not all books are shaped like these or are made of the same materials. When I show friends a book from ancient Ceylon that I have in my collection, written on dried banana leaves each about two inches wide by fourteen inches long and held together by string running through two holes in each leaf and two painted wooden end pieces, they have absolutely no idea what it is. Second, many people in nonliterate societies have never seen a book and would have no idea what one was even if they were shown one. Have you ever seen a very young child playing with a book? Babies have no idea what a book is or what to do with it until they have been taught by their parents how to deal with it.

Third, ask a physicist what a book is. He might tell you it is a book, but he might also tell you that each page is merely a collection of certain kinds of molecules held together by a force field, while a chemist might tell you that the individual pages are actually wood pulp with a certain rag content treated in certain ways, then rolled into long sheets, dried, and later printed on with certain dyes having such and such chemical content. Some people in the book-printing business, on the other hand, might see the binding, the quality of the paper, and the typeface. Some people collect books merely because they "look nice" as a decoration for a room.

Books are real enough, but each person who comes into contact with them will view them differently. The ideas contained in the books are also real—but they are much more abstract than the physical book itself and thus open to much greater variety of interpretation than the book is. The more abstract the reality, the greater the variety of interpretation one should expect.

What about people? Surely they exist, but what kind of person is anyone? Every term I show my classes a very old film starring Richard Conti called *The Eye of the Beholder*. In that film Conti plays a character named Michael Gerrard. The film asks the question, What kind of person is Gerrard? It then goes on to show several different people's perceptions of him. A waiter in a lounge sees him as a "ladies' man," a taxicab driver sees him as a "hood," his mother sees him as a "good boy" who works too hard, the landlord of the artist's studio he rents sees him as "a lunatic," and the cleaning woman in the building sees him as a "murderer." The movie replays what happened in a twenty-four-hour period from each of those different perspectives and then shows the audience how Michael Gerrard views himself and the events of that period from his perspective. What is very clear is that each person in the film—including Gerrard—attended to different bits of information in forming an opinion of what he was like and what happened that day. But even questions of "fact" change in each retelling. From Gerrard's perspective, he told the cab driver to "Please be quiet. I'm trying to concentrate." From the cabbie's telling of it, he said, "Shut up, Mac. I'm busy." Which is reality? I'm not certain that we could know unless there was a tape recorder to play it back as it happened. But even then we might not know. The words could have said, "Be quiet," but the tone could have said, "Shut up." Or the words could indeed have said, "Shut up." We don't always say what we intend to say.

We never truly know ourselves fully, let alone others. Since others know us less well than we know ourselves, it is inevitable that their perceptions of us (or our perceptions of them) will be very different from their perceptions of themselves. But whereas abstract concepts are open to more interpretation than are concrete concepts, so too, complex creatures like people are probably open to much more interpretation than are simple creatures like fish or dogs.

Somewhere out there, there is reality. Trying to know what that reality is, however, is not simple. In every age everyone has his or her own perceptions of what that reality is. In medieval times people behaved toward the world as though it were flat. It wasn't, but never mind that. They thought it was and therefore tended not to travel too far for fear of falling off. Now people know it is round and therefore treat it differently. They know that they can get east by traveling west, and they do. They also know that they can get to the moon by aiming not at where it is when they start the trip but at where it will be when they get there.

If we all have different perceptions of reality, how can we differentiate what is more nearly "true" from what is "less true"? After all, there are such things as hallucinations, and we do recognize when someone has "lost touch with reality" and believes (and behaves) as though he were Jesus Christ or Napoleon. One could, after all, argue that he merely had a different perception of reality. I know that there are some mental health theorists who might very well take that point of view. Others would argue that it is only the "insane" who see reality and that all the rest of us who think we do and call ourselves "sane" are in fact deceived. Yet intuitively we know that those kinds of answers simply will not do. Neither, it seems to me, can we resort to a vote to determine what reality is. Copernicus and Galileo would both have been overwhelmingly outvoted. So too would Hellenists and Christians in early Rome and heathens and heretics during the Inquisition in medieval Europe.

It seems to me that the scientific solution of observing and noting what our perceptions of reality are, of formulating a hypothesis that helps us to explain what it is we think we observe and then of monitoring data to test that hypothesis, may be the most useful approach. No hypothesis ever holds true indefinitely. Rather, prevailing views of reality are retained so long as they are useful in helping to explain phenomena. As soon as we start finding data that "don't fit" that view, we begin to try to formulate a different hypothesis that might better help explain what it is we are looking at. The same thing happens in trying to explain things, events, people, and ideas.

Trying to determine what reality is takes a great deal of time and hard work. This is particularly true of situations in which different individuals, groups, or nations have totally different perceptions about the same "reality," as they frequently do. But not all situations require that we test our perceptions of it. Indeed, very many probably do not. In most day-to-day situations in our life, nothing major is lost by trusting our perceptions of reality to be a fair assessment of what it really is—until we discover that we were wrong. When we do, then often no great harm has been done or will be done by changing our perceptions and searching for a new hypothesis that will better

explain the event or phenomenon we want to know about. This principle says: "Assume our perceptions of reality are correct until proven otherwise." In other cases it is terribly important to come as close to reality as possible before making a decision about whether our perceptions are correct, as in a murder trial or an international event that could lead to war. I would argue that in those cases it is wisest to assume that our perceptions of reality are probably *incorrect*—or at least different from the perception of reality held by others—and hence to keep working to determine what reality is until we are convinced "beyond a reasonable doubt" that we know.

The other device we should be careful to try to preserve is a constant level of analysis. Are we looking at a total system or merely at a subset of a system? Because "he" tends to carry a knife, does that mean that everyone in one of the subsets to which he belongs is also likely to carry knives? And which subset is it that best helps to categorize and describe his behavior? Is it the subset based on his skin color, his age, his height, his socioeconomic class, his level of education, his intelligence, his sex, his sexual orientation, his religious preference, his political preference, the food he eats, the movies he likes, the upbringing he has had, some "criminal personality," or his genes? Or is it some other subset that we have not yet thought of formulating?

Of course a book is a book at one level of analysis. But it is just as certainly a collectivity of molecules at another. Indeed it is precisely because of the existence of different levels of analysis that we must come to the conclusion that there is not just one but different "realities" out there, all of them, perhaps, equally valid. It may very well be the existence of these different realities on different levels of analysis, added to our differences of perception about reality—regardless of level—that makes for so much confusion.

If it is not possible for us to know reality directly, if we can know it only through our perceptions of it, and if each person's perceptions are inevitably different—and probably just as valid for him or her as mine are for me—then what are misperceptions? Doesn't the word itself imply that someone is "wrong" in the way he or she perceives reality? Not necessarily. That is one way to look at it, to be certain. But we could also argue that the word *misperceptions* most properly should be reserved for those situations when two (or several) individuals or groups are wrong about the way the other individuals or groups perceive an object, event, person, or idea. That is, it is not our, or their, perception of the event (or whatever) that is wrong but rather my perception of how they perceive the event that is wrong. In almost every conflict situation, for example, one group makes certain assumptions about why the other group is behaving the way it is. If those assumptions are incorrect—that is, if the other group is in fact not behaving the way it is because of the reasons the other group assumes, then that is a misperception. Not only why one group does what it does, but even what it does, may be misperceived.

If both you and I believe that the other is preparing to attack us, and neither of us is, that is a misperception. Further, if because I believe that you are about to attack I pick up a gun to defend myself, you are very likely to believe that your perceptions of me were correct and to point to my taking a gun as proof of my intention to attack you. Unfortunately this is precisely how most wars start. My reaching for a gun may indeed have been completely defensive, but can you take a chance in a situation like that? There is, after all, the chance—no matter how remote—that in fact I do intend to attack. Doesn't one have to do something to protect oneself? Of course. Since you can never know reality for certain, you have no alternative but to prepare for the worst. The only trouble is that as you prepare, I take that as further proof that it is you who are preparing to attack me.

The point is that people can be, and often are, wrong in the way they perceive situations, motives, or intentions. Whenever they are, we have to refer to that as a "misperception."

There are a great many things external to myself that I cannot know about for certain. But things about myself, in particular, I can know. When someone attributes actions or motives to me that are incorrect, that is a misperception and ought to be clarified as

quickly as possible. Just because you and I perceive each other correctly will in no way assure that I will like you or that we won't have conflicts. But at least if misperceptions are clarified, we will know what it is we are disagreeing about and may be able to resolve our conflict peacefully. I submit, however, that in the overwhelming majority of cases of conflict situations, neither party really knows what it is precisely that they are fighting over because the misperceptions tend to obscure everything else.

Allow me to relate a true story about differing perceptions of reality to illustrate just how important such differences can be to successful intercultural communication.[26] Many years ago a successful American businessman by the name of Sam Green retired to the mountains of Guatemala, near Lake Attitlan. He had made his fortune doing business in Guatemala and had fallen in love with the land and its people. Every evening after sunset when the Indians in the region returned from the fields to their villages, he would ride out to their villages on his horse and sit for hours talking with them. He came to know and trust them very much, and they him. He had learned their language, their culture, and their reality world very well. They would tell him of their needs and their dreams. It seemed to him that many of the things these simple people wanted were the same things that people everywhere wanted: health, safety, food, security. He discovered that one of the problems they had in obtaining these basic things was lack of cash—sometimes very small quantities at that. To the peasants in those small villages a hundred dollars or a thousand dollars seemed like an inordinate amount of money—and given their reality world, it was. But he also learned that these Indians did have a little surplus cash, maybe only a penny or two per person, per day, but they did have some cash. Accordingly he hit upon the idea of loaning them the money to dig the well they needed, or buy the medicine, or whatever (never a lot of money—usually on the order of magnitude of a few hundred dollars). They, in return, promised to pay him back a penny, per day, per family, until the loan was repaid. Because these were a very honest people whose word was their bond, Sam Green was always repaid in full for every loan he made. Indeed, his efforts with the Indians were so successful that he established what came to be known as the Penny Foundation in Guatemala to institutionalize this practice.

One year Mr. Green returned to the United States for an extended period. Very shortly after he returned to Guatemala he was met by a representative of the Guatemalan government who wanted to know why it was that he—a foreigner—could get those Indians to pay back loans he made, but they, the government of Guatemala, could not. It seems that in his absence, one of the drinking wells in a village had gone dry, and the Indians had approached the government asking them if they would supply water. Since the village next to the one in question had a more than ample water supply, the government arranged to pipe the water from the oversupplied village to the dry village. The government thought that the villagers had agreed to pay back the government for this service, but when the government tried to collect, the villagers refused. Mr. Green said that he couldn't explain why that had happened until he spoke to the villagers in question. When he rode out to the village and asked what had happened, he was told that yes, the village well had run dry, but that now the government was trying to make them pay for the water they used—the government had imposed a water tax to recover the loan—and everyone knew that God gave water free. Mr. Green agreed that was so but pointed out to the villagers that while God gave water free, metal pipes were made by man, and they cost money. He asked if the villagers would mind paying the government back for the pipe it had bought and installed to bring the water to the village. Of course, the villagers had no problem at all agreeing to pay for the pipe, and thus the issue was resolved.

I think the story illustrates well my contention that for intercultural communication, perceptions of reality may be more important than trying to establish any intrinsic reality itself.

ENDNOTES

[1]This concept was presented first in an article entitled "Culture: A Perceptual Approach," published originally in *Vidya*, No. 3, Spring 1969, and more recently reproduced in Larry A. Samovar and Richard E. Porter, eds., *Intercultural Communication: A Reader*, 4th ed. (Belmont, CA: Wadsworth Pub. Co., 1985).

[2]From *Collected Papers on Metalinguistics*, quoted by Franklin Fearing in "An Examination of the Conceptions of Benjamin Whorf in the Light of Theories on Perception and Cognition," in Harry Hoijer, ed., *Language in Culture* (Chicago: University of Chicago Press, 1954), 48.

[3]Here I am using *language* in the broadest sense. It may include the jargon or symbols used by social scientists or mathematicians, for example, to express the concepts peculiar to their group, or it may include the myriad of nonverbal gestures sometimes referred to as body language.

[4]Ruth Benedict, *Patterns of Culture*, 1934; reprint (New York: Mentor Books, 1959), 18.

[5]C. T. Patrick Diamond, "Understanding Others: Kellyian Theory, Methodology and Applications," in *International Journal of Intercultural Relations*, 6 (1982), 401.

[6]Harry Hoijer, "The Sapir-Whorf Hypotheses," in Harry Hoijer. ed., *Language in Culture* (Chicago: University of Chicago Press, 1954), 94.

[7]Diamond, "Understanding Others," 403.

[8]Paraphrased in *ibid.*, 396, 397.

[9]Milton Rokeach, *The Nature of Human Values* (New York: Free Press, 1973), 5.

[10]*Ibid.*, 7.

[11]Although drawn heavily from anthropological and social-psychological literature, this way of viewing culture is my own and can be used at every level of analysis—personal, group, or national.

[12]Richard W. Cottam and Ole R. Holsti are two scholars who come to mind. Cottam in particular, in personal communication to this author, argued the importance of temperament.

[13]Bernard Berelson and Gary A. Steiner, *Human Behavior: An Inventory of Scientific Findings* (New York: Harcourt, Brace & World, 1964), 104.

[14]Cited in D. Price-Williams, "Cross-Cultural Studies," from Brian M. Foss, ed., *New Horizons in Psychology* (New York: Penguin Books, 1966) and reprinted in Larry A. Samovar and Richard E. Porter, eds., *Intercultural Communication: A Reader*, 2nd ed. (Belmont, CA: Wadsworth Publishing Co., 1976), 34.

[15] All figures used in this example are completely hypothetical and are included merely to illustrate a concept. They are not based on any known research.

[16] An interesting variation occurred when I did that exercise in Pittsburgh some time ago. A Japanese student did *not* see the number 10, even though the Japanese write the number 10 the same way the Chinese do. Later when I asked him why, he said that it never occurred to him in the context of a Pittsburgh classroom that an American professor would know Japanese.

[17] Daryl J. Bem, *Beliefs, Attitudes, and Human Affairs* (Belmont, CA: Brooks/Cole Publishing Co., 1970), 14.

[18] See A. H. Maslow, "A Dynamic Theory of Human Motivation," in Charles R. Lawrence, ed., *Man, Culture and Society* (New York: Brooklyn College Press, 1962).

[19] *Ibid.*, 2–11.

[20] Milton Rokeach, *Nature of Human Values*, 20.

[21] Milton Rokeach, *The Open and Closed Mind: Investigations into the Nature of Belief Systems and Personality Systems* (New York: Basic Books, 1960), 33.

[22] *Ibid.*, 40–41.

[23] *Ibid.*, 43.

[24] *Ibid.*, 45–46.

[25] *Ibid.*, 47.

[26] Personal communication to the author by someone directly involved in the situation.

5

Intercultural and Interracial Communication: An Analytic Approach

Andrea L. Rich and Dennis M. Ogawa

In our internationally troubled world and racially tense society, the study of intercultural and interracial communication has become critically important to researchers concerned with the processes and effects of human interaction. This paper is designed to provide a hitherto absent structure within which concepts and hypotheses concerning cross-cultural and cross-racial communication can be tested and analyzed.

To provide some framework for the analysis of intercultural and interracial communication, we must explore factors in the macrocosm or larger environment in which this communication occurs. Specifically, our paper will attempt to answer the following questions:

1. What are the defining societal and interpersonal patterns and relationships which distinguish the terms "intercultural," "contracultural," "interracial," and "interethnic" communication?

2. What are some of the major factors which may influence patterns of interracial communication?

Reprinted from *Intercultural Communication: A Reader,* 3rd. ed. eds. L. A. Samovar and R. E. Porter, 43–49. Los Angeles County Museum of Art, 1982.

By suggesting the defining patterns and relationships of these terms and by delineating some of the factors influencing interracial communication, we hope to clear up the confusion and looseness with which the terms have been employed.

DISTINGUISHING SOCIETAL AND INTERPERSONAL PATTERNS AND RELATIONSHIPS

Intercultural Communication

"Culture is the sum total of the learned behaviors of a group of people which are generally considered to be the tradition of that people and are transmitted from generation to generation."[1] By "intercultural communication" we mean communication[2] between *peoples* of different cultures (as opposed to communication between official representatives of nations, i.e., international communication). Figure 1 represents our concept of intercultural communication.

A and *B* represent the two communicating cultures. (A_1 and B_1 would represent the individuals within those cultures who are actually interacting.) The important assumption here is that these cultures do not have and have not historically existed in a colonial relationship where one of the cultures has taken over or dominated the other for any long period of time. (Hence, the circles do not overlap.)

The communicators may or may not share a symbolic system in intercultural communication. When the system is shared (e.g., an American speaking with an Australian), the *X* of our diagram would refer to that shared system (the English language). When communication is conducted between people of different cultures who do not share a symbolic system (a Frenchman and a German, for example), the *X* portion of the diagram represents whatever improvised system they invent to make contact.

As we shall see in sections on interracial and contracultural communication, the important distinction between intercultural, contracultural, and interracial communication is the interpersonal relationship of the communicating individuals. In intercultural com-

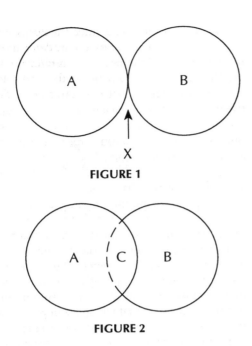

FIGURE 1

FIGURE 2

munication situations, individuals are strange to each other; they have had a relatively separate historical development. As such, they tend to communicate more or less as equals.

Interracial Communication

Figure 2 applies to interracial communication as it occurs in the United States. Circle A represents the dominant power structure, or, specifically, "white America." A includes the physical, social, and psychological space occupied by white America. The individuals who occupy that space we shall refer to as A_1.

Circle B represents the non-white racial group as it exists in its purest form, uninfluenced by the structure of white America. For example, B_1 (the individual who occupies the physical, social, and psychological space of B) could be the immigrant Japanese *before* he reaches the shores of America or the Mexican *abuela* (grandmother) who was brought to the United States by her family to dwell in the ethnic shelter of an East Los Angeles barrio. She speaks no English and may have created her own pure and unaffected racial subculture. There is some doubt, however, as to whether one may dwell in the United States and still be unaffected by the white structure. It is possible that B may exist only on its native

soil or as an idealized concept of the mind of C_1 (to be defined shortly).

Circle C represents the experience of being a racial minority in a white-dominated structure. It is the geographical, social, and psychological space allotted to the non-white American. C_1 (and C_2, C_3, etc.) are the individuals confined to that space, the ethnic-American (Mexican-American, Black-American, Japanese-American, etc.). The line of C traversing A is broken, not to suggest the possibility of C_1 ever entering into A, but to demonstrate that the size of C is elastic; it may vary depending upon the whim of A and, to a certain extent, upon the tenacity of C to remain close to B. For example, when Congress passes certain civil rights legislation, it enlarges the size of C. Such expansion of C into the domain of A, however, is under the control of A; the outside limit to which C can intrude upon A is dictated by A.

On the other hand, C could, by its own choice, choose to remain small and closer to B. Members of certain Mexican-American barrios, for example, have attempted to keep Mexican culture intact by speaking the Spanish language and generally preserving Mexican custom rather than white Anglo-Saxon custom. The size of C will also vary depending upon which group we consider as occupying C at any given time. Let us say, for example, that C_1 represents Black America and C_2 represents Mexican America (Figure 3). C_1 may be larger than C_2 because, at least until recently, Black America has depended more upon white American for its culture (language, customs, etc.) than has Mexican America.

There are certain assumptions which can be drawn from Figure 3. First, a member of C can never totally move within the realm of A. This is, at present, a fact of life in white-dominated America. Despite the thrust toward

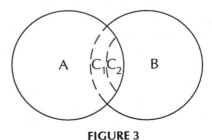

FIGURE 3

integration, white America has tenaciously maintained a portion of A into which, on the basis of color, non-white Americans may not enter. As long as a member of C can be identified as non-white, he cannot pass completely into the realm of A.

On the other hand, a member of C can move within his allotted space of C, and also within B, unless he has rejected B or has been rejected by B. That is to say, a Japanese-American is relatively free to return to Japan and drop the hyphenate of being a Japanese-American, if he so desires. Though his ethnic minority experience in the United States may cause him certain problems in acculturation within his new environment, in most cases there are few or no legal or social barriers preventing a member of C from entering into B, such as there are racial barriers preventing a member of C from entering into A in the United States.

A third and significant assumption for interracial communication is that a member of A can never become a member of C. A white American, despite his good intentions, can never fully contemplate the experience of being a racial minority in a white-dominated America. Communication between members of A and members of C, or between white and any non-white groups, is therefore highly difficult because of this lack of shared experience. The outstanding characteristic of communication between members of A and C (interracial communication, as opposed to international or intercultural communication) is that the very existence of C (a segregated physical and psychological space dictated by A) has to cause hostility and resentment on the part of C members; therefore, tension and great strain arise in any attempts at communication between individuals in A and C.

On the other hand, communication between C_1, C_2, C_3, C_4, etc. (Black-Americans, Mexican-Americans, Japanese-Americans) stands a better chance of positive response because all these non-white groups, to some degree, share C. While their C's may vary in size, they all have experienced being a racial minority in a white-dominated culture. Sitaram calls communication between C's *minority communication*.[3] Since the terms "minority" and "majority" are so relative, based on one's sys-

tem of classification, and since the term "minority" tends to cause abrasive reactions among those who regard themselves as a minority in the United States but a majority in the world, we would prefer to call communication between C's *interethnic communication*. Groups also to be included in the C classification of interracial communication in the United States are the American natives (Eskimos, Indians, and Hawaiians) who have been forced into C space by the white structure.

"Interracial communication," then, is communication between white and non-white in the United States and is characterized by strain and tension resulting from the dominant-submissive societal and interpersonal relationship historically imposed upon the non-white by the structure of white America. "Interethnic communication" is that which occurs between members of different non-white groups in America, groups which have in common the sharing of a peripheral societal and interpersonal space to which they have been relegated by the white structure.

Contracultural Communication

Figure 4 shows that contracultural communication occurs when intercultural communication is transformed, by continued contact of cultures and the imposition of one culture upon the other, into interracial communication. In other words, what began as a simple egalitarian interaction between two strange but relatively equal cultures becomes a colonial relationship where one culture is forced to submit to the power of another. The X of the intercultural model, that area of shared or improvised means of communication, becomes the C of the interracial model, an area in which individuals are relegated to a position and their mobility to move out of that position is dictated by a dominant structure. When Columbus first landed on the shores of the New World, for example, he undoubtedly engaged in intercultural communication with the natives he encountered. He improvised a system (exchanged gifts, etc.). As the colonization progressed, however, the white Spaniards came to occupy A space and allowed certain of the Indians (from B) to form a C group. Had the

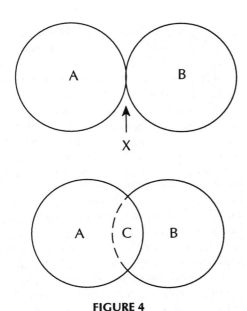

FIGURE 4

Indians maintained control and enslaved the Spaniards, according to our theory, the Indians would then have occupied the A circle with the Spaniards relegated to C. (And those Spaniards remaining safely in Spain composing the B circle.)

The interracial diagram, then, also describes contracultural communication. As long as a power relationship exists between cultures, where one has subdued and dominated the other, a C circle exists, and as long as a C area exists, hostility, tension, and strain are introduced into the communication situation. Communication between an Englishman and an Indian, or between a Belgian and a Congolese, serves to exemplify what we mean here by contracultural communication.

SOME MAJOR FACTORS INFLUENCING INTERRACIAL COMMUNICATION

Economic and/or Class Parameters

To test the real extent to which racial and cultural differences influence communication between individuals, it is also interesting to hypothesize as to the effects of the introduction of economic and/or class parameters into interracial communication (Figure 5). Since in America class position is frequently determined by economic position, let us, for the sake of discussion, combine the two, and consider X the highest economic/social class, Y the middle economic/social class and Z the lowest economic/social class. An AX individual in our society would be someone occupying the position of Nelson Rockefeller or Richard Nixon (Nixon, a rather new member of X; Rockefeller, a comfortable inheritor of position X). A CX in our society might be Thurgood Marshall or Edward Brooke. A BX would be a Japanese financier from Tokyo or a Prime Minister from Ghana.

Several interesting questions arise from such a structure that could be translated into testable hypotheses for future research. For example, would Richard Nixon be more comfortable with and successful in eliciting a desired response from CX Edward Brooke (a fellow Republican, though black), an AY (middle class clerk), or an AZ (poor coal miner)?[4] Would an American banker (AX) have a more successful business transaction with an African industrialist (BX) than he would with an American black capitalist (CX)? Do the tensions and strains in interracial communication resulting from the very existence of area C diminish as an individual member of C climbs the social/economic ladder from Z to X, or do tensions take other more subtle forms of expression? (It should be pointed out at this time, that a member of C has upward mobility in this model; he may move from Z to X, but he still has no lateral mobility to the left; that is, a CX can still not become an AX, or even an AZ, for that matter.) These are just a few of the many questions suggested by the introduction of an economic/social parameter.

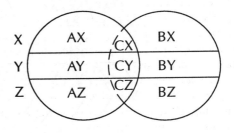

FIGURE 5

White Ethnic Parameter

One of the misleading assumptions of the interracial diagram (Figure 3) thus far has been in the classification of all members of A as one unit. From the non-white point of view, all whites are very much alike in the structure of our society. They do, by virtue of their color alone, enjoy many, many benefits and advantages that non-whites do not. On the other hand, there are ethnic differences between those occupying the A space in our model. Attempting, for example, to place Jews within the model of interracial communication posed a problem. The majority of C members (Black-Americans, for example) perceive Jews as white and as a part of the white power structure. In fact, much of black hostility against the white man is aimed at the Jew specifically, since often the Jew is spatially the closest to the black. Yet, the white society does not altogether regard the Jew as a member of the A group, and the Jew himself tends to identify with the more oppressed non-white groups. It seems appropriate, therefore, to add another dimension to the interracial communication model, that of white ethnic groups. For example, in Figure 6, we have arbitrarily divided A into three slices (it could conceivably be divided into as many slices as there are white ethnic groups in the United States). The closer the A slice is to C, the more tenuous is its position in the A circle. Jews, for example, would occupy position 3, the closest to the

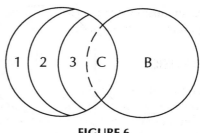

FIGURE 6

realm of C. Slice 2 might be occupied by Irish, Polish, and Italian Catholics, etc., and slice 1 would most likely be reserved for white Anglo-Saxon Protestants.[5]

Figure 7, finally, is a rather complex attempt to include, in their various combinations, all the racial, ethnic, social, and economic variations that will influence the manner in which individuals in a complex society can interact. The ABC parameter represents racial groups. The XYZ parameter represents social/economic class. The 1234 notation in the A circle represents white ethnic groups (the higher the number, the less the group is regarded by the A circle). The 1234 notations in the C circle have no values placed upon them; they simply represent different non-white groups (e.g., CX_1 would represent a wealthy black man, while CX_2 could represent a wealthy Japanese-American). The numbers merely denote the difference between the two racial groups. Circle B is not divided into complex ethnic subdivisions, since the focus of this paper has been primarily upon racial and

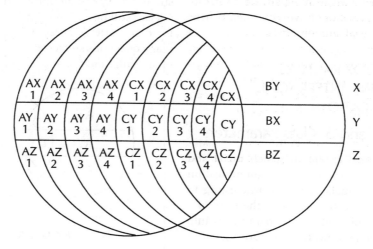

FIGURE 7

ethnic compositions that structure human interaction in the United States.

CONCLUSION

We have attempted, in this paper, to embrace the concepts of "intercultural" and "interracial" communication from a broad perspective. We first addressed ourselves to a discussion of the defining societal and interpersonal patterns and relationships that distinguish the various terms frequently used to apply to cross-group communication. In so doing, we sought to clarify and give meaning to these often loosely employed terms. Through our discussion of such societal and interpersonal relationships, we have defined "intercultural communication," "contracultural communication," "interracial communication," and "interethnic communication."

The second aim of our paper was to suggest some of the major factors that may influence patterns of interracial communication. Here we discussed how the dimensions of class and economic stratification and the multiethnic composition of the white and non-white populations of the United States further complicate the possibilities for interracial communication. Our exploration of a possible framework within which to view the many possible communication patterns arising in such an ethnically and racially diverse society has enabled us to propose certain interracial communication hypotheses and questions. For example: Are individuals more attracted to communication situations involving members of their own racial and/or ethnic group or to situations involving interaction with members of their own class and/or economic strata? Does tension in interracial communication diminish as the communicators ascend the economic and class ladders of the society?

These questions are a minute sample of the many relevant communication research areas suggested by the complex structure of our society. In asking such questions, and in attempting to provide a large framework within which we can view the multi-dimensional qualities of intercultural and interracial communication, we hope to gain a better understanding of the interaction between the various conflicting forces in our nation and our world.

ENDNOTES

[1] K. S. Sitaram, "Intercultural Communication: The What and Why of It," International Communication Association, Division V: Intercultural Communication Division, Minneapolis, Minnesota, May 7–8, 1970, 2.

[2] By "communication," we mean a process whereby a source elicits a response in a receiver through the transmission of a message, be it sign or symbol, verbal or nonverbal. We find it necessary for our purposes to include nonverbal and sign behavior in our definition of communication, since intercultural communication frequently occurs without the benefit of a symbolic system shared by the communicators.

[3] Sitaram, op. cit., 7.

[4] Milton Rokeach, in Beliefs, Attitudes, and Values (San Francisco: Jossey-Bass, 1968), pp. 62–81, suggests in his findings on race, attitudes, and interpersonal choice, that individuals are more likely to choose as partners those who hold common beliefs with them rather than those who are of the same color. This study was conducted only in the North, which may have influenced its validity. Rokeach also states that discrimination is institutionally sanctioned.

[5] Certain religions tend to be associated with given ethnic groups—Italian Catholics, for example. Though religion could be introduced as an entirely separate parameter, we have decided, for the sake of brevity, to combine ethnic background and religious affiliation into one graphic structure.

6

American Identity Movements: A Cross-Cultural Confrontation

Gary R. Weaver

If we were to assess the significant, long-term results of the civil rights and anti-Vietnam war movements of the 1960's, we would probably place at the top of our list the numerous court decisions barring discrimination, the development of massive opposition to the Vietnam war, and the 18-year-old right to vote. While all of these developments are indeed important, I suggest that by far the most significant long-term consequence of both movements is the growth of popular questioning of cultural assumptions held by Americans for generations. Rather than having values of a subcultural group dissipated and absorbed by the dominant culture, these two groups have undermined the values and assumptions of the dominant culture.

The net result of these two movements has been a drive toward true pluralism of cultures and subcultures—including such "subcultural" identity groups as Women's Lib, Gay Lib, Chicano, American-Indian, and many other groups. No longer are individuals denying their identities to fit into an abstractive, Anglo-male society. They are asserting their uniqueness and wholeness while taking it for granted that they are entitled to their fair share of society's benefits.

Reprinted from *Intellect* (March 1975): 377–380, copyright © 1975, Society for the Advancement of Education.

THE MELTING POT MYTH

Foremost among the numerous assumptions which are now questioned by many Americans is the long-standing "melting pot" myth of cultural equality of people of all races. We would have to search diligently to find evidence of Chinese, Latin, Middle Eastern, Indian-American, African, or of even Eastern or Southern European ethnic patterns of behavior and thought being absorbed into the American culture. The pot melted no further than corn, chop suey, spaghetti, pork chops, and shish kebab. Each ethnic group has not contributed its own cultural traits equally to the whole. Rather, there has been a cultural shaping by a white, male, Protestant, Anglo-Saxon cookie cutter. This leveling (not "melting") has now been challenged by numerous subcultural groups as they fight for their own life styles, values, perceptions, and interests, which are often contrary to the mainstream mold.

This cultural imperialism (not cultural pluralism) was a result of racism, liberalism, and rapid technological and urban growth. It was obviously easier to identify non-whites and to reject not only their cultural, but also their individual identities. The dynamics of racism are now apparent to most Americans. The more subtle effects of liberalism are less apparent. In fact, the community-focused, equality-directed characteristics of liberalism seem to be contrary to any sort of racism or cultural imperialism. Yet, the belief that all men are equal is perhaps as responsible for this cultural leveling as any sort of overt racism, primarily because it denies the reality of physical, cultural, and psychological differences among men.

Let us contrast the positions of the overt racist and the so-called liberal regarding racial attitudes. The racist would maintain that whites and non-whites are inherently different, and that non-whites are inferior to whites. The liberal would maintain that whites and non-whites are basically the same, except that non-whites have not been treated equally. This liberal contention appears very humane, yet could easily be translated to mean the only reason non-whites are different is that they are pathologically white. If their culture were the same as the white culture, everyone would be equal. This denies the very real fact that there are non-white subcultures and that non-whites are not only physiologically different, but also culturally different. Accepting these differences does not lead us back to racism, because there is no current need to assume superiority or inferiority.

The break-up of fairly isolated communities and ethnic groups by industrialism, urban growth, and technological advancement, especially in the mass media, has abetted the liberal drive for homogeneity and the consequent imposition of an Anglo-Saxon cultural cookie cutter. This shaping and leveling is expressed by Daniel P. Moynihan as he suggests that the lack of a biological father in many black homes is responsible for much of the economic and social ills in ghettos around the country.[1] The assumption is that the Western model of the family is ideal, and that the black model is pathological. There are literally millions of families around the world that do not have the biological father present, yet there is a low incidence of crime, few riots, and the social fabric seems quite healthy. Thus, it is anthropologically unsound to assume that the Western family model is "normal" or best. Indeed, numerous scholars are beginning to feel that the Western family model may be responsible for many contemporary ills in Western society today.

THE QUALITATIVE REVOLUTION

Blacks and students towards the mid-1960's began to resemble each other in terms of opposition—they were against *the system*. Until then, this was not necessarily true—that is, the black civil rights movement was geared to allow increased participation in the system. To this extent, it was very much like the labor movement and previous revolutionary movements. Its objective was *quantitative*—a piece of the socio-economic and political pie. The student movement, on the other hand, was primarily *qualitative*. For many, the pie was not worth eating in the first place. By the mid-1960's, however, black leaders began to question the quality of the pie and, indeed, began to develop cultural styles in opposition to the pie.

This opposition to the system extended throughout the student movement around the technologically advanced world. Regardless of nationality, students seemed to oppose any way of life or thought which appeared systematic, rule-bound, and impersonal, as opposed to the spontaneous, the free, the intensely and, therefore, personally felt. However, this opposition is true mainly of the technologically developed cultures. In the less technologically developed countries, student revolts were much less qualitative. For example, in January, 1972, there was a university student revolt in Sierra Leone, in which the major issues included ironing boards in the dormitories, more allowance, and better food. There was little effort to change "the system" of Sierra Leone.

Whereas the 1950's was the era of conformity, the 1960's was the era when nonconformity was paramount. In the late 1950's "everyone" smoked Marlboros, college men (black and white) wore Ivy League clothes, and, while McCarthy purged, the Korean War killed hundreds of thousands, an economic crisis pervaded, and Emmett Till was killed, young people ran through college dormitories yelling for panties before rushing to their favorite fraternity or sorority parties. In the 1960's, cigarettes became available for the *exceptional* man or woman, students could come to class nearly nude without arousing more than a hearty ho-hum, a President announced that he wanted to make the world "safe for diversity," and massive movements were led against racial discrimination and war. Students occupied the university president's office to protest discrimination, war, and lack of participation in decision-making. Fraternities and sororities were dying.

I suggest that many of these phenomena were not only reactions to the leveling process of the pre-1950's, but an effort to retain subcultural and personal identity, and to prevent the sense of meaninglessness and the rush toward an Orwellian *1984* from becoming a reality. That is, they were not signs of cultural disintegration, but, rather, efforts to truly maintain cultural integration of all ethnic and subcultural groups without the cultural imperialism of the past overwhelming individual and group identity.

No longer are various subcultural groups willing to pay the price of loss of individual and cultural identity to get their fair share of the systemic pie. If gaining a quantitative advance means qualitative loss in lifestyle to accommodate the mass-society cookie-cutter, then the alternative is no longer one of copping out, as the Beat Generation did, but one of altering the dominant cultural system to allow for retention and enhancement of cultural identity while offering a share of the pie. This new awareness may be termed "Consciousness Level III" or a "prefigurative culture," but the net result is that, with the 1970's, it has grown to include Women's Lib, Gay Lib, the Chicano movement, the American-Indian movement, and even various communal efforts.

THE ASSOCIATIVE VS. ABSTRACTIVE CULTURE

What is the qualitative American cultural revolution all about? It is a struggle between two modes of thought, reflecting two cultures which seem in opposition. More importantly, it represents a struggle between two ways of organizing society, its values, and perceptions. It has been described as a struggle between associative and abstractive cultures, relational and analytic thought, or as a struggle between members of a *Gemeinschaft* or community and members of a *Gesellschaft* or more complex society.

The struggle is very much analogous to the culture clash of technologically advanced mass societies and non-technologically advanced, community-oriented cultures. Although this clash has been described as occurring between East and West, this is greatly oversimplified and misleading. In actuality, it has no absolute geographic parameters, but, rather, socioeconomic, philosophic, and experiential demarcations, with no sharp line dividing one culture into the associative grouping and another into the abstractive grouping. While the associative, non-Westernized grouping might include parts of Latin America, Asia, and Africa, there are "hybrids" of sorts—such

as Japan, urbanized Latin America, and perhaps even urbanized Nigeria.

This oversimplified model of culture is intended to offer a way of contrasting and comparing two basic culture-and-personality systems. It is primarily descriptive, yet may lead us to understand that the clash between generations, races, and identity groups today is indeed a culture gap, not a generation gap. It is no accident that young people today have developed music styles similar to the realism of blues or the free-style of jazz, that youth prefer bright clothing, or that self-actualizing students use Eastern philosophies to guide their lifestyles while young blacks seek their African roots.

To illustrate this, let us consider the following linguistic example. As an undergraduate, I often joined my fraternity brothers at Howard University as they met outside one of the women's dormitories to evaluate the quality and quantity of incoming coeds during the first few days of the fall semester. This was a popular male, chauvinistic activity which allowed the brothers to get together and talk. As we sat there, I noticed that a particular brother, John, was not with the group. I asked a fellow brother, "Where's John?" "Oh he's not hanging out. He's got a nose job." At the moment I thought it extremely odd that John, who was fairly handsome, would have his nose altered surgically. A few weeks later, I again noticed that John was not hanging out at a local bar with his fraternity brothers. Again, I inquired as to the whereabouts of John. Again, the reply was, "He's got a nose job." Finally, I broke down and asked, "What do you mean, a nose job?" "You know, a young lady has him by the nose." To have a "nose job" was to be deeply involved with a girlfriend, consequently being unable to hang out with his friends. Out of cultural context, and translated literally, the phrase made absolutely no sense.

Here we find a characteristic of associative or relational language. It is a product of small, intimate groups or people who subconsciously share similar experiences. For example, every language has a standard and nonstandard form—the so-called King's English and patois. The non-standard form is usually a subcultural form. In no way is the non-standard language a sign of lack of intelligence. In fact, it is often more sophisticated than the standard language in its verbal, spoken form. Seldom is it written, making it necessary to communicate face-to-face vocally, sharing more than simply words, but also the physical presence of another. Body language, tone of voice, and who is speaking to whom are all important. Everything is *associated* with everything. It is more intimate than standard language, which can be written and translated quite easily to everyone, regardless of who wrote it, where only *words* are relevant and *abstracted* or selected out of the communications scenario.

BLACK DIALECT: AN ASSOCIATIVE LANGUAGE

Let us consider a non-standard form with which we are all somewhat familiar—black dialect, or black patois (sometimes termed ghettoese). Not only does it have a very consistent grammatical form, but, in terms of verbal usage, it is much more sophisticated than standard English. For example, if a teacher asked a child to have his mother come to school tomorrow, the child might respond, "No, she can't. She be sick." The teacher then asks, "Would you please have her come in next week, then?" The child responds, "No. She can't. She be sick." What is happening? Is the child making up an excuse? On the contrary, the child is expressing himself very clearly, using the verb "to be" in a tense which is no longer used in the English language, but is found in Shakespearean English, to indicate an ongoing process—that is, his mother is ill, and will be ill, an ongoing process. This verb tense is found in many non-written languages around the world and in many non-Western languages such as Greek. Interestingly, "to be" (ascription) is the most common verb in black dialect and many non-Western languages, while "to do" (achievement) is the most common verb in standard English.

Associative verbal interaction is highly developed. A popular activity among children in ghetto areas is an activity called Joning, the Dozens, or the Numbers. It is a form of interaction where one child tries to out-insult an-other, usually poetically, by referring to his mother. Often, this game can go on for hours and requires a good verbal command, the ability to tie words together associatively, use of vocal and body messages, and a very quick wit. Few standard-speaking children could handle the English language as deftly as these children do.

"Toasting" is another very common usage of non-standard English. A toast is a very long story in poetry fashion which is passed on and added to as it is passed along. Many famous toasts, such as "Stagger Lee," were developed in jail. Not only are toasts indicative of a highly sophisticated language form, they often have been passed down in perfect iambic pentameter form. The same is true of many of the lyrics to blues music.

In fact, all artistic work is, by definition, associative. That is, a work of art is meaningful because it sets off a series of emotional associations in the viewer/listener. It is somewhat misleading to term such modern art "abstract art." Although it does abstract from a totality of lines, colors, and forms only those which are basic to a particular theme, feeling, tone or mood, abstract art is art because the viewer can associate spontaneously with the message of the artist, without the clutter of extraneous lines, colors, and forms. To a great extent, this is perhaps the purest form of association, similar to the glass bead game of Herman Hesse.

Poetry and music are whole works which can not be divided into separate parts, however much pedantic critics might wish to do so. They ignite a series of deep associations in the listener's head, and he feels what the poet or composer felt. The words and sounds bring to his conscious mind feelings which were long buried in the unconscious. Is it any wonder that poetry is perhaps the most difficult written form to translate into another language?

A contrast of mainstream, white poetry and black poetry illustrates the associative element in the black culture. Black poetry is usually read aloud, and voice tone, gestures, and the presence of both poet and listener is essential (*e.g.,* Gill Scott Heron, Nikki Giovanni). White poetry is usually not read aloud, but, if it is, it is done in a monotone, non-emotional voice.

Lastly, we all speak associative languages with loved ones and friends. Labels we give loved ones have developed by usage and are intimate ways of expressing feelings. Most of us would be offended if a stranger called our wife "bunny," or our husband "sugar." Who says what to whom is vital, and the meaning is all in the situation.

MASS SOCIETY: THE ABSTRACTIVE CULTURE

Of course, we all can speak abstractive language. It is technical and provides a common language for performing tasks without considering who is saying what to whom. The message, not the communicator, is all that is important. Thus, it can be easily written, but communicates little feeling. It is eminently rational, logical, practical, and simple. In fact, much of what the Anglo-male culture values is typically abstractive (objectivity, aloofness, rationality), and is exactly the opposite of what is considered associative—and often feminine (subjectivity, personal and emotional involvement).

These two styles of expression not only represent two ways of thought, but two ways of organizing society. The abstractive is typical of complex societies, where individual differences or subgroup differences are leveled to provide a common mode of communication. The associative represents a homogeneous community, where everyone shares the same collective unconscious, has similar values and perceptions, and has similar childhood experiences. The small, isolated village would be an associative community, while the larger urban areas or the total U.S. would be an abstractive mass society.

People come together in groups because they either trust each other or because there is mutual predictability. In a community, there is natural predictability, because all share the same collective values and behavior patterns. Everyone knows his or her place and belongs to the community. There are spontaneous similarities between all members of the community, and one can therefore infer from one's own behavior the behavior of others. This is very common in all homogeneous groups where there is no need for written rules to govern behavior, because what is proper is unconsciously known.

Ten years ago, in a small, white community, roles were *ascribed*. If you came from a wealthy, landed family or one with a long "noble" heritage, you could be the dumbest citizen in the community and still have the highest status. On the other hand, even if you were the most intelligent black in the community, your role would be ascribed as having the lowest status. Communities are in-group oriented, unconsciously very tradition-directed, rigid, and difficult to belong to unless you were born into the culture. This is very illogical for organizing talents in the culture, but very *human*.

Abstractive societies are made up of groups of people who do not know each other well enough to trust one another spontaneously. People come from various ethnic groups, value systems, perceptual systems, etc. Status, ideally, is achieved generally in economic terms, and social trust is maintained through a system of explicit rules, which every member of the society must learn, and which must be enforced to protect the rights of all. Thus, what a person *is* becomes irrelevant to the system—only what a person *does* is important. This is much more logical and humane than the associative community, but much less human. In fact, it is a schizoid organization, where the totality of a person is discarded—whether he is Protestant, black, sad, happy, etc., is of no consequence unless it interferes with his task.

This schizoid nature of abstractive societies has led to the sense of alienation one feels. The boss really doesn't give a damn if your mother died last night. We have difficulty communicating feelings, and, in fact, we find we cannot really feel anything. It has reached the point where the schizoid nature of the abstractive system has created inefficiency. Thus, businesses and government are supporting such devices as sensitivity sessions to break down the inability of people to relate as human beings, instead of merely as task performers.

In many ways, the abstractive society is more humane—that is, it is more objective and not as in-group oriented. A black would not be logically rejected simply for being black, because blackness is irrelevant to task performance. There is a larger and less rigid frame of reference, but, also, there is an inability to grant the wholeness of people and to take into account such supposedly irrelevant criteria as ethnic identity, personal feelings, and individual egos.

The associative community is more human—it gives a sense of wholeness and belonging—but it also excludes the outsider and is often very inhumane. The abstractive society is more humane—it does not necessarily reject the outsider and allows for advancement in terms of achievement, but it is also less human, as it treats individuals in a schizoid manner. The associative community seems very illogical, because behavior is determined by custom and numerous factors are associated with particular behavior, whether logically or not. For example, a few years ago I was in Honduras, visiting a Peace Corps contingent there. Numerous women volunteers were having trouble in their village. The men no longer respected them, yet they had done nothing to earn this disrespect. Upon closer analysis, it was found that the American women chose to wear slacks, because they were much more practical in the jungle. However, the local culture frowned upon women who wore slacks. Generally, women who wore slacks were prostitutes. Thus, associated with wearing slacks was the suggestion of prostitution, and the American women were being associated with these so-called "bad" women.

TRUE PLURALITY TODAY

Both the abstractive and associative cultures have their excesses. The associative community gives a sense of belonging, spontaneity, wholeness, predictability, in-group identity, and is very human, but it also is often rigid, ascriptive, exclusive of outsiders, inhumane in extreme, and can even be turned fascistic. The abstractive society is very logical, achievement-oriented, and humane, but it also leads to alienation, lack of whole self-identity, a schizoid personality, and, consequently, is very inhuman. Economically (capitalism), politically (liberalism), and socially (mass societies of heterogeneous ethnic groups), the abstractive culture has clearly conquered most subcultural groups. However, the student movement was certainly a reaction to this system, as are the ethnic minority and various identity movements today.

Young people have asked themselves what price one has to pay to become a member of the abstractive system. Is life really meaningful if one earns $50,000 per year, but has sacrificed his individual identity and feels like an insignificant cog in a societal machine that determines his worth by what he *does* rather than who he *is*? Blacks and other minority groups have also asked themselves whether they must necessarily give up their individual and group identities to melt into the pot—cannot one be black, and still be American? Was it an accident that other ethnic groups that melted so easily were termed Italian-American or Irish-American, while, until recently, those who could not melt were termed American Indians and American Negroes? Clearly, certain identifiable groups were treated as castes within the class system, and getting into the system seemed paramount. Thus, many blacks did straighten their hair and attempt to lighten their skin, many women did feel as if they must sacrifice their femininity to become achievers, and many homosexuals did marry and live miserable lives to keep their jobs and status in the society.

Presently, the qualitative revolution demands that these groups participate with equal opportunity in the class system without giving up group or sub-cultural identity, because the white, male, Protestant, Anglo-Saxon mold is increasingly questioned and challenged in terms of its quality and worth. In fact, even white, male, Protestant, Anglo-Saxons have begun to join the revolution.

ENDNOTE

[1]"The Moynihan Report" was a document prepared by Daniel P. Moynihan, titled *The Negro Family: The Case for National Action*, U.S. Department of Labor, U.S. Government Printing Office, Washington, D.C., 1965.

7

On *Gemeinschaft* and *Gesellschaft*

Ferdinand Tönnies[1]

1. ORDER—LAW—MORES

There is a contrast between a social order which—being based upon consensus of wills—rests on harmony and is developed and ennobled by folkways, mores, and religion, and an order which—being based upon a union of rational wills—rests on convention and agreement, is safeguarded by political legislation, and finds its ideological justification in public opinion.[1]

There is, further, in the first instance a common and binding system of positive law, of enforcible norms regulating the interrelation of wills. It has its roots in family life and is based on land ownership. Its forms are in the main determined by the code of the folkways and mores. Religion consecrates and glorifies these forms of the divine will, i.e., as interpreted by the will of wise and ruling men. This system of norms is in direct contrast to a similar positive law which upholds the separate identity of the individual rational wills in all their interrelations and entanglements. The latter derives from the conventional order of trade and similar relations but attains validity and binding force only through the sovereign will and power of the state. Thus, it becomes one of the most important instruments of policy; it sustains, impedes, or furthers social trends; it is defended or contested publicly by doctrines and opinions and thus is changed, becoming more strict or more lenient.

Reprinted from *Sociology: The Great Statements,* ed. Marcello Truzzi (New York: McGraw Hill, 1971), 145–153.

There is, further, the dual concept of morality as a purely ideal or mental system of norms for community life. In the first case, it is mainly an expression and organ of religious beliefs and forces, by necessity intertwined with the conditions and realities of family spirit and the folkways and mores. In the second case, it is entirely a product and instrument of public opinion, which encompasses all relations arising out of contractual sociableness, contacts, and political intentions.

Order is natural law, law as such = positive law, mores = ideal law. Law as the meaning of what may or ought to be, of what is ordained or permitted, constitutes an object of social will. Even the natural law, in order to attain validity and reality, has to be recognized as positive and binding. But it is positive in a more general or less definite way. It is general in comparison with special laws. It is simple compared to complex and developed law.

2. DISSOLUTION

The substance of the body social and the social will consists of concord, folkways, mores, and religion, the manifold forms of which develop under favorable conditions during its lifetime. Thus, each individual receives his share from this common center, which is manifest in his own sphere, i.e., in his sentiment, in his mind and heart, and in his conscience as well as in his environment, his possessions, and his activities. This is also true of each group. It is in this center that the individual's strength is rooted, and his rights derive, in the last instance, from the one original law which, in its divine and natural character, encompasses and sustains him, just as it made him and will carry him away. But under certain conditions and in some relationships, man appears as a free agent (person) in his self-determined activities and has to be conceived of as an independent person. The substance of the common spirit has become so weak or the link connecting him with the others worn so thin that it has to be excluded from consideration. In contrast to the family and co-operative relationship, this is true of all relations among separate individuals where there is no common understanding, and no time-honored custom or belief creates a common bond. This means war and the unrestricted freedom of all to destroy and subjugate one another, or, being aware of possible greater advantage, to conclude agreements and foster new ties. To the extent that such a relationship exists between closed groups or communities or between their individuals or between members and nonmembers of a community, it does not come within the scope of this study. In this connection we see a community organization and social conditions in which the individuals remain in isolation and veiled hostility toward each other so that only fear of clever retaliation restrains them from attacking one another, and, therefore, even peaceful and neighborly relations are in reality based upon a warlike situation. This is, according to our concepts, the condition of *Gesellschaft*-like civilization, in which peace and commerce are maintained through conventions and the underlying mutual fear. The state protects this civilization through legislation and politics. To a certain extent science and public opinion, attempting to conceive it as necessary and eternal, glorify it as progress toward perfection.

But it is in the organization and order of the *Gemeinschaft* that folk life and folk culture persist. The state, which represents and embodies *Gesellschaft,* is opposed to these in veiled hatred and contempt, the more so the further the state has moved away from and become estranged from these forms of community life. Thus, also in the social and historical life of mankind there is partly close interrelation, partly juxtaposition and opposition of natural and rational will.

3. THE PEOPLE *(VOLKSTUM)* AND THE STATE *(STAATSTUM)*

In the same way as the individual natural will evolves into pure thinking and rational will, which tends to dissolve and subjugate its predecessors, the original collective forms of *Gemeinschaft* have developed into *Gesellschaft* and the rational will of the *Gesellschaft*. In the course of history, folk culture has given rise to the civilization of the state.

The main features of this process can be described in the following way. The anonymous mass of the people is the original and dominating power which creates the houses, the villages, and the towns of the country. From it, too, spring the powerful and self-determined individuals of many different kinds: princes, feudal lords, knights, as well as priests, artists, scholars. As long as their economic condition is determined by the people as a whole, all their social control is conditioned by the will and power of the people. Their union on a national scale, which alone could make them dominant as a group, is dependent on economic conditions. And their real and essential control is economic control, which before them and with them and partly against them the merchants attain by harnessing the labor force of the nation. Such economic control is achieved in many forms, the highest of which is planned capitalist production or large-scale industry. It is through the merchants that the technical conditions for the national union of independent individuals and for capitalistic production are created. This merchant class is by nature, and mostly also by origin, international as well as national and urban, i.e., it belongs to *Gesellschaft,* not *Gemeinschaft.* Later all social groups and dignitaries and, at least in tendency, the whole people acquire the characteristics of the *Gesellschaft.*

Men change their temperaments with the place and conditions of their daily life, which becomes hasty and changeable through restless striving. Simultaneously, along with this revolution in the social order, there takes place a gradual change of the law, in meaning as well as in form. The contract as such becomes the basis of the entire system, and rational will of the *Gesellschaft,* formed by its interests, combines with authoritative will of the state to create, maintain and change the legal system. According to this conception, the law can and may completely change the *Gesellschaft* in line with its own discrimination and purpose; changes which, however, will be in the interest of the *Gesellschaft,* making for usefulness and efficiency. The state frees itself more and more from the traditions and customs of the past and the belief in their importance. Thus, the forms of law change from a product of the folkways and mores and the law of custom into a purely legalistic law, a product of policy. The state and its departments and the individuals are the only remaining agents, instead of numerous and manifold fellowships, communities, and commonwealths which have grown up organically. The characters of the people, which were influenced and determined by these previously existing institutions, undergo new changes in adaptation to new and arbitrary legal constructions. These earlier institutions lose the firm hold which folkways, mores, and the conviction of their infallibility gave to them.

Finally, as a consequence of these changes and in turn reacting upon them, a complete reversal of intellectual life takes place. While originally rooted entirely in the imagination, it now becomes dependent upon thinking. Previously, all was centered around the belief in invisible beings, spirits and gods; now it is focalized on the insight into visible nature. Religion, which is rooted in folk life or at least closely related to it, must cede supremacy to science, which derives from and corresponds to consciousness. Such consciousness is a product of learning and culture and, therefore, remote from the people. Religion has an immediate contact and is moral in its nature because it is most deeply related to the physical-spiritual link which connects the generations of men. Science receives its moral meaning only from an observation of the laws of social life, which leads it to derive rules for an arbitrary and reasonable order of social organization. The intellectual attitude of the individual becomes gradually less and less influenced by religion and more and more influenced by science. Utilizing the research findings accumulated by the preceding industrious generation, we shall investigate the tremendous contrasts which the opposite poles of this dichotomy and these fluctuations entail. For this presentation, however, the following few remarks may suffice to outline the underlying principles.

4. TYPES OF REAL COMMUNITY LIFE

The exterior forms of community life as represented by natural will and *Gemeinschaft* were distinguished as house, village, and town.

These are the lasting types of real and historical life. In a developed *Gesellschaft,* as in the earlier and middle stages, people live together in these different ways. The town is the highest, viz., the most complex, form of social life. Its local character, in common with that of the village, contrasts with the family character of the house. Both village and town retain many characteristics of the family; the village retains more, the town less. Only when the town develops into the city are these characteristics almost entirely lost. Individuals or families are separate identities, and their common locale is only an accidental or deliberately chosen place in which to live. But as the town lives on within the city, elements of the *Gemeinschaft,* as the only real form of life, persist within the *Gesellschaft,* although lingering and decaying. On the other hand, the more general the condition of *Gesellschaft* becomes in the nation or a group of nations, the more this entire "country" or the entire "world" begins to resemble one large city. However, in the city and therefore where general conditions characteristic of the *Gesellschaft* prevail, only the upper strata, the rich and the cultured, are really active and alive. They set up the standards to which the lower strata have to conform. These lower classes conform partly to supersede the others, partly in imitation of them in order to attain for themselves social power and independence. The city consists, for both groups (just as in the case of the "nation" and the "world"), of free persons who stand in contact with each other, exchange with each other and cooperate without any *Gemeinschaft* or will thereto developing among them except as such might develop sporadically or as a leftover from former conditions. On the contrary, these numerous external contacts, contracts, and contractual relations only cover up as many inner hostilities and antagonistic interests. This is especially true of the antagonism between the rich or the so-called cultured class and the poor or the servant class, which try to obstruct and destroy each other. It is this contrast which, according to Plato, gives the "city" its dual character and makes it divide in itself. This itself, according to our concept, constitutes the city, but the same contrast is also manifest in every large-scale relationship between capital and labor. The common town life remains within the *Gemeinschaft* of family and rural life; it is devoted to some agricultural pursuits but concerns itself especially with art and handicraft which evolve from these natural needs and habits. City life, however, is sharply distinguished from that; these basic activities are used only as means and tools for the special purposes of the city.

The city is typical of *Gesellschaft* in general. It is essentially a commercial town and, in so far as commerce dominates its productive labor, a factory town. Its wealth is capital wealth which, in the form of trade, usury, or industrial capital, is used and multiplies. Capital is the means for the appropriation of products of labor or for the exploitation of workers. The city is also the center of science and culture, which always go hand in hand with commerce and industry. Here the arts must make a living; they are exploited in a capitalistic way. Thoughts spread and change with astonishing rapidity. Speeches and books through mass distribution become stimuli of far-reaching importance.

The city is to be distinguished from the national capital, which, as residence of the court or center of government, manifests the features of the city in many respects although its population and other conditions have not yet reached that level. In the synthesis of city and capital, the highest form of this kind is achieved: the metropolis. It is the essence not only of a national *Gesellschaft,* but contains representatives from a whole group of nations, i.e., of the world. In the metropolis, money and capital are unlimited and almighty. It is able to produce and supply goods and science for the entire earth as well as laws and public opinion for all nations. It represents the world market and world traffic; in it world industries are concentrated. Its newspapers are world papers, its people come from all corners of the earth, being curious and hungry for money and pleasure.

5. COUNTERPART OF *GEMEINSCHAFT*

Family life is the general basis of life in the *Gemeinschaft*. It subsists in village and town life. The village community and the town themselves can be considered as large families, the

various clans and houses representing the elementary organisms of its body; guilds, corporations, and offices, the tissues and organs of the town. Here original kinship and inherited status remain an essential, or at least the most important, condition of participating fully in common property and other rights. Strangers may be accepted and protected as serving members or guests either temporarily or permanently. Thus, they can belong to the *Gemeinschaft* as objects, but not easily as agents and representatives of the *Gemeinschaft*. Children are, during minority, dependent members of the family, but according to Roman custom they are called free because it is anticipated that under possible and normal conditions they will certainly be masters, their own heirs. This is true neither of guests nor of servants, either in the house or in the community. But honored guests can approach the position of children. If they are adopted or civic rights are granted to them, they fully acquire this position with the right to inherit. Servants can be esteemed or treated as guests or even, because of the value of their functions, take part as members in the activities of the group. It also happens sometimes that they become natural or appointed heirs. In reality there are many gradations, lower or higher, which are not exactly met by legal formulas. All these relationships can, under special circumstances, be transformed into merely interested and dissolvable interchange between independent contracting parties. In the city such change, at least with regard to all relations of servitude, is only natural and becomes more and more widespread with its development. The difference between natives and strangers becomes irrelevant. Everyone is what he is, through his personal freedom, through his wealth and his contracts. He is a servant only in so far as he has granted certain services to someone else, master in so far as he receives such services. Wealth is, indeed, the only effective and original differentiating characteristic; whereas in *Gemeinschaft* property it is considered as participation in the common ownership and as a specific legal concept is entirely the consequence and result of freedom or ingenuity, either original or acquired. Therefore, wealth, to the extent that this is possible, corresponds to the degree of freedom possessed.

In the city as well as in the capital, and especially in the metropolis, family life is decaying. The more and the longer their influence prevails, the more the residuals of family life acquire a purely accidental character. For there are only few who will confine their energies within such a narrow circle; all are attracted outside by business, interests, and pleasures, and thus separated from one another. The great and mighty, feeling free and independent, have always felt a strong inclination to break through the barriers of the folkways and mores. They know that they can do as they please. They have the power to bring about changes in their favor, and this is positive proof of individual arbitrary power. The mechanism of money, under usual conditions and if working under high pressure, is means to overcome all resistance, to obtain everything wanted and desired, to eliminate all dangers and to cure all evil. This does not hold always. Even if all controls of the *Gemeinschaft* are eliminated, there are nevertheless controls in the *Gesellschaft* to which the free and independent individuals are subject. For *Gesellschaft* (in the narrower sense), convention takes to a large degree the place of the folkways, mores, and religion. It forbids much as detrimental to the common interest which the folkways, mores, and religion had condemned as evil in and of itself.

The will of the state plays the same role through law courts and police, although within narrower limits. The laws of the state apply equally to everyone; only children and lunatics are not held responsible to them. Convention maintains at least the appearance of morality; it is still related to the folkways, mores, and religious and aesthetic feeling, although this feeling tends to become arbitrary and formal. The state is hardly directly concerned with morality. It has only to suppress and punish hostile actions which are detrimental to the common weal or seemingly dangerous for itself and society. For as the state has to administer the common weal, it must be able to define this as it pleases. In the end it will probably realize that no increase in knowledge and culture alone will make people kinder,

less egotistic, and more content and that dead folkways, mores, and religions cannot be revived by coercion and teaching. The state will then arrive at the conclusion that in order to create moral forces and moral beings it must prepare the ground and fulfill the necessary conditions, or at least it must eliminate counteracting forces. The state, as the reason of *Gesellschaft,* should decide to destroy *Gesellschaft* or at least to reform or renew it. The success of such attempts is highly improbable.

6. THE REAL STATE

Public opinion, which brings the morality of *Gesellschaft* into rules and formulas and can rise above the state, has nevertheless decided tendencies to urge the state to use its irresistible power to force everyone to do what is useful and to leave undone what is damaging. Extension of the penal code and the police power seems the right means to curb the evil impulses of the masses. Public opinion passes easily from the demand for freedom (for the upper classes) to that of despotism (against the lower classes). The makeshift, convention, has but little influence over the masses. In their striving for pleasure and entertainment they are limited only by the scarcity of the means which the capitalists furnish them as price for their labor, which condition is as general as it is natural in a world where the interests of the capitalists and merchants anticipated all possible needs and in mutual competition incite to the most varied expenditures of money. Only through fear of discovery and punishment, that is, through fear of the state, is a special and large group, which encompasses far more people than the professional criminals, restrained in its desire to obtain the key to all necessary and unnecessary pleasures. The state is their enemy. The state, to them, is an alien and unfriendly power; although seemingly authorized by them and embodying their own will, it is nevertheless opposed to all their needs and desires, protecting property which they do not possess, forcing them into military service for a country which offers them hearth and altar only in the form of a heated room on the upper floor or gives them, for native soil, city streets where they may stare at the glitter and luxury in lighted windows forever beyond their reach! Their own life is nothing but a constant alternative between work and leisure, which are both distorted into factory routine and the low pleasure of the saloons. City life and *Gesellschaft* doom the common people to decay and death; in vain they struggle to attain power through their own multitude, and it seems to them that they can use their power only for a revolution if they want to free themselves from their fate. The masses become conscious of this social position through the education in schools and through newspapers. They proceed from class consciousness to class struggle. This class struggle may destroy society and the state which is its purpose to reform. The entire culture has been transformed into a civilization of state and *Gesellschaft,* and this transformation means the doom of culture itself if none of its scattered seeds remain alive and again bring forth the essence and idea of *Gemeinschaft,* thus secretly fostering a new culture amidst the decaying one.

ENDNOTE

[1] Tönnies' major work, *Gemeinschaft und Gesellschaft* (first published in 1887), is available in English translation (edited and translated by Charles P. Loomis) as *Community and Society* (1957). It is also available in an earlier edition, which also contained some of Tönnies' later essays, as *Fundamental Concepts of Sociology* (1940). Tönnies' ten other books, of which the major work dealing with sociology is his 1931 *Einführung in die Soziologie (An Introduction to Sociology),* plus most of his essays, still await English translations. A full bibliography of Tönnies' work can be found in: *American Journal of Sociology,* 42 (1937): 100–101. He is best remembered for his distinction between two basic types of social groups. Tönnies argued that there are two basic forms of human will: the *essential will,* which is the underlying, organic, or instinctive driving force; and *arbitrary will,* which is deliberative, purposive, and future (goal) oriented. Groups that formed around essential will, in which membership is self-fulfilling, Tönnies called *Gemeinschaft* (often translated as *community*). Groups in which membership was sustained by some instrumental goal or definite end he termed *Gesellschaft* (often translated as *society*). *Gemeinschaft* was exemplified by the family or neighborhood; *Gesellschaft,* by the city or the state.

8

Contrasting and Comparing Cultures

Gary R. Weaver

MODELS FOR ANALYZING CULTURE

There are various ways of examining culture. For example, we can discuss each culture in terms of its components. We might begin with what we can observe—how people behave or what type of art and literature is most common. People in all cultures eat food and raise their children. However, the types of food they prefer and how the food is prepared and eaten many depend upon their culture—the majority of American may eat hamburgers with their hands. And, the ways in which people raise their children tend to be different in each culture.

This examination also allows us to explore why people of different cultures behave as they do. The dominant attitudes, values and beliefs shape or motivate behavior. In some cultures food is an important aspect of social life—who is invited to one's home to share a meal with the family may depend upon the person's age, gender or social class. Appropriate table manners are a way of showing respect for others.

We can contrast and compare these hidden parts of culture—traditional or mainstream attitudes, values, beliefs, ways of perceiving reality, types of discourse or interaction and so forth. One culture may emphasize individualism and independence while another values collectivism and interdependence.

When people from different cultures come together there is often misunderstanding and

conflict caused by these differences. We can often explain why people from other cultures behave as they do if we have a more comprehensive understanding of their culture. And, we can often understand why we behave as we do if we are consciously aware of own culture. More importantly, we can anticipate where misunderstandings and conflict will take place when we interact with those who are culturally different if we understand the process of intercultural communication.

THE ICEBERG ANALOGY OF CULTURE

There are hundreds of different ways to define culture. Nevertheless, most scholars agree that a culture is implicitly and explicitly learned, it is a system of interrelated parts and it is shared with others. People in the same society have roughly the same values, beliefs, behaviors, perceptions of reality and ways of communicating. Culture causes this to happen.

While culture is a concept, we know that is exists based upon inference. That is, we infer that people have a particular set of values or beliefs when we examine their artifacts—art, music or literature.

Personality is another concept that we infer exists based upon what we can observe. We might describe a person as shy or aggressive because that is the way he or she behaves in most situations. Sigmund Freud described personality as analogous to an iceberg with the largest part being unconscious. More importantly, he believed that the unconscious controls the conscious and if we really what to know what motivates behavior, we must delve into the unconscious which was largely formed during our preadolescent years.

Usually we are unaware of the importance of our unconscious until we experience a personal crisis which alters our everyday life or we undergo psychoanalysis where the normal rule of behavior and discourse are absent. During these situations we often begin to ask ourselves why we behave, think or feel as we do. According to Freud, the answers are often buried or repressed in our unconscious mind.

Edward T. Hall, an anthropologist, suggests that culture is also like an iceberg, the tip (or external culture) is really the smallest part.[1]

This article is first published here and was developed to help readers to conceptualize, organize and relate various cross-culture models discussed throughout this book.

The largest part of culture is inside our heads and unconscious—beneath the water level of awareness. This is internal culture. Hall also views internal culture or "mind" as dominant over external culture. If we are to understand what motivates behavior, we must explore internal culture.

We are usually unaware of our own culture until we leave it and interact with those who are culturally different. This interaction and conflict raises aspects of our own culture to our conscious awareness. The irony is that the way we often find our culture is by leaving it.

This vertical model of culture allows us to identify aspects of all cultures. We can add layers to the iceberg of culture and consider what happens when people from different cultures come together. When icebergs float together in the ocean, we first notice the tips, whereas they actually collide underwater. When people from different cultures come together they may be concerned about making mistakes on the external level—saying the wrong word or wearing inappropriate clothing. The real conflict occurs at the internal level when values, thought patterns, central beliefs, perceptions and attitudes clash.

Every culture has explicit and conscious behavioral aspects such as language or verbal communication, customs, and typical food or dress. This part of culture is external and can be acquired through observation, education or training. It is fairly easily learned and changed. However, these aspects of culture may be the least important.

Just as our unconscious mind may be the source for much of our behavior, thoughts and feelings, internal culture determines or motivates much of our overt or explicit cultural behavior. To explain why people from the same culture behave as they do we must examine their internal culture.

People in the same culture tend to share many common conscious beliefs—things we think are true or correct.[2] Some are learned overtly, primarily through formal education. They are specific, and thus similar to opinions because they often change with new information. For example, as a capitalist you think that government should not interfere in the economy. As you learn more about economics, you may change this belief because you find that sometimes government must interfere to insure a fair distribution of resources and opportunities for everyone.

Other beliefs are learned implicitly or unconsciously through interaction with others within a particular culture. They include likes

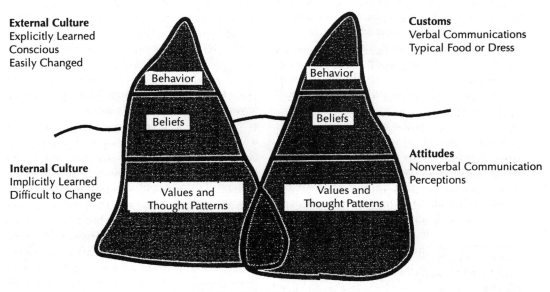

External Culture
Explicitly Learned
Conscious
Easily Changed

Customs
Verbal Communications
Typical Food or Dress

Behavior

Behavior

Beliefs

Beliefs

Internal Culture
Implicitly Learned
Difficult to Change

Attitudes
Nonverbal Communication
Perceptions

Values and Thought Patterns

Values and Thought Patterns

THE "ICEBERG ANALOGY" OF CULTURE

or dislikes (attitudes) and things that are important to us which we want or desire (values). Because these beliefs are learned so early in life, they are usually taken for granted until we encounter others who do not share our basic beliefs.

Our beliefs are interrelated and therefore we can speak of "belief systems." However, there are often inconsistencies and contradictions between our beliefs, especially between external and internal beliefs. We usually first become aware of these contradictions when we encounter others with different beliefs and we are must explain our beliefs.

The largest and the most hidden part of any culture includes basic values, ways of thinking and perceiving, and nonverbal communication. Because these aspects of internal culture are implicitly learned before adolescence, we are usually unaware of their existence. And, it is very difficult to change internal culture.

Some theorists claim that if we change someone's values, we will necessarily change his or her behavior.[3] People who value relationships or affiliations more than individual achievement may not be willing to leave their friends and family for job opportunities that require long hours away from home or travel to distant shores. However, when we reward individual achievement, with increased salary, the individual's productivity may increase along with the productivity of others in the society. In turn, the overall economy advances. In terms of economic development, this is almost the opposite of the Marxist approach which basically asserts that if we change the structure or means of production we will change the values of people.

On the other hand, we can perhaps change behavior which, in turn, alters attitudes, beliefs and values.[4] This is the basic premise of the theory of cognitive dissonance. If people engage in behavior that contradicts their beliefs, they feel dissonance. They cannot deny their behavior. To create consonance between the reality of their actions and their beliefs, most will change their beliefs.

This is the reason that many groups, such as fraternities and sororities, require new members to engage is some kinds of humiliating or humbling ritualized behavior (hazing) before they are given membership in the group. After engaging in such behavior, they convince themselves that they must surely value being a member of the group. This practice creates loyalty to the group and a strong sense of in-group membership.

CONTRAST CULTURE CONTINUUM

We can also consider horizontal models that allow us to contrast and compare cultures according to such characteristics as social structure, philosophic outlook, basic values and/or ways of interacting. These contrasts are oversimplifications and generalizations, but they allow us to consider the differences and similarities between cultures.

Cultures might be placed along a continuum ranging from the abstractive, low-context and urban to the associative, high-context and rural. Most cultures tend to fall on one side of the continuum or the other. However, no single culture falls completely within any one category. Differences between cultures are a matter of degree. For example, people in one culture may be more abstractive or low-context than people in another culture.

Theoretically, we could place the Swiss-German, urban American and rural Bedouin Arab cultures along this continuum as follows:

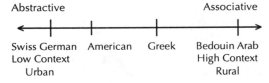

As with all typologies, these descriptions never apply to everyone in a particular culture at all times. For example, rural Americans from the South may fall on the right hand side of this continuum. Also, people from some cultures may be a combination of types. Greeks, Italians, Turks, Egyptians and other Mediterranean peoples could be described as both Eastern and Western or Dionysian and Apollonian. They may fall in the middle of the continuum.

While most people come from cultures that lean toward one end of the continuum, some are more bicultural or multicultural. For example, an American may have lived in a small, Southern rural village during his or her formative years and later adapted to the culture of Manhattan in New York City. Initially, there was a clash of values when this person arrived in Manhattan, but after years of acculturation, he or she can move easily and authentically between the two contrasting cultures.

Cultures might include gender or ethnic and racial groups within a particular society. Some authors would place Anglo-American males on the abstractive, low-context end of this continuum, while Anglo-American women and African Americans might be placed on the associative or high-context end.

This following chart is simply a heuristic device that can help us sort out the various contrasts and comparisons used by authors throughout this anthology. This list is neither totally inclusive nor comprehensive. We could add many other terms and categories. And, there is overlap between categories—social structure affects basic values and vice versa. In a society where the typical family is the nuclear family composed of the husband, wife and children and there is great physical and social mobility, independence and self-reliance may be significant values. These values, in turn, encourage people to be mobile and perhaps restrict the size of their family.

CHARACTERISTIC CULTURE

Abstractive	Associative[5]
Gesellschaft	*Gemeinschaft*[6]
Society	Community
Urban	Rural
Apollonian	Dionysian[7]
Heterogeneous	Homogeneous

SOCIAL STRUCTURE

Individualistic	Collective[8]
Small or nuclear family	Extended family
Overt social rules	Implicit social rules
Loose in-group/out-group distinction	Rigid in-group/out-group distinction
Achieved or earned status	Ascribed status[9]
Flexible roles	Rigid roles
Loosely integrated	Highly integrated
Class	Caste
Social and physical mobility	Little social or physical mobility
Low power distance	High power distance[10]

PHILOSOPHIC OUTLOOK

Mastery or control over nature	Harmony with or subjugation to nature[11]
Melodramatic/escapist	Tragic/realistic[12]
Humane/inhuman	Human/inhumane
Objective	Subjective
Quantitative	Qualitative
Alloplastic	Autoplastic[13]
Mind/body dichotomy	Union of mind and body

PSYCHOLOGICAL ORIENTATION

Psychology of abundance	Psychology of scarcity[14]
Schizoid or fragmented	Comprehensive or holistic[15]
Need for achievement	Need for affiliation[16]
Abstractive and logical	Anthropomorphic and complexic[17]
Masculine	Feminine[18]
Direct responsibility	Indirect responsibility
Great use of extensions	Little use of extensions
Extension transference	No extension transference[19]

Steep pleasure gradient	Flat pleasure gradient[20]
Weak uncertainty avoidance	Strong uncertainty avoidance[21]
Guilt-internal	Shame-external

THOUGHT PATTERNS

Analytic	Relational[22]
Theoretical learning and knowledge	Experiential or kinesthetic learning and knowledge
Dichotomous/divisions	Holistic/joining together
Linear-separations	Nonlinear-comprehensive
Abstractions/prose	Imagery/poetry

BASIC VALUES

Doing	Being[23]
Change/action	Stability/harmony
What/content	How/style
Individualism	Belongingness
Independence	Interdependence/dependence
Self-reliance	Reliance upon others

PERCEPTION

Mind/body dichotomy	Mind and body are one
Monochronic time/action	Polychronic time/action[24]
Linear or segmented time	Nonlinear or comprehensive time
Future orientation	Past or present orientation
Space/objects separated	Continuity of space/objects
Subject-object	Subject-subject
Nonsensual and non-senseful	Sensual and senseful

INTERACTION

Low-context	High-context[25]
Competition	Cooperation[26]
Verbal emphasis	Nonverbal and verbal
Written or electronic	Face-to-face
Impersonal	Personal
Schizoid/fragmented relationships	Holistic/interdependent relationships
Monological	Dialogical[27]
Practical/aloof	Nonpurposive/involved
Easy to break action chains	Difficult to break action chains[28]
Systematic	Spontaneous

ENDNOTES

[1]Edward T. Hall, *Beyond Culture* (Garden City, NY: Doubleday, 1976).

[2]See Milton Rokeach, *The Nature of Human Values* (New York: Free Press, 1973) and Marshall Singer's "The Role of Culture and Perception in Communication" in this section, 28–53.

[3]David McClelland, *The Achieving Society* (New York: Free Press, 1961) and Lawrence R. Harrison, *The Pan-American Dream: Do Latin America's Cultural Values Discourage True Partnership with the United States and Canada?* (New York: Basic Books, 1997).

[4]Leon Festinger, *A Theory of Cognitive Dissonance* (Stanford, CA: Stanford University Press, 1957). Also see Robert Jervis, "Cognitive Dissonance and International Relations" in Section V, 450–451. Once fighting begins, we are more likely to believe that our enemy deserved our aggression and that we are morally correct in our actions.

[5]Edmund S. Glenn, *Man and Mankind* (Norwood, NJ: Ablex, 1981).

[6]Ferdinand Tönnies, *Gemeinschaft and Gesellschaft* (Tubingen: Mohr, 1937). See also Ferdinand Tönnies' "En *Gemeinschaft* and *Gesellschaft*" in Section I, 66–71.

[7]Friedrich Nietzche, *The Birth of Tragedy* translated by William A. Haussmann, from *The Complete Works of Friedrich Nietzche,* Oscar Levy, editor (New York: Russell and Russell, Inc., 1964).

[8]Geert Hofstede, *Culture's Consequences: International Differences in Work-Related Values,* Abridged Edition (Beverly Hills:CA, Sage Publications, 1984). His framework is a multipolar rather than bipolar model and includes such continua as individualism/collectivism, masculine/feminine, high-/low-power distance and weak/strong uncertainty avoidance. Also see "The Cultural Relativity of the Quality of Life Concept" in Section II, 148–157.

A seven-dimensional model of national cultural differences is developed by F. Trompenaars, *Riding the Waves of Culture* (London: The Economist Books, 1993).

[9]Everett Hagen, *On the Theory of Social Change* (Homewood, IL: Dorsey Press/Massachusetts Institute of Technology, 1962).

[10]Hofstede, *Culture's Consequences.*

[11]Florence Kluckhohn and Fred Strodtbeck, *Variations in Value Orientations* (Evanston, IL: Row, Peterson, 1961).

[12]S.I. Hayakawa, *The Use and Misuse of Language* (Greenwich, CT: Fawcett, 1962).

[13]Robert Lindner, *Must You Conform?* (New York: Grove Press, 1956).

[14]Edward C. Stewart and Milton J. Bennett, *American Cultural Patterns: A Cross-Cultural Perspective* Revised Edition (Yarmouth, Maine: Intercultural Press, 1991).

[15]R.D. Laing, *The Divided Self* (London: Tavistock Publications; New York: Pantheon, 1960).

[16]McClelland, *The Achieving Society.*

[17]Jean Piaget, *Success and Understanding* (Cambridge, MA: Harvard University Press, 1978).

[18]Hofstede, *op. cit.*

[19]Hall, *Beyond Culture.*

[20]Philip Slater, *Earthwalk* (New York: Doubleday, 1974).

[21]Hofstede, *op. cit.*

[22]Rosalie A. Cohen, "Conceptual Styles, Culture, Conflict and Nonverbal Tests of Intelligence," *American Anthropologist,* 71, (1969): 828–856.

[23]Kluckhohn and Strodtbeck, *Variations in Value Orientations.*

[24]Hall, *op. cit.*

[25]*Ibid.*

[26]Theodore Isaac Rubin, *Reconciliations: Inner Peace in an Age of Anxiety* (New York: The Viking Press, 1980).

[27]Floyd W. Matson and Ashley Montagu, eds., *The Human Dialogue: Perspectives on Communication* (New York: The Free Press, 1967).

[28]Hall, *op. cit.*

9

Content Decisions in Intercultural Communication

Alfred G. Smith

By establishing a new Division of Intercultural Communication, SSCA (Southern Speech Communication Association) acknowledges that this field has graduated from an apprenticeship to a professional rank of scholarship and expertise. The inception of this new division also gives us a timely moment in the development of intercultural communication studies to reexamine what has been done and what can be done. We can consider the scope of the field and what it should include. We have this moment to make free and open decisions on the content and the priorities of this specialty, and to cast the die for the future.

SURVEY AND CHALLENGES

For this opportunity I reviewed the contents of many courses in intercultural communication: syllabuses from Virginia, Minnesota, Washington, and about thirty other institutions; I canvassed the textbooks by Prosser, Sarbaugh, Sitaram and Cogdell, Samovar and Porter and Jain, and half a dozen more; and I rechecked the programs and journals of ICA (International Communication Association), SIETAR (Society for International Education, Training, and Research), and other professional organizations in this field.

Alfred G. Smith (Ph.D., University of Wisconsin, 1956) is Professor of Speech Communication and Anthropology, University of Texas-Austin.

Reprinted from *The Southern Speech Communication Journal* 47, no. 3, (Spring 1982): 252–262, Appalachian State University.

Such a review can yield a meaningless miscellany unless we ask some specific questions about these courses and programs, questions that are basic to making content decisions for the future. One question might be, "What are the common denominators of these books, journals, and syllabuses?" A part of the answer is that the documents all cover some psychology of perception and prejudice, some anthropology of relativism and ethnocentrism, and some communication concepts like codes and channels. But at this moment of freedom we don't need common denominators, especially not the lowest and least common denominators. We can reach for the highest and most distinguished ideals.

Therefore we might rather ask, "Where do these courses fit in the ranks of the larger curriculum among French, physics, and philosophy?" A part of this answer is that intercultural communication is not a core liberal arts course like History of Western Civilization. Nor is it a specialized course with many prerequisites like Fluid Mechanics or Byzantine Architecture. At this turning point in the field, however, we don't need to make content decisions that merely fall into line with the rest of the curriculum. We can make decisions that lead to new planes of inquiry and new constellations of ideas.

Therefore, let us ask the bottom line question: "Why should we study intercultural communication?" The survey brought out three principal reasons: interpersonal adjustment; job skills; and cosmopolitanism. Let me size up each of these in turn, and let me look into alternatives. In that way let me present some challenges. For in general I found the content of intercultural communication courses to be timid, pale, and falling short of the promise.

In general I found that some scholars study role playing in order to learn what role expectations there are in another culture. Other scholars study nonverbal communication in intercultural contexts. To chemists, lawyers, and other professionals, studies of role taking and of body language may be interesting but they are also frothy and dilettantish. They are hardly a matter of life and death. The study of fidget patterns in intercultural communication is not an urgent matter like the doctor trying to save the victim of a heart attack; the cultivation of intimate entente is not an urgent matter like the physicist trying to control a nuclear chain reaction. In comparison with the concerns of other professions, some of the content of intercultural communication studies is rather effete and airy-fairy.

But that content can be significant. The world boils and belches with vital problems of intercultural communication. Often there is no freedom of speech on one side, or no access to information. Often there is injustice in the relations between the haves and have-nots. There is also war, that damned *doppelgänger* of intercultural communication. In the face of such problems some of the content of the field today is trivial. My challenge to the field is to change that content to what it can be: urgent and consequential.

INTERPERSONAL ADJUSTMENT

The most popular reason for studying intercultural communication is to "enhance individual capabilities for effective interaction in international and intercultural environments." These specific words happen to be SIETAR's but they speak for most of the syllabuses, journals, and texts. They focus on the individual and personal level of communication, the street floor of human interaction: face to face, eyeball to eyeball, nose to nose, and maybe heart to heart. At this level individual Boers interact with individual Bantu in South Africa, and the Turkish laborer in Germany tries to make out. As they seek some interpersonal adjustment on this intimate plane they face uncertainty and anxiety. Maybe a course in intercultural communication can help.

The world needs better human relations, but that depends on alleviating poverty, ignorance, injustice, and war, and that cannot be done on the interpersonal level. It takes better economic conditions, a job for everyone, freedom, and peace. The Turk has to leave his wife and children and hire out abroad because there is no work or money at home. Whatever intercultural accommodation he may manage in Germany is cold comfort and only hides the problem. To offer him interpersonal adjustment is to prescribe cough drops for tuberculosis.

Some Protestants and Catholics in Belfast may achieve some personal accord with one another, but that does not solve the basic discord in their country. Peace and justice between peoples are not gained at the level of personal adjustment. Intercultural communication between Black and White, Arab and Israeli requires rearrangements of political and economic institutions. When societal environments improve and people can take care of themselves and their families, then there is some foundation for better interpersonal relations.

The good souls who try to reduce bitterness and hate by reaching out in both directions across the intercultural no-man's land generally do not clear up underlying problems. They can't, not if they are ten thousand in a million, or even twenty thousand, that is, two percent. It probably takes a critical mass of twenty percent for interpersonal adjustments to have a significant impact on underlying differences between cultures. At that rate and at this level, the developing countries alone need a hundred million interpersonal adjustments. That would take at least ten million Peace Corps Volunteers from the United States plus millions of Japanese Overseas Cooperation Volunteers and more millions of French Volunteers for Progress and many more millions from every other country with a high standard of living. On an individual and personal level the job is so enormous and unwieldy, we had better think of approaching the problem at another level.

The critical mass for leaders may be lower because each of them can influence many people. Their interpersonal adjustments can trickle down and spread to all their staff and crew. Most leaders, however, do not think of intercultural communication as a personal matter. They look past their interpersonal adjustments and focus on the basic issues for their group: security and resources. Ronald Reagan and Jesse Jackson, or Deng Xiaoping and Ferdinand Marcos may well smile at one another; for them, however, thinking that better personal relations will improve intercultural conditions is like putting their shoes on first and then their socks.

Interpersonal adjustment is important to intercultural communication, and intercultural problems do affect people very personally. But these problems cannot be solved at an interpersonal level; they can only be solved at an intercultural level.

One of these problems, for example, is the invasion of privacy. The United States has laws against wiretapping, and we talk freely on telephones that are connected by microwave relays in the United States. The Cubans and the Russians, however, listened to our microwaved conversations quite openly from ships off our shores. Each country also has its own laws to protect personal information: our bank balances and medical files, our school records and tax payments, our votes and arrests. Different countries have different laws. Through the international network of computerized data banks, however, information that may not be available in one country may be available to some Big Brother in another country. Private information that becomes openly available in international communication is just one of the many personal problems that can make a great difference in the lives of millions of people but that can only be solved at the international level.

I challenge the notion that interpersonal adjustment is the most important reason for studying intercultural communication, and this raises the first of the content decisions to be made. Will these studies be radical in the sense of getting at the root of problems, or not? And will these studies get at the most important problems, those that affect most people the most?

JOB SKILLS

The syllabuses, books, and programs indicate that the second most popular reason for studying intercultural communication is to gain skills that are useful on the job. The skills these courses teach are for a general sensitivity to human relations and cultural differences. It is unmistakably valuable on any job to have such sensitivity. Is it, however, the most important skill if the job is to solve the major problems of intercultural communication?

Teaching students to be aware of empathy and discord depends on the kinds of students who take these courses. Today these students include an air traffic controller from India, a California businessman on his way to Nigeria, and a Peruvian studying pharmacy in Alabama. They all need some supplementary training in order to extend their main work to international settings. Some of these courses also have some students who make intercultural communication itself their principal field. These students tend to be generalists rather than technical specialists. As a whole, therefore, the intercultural job skills taught in these courses are less like an explicit discipline, such as computer programming or brain surgery, and more like an exploratory sensitivity, a general, supplementary, and non-technical awareness.

This keeps these courses from being as significant as they should be; even worse, it keeps them from dealing with the roots and causes of the major problems of intercultural communication. For in our wayward world, sensitivity training will not stop the saber rattling between the U.S.A. and the U.S.S.R., each one responding to the other by building bigger bombs. Sensitivity training will not solve the problems in Miami of young out-of-work Blacks, old and fading Whites, and recent arrivals from Cuba and Haiti. It will not help the starving refugees in Somalia. These problems call for reorganizing the frameworks of societies, rewriting the laws of countries, and changing the international policies of the powers of the world.

Some people may think it is utterly presumptuous to consider tackling such problems through communication. For the problems of saber rattling and starvation must be completely beyond the skills and resources of communication studies. Some people may think the problems in Somalia or El Salvador are simply not the function of communication studies. It is not their proper place. In the same way, some people once thought that the proper place for Blacks was in the back of the bus, and the proper place for women was at the kitchen sink.

The problems we face prescribe the skills we need. Air traffic controllers, pharmacists, and non-technical generalists face problems of interpersonal adjustment, and need skills of interpersonal sensitivity. American businessmen need skills in developing personal relationships with associates in Asia and Latin America. But these are relatively minor problems and skills. They are for intercultural communication what the common cold is for medicine. The serious problems of intercultural communication are brutal and deadly. They are problems of freedom and war, of equality and justice. They call for enormous technical skills.

For example, how should we make up our federal budget for international communication? Our annual military budget is at least five times greater than all other expenditures for foreign relations. This proportion of our military-to-civilian expenditures may convey an eloquent message itself; is this also the most effective budget mix? Would a ten percent increase in educational assistance, in Voice of America, and in other civilian services decrease the military expenditures by ten percent and reduce overall costs? This is a critical issue for intercultural communication studies, and it calls for great technical skills in cost-benefit analysis and risk-benefit analysis.

We also need rigorous skills for predicting what intercultural communication will be like in the future, and further skills for making decisions in the light of those predictions. For example, we enjoy a very favorable balance of trade in communication. Half the movies shown in the world at any time are from the United States. Our advertising agencies have half the billings on earth. We are the world's greatest exporters of communication. A number of independent investigations are beginning to show, however, that there is at least a leveling off in the international flow of broadcasts, films, books, and tapes. As business, science, and other undertakings mature, local communication increases but international communication decreases. As science develops in a country, the international citations in its scientific journals decrease. As television develops, imported programs decrease. This makes me wonder what our balance of communication trade will be five years from now. Will Hollywood become another Detroit? Is there something we should do today? This is another critical issue for intercultural communication studies, and it calls for great technical skills in economic forecasting.

The syllabuses, texts, and programs also neglect the skills of intercultural negotiation. What is our best strategy and tactic for negotiating with the other countries of the world? Consider a modest ninety-day bid for oil from the Middle East. We want the most favorable terms we can get in overall price, payment, and delivery for fifty thousand barrels a day of heavy high sulfur crude, and all the negotiations are conducted in Arabic.

The second reason for studying intercultural communication is to gain skills that are useful on the job. This raises the second of the content decisions to be made, and my second challenge. What is the main job and what skills does it require? Is it the job of the pharmacy student who needs some supplementary and non-technical skills for this personal adjustment? That is a relatively minor matter. Instead, is it the main job of intercultural communication to tackle the problems of negotiation and war, of sizing up today's communication budgets and tomorrow's communication traffic?

We face decisions not only about what skills to develop but also about how to develop them. At present, when the syllabuses, books, and programs aim to promote a general awareness of cultural differences, they always begin with the concept of culture, and they generally reify that concept. They make culture, which is an intangible abstraction, into a corporeal being. They say the culture does this and needs that. The Aibese culture glories in conflict while the Ceedese culture calls for an avoidance of conflict. This reification converts a conception into a physical body. It converts cultures into Airedale puppies that toddle around and need eyedrops. In Whitehead's terms, this commits the fallacy of misplaced concreteness; in statistical terms, it assumes behavior to be extremely skewed. Except in very special contexts, this is an unfortunate bit of nonsense and even dangerous. This and such further steps to a supplementary and non-technical awareness—precept and anecdote—fall short of being the most empirical and fertile ways of developing general skills.

If instead we aim to promote higher technical skills such as budget and traffic analyses for communication, then we will probably begin with the case method. Like business administration and law, intercultural communication is one of the policy sciences, and the case method is the best way we have for developing skills in these fields. This is a very demanding method. It took the Harvard Business School forty years and millions of dollars just to develop a good set of cases for its program. Legal scholars and practitioners are still developing the case study of law, nearly seven hundred and fifty years since Henry of Bracton. Intercultural communication needs a comparable effort of gigantic dimensions for its methodological development.

COSMOPOLITANISM

The survey also reveals a third reason for studying intercultural communication: to let us rise above our naive and simple provincialism and achieve a more worldly and sophisticated cosmopolitanism; to gain tolerance and charity for all peoples and to widen our opportunities to interact with them; and to let us feel at home everywhere, perhaps to find more congenial alternatives to our own ways of life.

This personal cosmopolitanism may fit an emerging world in which differences are disappearing. The Hilton here in Austin is just like the ones in Amsterdam, Nairobi, and Caracas. You can get a Big Mac and a Coke almost anywhere on earth. You can also see Toyotas and Panasonics everywhere, as well as Guccis and Fellinis. The world is being homogenized.

Personal cosmopolitanism may also fit an emerging world of interdependence. West Germans are buying up Texas real estate, and the price of Nebraska wheat depends on the size of the Russian harvest. The Ford Fiesta's windshields come from Tulsa, Oklahoma, its carburetors come from Northern Ireland, its spark plugs from England, its wheels from Belgium, its bumpers from West Germany, and it is put together in Spain. Everything the world over is becoming either integrated or homogenized.

Strictly speaking, the Cokes and carburetors represent the economic cosmopolitanism of multinational corporations. The personal cosmopolitanism of the texts, syllabuses, and programs is less concerned with Hiltons and Fords, and more with personal relations, open minds, and perhaps the free trade in thought. These, however, are not the heart's blood of intercultural communication.

A ghetto riot or an East-West summit meeting is a grim ordeal decided by fighting power and material resources. It is a battle about change, about improvements in the physical conditions of human existence, about greater opportunities to pursue worthwhile lives, about some people if not at all. Without actual change or secure expectations, cosmopolitan tolerance and sophistication are airy froth.

There are intercultural battles of belief and persuasion; they generally involve anti-cosmopolitans. Some Soviet commissars, for example, or some Islamic *imams* or fundamentalist preachers are persuaded they have the truth. Sometimes this is a political ideology, sometimes a moral theology, and sometimes some other light. For them foreign ideas are decadent and disruptive. Sometimes they think that such ideas have to be exterminated, with force if necessary, and no holds barred. For many cosmopolitans, these anti-cosmopolitans are themselves decadent and disruptive, and should be squelched. The zealous pot can become almost as black as the zealous kettle.

We do need a cosmopolitan view when we study intercultural communication, but for less personal or dogmatic reasons. We need it as a systems approach. We need to assess the state of the world system of intercultural communication to make content decisions about what to study and policy decisions about what to do. Does the world system today provide the highest quality of communication life for everybody, for senders and receivers, for Africans and Australians, for the once born and the twice born?

We need to find the strengths of that system, and also its weakest links. Stock market decisions are made in the same way. They are based on gauging the state of the economic system, and where it is soft or firm. Intercultural communication studies can gauge the weaknesses and strengths of the global communication system. These studies can also consider how to improve that system, how to develop and exploit its purpose. This calls for the heaviest decision and my third challenge: What kind of communication world do we want to promote?

One answer, for example, is democratic. It aims for public participation in determining the kind of communication world to be worked for. It calls for asking the people what they want, asking the Turks, the air traffic controllers, and commissars. It also calls for ways of resolving differences among the wants of different people. It aims for freedom and equality in communication everywhere, in the First, Second, and Third Worlds, and all the satellites in space.

Whatever view we have of the cosmopolitan communication system, it has problems to be studied and resolved. Can that view reconcile national sovereignty with international excellence? Does it understand the patterns of world communication well enough to make policies for them?

The problems are endless, and they make it clear that cosmopolitanism can be more than a jet-set sophistication. It can be a global view for assessing international conditions and for making world decisions.

Once more: the study of intercultural communications can be far more substantial and urgent than it is now. This study can contribute seriously to interpersonal adjustment on the international scene if it will focus on the bases for such adjustments, on the political and economic institutions of the world. This study can promote serious skills for work on the international scene if it will focus on highly technical skills, as in international finance, law, or transborder data flows. This study can promote serious cosmopolitanism if it will focus on the global system of communication. Across the board, the study of intercultural communication needs to focus on the serious problems of the international scene, problems that are morbid and malign: routine wretchedness and strife, transgression and injustice.

As professors and students we try to solve the problems of intercultural communication. I realize that very few of us will find the roots of these problems or the grail of our scholarly quest. It is the same in medicine: few professors or students will find the cause of cancer or cure for arthritis. In a world of complex troubles we can seldom be effective individually. But collectively we can. The shared enterprise of many scholars can indeed help to solve the serious problems of intercultural communication.

The birth of this new division can be a timely moment for making collective decisions. This turning point is the time to delineate the scope and content of the field. This is the time of decision, and of promise, for making an important difference.

10

Why Do We Study Intercultural Communication?

Paul E. Rohrlich

When talking to others of our professional interests, each of us has at some point been posed the question "Why do you study intercultural communication?" I have found that this question lingers in the conversation, and is supplemented by "Does it matter? Can it make a difference?" From the public, our colleagues, and ourselves, questions about the placement of this discipline abound. After all, intercultural communication has existed throughout history and never had a special course of study before, distinguishing here between international, among political units, and intercultural, among cultural groups. Answering these questions well is important because the strength and direction of inquiry in intercultural relations evolves directly from such answers. We can convince ourselves of the significance of the field, but unless society at large becomes convinced of its value its future is—and perhaps ought to be—in doubt.

Answers to these questions can take many approaches. Often I find myself taking the idealistic approach, answering that global peace depends partly upon our understanding of one another, and recognizing the cultural variety in the world enriches the observer. Sometimes a more practical answer suffices for the questioner: better interpersonal communication can clinch business deals and improve

Dr. Rohrlich is a professor at the University of Vermont.

Reprinted form *International Journal of Intercultural Relations* 2 (1987): 123–128, Elsevier Science Ltd., Oxford, England.

professional competence abroad. The response SIETAR offers on membership materials is to "increase (members') intercultural awareness and competence within and across disciplinary, professional and cultural boundaries." The important feature of each of these answers is that they address the concerns of the questioner. The individual can best recognize the importance of intercultural communication when it relates to his or her interests.

One widely noted assessment of intercultural communication as a discipline derides this "personal and practical" approach. Smith recognizes interpersonal adjustment, job skills, and cosmopolitanism as principle reasons for studying intercultural communications as an academic discipline. He insightfully calls for enhancing the methodology of intercultural communications courses, envisioning the field more as a policy science than study of psychodynamics, finding its present focus less significant than the policy science direction. The interpersonal and professional adjustment focus of the field he calls misplaced: "reaching out . . . across the intercultural no-man's land generally (does) not clear up underlying problems."[2] We need rearrangement of economic and political institutions far beyond the reach of improved interpersonal communications. We don't need interpersonal skills as much as political ability, nor job skills as much as predictive, policy-oriented insights. As for the individual's cosmopolitan view, the real concern remains the grim dispute over power and material resources and "without actual change or secure expectations, cosmopolitan tolerance and sophistication are airy froth."[3]

As a political scientist, I can agree that the economic and political contexts of world problems cannot and should not be forgotten; however, Smith's view neglects the importance of intercultural communication even in its present state of incomplete theory. By severing the connections between the interpersonal and the global, Smith weakens the field rather than strengthens it. We can all applaud his far-seeking goals towards which the field might evolve, but intercultural communication's present and continued interpersonal utility is real and equally important, not frothy or dilettantish as critics may hold. My belief is that the present study of intercultural communication *does* address global problems in three distinct ways—procedural, substantive, and informational—as well as benefit the person who studies it.

Does intercultural communication research in its present state "hide" the "real" problems, offering cosmetic treatment to problems demanding larger political cures? This in itself would not deny its value: a doctor is never disparaged for administering a pain-killer while the search for the cure progresses. Similarly, until the global economy is restructured to achieve employment opportunity for all in their own country, migrant workers will exist in many places, and it will be necessary to deal with their problems if social peace and the human condition are concerns. The problems of intercultural communication range from personal to global, and whether receiving a short-term palliative or the long-run cure, all the problems deserve to be addressed. Research on cultural assimilation and on the world communication order is equally valuable. Both the applied and the research sides of intercultural communications serve valuable functions, and there is no denying that they build upon each other. Clearly the root causes must ultimately be addressed, but we must have the pragmatism to apply theory wherever it can be useful. Therefore the issue is not whether intercultural communications solves the fundamental problems of the world community, but how our present knowledge can best be applied. The study of intercultural dynamics such as communication, youth exchange, negotiation, etc., does not pretend to replace political or economic science, but does serve to supplement them.

THE PROCEDURAL INSIGHT

Intercultural communication research can, in fact, contribute towards resolution of the larger problems in four ways. First, we have the procedural level of international relations. Reality forces us to admit that states never talk to one another: interstate relations always become interpersonal contacts at some stage in the communication process. Clearly intercul-tural communication is not limited to interstate contacts, but because of the nature of the international system organized around sovereign states ideally consisting of one ethnic nation (the nation-state), interstate relations necessitate interpersonal and usually intercultural contact. In the most critical example, on either end of the hotline linking Moscow and Washington remains a human mind. At this procedural level, intercultural theory applied in diplomatic and legal contexts can have a significant impact. Improving the effectiveness of communication between state representatives can only increase understanding of a counterpart's position, and while this may not necessarily increase agreement among them, certainly poor communication will hinder all progress to that end.

If war, as Clausewitz notes, is diplomacy by other means, diplomacy is actually war by other means, the ends for both being the pursuit of state interests. By expanding the efficiency and clarity of the verbal tools of politics such as diplomacy, we may hope to reduce the frequency of recourse to violent tools of politics. To claim that intercultural communication does not address the "real issue" is untrue. War is symptomatic of a world of divergent value systems and conflicting priorities, in brief, of cultural pluralism. Conditions of material shortages, limited land resources, and population density are simply the stage setting in which the drama of allocating who gets what occurs. The classic political questions of Lasswell are worth recalling: Who gets what, when and how?[4] Lacking a common cultural value system to facilitate the process, war is the ultimate response when diplomacy fails. The importance of personal training in intercultural communications should not be underestimated; halting the war without improving the diplomacy promises only a temporary truce. Avoiding the war altogether will surely take major political and/or economic steps, but this stage will never be reached if communication remains ineffective. Intercultural communication will never be the *sufficient* condition for solving the world's major ills, but it is undoubtedly a *necessary* one, even if "only" interpersonal.

THE SUBSTANTIVE INSIGHT

Second, intercultural communication theory gives us insight into the substance as well as the process of interstate contacts. By the substance of diplomacy we mean the claims that states advance in the interstate realm; the particulars of the land it protects, the characteristics of the welfare it guards, and the source of the ideology it follows are revealed in the culture of the state. The sensitivity to the cultural variable lent by intercultural training spreads to the interpretation of the issues themselves.

Whereas the procedural level noted miscommunication among individuals, the substantive level concerns us with the demands and perceptions of the state as a cultural unit. For example, what is the conception of a border to an Arab state? Recent research indicates the state borders serve a social function which may be variously perceived[5]; Arab states in particular may view inter-Moslem borders less critically than Moslem/non-Moslem boundaries because the legal conception of the state is based on being part of a larger Islamic reality[6]. Without this knowledge we may be misinterpreting their actions and statements regarding borders. While this communication of the "deep-culture" of a society far exceeds the information that verbal and non-verbal communication skills can give, being more anthropology than communication theory, process level sensitivity is the logical start for substance comprehension.

While insight on this score will probably not alter the demands made in the interstate political sphere, interculturally aware representatives of states may pursue these demands in more acceptable and persuasive ways and moderate their reactions to the reciprocal demands of other cultures. Diplomatically more successful states appear to do this: Austria, situated on the border between competing ideological and economic systems, moderates its political voice and demands to avoid alienating either side and thus maintains territorial integrity, welfare, and identity with little armed force or threat. Japan, another state with a highly "conditional" situation, observes an economic code culturally acceptable to its prime benefactor yet practices military and diplomatic conduct that recognizes the cultural and historic fears of its closest neighbors. It achieves its goals with a minimum of costs and maximum of anticipatory consideration. Sensitivity to the cross-cultural reception of state behavior brings intercultural theory into the substance of interstate relations.

THE INFORMATIONAL ASPECT

A third way in which intercultural communication relates to the larger problems of the world might be called informational. Smith points us in the right direction here: rather than intercultural learning to gain personal sophistication or promote a national ideology or outlook, we should use intercultural theory "to assess the state of the world system of intercultural communication to make content decisions about what to study and policy decisions about what to do."[7] In planning for the future we need to know the present state of the world communication order. This can be taken further however, because not only the world communication order but also the world economic, political, and business orders are subject to the intercultural context of decisionmaking. Each has been the focus of theories attempting to construct universal principles of judgment and norms of behavior without stopping to consider how universal the principles and norms may be. If we hope to solve the "real problems" of patterning more acceptable international relations, the intercultural aspects of all interstate relations must be squarely faced. Intercultural communication forces us to reassess the information to be used in problem solving. Incorporating intercultural criteria in decisionmaking will not be easily or willingly done. Are the universal economic criteria for the distribution of goods? How can we make international law interculturally valid? Who will judge when all cultures have been given due respect and a decision affecting them all can be made? Can there ever exist a trade-off between one culture's value, say of equal opportunity, and another's value, perhaps of equality of condition? Values are the baselines from which decisions are reached; if more decisions must be made internationally than ever before, conflicting value systems will be contended with more frequently.

None of these are easy questions; none of them are avoidable. The intercultural contexting of world problems is the informational aspect that current intercultural communication theory, even in its rudimentary state, contributes. The communications field is one of the few disciplines where actual experience and theory come together on the topic of cross-cultural interaction yielding concepts and tools that can be generalized to other spheres of world interaction. For the reason of research alone we could conclude that intercultural communication has a contribution to make to the "real" problems we face.

Finally, the utility of contemporary intercultural study on the personal level should not be discarded. Cosmopolitanism and sophistication may not be the goal, but interpersonal communicative ability and comfort should be. Study of intercultural contact addresses the basis for both science and the humanities: betterment of the human condition. Adjustment of the individual to his or her surrounding, be it native or foreign, at work or at home, is neither trivial nor secondary. In a world containing ethnic terrorism, massive flows of refugees, communal animosity, and personal anomie, the need for identity, a sense of self and an acceptance by others remains a human need as significant as food. Identity remains one of the five criteria by which the World Order Modelling Project evaluates the international system and attempts to construct improvements. Along with peace, welfare, social justice, and ecological balance, identity is a landmark by which life can be judge livable.[8] Generalizing intercultural awareness and acceptance through teaching intercultural communication may ultimately have a farther reaching impact than we think, but in no way should the education and sense of identity intercultural training imparts be considered trivial because it does not stop a war or raise GNP.

Why do we study intercultural communication? Because like a science it helps us understand the world around us, and like the humanities it helps us understand ourselves. It can help us with business, government, education, and language skills, all fields which ultimately depend upon interpersonal contact. As the crucial link between the individual and the larger world, intercultural communication as a field appeals to people precisely because it is interpersonal in how it addresses the "real issues." True, as a discipline it is ill-defined, and seems permeated by other fields. But then, most of economics was discounted as an intellectual gentleman's parlour game until the industrial revolution allowed its theories to be tested and verified. The ultimate utility of intercultural communication may extend significantly beyond its discipline as its theory accumulates and solidifies. Its immediate contributions, however, are recognizable and appealing; they address the concerns of people, which, at any level, is justification enough.

ENDNOTES

[1] A. G. Smith, Content Decisions in Intercultural Communications. *Southern Speech Communication Journal* 47 (1981): 252–262.

[2] *Ibid.,* 255.

[3] *Ibid.,* 260–261.

[4] H. D. Lasswell, *Who Gets, What, When and How?* (Cleveland: World, 1958).

[5] F. Kratoch and P. E. Rohrlich, *Peace and Disputed Sovereignty: Reflections on Conflict Over Territory* (Lanham, MD: University Press of America/Columbia University, Institute of War and Peace Studies, 1985).

[6] A. B. Bozeman, *The Future of Law in a Multicultural World.* (Princeton: Princeton University Press, 1971), 53–56.

[7] Smith, 261.

[8] S. Mendlovitz, *On the Creation of a Just World Order* (New York: Free Press, 1975).

II

Managing Diversity

The U.S. Labor Department and various other organizations that monitor demographic changes in the U.S. have all made similar projections—the United States is becoming more culturally and racially diverse and the vast majority of workers entering the labor force are minorities, immigrants and women.

Workforce 2000, a report prepared by the Hudson Institute on work and workers for the twenty-first century, claims that

> new workers entering the workforce between now (1988) and the year 2000 will be much different from those who people it today. Non-whites, women, and immigrants will make up more than five-sixths of the net additions to the workforce between now and the year 2000, though they make up only about half of it today.[1]

Hispanic Americans will replace African Americans as the largest minority group by 2010, and by 2050 there will be almost as many minorities as non-Hispanic whites, according to the U.S. Census Bureau.[2]

But, how do these minorities fit into the American society? While some might claim that the workplace should reflect the so-called "melting pot" of the American society, it is abundantly clear that the melting pot has been a myth. Rather than throwing their culture into a common pot and thereby changing the composition of the brew, immigrants have traditionally tried to fit into the "cookie cutter mold" of the dominant culture to advance into the so-called mainstream. There has always been a dominant culture with a distinct configuration of appropriate values, beliefs, behavioral norms, ways of thinking and perceiving.[3]

The workplace has also represented the mainstream cookie-cutter mold. Those who have advanced to management and supervisory positions usually have been white males or those who easily could change aspects of their culture to fit the shape of the mainstream mold. In fact, there is a "glass ceiling" above which minorities and women could not rise. Well over 95% of all top executives in the private and public sectors are white males. This glass ceiling has hardly cracked in the past twenty years.

In the 1970s and 1980s, as greater numbers of women entered the workforce, many companies offered "assertiveness training" courses. These courses were never designed for men, but were exclusively for women. The assumption was that women were simply not assertive enough to survive in the workplace, yet if they could be trained to act like men they could become perfectly competent workers, managers, and supervisors. They might even one day become executives.

Of course, this approach is not pluralism—this is "cookie cutterism." Worse still, it's cloning. In some organizations, Asians comprise a sizable proportion of gifted workers yet few make it to managerial positions. Often the excuse is that "they are too passive." Again, the basic argument is that Asians are unlike white mainstream American males. Many supervisors assume that "managing diversity" means helping "them" to become like "us." While this may make supervision easier, the net result is *decreased* productivity and creativity.

With the cookie-cutter approach, cultural aspects which do not fit the mold must be left outside the workplace. This diminishes self-esteem for many since only what one *does* is important. A part of their identity must be left at the door. Their gender, race, ethnicity or sexual orientation is denied, devalued or marginalized.

When a manager says, "I don't care if my secretary is white, black, Christian or Moslem, as long as he does the job," the implication is that one's race or religion is irrelevant. Yet, these attributes are essential to one's identity as a whole person. Anyone treated in this fragmented, fractionalized, schizoid manner cannot feel like a part of the team, and this sense of alienation will surely impact productivity.

Identity groups based upon gender, race or ethnicity may help to provide psychological and social support and decrease the sense of alienation as non-mainstream employees transition into the dominant work culture. These groups provide empathetic listeners with whom they may share their experiences. Co-national communities have helped immigrants from Asia or the Middle East to more effectively move into the mainstream American culture. Of course, these groups can also become havens where individuals avoid the stress of dealing with the dominant culture.

Supervisors can encourage employees to share their different ways of viewing problems that may be based upon their particular group. For example, how might women view a situation? Do Chicano employees value more hours to work overtime or do they prefer compensatory time? And, there may be opportunities for employees to bring their ethnicity into the workplace by having a diversity week or special events linked to ethnic heritage.

Today, diversity training is offered to employees and supervisors in almost all large companies in the U.S. The primary reason these businesses give for making diversity training part of strategic planning is the belief that it increases productivity. But, it may also increase creativity.

If everyone in an organization thinks alike and has the same basic values and beliefs, it is unlikely that the group will be very creative. When faced with a problem, the members may even suffer from groupthink.[4] However, when it comes to implementing solutions, the homogeneous group will be very efficient—they all think the same way and will move in the same direction.

On the other hand, a group composed of people from various ethnic or cultural backgrounds, male and female, is likely to come up with a long list of very creative solutions *if they are given enough time, and the group is managed to enable them to overcome the difficulties of diversity.* However, they may have difficulty coming to any agreements, and there may even be conflict as to how to choose a leader, when to get down to business and stop the chit-chat, or even how to develop an agenda. And, when it comes to implementation, the heterogeneous group will be like a herd of wild horses all going off in different directions.

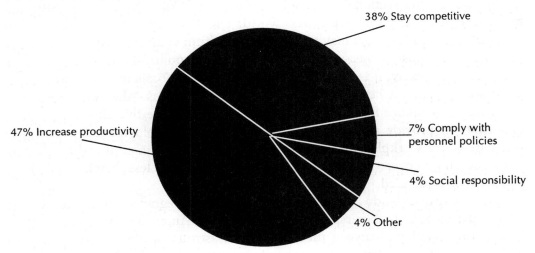

REASONS FOR DIVERSITY TRAINING

What businesses say are primary reasons for making divesity training part of strategic planning:

38% Stay competitive

47% Increase productivity

7% Comply with personnel policies

4% Social responsibility

4% Other

Source: The Conference Board, by Anne R. Carey and Dave Merrill, *USA Today,* August 15, 1995.

For example, Japan—a very homogeneous culture—was able to manufacture transistorized color televisions five years before Americans could get one off the assembly line. The Japanese are very good at implementation. However, Americans actually invented the transistor. Diversity in the United States has contributed to our innovative and creative approaches to problem-solving.

The word "manage" suggests manipulation or control, when in fact the objective is almost the opposite when it comes to diversity. To insure both productivity and creativity, a manager must bring about some sort of "cultural synergy"[5] or "diunitality"[6] where the whole is greater than the sum of its parts, and the process of decision-making elicits the widest array of opinions and ideas. We don't want to control or suppress these differences, we want to *facilitate or manage the process* the group takes in making decisions so that we can minimize the inefficiencies and frustrations that diversity causes and maximize the productivity and creativity of the group.

Lastly, in both the private and public sectors, the clientele that American organizations serve is also becoming much more diverse. The ability to relate effectively with people of various backgrounds is necessary for anyone dealing with the public—entrepreneurs, business executives, university professors and civil servants.[7] Knowledge of intercultural relations and the ability to communicate across cultures will be essential to almost everyone entering the workforce in the next century.

ARTICLES

This section examines the consequences of interaction between people of different races and ethnic backgrounds, especially in the workplace. What are the implications for managers and supervisors? How can we use our understanding of diversity and cultural differences to enhance productivity and creativity?

We begin this section by examining the impact of increased diversity and multiculturalism in the U.S. business world. The discussion is then expanded to consider organizations that may employ workers from countries around the globe.

One of the most pervasive and divisive social and political issues in America is race relations. Today, it is illegal to discriminate on the basis of race, and there is increased integration between black and white Americans—they are interacting with each other more frequently in the workplace and the overall society. Many organizations provide race relations and EEO (Equal Employment Opportunity) seminars in the workplace to decrease conflict and discrimination and to increase understanding between people of different races. Nevertheless, blacks and whites still seem to be divided.

According to Orlando Patterson, "The Paradox of Integration" is that blacks and whites have conflicting perspectives on racism in America today. Most blacks believe that relations between the races are disastrous, while most middle-class whites feel that things have gotten much better not only in the objective socioeconomic condition of blacks, but also in their improved attitude toward blacks. Patterson thinks that this paradox is a result of increased interaction between the races.

Jolie Solomon claims that "As Cultural Diversity of Workers Grows, Experts Urge Appreciation of Differences." Contrary to the melting pot assumption, as we increase diversity our culture and identity do not disappear, but instead become more important. In fact, as long as we remain in our own culture surrounded by those who think and behave the way we do, we take our culture for granted. Yet when we are surrounded by those who are culturally different, we become more consciously aware of our own culture. As the workforce becomes more diverse, cultural differences will also become more important.

Perhaps the study which has most dramatically raised awareness of the increasing diversity in the American workforce is *Workforce 2000*. William B. Johnston provides an executive summary of this book which not only describes the demographic trends, but perhaps even more importantly discusses the implications for management.

R. Roosevelt Thomas, Jr. ("The Concept of Managing Diversity") believes that affirmative action will die a natural death because most of its goals have been achieved. The question facing America today is how to take advantage of the diversity that exists and manage it in a way which makes it a strength. His position is close to that of Nancy J. Adler in her article, "Domestic Multiculturalism: Cross-Cultural Management in the Public Sector." She not only agrees that the melting pot has been a myth and the workplace is becoming more diverse, she asserts that we can create a kind of synergy if we acknowledge and manage diversity in a way that both values and rewards differences.

Organizations also have cultures, while people of different backgrounds bring their own cultures into the organization's culture. Nancy J. Adler and Mariann

Jelinek ask the question "Is 'Organization Culture' Culture Bound?" That is, are most organization cultures really reflections of the dominant American culture? Further, can a more robust multicultural organizational concept be developed which incorporates aspects of various cultures?

In the past two decades one of the most significant researchers to study dominant work-related values is Geert Hofstede. His research data on 53 countries and regions shows "The Cultural Relativity of the Quality of Life Concept." That is, what motivates or satisfies a worker in one country may be entirely different for a worker in another. We cannot assume that the same carrot or stick works for all workers, and if we are to manage a diverse workforce we must discover which values are most important for those from different countries or regions.

Linda S. Dillon explains how we cannot simply transfer management assumptions and techniques from one culture to another in her article "Adopting Japanese Management: Some Cultural Stumbling Blocks." She discusses "Theory Z" organizations which are typical in Japan. However, the assumptions and values which are found within these organizations do not necessarily exist in the United States. Consequently, Theory Z may not be useful for American managers.

Americans traditionally value individualism and independence while Chinese and other Asian managers encourage the development of connections between people. Both dependence upon others and interdependence with others is a fundamental aspect of traditional Chinese culture. M. Cordell Hart discusses the importance of interpersonal relationships imbedded in the concept of *guanxi* and its importance for understanding Chinese social and business behavior.

Lastly, Gary Althen uses Edward Hall's concept of "action chains" to explain why intercultural student meetings are often frustrating for everyone involved. Although Althen is discussing student groups, his findings would apply to any group involving participants from various cultural backgrounds. In his article "The Intercultural Meeting," Althen describes how participants carry with them unconscious assumptions as to how to select a leader, when to get down to business, how to set an agenda, and so forth.[8]

The workplace of the future will be more multicultural in both domestic and international or global organizations. Even if it is possible to create organizations that are monocultural where everyone shares the same behavior, attitudes, values and beliefs, both productivity and creativity would be diminished. The issue addressed in this section is not how to eliminate diversity, but rather how to use and manage it more effectively in the next millennium.

ENDNOTES

[1]William B. Johnston, *Workforce 2000: Executive Summary* (Indianapolis: Hudson Institute, Inc. 1987), 8.

[2]In 1997, nearly one in ten people in the U.S. was foreign-born, the highest rate in more than fifty years. In proportional terms, the foreign-born accounted for 9.3 percent of the total U.S. population, well below the high mark this century of 14.7 percent in 1910, but nearly double the rate since the low point in 1970 and continuing an upward trend since

then. William Branigin, "Nearly 1 in 10 in U.S. Is Foreign-Born, Census Says," *The Washington Post*, 9 April 1997, 18(A).

[3]The power to assimilate is controlled by the dominant culture. See Rich and Ogawa's "Intercultural and Interracial Communication: An Analytic Approach" in Section I, 54–59 and Benjamin Schwarz, "The Diversity Myth: America's Leading Export" in Section VI, 471–479.

[4]Irving Janis, *Groupthink*, 2d. ed. (Boston: Houghton Mifflin, 1982).

[5]R. T. Moran and P. R. Harris, *Managing Cultural Synergy* (Houston: Gulf Publishing Company, 1981).

[6]Gerald Jackson, "The Roots of the Backlash Theory in Mental Health," *The Journal of Black Psychology* 6, no. 1 (August, 1979): 17–45.

[7]A discussion of the impact of diversity on law enforcement can be found in Gary R. Weaver, "Law Enforcement in a Culturally Diverse Society," *FBI Law Enforcement Bulletin* (September, 1992): 1–7.

[8]Also see Gary R. Weaver, "The Multicultural Child Care Staff: Meeting the Needs of a Diverse Client Population," *CYCA* (Fall, 1988): 49–55.

11

The Paradox of Integration

Orlando Patterson

The traumas of the Million Man march and the O. J. Simpson verdict have forced America to focus its gaze once again on its lingering racial crisis. In sharpening our focus, they have done at least one good. By casting too bright a light on the realities of our unfinished racial agenda, they have scrambled the sordid use of coded and covert racial rhetoric by conventional politicians. We must now call a spade a spade, and, while pretending the opposite, it is far too risky to appear clearly to be doing so. But what exactly is the crisis upon which we again gaze?

For African Americans, these are genuinely the best and worst of times, at least since the ending of formal Jim Crow laws. What is odd, however, is that, in the current rhetoric of race, the pain completely dominates the gain. "Pain and predicament is driving this march," cried Jesse Jackson in a by now familiar African American refrain. The orthodox view among blacks at nearly all points in the political spectrum is that relations between the races are disastrous, whether it is the left, focusing on the political neglect of the devastated ghettos, or the right, condemning the abuses of affirmative action and failed government policies. Paradoxically, it is precisely the considerable success of America's experiment in integration that makes it almost impossible for black Americans to recognize what they

have achieved. This perceived lack of gratitude in turn fuels white resentment and gives public discourse on race today the bewildering quality of a dialogue of the deaf.

On the one hand, there is no denying the fact that, in absolute terms, African Americans, on average, are better off now than at any other time in their history. The civil rights movement effectively abolished the culture of post-juridical slavery, which, reinforced by racism and legalized segregation, had denied black people the basic rights of citizenship in the land of their birth. They are now very much a part of the nation's political life, occupying positions in numbers and importance that go well beyond mere ethnic representation or tokenism. Quite apart from the thousands of local and appointed offices around the country (including mayorships of some of the nation's largest cities), blacks have occupied positions of major national importance in what is now the dominant power in the world—as governors, senators and powerful members of Congress chairing major congressional committees, and as appointed officials filling some of the most important offices in the nation, including that of the head of the most powerful military machine on earth.

Even as I write, the Colin Powell phenomenon bedazzles. For the first time, a black man is being seriously considered for the nation's highest office, with his strongest support coming from people with conservative views on race. It would be ridiculous to dismiss these developments as mere tokens. What they demonstrate, beyond a doubt, is that being black is no longer a significant obstacle to participation in the public life of the nation.

What is more, blacks have also become full members of what may be called the nation's moral community and cultural life. They are no longer in the basement of moral discourse in American life, as was the case up to about thirty or forty years ago. Until then blacks were "invisible men" in the nation's consciousness, a truly debased ex-slave people. America was assumed to be a white country. The public media, the literary and artistic community, the great national debates about major issues, even those concerning poverty, simply excluded

Orlando Patterson is John Cowles professor of sociology at Harvard University and the author of a forthcoming book on black Americans.

Reprinted from *The New Republic*, 6 November 1995.

blacks from consideration. Even a liberal thinker like John Kenneth Galbraith could write a major discourse on the affluent society without much thought to their plight.

No longer. The enormity of the achievement of the last forty years in American race relations cannot be overstated. The black presence in American life and thought is today pervasive. A mere 13 percent of the population, they dominate the nation's popular culture: its music, its dance, its talk, its sports, its youths' fashion; and they are a powerful force in its popular and elite literatures. A black music, jazz, is the nation's classical voice, defining, audibly, its entire civilizational style. So powerful and unavoidable is the black popular influence that it is now not uncommon to find persons who, while remaining racists in personal relations and attitudes, nonetheless have surrendered their tastes, and their viewing and listening habits, to black entertainers, talk-show hosts and sit-com stars. The typical Oprah Winfrey viewer is a conservative white lower-middle-class housewife; the typical rap fan, an upper-middle-class white suburban youth. The cultural influence of so small and disadvantaged a minority on the wider society that has so harshly abused it finds few parallels in the history of civilization.

Closely related to the achievement of full political and cultural citizenship has been another great success of the post-war years: the desegregation of the military between 1948 and 1965. The extraordinary progress made in eliminating all formal discrimination, and a good deal of informal prejudice in promotions, has made the military, especially the Army, a model of successful race relations for the civilian community. With more than 30 percent of Army recruits and 10 percent of its officer corps black, the Army, and to a lesser extent the other services, stands out in American society as the only arena in which blacks routinely exercise authority over whites.

Most of these developments were helped along by another evolution in black life: the rapid growth in school enrollment and achievement at all levels. In 1940 there was a four-year gap in median years of schooling between whites and blacks; by 1991 this gap had been reduced to a few months. During the same

period, the proportion of blacks aged 25 to 34 completing high school almost caught up with that of whites: 84 percent compared to 87 percent.

The record is far more mixed, and indeed troubling, in the case of higher education. After rapid growth in college completion during the '70s, the numbers fell off considerably during the '80s, especially for black men. The long-term effect has been that, while the proportion of blacks completing college has grown from less than 2 percent in 1940 to almost 12.8 percent in 1994, this is still only about half the white completion rate of almost 25 percent.

Even so, a six-fold increase in college completion is nothing to sniff at. It is great absolute progress and, compared to white populations elsewhere, great relative progress. African Americans, from a condition of mass illiteracy fifty years ago, are now among the most educated persons in the world, with median years of schooling and college completion rates higher than those of most Western Europeans. The average reader might find this statement a shocking overstatement. It is not. It only sounds like an overstatement when considered in light of the relentless insistence of the advocacy community that the miseducation of black Americans is the major source of their present dilemmas.

The rise of a genuine black middle class over the past quarter of a century is another cause for celebration, although no group of persons is less likely to celebrate it than the black establishment itself. The term "black middle class" once referred dismissively to those black persons who happened to be at the top of the bottom rung: Pullman porters, head waiters, successful barbers and street-font preachers, small-time funeral parlor owners and the like. Today the term "black middle class" means that the segment of the nation's middle class which happens to be black, and it is no longer dependent on a segregated economy. These are without doubt the best of times for middle-class African Americans, who own more businesses and control a greater share of the national wealth than at any other period. At the most conservative estimate, they are between a quarter and a third of the black population, which means anywhere between 8 and 10 million persons. It is a mistake to overemphasize their shaky economic base, as is routinely done. Almost all new middle classes in the history of capitalism have had precarious economic starts. Seen from a long-term perspective, the important thing to note is that the children they produce will be second-and third-generation burghers with all the confidence, educational resources and, most of all, cultural capital to find a more secure place in the nation's economy.

And yet it is also no exaggeration to say that, both subjectively and by certain objective standards, these are among the worst of times, since the ending of Jim Crow, for the African American population.

Put in the starkest terms, the bottom third of the African American population—some 10 million persons—live in dire poverty, while the bottom 10 percent or so—the so-called underclass—exist in an advanced stage of social, economic and moral disintegration. The grim statistics are now familiar to anyone who pays even the most cursory attention to the news.

Thirty-one percent of all black families (in contrast with only 8 percent of non-Hispanic whites), comprising nearly a third of all African Americans, live in poverty. This is worse than in 1969. Children disproportionately bear the brunt of impoverishment. In 1994, 46 percent of all black children lived in poverty, nearly three times that of white children, and the situation is likely to get worse. Their parents and other adult caretakers experience Depression-level unemployment. The overall unemployment rate for blacks is 14 percent, more than twice that of whites (6 percent). But this obscures the fact that unemployment is concentrated in certain areas and among the young, where it tops 40 percent.

These figures tell only part of the plight of poor children. The other, grimmer aspect of the dilemma is the growing number of children born to female children with little or no social or economic support from the biological fathers or any other man, for that matter. The resulting abusive, mal-socialization of children by mothers who were themselves abused

and mal-socialized is at the heart of the social and moral chaos in what is called the underclass. The situation is one of complete social anarchy and moral nihilism, reflected in the casual devaluation of human life. Kids and young adults kill for sneakers, leather jackets, cheap jewelry and drugs; worse, they kill for no other reason than having been dissed by a wrong look or misstatement. Linked to this social and moral catastrophe are the other well-known pathologies: the high drop-out rate in inner-city high schools, the epidemic of drugs and crime resulting in a horrendous incarceration rate wherein one in three of all black men aged 25 to 29 are under the supervision of the criminal justice system. Although government action is needed, solving these problems will take considerably more than changes in the government policy. Clearly, the message of the Million Man March was long overdue.

There is undoubtedly much to outrage our sense of justice, but the condition of the bottom third should not obscure the extraordinary achievements of the upper two-thirds of the black population or the progress made in race relations over the past forty years. Black leaders' near-complete disregard of these hard-won achievements is obtuse and counterproductive.

This strange tendency to more loudly lament the black predicament the better it gets can be understood as a paradox of desegregation. When blacks and whites were segregated from each other there was little opportunity for conflict. The two groups lived in largely separate worlds, and when they did come in contact their interactions were highly structured by the perverse etiquette of racial relations. The system may have worked well in minimizing conflict, as long as both groups played by the rules, but it was clearly a pernicious arrangement for blacks since it condemned them to inferior status and excluded them from participation in the political life of their society and from nearly all the more desirable opportunities for economic advancement.

Desegregation meant partial access to the far superior facilities and opportunities open previously only to whites. Hence, it entailed a great improvement in the condition and dignity of blacks. All this should be terribly obvious, but it must be spelled out because it is precisely this obvious improvement that is so often implicitly denied when we acknowledge one of the inevitable consequences of desegregation namely that, as individuals in both groups meet more and more, the possibility for conflict is bound to increase.

Whites outnumber blacks eight to one, and this simple demographic fact has an enormous social significance often unnoticed by whites. Numerous polls have shown tremendous change in white attitudes toward blacks over the last thirty years. For example, the number of whites who hold racist beliefs, measured by unfavorable attitudes toward miscegenation, integrated housing and job equality, has declined from a majority in the '50s to a quarter of the total population today. For whites this is real progress, however one may wish to quibble over the meaning of the survey data. But, even with only a quarter of all whites holding racist beliefs, it remains the case that for every black person there are two white racists.

Furthermore, the vast majority of blacks will rarely come in contact with the 75 percent of whites who are tolerant, for simple socioeconomic reasons. More educated, more prosperous and more suburban, the tolerant three-quarters tend to live exactly where blacks are least likely to be found: in the expensive suburbs. On the other hand, it is the least educated and most prejudiced whites who tend to be in closest proximity to blacks.

Further, the behavior of the tolerant three quarters of whites, and their attempts to improve the condition of blacks, tends to intensify racist feelings among the whites most likely to come in contact with blacks. The cost of racial change is disproportionately borne by those whites who have traditionally been most hostile to blacks. Black improvement is invariably perceived as competition in the once-protected economic preserves of working-class whites. Hence, not only do racist whites continue to outnumber blacks but their racist behavior also finds more frequent and intense outlets.

Of special concern here is the behavior of law-enforcement agencies. The typical big-city police officer is the white person with whom the typical lower- and working-class black person is mostly likely to come in contact outside the workplace. Unfortunately, white police officers tend to come from precisely the working-class urban communities most likely to be hostile to blacks. And there is also abundant psychological evidence that they tend to conform to the authoritarian personality type which most closely correlates with racist behavior. At the same time, their profession brings them into contact with the most lawless members of the black community, continuously reinforcing their prejudices.

The result is that the typical white police officer holds all blacks in suspicion and treats them in a manner that constantly threatens their dignity and most basic rights. In some urban communities this amounts to life under a virtual police state for many law-abiding working-class and poor black Americans. Middle-class status makes some difference, but only in well-defined social situations. It can sometimes even be a disadvantage. The Mark Fuhrman tapes revealed what every bourgeois black person already knew: that in unprotected contexts—driving on the highway, visiting a white suburban friend or caught in some minor traffic or other infraction—they are likely to find themselves specially targeted by white police officers and detectives who resent their success and take malignant pleasure in harassing them, especially if they are in mixed relationships.

In this context, the speedy decision of the jury in the O. J. Simpson trial makes perfect sense. The type of lower-middle and working-class black people who sat on the jury have every reason to believe that white police officers are racists only too willing to plant evidence and lie in court. All this is in direct contrast to the experience of the typical white person, who views the police officer either as a friend or acquaintance from the neighborhood or as a protector and guardian of the suburban peace.

What exists, then, is a serious mismatch in racial perception of change. Most middle-class whites feel, correctly, that things have gotten much better not only in the objective socioeconomic condition of blacks but in their improved attitude toward blacks. The typical black person perceives and experiences the situation as either having not changed or having gotten worse.

The experience of Massachusetts is typical. By all objective criteria this is one of most racially liberal areas of America. Not only was it the first state to elect a black U.S. senator since Reconstruction, but its current two senators are among the most liberal and pro-black in the Senate. And yet, among blacks of all classes, the Boston area has the unenviable reputation of being one of the most racist parts of the country. Many African Americans, put off by its racist image, still refuse to move to the area. The fears of blacks are legitimate; but so is the bewilderment of whites in middle-class Boston or in neighboring cities such as Cambridge (arguably one of the most racially liberal cities in the nation) when black colleagues insist they would rather go back South than settle anywhere near Boston. The sad truth is that, even as the number of tolerant whites rapidly increased between the '60s and '70s, the amount of contact between blacks and racist working-class whites also increased, as did the racial animosity of these whites, expressed most notoriously in the anti-busing violence of South Boston.

To make matters worse, the hostile reaction of a small proportion of whites not only hurts a large proportion of blacks; but, given the adversarial and litigious nature of the culture, and the tendency of the media to highlight the exceptional, a small but active number of whites can disproportionately influence the perception of all whites, with consequences deleterious to blacks. The current political hostility to affirmative action is a perfect case in point.

Only a small portion of whites—7 percent, according to recent opinion-poll data—claim to have been personally affected in any way by affirmative action. Yet the point of affirmative action is to bring blacks into greater contact with whites at the workplace and other sites where they were traditionally excluded. Aggrieved whites who feel they have been passed over in preference for blacks react sharply to this experience, which in turn colors the views of many whites who are in no

way influenced by the policy. The result is the "angry white male" syndrome: increased hostility toward what are perceived as unreasonable black demands, and the conviction that the vast majority of whites are being hurt—78 percent of whites think so—when, in fact, only 7 percent can actually attest to such injuries from their own experience.

The experiential mismatch between blacks and whites is made still worse by what may be called the outrage of liberation. A formerly oppressed group's sense of outrage at what has been done to it increases the more equal it becomes with its former oppressors. In part, this is simply a case of relative deprivation; in part, it is the result of having a greater voice—more literate and vocal leadership, more access to the media and so on. But it also stems from the formerly deprived group's increased sense of dignity and, ironically, its embrace of the formerly oppressive Other within its moral universe.

The slave, the sharecropping serf, the black person living under Jim Crow laws administered by vicious white police officers and prejudiced judges, were all obliged, for reasons of sheer survival, to accommodate somehow to the system. One form of accommodation was to expect and demand less from the racist oppressors. To do so was in no way to lessen one's contempt, even hatred and loathing, for them. Indeed, one's diminished expectations may even have been a reflection of one's contempt.

It has often been observed that one of racism's worst consequences is the denial of the black person's humanity. What often goes unnoticed is the other side of this twisted coin: that it left most blacks persuaded that whites were less than human. Technically clever yes, powerful, well-armed and prolific, to be sure, but without an ounce of basic human decency. No one whose community of memory was etched with the vision of lynched, barbecued ancestors, no black person who has seen the flash of greedy, obsessive hatred in the fish-blue stare of a cracker's cocked eyes, could help but question his inherent humanness. Most blacks, whatever their outward style of interaction with whites, genuinely believed, as did the mother of Henry Louis Gates, that most whites were inherently filthy and evil, or as the poet Sterling Brown once wrote, that there was no place in heaven for "Whuffolks ... being so onery," that, indeed, for the most of them "hell would be good enough—if big enough."

Integration, however partially, began to change all that. By dis-alienating the Other, the members of each group came, however reluctantly, to accept each other's humanness. But that acceptance comes at a price: for whites, it is the growing sense of disbelief at what the nightly news brings in relentless detail from the inner cities. For blacks, it is the sense of outrage that someone truly human could have done what the evidence of more than three and a half centuries makes painfully clear. Like a woman chased and held down in a pitch-dark night who discovers, first to her relief, then to her disbelief, that the stranger recoiling from her in the horror of recognition had been her own brother, the moral embrace of integration is a liberation with a double take: outrage verging on incomprehension.

Increasingly exposed to the conflicts that result from integration, whites may rebel against affirmative action and other programs that bring them face to face with black anger.

But resegregation is neither plausible nor desirable. Instead, whites, who dominate America's powerful institutions, must address the roots of black rage by committing to black America's socioeconomic advancement.

But, despite this imperative, a painful truth (one seemingly recognized by the participants in last week's march) emerges from the comparative sociology of group relations: except for those now-rare cases in which a minority constitutes the elite, the burden of racial and ethnic change always rests on a minority group. Although both whites and blacks have strong mutual interests in solving their racial problem, though the solution must eventually come from both, blacks must play the major role in achieving this objective—not only because they have more to gain from it but also because whites have far less to lose from doing nothing. It is blacks who must take the initiative, suffer the greater pain, define and offer the more creative solutions, persevere in the face of obstacles and paradoxical outcomes, insist that improvements are possible and maintain a climate of optimism concerning the eventual outcome. Or, to paraphrase Martin Luther King, it is they, and often they alone, who must keep the dream of a racially liberated America alive.

12

As Cultural Diversity of Workers Grows, Experts Urge Appreciation of Differences

Jolie Solomon

At a workshop for American University lab assistants recently, a hot topic was Saddam Hussein: What motivates the Arab leader, and why doesn't he view negotiations the way George Bush does?

But the topic wasn't foreign relations; it was employee relations. Saddam Hussein and George Bush were being studied for insights into conflicts among about 80 university lab technicians, one-third of whom are foreign-born and many of whom are Arab-American. Some of the same cultural issues complicating the Mideast crisis have cropped up inside the lab.

The workshop was one of hundreds around the U.S. that focus on cultural differences affecting recent immigrants, as well as blacks, women and people whose U.S. roots may stretch back as far as the Mayflower.

White male corporate culture is disappearing, and the workplace is becoming less a melting pot than a mosaic. The white male share of the labor force will drop to 39.4% by the year 2000 from 48.9% in 1976, according to the U.S. Labor Department, while the share of women and people of African, Hispanic, Asian and Native American origin will rise. Even now, because the work force is growing

more slowly, employees of different cultures are in a position to demand more flexibility from management.

In the past, conformity was the rule—right down to shirt color. Even now, the average manager may think: "To be fair, I should assume that everyone is the same and treat them that way."

But experts on diversity disagree. At the American University lab, says Gary Weaver, the professor of intercultural communications who conducted the workshop, small disagreements have escalated into "real conflict, where someone was going to get fired." A major reason, he says, is cultural differences. When a manager from the dominant U.S. culture saw two Arab-American employees arguing, he figured he had better stay out of it. But the employees *expected* a third party intermediary, or *wasta* in Arabic, and without one the incident blew up.

The expectation goes back to the Koran and Bedouin tradition, says Prof. Weaver. While the dominant American culture is likely to take an individualistic, win-lose approach and emphasize privacy, Arab-Americans tend to value a win-win result that preserves group harmony but often requires mediation. The hope in cross-cultural communication, he adds, is not to decide "who's rational and who's irrational" but to understand both perspectives and become comfortable with them.

Cultural misunderstandings, usually far from overt, happen every day. Consider these scenarios, offered by human resource consultants:

—A female vice president says to a male vice president, "Do you think we should invite X to this meeting?" The woman really means, "I think we *should* invite X," but her colleague thinks he has been asked a question. Many women have learned to speak in tentative or questioning tones to avoid appearing too aggressive.

—A Latino manager starts a budget-planning meeting by chatting casually and checking with his new staff on whether everyone can get together after work. His boss frets over the delay and wonders why he doesn't get straight to the numbers. Latino culture teaches that building relationships is often critical to working together, while the dominant American culture encourages "getting down to business."

Ignoring such differences can hurt people and productivity. Managers who don't understand what's motivating a colleague or employee may provoke resistance or anger, says Toby Thompkins, a consultant at Harbridge House Inc., a Chicago-based human resources concern.

But before people can change their approach, says consultants, they have to reject a basic but wrongheaded idea. Most assume that "their human nature is everyone's human nature, and you're OK if you just get down to the human," says Barbara Deane, editor of Training and Culture Newsletter in Seattle.

Because negative stereotyping is so damaging, adds Lewis Griggs, a San Francisco-based producer of films on diversity, "we are taught" that we should ignore differences, or at best consider them irrelevant. But "real and relevant" differences exist, he argues, reflecting genuine cultural habits and values.

Consultants coach managers and employees to look for and talk about these differences, largely by presenting scenarios drawn from real life. For the most part, they aren't blatant cases of discrimination but the details of day-to-day life.

One territory that's ripe for misunderstanding is body language. Rules for eye contact, for example, differ among cultures.

"Say I'm interviewing an Asian woman, anywhere from first generation to third generation," says Mr. Griggs. Deferring to authority, she may keep her eyes down, rarely meeting his. But this goes against everything traditionally taught to American managers about interviewing. "Here I am," says Mr. Griggs, "thinking, 'She's not assertive, not strong enough, maybe she's hiding something, or insecure.'" Meanwhile, he adds, "she sees my persistent eye contact as domineering, invasive, controlling. We don't trust each other."

"First," Mr. Griggs says, "I have to understand that my penetrating eye contact isn't God's gift, or the 'right' way, it's just Anglo male Midwestern [habit]." Then, he says, "I can stay in neutral, be a little less judgmental" and meet the other person halfway.

One danger in such discussions is that dissecting differences may lead some people to adopt new stereotypes. The fear was demonstrated at a manufacturing plant in Dallas, when Bob Abramms, a consultant with ODT Inc. in Amherst, Mass., showed one of Mr. Griggs's films.

In one scene, portrayed by actors, a Native American woman is binding together wires in an electronics plant. The boss sees that she has come up with a better way to do the work, and, over her protests, makes a big fuss. "Hey, everybody, this is the kind of work I want to see!" he shouts to the other workers on the floor.

The boss, of course, thinks he was doing the woman a favor. The dominant American culture sees public praise as the best reward for a job well done. But in some cultures, where the emphasis is on group harmony and cohesion, singling someone out appears to threaten the group and causes the individual to suffer a loss of face.

In the next scene, the boss has learned his lesson. He offers the employee a letter of praise for her personnel file.

But the film's conclusion got an angry reaction from one viewer in the plant, another Native American. "She said, 'I don't know what tribe that woman is from, maybe Navaho, but I'm Cherokee and I want public praise as much as the next person,'" recounts Mr. Abramms.

"No matter how much we learn about cultures," he adds, "we have to be aware of differences" within a culture "and of personal idiosyncrasies and preferences." It may turn out that the person who wants private recognition is a blond California woman who just happens to be shy. "The bottom line," says Mr. Abramms, "is: Ask."

In addition to discussing cultural differences, consultants also bring up the reverse scenario: when someone from a minority group displays behavior common to many cultures but is scrutinized more closely than others would be.

"In a corporate setting, anything a person of color does is exaggerated," says Mr. Thompkins of Harbridge House, who is black. Especially at professional levels, he says, "they're usually the only one in the room. So if I show up late for a meeting once, it's noticed. If there are three [white] guys from finance and one is late, it's not much of an issue."

A white man may pound the table and be seen by others as emphatic or exuberant, adds Carmen Colin, a consultant at ODT. But if a black man raises his voice or gestures, she says, "it's immediately seen as a threat" by non-black colleagues.

Says a black manager at a cosmetics firm: "Do we face more animosity if we are confrontational in a meeting? Yes." Once, after a meeting where he vigorously argued his position, he recalls that a white colleague told him casually, "I've never met a black male who didn't have a chip on his shoulder."

Often, the hardest part of such training is getting people into it to begin with. Many people are frightened, say consultants, about bringing tensions to the surface in an organization that seems to be functioning well.

Even when people acknowledge problems, they often see them as someone else's affair. In preparation for a seminar on diversity, Mr. Abramms recently mailed orientation packages to about 200 executives of a large oil company.

Along with the date, location and other practical details, each kit included a reprint of a Harvard Business Review article called "Black Managers: The Dream Deferred," describing black corporate experiences. Dozens of the company's white middle managers, without reading the article, sent their copies to the one black manager in the group, thinking, with some good will, says Mr. Abramms, "Oh, this will interest Tom.'" When the group met, he chided them. "You're the ones that need to read it," he said. "Tom *knows* what it's like."

People laughed sheepishly, he says. "You begin to see the absurdity of it, and to realize that the best we'll ever be is recovering sexists and recovering racists."

13

Workforce 2000: Executive Summary

William B. Johnston

The year 2000 will mark the end of what has been called the American century. Since 1900, the United States has become wealthy and powerful by exploiting the rapid changes taking place in technology, world trade, and the international political order. The last years of this century are certain to bring new developments in technology, international competition, demography, and other factors that will alter the nation's economic and social landscape. By the end of the next decade, the changes under way will produce an America that is in some ways unrecognizable from the one that existed only a few years ago.

Four key trends will shape the last years of the twentieth century:

- *The American economy should grow at [a] relatively healthy pace,* boosted by a rebound in U.S. exports, renewed productivity growth, and a strong world economy.

- Despite its international comeback, *U.S. manufacturing will be a much smaller share of the economy in the year 2000* than it is today. Service industries will create all of the new jobs, and most of the new wealth, over the next 13 years.

- *The workforce will grow slowly, becoming older, more female, and more disadvantaged.* Only 15 percent of the new entrants to the labor force over the next 13 years will be native white males, compared to 47 percent in that category today.

- *The new jobs in service industries will demand much higher skill levels* than the jobs of today. Very few new jobs will be created for those who cannot read, follow directions, and use mathematics. Ironically, the demographic trends in the workforce, coupled with the higher skill requirements of the economy, will lead to both higher and lower unemployment: more joblessness among the least-skilled and less among the most educationally advantaged.

These trends raise a number of important policy issues. If the United States is to continue to prosper—if the year 2000 is to mark the end of the *first* American century—policymakers must find ways to:

- *Stimulate Balanced World Growth*: To grow rapidly, the U.S. must pay less attention to its share of world trade and more to the growth of the economies of the other nations of the world, including those nations in Europe, Latin America, and Asia with whom the U.S. competes.

- *Accelerate Productivity Increases in Service Industries*: Prosperity will depend much more on how fast output per worker increases in health care, education, retailing, government, and other services than on gains in manufacturing.

- *Maintain the Dynamism of an Aging Workforce*: As the average age of American workers climbs toward 40, the nation must insure that its workforce and its institutions do not lose their adaptability and willingness to learn.

- *Reconcile the Conflicting Needs of Women, Work, and Families*: Three-fifths of all women over age 16 will be at work in the year 2000. Yet most current policies and institutions covering pay, fringe benefits, time away from work, pensions, welfare, and other issues were designed for a society in which men worked and women stayed home.

- *Integrate Black and Hispanic Workers Fully into the Economy*: The shrinking

---

Reprinted from *Workforce 2000: Executive Summary*. Indianapolis: Hudson Institute, Inc., 1987.

numbers of young people, the rapid pace of industrial change, and the ever-rising skill requirements of the emerging economy make the task of fully utilizing minority workers particularly urgent between now and 2000. Both cultural changes and education and training investments will be needed to create real equal employment opportunity.

- *Improve the Educational Preparation of All Workers*: As the economy grows more complex and more dependent on human capital, the standards set by the American education system must be raised.

THE U.S. ECONOMY IN THE YEAR 2000

Because long-range forecasts are so uncertain, alternative scenarios are useful to help to bracket a range of possible outcomes. The three scenarios presented here are based not only on different rates of economic growth, but on different policy choices.

The baseline or "surprise-free" scenario reflects a modest improvement in the rate of growth that the nation experienced between 1970 and 1985. But despite improved trends in inflation and productivity, the U.S. economy does not return to the boom times of the 1950s and 1960s. Slow labor force growth is only partly offset by faster productivity gains, and imperfect coordination between the world's governments leads to only moderate rates of world growth. Economic turbulence causes periodic recessions in the U.S. that hold total growth to just under three percent per year.

In contrast, "world deflation" focuses on the possibility that a worldwide glut of labor and production capacity in food, minerals, and manufactured products could lead to a sustained price deflation and sluggish economic growth. World governments, chastened by a decade and a half of inflation, are slow to recognize the new economic realities and unwilling to undertake coordinated efforts to respond to them. The U.S., whose huge trade deficit has been the world's growth engine during the early 1980s, moves toward balance in its trade and fiscal accounts. Without U.S. stimulus, the rest of the world slides into a series of recessions that lead to increased protectionism and beggar-thy-neighbor trade, monetary, and fiscal policies that hold growth to only 1.6 percent per year over the period.

The third scenario, the "technology boom," outlines a powerful rebound in U.S. economic growth to levels that compare with the first two decades following World War II. Coordinated international monetary, fiscal, and trade policies succeed in smoothing world business cycles. Renewed public and private lending to developing nations and low oil prices trigger rapid growth in much of the Third World. In the U.S., high rates of investment in both physical and human capital, coupled with rapid productivity growth in services, low inflation, low resource prices, lower taxes, and less government intervention combine to produce a boom in productivity that causes the U.S. economy to surge ahead by 4 percent per year.

Table 1 summarizes the major assumptions and outcomes of the three scenarios. The table underscores several key points about the U.S. economy over the next 13 years:

- *U.S. Growth and World Growth are Tightly Linked:* The strong historical correlation between world growth and U.S. growth continues through the balance of the century. In the baseline forecast, the U.S. grows at about 2.9 percent, compared to 3.1 percent for the world.
- *U.S. Manufacturing Employment Declines While Services Grow:* Despite strong export growth and substantial production increases, manufacturing jobs decline in all scenarios. Whether the U.S. and world economies are booming in an open trading environment or growing slowly in an atmosphere of protectionism and nationalistic trading patterns, U.S. manufacturing jobs decrease. No pattern of growth enables manufacturing employment to return to the peak of 1979.

TABLE 1
The U.S. Economy in the Year 2000

	1985 Level	Base		Low		High	
		Level	Change*	Level	Change*	Level	Change*
				2000 (Three Scenarios)			
World GDP (bill. 82$)	7745	12204	3.1%	9546	1.4%	13057	3.5%
U.S. GNP (bill. 82$)	3570	5463	2.9%	4537	1.6%	6431	4.0%
GNP Deflator (1982-100)	111.7	182.4	3.3%	117.8	0.4%	196.4	3.8%
Employment (millions)	107.2	131.0	1.3%	122.4	0.9%	139.9	1.8%
Manufacturing	19.3	17.2	-0.8%	18.0	-0.4%	18.1	-0.4%
Commercial & Other Services	62.0	84.3	2.1%	76.5	1.4%	88.7	2.4%
Productivity (output/worker, 82$)	33.3	41.7	1.5%	37.1	0.7%	46.0	2.2%
Manufacturing	40.4	71.4	3.9%	58.0	2.5%	81.3	4.8%
Commercial & Other Services	29.9	34.1	0.9%	30.4	0.1%	38.2	1.6%
Fed. Surplus (bill. curr.$)	-200.8	-110.0	—	-170.1	—	-40.7	—
Curr. Acct. Bal. (bill. curr.$)	-116.8	14.0	—	12.5	—	32.6	—
Disp. Income Per Capita (thou. 82$)	10.5	13.5	1.7%	11.5	0.6%	15.6	2.7%

*Average Annual Gain
Source: Hudson Institute.

In addition to the decline in employment, manufacturing will decline as a share of GNP, measured in current dollars. Where manufacturing produced some 30 percent of all goods and services in 1955, and 21 percent in 1985, its share will drop to less than 17 percent by 2000.

The shift to services will bring with it broad changes in the location, hours, and structure of work. Service jobs tend to be located where and when the customer wants them, rather than centralized as are manufacturing jobs. Partly as a result, the typical workplace in the future will have fewer people, and the average workweek will become shorter with more people employed part-time.

The shift to services will also have a great impact on the economy and its employees. For example, the business cycle should moderate, since service industry growth is less volatile than manufacturing. Wages may become less equally distributed, since service jobs tend have more high and low earners, and fewer in the middle. Economic growth may be harder to achieve, because productivity gains are lower in most service industries.

Most importantly, the shift to services means that efforts to preserve or develop the nation's manufacturing base are swimming upstream against a powerful tide. Productivity gains, not Japanese competition, will gradually eliminate manufacturing jobs. Lower prices (relative to services) will gradually shrink manufacturing's share of the economy. Just as agriculture lost its central role in the American economy at the beginning of the century, so will manufacturing lose economic importance as the century draws to a close. Those who fail to recognize these inevitable trends—for example, states that try to capture new factories to boost their local economies or the Congress, which is threatening to legislate trade barriers to hang on to U.S. manufacturing jobs—will miss the most important opportunities of the future.

- *The Key to Domestic Economic Growth Is a Rebound in Productivity, Particularly in Services:* Throughout the 1970s and early 1980s, the United States managed to sustain a rising standard of living by increasing the number of people at work and by borrowing from abroad and from

the future. These props under the nation's consumption will reach their limits before the end of the century; there will be relatively fewer young people and homemakers who will enter the workforce during the 1990s, and the burden of consumer, government, and international debt cannot be expanded indefinitely. If the U.S. economy is to grow at its historic 3 percent per year average, the nation must substantially increase its productivity.

Output per worker during the 1990s is projected to double, from 0.7 percent per year to 1.5 percent, the same rate as the 1960s. A combination of older, more stable, and better-educated workers, and higher rates of investment will support this improvement. Better productivity performance by the service industries will be particularly important. Output per worker in manufacturing continues to show strong gains, but the most important productivity improvements come in services, where output per worker climbs from -0.2 percent over the last 15 years to +0.9 percent per year from 1985 to 2000. The keys to such advances will be more competition in traditionally noncompetitive industries such as education, health care, and government services, coupled with the application of advanced technologies to deliver more automated business, government, and personal services.

- *U.S. Trade Accounts Move Toward Balance:* Although the different scenarios show widely dispersed rates of growth of imports and exports, the U.S. current account balance improves under all conditions. This is due both to the devaluation of the dollar that has already taken place against other currencies and to improving productivity in manufacturing industries. Under the baseline scenario, by the year 2000 the U.S. current account balance is in the black by some $14 billion.

- *The U.S. Budget Deficit Declines:* Along with the improvement in the trade deficit comes a decline in the budget deficit. Even without any major tax increases, growth in GNP and a large surplus in the Social Security Trust Fund cut the federal budget deficit to $18 billion by 1995.

- *Inflation Moderates:* Under the baseline scenario, prices increase by an average of 3.3 percent per year over the 1985–2000 period. The excess world capacity in labor, goods, and services prevents inflation from resuming its pace of the 1970s.

- *Unemployment Remains Stubbornly High:* The baseline scenario forecasts unemployment at just over 7 percent in the year 2000, despite the relatively slow growth of the labor force projected over the period. In the deflation scenario, unemployment climbs above 9 percent, while even in the boom scenario unemployment is reduced only to 5.9 percent.

- *Disposable Income Increases Moderately:* Disposable personal income per person, the best single measure of how rapidly society is improving its standard of living, grows by 1.7 percent per year under the baseline scenario, almost precisely the rate at which it grew between 1970 and 1985.

WORKERS AND JOBS IN THE YEAR 2000

Changes in the economy will be matched by changes in the workforce and the jobs it will perform. Five demographic facts will be most important:

- *The population and the workforce will grow more slowly than at any time since the 1930s:* Population growth, which was climbing at almost 1.9 percent per year in the 1950s, will slump to only 0.7 percent per year by 2000; the labor force, which exploded by 2.9 percent per year in the 1970s, will be expanding by only 1 percent annually in the 1990s. These slow growth rates will tend to slow down the nation's economic expansion and will shift the economy more toward income-sensitive products and services (e.g., luxury

goods and convenience services). It may also tighten labor markets and force employers to use more capital-intensive production systems.

- *The average age of the population and the workforce will rise, and the pool of young workers entering the labor market will shrink:* As the baby boom ages, and the baby bust enters the workforce, the average age of the workforce will climb from 36 today to 39 by the year 2000. The number of young workers age 16–24 will drop by almost 2 million, or 8 percent. This decline in young people in the labor force will have both positive and negative impacts. On the one hand, the older workforce will be more experienced, stable, and reliable. The reverse side of this stability will be a lower level of adaptability. Older workers, for example, are less likely to move, to change occupations, or to undertake retraining than younger ones. Companies that have grown by adding large numbers of flexible, lower-paid young workers will find such workers in short supply in the 1990s.

- *More women will enter the workforce:* Almost two-thirds of the new entrants into the workforce between now and the year 2000 will be women, and 61 percent of all women of working age are expected to have jobs by the year 2000. Women will still be concentrated in jobs that pay less than men's jobs, but they will be rapidly entering many higher-paying professional and technical fields. In response to the continued feminization of work, the convenience industries will boom, with "instant" products and "delivered-to-the-door" service becoming common throughout the economy. Demands for day care and for more time off from work for pregnancy leave and child-rearing duties will certainly increase, as will interest in part-time, flexible, and stay-at-home jobs.

- *Minorities will be a larger share of new entrants into the labor force:* Non-whites will make up 29 percent of the new entrants into the labor force between now and the year 2000, twice their current share of the workforce. Although this large share of a more slowly growing workforce might be expected to improve the opportunities for these workers, the concentration of blacks in declining central cities and slowly growing occupations makes this sanguine outlook doubtful.

- *Immigrants will represent the largest share of the increase in the population and the workforce since the first World War:* Even with the new immigration law, approximately 600,000 legal and illegal immigrants are projected to enter the United States annually throughout the balance of the century. Two-thirds or more of immigrants of working age are likely to join the labor force. In the South and West where these workers are concentrated, they are likely to reshape local economies dramatically, promoting faster economic growth and labor surpluses.

In combination, these demographic changes will mean that the new workers entering the workforce between now and the year 2000 will be much different from those who people it today. Non-whites, women, and immigrants will make up more than five-sixths of the net additions to the workforce between now and the year 2000, though they make up only about half of it today:

	1985 LABOR FORCE	NET NEW WORKERS, 1985–2000
Total	115,461,000	25,000,000
Native White Men	47%	15%
Native White Women	36%	42%
Native Non-white Men	5%	7%
Native Non-white Women	5%	13%
Immigrant Men	4%	13%
Immigrant Women	3%	9%

Source: Hudson Institute.

Juxtaposed with these changes in the composition of the workforce will be rapid changes in the nature of the job market. The fastest-growing jobs will be in professional, technical, and sales fields requiring the highest education and skill levels. Of the fastest-growing job categories, all but one, service occupations, require more than the median level of education for all jobs. Of those growing more slowly than average, not one requires more than the median education.

Ranking jobs according to skills, rather than education, illustrates the rising requirements even more dramatically. When jobs are given numerical ratings according to the math, language, and reasoning skills they require, only twenty-seven percent of all new jobs fall into the lowest two skill categories, while 40 percent of current jobs require these limited skills. By contrast, 41 percent of new jobs are in the three highest skill groups, compared to only 24 percent of current jobs (see Figure 1). The changes ahead in the job market will affect different groups in the society in different ways. While young whites may find their jobs prospects improving, for black men and Hispanics the job market will be particularly difficult (see Figure 2). In contrast to their rising share of the new entrants into the labor force, black men will hold a declining fraction of all jobs if they simply retain existing shares of various occupations. Black women, on the other hand, will hold a rising fraction of all jobs, but this increase will be less than needed to offset their growing share of the workforce.

SIX POLICY CHALLENGES

These trends in the emerging economy suggest six policy issues that deserve the greatest attention:

Stimulating World Growth

For more than a decade, American policymakers have been concerned with the U.S. balance of trade, the nation's deteriorating ability to compete with other nations, and the presumed unfairness of the trading policies of other countries. These issues, while important, are not the most critical international concerns facing the nation. U.S. prosperity

FIGURE 1
Low Skilled Jobs Are Declining

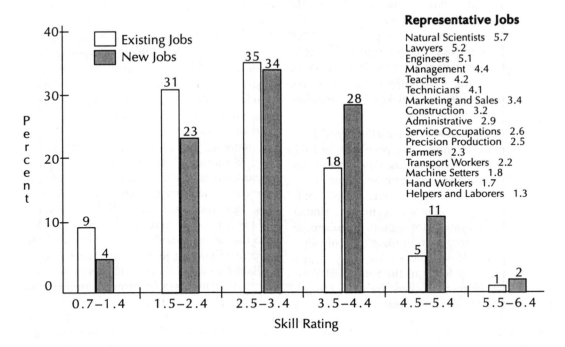

Representative Jobs

Natural Scientists 5.7
Lawyers 5.2
Engineers 5.1
Management 4.4
Teachers 4.2
Technicians 4.1
Marketing and Sales 3.4
Construction 3.2
Administrative 2.9
Service Occupations 2.6
Precision Production 2.5
Farmers 2.3
Transport Workers 2.2
Machine Setters 1.8
Hand Workers 1.7
Helpers and Laborers 1.3

between now and the end of the century will depend primarily on how fast the world economy grows and on how rapidly domestic productivity increases. It will depend very little on how open or closed the Japanese market is to American goods, or even on how soon U.S. trade accounts return to balance.

In particular, it is important for the United States, along with other industrial countries, to find ways to restimulate growth in the developing world. These nations that are still on the threshold of industrialization have the greatest opportunities for rapid growth that can stimulate the world and U.S. economies.

At the same time, efforts to improve U.S. competitiveness must always be undertaken within the context of strengthening the world economy. The envy and anger that many in the United States feel toward Japan's success should not blind policymakers to the reality that as Japan (and every other nation of the world) grows richer, the United States will benefit. Just as it is easier for a company to prosper in a rapidly-growing market than to capture market share in a shrinking one, so it will be easier for the United States to prosper

in rapidly-growing world markets than in static or shrinking ones.

Of course, the U.S. *share* of world growth is also important. But most of the steps that must be taken to improve U.S. competitiveness have little to do with changing the behavior of the Japanese or the Koreans. Instead, they involve changes in the propensity of Americans to borrow and spend rather than to save, major improvements in the educational preparation of large numbers of prospective workers, and reforms in the practices and laws that encourage America's best and brightest to provide legal advice in corporate takeovers rather than to build companies that exploit new technologies.

Improving Productivity in Service Industries: Manufacturing still controls the imagination, the statistics, and the policies of the nation, even though it now represents a small and shrinking fraction of national employment and output. The nation's mental image of progress continues to be one in which manufacturing plants produce more cars, computers, and carpets per hour. But services are a far larger segment of the economy and the sector whose

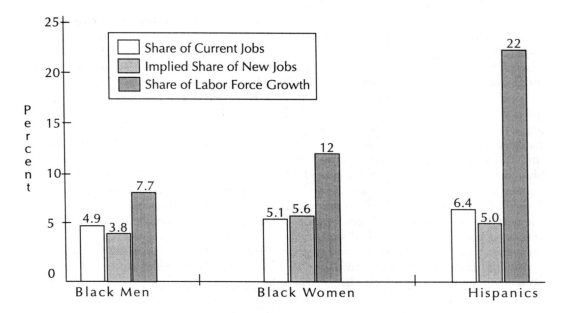

FIGURE 2
Black Men and Hispanics Face the Greatest Difficulties in the Emerging Job Market

productivity has actually declined in recent years. These industries—health, education, trade, finance, insurance, real estate, and government—must be the targets of government efforts to improve productivity.

To realize this objective, new efforts must be made to tear down the barriers to competition in many of the service industries where competition does not now exist. At the same time, new investments must be made in research and development targeted toward improving service industry productivity.

In education, for example, competition is needed at the elementary and secondary school level, where the monopoly position of the public schools has stifled innovation. In order to provide a benchmark for measuring gains, national standards and nationally comparable tests are essential. At the same time, new investments are needed in educational technology, in particular to develop a large base of public domain software to teach math, reading, science, and more advanced courses.

In health care, the steps taken to inject competition into the system must be extended, while new investments are made in productivity-enhancing technologies such as automated diagnostics. In a range of other government

services, privatization and competition promise to provide great productivity gains.

Improving the Dynamism
of an Aging Workforce

At the same time that the workforce is aging and becoming less willing to relocate, retrain, or change occupations, the economy is demanding more flexibility and dynamism. Despite general recognition of the importance of a flexible workforce, many national policies fail to promote this end.

For example, the nation's pension system is one in which most retirement benefits are tied to the job. In many cases, employees receive no benefits if they leave after a few years, and, by the time they reach mid-career, they would suffer major benefit losses if they switched employers. The current system tends to inhibit workers from changing jobs and to discourage companies from hiring older workers.

Similarly, the unemployment insurance system has been largely used to provide income support to workers who are laid off. Relatively little has been done to make the system one that promotes relocation, retraining, and job search.

Although worker retraining has become a catchphrase, and the federal government and private industry now spend billions of dollars for retraining, there is still no national consensus that all workers should expect to learn new skills over the course of their worklives. Except in a few companies, training is confined mostly to the top and bottom ranks of employees, with little systematic effort to insure that all workers are constantly reinvesting in themselves to avoid obsolescence. National policies that promote such corporate and individual attitudes toward retraining should be backed up with changes in the tax code to encourage lifelong education.

Finally, the goal of promoting dynamism requires reconsideration of national policies on immigration. The most careful studies of legal immigrants have concluded that they are a valuable asset to the nation and help to stimulate economic growth and change. The need for more, better-educated immigrants to help staff a growing economy will increase as the growth of the population and labor force slows in the 1990s. Despite the political and social objections, the nation should begin a program of gradually increasing its quotas and opening its doors to more individuals desiring to enter the country.

Reconciling the Demands of Women, Work, and Families

America has become a society in which everyone is expected to work—including women with young children. But many of society's institutions were designed during an era of male breadwinners and female homemakers.

What is needed is a thoroughgoing reform of the institutions and policies that govern the workplace, to insure that women can participate fully in the economy, and that men and women have the time and resources needed to invest in their children. For example, some formula is needed to provide parents with more time away from work. Flexible hours, the use of sick leave to care for children, more part-time work, pregnancy leaves for mothers and fathers, and other innovations are expensive, but ultimately necessary changes in the structure of work that will accommodate the combination of work and family life. Simi-

larly, the need for high-quality day care has not yet been fully addressed. Government and private mechanisms to provide for the care of the children of working parents need further development.

The increase in the numbers of working women also has implications for the current debate over welfare reform. The current stay-at-home welfare program was designed long before most women worked. Now that a majority of nonwelfare women with young children work, it no longer seems cruel to require welfare mothers to do so. The current system should be replaced with one that mandates work for all able-bodied mothers (except for those caring for infants), while providing training, day care, and job counseling.

Integrate Blacks and Hispanics Fully into the Workforce

For minority workers, the changes in the nation's demography and economy during the 1990s represent both a great risk and a great opportunity. With fewer new young workers entering the workforce, employers will be hungry for qualified people and more willing to offer jobs and training to those they have traditionally ignored. At the same time, however, the types of jobs being created by the economy will demand much higher levels of skill than the jobs that exist today. Minority workers are not only less likely to have had satisfactory schooling and on-the-job training, they may have language, attitude, and cultural problems that prevent them from taking advantage of the jobs that will exist.

If the policies and employment patterns of the present continue, it is likely that the demographic opportunity of the 1990s will be missed and that by the year 2000 the problems of minority unemployment, crime, and dependency will be worse than they are today. Without substantial adjustments, blacks and Hispanics will have a smaller fraction of the jobs of the year 2000 than they have today, while their share of those seeking work will have risen.

Each year of delay in seriously and successfully attacking this problem makes it more difficult. Not only will the jobs become more sophisticated and demanding, but the numbers of new workers entering the workforce will begin to increase after 1993. Now is the time to begin investing in education, training, and other assistance. These investments will be needed, not only to insure that employers have a qualified workforce in the years after 2000, but to finally deliver the equality of opportunity that has been America's great unfulfilled promise.

Improving Workers' Education and Skills

As the economies of developed nations move further into the post-industrial era, human capital plays an ever-more-important role in their progress. As the society becomes more complex, the amount of education and knowledge needed to make a productive contribution to the economy becomes greater. A century ago, a high school education was thought to be superfluous for factory workers and a college degree was the mark of an academic or a lawyer. Between now and the year 2000, for the first time in history, a majority of all new jobs will require postsecondary education.

Education and training are the primary systems by which the human capital of a nation is preserved and increased. The speed and efficiency with which these education systems transmit knowledge governs the rate at which human capital can be developed. Even more than such closely-watched indicators as the rate of investment in plant and equipment, human capital formation plays a direct role in how fast the economy can grow.

If the economy is to grow rapidly and American companies are to reassert their world leadership, the educational standards that have been established in the nation's schools must be raised dramatically. Put simply, students must go to school longer, study more, and pass more difficult tests covering more advanced subject matter. There is no excuse for vocational programs that "warehouse" students who perform poorly in academic subjects or for diplomas that register nothing more than years of school attendance. From an economic standpoint, higher standards in the schools are the equivalent of competitiveness internationally.

Promoting world growth, boosting service industry productivity, stimulating a more flexible workforce, providing for the needs of working families with children, bringing minority workers into the workforce, and raising educational standards are not the only items on the nation's agenda between now and the year 2000. But they are certainly among the most important.

More critically, they are issues that will not go away by themselves. If nothing unusual is done to focus national attention and action on these challenges, they are likely to be still unresolved at the beginning of the next century. By addressing them now, the nation's decision makers can help to assure that the economy and the workforce fulfill their potential to make the year 2000 the beginning of the next American century.

14

The Concept of Managing Diversity

R. Roosevelt Thomas, Jr.

For the past seven years, I have served as president of The American Institute for Managing Diversity, where we have been testing out a definition of managing diversity as distinct from affirmative action and valuing differences. In this article, I discuss highlights of the concept and relate it to questions that surface often about "diversity."

WHAT IS MANAGING DIVERSITY?

Essentially, managing diversity (MD) is a "way of thinking" toward the objective of creating an environment that will enable all employees to reach their full potential in pursuit of organizational objectives. It differs from affirmative action (AA) in at least five key ways.

Mutual Adjustment Process

Affirmative action assumes that the individual employee alone will do the necessary adjustment to assure a good fit with the organization. MD assumes that the manager and organization adjust, as well as the employee, to assure individual-organizational compatibility.

This mutual adjustment process, however, does have limits. For example, managers must do their adjustment around the absolute requirements for the success of the enterprise. These factors cannot be compromised. This means that some individuals will be too diverse for a given organization.

Reprinted from *The Bureaucrat,* Winter 1991–1992, 19–22.

Managers must be certain that what they label a requirement is indeed one and not a preference, convenience, or tradition. In the context of the analogy of catching a baseball, managers must be clear whether the requirement is to catch the ball a certain way or simply not to drop the ball.

Use of Potential

Affirmative action focuses on recruitment, upper mobility and retention, while MD centers on full utilization of employee potential. The assumption is that if you are fully utilizing an employee, you are also implicitly addressing upper mobility and retention issues.

Evolutionary Approach

Affirmative action says, "let's get relief from undesirable practices as quickly as possible, even if through artificial means," while MD places a priority on bringing about relief naturally. MD says, "let's make sure we address root causes; then we can stand back and watch the desired results evolve naturally." Also, it is assumed that when root causes are addressed, change will be easily sustained.

Helping the Manager

Affirmative action assumes that actions are taken for the benefit of individuals who are "disadvantaged" in some fashion. MD, on the other hand, sees the manager being the principal benefactor.

To say that MD is primarily for the manager is to say that it is not primarily about civil rights, moral responsibility or social responsibility. Neither is it about eliminating racism or sexism, leveling the playing field, making amends for past wrongs, or doing something for minorities and women. Managing diversity is about helping the manager learn how to tap the potential of all employees.

Business Issue

Unlike the situation with affirmative action, where the driving motives are legal requirements, moral prescriptions or social responsibility, the motive for moving forward with MD is that it is a business issue. MD is a business issue in several ways for many companies.

One is that corporations are burning a human resource fuel that is diverse and will become more diverse; those burning this fuel most effectively will have a competitive advantage. Another is that much of what is already on the plate of corporate America for the purpose of strengthening viability implicitly or explicitly calls for a managing diversity capability.

Systematic efforts to improve quality, for example, call for pushing decision-making down and for involving all employees. In the context of a diverse workforce, such quality approaches can not be implemented fully without managing diversity. Accordingly, pioneering corporations are beginning to coordinate their diversity and quality efforts.

High commitment work systems and teams, identified by some corporations as strategic, cannot be implemented with a diverse workforce without managing diversity capability. In one company, as managers sought to create teams, they found that only white males were enthusiastic about participation. This circumstance led them to explore how they might create an environment that would foster excitement and commitment on the part of all employees. In other words, they sought to learn how to manage diversity.

Running lean is becoming increasingly desirous for companies. This means that a premium is placed on utilizing fully the potential of all remaining resources. In the context of remaining human resources that are diverse, a premium is placed on managing diversity.

Finally, managing diversity is a business issue for companies because their external constituencies are becoming more diverse. An ability to manage internal diversity will enhance a corporation's ability to manage external diversity. Incidentally, this does not translate into minorities serving minority constituencies or women serving women, but rather into managers who can design strategies that work for the total mixture of both employees and external forces.

MD is an alternative that enables the manager simultaneously to move beyond AA, and to build upon its gains. Its potential is beginning to be recognized. One white male manager commented, "This is a different way of looking at old issues. I like it. There is something for everyone."

VALUING DIFFERENCES APPROACH

MD also differs significantly from an approach known as valuing differences. Valuing differences as a generic approach aims to bring about greater understanding and acceptance of people who are different, enhancement of interpersonal relationships, and minimization of blatant expressions of racism and sexism.

MD includes the improvement of relationships among people who are different, but recognizes that changes in organizational culture and systems may also be required to create an environment that enables all employees.

MD differs from both affirmative action and valuing differences in its definition of diversity. MD defines diversity as including white males and as being broader than race and gender. So when we say managing diversity, we are not talking about white males managing minorities and women, but rather about any manager managing whoever is in his/her workforce.

Consider a jar of red jelly beans, into which you place yellow and green jelly beans. Everyday language labels the yellow and green beans as "diversity," but managing diversity views the mixture of yellow, green, and red jelly beans to be "diversity." It recognizes further that the beans can differ in ways other than color, such as, taste, age, weight, and time in the jar. Even among all red beans there can be substantial diversity.

WHY "MANAGING DIVERSITY" NOW?

Why is the corporate manager beginning to talk more about managing diversity instead of the traditional affirmative action focus? Why the shift in perspective now? Three factors deserve mention: frustration with affirmative action, the growing tendency of employees to celebrate differences, and worldwide competitive realities.

Frustration with Affirmative Action

After more than 20 years of affirmative action effort, many managers find themselves frustrated with limited progress.

- We've spent some money and bought all kinds of programs; and we have committed people of goodwill. Yet, we're worse off than we've ever been.

- As I look over the landscape, I sense that we're all in the same boat—puzzled as to how to bring about equal opportunity.

- When I started out, I had some rather naive notions about how progress could be achieved with affirmative action. But now, I just do not know.

Looking to move beyond frustration, executives like these are willing to explore alternatives.

New Attitudes

Managers also are noting that employees are more inclined to celebrate differences, and less willing to "fit in." Recently, on a radio talk show, a caller asked, "Why can't we focus on what brings us together like the mission of the company, and leave everything else outside? We would be a lot better off."

The reality is that employees more and more desire to focus on the forces that bind as well as on the factors that make people different. They are less willing to leave differences at the door before entering the work arena.

This new attitude can be seen in various employee groups. It's true for new minority employees, who observe that their predecessors who "fitted in" have lost some of their "minority identity." It is true for new women employees, who see their predecessors wondering if the "loss of femininity" has been too great a cost for success. It is true for young workers, who find themselves questioning the wisdom of old men with out-of-date experience and see little value in learning to be like them. It is true for highly educated professionals, who come to their companies with expectations of participatory decision-making quite at odds with the usual hierarchical style. All of them, in their own way, are saying, "Don't assimilate me. Don't dilute my strengths."

This reluctance to adapt, even more than changing demographics, is the major force behind the increase in workforce diversity and the need to modify the traditional approach.

Competition

Finally, global and domestic competitive realities are prompting managers to rethink their approach to diversity. Few industries or corporations have not encountered the pressures of worldwide competition. Rare is the manager who can assume the continued viability of his/her industry or corporation.

In this competitive context, managers simply cannot afford to underutilize any resource. This means that they vigorously must seek ways to move beyond frustrations and the limitations of the "fitting in" approach. Creating a corporate environment that enables all employees to reach their potential is now no longer solely a legal, moral, or social responsibility issue, but also a matter of business survival.

SELECTED QUESTIONS AND RESPONSES

Doesn't It All Boil Down to Good Relationships?

Individuals raising this question believe that diversity challenges can be addressed by improving interpersonal relationships. Managers in this camp implement programs to enhance relationships and minimize blatant expressions of racism, sexism, and other isms.

Two examples of such programs would be multicultural days featuring the culture of a given minority group and support groups for minorities and women that function as liaisons between these employees and senior management. Generally, options like these produce few lasting results. People often feel better about themselves, colleagues, and their corporation, but the managerial challenges of fully utilizing the potential of all employees are not met.

Managers consequently are learning that there is no pot of gold at the end of the "better relationships" rainbow. Reasons as to why this is so can be found in the story of a particular giraffe and elephant.

A giraffe builds a house that is ideal for giraffes; for example, the ceilings are high, portals are narrow and the windows are high off the floor. One day, the giraffe widens his basement door and invites his elephant friend to share the house. The giraffe and the elephant like each other and relate well, but the elephant does not thrive in the house.

The portals are too narrow; the steps, walls, and floors will not support the elephant's weight; and the windows are too high off the floor. Both the giraffe and elephant are distressed by these circumstances. The giraffe and elephant, throughout the ordeal, continue to relate well, and the giraffe affirms his desire for the elephant to be at home in his house. Finally, in wisdom and understanding, the elephant notes "I do not think an elephant will ever be at home in a house built for a giraffe."

There is no malicious intent here, but rather a historical fact: the house was not designed with the elephant in mind. Given the significant differences between giraffes and elephants, a house meeting both sets of needs is likely to be much different than one designed solely around the giraffe.

Stated differently, the corporation wishing to create an environment that enables all employees to reach their full potential will have to work for better relationships and also change organizational practices as necessary.

What Are Some of the Major Differences?

This question suggests that certain behavior patterns or cultural traits can be identified as characteristics of a given minority group, and that an awareness of these factors would enhance the manager's ability to relate to members of the respective groups.

I am not convinced of the utility of this approach. We must keep in mind that we are managing individuals and not groups. Within any designated category of employees, there is enormous diversity. For example, blacks,

whites, Hispanics, and Asians differ among themselves significantly. Accordingly, any effort to understand group traits is likely to lead to a false sense of managerial security.

This reality makes the task of managing diversity very challenging.

What Value Is Added by Having Diversity?

Here, the suggestion is that if we can identify the value added by having diversity at the table, by including people who are diverse, we can more easily make the case for managing diversity.

This is an erroneous premise. Given the definition of diversity as encompassing more than race and gender, and given the reality of demographic projections of greater representation of minorities and women in the workforce, whether a manager values or seeks diversity he/she will have a diverse set of employees.

Whether to have a diverse workforce is not an option. Even in the absence of race and gender diversity, other dimensions will be present. So the issue is not to convince the manager to have a diverse workforce, but rather to help the manager develop the managerial wherewithal to secure from a pluralistic group the required level of productivity.

What Managerial Skills Are Required for Managing Diversity?

The approach most compatible with MD is the empowerment model. This model defines the task of managing as enabling employees to behave in ways required to achieve business objectives. In this model, the duality between "business issues" and "people issues" is absent. Instead, the empowerment of employees is linked directly to or with business objectives.

Under the empowerment model, managing is the priority, while doing is a secondary focus. Empowerment managers of accounting, for example, worry about whether they have done everything possible to fully enable accountants to do accounting. They're less concerned with doing accounting themselves.

However, our research findings indicate that what we call the "doer model" prevails in corporations, rather than the "empowerment" approach.

"Doer" managers value serving as models of how work should be done, and consider the "best" employees to be those who come closest to being clones of the boss. For these managers, managing the business, managing means doing the work. For the accounting manager, for example, this means practicing accounting. Doer managers make statements such as "I wouldn't ask my people to do anything I wouldn't do myself; I roll up my sleeves and get in the trenches."

Doer managers perceive themselves as the center of the action—the "chief doers." They believe that the corporation values their abilities to do so much that other people have been assigned to them as a way of expanding their personal capability to perform. They believe, in other words, that employees are there to function as their extensions so that their ability to do is enlarged.

Doer managers see their job as two dimensional: they must manage the business and manage people. They often fail to integrate the two. Typically they talk of "people" and "business" issues as if they were unrelated. Furthermore, they see "doing" as their major task and taking care of people as secondary. They cherish the "real work" of doing (accounting, for example) and minimize the "managing people" activity. Any hint of a "people challenge" is referred immediately to the human resources department.

When we look at the function of a manager this way, it is easy to see why the doer model is such a barrier to any attempt at managing diversity. First, it discourages acceptance of diversity. Doer managers seek people who can predictably clone their behavior. They are not interested in the ways in which differences can enhance corporate profits. Second, doer managers do not see managing people as a legitimate activity. They will always have difficulty managing a diverse workforce because they place no priority on managing people in general.

Does Meritocracy—the Presumption that "Cream Will Rise to the Top"— Fit in with the Concept of Managing Diversity? Are They in Conflict?

No, our research suggests that merit promotions have three dimensions:

- task merit: demonstrated capability to perform a given task sufficiently;
- cultural merit: demonstrated capability to conform to the major requirements of the corporation's basic assumptions or roots; and
- political merit: demonstrated capability to attract the endorsement of someone with sufficient clout to minimize doubt about an individual's qualifications.

People who are "different" often are able to meet the first condition but not the second or third.

Managing diversity simply calls for the manager to ensure that cultural and political realities do not advantage or disadvantage anyone because of irrelevant considerations. In this sense, then, there is no conflict between the two ideas.

Notice that this merit framework makes it clear that cream does not rise naturally. All employees, even "self-made" individuals, benefit from political assists. This is the nature of organizational reality. This explains why "just do your job, don't get involved in politics" is bad advice. New managers who follow this advice often wonder why they are overlooked for promotions. There is no substitute for fulfilling all three requirements of the merit framework.

SUMMARY

In this article, I have provided highlights of a managerial perspective required for enabling an increasingly diverse workforce. I have contended that managing diversity, valuing differences, and affirmative action are different. Organizations, for the foreseeable future, will need to use all three approaches, although eventually (roughly in 20 years for most organizations) MD will make AA and valuing differences unnecessary.

My intent has been to give the reader an awareness of what will become dominant managerial considerations, as the workforce becomes more diverse and organizational environments become more competitive.

15

Domestic Multiculturalism: Cross-Cultural Management in the Public Sector

Nancy J. Adler

The Women's Health Van is a traveling clinic for women who cannot afford to see a private physician. Initial visits to Anglo areas of a major American city were highly successful. Anglo women made full use of the consultation and testing services. The public health director was surprised and disappointed to discover that few women were visiting the van during its stops in Hispanic areas. Why? The service was the same. The announcements had been in both Spanish and English. What went wrong?

Again and again in the Post Office Department Anglo supervisors failed to promote Filipino workers. When questioned, the supervisors described the Filipinos as "lacking the maturity necessary for higher positions." As one supervisor cited, "Filipino workers have come to me numerous times with small questions about their

Nancy Adler is a Professor in the Faculty of Management at McGill University in Montreal, Canada. Dr. Adler conducts research and consults on strategic human resource management, global women leaders and managers international negotiating, and global organization development.

Reprinted from *Handbook of Organization Management,* ed. William B. Eddy, Spring 1986, 25, no. 1, 481–499, Marcel Dekker, Inc.

personal lives. One asked me what present he should buy his daughter for her graduation. Another asked me how many guests he should invite to a party. These men are clearly too immature to be considered for promotion. . . ." Are they? Is the situation that clear?

In both cases, cultural differences might best explain the situation. In the first case, the public health director should recognize that the norms around privacy are quite different in the Anglo and Hispanic communities. Women in the Hispanic community tend to be much more hesitant than Anglo women to let it be known that they are seeing a doctor; that they are being examined; or that they may have a disease. The Woman's Health Van would have a possibility of success only if the privacy norms of the Hispanic women were recognized.[1] In the second example, the Anglo supervisor should recognize that the Filipino community tends to show respect for people in authority by seeking and following their advice. In addition, the Filipino community tends to draw less distinct lines between private and professional life than does the Anglo community. There are very different consequences from the supervisor's interpretation of the Filipino's behavior as "immature" than from an interpretation of "cultural differences."

In the United States, we have tended to make the assumption that all Americans are pretty much like all other Americans. The fact is, all Americans are Americans, but they are *not* just like all other Americans. All Americans do not act the same, nor live the same, nor have the same personal or professional goals in life. Given that the role of government is to provide goods and services to the public, government officials and employees must both understand the needs of a culturally diverse public and respond to those needs by providing culturally appropriate services.

The purpose of this chapter is to highlight the extent to which ethnic communities still exist within the United States; to examine the cultural assumptions Americans make about other Americans; and to identify the role of government within a culturally diverse environment.

I. DOMESTIC MULTICULTURALISM: AREN'T ALL AMERICANS AMERICAN?

You do not have to go overseas to meet someone who is culturally different, nor do you have to work for the U.S. Department of State to be concerned with the effect of cultural diversity on government. Culturally distinct populations exist in all parts of the United States. Each of these populations has a culturally unique lifestyle. Most of us are familiar with the typical foods of the major ethnic groups. No one thinks that spaghetti is Chinese, or that tortillas are Russian, or that sushi is Ghanian. But many of us are unaware of the extent to which the lifestyles of members of other cultural groups differ from our own. Further, many of us fail to appreciate the percent of the population in North America that is not white, Anglo-Saxon, and English speaking; that is not stereotypically "American."

Taking California as an example, the trends are telling. According to one Lieutenant Governor of California, there is one central, inevitable fact: "If the present trends continue, the emerging ethnic groups will constitute more than half the population of California by 1990, and we will become the country's first Third World state."[2] In 1950, the white population of Los Angeles was 80.9 percent; by 1960, it had dropped to 71 percent; and by 1980, it had fallen again to 44.4 percent, half the percentage of whites that had lived in Los Angeles a generation ago.[3] Total minority population is estimated at 8.4 million people, a solid 33 percent of the California population.[4] We know that at least a quarter of the population in California, about 6.3 million, is black, Hispanic, or Asian background.[5] Metropolitan Los Angeles has a population of 7 million; 1.6 million are Hispanic. Los Angeles is the second largest Mexican agglomeration after Mexico City.[6] In Los Angeles County, in a single decade (1960–1970), the Japanese population increased 34.6 percent, Chinese increased 111.5 percent, Filipino increased 176 percent, and Native Americans increased 202.2 percent.[7] There are currently more Samoans in Los Angeles than on the island of Samoa 4,000 miles away;[8] more Israelis than in any other city outside of Israel; and, already by 1979,

more than 100,000 Iranians were living in the Southern California area.[9] The character of Hollywood has changed dramatically. The Asians, most visibly Koreans, have increased from 6,000 to 20,000; the Armenians from 10,000 to at least 25,000, and those with Spanish surnames, many from Central and South America, from 20,000 to 35,000. This is already half of Hollywood's population.[10]

The story is the same for other cities and states. Of the 700,000 largely middle-class Cubans who had left Cuba by 1978, more than 430,000 have settled in Dade County, Florida.[11] More than 1.3 million Puerto Ricans now live in the greater New York City area.[12] And, in the past quarter-century, the number of black Americans has grown by 10 million.[13] In addition, there has been a resurgence of ethnic self-identity among European populations that had seemed all but assimilated.[14] It is clear from these and dozens of other statistics that multiculturalism is a fact of domestic life. Multiculturalism is not a topic that can be relegated solely to students of international politics or forgotten. The problem is that historically we have tended to ignore domestic multiculturalism and therefore have failed to incorporate it fully into our governmental perspective. Why? What role does multiculturalism play in the effective functioning of governmental bodies?

II. THE ROLE OF GOVERNMENT IN A MULTICULTURAL ENVIRONMENT

Government is a provider of public goods and services. It is the role of government to understand the needs of the public and to create and deliver services to meet those needs. Given the demographics of the United States, the government must be able to understand the diverse needs of a multicultural population and be able to provide services that are appropriate to each cultural constituency. In addition, it must be able to manage government employees from a wide variety of backgrounds if it is to meet its public commitments. As stated in Nigro and Nigro:

> Important as international relationships are, understanding of the cultural factor is also essential in the formulation

and execution of programs for different ethnic groups within a particular country. Cultural barriers create numerous problems in relationships between public officials and such groups as the American Indians, the Mexican and Spanish Americans, and the Puerto Ricans. Of course, all of these people are Americans, and they represent one of the greatest values in our society—cultural diversity. In order to serve them effectively, public employees who have contact with them should understand why and how they are in some respects different from other Americans.[15]

Thus both the external function of government—serving the public—and the internal functioning of government—managing government employees—are strongly influenced by cultural diversity.

A. Serving the Public

In order to survey accurately a multicultural domestic environment and provide appropriate services to a culturally diverse constituency, the government should have cross-cultural awareness.[16] The government should be able to identify the public service needs of culturally distinct groups. In order to understand the cultural implications of its own practices, the government should have cultural self-awareness. The government should be able to recognize the culture-specific aspects of the public programs and services it offers. In order to communicate to its diverse cultural constituencies, government officials should have cross-cultural communications skills. The government should learn to communicate through the language and customs of the people it is trying to reach.

An example is given by Saunders in his study entitled *Cultural Differences and Medical Care*.[17] He describes how irritated Anglo officials become because the Spanish-speaking people seem to be willing to accept a status of dependency on local government welfare services.

> Americans are reared in a culture that emphasizes self-help; we feel guilty and ashamed if we have to ask the govern-

ment to satisfy our vital needs for any long period of time. So when we have contact with someone who seems to think nothing of accepting such services and a prolonged status of dependency, we are prone to regard him as irresponsible.

> Yet for many years the Spanish-speaking people have lived in social relationships where asking for help from others and expecting to receive it is the accepted mode of conduct. For centuries they lived in isolated, self-contained communities in which the members were drawn together by close family and personal ties. Most everyone had frequent face-to-face contact with his neighbors; there was no institution of government as we know it today, with its welfare services, hospitals, and the like. When someone was in trouble or needed something, he sought and received the protection and help of his relatives and friends. Many of the Mexican and Spanish Americans continue to live in relatively isolated communities where this same pattern of conduct is preserved. Even those who have moved to the urban centers still basically maintain some of these same attitudes. Thus when government services of various kinds are made available to them today, they will accept such help in ways that indicate they see nothing wrong in doing so. To the Anglo who has no knowledge of their background or customs, this is "peculiar" behavior. To the Anglo who understands their traditions, it is just as normal as the typical American's uneasiness over accepting such help. . . .

> Above all, more personal relationships should be established with the patient. Rigid time schedules for appointments should not be followed, and if possible, all matters relating to a single illness should be taken care of during one visit. Doctors and nurses should be chosen not only on the basis of professional qualifications, but also for their personal qualities and ability to establish rapport with the patients. While "in the treatment of disease there can be no compromise with the highest professional standards . . . in the treatment of people there may have to be more com-

promise if the treatment relationship is to be accepted."[18]

B. Managing Employees

The government, like all other forms of organization in the public and private sectors, must manage the behavior of people in order to achieve its goals. Government officials should recognize that employees from different cultures will have different ways of working. The role of management in a multicultural organization includes the recognizing and managing of cultural differences.

These two functions—serving the public and managing employees—are central. As stated earlier, the problem is that historically we have tended to ignore domestic multiculturalism. We have therefore failed to incorporate fully a multicultural perspective into the government. Unfortunately, many government departments and agencies have tended to see the public and employee populations as homogeneous. They have tended to assume that there is one best way to deliver government services. They have not tended to see the need for culture-specific approaches to serving the public. Why? The answer is in the assumptions we make about people.

III. AMERICAN ASSUMPTIONS ABOUT AMERICANS

All of us use assumptions to explain our world to ourselves. When an assumption no longer fits the reality that it is supposed to help us to understand, it becomes dysfunctional. The following four assumptions are often used by Americans to help them to understand the United States. Each is functional in that it simplifies a complex situation and makes it understandable. Each is dysfunctional in that it leads us to draw incorrect conclusions and to act in ineffective and often counterproductive ways. As shown in Fig. 1, the four involve assuming a homogeneous population, assuming similarity among citizens, assuming that our way is the only way, and assuming that our way is the best way to approach a situation. Each assumption will be discussed separately, along with suggestions for replacing these traditional assumptions with more appropriate assumptions for governing today's reality.

A. Assumption One: Homogeneity or the Melting Pot Myth

This first assumption, homogeneity, was briefly referred to earlier. Homogeneity is the belief that we are all the same. It is the belief that most Americans are like most other Americans, that most Americans are white, Anglo-Saxon, Protestants, and that all of the other peoples form a small minority of the population. Homogeneity is a belief in the "melting pot" myth; a belief that even though the United States is the land of immigrants, those immigrants have integrated into the rest of America and have become like everyone else. It is the belief that everyone is and wants to be like the majority.

The problem is, as pointed out above, that America is a nation of many distinct cultures. Domestic multiculturalism is the reality; the melting pot is a myth. Cultural pluralism has guided our behavior even if the melting pot has been our public intention. In place of homogeneity, the more appropriate assumption is heterogeneity. *Heterogeneity* is the assumption that we are not all the same—that society is composed of many different groups. Heterogeneity allows one to see society as it is, rather than as we simplistically assumed it to be.

B. Assumption Two: Similarity or the Myth that You Are Just Like Me

Similarity is the belief that other people are like you. It is the assumption that other people have the same life goals and career aspirations as you, that they enjoy the same activities as you, and that they behave in similar ways to you. The Golden Rule is based on the assumption of similarity: "Do unto others as you would have them do unto you." As with the assumption of homogeneity, the assumption of similarity is a natural tendency. In a recent research study, Bass and Burger discovered that in all 14 countries studied, participants saw people from other cultures as having values,

FIGURE 1
Misleading Assumptions in a Multicultural World

Common and Misleading Assumptions		Less Common and More Appropriate Assumptions
HOMOGENEITY The Melting Pot Myth We are all the same.	HETEROGENEITY	The Image of Cultural Pluralism We are not all the same; there are many culturally different groups in society.
SIMILARITY The Myth that they are all just like me.	SIMILARITY AND DIFFERENCE	They are not just like me. Many people are culturally different from me. Most people have both cultural similarities and differences when compared to me.
PAROCHIALISM The Only-One-Way Myth Our way is the only way. We do not recognize any other way of living, working or doing things.	EQUIFINITY	Our way is not the only way. There are many culturally distinct ways of reaching the same goal, or of living one's life.
ETHNOCENTRISM The One-Best-Way Myth Our way is the best way. All other ways are inferior versions of our way.	CULTURAL CONTINGENCY	Our way is a way. There are many other different and equally good ways to reach the same goal. The best way is contingent on the culture of the people involved.

attitudes, and behaviors that were more similar to their own than was actually the case.[19] In reality, people from other cultures tend to be more different from us than we assume them to be.

The first problem with the assumption of similarity is that we expect people from other cultures to act as we do and we are surprised—and often angry or disappointed—when they do not act as we expect. Most people feel much more comfortable with people who are more similar to them than with those who are different from them. Social psychological research has shown that people tend to be attracted to people who hold the same beliefs as they do,[20] to people whom they perceive to be most similar to themselves. It appears that in ambiguous situations, in order to avoid the threat of difference, we tend to assume similarity when no information exists.[21]

The second problem with assuming similarity between ourselves and people from other cultures is that it fundamentally denies individuality. People, as cultures, have aspects that are both similar to each other and different from one another. By seeing only the ways in which others are similar, one negates their characteristics. One simply sees and likes a projection of himself in the other person. Similarly, by focusing strictly on universal human qualities, one denies the other person's unique qualities. The question is *not* to determine if individual differences exceed similarities, nor if cultural differences exceed similarities. It is rather the challenge of attempting to recognize both similarities *and* differences at the same time.

Replacing the assumption of similarity, the more appropriate assumption is difference. As Triandis so wisely stated at the American Psychological Association conference (1980), "instead of assuming similarity until difference is proven, we should assume difference until similarity is proven." Assuming difference means assuming that other people are not just like me. It means assuming that many people are culturally different from me. As a government official, it means assuming that all people will probably not want the same services as I would want, nor would they want those services delivered in the same way. What

is desired by me may not be desired by others. What is appropriate for me may not be appropriate for others. Or, to modify the Golden Rule, the culturally appropriate assumption is "Do unto others as they would like to be done to; not as you would have them do unto you."[22]

The implications of these first two assumptions can be combined. The first assumption, heterogeneity, suggests that government officials regard society as culturally pluralistic, as being made up of many different distinct groups. The second assumption—difference—suggests that government officials do not project their values and goals onto the public. Together, the two assumptions suggest that officials begin by assuming that the various cultural groups within the population are neither necessarily similar to each other nor necessarily similar to the culture of the government officials.

C. Assumption Three: Parochialism or the Myth that My Way Is the ONLY Way

Parochialism is the assumption of a narrow perspective. It is the assumption that there is only one way, my way, of doing anything. Parochialism leads to the belief that my way of living is the only way of living, that all other ways of living are inferior attempts to live life my way. Parochial views tend to lead to negative evaluations of people who are culturally different. A poignant example comes from Hawaii, where an Anglo social worker was horrified by the response of a Samoan mother to a question about the whereabouts of the woman's child. The mother responded, "Oh it's evening. I am sure that the child is having dinner with one of the neighbors. And, if it gets much later, I am sure my neighbor will put the child to sleep." The social worker needed no further evidence of the mother's unfit behavior as a parent: "Imagine a mother not giving her child dinner! Imagine a mother not knowing where her child was at 8 o'clock at night! Imagine a mother not knowing where her child would spend the night!" Unfortunately, the social worker did not understand that the Anglo norms of a nuclear family in which the mother and father of a child are responsible for the child's food, shelter, and safety were not replicated in this Samoan community. In the Samoan community, the extended family was the norm. All adults felt a responsibility to take care of the children in the community. As the mother later explained, "If it is meal time and there are children around, you feed them. That's it. You do not ask if the child is yours and deny him or her food if the child is not yours." Evidently, the Anglo behavior of having children eat in their own homes unless a prior arrangement had been made was as bizarre to the Samoan woman as was the Samoan's behavior to the Anglo social worker. The unfortunate aspect is that the Samoan woman was labeled by the social service department as an unfit mother as a result of a cultural misunderstanding.

Replacing the parochial myth that there is only one way to live is a more appropriate assumption that there are many culturally distinct ways to live life, or to reach a particular goal. Our way is *not* the only way. The belief that there are many ways of achieving a particular goal is called equifinality. *Equifinality* is the understanding that there are many, equivalent ways to reach a final goal. The assumption of equifinality in the prior example would have allowed the social worker to understand that the goal for the child (a healthy, happy, safe life) could have been reached in many ways. It could have been reached by having the parents provide the majority of the child's basic needs (Anglo) or by having the community provide many of the child's basic needs (Samoan). Both systems can be used to provide a good life for the child. Neither system is inherently better than the other system.

D. Assumption Four: Ethnocentrism or the Myth that My Way Is the BEST Way

Ethnocentrism is the assumption that, although there are many ways of accomplishing anything, my way is the best way. Difference, although recognized, is seen as an inferior version of my way of doing things. Ethnocentrism tends to lead to judging the other people

and groups as inferior: I do not see you as unique, I see you as an inferior version of me.

According to Thompson:

Each society molds the potentialities of its constituents, but it can do so to their full potentialities only if allowed cultural autonomy. . . .[23]

Exotic, arbitrarily imposed types of administration may be expected, in the long run, to be unsuccessful and psychologically unhealthy in human terms because they attempt to superimpose arbitrary, rigid, and foreign culture structures on the community and tend therefore to dislocate critically indigenous structures and to engender culture crisis.[24]

A typical example is a Latin official of the Internal Revenue Service who became annoyed with his Anglo manager. The manager had glanced continually at his watch during their conversation and had announced finally that he had another meeting to attend, and had left the room. The Latin felt that the Anglo manager had been rude and took his behavior as a personal insult. Both the Latin and the Anglo were guilty of ethnocentrism. The Latin expected the Anglo to behave according to his own cultural standards and became annoyed when the Anglo behaved according to different cultural values. Culturally, Latins tend to value developing a personal relationship between business partners and place less importance on punctuality. These values are in direct conflict with the Anglo's stress on efficiency, punctuality, and conducting business prior to developing social relations. Neither system is inherently better than the other. They are simply different.

Replacing ethnocentrism, the myth that my way is the best way, is the *cultural contingency* approach. Cultural contingency suggests (as does equifinality) that there are many equally valid ways to reach a final goal, and that the best way depends on the cultural mix of people involved. Our way of doing things is only *a* way. The best way is dependent on the particular situation. In many situations, there may not be a single best way.

IV. CULTURE'S IMPACT ON PEOPLE AND GOVERNMENT ORGANIZATIONS

From the previous discussion, it is clear that the United States is a multicultural population and that the tendency of people is to make assumptions that lead them to ignore cultural diversity. The question of the impact of culture on the functioning of governmental organizations has yet to be addressed. What is culture? How does it influence the attitudes and behaviors of people? What is the impact of cultural differences on the behavior of people within governmental organizations? These questions will be examined in the following section.

A. What Is Culture?

Culture has been defined in many ways. The most commonly used definition of culture is given by Kroeber and Kluckhohn.

> Culture consists of patterns, explicit and implicit of and for behavior acquired and transmitted by symbols, constituting the distinctive achievement of human groups, including their embodiment in artifacts; the essential core of culture consists of traditional (i.e. historically derived and selected) ideas and especially their attached values; culture systems may, on the one hand, be considered as products of action, on the other as conditioning elements of further action.[25]

Culture is "that complex whole which includes knowledge, belief, art, morals, law, custom, and any other capabilities and habits acquired by man as a member of society."[26]

For the purpose of this chapter, culture can be considered the unique lifestyle of a particular group of people.[27] Culture gives people their view of reality. It includes what they know and how they express it, as well as their values and standards of behavior. Each culture has its own orientations to political, social, and economic action. And each culture has a common structure of feeling.[28]

B. How Does Culture Influence Behavior?

As anthropologist Edward T. Hall has described:

> Deep cultural undercurrents structure life in subtle but highly consistent ways that are not consciously formulated. Like the invisible jet streams in the skies that determine the course of a storm, these hidden currents shape our lives; yet their influence is only beginning to be identified.[29]

The influence of culture, as shown in Fig. 2, can be looked at as a circle: culture affects values, which affect attitudes, which affect behavior, which in turn affects the culture itself.[30] It is important to note, however, that although the influence of the collective cul-

FIGURE 2
Influence of Culture on Behavior
(Adapted from Rhinesmith, 1970)[31]

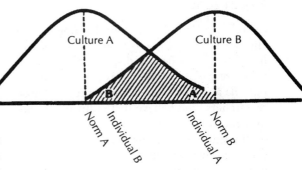

FIGURE 3
Cultural Norms and Individual Diversity
Although the overall norms of any two cultures are different, specific individuals within each culture express a full range of behaviors. Descriptions of cultures strictly show central tendencies, or norms. They portray what the majority of people do, not what all people do.

ture within a particular ethnic group can be substantial, it is not all-determining. Individual differences exist within all cultures. As Fig. 3 illustrates, descriptions of cultural influences and behaviors portray only the norm, or the average, for a particular group. Cultural descriptions are never intended to describe accurately the behavior of any single member of the group. For example, one can say that the Japanese tend to be more group-oriented whereas Americans tend to be more individualistic.[32] But it is also possible to find individual Japanese who are less group-oriented than individual Americans. The difference is that, on average, Japanese tend to be more group-oriented than Americans. Cultural descriptions strictly describe central tendencies, or norms. Cultural descriptions portray what the majority of people do, not what all people do. If a person is born in Sweden, my best prediction—prior to knowing the individual—is that he or she will speak Swedish. Cultural definitions therefore give us the image of a society before we have had a chance to meet the individual members within the society. Cultural definitions help us to make the best predictions about behavior given that we have no specific knowledge about the individual to be encountered.[33]

C. How Does Culture Influence the Behavior of People in Organizations?

As reflected in the title of Lammers' and Hickson's book, *Organizations Alike and Unlike*,[34] there has been a dispute for years between researchers who believe that organizations *do* and *do not* vary across cultures. Those researchers who believe that culture does *not* influence organizations have tended to focus on the similarities in the overall structures of the organization across cultures—on the macro-level variables—rather than on the behavior of people within the organization structure.[35] They have shown how similar technologies (e.g., automobile plants) tend to be in similar organizations the world over. They have also highlighted the extent to which organizations vary according to the political systems and the level of economic development of the country in which they are located. These researchers posit that organizations in economically developing countries have more in common with each other than they do with organizations in economically developed countries, regardless of the countries' cultures. Similarly, they have pointed out the greater similarity between organizations in democratic countries versus those in countries with socialist or communist regimes. A number have strongly suggested that with improvements in communication and the increasing transfer of technology, structures of organizations are tending to converge. Organizations are becoming more and more similar rather than maintaining their differences.[36] The important element to note in these arguments is that they refer to the overall organization design, not to the behavior of people within the organization.

Crozier, author of *The Bureaucratic Phenomenon*, poses the counter-argument:

> Intuitively, however, people have always assumed that bureaucratic structures and patterns of action differ in different countries of the western world and even more markedly between East and West. Men of action know it and never fail to take it into account. But contemporary social scientists . . . have not been concerned with such comparisons.[37]

Whereas the macro-level organizational variables, such as organization structure, appear not to be highly influenced by culture, managers report that culture does affect the day-to-day lives of employees within their organizations. There have now been many studies indicating that the behavior of people in organizations varies across cultures.[38] Studies comparing the behavior of employees in different cultures has shown that their styles of decision making vary,[39] their leadership behavior varies,[40] their attitudes toward delegation vary,[41] their emphasis on competitive behavior varies,[42] their risk-taking behavior varies,[43] the characteristics they attribute to good managers vary,[44] and so on. These studies show that the values people hold, their ways of managing others, their ways of resolving conflict, as well as their ways of planning vary across cultures. The organizational life of the Japanese is not the same as that of the

Americans,[44] which is not the same as that of the Russians, nor the Spaniards, nor the Israelis, nor the Kenyans, among others. Although the structures of organizations across cultures are relatively similar, it appears that the ways in which people work within those structures differ according to the cultural backgrounds of the specific employees involved.

These differences are not confined to a certain type of organization. Cultural differences are found in public as well as private organizations, in for-profit as well as not-for-profit organizations. The challenge to the manager of a multicultural organization is to manage the interaction of employees and clients across cultures—to manage the cross-cultural interaction.

V. MANAGING THE INTERACTION OF EMPLOYEES FROM DIFFERENT CULTURES

When do people behave in ways specific to their own culture? When can cultural differences be ignored? When can they be transcended? All of us can cite examples of happily married couples in which the man is from one culture and the woman is from another culture. Most of us can cite examples of formal public occasions—such as award ceremonies—in which the cultures of the participants were irrelevant to the discussion. Yet, from the previous discussion, it is clear that much of the behavior within organizations is culture-specific. Why?

As shown in Fig. 4, it appears that the potential for cross-cultural problems varies with the frequency and intimacy of the people involved. If, as in the case of lovers, the relationship is intimate and frequent, it is often possible to transcend cultural differences and to create a deep relationship based on both the similarities and differences in the two individuals. If, as is the case with public meetings, the relationship is infrequent and not intimate, then it is usually possible to ignore the cultural differences temporarily. If I attend a banquet given for officials of the Hawaiian state government, and am served food that is new and strange to me—as is poi for many non-native Hawaiians—it is possible for me to taste it and either enjoy it for the evening or ignore it for the evening. I know, because the situation is infrequent and the relationship with the people is not intimate, that I shall not be forced to alter my lifestyle—to eat poi regu-

FIGURE 4
Universal versus culturally specific behavior—When do they act like foreigners and when do we reject them for being foreigners?

FIGURE 5
Approaches to Managing Culturally Diverse Employee and Client Populations

Approach	Description	Focus	Response from Non-dominant Culture	Potential Effectiveness *vis-à-vis* a Unicultural Organization
Traditional	Organization ignores cultural diversity and uses the approach of the dominant culture to manage all situations.	Unicultural Solutions	Resistance	Below par
Culturally Aware	Organization recognizes cultural similarities and differences but chooses to attempt to minimize the diversity by imposing single one-best-way solutions on all management situations.	Unicultural Solutions	Resistance	Below par
Equifinality	Organization recognizes cultural similarities and differences and allows a variety of parallel approaches based on members' cultures to be used simultaneously in each management situation.	Simultaneous Parallel	Acceptance	Par
Synergy	Organization recognizes cultural similarities and differences and uses them to create new integrative solutions to organizational problems that go beyond the individual cultures of any single cultural group.	Integrative Solutions	Challenge	Above par

larly—following the banquet. It is possible for me to be polite, to accept temporarily the other culture's behaviors, without threatening my own essential values or lifestyle. It is possible for one or the other culture's ways to be dominant for the evening without threatening the integrity of the second culture's values.

Problems arise in cross-cultural interaction when the relationship is either frequent yet not intimate—as is the case of employees within the organization—or when the relationship is intimate yet not frequent—as is the case of many couples' relationship with out-of-town relatives. Within the organization, employees are in day-to-day contact with each other. The patterns of relationship that they establish determine to a significant extent what the quality of their working life will be like. Unlike public relationships that are infrequent, it is usually not possible for employees to accept the culture of other employees (or bosses) on a daily basis. Since the work relationship is not temporary, the employees must establish relationships that are satisfying to participants from all other cultures. But, unlike the relationship between lovers, there is usually not sufficient intimacy in the work relationship for employees from different cultures to be motivated to transcend their cultural differences and establish a relationship based on individual similarities and differences. Because of the frequent yet not intimate nature of the working relationships, it is easy to understand why culturally distinct behavior is common and cross-cultural interaction, if not properly managed, can become a problem.

VI. WHAT TO DO?: MANAGING THE GOVERNMENT AS IF CULTURE MATTERED

Given the inherent problems of managing a multicultural organization (e.g., the government) in a multicultural environment—the United States—what can be done to increase the cultural sensitivity and effectiveness of government departments and agencies? As shown in Figs. 5 and 6, the government can take a traditional approach, which ignores cultural differences or treats them as problems, or, it can take a culturally aware approach and use cultural diversity to create both culturally appropriate and parallel synergistic solutions to the problems encountered in working with a culturally diverse domestic population. Each of these approaches will be discussed separately.

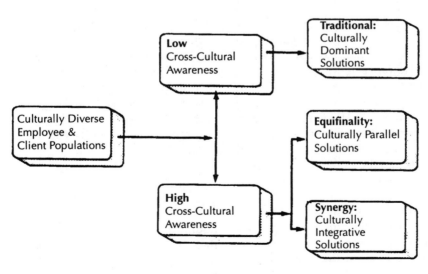

FIGURE 6
Solutions to Managing Cultural Diversity

A. The Traditional Approach

The traditional approach treats cultural diversity as a problem, as something to be ignored or minimized. As Caiden states in his chapter on the obstacles to administrative reform:

> Cultural diversity is a handicap in administrative cooperation as is well illustrated in national administrations embracing diverse cultures. . . . Administrative subcultures are quite different, and when they come together without any overriding uniformity of preparedness to compromise for mutual goals, the results are often haphazard, sometimes tragically comic. For a start, people cannot communicate with one another, even when one common language is accepted and employment is confined to a select group who knows that language sufficiently to be able to think in it. . . . Most other cultural factors (beyond language and religious moral codes) contain obstructive features. . . .[46]

Organizations using a traditional approach often attempt to superimpose the dominant culture's ways of managing on all situations with employees and clients from all cultural backgrounds. This has frequently led to perceived and actual discrimination against members of the nondominant culture. As Lane cites: "Historically, much governmental action in the United States has been not simply discriminatory, but massively and harshly so. Much government action has also, however, been directed toward achieving equality: paradoxically, action to secure assimilation and uniformity also has sometimes been insensitive and coercive. . . ."[47] Herbert notes further that: "For almost two centuries, minority groups have been systematically excluded from making inputs into the administrative process of government as both decision makers and policy implementors."[48] This traditional approach of ignoring or attempting to minimize cultural differences often causes resistance and disenfranchisement, which leads the government to operate in a less than fully effective manner.

B. The Culturally Aware Approach

Cultural awareness is a prerequisite to the more culturally effective approaches to government (equifinality and synergy, both of which will be discussed more fully in the following section). The culturally aware organization recognizes the cultural diversity in the population and is cognizant of the need to address that diversity. Many government officials and researchers have noted the increasing awareness of cultural diversity on the part of public organizations. As Lane states: "Indeed, whether one is black, brown or red, the visible presence of an administrator with whom . . . [the minority person] can identify causes at least greater initial security that someone is listening who can understand the needs, realities, and perceptions being described [by members of minorities' communities], and who will help if at all possible."[49] The U.S. Civil Service Commission has noted that already a decade ago, "federal government employment data . . . revealed that despite the continued decline in total federal employment, minority employment has continued to increase.[50] Lane further notes that "the issues of equality of treatment, especially for blacks, is . . . centrally and intimately involved in programs in such areas as education, housing, and employment; smaller agencies are created that do have quality of treatment as their central mission; and in the administration of government personnel programs, the issue of equal treatment is, as such, an increasingly important issue."[51] Cultural awareness means that the government recognizes the similarities and differences in the public and in its employee populations. Cultural awareness is not sufficient to address properly the issues raised by cultural diversity; it is simply a necessary first step to more effective action.

C. Equifinality— The Parallel Approach

Equifinality, as discussed earlier, means that there are many, equally valuable ways of reaching a particular goal or end point. Public organizations using an equifinality approach create parallel ways of reaching their goals based on the cultural diversity of the client and employee populations. For example, a court clerk might address Anglo clients in English, newly arrived Iranian clients in Farsi, and Vietnamese clients in Vietnamese. The three languages being used with culturally different clients in the same situation represents an equifinal solution to the problem of communicating effectively with a culturally diverse population. This approach demands that government officials *not* assume that there is only one best way to conduct business. It demands that they allow various ways of conducting business to be used simultaneously to solve the same problem. Whereas this approach can be very effective, it does demand that extensive resources be made available for creating and maintaining parallel programs for different cultural constituencies.

D. Synergy— The Integrative Approach

Cultural synergy is a process in which organization policies and practices are formed on the basis of, but not limited to, the cultural patterns of individual organization members and clients.[52] The cultural synergy approach recognizes both the similarities and the differences between the ethnic backgrounds that compose the multicultural government department or agency. This approach suggests that cultural diversity be neither ignored nor minimized, but rather viewed as a resource in the design and development of organizations. Cultural synergy, unlike the parallel approach of equifinality, is an approach to the management of cross-cultural interaction. Using this approach, the public organization uses cultural similarities and differences to create a new integrative organizational culture that goes beyond the individual ways of managing of any of the organization members or clients.

The process of creating synergistic solutions is challenging because it is not based on past patterns. It demands that government officials ask such seemingly absurd questions as "How can we both start meetings on time (Anglo norms) and start meetings when everybody arrives (Hispanic norms)?" "How can

we have set prices for government services (Anglo norms) and allow clients to negotiate the price (Middle Eastern norms)?" Employees involved in creating synergistic solutions must (1) recognize that cultural diversity exists, (2) have an awareness of the cultural similarities and differences in the population involved, (3) recognize that there is no one best way to manage (that parallel "equifinal" solutions are possible), and (4) be able to integrate culturally distinct approaches into new synergistic approaches. Although the specific process for creating such integrative solutions has been described elsewhere,[53] it should be noted that such solutions generally demand a creative problem-solving or "right brain" approach. The benefit to government is that synergistic approaches can work well with employees who must work on a day-to-day basis with other employees and clients who are from other cultures. And, unlike the parallel "equifinal" approach, synergy does not demand that government employees attempt to become conversant and proficient with the full range of cultures in which they work.

E. Culturally Appropriate Approaches

As suggested by the above discussion, the most effective approach that a government agency or department can take is to cultivate cross-cultural awareness in all employees and then develop a set of culturally parallel and culturally synergistic approaches depending on the demands of the particular situation. The goal is *not* to use one approach exclusively, but rather to use the approach that is most culturally appropriate for any given situation.

ENDNOTES

[1]B. D. Paul, ed., *Health, Culture and Community* (New York: Russel Sage Foundation, 1955).

[2]J. Kirsch, "Chicano Power," *New West* 3(19), 1978: 35.

[3]"It's Your Turn in the Sun: Now 19 Million and Growing Fast, Hispanics Are Becoming a Power," *Time* 112(16), 1978: 52.

[4]Kirsch, 35.

[5]*Ibid.*

[6]*Time*, 52.

[7]Los Angeles County Department of Regional Planning, *Quarterly Bulletin,* 116 (April 1, 1972).

[8]"The Samoans Among Us," *Los Angeles Times* 2 January 1979: 1.

[9]Personal conversation with immigration official, U.S. Office of Immigration, Los Angeles, California, November 1979.

[10]S. Kaplan, "New Immigrants of Hollywood," *Los Angeles Times,* 4 January 1979, part 2.

[11]*Time*, 51.

[12]*Ibid.,* 55.

[13]"Blacks in America: 25 Years of Radical Changes," *U.S. News and World Report,* 14 May 1979: 48–68.

[14]M. Novak, *The Rise of the Unmeltable Ethnics,* 1972, New York: Macmillan, as cited in F. S. Lane, ed., *Current Issues in Public Administration* (New York: St. Martin's Press, 1978): 543.

[15]F. A. Nigro and L. G. Nigro, *Modern Public Administration,* 3d ed. (New York: Harper & Row, 1973): 50–51.

[16]M. J. Feldman, "Training for Cross-cultural International Interaction," *Training & Development Journal 30* (11), 1976: 19–23.

[17]Nigro and Nigro, 62–64.

[18]*Ibid.,* 64. *See also* L. Saunders, *Cultural Differences and Medical Care,* (New York: Russell Sage, 1954).

[19]B. M. Bass and C. Burger, *Assessment of Managers: An International Comparison* (New York: Free Press, 1979).

[20]D. Byrne, *The Attraction Paradigm,* (New York: Academic Press, 1971).

[21]H. C. Triandis, "Culture as a Boundary to Organizational Theories." Paper presented at the American Psychological Association Meetings in Montreal, Canada, September 1980.

[22]R. T. Moran, *Crosscultural Communication Lecture,* Glendale, AZ: American Graduate School of International Management, 1977.

[23]L. Thompson, *Culture in Crisis: A Study of the Hopi Indian* (New York: Harper & Row, 1950): 148.

[24]*Ibid.,* 181.

[25]A. L. Kroeber and C. Kluckhohn, *Culture: A Critical Review of Concepts and Definitions,* Papers of the Peabody Museum of American Archaeology and Ethnology, vol. XLVII, no. 1, Cambridge, MA: Harvard University, 1952: 181.

[26]E. B. Tylor, *Primitive Culture,* (New York: Henry Holt, 1977).

[27]P. R. Harris and R. T. Moran, *Managing Cultural Differences* (Houston: Gulf Publishing, 1979): 2.

[28]E. R. Tannenbaum, *1900: The Generation Before the Great War* (New York: Anchor, Doubleday, 1977).

[29]E. T. Hall, *Beyond Culture,* (Garden City, NY: Anchor, Doubleday, 1977).

[30]S. H. Rhinesmith, *Cultural-Organizational Analysis: The Interrelationship of Value Orientation and Managerial Behavior* (Cambridge, MA: McBer, 1970).

[31]*Ibid.,* 7.

[32]D. C. Barnlund, *Public and Private Self in Japan and the United States: Communicative Styles of Two Cultures* (Tokyo: Simul Press, 1975).

[33]B. M. Bass, "The American Adviser Abroad," *Journal of Applied Behavioral Science* 7 (3), 1971: 285–307.

[34]C. J. Lammers and D. J. Hickson, *Organizations Alike and Unlike: International and Inter-institutional Studies in the Sociology of Organizations* (London: Routledge & Kegan Paul, 1979).

[35]J. Child, "Culture Contingency and Capitalism in the Cross-national Study of Organizations," in *Research in Organizational Behavior,* vol. 3, B. M. Staw and L. L. Cummings, eds., (Greenwich: JAI Press, 1981): 303–356.

[36]R. A. Webber, "Convergence or Divergence?" *Columbia Journal of World Business* IV (May/June, 1969): 75–83.

[37]M. Crozier, *The Bureaucratic Phenomenon,* (Chicago: University of Chicago, 1964).

[38]Bass and Burger; G. Hofstede, *Culture's Consequences: International Differences in Work-Related Values* (Beverly Hills, CA: Sage, 1980); A. Laurent, "The Cultural Diversity of Western Management Conceptions," *International Studies of Management and Organization,* Spring 1983.

[39]P. Hessling and E. E. Konnen, "Culture and Subculture in a Decision-Making Exercise," *Human Relations 20,* 1969: 31–51.

[40]*Ibid.*

[41]E. McCann, "Anglo-American and Mexican Management Philosophies," *MSU Business Topics 18*(3), 1970: 23–38.

[42]M. H. R. Hoekstra, "Corporate Objectives: A Cross-cultural Study of Simulated Managerial Behavior," *Proceedings of the 16th International Congress of Applied Psychology* (Amsterdam: Swets and Zeitlinger 1969); G. V. Barrett and E. C. Ryterband, "Life Goals of United States and European Managers," *Proceedings of the 16th In-*

ternational Congress of Applied Psychology, (Amsterdam: Swets and Zeitlinger, 1969).

[43]K. M. Thiagrajan and B. M. Bass, "Differential Preferences for Long- Versus Short-Term Payoffs in India and the United States," *Proceedings of the 16th International Congress of Applied Psychology* (Amsterdam: Swets and Zeitlinger, 1969).

[44]E. C. Ryterband and G. V. Barrett, "Managers' Values and Their Relationship to the Management of Tasks: A Cross-cultural Comparison," in *Managing for Accomplishment,* B. M. Bass, R. C. Cooper, and J. A. Haas, eds. (Lexington, MA: Heath Lexington, 1970).

[45]M. J. Esman, "Japanese Administration—A Comparative View," *Public Administration Review VII* (2), 1947: 100–112; W. Ouchi, *Theory 2: How American Business Can Meet the Japanese Challenge* (Reading, MA: Addison-Wesley, 1981).

[46]G. E. Caiden, *Administrative Reform* (Chicago: Aldine, 1969): 173–175.

[47]F. S. Lane, ed., *Current Issues in Public Administration,* (New York: St. Martin's Press, 1978): 543–544.

[48]A. W. Herbert, "The Minority Administrator: Problems, Prospects, and Challenges," in *Current Issues in Public Administration,* F. S. Lane, ed., (New York: St. Martin's Press, 1978): 201.

[49]Lane, 196.

[50]U.S. Civil Service Commission, *Minority Group Employment in the Federal Government* (Washington, D.C.: U.S. Government Printing Office, 1974).

[51]Lane, 544.

[52]N. J. Adler, "Cultural Synergy: The Management of Cross-cultural Organizations," in *Trends and Issues in OD: Current Theory and Practice,* W. W. Burke and L. D. Goodstein, eds., (San Diego, Calif.: University Associates, 1980): 163–184.

[53]*Ibid.*

16

Is "Organization Culture" Culture Bound?

Nancy J. Adler and Mariann Jelinek

With increasing global competition, the evolution of multinational firms' structures has become legendary: Organizing principles alternately emphasize function, product, and territory. From the macro perspective of structure, technology, and resource, product, and financial markets, it is clear that executives have a choice, if not a mandate, to "go global." From the micro perspective of managing people within those structures, the choice to transcend national boundaries is by no means clear.

How should executives manage a multinational workforce? Must human resource professionals modify selection, development, appraisal, and reward systems to reflect the diversity of employees' cultural backgrounds? Can we ignore employees' national cultural differences, as Levitt[1] suggests? Is management analogous to internal transfer prices, which have successfully masked the impact of national financial differences, and improved transportation and communication, which have reduced the influence of physical distance? We think not. The history of international human resource policies has been defined by the interplay of parent-, host-, and third-country nationals and punctuated by decisions on alternative expatriate benefits packages. It falls far short of guiding today's executives in identifying appropriate approaches to managing people worldwide.

Reprinted from *Human Resource Management*, 25, no. 1 (April 1986): 73–90. Copyright © 1986 by John Wiley & Sons, Inc.

"Organization culture" has become a favored focus of American[2] human resource managers as well as many of their western colleagues. Could "organization culture" become a viable paradigm for approaching global human resource issues?

Listening to our American colleagues struggle with, and often reject, the concept of national cultural differences has made us suspicious that seeing, managing, and using cultural differences is an illegitimate process when viewed from within the American cultural paradigm. In contrast, creating, managing, maintaining, and changing organizational cultures seems somehow more acceptable. Why? This paper investigates the cultural roots of the organization culture concept, and questions its ability to integrate culturally diverse perspectives within its current conceptual framework. The paper is divided into three sections. First, it introduces a model for explaining cultural variance and locates the American cultural perspective within that model. It then reviews the organization culture concept and investigates the ways in which it appears to be rooted in American cultural concepts. In the final section, it suggests some assumptions that would need to be made to incorporate the role of national culture within the organization culture paradigm, and thus make it relevant to the global corporation.

CULTURE

Culture, whether organizational or national, is frequently defined as a set of taken-for-granted assumptions, expectations, or rules for being in the world. As paradigm, map, frame of reference, interpretive schema, or shared understanding, the culture concept emphasizes the shared cognitive approaches to reality that distinguish a given group from others.

That cultures vary in their assumptions about the world has long been accepted by the anthropological community. While national cultural differences have tended to be ignored by many management researchers,[3] recently they have begun to be accepted by a subset of the management community.[4] Most notably, the Japanese style of management has been delineated as an alternative, contrasting, and highly effective approach,[5] very different from the traditional American approach.

Anthropologists assert that the full range of human attitudes and behaviors exists within any society, but that each society favors certain behaviors and attitudes over others.[6] There is no single, universal pattern (as Harris eloquently reiterates[7]). Instead, each society develops a cultural orientation that is descriptive of the attitudes of most of its people most of the time. Culture both shapes individual attitudes and in turn, is continued by the actions, beliefs, and behaviors of individuals: it is the anthropological "common denomination," or norm. Nevertheless, a range of attitudes and beliefs is typically present in any culture.

Between and within cultures there is much diversity. Anthropologists Kluckhohn and Strodtbeck[8] suggest a set of propositions which allows us to understand the cultural orientation of a society without doing violence to the diversity within it. These propositions (as adapted by Rhinesmith[9]) are that:

1. There are a limited number of common human problems for which all peoples at all times must find some solutions. For example, each society must decide how to clothe, feed, house, educate, and govern its people.

2. There are a limited number of alternatives which exist for dealing with these problems. For example, people may house themselves in tents, caves, igloos, single-family dwellings, or apartment buildings; but, in most climates, they cannot survive the winter without some form of shelter.

3. All alternatives are present in all societies at all times, but they are differentially preferred. For example, businessmen can purchase business suits in all colors of the rainbow; but on Wall Street, dark blue, grey, and black are preferred.

4. Each society has a dominant profile or values orientation, and in addition, has numerous variant or substitute profiles. In both dominant and variant profiles, there is a rank-ordering of preferences for alternatives. For example, people may cure disease with chemotherapy, surgery, acupuncture, acupressure, prayer, or nutrition. While many Chinese prefer acupres-

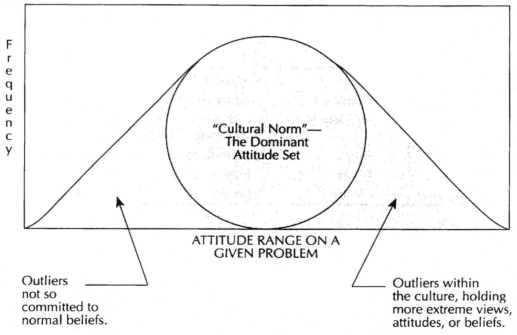

Frequency

"Cultural Norm"—
The Dominant
Attitude Set

ATTITUDE RANGE ON A
GIVEN PROBLEM

Outliers not so committed to normal beliefs.

Outliers within the culture, holding more extreme views, attitudes, or beliefs.

FIGURE 1

sure and acupuncture, the British prefer chemotherapy and surgery, and Christian Scientists worldwide prefer prayer.

5. In societies undergoing change, the ordering of preferences will not be clear. For example, as the computer revolution changes society, organizations' preferred mode of communications—telex, telephone, electronic mail, or the postal system—become unclear; organizations and individuals within the same culture make different choices.

Kluckhohn and Strodtbeck use five basic dimensions to describe the primary variability of societies' cultural orientations, including: the nature of human beings, their relationship to nature (the physical environment and the supernatural), their relationship to other human beings, their primary mode of activity, and their temporal orientation.[10] Some scholars have added a spatial orientation as the sixth dimension. Each orientation is a values statement having attitudinal and behavioral implications. Each in turn has implications for management.

THE AMERICAN CULTURAL ORIENTATION

For Americans, the five dimensions describe what most Americans do most of the time. In particular, they specify how most Americans would answer the questions: Who am I? How do I view other people? How do I see the world? What do I do? And how do I use time? While the United States is certainly not homogeneous, the orientations represent the norm based on Americans' shared history.[11] As summarized in Table 1, the following section describes the American cultural perspective and gives examples of contrasting perspectives.

Good-and-Evil and Changeable: How Americans See Themselves

What is the nature of the individual: good or evil? Americans have traditionally viewed people as a mixture of good and evil, and therefore as needing to choose good over evil. Other cultures see people as basically evil—as was reflected in the puritans' orientation—or as basically good—as has been reflected in utopian societies throughout the ages. Societies which consider people good tend to trust them a great deal. Societies which consider people evil tend to suspect and mistrust them. In high trust societies, people leave doors unlocked and do not fear being robbed. In low trust societies, they bolt lock their doors, may keep guard dogs, and own hand guns "for protection." People in high trust societies expect to receive the merchandise they have ordered; they do not expect to be cheated. In low trust societies, *caveat emptor* (let the buyer beware) rules the marketplace; one can only trust oneself. As cross-cultural management expert Joseph diStefano described:

> Recently, a North American businessman on his first trip to Saudi Arabia was surprised to see a "vendor" in an open air market with what looked like a quarter of a million dollars clipped to a money board. The North American was even more surprised when he saw the "vendor" get up, leave his stall, and go to have tea with a friend. As he reported,

TABLE 1
Values, Orientations, Dimensions

Perception of:	Dimensions		
Individual	Good	Good & Evil	Evil
World	Dominant	Harmony	Subjugation
Human Relations	Individuals	Laterally Extended Groups	Hierarchical Groups
Activity	Doing	Controlling	Being
Time	Future	Present	Past
Space	Private	Mixed	Public

"In New York, people would think that this man was crazy, and no one would have sympathy for him when his money was stolen. In Saudi Arabia, it is different. People do not expect others to steal, and thieves are severely punished (under Islamic law, a thief's hand is cut off). In Saudi Arabia it is different: nobody took the money!"[12]

Evidence of Americans' distrust of each other abounds. To stop motorists from driving away without paying, gas stations in major U.S. cities now require prepayment or a signed credit slip before unlocking the gas pump. A Minneapolis firm, National Credential Verification Service, today makes a profitable business exposing resume deception. Out of 233 personnel officers responding to a survey of Fortune 500 firms, only one said that deception by applicants for executive posts was diminishing.[13] The contrast between trusting Arabs and mistrusting Americans is a stark reminder of basic social-cultural differences in assumptions about people.

In addition to good and evil, societies vary in their belief in individuals' ability to change. Reviewing the founding of the United States, Newman has pointed out Americans' guiding events and myths.[14] The founders wanted something new; they broke away from England, conquered the wilderness, and created communities in which to live. When situations changed, they moved on West, continuing to create new lives and new homes. Inherent in this history is the strongly embedded notion that change is not only possible, but good. In the literal sense, the United States is not a conservative society. It does not attempt to conserve the ways of the past; rather, it overwhelmingly embraces the new, the possible.

For managers, this means viewing organizations as changeable—a basic tenet of the organization culture paradigm. Change within organizations is seen as brought about through the conscious decision of management. For example, managers who believe employees can change will emphasize training. Those who believe that people's ways are fixed will emphasize selection instead. With over 600 accredited programs, Americans' emphasis on the M.B.A. and executive education (training)

strongly reflects their belief that change is both possible and good.

Dominant: Americans' Relationship to Their World

What is a person's relationship to the world? Are people dominant over their environment, in harmony with it, or subjugated by it? Americans tend to see themselves as dominant over both the man-made and the natural environments. American executives have traditionally seen their relevant external environments— economic, social, cultural, political, legal, and technological—as relatively stable and predictable. They do not expect the U.S. dollar to become suddenly worthless, nor a coup to topple the Reagan administration, nor the judicial system to cease enforcing laws. Although we are going through a period of rapid change, Americans maintain a higher degree of certainty and predictability than many of their foreign colleagues. Indeed, one reason for U.S. managers' discomfort in the present situation of turbulence is precisely this expectation of stability: when so much changes, the times seem out of joint.[15]

Anticipating stability, Americans also anticipate that they shall master the environment around them. Examples of Americans' dominance orientation are everywhere: in space, Americans walked on the moon. In health care, life is prolonged with artificial organs, and the now highly controversial techniques of bioengineering and genetic programming. In marketing, campaigns are developed based on consumer research and psychologically sophisticated advertising approaches for everything from industrial products to political candidates. In international affairs, Americans are notorious for making their "presence" felt worldwide.

Americans' fundamental orientation, toward problem solving, is also indicative of their dominance orientation. Americans see situations as problems to be solved. By contrast, many people in other parts of the world see situations as realities to be accepted: *Que será, será* (What will be, will be). They do not expect to influence or change their external environment. When the American says "Can do!," the Arab says

En Shah Allah (If God is willing), and the Inuit (Eskimo) says *"Ayorama"* (It can't be helped): dominance, harmony, subjugation, three very different orientations.

Individualistic: Americans' Relation to Others

Hofstede found Americans to be one of the world's most individualistic peoples.[16] As he describes, people in individualistic cultures use personal characteristics and achievements to define themselves. They value individual welfare over that of the group. By contrast, in group oriented societies, people define themselves as members of clans or communities and consider the group's welfare as most important. Given its individualistic orientation, Warren Bennis and Philip Slater have described the United States as a temporary society with temporary systems, characterized by uprootedness, disconnectedness, non-permanent relationships, and mobility.[17] America is a country of people no longer connected to specific locations or specific other people. More group oriented societies, such as Japan, China, or the Israeli *Kibbutzim* emphasize group harmony, unity, and loyalty. Individuals fear being ostracized for deviating from the norm. In Asia, "saving face" is important because it allows both parties to remain respected members of the group, even when they disagree. (A contrasting American attitude is captured in the movie sheriff's demand that outlaws "get out of town"—or the challenge between outlaws that "This town isn't big enough for both of us." These myths, while extreme, highlight American solutions, departure or violence.)

Personnel policies often reflect a society's values orientation. Individual oriented personnel directors tend to hire those best qualified to do the job according to technical or task criteria, that is, based on the individual's skills and expertise. Individualistic applicants submit resumes listing their personal, educational, and work-related achievements. Group oriented personnel directors also tend to hire those they believe most qualified. However in their minds, the primary qualifications are trustworthiness, loyalty, and compatibility with co-workers. They often hire other employees'

friends and relatives. Rather than presenting well-prepared resumes listing personal achievements, applicants seek introductions to the personnel director through friends or relatives, and center initial discussions on mutual acquaintances. In a group oriented company in Ghana, management believes that only people who are known by other employees in the company will act responsibly (and therefore can be trusted). Group membership is equated with trustworthiness. In the United States, by contrast, Civil Service job applicants are deemed acceptable for employment based on anonymous exam scores. In the U.S., hiring friends, acquaintances, or family members is considered unfair favoritism, or nepotism. It is thought to be corrupt practice, and is even illegal in some instances.

Doing and Achieving: Americans' Primary Mode of Activity

Americans are DOers. Their striving orientation stresses accomplishments measurable by standards believed to be objective, and external to the individual. American managers use promotions, raises, bonuses, and other forms of individual, public recognition to motivate employees. Consequences are expected to follow actions, and "fairness" equates with appropriate external rewards seen as commensurate with effort. A widely held belief is that a "psychological contract"[18] exists between superior and subordinate, obligating responsible, continued contribution by the employee in return for fair treatment. In contrast, an alternate orientation is that of BEING. People in being-oriented cultures accept people, events, and ideas as flowing spontaneously. They stress release, indulgence of existing desires, and working for the moment. If managers in being oriented cultures do not enjoy their work, they quit: they will not work strictly to achieve future goals and rewards. They are not motivated by a sense of on-going obligation and responsibility to the firm.

As DOers, Americans plan their work, deciding what they will get accomplished by when. By contrast, people from more being oriented cultures tend to accept the natural pace of life without trying to force or influence it. In this orientation, planning is not so important—the plant will be completed when it is completed, the work will be done when it is done. Being oriented managers believe it is neither good nor possible to try to hurry the natural order of events. While the DOer "lives to work," the BEing oriented person "works to live."

Present to Future: Americans' Use of Time

How do societies use time? Are they oriented to the past, present, or future? Managers in past oriented cultures believe that they should evaluate plans based on societal customs and traditions. Innovation and change can be justified only to the extent that currently contemplated actions follow precedent. By contrast, managers in future oriented cultures often use projected costs and benefits to evaluate plans. Seeing change as good in and of itself, they easily justify innovation and change in terms of future economic payoffs, with less regard for past social or organizational customs and tradition.

Americans have a present to slightly future time orientation. For them, improvement, progress, and discernible movement toward identified future goals is of primary importance. The past is either ignored, viewed as relatively unimportant (because its impact is minimal), or seen as essentially consistent with management's present view. One important consequence of this assumption is an ahistorical bias in much organization theory, and with it, a spurious claim to universality.

Americans talk about achieving five-and ten-year plans, but work for this quarter's results. American employment practices are similarly short-term. Managers who do not perform well during their first year are fired or, at best, not promoted. Companies do not give them ten years to demonstrate their worth, nor do new employees, especially new MBAs, give the organization a decade to recognize their contribution. By contrast, major Japanese companies use a more long-term, future oriented time horizon: when hiring new employees, the commitment on both sides is for life. Europeans, compared with Americans,

frequently have a more past orientation; they tend to conserve past traditions and rarely embrace change for its own sake.

ORGANIZATION CULTURE

"Organization culture" has recently taken center stage as a major concern in organization studies, and is an idea of much promise as emphasized in this journal over the last couple of years.[19] Implicit in the organization culture notion as it is widely used is a fundamental set of assumptions, which, as will be argued, coincides with American cultural assumptions. This coincidence makes the assumptions difficult for Americans to see, if not outright invisible. Because the assumptions are "taken for granted," they are typically unexamined. They reside in what is, for most Americans, a cultural "blind spot." This blind spot also profoundly limits the power of the organization culture construct when applied in other than domestic United States settings.

Organization culture is a widely acclaimed metaphor for understanding how organizations differ, how their members cohere, and how organizations and members interact. An avalanche of recent books and articles have been dedicated to culture in organizations.[20] The idea is by no means new: Tagiuri and Litwin explored "organization climate" almost two decades ago,[21] and the very first issue of *Administrative Science Quarterly*, in 1956, carried an appeal by Talcott Parsons for attention to the "cultural-institutional" perspective on organizations. One central focus of the new interest is in the way organization culture, like national or ethnic culture, shapes people's perception and thinking, affecting what they notice and how they interpret it.

Organization culture has been defined similarly by many social scientists. One comprehensive definition posits that:

Organization culture is the pattern of basic assumptions that a given group has invented, discovered or developed in learning to cope with its problems of external adaptation and internal integration, which have worked well enough to be considered valid, and, therefore, to be taught to new members as the correct way to perceive, think, and feel in relation to those problems.[22]

This description underlines the shared quality, and the interpretive function of culture. Other descriptions emphasize values,[23] meaning structures,[24] and artifacts like myths,[25] rituals,[26] or social structures.[27]

ORGANIZATION CULTURE'S IMPLICIT AMERICAN ROOTS

Fundamental to the organization culture concept is the belief that top management can create, maintain, and change the culture of an organization. This belief is based in turn on the assumption of free will. Individuals, usually top management, are seen as capable of affecting the ways in which people think, feel, and behave at work. Management's influence is seen as capable of changing or erasing other influences on employees' behavior. Similarly, work environment influences are seen to dominate private life conditioning in creating and modifying work-related behavior. Like work in Weber's bureaucracy, one's work in the culture concept is seen as an all-encompassing, full-time endeavor. Moreover, employees are seen as capable of changing; and change, in and of itself, is seen as basically good. In short, many management theorists envision culture as a method for affecting performance, productivity, and experience in the organization. Whether implicitly or explicitly, organization culture is most typically seen as an implement for managerial manipulation and control. Let's look more closely at its assumptions.

FREE WILL VS. DETERMINISM

Consistent with assumptions of free will and dominance, Americans see themselves as "in control" of their environment. They see individuals as capable of creating and selecting their own values, attitudes, behaviors, and directions in the world. While recognizing the influence of nature and nurture, Americans do not see themselves as ultimately constrained by their biological or psychological inheritance, by their childhood socialization, or even their prior experience. Instead, they see themselves as almost infinitely capable of self-change, as evident from the number of self-help books lining the shelves of popular American bookstores. Self-change can address anything from acquisition of social skills to major psychological change, weight loss or religious conversion, improved golf or better child rearing.

By contrast, many other cultures see a substantial portion of human values, attitudes, behaviors, goals, and accomplishments as set by factors beyond the individual's control. They believe in a different balance between free will and determinism. Depending on the culture, god, fate, history, social class, or luck may seem to determine one's fate to a substantial degree.

While the organizational culture concept accepts a limited amount of determinism (that imposed by the organization's culture), its fundamental underpinnings are those of free will. These differences can be portrayed as a spectrum. From this portrayal, it is clear that the organization culture concept is not rooted in fundamental determinism—neither theological, biological, (national) cultural, or societal (whether political, economic, or sociological). Indeed, perhaps ironically, these contexts are largely excluded in much management research. Based on their survey of cross-national organizational researchers, Roberts and Boyacigiller found that "no investigations simultaneously embedded people into organizations and organizations into their environments," although, "the very reason to do cross-national organizational research is just that, examining how behaviors are embedded into organizations, and organizations into their environments."[28] Instead, organizations and their members are often seen in splendid isolation from the culture around them.

This severing of linkages between the external environment, the organization, and the individual employee makes apparent a widespread view among management researchers that individuals enter the organization as *tabula rasa*. As blank slates, they are ready to receive organization culture conditioning, or, without such conditioning, strictly to express their unique personalities. The manager of *tabula rasa* employees can create an organization cul-

FIGURE 2
Spectrum of Determinism

ture and manipulate it. However, he or she, too, enters the organization essentially isolated from external influences, free from external roles or enculturation from the societal culture outside.(Perhaps the greatest present day fulfillment of this model is the robot, programmable and reprogrammable at will.)

In contrast, a true cross-cultural approach must accept the importance and influence of cultural differences, and assign them a greater role in affecting beliefs, attitudes, and behavior. The cross-cultural approach, being further down the spectrum, accepts a greater degree of determinism than does the organization culture concept. Far from viewing the individual as entering the organization *tabula rasa,* cross-cultural adherents stress the indelible influence of national culture on adult behavior. Contrary to the image of multinational managers as being "beyond passport,"[29] the culturalist sees managers and employees as fundamentally conditioned by national culture. Americans' rejection of most types of determinism may also explain in part why the burgeoning popularity of the organization culture concept has not, as yet, been integrated with a commensurate interest in cross-cultural approaches to management. Perhaps it is not surprising that much of the most significant cross-cultural management research has been conducted by non-U.S. based scholars,[30] while most of the organization culture research has come out of the United States.

One useful model for expanding our view is Kluckhohn and Strodtbeck's cultural variance model. When viewing the spectrum of deter-

minism from within it, freewill is fairly consistent with several key American orientations:

- dominance—over the external environment
- change—as both possible and good
- individuals—as problem-solvers and prime movers (and self-selected groups)
- doing and changing—rather than accepting situations
- future—as better than the past.

A belief in free will allows people to see themselves as dominant. They assume that they are separate from the environment and can act upon and change it. Unlike subjugated individuals, dominance oriented managers do not see themselves as determined by things external to them. They tend to see themselves as "in control." Not surprisingly, Louis found that American MBAs have a highly internal pattern of attribution, whereas international MBAs demonstrate the entire range of orientations, from highly internal to highly external.[31] American managers believe that they can control their own environment and what happens to them within that environment. In some instances, this belief can be carried to extremes, and U.S. managers may feel themselves responsible for matters clearly outside their control (e.g., distant strikes, acts of God, or economic trends). Their international colleagues balance internal with external attribution: they believe in their own efficacy, but also accept that much is beyond their control. For them, change is seen as being brought about by a combination of personal initiative and positive enabling conditions.

The concept of organization culture, as currently used, focuses on the inside of the organization and treats the organization as *if* it were separate from the societal environment in which it is embedded. Many researchers seem blind to the context within which any organization's culture must exist. Despite frequent proclamations of the importance of "open systems" perspectives, they are rarely seen in practice. The spate of organization culture research is little improvement. Like most organization theory, organization culture, too, views organizations, their cultures, and members as closed off from the influence of the society around them. Even where social culture is drawn upon, it is often in a limited fashion. Studies of organizational myths and stories make no attempt to relate organizational stories to societal culture, even when using myths derived from the societal culture.[32] This organization/environment separation is another manifestation of an implicit rejection of determinism and acceptance of freewill. As we have argued, this view is both coincident with the American culture, and rooted deep within its assumptions of dominance and free will.

A MORE ROBUST MULTICULTURAL ORGANIZATION CULTURE CONCEPT

Has the American belief in free will and in our own ability to shape our environment and our organizations to our liking inhibited our willingness to see the extent to which environments are fixed and we, ourselves, determined? Perhaps because we insist on seeing ourselves as effective actors, we ignore conflicting evidence—which if truly recognized might impose cognitive dissonance[33] or even compel us to revise our world view.[34] Perhaps we also find it necessary to limit our ability to see, let alone to study, the impact of societal culture—because it seems far more difficult to change.

At this point it is clear that expanding our perspectives to transcend the limitations of the culture-bound model or organization culture requires looking across organizational and national boundaries. More importantly, perhaps, it requires looking within, examining our own mental frameworks.

Interpretive approaches to the study of organizations and culture underline the complex nature of culture: it is both product and process, external reality and internal guide, existing in tension with the individual and evolving over time.[35] Individuals can and do act apart from cultural demands—but most people in a culture, most of the time, act in consonance with their culture. Culture itself is indeed subject to change, but typically any single individual is relatively powerless to affect culture. Culture changes, but only slowly, as the cumulative result of many individuals' changes. Culture is not fixed, but neither is it infinitely or immediately malleable.

The alternative approach sketched here suggests an inclusive view that may be more appropriate for managing of global organizations. That view is based on the assumption that a collective culture evolves within each organization. That culture is necessarily based on both the culture(s) of the organization members and the overarching goals and directions of organization management. People enter organizations—as managers or employees—with much societal conditioning, many attitudes and beliefs, much prior culture already in place. The emergent collectivity, which affects the way work is done, how relationships structured, or events perceived and interpreted is not wholly management's creation. While subject to some managerial control, such a collective culture is by no means simply determined by managerial intentions, nor is it quickly changeable by management fiat.

Perhaps the organization culture concept would become more robust in the multinational and even in the pluralistic domestic American environment if we asked ourselves:

1. What if organizations and their environments merged; what if the boundaries were assumed to be more permeable, if people brought their ethnicity into the workplace?

2. What if people could not change and managers could not change them; what if managers could only select the right

people but could not shape them after selection?

3. What if situations had to be accepted; if managers did not solve problems; but rather asked only how best to live with situations as they are?

4. What if time was cyclical, if tomorrow was assumed to be different, but not necessarily better than today, not necessarily a progression beyond yesterday?

5. What if determinism was accepted, if the limits to free will were respected?

Such questions, because they direct us to examine the underpinnings of our beliefs and assumptions, are both difficult and potentially enlightening. Drawn from contrasting cultures, they illuminate the unconsidered alternatives so often invisible to American cultural perspectives. They suggest non-stereotypic reactions that may enable managers to understand and draw upon a richer palette of responses.

An expanded model of organization culture would include both free will and determinism. At minimum it would recognize far more persistent and enduring, pervasive commonalities. It would provide a means for including important aspects of reality ignored by the more limited model.

Culture within the organization is by no means wholly within the control of management. At the same time, there is abundant evidence to demonstrate that management can encourage an identifiable "culture" within the organization.[36] Such a culture can provide a powerful means of guidance and support for organization members. (We would speculate that this is especially so where the organization culture satisfies deep needs perhaps unaddressed by the surrounding societal cultural matrix.) Such a perspective creates the opportunity for investigating the benefits of cultural synergy, the positive interaction between multiple national and ethnic cultures within a single organizational context.[37] While synergy is beyond the scope of this paper, it is certainly suggestive of some alternative approaches, quite different from the typical American "melting pot" view of amalgamation, or the image of a consistent "strong" corporate culture over-whelming ethnic differences.

The dual free will–deterministic model allows management to recognize the societal culture within which the organization is embedded and see its impact on the organization. By careful attention to societal culture, managers can more effectively act to create an organizational culture in harmony with societal culture—or work toward a transcendent organizational culture, drawing on multiple cultures, rather than warring with them.

In an era of increasingly global competition, multinationals—including or especially American multinationals—can no longer ignore others' cultures. Governments of countries around the world (and most notably third-world countries) now routinely insist upon significant control of organizations operating within their borders. Significant host national participation at all levels is also routine. Along with the increasing pace of technological competition and the expansion to global markets, such ecumenical participation defines a new global reality. To compete effectively, or even to be allowed to participate in many important markets, corporations must recognize the influence of cultural orientations other than their own. It is not so much that the American construct of organization culture is wrong or wholly dysfunctional, but that it is incomplete. To sensibly advise managers, or indeed to understand the new global realities, organization theorists must transcend the limitations of culture-bound models, including the present limited construct of organization culture.

ENDNOTES

[1]Theodore Levitt, "The globalization of markets," *Harvard Business Review,* May/June 1983: 92–102.

[2] The term American accurately refers to the peoples of both North and South America. In this paper, for purposes of brevity only, the term American will be used to refer to the citizens of the United States.

[3]Nancy J. Adler, "Cross-cultural management: the ostrich and the trend." *Academy of Management Review,* 8(2), April 1983: 226–232.

[4]Geert Hofstede, "Motivation, Leadership and Organization: Do American Theories Apply

Abroad?" *Organizational Dynamics*, Summer 1980: 42–64; G. W. England, *The Manager and His Values: An International Perspective from the USA, Japan, Korea, India and Australia*. Cambridge, MA: Ballinger, 1975; Andre Laurent, "The Cultural Diversity of Western Management Conceptions." *International Studies of Management and Organization*, Vol. XIII, No. 1–2, Spring/Summer 1983: 75–96.

[5]William Ouchi, *Theory Z*, Reading, MA: Addison-Wesley, 1981; Richard Tanner Pascale and Anthony G. Athos, *The Art of Japanese Management*, New York: Simon & Schuster, 1981.

[6]Talcott Parsons, *Structure and Process in Modern Societies*, Glencoe, IL: The Free Press, 1960.

[7]Marvin Harris, "The Sleep-Crawling Question." *Psychology Today*, 24, May 1983: 26–27.

[8]F. R. Kluckhohn and F. L. Strodtbeck, *Variations in Value Orientations*, New York: Row, Peterson, 1961.

[9]Stephen H. Rhinesmith, *Cultural Organizational Analysis: The Interrelationship of Value Orientations and Managerial Behavior*. Cambridge, MA: McBer Publications Series Number 5, 1970.

[10]Kluckhohn and Strodtbeck, *op. cit.*

[11]William H. Newman, "Cultural Assumptions Underlying U.S. Management Concepts," in J. L. Massie and S. Laytje, eds., *Management in an International Context*. New York: Harper and Row, 1972: 327–352; E. C. Stewart, *American Cultural Patterns: A Cross-Cultural Perspective*, Chicago, IL: Intercultural Press, Inc., 1971.

[12]Based on the personal obsevation of Professor Joseph diStefano, Faculty of Business Administration, University of Western Ontario, London, London, Ontario, Canada, 1985.

[13]Mark McCain, "Resumes: separating fact from fiction," *American Way*, December 1983: 85.

[14]Newman, 327–352.

[15]Ezra Vogel, *Japan as Number One*, Cambridge, MA: Harvard University Press, 1979; *Comeback*. New York: Simon & Schuster, 1985.

[16]Geert Hofstede, *Culture's Consequences: International Differences in Work-Related Values*, Beverly Hills, CA: Sage Publications, 1980; "Motivation, Leadership and Organization: Do American Theories Apply Abroad?" *Organizational Dynamics*, 42–64; Summer 1980.

[17]W. Bennis and P. Slater, *The Temporary Society*, New York: Harper & Row, 1968: 124.

[18]The concept of a "psychological contract" is attributed to Kotter.

[19]Charles J. Fombrun, "Corporate culture, environment, and strategy," *Human Resource Management*, 22(1/2), Spring/Summer 1983: 139–154; Philip H. Mirvis, "Formulating and implementing human resource strategy: A model of how to do it, two examples of how it's done," *Human Resource Management*, 24(4), Winter 1985: 385–412; Barry Z. Posner, James M. Kouzes, and Warren H. Schmidt, "Shared values make a difference: An empirical test of corporate culture," *Human Resource Management*, 24(3), Fall 1985: 293–309; Sydney L. Solberg, "Changing Culture through Ceremony: An Example from GM," *Human Resource Management*, 24(3), Fall 1985: 329–340; Alan L. Wilkins, "The creation of company cultures: The role of stories and human resource systems," *Human Resource Management*, 23(1), Spring 1984: 41–60.

[20]Howard Schwartz, and Stanley Davis, "Corporate Culture and Business Strategy," *Harvard Business Review*, 1980; Terrence E. Deal and Alan A. Kennedy, *Corporate Cultures: The Rites and Rituals of Corporate Life*, Reading, MA: Addison-Wesley, 1982; Vijay Sathe, *Culture and Related Corporate Realities*, Homewood, IL: Richard D. Irwin, Inc., 1985; Edgar H. Schein, *Organization Culture and Leadership*, San Francisco: Jossey-Bass Publisher, 1985.

[21]Renato Tagiuri and G. H. Litwin, *Organizational Climate: Explorations of a Concept*, Boston, MA: Division of Research, Harvard Business School, 1968.

[22]Edgar H. Schein, "Coming to a New Awareness of Organizational Culture," *Sloan Management Review*, Winter 1984: 3–16; *Organization Culture and Leadership*, San Francisco: Jossey-Bass Publisher, 1985.

[23]Talcott Parsons, "Suggestions for a Sociological Approach to the Theory of Organizations," *Administrative Science Quarterly*, 1(1), 1956: 63–85.

[24]David Silverman, *The Theory of Organizations*, New York: Basic Books, 1970.

[25]Bo Hedberg, "How Organizations Learn and Unlearn," in P. C. Nystron and W. H. Starbuck, eds., *Handbook of Organization Design*, Vol. 1, Oxford University Press, 1979.

[26]Harrison M. Trice and Janice Beyer, "The Ceremonial Effect: Manifest Function of Latent Dysfunction in the Dynamic Organization," Paper presented at the Conference on Myths, Symbols and Folklore: Expanding the Analysis of Organi-

zations. University of California at Los Angeles, March 1983.

[27]Marvin Harris, *Cultural Materialism: The Struggle for a Science of Culture,* New York: Random House, 1980.

[28]Karlene Roberts and Nakiye Boyacigiller, "A survey of cross-national organizational researchers: Their views and opinions," *Organizational Studies,* 1983: 12.

[29]David A. Heenan and Howard V. Perlmutter, *Multinational Organizational Development* (Reading, MA: Addison-Wesley Publishing Co., 1979).

[30]M. Crozier, *The Bureaucratic Phenomenon.* Chicago: University of Chicago, 1964; G. B. Groenendijr, *De Kunst van het Vergelijken,* Amsterdam: Free University, 1981; Pat Joynt and Malcolm Warner, *Managing in Different Cultures.* Oslo, Norway: Universitetsforlaget AS, 1985; C. J. Lammers and D. J. Hickson, eds. *Organizations Alike and Unlike: International and Inter-Institutional Studies in the Sociology of Organizations.* London: Routledge & Kegan Paul, 1979; James R. Lincoln, Mitsuyo Hanada and Jon Olson, "Cultural orientations and individual reactions to organizations: A study of employees of Japanese-owned firms," *Administrative Science Quarterly,* 26, 1981: 93–115; S. G. Redding, "Some perceptions of psychological needs among managers in South East Asia," in Y. H. Poortinga, ed., *Basic Problems in Cross-Cultural Psychology,* Amsterdam/Lisse: Swets & Zeitlinger, 1977; "Cognition as an aspect of culture and its relation to management processes: An exploratory view of the Chinese case," *Journal of Management Studies,* 17, 1980: 127–148; Laurent, *op. cit.*

[31]Meryl Louis, "How MBA graduates cope with early job experience: An expectation–attribution approach," UCLA Dissertation (unpublished), Los Angeles, 1978. Based on the unpublished research of Nancy J. Adler on internal and external attribution, conducted at the American Graduate School of International Management, Phoenix, Arizona, 1977.

[32]Joanne Martin, Martha Feldman, Mary Jo Hatch and Sim Sitkin, "The uniqueness paradox in organization stories," *Administrative Science Quarterly*, 28(3), September 1983: 438–453.

[33]Leon Festinger, *A Theory of Cognitive Dissonance,* Evanston, IL: Row, Peterson and Co., 1957.

[34]Thomas S. Kuhn, *The Structure of Scientific Revolutions.* Chicago, IL: University of Chicago Press, 2nd edition, 1970.

[35]Peter L. Berger and Thomas Luckman, *The Social Construction of Reality,* New York: Doubleday, 1956.

[36]T. J. Peters and R. Waterman, *In Search of Excellence,* New York: Harper & Row, 1983.

[37]Nancy J. Adler, "Cultural synergy: The management of cross-cultural organizations," in W. Warner Burke and Leonard D. Goodstein, eds., *Trends and Issues in OD: Current Theory and Practice,* San Diego, CA: University Associates, 1980: 163–184.

17

The Cultural Relativity of the Quality of Life Concept

Geert Hofstede

What people see as the meaning of their lives and the kind of living they consider desirable or undesirable are matters of personal choice par excellence. However, personal choices are affected by the cultural environment in which people are brought up. Thus one can expect definitions of the quality of life concept to be culturally dependent as well. For example, in some cultures the quality of life is strongly associated with the degree of satisfaction of material needs. In others, it is associated with the degree to which people succeed in subduing and reducing their material needs.

One facet of a people's quality of life is their quality of work life. The relative contribution of the quality of work life to the quality of life is, in itself, a matter of personal and cultural choice. Charles F. Lettering is quoted as saying:

> I often tell my people that I don't want any fellow who has a job working for me. What I want is a fellow whom a job has. I want the job to get the fellow and not the fellow to get the job. And I want that job to be holding of this young man so hard that no matter where he is the job has got him for

keeps. I want that job to have him in its clutches when he goes to bed at night, and in the morning I want that same job to be sitting on the foot of his bed telling him it's time to get up and go to work. And when a job gets a fellow that way, he's sure to amount to something.[1]

This statement is attributed to a classical U.S. businessman. It is an extreme of a manifestation of a culture in which the quality of work life is associated with a very central place of work in a people's life concepts. It is a product of a society stressing job challenge, achievement, and the satisfaction of intrinsic needs. However, there are other societies in which the primary loyalties of individuals are to their parents, relatives, or clan. Life fulfillment consists of living up to those loyalties. In such a society, a high quality job is one allowing individuals to fulfill obligations to their families.[2]

This paper deals primarily with cultural aspects of the quality of *work* life. However, *work* first must be placed in the wider context of total life patterns; that is, the quality of (total) life must be kept in mind. At the level of culture, work and life cannot and should not be separated. "Quality," by definition, is a matter of values. It relates to standards for "good" and "bad." Values depend partly on personal choices, but to a large extent what one considers good or bad is dictated by one's cultural context. In this paper, conclusions about the cultural relativity of the Quality of Life concepts are based on data about the cultural relativity of values.

VALUE PATTERNS

A shorthand definition of a value is a broad preference for one state of affairs over others. Culture can be defined as the collective programming of the mind which distinguishes the members of one category of people from those of another. Elsewhere the present author has reported on research into national differences in work-related value patterns in 40 countries.[3] Later on, this research was extended to another 10 countries and 3 multi-country regions, so that it now encompasses 50 countries and 3 regions.[4] Paper-and-pencil

Geert Hofstede is Director of the Institute for Research on Intercultural Cooperation, The Netherlands.

Reprint originally published in *Academy of Management Review* 9, no. 3 (1984): 389–398.

answers on 32 value questions by matched samples of employees of subsidiaries of the same multinational business corporation in all these countries were used to study the relationship between nationality and mean value scores. In a factor analysis of 32 mean scores for each of the 40 countries (an ecological factor analysis), three factors together explained 49 percent of the variance in means.[5] Afterwards, several reasons led to the splitting of one of these factors into two parts. Thus four dimensions were created. Together they explained about half of the differences in mean value scores among the 40 nations. Each country could be given an index score on each of these four dimensions.

The subsequent phase of the research was devoted to the validation on other populations of the four dimensions. This showed their meaningfulness outside the subsidiaries of this one multinational corporation. About 40 other studies were found that compared conceptually related data for between 5 and 40 of the countries involved. These studies produced qualitative outcomes that correlated significantly with one or more of the four dimensions scores.[6]

The labels chosen for the four dimensions, and their interpretations, are as follows:

1. *Power distance*, as a characteristic of a culture, defines the extent to which the less powerful person in a society accepts inequality in power and considers it as normal. Inequality exists within any culture, but the degree of it that is tolerated varies between one culture and another. "All societies are unequal, but some are more unequal than others."[7]

2. *Individualism*, as a characteristic of a culture, opposes collectivism (the word is used here in an anthropological, not a political, sense). Individualist cultures assume individuals look primarily after their own interests and the interests of their immediate family (husband, wife, and children). Collectivist cultures assume that individuals—through birth and possibly later events—belong to one or more close "in-groups," from which they cannot detach themselves. The in-group (whether extended family, clan, or organization) protects the interest of its members, but in turn expects their permanent loyalty. A collectivist society is tightly integrated; an individualist society is loosely integrated.

3. *Masculinity*, as a characteristic of a culture, opposes femininity. Masculine cultures use the biological existence of two sexes to define very different social roles for men and women. They expect men to be assertive, ambitious, and competitive, to strive for material success, and to respect whatever is big, strong, and fast. They expect women to serve and to care for the nonmaterial quality of life, for children, and for the weak. Feminine cultures, on the other hand, define relatively overlapping social roles for the sexes, in which neither men nor women need to be ambitious or competitive. Both sexes may go for a different quality of life than material success and may respect whatever is small, weak, and slow. In both masculine and feminine cultures, the dominant values within political and work organizations are those of men. In masculine cultures these political/organizational values stress material success and assertiveness. In feminine cultures they stress other types of quality of life, interpersonal relationships, and concern for the weak.

4. *Uncertainty avoidance*, as a characteristic of a culture, defines the extent to which people within a culture are made nervous by situations that they consider to be unstructured, unclear, or unpredictable, and the extent to which they try to avoid such situations by adopting strict codes of behavior and a belief in absolute truths. Cultures with a strong uncertainty avoidance are active, aggressive, emotional, security-seeking, and intolerant. Cultures with a weak uncertainty avoidance are con-

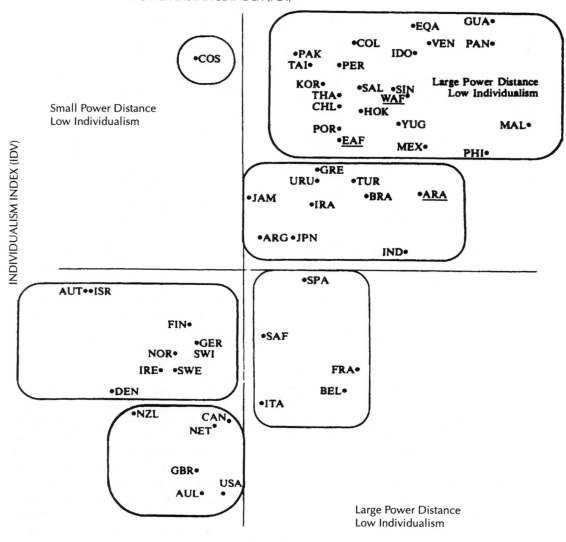

FIGURE 1

A Power Distance x Individualism/Collectivism Plot for Fifty Countries and Three Regions
(For country abbreviations see Exhibit 1.)

templative, less aggressive, unemotional, accepting of personal risk, and relatively tolerant.

Country scores on the four dimensions have been plotted in Figures 1 and 2. Exhibit 1 lists the countries and regions and the abbreviations used. Figure 1 plots power distance against individualism/collectivism. There is a statistical association between power distance and the collectivist end of the individualism/collectivism (I/C) dimension (*r* = −.67 across

the original 40 countries). This association, however, is caused by the correlation of both power distance and individualism with national wealth. (The countries' per capita GNP correlates −.65 with the power distance index and .82 with the individualism index.) If one controls for national wealth, the correlation between power distance and collectivism disappears. In the ecological factor analysis of 32 values questions mean scores for 40 countries, power distance plus collectivism showed up

EXHIBIT 1
Country Abbreviations
(for Figures 1 and 2)

ARA	Arab countries (Egypt, Lebanon, Libya, Kuwait, Iraq, Saudi-Arabia, U.A.E.)	GBR	Great Britain	PAN	Panama
		GER	Germany	PER	Peru
		GRE	Greece	PHI	Philippines
		GUA	Guatemala	POR	Portugal
ARG	Argentina	HOK	Hong Kong	SAF	South Africa
AUL	Australia	IDO	Indonesia	SAL	Salvador
AUT	Austria	IND	India	SIN	Singapore
BEL	Belgium	IRA	Iran	SPA	Spain
BRA	Brazil	IRE	Ireland	SWE	Sweden
CAN	Canada	ISR	Israel	SWI	Switzerland
CHL	Chile	ITA	Italy	TAI	Taiwan
COL	Colombia	JAM	Jamaica	THA	Thailand
COS	Costa Rica	JPN	Japan	TUR	Turkey
DEN	Denmark	KOR	South Korea	URU	Uruguay
EAF	East Africa (Kenya, Ethiopia, Zambia)	MAL	Malaysia	USA	United States
		MEX	Mexico	VEN	Venezuela
		NET	Netherlands	WAF	West Africa (Nigeria, Ghana, Sierra Leone)
EQA	Equador	NOR	Norway		
FIN	Finland	NZL	New Zealand		
FRA	France	PAK	Pakistan	YUG	Yugoslavia

on one factor. Their joint relationship with wealth and the disappearance of their inter-correlation when the author controlled for wealth is one of the two reasons why he split this factor into two dimensions. The other reason is that power distance (inequality) and collectivism (social integration) are conceptually two different issues.

Figure 2 plots masculinity/femininity against uncertainty avoidance. In this case there is no statistical association between the two dimensions (correlation across the original 40 countries, $r = .12$). These two dimensions are directly based on two separate factors in the ecological factor analysis of 32 values questions mean scores for 40 countries.

Because of the joint association of power distance and collectivism with national wealth, the Third World countries in Figure 1 tend to be separated from the wealthy countries. The former are in the upper right hand corner and the latter are in the lower part of the diagram. However, masculinity and uncertainty avoidance are both unrelated to national wealth. Thus, in Figure 2 wealthy countries and Third World countries are found in all four quadrants of the diagram.

Work-related values differ by occupation as well as by nationality.[8] There are striking differences in the saliency of work goals if one goes from unskilled workers via clerical workers and technicians to professionals and managers. Professionals, technicians, and managers stress the content of their jobs. Clerks, managers, and technicians stress the social context (interpersonal relationships). Skilled workers and technicians stress security and earnings; and unskilled stress only benefits and physical conditions.[9] These occupational differences affect attempts at "humanization of work."[10] The dynamics of the humanization of work movements are such that the "humanizers" tend to be managers and professionals. But the people whose work is to be humanized tend to be clerks and unskilled workers. Thus, there is a real danger of the humanizers trying to increase the quality of work life of these other employees (clerks and unskilled) based on their own (the humanizers') work values of what represents a high quality job; in particu-

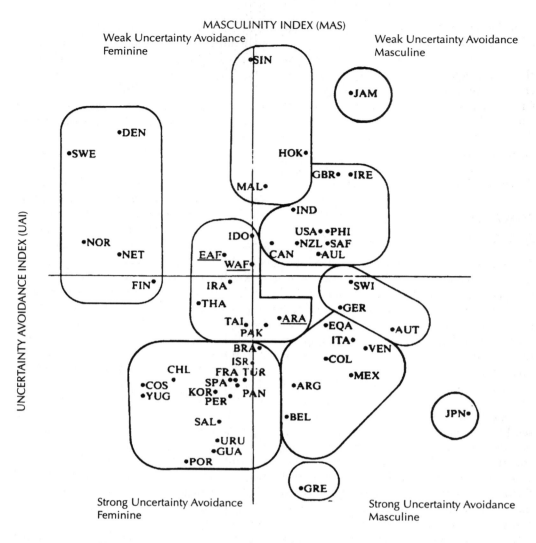

MASCULINITY INDEX (MAS)

FIGURE 2
A Masculinity/Femininity x Uncertainty Avoidance Plot for Fifty Countries and Three Regions
(For country abbreviations see Exhibit 1.)

lar, by trying to make the jobs more interesting. This helps to explain the lack of support for many attempts at improving the quality of work life from the workers and the unions that represent them.[11] In spite of the low priority that workers tend to give to job content factors, however, making the job more interesting *does* increase the workers' satisfaction with it.[12] If an increase in job satisfaction is wanted, the humanizers' attempts at making jobs more interesting are justified. Their problem becomes one of what is the best strategy to adopt in order to gain the support of employees and

unions, without which support the humanization revolution is unlikely to succeed.

Occupational differences in work values can be seen as superimposed on the national patterns.[13] In the cross-national research referred to earlier, the occupation effect was eliminated because the comparison was based on matched samples of people in the same occupation from country to country. In any practical quality of work life problem, an account should be taken of both the nationality and the occupational level of the people involved. A useful way of measuring the occupational level is by the number of years of formal education necessary for their occupation.[14]

In addition to the differences due to nationality and occupation, one is likely to find differences between one organization and another. Organizations have their own subcultures,[15] which reflect the values of their founders and the ways in which they were set up. Particular organizations may have particular objectives related to the quality of life that are reflected in the needs of the people who work for them.[16]

POWER DISTANCE, INDIVIDUALISM, AND QUALITY OF LIFE

Although occupational and organizational differences have to be considered, the focus of this paper is on the dimension of power distance and I/C (Figure 1). A society's position on the I/C continuum will have a strong impact on the self-concept of its members and on the way in which they define the quality of their lives.[17]

In an individualistic society (lower part of Figure 1) a high quality life means individual success, achievement, self-actualization, and self-respect. The capitalist economic system prevalent in and originating from these countries is based on enlightened self-interest. However, in a collective society (upper half of Figure 1), a high quality life is defined much more in family and group terms. Children in collectivistic societies learn to think of themselves as "we" rather than "I." Whoever has success and wealth is supposed to let his/her relatives and friends share in it. The satisfaction of a job well done (by one's own standard) is an individualistic goal. In a collectivistic society, people seek the satisfaction of a job well recognized. Students are less motivated by a need to master their subject and more by a desire to pass their examinations and acquire the status that a degree can provide. Preserving face—that is, preserving the respect from one's reference groups—is the collectivistic alternative to preserving self-respect in the individualistic cultures. Avoiding shame in the collectivistic society takes the place of avoiding guilt in the individualistic one. In Southeast Asian cultures, such as Indonesia (upper right-hand corner of Figure 1),

preserving harmony with one's social environment is a powerful motivator. People would probably define a high quality life as one in which harmony is achieved and preserved. In many Third World countries, national unity is an important symbol. A criterion for a high quality job will be the degree to which they can serve their country.

In the individualistic society, job life and private life are sharply set apart, in both time and mind. Not so in the collectivistic society. People accept the job invading their private life. But they also expect the employer to take account of family problems and allow time to fulfill family duties, which may be many. Most importantly, in individualistic work organizations, the task comes before the relationship. In collectivistic work organizations the relationship has precedence over the task. This is because a society in which people think of themselves as "we," not "I," also will teach people to distinguish between "us" and "them." Others are classified as belonging to "our" ingroup, or not belonging, and the way others are treated depends on their group membership. In order to perform a task together, or to do business together, there must be time to develop a relationship with the other person, allowing him/her to be "adopted" into the ingroup. Developing such a relationship will take time—anything from two minutes to two years—but it is an essential precondition for achieving the task.

A society's position on the power distance continuum is correlated largely with its position on I/C (Figure 1), although there are exceptions, such as Austria, France, and India. Power distance, among other things, indicates the strength of the need for dependence on more powerful people among the adult members of a society. If this is low (left side of Figure 1), the norm of subjecting oneself to the power of others is undesirable. Everyone should have a say in everything that concerns them. This may be difficult to realize in practice. Small power distance societies, such as Denmark and Sweden, often go through considerable rituals of democratization to satisfy the need for consultation without necessarily contributing much to actual decisions. Status differences are suspect in small power distance societies. Ideal leaders are "democrats" who loyally execute the will of their groups.

In medium power distance societies such as the United States and Canada, consultation is usually appreciated but not necessarily expected. "Participative leadership" is initiated by the participative leader, not by the rebellious subordinate. Ideal leaders are resourceful "democrats"—that is, individuals with some outstanding characteristics people enjoy. Moderate status differences and privileges for leaders are socially acceptable. However, laws and rules are expected to apply to superiors and subordinates alike.

In large power distance societies (right of the vertical line in Figure 1), subordinates have strong dependence needs. They usually aspire to democracy as an impersonal ideal. Subordinates expect superiors to behave autocratically and not to consult them. They may even be uncomfortable if superiors consult them. Ideal superiors in such a culture are benevolent autocrats or paternalists, "good fathers" on whom they like to depend. Everybody expects superiors to enjoy privileges. Moreover, laws and rules differ for superiors and subordinates. In addition, status symbols are widely used and contribute to the superiors' authority in the eyes of subordinates.

This set of connotations should make it clear that equality, participation, industrial democracy, and leadership mean different things for the quality of work life in societies at different positions on the power distance scale. North Americans are often appalled and uncomfortable at the legally required codetermination procedures in countries such as Sweden or Germany. They suppose a degree of subordinate initiative and basic equality not in the American book.

On the other hand, North and West Europeans have trouble with the vertical society of nearly all Third World countries. They believe the first thing these Third World countries need is the elimination of their power inequalities. However, after a certain time in those countries they usually adopt "neocolonial" attitudes. This means the North and West Europeans start behaving towards the native lower classes just as does the native ruling class. Third World citizens in Western countries often initially feel

lost. This is because of the lack of dependable superiors to take a personal attitude towards them and give clear orders.

Differences in I/C and power distance affect the feasibility of socio-technical interventions. This is because different societies define the "socio" element in the system quite differently, as should be clear from the previous paragraphs. Should the "system" include family relationships? What degree of consultation and visible leadership makes people feel comfortable? These are missing considerations in the classical Anglo-American imported socio-technical approach. Changes in the system are brought about in various ways in different cultures. In small power distance societies people can accept new and less powerful roles and still continue functioning. The larger a society's power distance the more the system is identified with one or more powerful individuals. Thus, change comes about by decree from the center of power or by revolution, changing the center of power.

Kanungo suggests that differences in the cultural environment also affect the appropriateness of research instruments.[18] Instruments developed by and for the North American mind are too often exported indiscriminately to other cultures. These instruments overemphasize items related to North American (individualist, medium power distance) values and lack items related to other cultures' values. As an example, Kanungo uses the emphasis on intrinsic need satisfaction of most instruments for measuring the quality of work life. Even the classification of needs as "intrinsic" and "extrinsic" ceases to make sense in cross-national research.[19] These instruments need to be redesigned and the entire research paradigm merits redefinition.[20]

So far, this paper has presented a static view of the cultural choices of nations. Obviously, cultures do change over time. For the indices plotted in Figures 1 and 2, shifts have been measured over a 4-year period, 1968–1972.[21] These show a consistent increase in individualism, which can be proven to follow, rather than precede, the increase in wealth in the countries concerned. These countries show a mixed picture for power distance. On the one hand, greater equality is expected. On the other hand, these are signs that the powerful are not prepared to reduce their power, at least in the large power distance societies. The stress in the large power distance systems increases. There is no sign whatsoever of a convergence among countries. Although cultures change, their differences remain remarkably stable.

MASCULINITY, UNCERTAINTY AVOIDANCE, AND THE QUALITY OF LIFE

Figure 2 shows the masculinity/femininity x uncertainty avoidance plots. These plots denote the prevalent standards in a country for the quality of work life in different ways than Figure 1. The differences among countries in Figure 2 are unrelated to whether the country is wealthy or poor. Both dimensions relate to human motivation. Masculinity in society relates to the desirability of achievement; femininity relates to interpersonal relationships (not, as in the case of collectivism, with relatives and in-group members, but with people in general). Uncertainty avoidance relates to the acceptability in a society of personal risk-taking (weak uncertainty avoidance) versus an emphasis on personal security (strong uncertainty avoidance).

The consequence of country differences along these two dimensions is that management conceptions about the motivation of employees, common in North America, do not necessarily apply abroad. To illustrate consider the cultural limitations of two North American motivation theories highly popular among managers: McClelland's achievement motivation theory and Maslow's hierarchy of human needs. Both are either implicitly or explicitly considered by many managers as applying universally to the human race.

McClelland has published scores for the need for achievement (n_{Ach}) in a large number of countries, based on a content analysis of children's readers from around 1925 and around 1950.[22] Across 22 countries, McClelland's n_{Ach} scores (1925 data) show a multiple correlation of $r = .74$ with a low uncertainty avoidance index and a high masculinity index. That is, what McClelland identified as n_{Ach} follows a diagonal in Figure 2 from lower left (low n_{Ach})

to upper right (high n_{Ach}).[23] It is remarkable that McClelland's 1925 data, not his 1950 data, show significant correlations. It is likely that the traditional children's readers from 1925 reflected basic national values more purely than do the modernized readers from 1950.[24] The countries in which McClelland's n_{Ach} is strong are characterized by weak uncertainty avoidance (personal risk-taking) and strong masculinity. McClelland's n_{Ach} may represent one particular combination of cultural choices. Defining n_{Ach} as a desirable end-state for the world as a whole is McClelland's personal values choice. It is also a highly ethnocentric one. McClelland predicted the fastest economic growth for countries with high n_{Ach} scores. This prediction did not come true in the 1960–1980 period.

With the help of Figure 2, another theory that can be unmasked as ethnocentric is Maslow's hierarchy of human needs.[25] Empirical evidence of its cultural limitations is found in the classical 14-country study by Haire, Ghiselli, and Porter.[26] In Haire et al.'s study, managers were asked to rate the importance to them of, and their satisfaction with, the fulfillment of a number of needs. These needs were chosen to represent the five levels of Maslow's hierarchy (from low to high: security–social–esteem–autonomy–self-actualization). Although Haire et al. never drew this conclusion from their data, the only nationality group that ordered their need importance almost, and their need satisfaction exactly, in the Maslow order was the U.S. managers. The other nationalities showed more or less deviant patterns. The present author concluded the ordering of needs in Maslow's hierarchy represents a value choice—Maslow's value choice.[27] This choice was based on his mid-twentieth century U.S. middle class values. First, Maslow's hierarchy reflects individualistic values, putting self-actualization and autonomy on top. Values prevalent in collectivist cultures, such as "harmony" or "family support," do not even appear in the hierarchy. Second, the cultural map of Figure 2 suggests even if just the needs Maslow used in his hierarchy are considered—the needs will have to be ordered differently in different culture areas. Maslow's hierarchical ordering (self-actualization on top) corresponds to the upper right-hand quadrant of Figure 2. In the lower right-hand quadrant (strong uncertainty avoidance and masculinity), a combination of security and assertiveness needs should be placed on top of a need hierarchy. In the upper left hand quadrant (weak uncertainty avoidance and femininity), social (relationship) needs should be placed on top. In the lower left hand quadrant (strong uncertainty avoidance and femininity), security and relationship needs should be placed on top.

For managers operating internationally it is important for them to realize what countries tend to order human needs differently. Moreover these countries are not necessarily inferior technologically, economically, or in the quality of their management. Some countries may even be superior in some or all of these respects. Japan, a country in which security needs rank very high, has been outperforming the world in recent years. Other East Asian countries follow closely. However, the dominant motivation patterns may affect the type of economic and technological activities at which a country is best. Masculine cultures may have an advantage when it comes to mass production. Feminine cultures may have an advantage when it comes to providing services (such as consulting) and to growing things rather than mass producing them (such as high quality agriculture and biochemistry). For example, the leading companies in the world in the field of penicillin and enzymes are in the Netherlands and Denmark. A truly international management should be able to recognize the strengths and the weaknesses in any country's culture pattern, including the home culture.

Improving the quality of work life often has been interpreted as offering to people satisfactions of needs higher on their need hierarchy. Thus, it should be recognized that different cultures have different need hierarchies. In the lower half of Figure 2, improving the quality of work life probably implies offering more security and possibly more task structure on the job. In the left half of Figure 2, improving the quality of work life implies offering opportunities for creating relationships on the job. In this context a difference is noted between the North American and the North European school of improving the quality of work life (humanization of work, job restructuring). In North America, the dominant objective is to make individual jobs more interesting by providing workers with an increased challenge. This grew out of the earlier "job enlargement" and "job enrichment" movements. In countries such as Sweden and Norway, the dominant objective is to make group work more rewarding by allowing groups to function as self-contained social units (semiautonomous groups) and by fostering cooperation among group members. Humanization of work means "masculinization" in North America, but "femininization" in Sweden.[28] This shows another aspect of the cultural relativity of the quality of work life.

To the extent the data permitted measurement, the shifts over time on the masculinity-femininity and uncertainty avoidance dimensions were relatively small and inconsistent. There was no sign of convergency among countries, rather there was an indication of increasing divergence.[29] This means there are not changes permitting one culture's standards for the quality of work life to prevail.

FAREWELL TO ETHNOCENTRISM

Concern for the quality of life is a worthwhile issue in any culture.[30] However, researchers approaching the issue in Third World countries have relied too much on definitions of "quality" derived from North American and, to a lesser extent, West European values. Many Third World social scientists have been educated in North America or Western Europe. It is difficult for them to free themselves from the ethnocentricity of the Western approaches. This ethnocentricity is never explicit but is hidden behind "scientific" verbiage. U.S. social scientific theories and instruments, especially have a high status value. It takes considerable personal courage and independence of thought of a Third World researcher—or of an expatriate Western researcher—to suggest these theories and instruments may be wholly or partly inapplicable and irrelevant to another situation. Science approaches are never purely "objective." They always have a quasi-religious, symbolic meaning to the initiated. It is highly flattering to the designers of social science theories in the United States and in Western Europe if their ideas become religion to followers in faraway parts of the world. For the longer term this situation serves neither those followers nor their Third World countries. Even social scientists are children of their culture. The patterns of collectivism (loyalty to the scientific reference group at their U.S. or European university) and large power distance (intellectual dependency on the brilliant professor) are more likely among Third World social scientists than among those from Western countries.

There are counterforces, however. Western ethnocentrism has become too evidently untenable. Countries trying to transfer Western ideas wholesale have been in trouble—Iran, for example. Countries translating them in a way consistent with their own cultural traditions are now outperforming the West—Japan and Singapore, for example. It is time to bid farewell to ethnocentrism in social science theories in general, and in definitions of the quality of life in particular.

ENDNOTES

[1] W. F. Whyte, "Culture and Work," in R. A. Webber, ed., *Culture and Management* (Homewood, IL: Irwin, 1969): 31.

[2] M. Kiggundu, "The Quality of Working Life in Developing Countries: Beyond the Sociotechnical System Model," Paper presented at the 20th International Congress of Applied Psychology, Edinburgh, Scotland, 1982.

[3] G. Hofstede, "Value Systems in Forty Countries: Interpretation, Validation, and Consequences for Theory," in L. H. Eckensberger, W. J. Lonner, and Y. H. Poortinga, eds., *Cross-Cultural Contributions to Psychology* (Lisse, Netherlands: Swets and Zeitlinger, 1979): 398–407; *Culture's Consequences: International Differences in Work-Related Values.* (Beverly Hills, CA, and London: Sage, 1980).

[4] G. Hofstede, "Dimensions of National Cultures in Fifty Countries and Three Regions," in J. B. Deregowski, S. Dziurawiec, and R. C. Annis, eds., *Explications in Cross-Cultural Psychology* (Lisse, Netherlands: Swets and Zeitlinger, 1983): 335–355.

[5] G. Hofstede, *Culture's Consequences: International Differences in Work-Related Values.* (Beverly Hills, CA, and London: Sage, 1980).

[6] *Ibid.*

[7] *Ibid.*, 136.

[8] G. Hofstede, "The Colors of Collars," *Columbia Journal of World Business,* 7(5), 1972: 72–80; "Humanization of Work: The Role of Values in a Third Industrial Revolution," in C. L. Cooper and E. Mumford, eds., *The Quality of Working Life in Eastern and Western Europe* (London: Associated Business Press, 1979): 18–37.

[9] G. Hofstede, "The Colors of Collars," *op. cit.*

[10] G. Hofstede, "Humanization of Work," *op. cit.*

[11] J. P. Singh, "QWL Experiences in India: Trials and Triumph," Paper presented at the 20th International Congress of Applied Psychology, Edinburgh, Scotland, 1982.

[12] G. Hofstede, "Humanization of Work,"

[13] G. Hofstede, *Culture's Consequences.*

[14] *Ibid.*

[15] G. Hofstede, "The Interaction between National and Organizational Value Systems," Paper presented at the 20th International Congress of Applied Psychology, Edinburgh, Scotland, 1982; "The Individual among National, Occupational and Organizational Cultures," Paper presented at the 20th International Congress of Applied Psychology, Edinburgh, Scotland, 1982.

[16] L. A. DeBettignies and G. Hofstede, "Communauté de travail 'Boimondau,'" A case study on participation. *International Studies of Management Organization,* 7, 1977: 91–116.

[17] R. N. Kanungo, "Work Alienation and the Quality of Work Life: A Cross-Cultural Perspective," Paper presented at the 20th International Congress of Applied Psychology, Edinburgh, Scotland, 1982.

[18] *Ibid.*

[19] G. Hofstede, *Culture's Consequences.*

[20] P. C. Morrow, "Concept Redundancy in Organizational Research: The Case of Work Commitment," *Academy of Management Review,* 8, 1983: 486–500.

[21] G. Hofstede, *Culture's Consequences.*

[22] D. C. McClelland, *The Achieving Society* (New York: Van Nostrand Reinhold, 1961).

[23] G. Hofstede, *Culture's Consequences.*

[24] *Ibid.*

[25] A. H. Maslow, *Motivation and Personality* (New York: Harper & Row, 1954).

[26] M. Haire, E. E. Ghiselli and L. W. Porter, *Managerial Thinking: An International Study* (New York: Wiley, 1966).

[27]G. Hofstede, *Culture's Consequences.*

[28]*Ibid.*

[29]*Ibid.*

[30]N. J. Adler, "Cross-Cultural Management Research: The Ostrich and the Trend," *Academy of Management Review,* 8, 1983: 226–232.

18

Adopting Japanese Management: Some Cultural Stumbling Blocks

Linda S. Dillon

William G. Ouchi, whose research into Japanese management practice has been largely responsible for the current interest in Japan's highly productive management methods, is fond of telling the story of three men sentenced to die in front of a firing squad. The executioner asked the men—a Frenchman, a Japanese, and an American—if they had any last requests. "Oui," replied the Frenchman, "I would like to sing *La Marseillaise* once more before I die." "Granted," said the executioner. "I would like to give my discourse on quality circles one last time," said the Japanese. "Granted," said the executioner, who then turned to the American. "Please," said the American, "Shoot me before the Japanese has a chance to talk about quality circles again."

Ouchi's story illustrates the extent to which American business has bought into the Japanese model—in theory, if not in practice. Ouchi's work describes the American organizations labeled "Type A," which are characterized by short-term employment, rapid evaluation and promotion, specialized career paths, explicit control mechanisms, individual decision making and responsibility, and segmented concern. He compares these with "Type J" (Japanese) organizations,

Reprinted by permission of publisher, from *Personnel* 60 (July/August 1983): 73–77. Copyright © 1983, American Management Association, New York. All rights reserved.

which practice lifetime employment, slow evaluation and promotion, nonspecialized career paths, implicit control mechanisms, collective decision making and responsibility, and a holistic concern.

"Theory Z" organizations are those identified by Ouchi as having been able to make the cultural crossover—that is, American firms that have foregone the mistrust of employees and autocratic management style so typical in Type A organizations in favor of the Type J approach, which views employees as the company's greatest resource and assumes that, given the opportunity, employees want to and will do good work. Many writers have examined why Theory Z has worked well for Motorola, Westinghouse, Hewlett-Packard, and the other highly touted Theory Z models. But few have asked why Type J organizations function so well in Japan. An understanding of this cultural perspective should help American managers trying to introduce a Japanese approach into an American organization.

LIFETIME EMPLOYMENT AND THE NONSPECIALIZED CAREER PATH

The willingness of Japanese managers to think of their employees as the company's greatest asset is not so much an example of humanistic concern as an example of their ability to deal with the unpleasant truth. Japan is a resource-poor nation whose land and raw materials are in extremely short supply. Over the past century, Japan's military efforts to alleviate that problem have ended disastrously, and the memory lingers. If the 30 percent of Japan's major corporations who offer lifetime employment do value their employees, it is because they know that they have to compete to get quality and that lifetime employment precludes the availability of a trained labor force from which to choose in filling current needs. This, of course, leads quite naturally to the practice of job rotation. Individuals may not be so apt to balk at being asked to fill a job they are unqualified for if that requirement is part of the company's basic approach to personnel planning.

But how can you offer lifetime employment when workforce needs vary with the supply-and-demand cycle? The answer in Japan is to use the participation of women in the labor force to buffer the lifetime employment of men. Women are hired as temporary or part-time workers and discarded when demand decreases. This system works well in Japan because 94 percent of the population over 30 years old is married. In this way the majority of women receive financial security in one form or another. But even if we disregard the illegality of institutionalizing a similar approach in the United States, it is easy to imagine the economic and social chaos of using women as a disposable workforce in a country where just 13 percent of the population lives in conjugal units.

SLOW EVALUATION AND PROMOTION

The Japanese practice of slow evaluation and promotion takes on special meaning when seen in terms of another infamous Japanese practice, the examination system. Examinations, which begin in junior high school, are used to determine both high school and college placement. Since the most prestigious firms hire from the most prestigious schools, children realize that their futures may be irreversibly decided at a very early age.

This practice has caused the Japanese to adopt a Japanese counterpart to a uniquely American concept: the "show biz mother." The Japanese alternative, *Kyoeku Mama* or "education mother," spends her day juggling the food budget to pay for after-school classes and hounding her children to do their homework. In feudal times, the Samurai who lost his retainer was called a "ronin" to indicate his predicament as a soldier without a master. Today, "ronin schools" provide extracurricular help for students who score low on examinations, and suicide is still an acceptable way to atone for this failure. The excruciating pace that children are forced to keep eventually pays off: when they achieve lifetime employment with a good firm. The slower pace which follows entrance into the workforce is the logical reward for the years of struggle it requires.

COLLECTIVE DECISION MAKING AND RESPONSIBILITY

Some of Japan's highly productive methods result from efforts to compensate for some very difficult features of her culture. Japan's love of consensus decision making and the use of quality control circles are reasonable reactions to the difficulties of the Japanese language. The Portuguese missionaries who first attempted to translate Japanese termed it "The Devil's Language" when they began to settle in Japan during the seventeenth century. Japanese is normally written with a mixture of two syllabaries (*Kana*) and Chinese characters (*Kanzi*). There are verb forms representing levels of formality and politeness for any situation you might encounter in addressing the Emperor or your pet cat and all points on the spectrum in between. There are two sets of ordinal numbers that use suffixes to reveal whether you are counting hotels or cows. To be able to read a Japanese newspaper requires knowledge of 2,000 *Kanzi,* each symbol having several meanings and pronunciations.

The difference between male and female speech is so pronounced that Japanese schools which train seeing-eye dogs for the blind use English commands and teach the blind people English, instead of training a dog in Japanese and thus limiting it to use with just one sex. In the face of this incredibly difficult system of written communication, it is hardly surprising that Japan has come to rely on verbal communication in the form of quality circles and an office seating arrangement that features all employees in one work unit sharing a common office, with desks arranged so that everyone is forced to be aware of what everyone else is doing.

HOLISTIC CONCERN AND IMPLICIT CONTROL MECHANISMS

An organization that maintains a holistic approach to company decision making forces employees at all levels to deal with each other as human beings and creates a condition in which open communication, trust, and com-

mitment can flourish. Theory J management seeks more than a vote; it seeks agreement. A group member may be asked to accept responsibility for a decision he does not prefer, but which has been arrived at through a collective process.

To be able to put personal preference aside and commit oneself wholeheartedly to company goals is the essence of a holistic approach. "Labor, not the art of management, is the key to Japan's ascendancy," writes B. Bruce-Briggs in his critique of Theory Z, ". . . labor does what is expected of it. It is expected to work hard, work right, and not block productive improvements. American labor is told what to do but does not do it reliably; that is the difference."

A holistic approach to corporate decision making and business activities is made easy in Japan by the homogeneity of the Japanese culture and the implicit philosophy that employees share. Japan has one of the lowest interracial marriage rates of any nation, and even today there is social discrimination against Koreans, Chinese, and the *burakumin*, the descendants of butchers and leather workers who were historically outcast because of the Buddhist prejudice against the taking of animal life. The Japanese today are the most thoroughly unified and culturally homogeneous large block of people in the entire world, with the possible exception of the North Chinese. To say that the Japanese people are all Japanese has no equivalent concept in American culture.

The Christian religions that have dominated American life over the last 200 years have created a "guilt culture" in the United States wherein judgment before the eyes of God is the primary conditioning force. Japan's culture has been characterized as a shame culture rather than a guilt culture. The Japanese fear shame from the judgment of family or society over all else and have developed elaborate systems of duty (*giri*) and obligation (*on*) which represent their shared cultural values. These value systems apply equally to business concerns and family matters, and operate efficiently to provide a unified labor force that can easily be motivated toward a common goal. Many of the judgment calls that managers and workers make are made on the basis of a company philosophy that is implicit rather than explicit, communicated by a common cultural perspective that all share. Of course, slow promotion and the common practice of yearly bonus systems that reward all employees on the basis of company profitability combine to ensure that the only way for individuals to profit personally is for the total company to prosper—another factor that rewards a holistic approach.

CONCLUSION

Examination of concepts unique to Japanese management reveals just how closely they are tied to the Japanese culture. Equally apparent is the interrelatedness of each factor with the other. It is not surprising that so few American firms have been able to successfully adapt the Theory Z approach. The real success of the Japanese approach lies in what they were able to learn from the United States in the early postwar years: the value of controlling cost, working hard, saving money, and giving the customer value for his dollar. It was their ability to adapt those concepts to a Japanese culture that led to their productivity gains and subsequent worldwide envy. But it would be a mistake to assume that these techniques can be borrowed and used productively as easily as Japan has "borrowed" American technology in the past. It will take the most creative efforts of America's most skilled managers to adapt the Japanese approach to the American culture.

19

The Chinese Practice of *Guanxi*

M. Cordell Hart

Guanxi is translated into English as "relationship" or "connections," but it also has the meaning of "intercourse." Just as when using the latter English word, one must be careful in speaking Chinese to use the term in the intended way. For example, while a Chinese man may openly ask another if he has business connections with another man, one would never ask a person of one sex whether they have *guanxi* with a person of another sex—unless one intends to boldly ask about sexual relations.

The Chinese social practice of *guanxi* is similar in some ways to what we of the west have in mind when we say that we "have a friend at city hall." But the Chinese practice is so pervasive, so fundamental to their social ways, that it should be considered a distinguishing feature of the Chinese mindset. Indeed, it is exactly the feature that underlies the primary difference between western man's sense of self and that of the Chinese.

Western man is imbued with the idea of independence and individualism, of the knight errant, of the Lone Ranger, of Polonius's admonition in Shakespeare's "Hamlet": "This above all: to thine own self be true." Western man forms associations, to be sure, but he does so for benefits that are specific, definable, not obtainable by his individual self and considered to be of temporary duration—though they may last a lifetime. For Chinese, constant and close identification with a variety of groups

beyond the family is the norm. Conversely, a Chinese person will consider acting independently with about the same frequency and trepidation that a western man will join a fraternal organization or enter into a binding contract.

AN ANCIENT PRACTICE

Guanxi is an ancient consideration among Chinese. The earliest record of the concept comes from the Chou Dynasty, when it was used around 500 B.C. in describing the ethics of certain "natural relationships": between prince and minister, between father and son, between husband and wife, between brothers, and between friends. However, the *guanxi* addressed in this paper, has rather to do with other, more distant relationships. Even so, note the dates in the several references to *guanxi* (pertinent to this paper) found in just one history text.

    a. *Commenting on the use of the examination system for the recruitment of officials during the Sui-Tang era (589–907 A.D.):* The examination system "did not dominate the process whereby officials were recruited. Recruitment was a social rather than a legal process because in the social scene personal connections (*guanxi*) formed the fluid matrix in which candidates for office were advanced and family status was maintained. For example, the Northern Wei established its own list of major clans and made them equivalent to the Chinese list, so that families of nomad background could now move into Chinese life at the top level."[1]

    b. *Commenting on the great Ming emperor, Hongwu, who reigned 1368–1398:* "Finding his prime minister plotting against him in 1380, he had him beheaded, along with everyone in his family or remotely connected, which totaled over the years about 40,000 persons. (*Guanxi* networks have their dangers!) Continued beheading of officials and several later purges may have swelled this total to 100,000 victims."[2]

This original essay appears here in print for the first time. M. Cordell Hart is a senior analyst of the U.S. Department of the Treasury and a Chinese linguist who has lived many years in Asia.

c. *Commenting on certain tax surcharges during the reign of Yongzheng, the Manchu emperor who reigned 1722–1736:* "Provinces used the proceeds partly to pay higher official salaries to 'nourish honesty.' But the networks of personal connections or *guanxi* that helped each individual's career were far too deeply inlaid in the structure of government to be eliminated. Today they are still a problem."[3]

d. *Commenting on the emergence of new leaders of the Chinese Communist Party in the 1950s:* "Unlike the democratic egalitarianism and plural opportunities of the American experience, these new power-holders were adept in the creation of *guanxi* (networks or connections), sycophantic ingratiation with superiors, and authoritarian exploitation of inferiors in the traditional Chinese style."[4]

e. *Commenting on production team leaders in modern China:* "The team leader was thus the ultimate broker in the grain procurement system, mediating between his team-member inferiors and his brigade-cadre superiors. This function was as old as China's history, a main focus of rural politics and interpersonal village relations. Quite naturally the team leader was involved in patron-client relations with others both above and below his status level. Here was where his connections (*guanxi*) came into play. Here was where corruption occurred and often flourished."[5]

It is all too typical of western man to offer value judgments on the phenomenon of *guanxi* as did the eminent and late sinologist John King Fairbank in paragraphs a.-e. above. And a western generalization regarding organizations holds that inefficiency is present in the degree to which the actual lines of communication and authority do not conform to the prescribed lines, as can be seen in "plumbing" charts. But the Chinese mindset is different, and China's fortunes over the ages seem to have fluctuated for reasons quite apart from the continued practice of *guanxi*. An understanding of *guanxi*, and the other social forms brought to the west by Chinese, may benefit us all.

Surely referring, at least in part, to the criminal manifestations of *guanxi*, one writer notes that "In Chinatown, there is a social order so ruthless that its very existence seems to be against the law . . . but most of the people who live here accept it as normal."[6]

WE AND THEY

Compared to Americans, Chinese make a sharp distinction between their behavior towards strangers and their behavior towards acquaintances. To put it simply, Chinese distrust strangers and trust associates to a greater degree and for other reasons than do Americans. While there are occasions in which strangers are the subject of unabashed curiosity, Chinese generally will ignore or avoid them, especially those of a different ethnicity or from a different background. To minimize the necessity for dealing with strangers, Chinese develop a multitude of personal relationships called *guanxi*. *Guanxi* is a bond established between two or more persons for the purpose of assuring the provision of goods and services. Each party to the bond specifies the general kinds of things he can and will do for the benefit of the others.[7]

Though the Chinese language has all the necessary terms to discuss *guanxi*, and Chinese use them frequently in conversation, many Chinese are oblivious to their own frequent practice of *guanxi*. In some cases, Chinese have simply been unwilling to discuss their social practices with foreigners. According to one ethnic Chinese author, there is something of a collusive mindset among Chinese, at least in their business networks. "The Chinese don't like to talk about networking. It's like they're a sect," he said. "They don't like to be intellectually analyzed. When you describe it, the mystique value is lost. They think their practices can be learned and used against them.[8] But many Chinese are truly unaware of what they do so naturally. One Chinese police official responded to this writer's request for examples of *guanxi* by stating that he never practices it—but he offered to check the matter out with certain of his colleagues on the force who were of the same ancestral home as he. He could trust them to be candid, he explained.

It is not enough, however, to be merely acquainted with other persons: one must have the mutually-agreed-to privilege of making demands of others. Each party to the *guanxi* bond is convinced that the other(s) has like agreements with still other persons, in sufficient number and of adequate quality, to make this agreement worthwhile. The effectiveness of an individual's "connections" is measured by the amount of his "face" (*mianzi*). Strong *guanxi* gives much *mianzi*. If A has *mianzi* with B, he can be certain that B will render him services on occasion. This bond ensures reciprocity, so that the greater the circle of those with whom "one has *mianzi*," the better one can encounter adversity.[9]

CONTINUING NEEDS

Because a Chinese depends almost exclusively on his *guanxi* connections to sustain him, he must forever seek to maintain and expand his network of connections. It is most unusual for a Chinese to seek help from an official unknown to him or to expect reliable information from anyone to whom he has not been properly introduced. Since little of consequence is likely to be transacted through anyone outside his network, an individual's *guanxi* relationships will ideally be established in anticipation of foreseeable needs.[10]

One Chinese businessman explained,

An individual wishing to open a Chinese restaurant knows, as a result of existing *guanxi*, many contractors who are able to do remodeling work, for example. But the restaurant owner must be careful to choose the right contractor. He must choose one who has done remodeling and construction work in the restaurant business. He could choose a contractor who had recently done work for a fruit stand or a butcher shop, and one of the persons he employs only works for him part-time and has a full-time job as a waiter. The waiter, in turn, has a sister-in-law whose father owns an accounting firm which has as a client a restaurant supply store. Another contractor that the restaurant owner may know has done work on some restaurants, but concentrates mostly on residential homes. This contractor may have a son who is a doctor, who is married to a computer salesperson. This contractor may also have a good friend in a car dealership. Obviously, the first contractor would be the better choice, because the restaurant owner can then use his *guanxi* with the contractor to obtain the other services and goods that he will need in the restaurant business. The selection of people with different *guanxi* for different purposes is key to obtaining goods and services. Also, a fair amount of planning is required to forecast future needs of this project.[11]

Obviously, however, some Chinese will achieve such financial prosperity and wealth of connections that they can afford to relax their efforts to establish new *guanxi*. In those cases, as with the rich and powerful anywhere, they will deign to accept party invitations and other overtures primarily out of a sense of obligation, almost a sense of *noblesse oblige*. In the case of a ranking, but not highly paid, Chinese official who needed to guarantee sufficient funds for his son to attend college in the United States, however, the official needed to find a contact who did have the money and who could serve as his son's guarantor. The fact that guarantor actually signed as the father made the transaction fraudulent according to U.S. law and somewhat dangerous to the official for having to rely on someone in a foreign country. The Chinese attitude towards all this could be expressed as "But what are friends for, if not to get things done which cannot be done entirely legally?" Obviously, the guarantor in the United States acted not out of friendship, but out of his obligation to a *guanxi* partner.

SENIOR-SUBORDINATE RELATIONSHIPS

The main purpose of senior-subordinate relations in *guanxi* is to facilitate the original agreement of terms. Once the senior partner has determined the types of goods and services to be exchanged, the ranking system assumes a passive function. Each partner has equal obligations to honor the agreement. Neither partner may make demands of a type not originally specified. The subordinate partner need not respond to unreasonable requests by the senior.[12]

One investigation of smuggling clearly showed a senior-subordinate relationship: One Mr. Lee "orchestrated an international smuggling ring that included catcher vessels, transport vessels, and holding facilities. Unfortunately, Mr. Lee had no system in place to secretly move large sums of money in foreign commerce. To meet his needs . . . Mr. Lee enlisted the assistance of one Mr. Hsu a graduate from the same school which Mr. Lee had attended. Mr. Lee was older than Mr. Hsu, and had graduated from the school several years before Mr. Hsu . . . Mr. Hsu was an established businessman, and gave up an honorable life style to accommodate the needs of his higher classmate. It appeared . . . that Mr. Hsu has some sense of 'duty' to help his higher classmate. After Mr. Lee and Mr. Hsu were arrested, guanxi dictated that . . . Mr. Lee confess before the junior member, Mr. Hsu, could talk."[13]

As in guanxi, concern for relative rank carries over into other Chinese interpersonal relationships. The Chinese friend of one American sociologist told the American, "I want to be an elder brother to you." The American explained the incident as follows: In order to sustain the role equality that Chinese value in friendship for the emotional involvement it allows, my friend had to apply power differences belonging to the kinship model of voluntary brotherhood in his definition of friendship. He was called upon to enforce predictability in that very relationship he valued for its equities and changes of affect. In Chinese friendship, the senior partner is obliged to police the relationship for its social content, making sure that it shall in fact contain role equality. The norm of reciprocity reserved for friendship is ratified by a non-reciprocal obligation on the part of the person in charge of

the definition, even though the definition repudiates unequal responsibility.[14]

GUANXI EQUALS FACE

Although guanxi is most easily understood as it exists between two persons, it is most often found among several, and each member's position in a guanxi is his "face" or mianzi. The rules prescribed for "face" behavior differ with each rank, but each has its rules. One rule that all ranks have in common is that each individual must act so as to maintain the structure. Once a guanxi arrangement has been established, it is expected to endure a lifetime. No change in positions is envisioned, and no reneging on performance is expected. One of the easiest ways to lose "face" or position in a network is to go bankrupt. Word of such loss spreads slowly in Mainland China, but quickly elsewhere. It is interesting that word is passed among Chinese subtly, not like the harsh words found in western credit reports. For example, reference to one bankrupt businessman was simply that it "wasn't his own money."

But some people become greedy or selfish or ambitious. If the person who initiates a struggle does not succeed in unseating his adversary, their relationship does not merely return to its previous state. The initiator suffers a loss of "face." If the initiator does succeed, his adversary loses "face." In either case, a loss of "face" means a loss of position, and the loser is ejected from the structure. The outcome of a contest is usually the restructuring of the interrelationships between the remaining members. One possible, though infrequent, outcome is that the entire structure will be dissolved, or transformed drastically.[15] This is utter disaster for all as they can no longer count on the network of social relationships to help them out. That explains many business alliances among Overseas Chinese business people.

One thing for sure: it is dangerous not to take sides in a "face" fight. If the challenged person succeeds in saving "face," those who should have helped him but did not, will probably be cut out of the victor's guanxi net. On the grounds that he who is not for me is against me, remaining neutral is equivalent to joining the attack. If the challenger forces his adversary to lose "face," thereby winning the contest, he too will show little enthusiasm towards anyone who stood by quietly on the sidelines. Everyone having a vested interest in the outcome of these attempts at impeachment (except those who may choose to benefit from playing mediator) must choose sides early. As soon as the wall begins to tilt, everyone must start either pushing or pulling.[16]

Note that "face" is situationally defined. It is a semantic construct applicable to a single and specific *guanxi* relationship. What can be created by words can be destroyed by words. For a Chinese, it is not sticks and stones, but words, that break one's bones.[17]

GUANXI IS NEITHER FRIENDSHIP NOR GO-BETWEENS

Americans in particular are prone to confuse *guanxi* with friendship. Chinese use *guanxi* to provide and receive goods and services, while Americans value friendship for its emotional content and, only incidentally, for the practical benefits that may obtain. Although the American's supposed Chinese "friend" in a *guanxi* relationship may be sincere in his relations with the American, it is not affection that he is sincere about.[18] More succinctly, Americans give and take away love; Chinese give and take away face.[19]

The common American explanation for the Chinese use of go-betweens is, understandably, based on American logic. One theory holds that the use of a go-between avoids embarrassment. Another has it that go-betweens present requests in a more persuasive manner than do their sponsors. But go-betweens are employed for rather infrequent matters, such as marriages and, anyway, *guanxi* has neither of the above benefits in mind. A request for services under a *guanxi* arrangement may require the assistance of several people intervening between the requester and the person who has the ability to honor the request, but those intervening are not middlemen or go-betweens, they are members of a *guanxi* network.[20] The compradore system used by European traders until the 1950's was the most successfully institutionalized *guanxi* in business—and reasonably respectable, too.

A Chinese businessman in the United States once solicited investment money from other ethnic Chinese in order to finance a shopping center. One wary potential investor thought to check up on the developer, but he did not contact a credit bureau or a business service such as Dun & Bradstreet. Rather he called an acquaintance in Hong Kong to ask about the developer. The contact in Hong Kong made inquiries of other contacts in other Asian cities and responded to the potential investor that the businessman was a bad risk.

American businessmen in China often do hire go-betweens, primarily because they are not sufficiently adept at playing the *guanxi* game. Although American companies operating abroad still have to abide by the strict corruption codes of their country, many apparently hire agents in China who are called upon to do whatever is necessary to make a deal go ahead.[21]

IS *GUANXI* PRACTICED BY WESTERNERS?

By this point, western readers will surely (but mistakenly) be thinking that maybe *guanxi* is not such a foreign idea. Before considering the specifics of how Asians practice *guanxi*,—and therein lies the real difference between east and west in this matter—let's consider our own ways. Do we of western cultures also have such "bundles" of ties, favors, and obligations as noted above? You bet we do! Beyond blood relations, we have "old Army buddies," classmates, sports teammates, etc., and we participate in unions, fraternities, alumni associations, police fraternal orders, civic associations, political parties, etc.—and we understand what it means to "marry the boss's daughter," to "have a friend at city hall," to "know someone who can get it for you wholesale," and that "a friend in need is a friend indeed." It is not so much that Asians and westerners have any exclusive activities, it is more than the two groups apply varying amounts of resources and degrees of emphasis and skill in doing similar things.

ENDNOTES

[1] John King Fairbank, *China—A New History* (Massachusetts: Belknap Press of Harvard University Press, 1992), 84.

[2] *Ibid.,* 129.

[3] *Ibid.,* 150.

[4] *Ibid.,* 353.

[5] *Ibid.,* 356.

[6] Gwen Kinkead, *Chinatown: A Portrait of a Closed Society,* (New York: Harper Collins Publishers, 1993).

[7] Anonymous, *Essays on Chinese Behavior,* Undated U.S. Government publication.

[8] Karl Shoenberger, "Networking Pays Off for Chinese," *Los Angeles Times*, April 6, 1994.

[9] Hu Hsien-chin, "The Chinese Concepts of Face" in Douglas Haring, *Personal Character and Cultural Milieu* (Syracuse University Press, 1956).

[10] Anonymous.

[11] Account of Special Agent Neil Pitagno, U.S. Customs Service.

[12] Anonymous.

[13] Account of Special Agent Richard Severtson, U.S. Department of Commerce.

[14] Leon E. Stover, *The Cultural Ecology of Chinese Civilization* (New York Pica Press, 1974).

[15] Anonymous.

[16] Anonymous.

[17] William K. Carr, "The 'Face' of Mao Tse-tung," *World Affairs,* vol. 131, no. 3, (1968).

[18] Anonymous

[19] Stover.

[20] Anonymous.

[21] John Kohut, "Going to War on Graft," Los Angeles *Sunday Morning Post*, April 17, 1994.

20

The Intercultural Meeting

Gary Althen

A common source of frustration for administrators of foreign student programs is the "international student club," or whatever the local organization of foreign (and sometimes U.S.) students is called. "We sent out a notice about an organizational meeting," an FSA might report, "and a reasonable number of students showed up. But the meeting went on and on, and got nowhere." Or, "We have an international student club, but it doesn't do much. The meetings are exercises in frustration."

From the viewpoint of the adviser who believes it would be salutary to have an active international student club on a campus, it is usually the club's meetings that are the focus of the greatest discontent. The meetings tend to be long, unproductive and often disputational. Why should this be? A look at people's culturally based ideas about meetings might suggest some answers to that question. Before looking at those ideas, though, it is important to mention other possible explanations for the problems advisers face in fostering the development of international student clubs. These have to do with the adviser's and the students' discrepant assumptions concerning such clubs.

An adviser who decides to call an organizational meeting for an international student club is probably making most, if not all, of the following assumptions:

- It would be constructive to have an international student club, to foster interaction between foreign and U.S. stu-

dents and/or to provide social activities for foreign students.
- It is possible to have an international student club that is divorced from the political interests and viewpoints of the students.
- Students view the staff of the foreign student office as benevolent, apolitical and capable of organizing situations that benefit most foreign students.
- Students from diverse countries see themselves as having important interests in common. They will be able to agree upon objectives for an organization, and will willingly cooperate with each other in seeking those objectives.

All of these assumptions are open to question. But even if they were all accurate, and the international student club idea gets to the point where meetings are held, the problems are only beginning. People with differing cultural backgrounds bring such diverse assumptions and behaviors to meetings that their gatherings are often rife with misunderstandings.

In *Beyond Culture*, anthropologist Edward Hall offers the notion of "action chains." An action chain is a series of behaviors which people who grow up in a particular culture are taught (usually implicitly) to view as appropriate for a particular situation. People follow their action chains without having to think about what they are doing, or why they are doing it. The situation evokes the behavior.

One situation that evokes certain behaviors is a "meeting." What does the concept of meeting mean to people from different cultures? What behavior is appropriate at a meeting?

To Americans, it seems quite sensible to summon interested people to an organizational meeting for an international student club. It is assumed that interested people will appear at the appointed time and place. There will be a leader, probably elected in some way, or appointed for a temporary period by someone in authority. The leader will moderate the discussion, recognizing people who wish to speak, summarizing people's comments and keeping speakers on the track.

There will be discussion at the meeting. Everyone who wants to talk will have an op-

Reprinted from *National Association of Foreign Students Affairs Newsletter*, (November 1981): 34, 41, 46, 47. Copyright © 1981 by the National Association of Foreign Students Affairs.

portunity to do so. People attending the meeting will seek a common ground (that is, they will compromise), establishing a foundation for subsequent joint action. Agreement will be ratified, probably by means of a vote. If the group is large or the issue complicated, Robert's Rules of Order will be employed to manage the discussion. Otherwise, informality will prevail.

Not everyone has this same action chain concerning meetings. There can be diverse assumptions about several aspects of meetings: why they are held; the means of selecting a leader; the leader's role; and the role and behavior of those attending the meeting. Some of the various assumptions that people from different cultures make about these topics are discussed here.

WHY MEETINGS ARE HELD

Americans typically hold meetings in order to share information or to make decisions. More often than Americans, people from elsewhere might hold meetings in order to ratify or formalize decisions that are made elsewhere, or to give people an opportunity to air their views in the absence of an intention to make any decisions. Of course, people who go to a meeting with the assumption that some decisions are to be made will be frustrated if there are others who are at the meeting merely to express their opinions.

MEANS OF SELECTING A LEADER

Most people make the assumption that a meeting needs a leader, although there are people who do not assume that. Among those who do suppose there should be a leader, there are diverse views about the means by which the leaders should be designated. In some cultures, a person's age and/or social standing would automatically make him or her the leader in the eyes of all those present. In other cultures a formal nomination and election procedure would be employed. Other possibilities for selecting a leader include having someone volunteer to be the leader, waiting for a leader to emerge from the proceedings or having the leader appointed by someone in authority.

At a meeting of students from different countries, especially one held for the purpose of organizing an international student club, these diverse ideas about leadership selection are likely to cause problems. A leader chosen by some people's method may not have legitimacy in the eyes of others. In fact, the others might not even realize that some of the people at the meeting believe a leader has been recognized.

THE LEADER'S ROLE

Americans typically suppose that a leader who is acting appropriately in the context of a meeting will serve as a moderator—keeping order, calling on speakers, preventing anyone from dominating the proceedings, assuring that everyone who wishes to speak has the opportunity to do so, keeping people's remarks on the subject and helping the group reach decisions. It is often expected that the leader will be neutral with respect to topics of disagreement that arise during the meeting.

In many other societies, the leader is expected to exercise much more authority, and even to make important decisions on behalf of the group. In the eyes of people from such societies, the "democratic" style of group leadership that Americans tend to idealize is likely to seem unsatisfactory. It may give members so much opportunity to present diverse comments that the result seems like chaos. Or the leader's presumably greater wisdom may be seen as getting too little attention.

On the other hand, in societies where it is the norm to reach decisions by consensus, a U.S.-style chairman might seem too obtrusive.

ROLE AND BEHAVIOR OF MEETING PARTICIPANTS

It is probably the culturally influenced differences in group members' action chains for meetings that account for most of the difficulty at international student club meetings. First, there is the question of the role of people who attend meetings. In general, when a person comes to a meeting, he or she makes some assessment of his or her status in the group, because one's status within the group does much to determine how one is supposed to behave during the meeting. Determining one's status in a meeting of students from diverse countries is essentially impossible because there is no agreed-upon criterion or set of criteria for deciding where group members stand vis-à-vis each other. Possible criteria include age, sex, period of time as a student at the school, previous leadership position within the group, being from a rich or large country, being from the country or region with the largest number of foreign students at the particular school, being an officer in a nationality organization at the school, having a charismatic personality or having some special affiliation with the foreign student office.

With all of these (and no doubt other) criteria being used by different people at the meeting to determine how they fit in, and with these determinations being made in the absence of conscious thought, discrepant conclusions are inevitable. Some people at the meeting will think that others are out of line.

Second, there is not likely to be a shared assumption about the overall function of the meeting. For Americans, as has been said, the unspoken assumption is that people at a meeting will "give and take" to reach compromise agreements that serve as the basis for action. For many others, though, compromise is not seen as natural or desirable. And there is less of an orientation to action. The purpose of the meeting may be to win all arguments, or at least block the progress of those with opposing views or to display one's rhetorical talent. Engaging in what Americans are likely to consider "mere talk" may be, according to some people's assumptions, the basic function of the meeting. People who behave according to these assumptions often seem dogmatic, insensitive and obstructionist in the eyes of those who want to find compromises and make decisions.

A third source of disharmony in meetings of foreign students is differences in what Dean Barnlund calls "communicative style."[1] Only two aspects of communicative style will be discussed here. They are the general manner of interaction in a discussion, and the means by which people reach conclusions in their arguments.

Americans generally prefer a style of interaction that Barnlund labels "repartee." According to that style, no one speaks for very long. A speaker gets to the point quickly, then gives way to another speaker. A person who talks for too long gets a disapproving reaction.

A style prevalent in many other societies encourages much longer presentations from each speaker. Students from those societies are likely to view American-style presentations as superficial, and perhaps lacking in rhetorical skill.

Meetings of foreign students nearly always include some students who, from the viewpoint of others who are present, talk too long. Impatience results.

People from different cultures are likely to manifest different ways of presenting their arguments. In a meeting of foreign students, one student's logic is likely to be another's nonsense. Some speakers will cite what they consider objective evidence to support their views. Others will invoke authorities of some kind. Others will make appeals to sentiment or emotion. Still others will endorse philosophical principles they wish the group to follow.

With two or more different ways of arguing in use at once, failures to understand are inevitable. Impatience and frustration result.

Given all the difficulties confronting an intercultural meeting, it is little wonder that international student clubs are so often dominated by one energetic leader *and* his or her compatriots. They have the same action chain for meetings.

There are things advisers can do to make intercultural meetings more productive. What they can produce at a minimum is learning about cultural differences. If the students attending the meeting can be helped to understand the ideas that appear in this article, they will have learned a good deal about themselves, about other cultures, about the influence of culture on their own and other people's behavior and about the difficulties that beset intercultural encounters. They might be able to work together to surmount those difficulties.

Advisers could use various approaches to helping students learn from the cultural differences that are manifest in intercultural meetings. They could attend the international student club's meetings and offer observations about culturally based behavior they see taking place there. They could have students from a particular country describe to others their action chain for meetings. Better yet, students from particular countries could conduct brief mock meetings that other students could observe, and then there could be discussion of what has been seen. Such an exercise could sharpen students' ability to observe and analyze manifestations of cultural differences.

Another possibility is to have students from a particular country describe and show how they customarily conduct meetings, and then have all students use that action chain for the meeting. Different groups' action chains could be used at different meetings.

Still another possibility is to have the club's leader explain his or her conception of the leader's role, and his or her expectations of group members. Making these conceptions and expectations explicit can reduce the amount of frustration and anger that result from behavior that others do not understand.

A relatively common approach to the problem of unsatisfactory international student clubs is to try to teach the students the idealized American action chain for meetings. This often takes the name of "leadership training" or "organizational behavior consulting." Such training is best accompanied by explicit acknowledgment of the U.S. cultural assumptions and values on which it is based.

Given all the cultural differences that are manifest in meetings of international student clubs, it is to be expected that such meetings will be unsatisfying for many of the people who attend them. If they are used as occasions for learning about cultural differences, they can be made more productive. If those in attendance are able to find ways to overcome the difficulties that their diverse cultural backgrounds cause them, some very important lessons will have been learned.

ENDNOTE

[1]Dean Barnlund, *Public and Private Self in Japan and The United States* (Tokyo: Simul Press, 1975).

III

Cross-Cultural Adaptation

Change, in and of itself, is stressful for all living things.[1] Transplanting plants or animals to new locations sometimes causes so much trauma that it kills the organism. Of course, the same is true for human beings. During the period of adaptation to a new environment, special care or support must be given to help the individual through the transition period.

Everyone has adapted to new social environments—the first few weeks at a new school, summer camp, or a new job. Some have had great difficulties while others encountered only a brief period of discomfort. Nevertheless, anyone who adapted to a new social environment went through a stressful period.

If the adaptation involves a new culture, we often refer to the stress as "culture shock." The experience might be on a domestic level, such as a male entering an all-female workplace or an individual moving from one city to another. It can also be international, such as moving overseas or working for an international organization.

Most people eventually adjust and adapt to the new culture. However, upon returning to their native culture they go through another type of stress referred to as "reverse culture shock" or reentry/transition stress. This stress is usually even more severe than culture shock.

CROSS-CULTURAL TRAINING

The primary reason for training people to work overseas is to help them become more effective and to minimize the severity and duration of cross-cultural adjustment stress. There are various studies which show that cross-cultural training increases effectiveness, helps with adjustment, and decreases the rate of those returning home before they complete their assignments.

This training may involve pre-departure *briefing* to give sojourners some basic information about the new culture before they leave home. The briefing may give them confidence that they will not make a major social mistake, thereby decreasing their anxiety. More importantly, the briefing may paint a realistic picture of people in the new culture, and thus decrease stereotypes. By humanizing people in the new culture, there may be less of a tendency to be prejudicial, especially during the stressful period of entry.

Pre-departure training might also help sojourners anticipate the stress of leaving a familiar culture to enter a new culture and the difficulty of interacting with people in the new culture. This more culture-general *orientation* might consider the process of adaptation and communication in a new social environment and help sojourners develop some cross-cultural communicative, interpretative and analytical skills. This type of training is likely to be more experiential because these skills require participatory, as well as didactic, learning.

There are many other types of training and education programs provided for sojourners—arrival orientation, evaluation and briefing during the sojourn, pre-departure orientation and reentry training. While these programs may have different purposes that require different approaches and methodologies, they often overlap and include similar information and training techniques. A briefing may be more didactic and emphasize information while an orientation may be more interactive and emphasize the development of skills.

The timing of each type of training may be important. For example, six months before departure many sojourners are interested in the dynamics of cross-cultural communication and adapting to a new culture. They have *interaction information needs*. On the other hand, just before departure, they are more concerned with basic *survival information needs*—how to use public transportation, the cost of living, visa requirements and so forth. If we are conducting an entry orientation program when people arrive in a new country, it is important to realize that there is a hierarchy of training needs and more basic survival needs must be considered before providing for social or interactive needs.

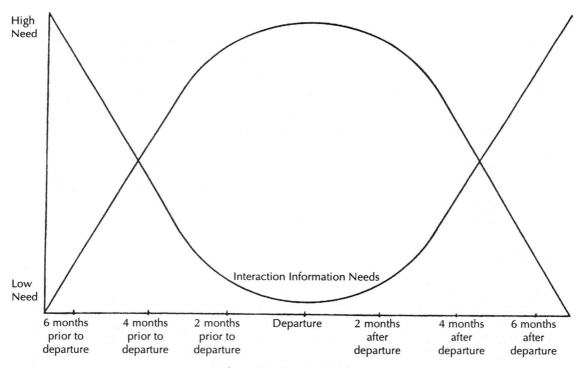

Information Needs of Trainees
(From Gudykunst and Hammer[2])

Impact on the Family

The stress of adapting to a new region of the U.S. or working for a new organization may be akin to culture shock overseas. Many of the reactions to these changes are comparable. However, because of the distance and greater cultural differences we can assume that it is likely to be much more stressful to relocate overseas for the employee and the family.

Some organizations provide cross-cultural training for the entire family, not simply the employee working abroad. Employees often want to go overseas to further their careers.[3] And, they usually do the same type of work overseas that they were trained to perform at home. The rest of the family are sometimes reluctant sojourners who find that their life has changed dramatically and they must do most things differently overseas.

While the employed family member enjoys a daily routine similar to that at home, for spouses and children everything may be different. The children have the continuity and routine of school but they still must develop new friendships at a strange school, sometimes in a different language. Spouses also leave their friends and activities at home and the continuity of their lives are disrupted. They may be forced to leave or restructure a job or career in order to follow their partner overseas.

The social role of wife and mother may not be the same as at home. Shopping and arranging social events may be very different than in one's native country, and managing the household may require intense and prolonged interaction with local nationals. All of this leads to greater stress or culture shock for the spouse than the employee. In fact, the most common reason for a premature return home is an unhappy spouse.[4]

Not only do husband and wife experience culture shock differently, but each child may experience this stress in ways that vary with age, gender, and personality. Pre-adolescent children may adjust very well overseas because they have not been fully enculturated in their home culture, while adolescent children may have a very difficult time because they must leave their peers to go abroad. Rather than being part of their parents' culture or the overseas culture, pre-adolescent children who grow up overseas appear to be members of a "third culture."

Because members of the family experience culture shock differently when overseas, each goes through reentry stress or reverse culture shock differently upon returning home. Ironically, those who adjust best overseas usually experience more severe stress for a longer period of time when they return home.

ARTICLES

The section begins with a series of articles on cross-cultural training. Authors discuss the many types of training and their effectiveness for preparing sojourners to work and live overseas.

Joann S. Lublin describes how "Companies Use Cross-Cultural Training to Help Their Employees Adjust Abroad." Nearly half of all major U.S. companies give some of their executives cross-cultural training before they leave to work overseas. They also provide training when they arrive overseas and even upon their return home. Most companies believe that this training improves effectiveness overseas and prevents failed overseas assignments. In his piece, "The Importance of Cross-Cultural Training in International Business," Mitchell R. Hammer provides evidence that cross-cultural training does improve effectiveness of Americans working outside the U.S.

There are many ways to measure "effectiveness" overseas. We can consider drop-out rates or premature returns, the severity and duration of stress that accompanies cross-cultural adaptation, or even the number of incidents that are caused by cross-cultural ignorance or insensitivity which jeopardize the organization's efforts overseas. Regardless of how effectiveness is measured, both Lublin and Hammer agree that it is increased with cross-cultural training.

We then consider the process of cross-cultural adaptation overseas and readaptation to our home culture. There is a cycle of adjustment stress that is ongoing. It begins when we prepare to leave our culture, intensifies when we are overseas and occurs again when we return home. Should we leave home and adapt to another culture, the cycle begins again.

The stress of adapting to a new culture is popularly known as "culture shock." Kalvero Oberg was one of the first persons to use the term "culture shock" to describe cross-cultural adaptation stress. Since the 1950s, when he first described the phenomenon, there have been a number of other studies which support Oberg's original explanation of the causes and dynamics of cross-cultural adaptation stress.

My chapter, "Understanding and Coping With Cross-Cultural Adjustment Stress," summarizes many of these studies and considers their implications for cross-cultural training. I also suggest that Oberg may have inadvertently misled us by describing culture shock as an "ailment" of some sort, thereby implying a medical, disease, or pathological model for this phenomenon. Culture shock is not an illness with physiological causes or remedies. Rather it primarily has psychological causes and manifests itself in various forms of reactions to stress.

One of the common symptoms or manifestations of culture shock is a sense of being out-of-control. We cannot control our feelings or the situations in which we find ourselves. Often we feel childish or incompetent and our self-esteem is lowered.

During the initial phase of culture shock, most people simply want to leave this painful social situation. However, if they cannot leave, they become trapped in a painful situation that is usually accompanied by irrational aggression or anger. This anger is to be expected, especially when we feel helpless and our normal ways of behaving and communicating are no longer rewarded or reinforced.

Research psychologist Nathan Azrin conducted a famous experiment with rats that demonstrated the first two phases of culture shock.[5] He placed a rat in a cage with an electric grid on the bottom. When the electricity was turned on, the rat ran out of the cage—*flight* or avoidance behavior. When we experience the psychological pain of culture shock, one of the first reactions is to flee or escape the painful situation or those who cause us pain.

Azrin then placed two rats in the cage, closed its doors, and turned on the electricity to produce pain. The rats tried to escape but could not. Within minutes they began to attack each other. Azrin hypothesized that when we are trapped in a painful situation where there is no escape, the second reaction sets in—*fight* behavior or irrational aggression. Most sojourners cannot easily return home. Like Azrin's rats, they are trapped in a painful situation and consequently become angry.

While culture shock may be painful and frustrating, it also offers enormous opportunities for personal growth. Many researchers have discovered that those who go through culture shock tend to come out of it with a greater sense of self-esteem, self-confidence, and self-awareness.

"The Shattered Language of Schizophrenia" by Brendan A. Maher, and "When Schizophrenia Helps" by Julian Silverman, describe how an acute schizophrenic episode can be a form of "positive disintegration." Also, culture shock may be a form of acute or reactive schizophrenia. It allows us to transcend our own culture and try new ways of solving problems, perceiving reality and behaving. Somewhat like any identity crisis, we must give up an inadequate identity or expand it so that a more mature and flexible one can emerge.

This death-rebirth cycle actually becomes a growth cycle. However, no one grows without experiencing some pain. As William H. Blanchard points out, "Ecstasy Without Agony Is Baloney." From this perspective, culture shock is a positive phenomenon. The objective is not to avoid experiencing culture shock, but rather to make it an even more positive and rewarding experience.

Reverse culture shock occurs when sojourners return to their home or native culture. But, Richard W. Brislin and H. Van Buren, IV, ask, "Can They Go Home Again?" This article examines the issue of reentry/transition stress. Reentry stress or reverse culture shock has not been as fully researched as culture shock. However, most preliminary data suggest that it is more severe and lasts longer than culture shock, and those who adjust best overseas often have the greatest difficulty returning home. My article, "The Process of Reentry," briefly describes this phenomenon.

This section concludes with articles exploring the phenomenon of children raised outside their parents' culture and persons who have adapted to numerous cultures. The numbers of multicultural people are dramatically increasing today with the increased interaction of people from around the world. These "global citizens" have unique cultures and identities which allow them to become bridges between different cultures. But, they also have some personal psychological and interpersonal difficulties which monocultural people do not experience.

Nina Killham explores cross-cultural adaptation in her article "World-Wise Kids," with a special emphasis on children who spent their formative years overseas. These so-called "third-culture kids" (TCKs) or "global nomads" have grown up in cultures different than their parents and yet return to their parents' culture. Consequently, they have very special gifts and difficulties which differentiate them from monocultural children.

The most recent research on TCKs is presented in Kathleen Jordan's article, "Third Culture Persons." While the overseas experience contributes to a sense of loneliness for these children, it can also cause the family to become even closer. TCKs often say that their best friends are their parents, and they tend to feel closer to their teachers than they would in their home culture.

Immigrant children and children raised in an urban society whose parents grew up in a rural community must have experiences similar to those of TCKs. Perhaps the gang activity of many immigrant children is their attempt to form a third-culture community similar to groups such as "global nomads" created by third-culture students on American university campuses. Even the African-American child whose parents come from a predominantly black community and who is raised in a white suburban community must share many of the frustrations, identity questions, and struggles that we find to be common for TCKs.

The multicultural individual is a new kind of person who is both a part of, and apart from, numerous cultures. This person may have grown up in various cultures. Peter S. Adler's "Beyond Cultural Identity: Reflections on Cultural and Multicultural Man" is a provocative and thoughtful discussion of the mixed blessing which multiculturalism offers.

If we never leave our culture or interact with those who are culturally different, we tend to be unaware of our own culture. We take it for granted. But, those who adapt to numerous cultures are constantly in search of their personal and cultural identity. The existential fluidity of the multicultural person provides enormous personal freedom but also creates psychological stresses that are relatively unknown to those who remain in a single culture throughout their lives.

As our societies become more diverse and as we increasingly interact with people from around the globe, the stress of adaptation will be a part of most people's lives. It is a natural, normal consequence of interacting with people who are different. In fact, one could argue that if we are living or working with those who are culturally different than ourselves and we do not experience this stress, we are probably doing something wrong. Only those who do not leave their own culture or interact with people who are culturally different do not experience cross-cultural adaptation stress.

ENDNOTES

[1]Hans Selye, "Overview of Stress," in *Readings in Experimental Psychology Today,* ed. Norman T. Adler (Del Mar, CA: CRM Books, 1970), 157–159.

[2]From William B. Gudykunst and Mitchell R. Hammer, "Basic Training Design: Approaches to Intercultural Training," in the *Handbook of Intercultural Training,* vol. 1, eds. Dan Landis and Richard W. Brislin (New York: Pergamon Press, 1983), 145.

[3]Less than 10 percent of the current North American expatriate managers are female. Thus, the employee is usually male while the spouse tends to be female. This is changing as more females develop international careers. Nancy Adler, *International Dimensions of Organizational Behavior:* 3d ed. (Cincinnati: South-Western College Publishing, 1997), 308.

Because of the rigidity of ascribed gender roles in high-context or traditionally associative cultures, we might expect that American female managers would be impeded in their effectiveness in these cultures. However, Adler has found that expatriate female managers tend to be more effective than males when sent to many of these cultures.

There are various explanations for this effectiveness. Local men tend to view the manager as a North American manager first and a female second. Because females are more carefully selected, they are usually more highly qualified to work overseas. Most females speak at least two languages. Lastly, many of the cultural characteristics of high-context cultures are also those attributed to women by some researchers. Thus, North American women may be more comfortable with traditional styles of interaction and doing business than North American men. See Nancy Adler and D. Izraeli, eds., *Women in Management Worldwide,* (New York: M. E. Sharpe, Inc., 1988).

[4]Adler, *International Dimensions,* 263.

[5]Nathan Azrin, "Pain and Aggression," in *Readings in Experimental Psychology Today,* ed. Norman T. Adler (Del Mar, CA: CRM Books, 1970), 103–107.

21

Companies Use Cross-Cultural Training to Help Their Employees Adjust Abroad

Joann S. Lublin

Dale Pilger, General Motors Corp.'s new managing director for Kenya, wonders if he can keep his Kenyan employees from interrupting his paper work by raising his index finger.

"The finger itself will offend," warns Noah Midamba, a Kenyan. He urges that Mr. Pilger instead greet a worker with an effusive welcome, offer a chair and request that he wait. It can be even trickier to fire a Kenyan, Mr. Midamba says. The government asked one German auto executive to leave Kenya after he dismissed a man—whose brother was the East African country's vice president.

Mr. Pilger, his adventurous wife and their two teen-agers, miserable about moving, have come to this Rocky Mountain college town for three days of cross-cultural training. The Cortland, Ohio, family learns to cope with being strangers in a strange land as consultants Moran, Stahl & Boyer International give them a crash immersion in African political history, business practices, social customs and nonverbal gestures. The training enables managers to grasp cultural differences and handle culture-shock symptoms such as self-pity.

Cross-cultural training is on the rise everywhere because more global-minded corpo-

rations moving fast-track executives overseas want to curb the cost of failed expatriate stints. "Probably between $2 billion and $2.5 billion a year is lost from failed assignments," says J. Stewart Black, an associate professor of business administration at Dartmouth's Tuck School. Nearly half of major U.S. companies now give executives cross-cultural training before foreign transfers, compared with about 10% a decade ago, consultants estimate.

The number of cultural-training providers also is growing. Berlitz International Inc. will set up a cross-cultural division this year, officials say, because a recent survey of 200 corporate clients found they needed cultural orientation more than its foreign-language training.

American businesses "are dumb if they don't use cross-cultural training," says Richard B. Jackson, personnel vice president of Reynolds Metals Co.'s overseas arm. The big aluminum maker's high rate of expatriate burn-out fell "to almost zero," Mr. Jackson notes, after the company began using cross-cultural training in the late 1970s. Other concerns train U.S.-based executives as well because their global duties often take them abroad.

GROWING CRITICISM

But as cross-cultural training gains popularity, it attracts growing criticism. A lot of the training is garbage, argues Robert Bontempo, assistant professor of international business at Columbia University. Even customized family training offered by companies like Prudential Insurance Co. of America's Moran Stahl— which typically costs $6,000 for three days— hasn't been scientifically tested. "They charge a huge amount of money, and there's no evidence that these firms do any good" in lowering foreign-transfer flops, Prof. Bontempo contends.

"You don't need research" to prove that cross-cultural training works because so much money has been wasted on failed overseas assignments, counters Gary Wederspahn, director of design and development at Moran Stahl.

General Motors agrees. Despite massive cost cutting lately, the auto giant still spends

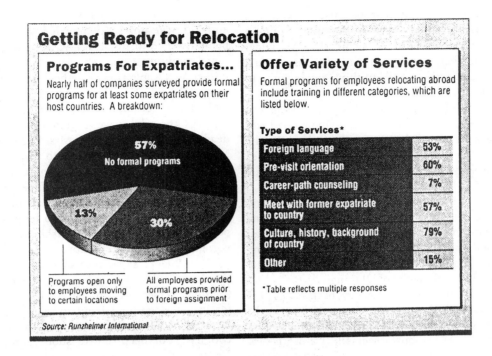

Getting Ready for Relocation

Programs For Expatriates...

Nearly half of companies surveyed provide formal programs for at least some expatriates on their host countries. A breakdown:

57% No formal programs

13%

30%

Programs open only to employees moving to certain locations

All employees provided formal programs prior to foreign assignment

Offer Variety of Services

Formal programs for employees relocating abroad include training in different categories, which are listed below.

Type of Services*

Type of Services*	
Foreign language	53%
Pre-visit orientation	60%
Career-path counseling	7%
Meet with former expatriate to country	57%
Culture, history, background of country	79%
Other	15%

*Table reflects multiple responses

Source: Runzheimer International

---

nearly $500,000 a year on cross-cultural training for about 150 Americans and their families headed abroad. "We think this substantially contributes to the low [premature] return rate" of less than 1% among GM expatriates, says Richard Rachner, GM general director of international personnel. That compares with a 25% rate at concerns that don't properly select and coach expatriates, he adds.

The Pilgers' experience reveals the benefits and drawbacks of such training. Mr. Pilger, a 38-year-old engineer employed by GM for 20 years, sought an overseas post but never lived abroad before. He finds the sessions "worthwhile" in readying him to run a vehicle-assembly plant that is 51% owned by Kenya's government. But he finds the training "horribly empty . . . in helping us prepare for the personal side of the move."

SCANT KNOWLEDGE

Dale and Nancy Pilger have just spent a week in Nairobi. But the executive's scant knowledge of Africa becomes clear when trainer Jackson Wolfe, a former Peace Corps official, mentions Nigeria. "Is that where Idi Amin was from?" Mr. Pilger asks. The dictator ruled

Uganda. With a sheepish smile, Mr. Pilger admits: "We don't know a lot about the world."

The couple's instructors don't always know everything about preparing expatriates for Kenyan culture, either. Mr. Midamba, an adjunct international-relations professor at Kent State University and son of a Kenyan political leader, concedes that he neglected to caution Mr. Pilger's predecessor against holding business dinners at Nairobi restaurants.

As a result, the American manager "got his key people to the restaurant and expected their wives to be there," Mr. Midama recalls. But "the wives didn't show up." Married women in Kenya view restaurants "as places where you find prostitutes and loose morals," notes Mungai Kimani, another Kenyan trainer.

The blunder partly explains why Mr. Midama goes to great lengths to teach the Pilgers the art of entertaining at home. Among his tips: Don't be surprised if guests arrive an hour early, an hour late or announce their departure four times.

The Moran Stahl program also zeros in on the family's adjustment (though not to Mr. Pilger's satisfaction). A family's poor adjustment causes more foreign-transfer failures than a manager's work performance. That is the

Pilgers' greatest fear because 14-year-old Christy and 16-year-old Eric bitterly oppose the move. The lanky, boyish-looking Mr. Pilger remembers Eric's tearful reaction as: "'You'll have to arrest me if you think you're going to take me to Africa.'"

While distressed by his children's hostility, Mr. Pilger still believes living abroad will be a great growth experience for them. But he says he promised Eric that if "he's miserable" in Kenya, he can return to Ohio for his last year of high school next year.

To ease their adjustment, Christy and Eric receive separate training from their parents. The teens' activities include sampling Indian food (popular in Kenya) as well as learning how to ride Nairobi public buses, speak a little Swahili and juggle, of all things.

By the training's last day, both youngsters grudgingly accept being uprooted from friends, her swim team and his brand-new car. Going to Kenya "no longer seems like a death sentence," Christy says. Eric mumbles that he may volunteer at a wild-game reserve.

But their usually upbeat mother has become increasingly upset as she hears more about a country troubled by drought, poverty and political unrest—where foreigners live behind walled fortresses. Now, at an international parenting session, she clashes with youth trainer Amy Kaplan over whether her offspring can safely ride Nairobi's public buses, even with Mrs. Pilger initially accompanying them.

"All the advice we've gotten is that it's deadly" to ride buses there, Mrs. Pilger frets. Ms. Kaplan retorts: "It's going to be hard" to let teen-agers do their own thing in Kenya, but then they'll be less likely to rebel. The remark fails to quell Mrs. Pilger's fears that she can't handle life abroad. "I'm going to let a lot of people down if I blow this," she adds, her voice quavering with emotion.

The Pilger's experience suggests that U.S. managers and their families may need extra training overseas. At Procter & Gamble Co., for instance, cultural familiarization doesn't even begin until expatriates reach a foreign country. "For deep-rooted, subtle concepts, it's more effective" to train people that way, says Dartmouth's Prof. Black. "But it's more effective to do it before" expatriates leave home "than not at all."

22

The Importance of Cross-Cultural Training in International Business

Mitchell R. Hammer

Two of the most frequently asked questions by both potential users of intercultural expertise as well as new members to the profession are: (1) is there really a need for cross-cultural training? and (2) what is the value of cross-cultural training? I thought I would address these questions by focusing on one particular context in which cross-cultural training is practiced: the arena of multinational business. While I am limiting my own comments to the international business situation, an equally important argument can be made for the need and value of multicultural expertise in the many other arenas in which we practice our profession (e.g. education, counseling, immigrant, refugee resettlement, international student advising).

THE NEED FOR CROSS-CULTURAL TRAINING

The success of international business depends on many factors, ranging from capitalization strategies to attitudes of host country nationals toward the "foreigner" operations. One factor, however, which has received little attention concerns the cross-cultural training

Reprinted from *SietarCommuniqué*, 21, no. 2 (February/March 1991): 5–6. Reprinted with permission from the author.

of organizations' human resources. It is this area of human resource management that can have a strong positive impact on the long-term success of the international firm. Yet, effective cross-cultural training is not easily developed nor implemented because it is fraught with a variety of "intercultural" interaction difficulties.

The results from research conducted predominately on U.S. international firms may be instructive. Cross-cultural difficulties often can lead not only to poor overseas job performance, but ultimately to premature return back home. Henry, for instance, reported that 30% of U.S. multinational corporations (MNC's) expatriate placements were unsuccessful due to cross-cultural adjustment problems.[1] These findings have been confirmed in more recent studies by Lanier and Tung.[2] In more graphic terms, Feldman describes the experience of two U.S. MNC's then under contract to Iran. These companies had hundreds of employees (a total of 2500 expatriates, including members of families). Each company suffered, respectively, a 50% and 85% premature return rate among their U.S. hired employees and families, the cost of which was estimated at $55,000.00 per returned family.[3]

Schaaf estimates that the average cost of an overseas assignment ranges from $75,000.00 to $150,000.00[4] while Harris and Moran suggest a range of $50,000.00 to $200,000.00.[5] Tucker and Wight conclude that if proper assessment and training for international assignments result in preventing just one family's premature return, the cost savings will pay for assessment and training of an additional 35 managers and their families.[6]

Further, the results from research suggest that the predominant reason for such premature return rates and difficulties encountered in effectively managing and living in a foreign culture is not due to a low level of technical competence of the managers (in fact, it is typically quite high), but to the dynamics of the intercultural experience—the fundamental concern of cross-cultural training activities (e.g., Dinges; Kealey and Ruben; Brislin; and Tung).[7]

Clearly, the costs of cross-cultural incompetence are severe and one of the critical and predominate reasons for failure in this area is due to cultural differences in the communication and interaction patterns that take place between the expatriate manager and host nationals. Certainly there is a need for cross-cultural training in multinational operations.

THE VALUE OF CROSS-CULTURAL TRAINING

How effective, though, is cross-cultural training for the organization? In one recent example, a comprehensive training program lasting for approximately one year was conducted for American and Japanese managers of an American-owned subsidiary in Japan. By the company's own estimates, the training was responsible for a substantial dollar savings and resulted in the start-up of a new plant in Japan one year earlier than projected. These positive outcomes occurred, according to the company, as a direct result of the improved transfer of technology and management competence of the American and Japanese managers which in turn was due to the effectiveness of the cross-cultural training program conducted for the managers.[8]

An exhaustive review of cross-cultural training effectiveness studies was recently completed by Black and Mendenhall. Their findings clearly indicate that cross-cultural training has great impact on the overall success of international firm operations. They examined the findings of *29 empirical studies of cross-cultural training effects*. Their summary suggests a clear, positive "relationship between cross-cultural training and the following dependent variables: cross-cultural skill development, cross-cultural adjustment, and performance in a cross-cultural setting."[9] In short, cross-cultural training can develop cross-cultural skills which have been shown to impact on subsequent success in an overseas assignment; improve expatriates' psychological comfort and satisfaction with living and working in a foreign culture; and improve task

accomplishment in the cross-cultural environment. Clearly, there is a strong positive value of cross-cultural training for the international firm.

ENDNOTES

[1] E. R. Henry, "What Business Can Learn from Peace Corps Selection and Training." *Personnel, 42,* 1965: 17–25.

[2] A. R. Lanier, "Selecting and Preparing Personnel for Overseas Transfers." *Personnel Journal, 58* (3), 1979: 160–163; R. L. Tung, "Selection and Training Procedures of U.S., European and Japanese Multinationals." *California Management Review, 25* (1), 1982: 57–71.

[3] M. J. Feldman, "Training for Cross-Cultural International Interaction in the Federal Government." *Training and Development Journal, 30* (11), 1976: 19–23.

[4] D. Schaaf, "The Growing Need for Cross Cultural and Bilingual Training." *Training/HRD,* January 1981: 85–86.

[5] P. Harris and R. T. Moran, *Managing Cultural Differences* (Houston, TX: Gulf Publishing, 1987).

[6] M. F. Tucker and A. Wight, "A 'Culture Gap' in International Personnel Programs." *The Bridge,* Winter 1981: 11–13.

[7] D. J. Kealey and B. D. Ruben, "Cross-Cultural Personnel Selection Criteria, Issues, and Methods," in D. Landis and R. W. Brislin, eds., *Handbook of Intercultural Training, Volume 1: Issues in Theory and Design* (New York: Pergamon, 1983): 155–175; R. Brislin, *Cross-Cultural Encounters: Face-to-Face Interaction* (New York: Pergamon, 1981); N. Dinges, "Intercultural Competence," in D. Landis and R. W. Brislin, *Handbook:* 176–202.

[8] M. R. Hammer and C. Clarke, "Predictors of Japanese and American Managers' Job Success, Personal Adjustment, and Intercultural Interaction Effectiveness," unpublished manuscript, 1990.

[9] J. S. Black and M. Mendenhall, "Cross-Cultural Training and Effectiveness: A Review and a Theoretical Framework for Future Research." *The Academy of Management Review, 15* (1), 1990.

23

Culture Shock and the Problem of Adjustment in New Cultural Environments

Kalvero Oberg

Culture shock might be called an occupational disease of people who have been suddenly transplanted abroad. Like most ailments, it has its own symptoms and cure.

Culture shock is precipitated by the anxiety that results from losing all our familiar signs and symbols of social intercourse. Those signs or cues include the thousand and one ways in which we orient ourselves to the situation of daily life: when to shake hands and what to say when we meet people, when and how to give tips, how to make purchases, when to accept and when to refuse invitations, when to take statements seriously and when not. These cues, which may be words, gestures, facial expressions, customs, or norms, are acquired by all of us in the course of growing up and are as much a part of our culture as the language we speak or the beliefs we accept. All of us depend for our peace of mind and our efficiency on hundreds of these cues, most of which we do not carry on the level of conscious awareness.

Now when an individual enters a strange culture, all or most of these familiar cues are removed. He or she is like a fish out of water.

Reprinted from *Practical Anthropology* 7 (1960): 177–182, Society for Applied Anthropology.

No matter how broad-minded or full of goodwill you may be, a series of props have been knocked from under you, followed by a feeling of frustration and anxiety. People react to the frustration in much the same way. First they reject the environment which causes the discomfort. "The ways of the host country are bad because they make us feel bad." When foreigners in a strange land get together to grouse about the host country and its people, you can be sure they are suffering from culture shock. Another phase of culture shock is regression. The home environment suddenly assumes a tremendous importance. To the foreigner everything becomes irrationally glorified. All the difficulties and problems are forgotten and only the good things back home are remembered. It usually takes a trip home to bring one back to reality.

Some of the symptoms of culture shock are excessive washing of the hands, excessive concern over drinking water, food dishes, and bedding; fear of physical contact with attendants; the absent-minded stare; a feeling of helplessness and a desire for dependence on long-term residents of one's own nationality; fits of anger over minor frustrations; great concern over minor pains and eruptions of the skin; and finally, that terrible longing to be back home.

Individuals differ greatly in the degree in which culture shock affects them. Although not common, there are individuals who cannot live in foreign countries. However, those who have seen people go through culture shock and on to a satisfactory adjustment can discern steps in the process. During the first few weeks most individuals are fascinated by the new. They stay in hotels and associate with nationals who speak their language and are polite and gracious to foreigners. This honeymoon stage may last from a few days or weeks to six months, depending on circumstances. If one is very important, he or she will be shown the show places, will be pampered and petted, and in a press interview will speak glowingly about goodwill and international friendship.

But this mentality does not normally last if the foreign visitor remains abroad and has seriously to cope with real conditions of life. It is then that the second stage begins, characterized by a hostile and aggressive attitude toward the host country. This hostility evidently grows out of the genuine difficulty which the visitor experiences in the process of adjustment. There are house troubles, transportation troubles, shopping troubles, and the fact that people in the host country are largely indifferent to all these troubles. They help, but they don't understand your great concern over these difficulties. Therefore, they must be insensitive and unsympathetic to you and your worries. The result, "I just don't like them." You become aggressive, you band together with your fellow countrymen and criticize the host country, its ways, and its people. But this criticism is not an objective appraisal. Instead of trying to account for the conditions and the historical circumstances which have created them, you talk as if the difficulties you experience are more or less created by the people of the host country for your special discomfort.

You take refuge in the colony of your countrymen which often becomes the fountainhead of emotionally charged labels known as stereotypes. This is a peculiar kind of offensive shorthand which caricatures the host country and its people in a negative manner. The "dollar grasping American" and the "indolent Latin Americans" are samples of mild forms of stereotypes. The second stage of culture shock is in a sense a crisis in the disease. If you come out of it, you stay; if not, you leave before you reach the stage of a nervous breakdown.

If the visitor succeeds in getting some knowledge of the language and begins to get around by himself, he is beginning to open the way into the new cultural environment. The visitor still has difficulties but he takes a "this is my problem and I have to bear it" attitude. Usually in this stage the visitor takes a superior attitude to people of the host country. His sense of humor begins to exert itself. Instead of criticizing, he jokes about the people and even cracks jokes about is or her own difficulties. He or she his now on the way to recovery.

In the fourth stage, your adjustment is about as complete as it can be. The visitor now accepts the customs of the country as just another way of living. You operate within the new surroundings without a feeling of anxiety, although there are moments of social strain. Only with a complete grasp of all the cues of social intercourse will this strain disappear. For a long time the individual will understand what the national is saying, but he is not always sure what the national means. With a complete adjustment you not only accept the food, drinks, habits, and customs, but actually begin to enjoy them. When you go home on leave, you may even take things back with you; and if you leave for good, you generally miss the country and the people to whom you became accustomed.

24

Understanding and Coping with Cross-Cultural Adjustment Stress

Gary R. Weaver

WHAT IS "CULTURE SHOCK"?

The phrase "culture shock," coined by Cora DuBois in 1951, was first used in the cross-cultural literature by anthropologist Kalvero Oberg to describe problems of acculturation and adjustment among Americans who were working in a health project in Brazil. He viewed it as "an occupational disease of people who have suddenly been transported abroad [which] is precipitated by the anxiety that results from losing all our familiar signs and symbols of social intercourse."[1] Oberg viewed culture shock as a specific ailment with its own symptoms and cures. However, in the past thirty years the phrase has become a basic part of the international sojourner's jargon and is now commonly used to describe almost any physical or emotional discomfort experienced by those adjusting to a new environment. "Homesickness," "adjustment difficulties" "uprooting"[2] and numerous other terms are often used to describe the same phenomenon as culture shock. While that term may be a bit too strong, the other labels fail to focus on cultural factors and are overly euphemistic. Most cross-cultural trainers use the term culture shock because of historical tradition and the attention-getting value of the words.

Reprinted from *Education for the Intercultural Experience,* ed. R. Michael Paige (Yarmouth, Maine: Intercultural Press, Inc., 1993), 137–167.

Symptoms may range from mild emotional disorders and stress-related physiological ailments to psychosis. The types and intensity of reactions to a new cultural environment depend upon the nature and duration of the stressful situation and, more importantly, the psychological makeup of an individual. Some people quickly develop useful coping strategies which allow them to adjust easily while, at the other extreme, some resort to the use of progressively more inappropriate and maladaptive neurotic defense mechanisms which may eventually develop into such severe psychological disorders as psychosis, alcoholism, and even suicide.

Most studies suggest that such severe reactions account for less than 10 percent of all sojourners, and it may well be that they were predisposed to an inability to cope with sudden traumatic stress before they traveled overseas. The vast majority of sojourners experience moderate reactions and successfully overcome culture shock. In fact, some may actually come through culture shock more psychologically sound than before they left their own culture.

In the past decade severe culture shock has also been measured in terms of a so-called "dropout rate." It has been informally estimated, for example, that the Peace Corps has a dropout rate of between 30 and 40 percent. These are volunteers who return home before completing their term of service overseas. The implication is that these volunteers terminated their stays because of the stress of cross cultural adjustment or an inability to adapt overseas. Of course, there may be many other factors to account for such termination including family difficulties, health problems unrelated to stress, or differences with management overseas.

The severity of culture shock is generally much greater when the adjustment involves a completely different culture, because there is a greater loss of Oberg's "familiar signs and symbols of social intercourse" in an entirely new environment. On the other hand, anticipation of a stressful event also affects the severity of the reaction. It seems that if we do not anticipate a stressful event we are much less capable of coping with it. This would explain why we still experience culture shock when entering a slightly different cultural environment or when returning home to our native culture. Most Americans do not anticipate stress when adapting to London and few anticipate the stress of reentering their home culture.

Ultimately the psychological makeup of the individual may be the most important factor. Some people can tolerate a great deal of stress caused by change, ambiguity, and unpredictability while others demand an unchanging, unambiguous, predictable environment to feel psychologically secure. Psychological traits, rather than cross-cultural adjustment skills or cultural awareness, may be of primary importance in determining the success with which one adapts to another culture.[3]

While Oberg considered culture shock to be a separate "ailment," thereby suggesting a medical disease model to explain the phenomenon, some have come to consider it a normal and natural growth or transition process as we adapt to another culture.[4] As with growth or adaptation there is disorientation, ambiguity, and pain, but we often come through this state more stable and centered than ever before. The object is not to eliminate or avoid culture shock but rather to make it a less stressful and more positive experience. Culture shock is most probably the result of a normal process of adaptation and may be no more harmful than the psychological reactions we experience when adapting to such new environmental situations as entering college or moving to another city in our own culture. Those who claim they have never experienced any form of culture shock overseas are either fairly unaware of their own feelings or have never really cross-culturally adjusted. Tourists and those who remain enmeshed within conational groups generally do not experience culture shock.

WHY DOES CULTURE SHOCK OCCUR?

In the literature on culture shock there are three basic causal explanations: (1) the loss of familiar cues, (2) the breakdown of interpersonal communication, and (3) an identity crisis. All three disorienting states occur in adjustment to any new social environment. However, in a cross-cultural situation they are greatly exaggerated and exacerbated by cultural differences. While each of these explanations takes a slightly different approach, they are not mutually exclusive nor is any single one adequate to fully understand the phenomenon. Indeed, they overlap and complement each other.

Loss of Cues or Reinforcers

This explanation is the most behavioral in that it primarily focuses on that which is tangible and observable. Everyone is surrounded by thousands of physical and social cues which have been present since childhood and therefore are taken for granted until they are absent. Behavioral or social cues, which Oberg refers to as signs and signals, provide order in interpersonal relations. Physical cues include objects which we have become accustomed to in our home culture which are changed or missing in a new culture. These familiar cues make us feel comfortable and make life predictable. When they are absent we begin to feel like a fish out of water.

Cues are signposts which guide us through our daily activities in an acceptable fashion which is consistent with the total social environment. They may be words, gestures, facial expressions, postures, or customs which help us make sense out of the social world that surrounds us. They tell us when and how to give gifts or tips, when to be serious or to be humorous, how to speak to leaders and subordinates, who has status, what to say when we meet people, when and how to shake hands, how to eat, and so on. They make us feel comfortable because they seem so automatic and natural.

Cues serve as reinforcers of behavior because they signal if things are being done inappropriately. In a new social environment, behavior is no longer clearly right or wrong, but instead becomes very ambiguous. This ambiguity is especially painful for many Euro-Americans because they are accustomed to clear verbal messages and feedback, explicit rules of behavior, and the ability to predict the behavior of others. In many other cultures, people may say yes when they mean maybe because they seek to please. Or they may say maybe when they mean no because they don't want to give negative feedback to another person.

The low-context, loosely integrated, and heterogeneous nature of Euro-American societies is built upon clear, explicit, overt rules of behavior which ensure predictability.[5] In high-context, non-Western cultures, rules of behavior are often vague, implicit, and tacitly learned simply by growing up in that culture. They are buried or embedded deeply within the context of the culture. The society is usually more tightly integrated and homogeneous. Thus, one can infer from his or her own behavior what is appropriate for everyone else. For Euro-Americans, on the other hand, there are fewer rules of behavior and they are less easily identified. Consequently, there is less predictability. When familiar cues or reinforcers are no longer elicited by their behavior, they experience pain and frustration. In fact, the loss of a reinforcer or cue is actually a form of punishment in terms of their psychological reactions.[6] Thousands of times Euro-Americans deposit coins into a soft drink machine which results in the drop of a can or cup. If one day no can or cup drops down after depositing their money, they may react to this lack of an expected reinforcer by irrationally kicking the machine. It usually does not cause the can or cup to drop down nor does the machine return the money. But they may feel better because they have vented their anger over the loss of the reinforcer.

In a new culture, our messages of "good morning," "thank you," "how are you," no longer bring the response we are accustomed to in our native culture. It is not even clear when one should smile or laugh. These simple behaviors that we have used to interact with others no longer elicit the reinforcers we have received throughout our lives. And the reaction is often frustration and anger which is irrationally displaced onto others whom we perceive to be lower in our social hierarchy, such as taxi drivers, waiters, porters, and secretaries.

Cues also involve how we use time and space.[7] They include the very rhythm or synchrony of speech and movement which we acquire during the first few weeks of life and the social distance we maintain between ourselves and others.[8] How late we can arrive without making an apology; the rhythm of conversation including pauses between words and phrases; and the appropriate pace, amount, and kind of body movement are learned implicitly or tacitly from the social or cultural environment during the first few years of life.

When we enter another culture we feel out of sync and, yet, we often do not realize the cause of our awkwardness because we learned our own kinesic, proxemic, and chronemic cues simply by growing up in our own culture. This silent language, or nonverbal communication, is especially important for the communication of feelings and yet is almost totally beyond the conscious awareness of the average person.[9]

The very act of changing physical environments causes stress. It is true that we are adaptable, but within limits. Moreover, adaptation always produces some stress, whether it is to a better or a worse a condition. As both Alvin Toffler and Philip Slater point out, there is a direct correlation between the number of major changes experienced in a given period and the likelihood of the person falling ill.[10] Selye's and Barna's research on stress as it relates to change clearly suggests that change of physical environments in and of itself produces much of the stress that may be attributed to culture shock.[11]

There probably is a form of "object loss" when we experience loss of cues and reinforcers, and one may actually go through various stages of acute grief.[12] Disorientation can lead to a form of "learned helplessness"[13] which often results in depression. While everyone going through culture shock feels disoriented, some people panic psychologically and become extremely self-destructive.

Fortunately, most of us adapt to new environments and, in the process, acquire new skills and ways of looking at the world. Through the process of adaptation we often gain insights into our own personality and the great impact our culture has had in shaping it. But this awareness and personal growth necessarily involves some pain.

The Breakdown of Communication

Identifying a breakdown of communication as a cause of culture shock emphasizes the process of interpersonal interaction and is much less behavioral than the other possible causes. In fact, it approaches humanistic psychology with its emphasis on the psychodynamics of human interaction. A basic assumption in this explanation is that a breakdown of communication, on both the conscious and unconscious levels, causes frustration and anxiety and is a source of alienation from others.

Proponents of this explanation may emphasize any part or link in a communication system. Some might concentrate on the inefficiency and misunderstandings brought about by different meanings given to messages. Others might carry this approach into the areas of transactional analysis or even existential psychology, stressing the inability to communicate on an "authentic level" with others as the source of stress.[14] These latter theorists dovetail into the third explanation of cause—an identity crisis—with their emphasis on self and human interaction.

From a cross-cultural or orientation-training standpoint, the communication-breakdown explanation allows for an understanding of the process of cross-cultural adjustment and provides a paradigm for identifying the various components of any cross-cultural interaction. One may begin with a simple cybernetics model of communication to illustrate how the breakdown of communication inevitably takes place as one interacts with people in a new culture. The simple model below may serve as an illustration.

Basic Cybernetics Model of Communication

SENDER—>ENCODER—>MEDIA—>DECODER—>RECEIVER

FEEDBACK

As this cybernetics model suggests, the breakdown of any part or link between parts in the system causes the entire system to break down, somewhat like a tube blowing on an old radio.

For example, focusing on the *sender* and *receiver*, it is clear that we send messages, not meanings. If the sender and receiver come from different cultures, the same messages may elicit completely different meanings in their respective minds.

At the *encoder* and *decoder* stages, the obvious source of breakdown involves different languages. However, nonverbal codes are probably even more significant in cross-cultural communication because these codes are learned implicitly and thus are generally unconscious. They are mostly culture-specific and are used primarily for communicating messages regarding feelings.[15] One can easily identify the breakdown of verbal messages, whereas the breakdown of nonverbal messages is less obvious but more significant in that we feel emotionally confused and cut off from others.

Feedback involves both verbal and nonverbal messages and certainly varies with each culture. In many non-Western cultures, feedback is circuitous and subtle, whereas Americans prefer direct and unambiguous feedback. Americans want a clear yes or no, not "it is the will of God," "it is difficult," or "maybe."

When communication breaks down or becomes ineffective, we experience pain. Passive-aggressive individuals are especially effective at cutting off communication with others to induce frustration and pain. Victims of this aggression often have no conscious awareness of why and how the passive-aggressive causes them so much distress. Because most humans communicate quite effectively before the age of three or four, we take the ability to communicate for granted and seldom are consciously aware that the source of much of our pain in human interaction is the breakdown of communication.

When any animal experiences pain, it reacts by fleeing the source of pain (escape or avoidance behavior), displacing aggression (fight behavior), or distorting, simplifying, and denying the complexity and reality of the painful situation. Note that, in human beings, all of these reactions when carried to extremes, are both unconscious and highly neurotic. People going through culture shock are not aware of what is causing them pain nor why they often behave in such irrational ways. They have a sense of hopelessness and helplessness. The situation is controlling them, and, unless they understand the process of communication breakdown, they fail to develop coping strategies, lose their sense of control, and cannot find alternative ways of behaving. Instead of acting, they end up reacting.

By considering culture shock as a result of the breakdown of communication, one can apply many psychological constructs to explain the behavior of those going through the stress of cross-cultural adjustment. These include learned helplessness, autistic hostility, psychosomatic reactions, displacement of aggression, projection, the conflict cycle, image theory, and attribution theory.

This explanation is especially useful for helping sojourners understand the underlying dynamics of culture shock. Furthermore, it suggests that culture shock is an inevitable but natural process of cross-cultural adjustment which can be overcome with conscious awareness of one's own reactions. While this explanation offers no specific answers for overcoming culture shock, it does help sojourners replace neurotic reactions with coping strategies.

AN IDENTITY CRISIS

This explanation of culture shock draws together behavioral, psychoanalytical, and existential approaches with an overlay of cognitive theory. This is by far the most complicated yet the most fascinating explanation of culture shock, because it implies that there is genuine psychological growth that occurs when one successfully overcomes culture shock.

The loss of cues or reinforcers is disorienting, but the disorientation frees people from habitual ways of doing and perceiving things and allows them to perceive and adopt new cues. It also brings to conscious awareness the grip that our culture has on our behavior and personality.

We might consider culture as analogous to a computer program, that is, our culture determines what information gets into our heads and how we use that information to solve problems. To this extent, culture is indeed synonymous with mind.[16] This culture "program" in turn determines our behavior. To understand someone's behavior (output) it is necessary to understand how the person experiences or perceives the world (input) and how that person has learned to organize and utilize that information (program).

Computer Analogy of Culture

INPUT ──────→ PROGRAM ──────→ OUTPUT
selective perception   thought pattern   behavior
information   values   actions and reactions

When we enter another culture, the program which has worked so well since childhood no longer is adequate. The system of selective perception and interpretation no longer wards off the bombardment of millions of new stimuli or cues, and it is no longer clear what one should pay attention to or what the stimuli mean.[17]

The ways in which we have been programmed by our culture to solve problems or to think no longer work effectively. The environment makes new demands upon us. Finally, we are overwhelmed by the bombardment of stimuli and demands and must temporarily experience the sense of confusion of not knowing what to pay attention to or how to solve problems. This period may be similar to the transitional stages we experience during other life crises such as adolescence. The ways in which we select out that which is relevant or abstract from our social and physical environment, that which is significant, are obsolete. We are overwhelmed and can no longer cope.

The transitional period is very associative or relational in that everything seems to flow together somewhat chaotically.[18] But this is how we begin to see new relationships and new ways of ordering our perceptual and intellectual world. We are gradually expanding our cultural program, image system, and subjective knowledge structure.

As with any other identity crisis, culture shock allows us to give up an inadequate perceptual and problem-solving system to allow another more expanded and adequate system to be born. It is somewhat of a death-rebirth cycle.

In her book *Passages*, Gail Sheehy suggests that we human beings are similar to hardy crustaceans. "The lobster grows by developing and shedding a series of protective shells. Each time it expands from within, the confining shell must be sloughed off. It is left exposed and vulnerable until, in time, a new covering grows to replace the old." As with the passages from one stage of human growth to the next, when we go through culture shock, "we must shed a protective structure and are left exposed and vulnerable—but also yeasty and embryonic again, capable of stretching in ways we hadn't known before."[19] Fundamentally the lobster is still the same except more mature. And when we come through culture shock, we are fundamentally still the same except that we may now see the world in different ways and have a host of new alternatives for solving problems and considering reality.

The breakdown of communication may be more of a breakthrough to new ways of interacting with others, and it might give us insight into our own need for human interaction on an authentic level. Ways of accomplishing tasks, solving problems, and thinking which may have worked effectively all our lives may be ineffective in a new culture. When we go through culture shock, we become aware of how our culture has shaped our thinking and perception, and we may become more conscious of our "hidden culture"[20] and, in turn, transcend it.

As with the psychoanalytic cathartic event and the existential crisis, there is pain and risk involved in the culture-shock experience.[21] Some do not want to be freed from the cultural prison they have been born into, and not all make it to the other side when they take an existential leap. A certain percentage of people will be unable to tolerate the stress of giving up an inadequate problem-solving system or an identity which gave them a sense of security and predictability for so long. Every soldier who goes into battle does not experience the kind of acute psychosis associated with shell shock. And everyone who goes through culture shock does not experience the reactive or acute psychosis associated with severe adjustment difficulties. A great deal depends upon the predisposition of the individual and his or her psychological makeup.

The overseas experience, like that of an encounter or sensitivity group, offers a new social milieu in which to examine one's behavior, perceptions, values, and thought patterns. An experience close to psychosis may be required to take one outside the collective pressures and assumptions of our culture. We may discover things about ourselves that allow for great personal growth. Yet it may be an ego-shattering experience. Great personal insight can occur for many, while others may find it very destructive.[22] Whether the experience will eventually become positive or negative, a source of personal growth or destruction, depends upon one's expectations, adaptability, tolerance for ambiguity and stress, and an understanding that there inevitably will be pain which can be handled and overcome.

The analogy between the overseas experience and the encounter group is even more apropos when we consider that both involve emotional and somewhat irrational situations. Moreover, both demand full participation and emotional involvement. Frustration is only heightened when one attempts to cope with the situation as an aloof, rational, objective observer. It is a total experience of mind and body, the intellectual and sensual, and the objective and subjective person.

It is not so much that the individual is a fish out of water as it is that he or she is a youngster being thrown into the water who must learn how to swim. People cannot intellectualize the experience nor simply observe others swimming. They must try to swim by moving their arms and legs in the water, by participating kinesthetically in the aquatic environment. This is not a simple theoretical or intellectual exercise. Eventually most will experience the ecstasy of being able to swim. Some, however, rush to the shore, never to set foot in the water again. Some even drown.

CULTURE SHOCK IS NOT A DISEASE

For over a hundred years psychologists have been trying to overcome the medical model of emotional disorders which originates with Sigmund Freud. The problem with the model is that it suggests that an emotional disorder is actually an illness or disease which you can catch like a cold or tuberculosis. It implies that it has a distinct set of symptoms which can be cured. This relieves the person and others in his or her life of any responsibility for the disorder, it ignores the reality that most disorders are directly related to complex interpersonal relationships, and it suggests that we may find a magic-bullet cure of some sort. Worst of all, it causes both the observer and the participant to focus on the pathological aspects of emotional disorder rather than the growth process and positive benefits.

The medical model also leads us to label emotional disorders and identify specific pathological symptoms. Once the label is applied to an individual, it is very difficult for that person to convince others that he or she is not schizophrenic, psychotic, or neurotic.[23] That is, people tend to perceive selectively that behavior which fits the label while ignoring behavior which contradicts the label. Even worse, the individual often adjusts his or her behavior to fit the label, thereby creating a self-fulfilling prophecy.

As noted earlier, Oberg described culture shock as an ailment with distinct symptoms and cures, thereby establishing a medical model to explain cross-cultural adjustment stress. Orientation trainers often uncritically accept this model and seek to give trainees a clear diagnosis, set of symptoms, prognosis, and cure. They may resort to using flip charts listing distinct symptoms ranging from diarrhea to insomnia. Sometimes they produce U- and W-curve charts to illustrate a clear pattern of progression or phases of the disease. Some even suggest a list of cures or specific ways of overcoming culture shock.

When someone in our own family has an emotional disorder, we really like to believe that it struck the person arbitrarily, like some mysterious germ. When we discuss the disorder with a therapist, most of us are not interested in hearing all the theoretical explanations of cause or responsibility. We would like a clear diagnosis, a label for the disease with a list of specific symptoms which can be cured by following concrete procedures. Ideally, we would like to hear that it is biochemically caused and thus can be biochemically cured. That is, give us a simple explanation of cause, a clear description of symptoms, and some prescription to cure the illness.

The medical, or illness, model of culture shock is counterproductive and misleading, yet is an unfortunate result of the desire of many sojourners to have a simple formula for dealing with it. Of course, when they get overseas they find they may not have all the symptoms, and stress may manifest itself in complex psychological disorders such as depression, confusion, irrational behavior and thoughts, and a sense of lacking control. These are all internal, not external, symptoms. The distress does not follow any particular pattern and the sojourners are not sure where they are on the so-called U- or W-curve of adjustment. The resultant confusion adds to their stress and gives them a lack of confidence in their predeparture training.

Most people going overseas are not really interested in understanding the causes of culture shock or the process of cross-cultural adjustment. They want specific information, not analysis and interpretation. They want cookbooks and a list of do's and don't's for dealing with the new culture and cross-cultural adjustment stress. And some cross-cultural trainers will sell them their favorite cookbook with catchy labels and simple, concrete examples of symptoms and cures.

New situations often come up that were not covered in the training, and their vague psychological malaise fits into none of the distinct categories on the trainers' charts. The sojourners mentally thumb through the index of their cookbook but to no avail. At this point, panic often sets in. It would have been much more useful to have a broad framework within which they could analyze and interpret their reactions. Knowing the causes of culture shock and the process of cross-cultural adjustment would have helped them understand that it is a normal reaction which does, in fact, end—sooner or later.

No cure will work for everyone because there are so many variables involved. What might work for one person in a specific environment may not work for others in different environments. Wives may react differently from husbands, and children differently from adults. Rather than traveling overseas with a false sense of confidence in cure-alls, it would have been much more helpful to develop coping strategies which allow each individual to find his or her own way of dealing with and overcoming the stress of cross-cultural adaptation.

The most common symptom of culture shock is a lack of control or helplessness. Unconscious reactions to the situation control us unless we understand what is going on. Thus, simply understanding the process of cross-cultural adjustment or adaptation is probably the best way of overcoming culture shock. Then we have a sense of control and can act instead of reacting.

Culture shock is primarily an unconscious phenomenon. Most people have no idea why they are behaving as they are or feeling as they do. By understanding the process of adaptation, one sees that it is a normal reaction to a new cultural or social environment which everyone goes through to some extent. Furthermore, it can be a very positive experience which allows for personal insight and growth.

COPING WITH CROSS-CULTURAL ADJUSTMENT STRESS

The various reactions to the stress of cross-cultural adjustment are much akin to what Sigmund Freud and his daughter Anna described as defense mechanisms—unconscious steps we take to protect our ego or self from a painful reality.[24] Most neurotics have a sense of hopelessness, helplessness, and lack of control. They are victims of a situation that they cannot realistically change, and they are controlled by their unconscious reactions.

Of course, many neurotics fully understand the cause and process of their neurosis but they are still highly neurotic. Understanding is the beginning step in overcoming a neurosis, but ultimately each individual must develop a sense of control over his or her reactions and must cope with a painful reality which cannot be changed.

A conscious understanding of the process of adaptation and the expectation that culture shock will occur eliminates a great deal of the pain caused by uncertainty and lack of predict-ability. It helps if we know that our reactions are part of the process of adjustment to the reality of another culture which we cannot change. However, this knowledge is not enough. There are conscious steps we can take which allow us to control our reactions and minimize the length and severity of the stress. These coping mechanisms or strategies[25] permit sojourners to *act* instead of simply *reacting* to the new culture, to face reality and decide what to do about it, and to find various alternative ways of dealing with the adjustment problems.

It is important to distinguish between *coping* and *defense* mechanisms. Defense mechanisms are unconscious reactions to a stressful or painful reality. The situation controls the individual by causing the reactions. These defenses help one avoid the painful reality through such unconscious processes as denial, distortion, withdrawal, and repression. They are normal and explicable, but ineffective, ways of dealing with the situation and the resultant stress.

Coping mechanisms are actions, not reactions, which one consciously takes to give one a sense of self-control and to respond effectively to a situation. They provide strategies, methods, or steps for dealing with the stressors and the stress, and they increase effectiveness. One cannot change another culture, and the goal of cross-cultural adaptation is not to avoid the source of stress (people in the host culture) but to increase interaction with the local people. Thus, one of the primary ways to minimize defensive reactions, to provide greater self-control, and to maximize effective interaction in another culture is to develop coping strategies.

While each person must develop his or her own ways of coping, the following brief list of broad strategies may be applied by most sojourners. They are a logical extension of the discussion of the process of cross-cultural adjustment.

UNDERSTAND THE PROCESS OF ADJUSTMENT

By understanding the process of adjustment, we can anticipate stress and this, in and of itself, helps minimize the severity of our reactions. Furthermore, this understanding gives sojourners a way to make sense out of the confusion, ambiguity, and disorientation which are symptomatic of culture shock. It suggests that there are strategies one may take to cope with the stress and more effectively overcome the causes of culture shock. And, most importantly, it makes the pattern of cross-cultural adjustment predictable and clearly shows most people that they will overcome the stress and may even be better for having gone through it.

Loss of control, helplessness, and hopelessness are some of the more obvious symptoms of culture shock, and they result from a lack of understanding of what is happening. These symptoms cannot be controlled unless there is an understanding that culture shock is not some mysterious disease. Moreover, most sojourners will realize that they have gone through this process before, such as their first day of school, summer camp, or military training. These parallel experiences were overcome and some of the same reactions and coping strategies will work again. We can build upon this reservoir of experience much as reverse culture shock or reentry/transition stress can be overcome by building upon the experience of having gone through culture shock.[26]

If you understand the process of cross-cultural adjustment, it is fairly easy to recognize the symptoms of culture shock. Withdrawal, displacement of anger, building little American communities, going native, and various psychosomatic illnesses are all obvious symptoms which can be controlled. Simply knowing that these are symptoms and not causes eases a great deal of the stress.

Control the Symptoms or Reactions to Cross-Cultural Adjustment Stress

Before you can treat the root causes of culture shock, it is necessary to control the symptoms. If one is paralyzed with frustration and anxiety and feels overwhelmed by the stress, it is difficult to perceive alternative ways of behaving or coping. Thus, the first step is to develop first-aid techniques which will allow for greater control of reaction to stress.

From our understanding of culture shock, it is obvious that some behavior is counterpro-ductive and will only inhibit adjustment. For example, if culture shock results from a breakdown of communication, withdrawing from host nationals may alleviate the pain temporarily but ultimately will not help one adjust. The withdrawal behavior is defensive, and extreme withdrawal and paranoia are danger signs that culture shock may be getting worse.[27]

Some sojourners decide to leave behind all reminders of home and start off anew in another culture. However, from our understanding of what happens in the loss of familiar cultural cues, this will actually increase the stress of adjustment. Transferring potent reminders from one's home culture, such as favorite CDs or photographs, may be an effective coping strategy to temporarily ease the pain of loss of cues until new potent ones are adopted.[28] Modifying things in the host environment so that they are somewhat similar to those in the home culture is another coping strategy that may ease the stress. One can make a hamburger of sorts out of almost any meat.

According to research on reactive or acute schizophrenia, interfering with the normal death/rebirth or growth process can make the situation worse.[29] If culture shock is understood as an identity crisis, then abruptly interfering with the process, such as returning home during the crisis period, is not a wise course of action. Rather, intensifying the sharing of feelings with others who understand the process of adaptation helps one through the transition. Temporarily cutting down stimuli by withdrawing somewhat from host nationals may be a wise conscious strategy in light of this paradigm. But that is not an unconscious retreat from a painful reality—it is a strategic withdrawal. There is a clear difference.

Often, people intuitively adopt coping strategies which help control the symptoms of culture shock. For example, during the first few weeks or months of an overseas experience, sojourners write numerous long letters to their loved ones at home. Certainly people back home are not all that interested in every meal or experience the sojourner has had. However, for the sojourner it provides a way of communicating authentically with those who share the same meaning system. That is, it may be an unconscious form of compensation for the breakdown of communication overseas. And, as one gradually adjusts to the new culture and begins communicating effectively with host nationals, the letter writing usually decreases. Loved ones back home may be concerned that something has happened when letters stop coming with such frequency and detail, but, in fact, the sojourner is probably happier than when the copious letter writing was taking place.

As with any stressful situation, relaxation, desensitization, and counterconditioning techniques are very useful for minimizing reactions.[30] Knowing that too much stress and overstimulation can be traumatic allows one to develop stress-control techniques such as decreasing stimuli, relaxing, minimizing the number of changes in a short period of time, and withdrawing temporarily.

These first-aid strategies ultimately do not treat the root causes of culture shock or help one adjust to another culture. However, they do give sojourners a greater sense of control and prevent the symptoms from overwhelming them.

Developing Coping Strategies That Facilitate Adjustment

Just as understanding the process of cross-cultural adjustment leads to logical methods for controlling the symptoms of culture shock, it also leads to ways in which we can more quickly and effectively adjust to another culture. Cross-cultural adjustment is the final goal.

If withdrawing from others is ultimately maladaptive, increased communication with host nationals is ultimately adaptive. Temporarily this may actually increase stress because host nationals are the stressors.[31] But in the long run it will speed up the process of adjustment. Learning the verbal and nonverbal language in the context of the culture and consciously placing oneself in situations where there is greater likelihood of interacting with host nationals are coping strategies which lead toward greater cross-cultural understanding. Furthermore, they will allow for the development of cross-cultural communication skills.

In researching the process of cross-cultural adjustment with over a thousand Nigerian students who studied in the U.S.[32] and with hundreds of international students at American University, it was found that most identified a fairly clear U-curve pattern with an initial high or honeymoon period followed by a sharp emotional downturn.[33] Almost all came out of the slump with an emotional upswing as they adjusted to American culture. When asked what single event seemed to be most responsible for the upturn, the vast majority responded that they had developed a friendship with a host national. Interpersonal communication with host-national friends seemed to turn the tide.

When we go through culture shock, there is often a sense that there is some personal weakness or inadequacy on our part which inhibits our adjustment. Sometimes irrational behavior such as displacement of anger causes feelings of guilt. The apparent lack of concern by host nationals for our misery may be interpreted as enjoyment of our discomfort.

To overcome this sense of personal inadequacy and paranoia, it is helpful also to associate with those who have gone through culture shock. Host nationals may have never experienced culture shock and are actually quite unaware of what is happening to us. Experienced sojourners have gone through this before and can provide assurance that it is both normal and transitional. They also may model strategies to overcome the stress and successfully adapt. Caution must be taken that this association with other sojourners not be exclusively conational or reactionary in nature (i.e., gripe sessions). Otherwise, it may lead to avoidance of host nationals and inhibit successful adjustment.

Learn Something About the New Culture Before Leaving Home

Just as it helps to anticipate reactions to stress, it helps to have some knowledge of the new culture before departure. It is fairly easy to acquire information on history, geography, food, customs, dress, language, and religion before leaving. This information, if understood as incomplete and simply a descriptive set of broad generalizations, may help diminish negative stereotypes and give some confidence that you will know what is going on. Having realistic expectations of the new culture obviously helps decrease stress.

This culture-specific knowledge also provides conversational currency. It helps sojourners coming to the U.S. if they already know something of American sports, politics, history, and music. They then have the basis for a conversation with almost any American. This predeparture, culture-specific knowledge also communicates to host nationals that you care enough about them to gather the information.

While no "cookbook" for another culture can be written, we can acquire a list of basic do's and don't's which at least get us started on the right foot, helping us avoid grossly offensive behavior and giving us the confidence that we can at least greet people correctly, know when and how to tip, avoid gestures that will be interpreted as obscene, and eat in a manner that does not upset everyone else present. As long as this knowledge does not become a security blanket or crutch which inhibits our ability to accept its incompleteness and even inaccuracy, it is useful during the transition period.

The tendency to judge others in terms of one's own cultural experiences and expectations (ethnocentrism) is diminished if we have some predeparture, culture-specific knowledge. We are more likely to understand the behavior of our hosts in terms of their cultural experiences. While complete empathy is almost impossible unless we actually grew up in that culture, we can at least become less ethnocentric and rein in our prejudices. In a lecture some years ago, if my memory hasn't betrayed me, Edmund Glenn defined prejudice as "being down on that which you are not up on." It is more difficult to be down on people in the new culture if you have more culture-specific information about them which explains their behavior.

This knowledge also helps to lessen the tendency sojourners have of making trait attributions of host-national behavior instead of situational attributions.[34] When we behave negatively, we usually explain the behavior in terms of the particular situation—normally,

we don't behave badly. But, when *they* behave negatively it is because of innate personality traits. For example, "*I* cheated because it was a surprise exam and the professor didn't give me a chance to study for it. *They* cheat because they are basically dishonest people." If we understand their culture we can see that their behavior is simply a matter of cultural background, and they behave in ways we consider negative in many cases because of particular situations.

Caution must be taken when gathering culture-specific, predeparture information. It can never be complete or accurate in every situation. Even worse, it may predispose you to have expectations which are not met. The consequence is that some people, after they arrive in-country, may take perverse pleasure in selecting out that which contradicts what they learned before coming. This distortion and selective attention may inhibit successful adjustment and true understanding of the culture.

Develop Skills Which Will Facilitate Cross-Cultural Understanding, Communication, and Adaptation

Personality may be the most important determinant of successful cross-cultural adaptation. There are skills, however, which can be developed through cross-cultural training or orientation which will allow one to cope more effectively with culture shock and understand the new culture without memorizing lists of do's and don't's.

These skills can best be developed experientially. One need not go overseas to experience the disorientation, confusion, and ambiguity of entering another culture. There are enough subcultural communities in the U.S. to experience the same feelings without going overseas. This kind of experience can serve as an inoculation against culture shock. The various ethnic communities of metropolitan areas provide excellent opportunities for this type of experience, and the coping strategies developed during these brief encounters can be transferred overseas.

These domestic experiences also allow for the development of analytical, interpretive, and communicative skills. What causes the behavior of people within the ethnic community? Why do they take offense at particular expressions? What do particular nonverbal and verbal messages mean in the context of their community? And what causes the conflict between members of this community and outsiders? We could go on and on considering questions which aid in the development of cross-cultural understanding and cross-cultural adaptation and communication skills.

Of course, language ability is a basic skill which can be developed before departure. However, it is especially important to remember that nonverbal messages cannot be learned effectively outside the context of the culture. In fact, most people in the culture are unaware of how they give meaning to particular messages. Sometimes sojourners are overconfident that they can communicate effectively when they have studied the host culture's language before departure. Because they do not anticipate any stress in communicating, their culture shock is sometimes even more severe than those with little prior knowledge of the language.

SOME IMPLICATIONS FOR CROSS-CULTURAL ORIENTATION OR TRAINING

Cross-cultural trainers are often expected to give advice on how best to adjust quickly and painlessly to another culture. Furthermore, they are to describe the other culture in a colorful manner without ambiguity or complexity. Many sojourners do not want theoretical or abstract culture-general presentations which emphasize process. Rather, they want their training short, concrete, painless, entertaining, and simple.

It is very tempting to give these sojourners what they want—cookbooks, do's-and-don't's lists, fancy charts and graphs, and a multitude of clever anecdotes. Some might even prefer to watch slick, fast-paced films which they feel can eliminate the trainer altogether.[35] The films are often simplistic and humorous, thereby suggesting that there is little pain involved in cross-cultural adjustment. They usually offer clear-cut advice on

how to minimize the stress of culture shock and quickly adjust overseas.

Like the self-help psychology books and the various forms of sensitivity training of a couple of decades ago, it is doubtful that these quickie, cure-all, painless approaches are productive. In fact, they may be quite counterproductive[36] in giving sojourners a false sense of confidence in their abilities, false expectations about the ease of cross-cultural adjustment, misleading and inaccurate stereotypes about other cultures, and a lack of true understanding of the dynamics of culture shock.

Of course, trainers must be entertaining simply to get and hold the attention and interest of clients who may not be accustomed to didactic presentations or complex conceptual frameworks. Stage presence, anecdotes which make a point or concretely illustrate a concept, and sometimes even graphs, charts, and films are necessary. Even stereotypes are useful so long as they are accurate and lead to conceptual understanding. But all of these should have the clear purpose of (1) helping the client anticipate the stress of cross-cultural adaptation and his or her reactions to the stress, (2) facilitating the development of coping strategies, (3) giving the sojourner confidence that he or she can adjust to another culture and interact effectively with host nationals, and (4) helping the client understand the process of cross-cultural adaptation.

While there is no one formula which is best for orienting sojourners, a solid training program should include many of the following guidelines, approaches, and goals which flow logically from our discussion of cross-cultural adaptation.

Understand the Concept of Culture

Culture is an abstraction which must be understood before we can begin discussing our own culture, the cultures of others, or the process of cross-cultural adaptation and interaction. Just as we cannot discuss individual human behavior without understanding the concept of personality, it is almost impossible to discuss intelligently the behavior of people in particular societies without understanding the concept of culture.

Many, if not most, people think of culture as what is often called "high culture"—art, literature, music, and the like. This culture is set in the framework of history and of social, political, and economic structures. Sojourners often think that if they have learned about these aspects of a culture they are prepared to enter it.

Actually, the most important part of culture for a sojourner is that which is internal and hidden,[37] but which governs the behavior they encounter. This dimension of culture can be seen as an iceberg with the tip sticking above the water level of conscious awareness. By far the most significant part, however, is unconscious or below the water level of awareness and includes values and thought patterns.

Knowledge of internal culture gives a framework for analyzing and interpreting behavior and customs both of others and of ourselves. For example, individualism, the achievement motive, and the linear time orientation of Americans causes them to be competitive and concerned about actions and earned status rather than with harmony and ascribed status. These values also explain the American concern with punctuality, time scheduling, and the future. Unless there is some understanding of these basic values, it is almost impossible to explain why Americans behave as they do.

Another example is patterns of thinking. There is a particular way of solving problems or thinking which is logical to people in each culture. Americans tend to be low-context,[38] abstractive,[39] analytical[40] thinkers, typical of complex, loosely integrated, urban or Gesellschaft societies.[41] At the other end of the continuum are high-context, associative, relational thinkers, typical of traditional, homogeneous, rural communities or Gemeinschaft societies.

This kind of cross-cultural analysis offers analytical and interpretive tools which can give sojourners confidence in their ability to explain their own behavior and that of others in cross-cultural situations.

All of this is to suggest that cross-cultural training ought to help sojourners move from the overt and descriptive level to the analytical and interpretive. This requires didactic presentations to provide a framework or system for understanding the interrelationship of the various facets of cultures and the process of cross-cultural interaction. These concepts provide keys to understanding and even to predicting individual behavior within the context of particular cultures.

Understand the Dynamics of Cross-Cultural Communication and Adaptation

If the breakdown of communication is one of the primary causes of culture shock, sojourners must understand the dynamics of interpersonal communication. The cybernetics model already mentioned helps them conceptualize the process of communication and identify the basic parts and links in a face-to-face communication system. Furthermore, it helps participants identify why, where, and how communication breaks down and anticipate reactions to it.

Basic to any discussion of cross-cultural communication is nonverbal communication. If the vast majority of messages which communicate feelings are sent nonverbally[42] and the meanings we give to nonverbal messages are culture-specific and unconsciously acquired, then it is vital that considerable attention be paid to nonverbal communication.

There are many tangential concepts which add breadth and depth to the discussion of cross-cultural interaction. For example, synchrony, the rhythm of body movement and speech, helps explain how each culture has its own rhythm which members learn within the first few hours or days of birth. When we enter another culture, much of the discomfort we feel may be because we are out-of-sync with movement in the culture.[43]

Action chains are culture-specific sequences of behavior which we unconsciously follow to reach goals.[44] They include courting behavior, the way conflict escalates or is resolved, and even how friendships develop. Perhaps one reason multicultural meetings seem to get out of hand is that each participant carries unconscious assumptions about the pertinent action chain, how a leader is selected, how discussion ought to progress, or how an agenda should be developed.[45] As with synchrony, action chains are unconscious and acquired simply by growing up in a particular culture.

THE "ICEBERG ANALOGY" OF CULTURE

Understanding the dynamics of cross-cultural adaptation or culture shock, including the three explanations of cause, is essential to realizing that one's reactions are normal and that there are steps one can take to cope with both the stress and stressors. Again, it is important to focus on internal or subjective culture.[46] When one enters another culture, it is somewhat like two icebergs colliding—the real clash occurs beneath the water where values and thought patterns conflict. This model serves as a device for explaining a fairly complex concept and causes participants to focus on culture as a system, rather than trying to memorize lists of culture-specific behaviors.

The terms "internal" and "external" culture are used by Edward T. Hall in his book *Beyond Culture*.[47] He suggests that what we normally refer to as "mind" is actually internal culture which we have embodied here in the iceberg analogy of culture. This is similar to Freud's concept of personality which he also compares to an iceberg with conscious mind represented by the tip and unconscious or subconscious mind represented by the part below the water level. Hall argues that the only way to really learn the internal culture of others is on a gut level by actively participating in their culture In the process one becomes more aware or conscious of his or her own internal culture. That is, the collision of culture causes one to raise to the conscious level that part of culture which is internal or unconscious.

THE SEQUENCE OF TOPICS IS VERY IMPORTANT

Training programs which begin with culture-specific information alone suggest that the focus is on "those people," and participants naturally expect to be given a cookbook, which starts them off on the wrong foot.

Training programs which move from the culture-general to the culture-specific finesse this desire for cookbooks. In turn, sojourners are, more likely to develop coping strategies and gain understanding rather than simply amassing questionable information. Culture-specific knowledge is important and should be available with as much depth and breadth as possible. But the mind-set which aids cross-cultural adaptation best is one oriented toward interaction and process and focused on "us" rather than simply "them."

Training which begins with the study of "those people" also implies we need not examine or understand our own culture. How can sojourners understand the impact of culture on the behavior, perceptions, values, and thought patterns of "those people" if they do not understand the impact of their own culture on their personality? An admonition that might be taken to heart by all trainers is "know thy own culture first."

For Americans, this is a special problem because most people are culturally unaware. They may have studied American literature and history; few have systematically studied their own culture. Because of geographic isolation during the formative period of the United States, the unique background of early immigrants, the frontier experience, the continually expanding economy, the seemingly unlimited natural resources, and the economic and political success of the United States, Americans are fairly parochial and take their own culture for granted.

Surely any training program designed for Americans would raise consciousness of their own culture. That in turn would tend to decrease ethnocentrism and make it clear that American behaviors, values, thought patterns, and ways of viewing the world are a result of their historical experiences and not necessarily appropriate or normal for the rest of the world.

The contrast-culture approach of Kluckhohn and Strodtbeck and Stewart, deals by necessity with oversimplifications and even stereotypes.[48] Nevertheless, it provides a solid conceptual framework which focuses on values and thought patterns as the determinants of behavior. Once the interrelatedness of

American values and behaviors is understood, they can be contrasted quite easily with non-Western cultures such as those of the traditional Middle East, Africa, and Asia. The model can then be expanded to suggest a continuum moving from high to low context, associative to abstractive, and analytical to relational cultures, and sojourners can place themselves and others along such a continuum. Consequently, they move beyond the simple contrasts to understand that there are also similarities among various cultures around the globe and that differences along the continuum are a matter of degree.

USE PARTICIPATORY OR EXPERIENTIAL EXERCISES

While many of the basic concepts require some didactic presentation and every trainer must have a sound command of theoretical frameworks and concepts, a good training program ought to allow each participant an opportunity to experience some of the ambiguity, confusion, uncertainty, and frustration involved in cross-cultural adaptation and intercultural communication. If culture can only be learned at a gut level (as Hall argues; see above), then participatory exercises, such as role playing, are extremely useful in facilitating learning.

These exercises also provide a laboratory experience in applying the various concepts and approaches discussed here and in the development of coping, interpretive, analytical, and communicative skills. In fact, unless they have these clear purposes they may be perceived as childish and meaningless.[49]

A trainer should be able to model analytical and interpretive skills which may be adopted by participants as they develop their own techniques. In no way should the trainer cause a dependency relationship to develop where sojourners expect advice which they feel must be followed if they are to succeed overseas. Rather, the ultimate goal of training is that each sojourner assume the responsibility of developing his or her own strategies for cross-cultural adjustment and communication.

A trainer is then a facilitator who provides the conceptual frameworks for understanding as well as the opportunities to apply them in a participatory manner. Experiential exercises can include contrast-culture games such as *Bafá Bafá* or other contrast-culture simulation exercises. Because of their ambiguity, they produce stress and force participants to apply conceptual frameworks which help them interpret and analyze their own reactions and the behavior of others. Furthermore, they encourage the development of communication and coping skills.

Again, it is important that these exercises be culture-general and that only afterward does the trainer move to a culture-specific focus. Seldom do culture-specific role plays and exercises actually replicate situations or persons in the actual overseas culture, and they encourage cookbook thinking, provide false and misleading stereotypes, and promote unrealistic expectations. The major goal of the exercises is not to enable the participants to fully understand another specific culture but rather to help them develop strategies for understanding any other culture they might encounter and to examine their reactions to the stresses of cross-cultural communication and interaction.

Contrast-culture models are especially useful because they are ambiguous and culture-general. For example, the famous Khan contrast-culture simulation involves rather open-ended scenarios in which Khan plays the role of a person who comes from a culture and behaves in a way that is generally non-Western, associative, high-context, and relational.[50] "Mr. Khan" (not his real name) is a man of non-European background specifically trained by Stewart and his colleagues to play this role—commonly referred to as "contrast American"—in interactions with American participants. The role-play scenarios were originally created for American advisors going abroad on technical assistance projects but are now used for a variety of cross-cultural training purposes. If Khan were to represent a member of a particular culture with which participants were familiar, they would probably resort to their stereotypes of that culture to explain his behavior. Rather than applying the conceptual models, developing coping skills, or examining their reactions, they would mentally leaf through the cookbook for that country. When Khan is culture-general and simply a contrast to the mainstream. American culture, he acts as a cultural Rorschach inkblot upon which Americans project their unconscious assumptions regarding people from other cultures. This in turn brings out revealing thoughts and behavior from the Americans.

Inoculate Sojourners

Just as one inoculates people against physical disease by giving them a little dose of the disease to build up their resistance, training should inoculate sojourners to the stress of cross-cultural adaptation and the difficulties of cross-cultural communication This may be done with participatory exercises which allow participants to experience the discomfort, uncertainty, and ambiguity of dealing with someone who behaves and thinks differently.

Barna refers to this as "stress inoculation training" and finds that "an underlying premise of this approach is that the effective management of stress and anxiety is the goal, not stress avoidance."[51] Consequently, various coping strategies can be used such as modeling desired behaviors, imagery rehearsal, relaxation training, desensitization, and counterconditioning. But, first of all, the client must understand the nature of stress and reactions to stress and have an opportunity to experience a stressful situation to practice coping skills. These skills give the sojourner a sense of greater control over his or her behavior in a stressful situation.

Inoculation also involves helping sojourners anticipate the stress of cross-cultural adaptation and communication and their reactions to it. Thus, they begin to worry somewhat as they proceed through the training program. The training normally raises the anxiety levels of sojourners because they have become more aware of communication and adaptation difficulties.

They also have been helped in developing the skills to cope with these difficulties and the confidence to overcome them. The anxiety produced through inoculation should be balanced by the assurance and confidence that sojourners have within themselves adequate knowledge and skills to cope with these stresses.

CONCLUSION

If there is a medical or illness analogy for culture shock, the common cold is probably it. Like the common cold, there is no way to prevent culture shock and one can catch it over and over again. Each time we adjust to another culture or readjust to our own culture, we go through culture shock.

The symptoms of a cold are relatively harmless unless we fail to take minimal precautions to prevent the cold from weakening our immune system. The body can only take so much physical stress at any one time. A certain percentage of people who get colds experience severe reactions. The same is true of culture shock—the symptoms are relatively harmless unless we have experienced too many life changes in too short a time period and a certain percentage of people going abroad may be unable to tolerate the additional stress of cross-cultural adaptation.[52]

A cold follows a somewhat regular pattern; it will eventually come to an end, and you will eventually be as healthy as ever. Knowing the "cold process" prevents you from thinking that every cough, sniffle, or pain is symptomatic of some more severe, or perhaps even terminal, disease. And you can control the symptoms by getting rest, drinking plenty of liquids, eating chicken soup, etc. However, there is no one cure for a cold, and each person probably has a personal remedy that seems to work.

In the end, each of us will develop our own set of coping strategies. We can manage culture shock. Like the cold, there is no real cure or prevention, but understanding the process gives us a sense of control and predictability and allows us to cope better with the symptoms an achieve some new level of cross-cultural skill.

ENDNOTES

[1]Kalvero Oberg, "Cultural Shock: Adjustment to New Cultural Environments," *Practical Anthropology* 7 (1960): 177–182.

[2]Charles A. Zwingmann, and A.D.C. Gunn, *Uprooting and Health: Psycho-Social Problems of Students from Abroad,* Geneva: World Health Or-

ganization, Division of Mental Health (WHO/MNH/83.8), 1983.

[3]Richard W. Brislin, *Cross-Cultural Encounters: Face-to-Face Interaction* (Elmsford, NY: Pergamon, 1981): 40–71.

[4]Nancy J. Adler, *International Dimensions of Organization Behavior* (Cambridge, MA: Kent. 1985); Peter S. Adler, "Beyond Cultural Identity: Reflections on Cultural and Multicultural Man," *Topics in Culture Learning* 2 (August 1974): 23–71.

[5]Edward T. Hall, *Beyond Culture* (New York: Doubleday, 1976).

[6]Nathan Azrin, "Pain and Aggression," in N. T. Adler, ed., *Readings in Experimental Psychology Today* (Del Mar, CA: CRM Books, 1970): 103–107.

[7]Hall, *Beyond Culture* (Garden City, NY: Anchor Press/Doubleday, 1976); *The Hidden Dimension,* New York: Doubleday, 1966; *The Silent Language,* (New York: Doubleday, 1959).

[8]Hall, *The Dance of Life* (New York: Doubleday, 1983).

[9]Albert Mehrabian, "Communication without Words," *Psychology Today* 2(4), 1968: 53–55.

[10]Alvin Toffler, *Future Shock* (New York: Bantam, 1970); Philip Slater, *Earthwalk,* 1974 (Garden City, NY: Doubleday, 1974).

[11]Hans Selye, *The Stress of Life* (New York: McGraw-Hill, 1956); *Stress without Distress* (Philadelphia, PA: Lippincott, 1974); LaRay M. Barna, "The Stress Factor in Intercultural Relations," in Dan Landis and Richard T. W. Brislin, eds., *Handbook of Intercultural Draining,* vol. 2 (Elmsford, NY: Pergamon, 1983): 19–49.

[12]E. Lindemann, "Symptomatology and Management of Acute Grief," *American Journal of Psychiatry* 101(1944): 141–148.

[13]Martin E. P. Seligman, *Helplessness* (San Francisco: Freeman, 1975).

[14]Roland D. Laing, *The Divided Self* (New York: Pantheon, 1967, originally published, 1959).

[15]Mehrabian, *op. cit.*

[16]Hall, *Beyond Culture.*

[17]Nancy J. Adler, *op. cit.*

[18]Gary Weaver, "American Identity Movements: A Cross-Cultural Confrontation," *Intellect* (March 1975): 377–380.

[19]Gail Sheehy, *Passages: Predictable Crisis of Adult Life* (New York: Bantam, 1977): 29.

[20]Hall, *Beyond Culture.*

[21]William H. Blanchard, "Ecstasy without Agony Is Baloney," *Psychology Today* 3(8), 1970: 8, 10, 64.

[22]*Ibid.*

[23]D. L. Rosenhan, "On Being Sane in Insane Places," *Science* 179 (1973): 250–258.

[24]Sigmund Freud, *The Problem of Anxiety* (New York: W. W. Norton, 1936); *Little Hans* (London: Hogarth Press, 1955); Anna Freud, *The Ego and the Mechanisms of Defense,* rev. ed., (New York: International Universities Press, 1970).

[25]Gordon W. Allport, *Pattern and Growth in Personality* (New York: Holt, Rinehart & Winston, 1961); Abraham Maslow, *Motivation and Personality,* 2nd ed. (New York: Harper and Row, 1970).

[26]Gary Weaver and Philip Uncapher, "The Nigerian Experience: Overseas Living and Value Change." Paper and workshop presented at Seventh Annual SIETAR Conference, Vancouver, BC, Canada, March 11, 1981.

[27]J. Silverman, "When Schizophrenia Helps," *Psychology Today* 4(4), 1970: 63–66, 68, 70.

[28]Kenneth H. David, "The Use of Social-Learning Theory in Preventing Intercultural Adjustment Problems," in Paul Pedersen, W. J. Lonner, and J. G. Draguns, eds., *Counseling Across Cultures,* (Honolulu: University of Hawaii Press, 1976): 123–138.

[29]Silverman, *op. cit.*; B. Maher, "The Shattered Language of Schizophrenia," *Psychology Today* 2(6), 1968: 30–33, 60.

[30]Barna, *op. cit.*; S. Walton, "Stress Management Training for Overseas Effectiveness," *International Journal of Intercultural Relations* 14(4), 1990: 507–527.

[31]Barna, 19–49.

[32]Weaver and Uncapher, *op. cit.*

[33]Oberg, *op. cit.*

[34]Brislin, 72–108; R. P. Martin, "Consultant, Consultee, and Client Expectations of Each Other's Behavior in Consultation," *School of Psychology Review* 12(1), 1983: 35–41.

[35]Michael Duncan, "American Corporations Learn a Lesson in Cross-Cultural Business." *OAG Frequent Flyer* (Part 2, OAG Pocket Flight Guide). (March 1985): 59–62.

[36]Blanchard, *op. cit.*

[37]Hall, *Beyond Culture.*

[38]*Ibid.*

[39]Edmund S. Glenn, "The University and Revolution: New Left or New Right?" in G. R. Weaver and J. H. Weaver, *The University and Revolution* (Englewood Cliffs, NJ: Prentice-Hall, 1969); Weaver, *op. cit.*

[40]R. A. Cohen, "Conceptual Styles, Culture Conflict and Nonverbal Tests of Intelligence," *American Anthropologist* 71 (1969): 828–856.

[41]Ferdinand Tönnies, *Gemeinschaft and Gesellschaft* (Tubingen, Germany: Mohr, 1937). C. P. Loomis (trans.), *Fundamental Concepts of Sociology* (New York: John Wiley and Sons, 1940).

[42]Mehrabian, *op. cit.*

[43]Hall, *The Dance of Life.*

[44]Hall, *Beyond culture.*

[45]Gary L. Althen, "The Intercultural Meeting," in *The Handbook of Foreign Student Advising* (Yarmouth, ME: Intercultural Press, 1983).

[46]Harry C. Triandis, *The Analysis of Subjective Culture* (New York: John Wiley and Sons, 1972).

[47]Hall, *Beyond Culture.*

[48]Florence R. Kluckhohn and Frederick L. Strodtbeck, *Variation in Value Orientations* (New York: Row, Peterson, 1961); Edward C. Stewart, Jack Danielian, and R. J. Foster, *Simulating Intercultural Communication Through Role-Playing,* Washington, DC: George Washington University Human Resources Research Office (HumRRO Division No. 7, Technical Report, May 1969): 69–77.

[49]Weaver and Uncapher, *op cit.*

[50]Stewart, Danielan, and Foster, *op. cit.*

[51]Barna, *op. cit.*

[52]Selye, *Stress without Distress* (Philadelphia, PA: Lippincott, 1974).

25

The Shattered Language of Schizophrenia

Brendan A. Maher

Somewhere in a hospital ward a patient writes: *"The subterfuge and the mistaken planned substitutions for that demanded American action can produce nothing but the general results of negative contention and the impractical results of careless applications, the natural results of misplacement, of mistaken purpose and unrighteous position, the impractical serviceabilities of unnecessary contradictions. For answers to this dilemma, consult Webster."* The document is never sent to anyone; it is addressed to no one, and perhaps intended for no reader.

Another patient, miles away, writes: *"I am of I-Building B . . . State Hospital. With my nostrils clogged and Winter here, I chanced to be reading the magazine that Mentholatum advertised from. Kindly send it to me at the hospital. Send it to me Joseph Nemo in care of Joseph Nemo and me who answers by the name of Joseph Nemo and will care for it myself. Thanks everlasting and Merry New Year to Mentholatum Company for my nose for my nose for my nose for my nose for my nose."*

A British patient writes: *"I hope to be home soon, very soon. I fancy chocolate eclairs, chocolate eclairs, Doenuts. I want some doenuts, I do want some golden syrup, a tin of golden syrup or treacle, jam. . . . See*

the Committee about me coming home for Easter my twenty-fourth birthday. I hope all is well at home, how is Father getting on. Never mind there is hope, heaven will come, time heals all wounds, Rise again Glorious Greece and come to Hindoo Heavens, the Indian Heavens. The Dear old times will come back. We shall see Heaven and Glory yet, come everlasting life. I want a new writing pad of note paper. . . ."*

Yet another writes: *"Now to eat if one cannot the other can—and if we cant the girseau Q.C. Washpots prizebloom capacities—turning out—replaced by the head patterns my own capacities—I was not very kind to them. Q.C. Washpots under-patterned against—bred to pattern. Animal sequestration capacities and animal sequestired capacities under leash—and animal secretions. . . ."*[1]

Experienced clinicians, when called upon to diagnose the writers of language like this, agree closely with each other (80 per cent of the time or more). The diagnosis: schizophrenia. Nearly every textbook on psychopathology presents similar examples, and nobody seems to have much difficulty in finding appropriate samples. It would seem obvious that there must be a well-established and explicit definition of what characteristics language must possess to be called schizophrenic. But when we ask clinicians to tell us exactly what specific features of an individual language sample led them to decide that the writer was schizophrenic, it turns out that they aren't exactly sure. Instead of explicit description, the expert comment is likely to be: "It has that schizophrenic flavor" or "It is the confusion of thought that convinces me."

Impressionistic descriptions abound. The language is described as *circumlocutious, repetitive, incoherent,* suffering from an *interpenetration of ideas, excessively concrete, regressed,* and the like. Doubtless, all of these descriptions have merit as clinical characterizations of the language. Unfortunately, they are quite imprecise, and they give us no adequate basis for developing theoretical accounts of the origin of schizophrenic language. This is, of course, hardly surprising. Quantitative stud-

Reprinted from *Psychology Today* (November 1968): 30–33, 60–61. Copyright © 1968, Sussex Publishers, Inc.

ies of language have been notoriously laborious to undertake. However, two recent developments in behavioral sciences have combined to change the situation quite significantly. The first of these is the development of language-analysis programs for computer use, and the second is the increasing sophistication of psycholinguistics as a framework for the study of applied problems in the psychology of language.

Before turning to look at the consequences of these developments, we should glance at the kinds of hypotheses that have already been advanced to account for schizophrenic language. The first of these might be termed the *Cipher Hypothesis*. In its simplest form this says that the patient is trying to communicate something to a listener (actual or potential) but is afraid to say what he means in plain language. He is somewhat in the same straits as the normal individual faced with the problem of conveying, let us say, some very bad news to a listener. Rather than come right out and tell someone directly that a family member is dying, the informant may become circumlocutious and perhaps so oblique that his message simply does not make sense at all.

In the case of the schizophrenic patient, however, it is assumed that the motives which drive him to disguise his message may be largely unconscious—that he could not put the message into plain language if he tried. Where the normal person is trying to spare the feelings of the listener by his distortions and evasions, the patient purportedly is sparing his own feelings by the use of similar techniques. This analogy can be stretched a little further. Just as the normal speaker is caught in a dilemma— the necessity to convey the message and the pressure to avoid conveying it too roughly— so the patient is caught in a conflict between the necessity of expressing himself on important personal topics and the imperative need to avoid being aware of his own real meanings. Thus, so the Cipher Hypothesis maintains, it is possible in principle to decipher the patient's message—provided one can crack the code. This hypothesis assumes, of course, that there really is a message.

Obviously, the Cipher Hypothesis owes its genesis to psychoanalytic theory. In essence, it is identical with Freud's interpretation of the relationship between manifest and latent dream content. Unfortunately, from a research point of view, this hypothesis suffers from the weakness of being very hard to disprove. No two patients are assumed to have the same code, and so the translation of schizophrenic language into a normal communication requires a detailed analysis of the case history of the individual writer. As the code that is discovered for any one case cannot be validated against any other case, the hypothesis rests its claim to acceptance upon its intrinsic plausibility vis-à-vis the facts of the life history of the patient. But plausible interpretations of a patient's language may reflect the creative (or empathetic) imagination of the clinician, rather than a valid discovery of an underlying process governing the patient's utterances.

One more or less necessary deduction from the Cipher Hypothesis is that language should become most disorganized when the topic under discussion is one of personal significance, and less disorganized when the topic is neutral. To date, no adequate test of this deduction has been reported. In the absence of this or other independent tests of the Cipher Hypothesis, it must be regarded for the time being as, at best, an interesting speculation.

A second explanation has been that the patient's communications are confusing and garbled precisely because he wishes to *avoid* communicating with other people. This hypothesis, which we shall call the *Avoidance Hypothesis*, interprets the disordered language as a response that is maintained and strengthened by its effectiveness in keeping other people away. Presumably, the normal listener becomes frustrated or bored with such a speaker and simply goes away, leaving the schizophrenic in the solitude he seeks. This theory rests, in turn, upon the assumption that the patient finds personal interactions threatening. We might expect that casual interactions—such as chatting about the weather—are relatively unthreatening and do not provoke avoidant disorder in language. The language disturbance should become more evident when the threat of personal involvement arises.

At this level, the Avoidance Hypothesis cannot be distinguished from the Cipher Hypothesis. The main difference between the two is that the Avoidance Hypothesis is concerned with a *dimension* of incomprehensibility and does not imply that the incomprehensible can be unscrambled. Both of these hypotheses have their attractions.

"For answers to this dilemma, consult Webster," wrote the first patient we have quoted. Is he just playing a word game with an imaginary reader or is there a meaning to his message? We might remark on the similarity of the prefix in many of the words he uses: *subterfuge, substitution; unrighteous, unnecessary; mistaken, misplacement; contention, contradiction.* His message might, indeed, sound like a random sampling from a dictionary.

Or did the dictionarylike nature of the "message" only occur to the patient himself toward the end—and hence the closing remark? In any event, the sample seems to fit plausibly into the notion that some kind of enciphering was going on between the patient's basic "message" and the language that he wrote.

Our fourth sample of schizophrenic language, on the other hand, seems to be absolutely incomprehensible. Fragments of phrases, neologisms ("girseau") and repetitions—*sequestration* and *sequestired*—combine into a jumble that seems to defy understanding. It is hard to believe that there might be a message in disguise here, or even that the language was uttered with any wish to communicate.

Although both hypotheses can be made to seem plausible, they are intrinsically unsatisfying to the psychopathologist. They do not deal with the most fascinating problem of schizophrenic language: why does a particular patient utter the particular words that he does, rather than some other jumbled-up sequence?

Some beginnings of an answer to this question have begun to emerge. Years ago, Eugen Bleuler commented on the presence of *interfering associations* in schizophrenic language. He suggested that the difficulty for the patient was that ideas associated with the content of his message somehow intruded into the message and thus distorted it. A patient of his, whom he had seen walking around the hospital grounds with her father and son, was asked

who her visitors were. "The father, son and Holy Ghost," she replied. These words have a strong mutual association as a single phrase and although the last item, "Holy Ghost," was probably not meant as part of her message, it intruded because of its strong associative links with other units in the message.

Bleuler also noticed the difficulty that patients seemed to have in *understanding* a pun, despite their tendency to talk in punning fashion. A patient asked about her relationships with people at home says, "I have many ties with my home! My father wears them around his collar." The pun on the word *tie* was unintentional, hence humorless.

Against the background of this general hypothesis of interfering associations, my students and I began investigations of schizophrenic language some years ago in Harvard's Laboratory of Social Relations. Our first concern was with the original question of definition. What must language contain to be labeled schizophrenic? Our work began with a plea to over 200 hospitals for examples of patients' writings—whether the patients were schizophrenic or not. Colleaguial response was rather overwhelming, and we amassed a very large number of letters, documents, diaries and simple messages written in almost every state of the Union. (Many of these were inappropriate to our purposes. A carton load of documents in Spanish from a Texas hospital, some brief obscenities scribbled on match covers and dropped daily onto the desk of a colleague in a St. Louis hospital and other similar items were eliminated, of course.)

From this mass, we selected a set of documents that were legible, long enough to include several consecutive sentences—and written in English. These texts were then read by a panel of clinicians. Each text was judged independently, and then was classified as *schizophrenic language* or *normal language*. (We obtained typical interjudge agreements of around 80 per cent.) At this juncture we did not know whether the writers of the letters had been diagnosed as schizophrenic or not. Our concern was with the characteristics of the language—and with the clinicians' reactions to it.

Our two sets of texts then were submitted for computer analysis with the aid of the *Gen-*

eral Inquirer program. This program codes and categorizes language in terms of content, and also provides a summary of grammatical features of the language. Out of this analysis, we developed some empirical rules (or a guide on how to write a document that a clinician will judge schizophrenic). Two of the most reliable rules were:

1. Write about politics, religion or science. Letters dealing with global social issues of this kind are highly likely to be regarded as schizophrenic by clinicians.

2. Write more *objects* than *subjects* in sentences. Typical sentences consist of enumerations of classes of objects in a form illustrated in our second and third examples above: "send it to me, Joseph Nemo, in care of Joseph Nemo and me who answers by the name of Joseph Nemo"; or "I fancy chocolate eclairs, chocolate eclairs, doenuts." Or in chains of associations at the end of a sentence. When, for example, a woman patient writes: "I like coffee, cream, cows, Elizabeth Taylor," the associational links between each word and the one following seem obvious.

This kind of associative chaining already had been described clinically by Bleuler; hence it was hardly surprising that the computer should find it to be a reliable discriminator in our document samples. What began to interest us, however, was the fact that these associations interfere most readily at the end of a sentence. Why not chains of subjects or chains of verbs, and why not at the beginning or middle of a sentence? Furthermore, why is this kind of interference found clearly in some schizophrenic patients and yet never occurs at all in others?

For some time it has become increasingly apparent that, in schizophrenia, *attention* is greatly disrupted. It is hard for a patient to remain focused on any one stimulus for any length of time. He is unable to "tune out" or ignore other surrounding stimuli. These distract him; they enter consciousness at full strength and not in an attenuated fashion as they do with the normal person. Reports by the patients themselves make the point dramatically:

"Things are coming in too fast. I lose my grip of it and get lost. I am attending to everything at once and as a result I do not really attend to anything.

"Everything seems to grip my attention, although I am not particularly interested in anything. I am speaking to you just now but I can hear noises going on next door and in the corridor. I find it difficult to concentrate on what I am saying to you.

"I cannot seem to think or even put any plans together. I cannot see the picture. I get the book out and read the story but the activities and the story all just do not jar me into action."

Experimental tasks that require close attention, tasks that call for fast reactions to sudden stimuli, or any continuous monitoring of a changing stimulus field are almost invariably done poorly by schizophrenics. Sorting tasks, where the subject must organize objects or words into conceptual groups, are progressively more difficult for the schizophrenic if irrelevant or puzzling factors appear in the material.

We may regard the focusing of attention as a process whereby we effectively inhibit attention to everything but certain relevant stimuli in the environment. As attention lapses, we find ourselves being aware of various irrelevant stimuli—the inhibitory mechanism has failed temporarily.

It is possible that an analogous set of events takes place when we produce a complex sequence of language. Attention may be greater or lesser at some points in a language sequence than at others. The end of a sentence— the period point—may be particularly vulnerable to momentary attentional lapses: one thought has been successfully completed, but the next one may not yet have been formed into utterable shape. Within a single sentence itself, there may be other points of comparative vulnerability, though not perhaps as marked as at the sentence ending.

Uttering a sentence without disruption is an extremely skilled performance, but one that most of us acquire so early in life that we are unaware of its remarkable complexity. (However, we become more aware of how difficult it is to "make sense" when we are extremely tired, or ripped out of sleep by the telephone, or distraught, or drunk.)

Single words have strong associational bonds with other words—as the classic technique of word association indicates. We know that the word "black" will elicit the response "white" almost instantaneously from the majority of people. The associational bond between black and white is clearly very strong. Strong as it is, it will not be allowed to dominate consciousness when one is uttering a sentence such as "I am thinking about buying a black car." Our successful sentences come from the successful, sequential inhibition of all interfering associations that individual words in the sentence might generate. Just as successful visual attention involves tuning out irrelevant visual material, so successful utterance may involve tuning out irrelevant verbal static.

By the same token, disordered attention should lead to an increasing likelihood that this kind of interference will not be inhibited, but will actually intrude into language utterance. Its most probable point of intrusion is wherever attention is normally lowest.

"Portmanteau" words or puns provide unusually good occasions for disruptive intrusions. Consider, for example, the word "stock." This word has several possible meanings, each of them with its own set of associations. Financial associations might be *Wall Street, bonds, dividend,* etc. Agricultural associations might include *cattle, barn* and *farm*; theatrical associations might be *summer, company* and the like. Webster's Third International Dictionary gives 42 different definitions of the word *stock*, many of them archaic or unusual, but many of them common. If one set of meanings intrudes into a sentence that is clearly built around another set of meanings, the effect is a pun, and an accompanying digression or cross-current in surface content. The sentences—"I have many ties with my home. My father wears them around his collar,"—seem to skip, like a stone on a lake, from *ties* (bonds) to *home* to *father* to *ties* (neckties). On the surface, this is a witty statement, but the speaker had no idea of what was really going on inside or underneath the form of words. The statement was therefore unwitting and hence unwitty.

Loren Chapman and his associates, in work at Southern Illinois University, demonstrated that schizophrenics as a group are more open to interference from the most common meaning of a punning word. When we use a word like *stock* as a stimulus for word association, we discover that most normal respondents give financial associations first, and may find it difficult to respond when asked to "give associations to another meaning." Associations to the other meaning are weaker or less prepotent, and only emerge under special instructional sets. Chapman's work suggests that if the plan of a sentence calls for the use of a weaker meaning, the schizophrenic runs some risk that associational intrusions will interfere and actually produce a punning effect.

On the other hand, if the plan of a sentence involves the stronger meaning, then there may be no intrusion of associations. And if associations do intrude, these intrusions will appear relevant to the sentence and will not strike the listener as strange. Which meanings will be strong or weak will depend to some extent upon the culture from which the patient comes. (Personal experience may of course produce uniquely strong or weak associations in individual cases.) However, Chapman was able to predict correctly the direction of errors for schizophrenic patients as a group on the basis of estimates of strength obtained from normal respondents. Thus, some patients may have personal idiosyncrasies, but the associations that interrupt the schizophrenic are generally the same as those that are strong for the population at large.

A parallel investigation I conducted at the University of Copenhagen included a study of the language of Danish schizophrenics. I observed the same general effect: patients were liable to interference from strong meanings of double-meaning words. English is a language, of course, that is unusually rich in puns, homonyms, cognates and indeed a whole lexicon of verbal trickery. But it seems plausible to suppose that in any language in which double-meaning words are to be found, this kind of schizophrenic disturbance may be found.

From these observations we can begin to piece together a picture of what happens when schizophrenic intrusions occur in a sentence that started out more or less normally. Where a punning word occurs at a vulnerable point, the sequence becomes disrupted and rapidly disintegrates into associative chaining until it terminates.

We may look at schizophrenic utterances as the end result of a combination of two factors: the vulnerability of sentence structure to attentional lapses, and the inability of patients to inhibit associational intrusions, particularly at these lapse points. From this point of view, the problem of language is directly related to the other attentional difficulties which the schizophrenic has; he is handicapped in making language work clearly, just as he is at any other task that requires sustained attention. The emotional significance of what the schizophrenic plans to say may have little or no bearing on when an intrusion occurs, or what it seems to mean. Any sentence with vulnerable points in its syntactic or semantic structure may result in confusion, whether the topic is of great psychological importance or has to do with a patient's harmless liking for chocolate eclairs and doughnuts.

Serious and sustained difficulties in the maintenance of attention suggest a biological defect. Peter Venables at the University of London has suggested swimming or unfocusable attention in schizophrenia may be connected with low thresholds of physiological arousal—stimuli can be very weak and yet trigger strong physiological reactions. This low arousal threshold is found mostly in acute, rather than chronic, schizophrenia.

Evidence from studies of a variety of attentional tasks supports this interpretation. Additional and intriguing evidence was obtained by one of my students, Dr. Joy Rice at the University of Wisconsin. Using electrochemical (galvanic) changes in the skin as a measure, she found that schizophrenic patients who were most responsive to noise stimulation were also the patients who showed the most difficulty in dealing with the meaning of punning sentences. The magnitude of galvanic skin response to external stimulation is presumably greatest in patients with low initial arousal levels (and hence the most receptivity to external stimulation). Rice's data may therefore support the notion that verbal associational interference is part and parcel of a total syndrome of which biological control of attention is a crucial central focus.

Recent research into the effects of LSD has shown that it is people with low initial arousal systems who have the "good trips"; the most cursory glance at literary biography will reveal an extraordinary number of poets and writers who were "sensitive," "neurasthenic," and so on. Which leads me to a sort of Parthian speculation.

Look again at the four samples quoted in the beginning of this article. What you see there, I think, is the literary imagination gone mad, if I may use so unclinical a term here. The first sample, had it come from the pen of someone whose brain we trusted, might almost be a crude parody of ponderous political tracts or socio-economo-political gobbledygook of one sort or another. In the second, the fragment, "With my nostrils clogged and Winter here," is really not bad, and one wouldn't be terribly surprised to find it occurring in, say, the *Cantos* of Ezra Pound. In the third quotation, there are unmistakable echoes from the New Testament, Lord Byron, and Ralph Waldo Emerson, or rather echoes from an entire chamber of the literary heritage. The kind of wordplay indulged in throughout the fourth quote is not essentially different technically from that employed by the later James Joyce, or by the John Lennon of *In his own write*.

What is lacking from these samples, so far as we can tell, is context and control and the critical, or pattern-imposing, intelligence. It would seem, therefore, that the mental substrata in which certain kinds of poetry are born probably are associative in a more or less schizophrenic way. (In the case of poets like Dylan Thomas or Hart Crane, of course, these substrata had to be blasted open by liquor.) The intelligence that shapes, cuts, edits, revises and erases is fed by many conscious sources, most of them cultural; but the wellsprings seem to be, as poets have been telling us for centuries, sort of divine and sort of mad.

ENDNOTES

[1]These quotations are taken from McDonald Critchley, "The Neurology of Psychotic Speech," *British Journal of Psychiatry* 110 (1964): 353–360.

[2]These quotations are taken from McGhie and Chapman's "Disorders of Attention in Schizophrenia."

26

When Schizophrenia Helps

Julian Silverman

There are forms of schizophrenic experience that can be positively and creatively constructive. Karl Menninger, in 1959, put it this way: "Some patients have a mental illness and then get well and then they get weller! I mean they get better than they ever were. . . . This is an extraordinary and little-realized truth."

A handful of psychiatrists have recognized the validity of this observation—Harry Stack Sullivan, John Perry, R. D. Laing and others. But most psychiatrists find it hard to regard the bizarre disorganization of schizophrenia as anything but ominous, and they see the crazy disturbances as behaviors to be done away with as quickly as possible. When this cannot be done, they prescribe huge doses of antipsychotic drugs.

But there is mounting evidence that some of the most profound schizophrenic disorganizations are preludes to impressive reorganization and personality growth—not so much breakdown as breakthrough. Kazimierz Dabrowski has called it "positive disintegration." It appears to be a natural reaction to severe stress, a spontaneous process into which persons may enter when their usual problem-solving techniques fail to solve such basic life crises as occupational or sexual inadequacy. If this natural process is interrupted by well-intended psychotherapy or by antipsychotic medication, the effect may be to detour the patient away from the acute schizophrenic

Reprinted from *Psychology Today 4*, no. 4 (September 1970): 63–65. Copyright © 1970, Sussex Publishers, Inc.

episode, away from a process as natural and benign as fever. The effect can be disastrous—it can rob him of his natural problem-solving potential.

MAKE OR BREAK

Anton Boisen was one of the first to recognize the potentially beneficial aspects of psychosis. Boisen was a psychologist and chaplain who went through several brief schizophrenic periods himself. Acute schizophrenic reactions, he wrote, are "not in themselves evils but problem-solving experiences. They are attempts at reorganization in which the entire personality, to its bottom-most depths, is aroused and its forces marshaled to meet the danger of personal failure and isolation. . . . The acute disturbances tend either to make or break. They may send the patient to the back wards, there to remain as a hopeless wreck, or they may send him back to the community in better shape than he had been for years."

As Boisen indicates, while some patients are likely to recover—even benefit—from their psychotic experiences, others may be severely disturbed for the rest of their lives. There has been extensive research in recent years concerning which patients are which; usually this has involved collecting a quantity of data about many schizophrenic patients, waiting to see which ones get better, then rechecking the data to see if the improved patients were in any way systematically different from the unimproved patients.

One of the most common findings is that the patient who improved had a sudden onset of symptoms; he typically went from a moderately effective lifestyle to severe psychosis in a period of perhaps a few days or weeks. Further, there was typically a precipitating event, some life-crisis that immediately preceded the break. On the other hand the schizophrenic who has been developing his symptoms over a period of years, gradually becoming more withdrawn and out of touch with reality, is more likely to remain in a disturbed condition for many years.

DEATH

There are other typical characteristics of the "problem-solving schizophrenic." A reaction to personal failure or guilt often starts with high anxiety as the patient searches for any possible way to repair his self-esteem. With increasing emotional turmoil, he takes a highly subjective orientation to the problem and becomes preoccupied, socially isolated and withdrawn. He feels despair and hopelessness. As Sullivan has noted, he may finally think "that he is dead, that this is the state after death; that he awaits resurrection or the salvation of his soul. Ancient myths of redemption and rebirth seem to appear." Ideas of death-rebirth, world catastrophe and cosmic importance are common.

The patient may regress to childish behavior. He may go so far as to simulate the womb by wrapping himself in wet sheets. He may become extremely withdrawn—not eating or drinking, not talking, not blowing his nose, staying in bed all day, perhaps with eyes and mouth tightly closed. He might rock back and forth with strange, rhythmic movements. Occasionally he may pass from his catatonic stupor into violent, random excitement. In this state he may hurt himself or others, but only by accident. He is not mad at anyone else. In fact, persistent outright aggression toward others is a bad sign. It is as if such a patient has aborted his schizophrenic trip, has taken the easy way out by blaming his troubles on someone else. Harry Stack Sullivan has vividly described the implications:

> This is an ominous development in that the schizophrenic state is taking on a paranoid coloring. If the suffering of the patient is markedly diminished thereby, we shall observe the evolution of a paranoid schizophrenic state. These conditions are of relatively much less favorable outcome. They tend to permanent distortions of the interpersonal relations. . . .
>
> A paranoid systematization is, therefore, markedly beneficial to the peace of mind of the person chiefly concerned, and its achievement in the course of a schizophrenic disorder is so great an improvement in security that it is seldom relinquished. . . . It is for this

reason that the paranoid development in a schizophrenic state has to be regarded as of bad omen.

INTERFERENCE

Phenothiazine drugs—especially chlorpromazine—have made it possible to control the most difficult, craziest patients. But in certain individuals these drugs may interfere with recovery. In a recent study, Drs. Michael Goldstein, Lewis Judd and their colleagues at U.C.L.A. tested schizophrenic patients who had shown reasonably good psychological adjustments before they were hospitalized. The acute nonparanoid schizophrenic patients treated with chlorpromazine actually showed increases in thought disorder over a three-week period, while a similar group of patients, on placebos, showed decreases in thought disorder during the same period. This relationship did not hold in patients with the paranoid type of schizophrenic reaction.

Tranquilizers seem to reduce regressed and agitated schizophrenic behavior, and most psychiatrists take this as evidence of improvement. Unfortunately, regressed and disorganized behavior may be essential parts of schizophrenia's problem-solving process.

Several research studies have shown that chlorpromazine reduces the clarity of ordinary experience, and it disrupts a person's abilities to see alternatives and solve problems. It is no wonder then that in schizophrenic reactions that are essentially problem-solving processes, the use of chlorpromazine can make the psychosis worse.

LIGHT

This type of schizophrenic reaction bears an interesting relationship to the phenomenon of suicide. Suicide is also a radical response to a life-crisis situation. The suicidal person, unable to die the ritual death that the acute paranoid schizophrenic does, actually removes himself completely from this entrapment.

There is fascinating research that relates suicide to the autokinesis test in which one sits in a darkened room and looks at a small spot of stationary light several yards away.

After a few minutes in darkness, most persons report that the light is moving erratically. One explanation of this effect is that in darkness, in the absence of external references, we respond more to internal cues. Our eyes normally have a slight vibrating movement that we never notice, but in the darkness we are aware of the movement and conclude that the spot of light is doing it. Harold Voth and his colleagues found that persons who later commit or attempt suicide tend to see the light as stationary. In part this is because they are unable to respond to inner cues—their attention is primarily outside, on the external world. Conflict is not experienced as occurring within oneself but rather outside—between oneself and others. Such individuals find it very difficult to escape into fantasy where they might consider alternative solutions. This reduces the options available for mastering personal distress.

The important point here is that, while certain patients with nonparanoid schizophrenia see more autokinetic movement than normal persons do, paranoid schizophrenics are similar to suicidal groups in that they report relatively little movement. As we noted, it is the paranoid schizophrenic who has aborted the natural schizophrenic experience by directing his attention outward.

TRIPS

Research has indicated several similarities between the schizophrenia trip and the psychedelic-drug trip, with LSD for example. First of all such tranquilizers as chlorpromazine can make a bad trip worse, possibly in the same way that they interrupt the schizophrenic process. The development of paranoid ideas in a person under LSD is also ominous; they take him away from the ideal subjective orientation to the drug experience. We have also found that persons on either kind of journey have a more undifferentiated perceptual orientation than normal persons. For example, they respond to distracting stimuli which causes them to perform poorly on reaction-time tasks and on complex perceptual tasks.

Further, acute schizophrenics and persons under the influence of psychedelic drugs are highly sensitive to stimuli. Sights and sounds are experienced as brilliant, intense, alive, rich, compelling. This acute sensitivity of schizophrenia has gone unnoticed until recently because it is very hard to test. Schizophrenics do not respond well to complex directions; they are flooded by so many stimuli, and so easily distracted by minor sights and noises, that on many sensitivity tests ("press this button when you see the light") they appear unable to perceive stimuli as well as normal persons can.

Only in recent studies have we learned that certain schizophrenics can detect lights and sounds that are too weak for normal persons to sense. We are beginning to accumulate evidence that supports the acute schizophrenic's description of his overaroused world. He is overwhelmed by stimulation. He has difficulty in focusing attention for very long. While he is expressing an idea, a whole series of complicating ideas may come to his mind. He may be blocked in the act of speaking, or may give up the struggle and go mute.

Apparently the mechanism that filters out nonessential stimuli for the rest of us—the humming of the refrigerator, the rustling of the leaves—has ceased to function in the acute schizophrenic. In this distressed individual, who is groping for any possible answer to a life-crisis dilemma, heightened awareness may allow him to see alternative perspectives for making sense out of the life-crisis situation.

INSIDE

In the highly aroused state the schizophrenic may become aware of thoughts, images and feelings that would ordinarily be beyond the scope of the consciousness. Internal events and ideas may be experienced as vividly as if they were real.

With continued overstimulation, inhibition is built up against very strong stimuli. The individual may now be able to tolerate intense pain; he may not show a startle response to very loud sounds. This paradoxical situation of sharpening sensitivity to weak stimuli and reduced responsiveness to strong stimuli has also been reported in subjects on LSD.

Looked at in this perspective, the familiar symptoms of early schizophrenia—distractibility, thought-blocking withdrawal, loss of spontaneity in movement and speech—all may be understood as defensive reactions to overstimulation.

Some studies show that an acute schizophrenic may improve temporarily after being placed in a dark, sound-proofed room. Apparently the brief interlude of semirelief from overstimulation allows him to drop some of his automatically defensive reactions to overstimulation, at least for a while.

RITES

Cross-cultural research has reinforced the impression that the schizophrenic process is a universal one. There is a striking similarity between what we call schizophrenia and the behaviors observed in socially accepted initiation rites in some other cultures.

These transition ordeals clearly imply a ritual death followed by resurrection or a new birth—an image that closely parallels the death-rebirth experience that is so common in the schizophrenic reaction of Western culture. In some societies persons may become esteemed spiritual leaders or shamans after being possessed by religious experiences in which they explore the inner world.

In a survey of many such cases I found that these persons were often reported to be hypersensitive before their experiences and had unsolved or traumatic problems that aroused strong emotional reactions. Often they had felt personally inadequate and had built defensive barriers that protected them from intimate contact with others.

Many religious figures—St. Paul, St. Theresa and George Fox, the founder of the Quakers, for example—have gone through experiences that today would be regarded as full-blown psychoses. But since their personal disharmonies resonated with the society's disharmonies at that time, the individuals were valued for their special insights.

INITIATION

In many non-Western cultures the psychoticlike transition ordeal is accepted—there is no social stigma for the initiate. In our culture, however, the schizophrenic must make his fantastic voyage alone, ashamed, in the hands of hospital-ward personnel whose purpose is to interrupt his schizophrenic trip.

In tribal cultures the initiatory experience is guided by an old leader, a spiritual master or a guru. But in our culture we have certified doctors whose job all too often is to abort the schizophrenic process by powerful chemicals or any other means necessary.

At Agnews State Hospital in San Jose, California, I am working with other mental-health professionals who agree that this type of schizophrenic reaction should be encouraged and supported. With systematic clinical tests, electrophysiological measures and computer techniques we are attempting to identify those individuals who are on the schizophrenic trip. We are withholding antipsychotic medication from patients who ordinarily would be heavily drugged.

EMPATHY

A primary concern at our center is the attitude and orientation of the staff. Nurses, attendants and doctors are trained to encourage and support the acute schizophrenic episode; they are learning to understand deep regressive states and to live with their own fears and fantasies about madness. In collaboration with Richard Price, Vice President of the Esalen Institute at Big Sur, and the Esalen staff, our staff members participate in intensive group-work sessions that focus on awareness of their own feelings and openness to the feelings of others.

We have even begun extensive psychophysical and personality testing of ourselves to see which type of therapist has the most success with schizophrenic patients. And, of course, we are doing comparison studies to see if our program is more effective than traditional treatments in helping patients and returning them to the community. Our basic hypothesis is that the organism's wisdom is greater than our limited intellectual appreciation of it. The daemonic symptoms may, like fever, be benign responses to the deeper trials of life that the patient may never solve if the therapist encourages escape or drugs him into a permanent state of psychic helplessness.

It may be that one day acute schizophrenics of certain types will not go to hospitals but will go instead to asylums or sanctuaries to grapple with their otherwise unsolvable life-crisis problems. One hopes that in this kind of environment the schizophrenic patient who emerges "weller than before" will be more the rule than the exception.

27

Ecstasy Without Agony Is Baloney

William H. Blanchard

A middle-aged schoolteacher stands tense, eyes shut, on a hill. A flower has been placed in her hand. She opens her eyes. She looks at the flower reverently, stroking the petals with a delicate, smoothing touch, "It's a growing thing," she says, "It's alive, and I'm actually touching it—feeling what it's really like!" She has just completed a blind walk, one of many awareness-expanding techniques used by the modern growth center she is attending for the weekend. Her partner, a young corporation lawyer in sport shirt and tight cutoffs, is waiting for her. She smiles broadly, concealing a slight embarrassment: she is effusive. The schoolteacher stretches out her arms as though to encompass the other members of the group. "Oh the life there is in all of us," she exclaims. "Oh the humanity, the pure bliss of being alive!" Some members of the group pause to look at her, and smile approvingly. Others are doing their own thing.

All these people, refugees from the middle class, are attending one of the many centers or workshops for awareness and human growth that dot the coast of Southern California and are scattered more sparsely elsewhere in the United States. The great new industry of human growth began quietly at the Esalen Institute at Big Sur in Northern California in 1961, but since that time new growth centers have proliferated. Kairos at Rancho Santa Fe, near San Diego in southernmost California, the Topanga Center for Human Development in the Los Angeles area, Shalal in Vancouver, Amare in Bowling Green, Ohio, Evergreen

Institute in Littleton, Colorado, and the Aureon Institute in New York City are a few of the more than 60 centers now in existence. Most of them produce brochures that advertise various means, usually group interactions, for discovering one's full potential through expanded awareness. Their organization is, to use their language, "based on the belief that the natural state of the human organism is joy." They are designed to help one get in touch with an "inner rhythm," "release suppressed energies," and, more than anything, have a "peak experience."

The whole group scene has become dangerously easy to ridicule, almost like Southern California itself. Growth centers compete with one another to sign up leaders with the most prestige and to billboard the most impressive-sounding seminar titles. There is a rush to invent new and different awareness-enhancing techniques. The head of one center told Rasa Gustaitis, "I feel like Sol Hurok. I found this man who has really got something. I wish I could sign him up before someone else gets to him or steals his technique." As the centers vie with one another the workshop titles become more grandiose. William Schultz at Esalen began with a rather modest promise of "Joy" and followed it with "More Joy." Herbert Otto, now at the National Center for the Exploration of Human Potential in La Jolla, introduced "Peak Joy" when he was at the University of Utah. Then the Elysium Institute at Los Angeles countered with "Cosmic Joy" and "Advanced Cosmic Joy," for which the "Awakening Seminar" is a prerequisite. Any day now we can anticipate a program on Super Advanced Cosmic Joy. Like the makers of Tide, Bold and Ivory Soap, the seminarists are always improving their product. Middle-aged housewives and young corporation executives in Levis manage, after a series of announcements, arguments, tears, sensory saturation and rolling on the grass, to reach their weekend moments of ecstatic awareness or supreme consciousness. However, such experiences seldom occur just because one is chasing a fad and wants something nice to happen to him: it takes quite a lot of doing. Seminar leaders use various devices, sometimes encouraging participants to take off their clothes in order to be

Reprinted from *Psychology Today* 3, no. 8 (January 1970): 8, 10, 64. Copyright © 1970, Sussex Publishers, Inc.

more honest with themselves. But people who live in a mendacious society often find it difficult to get close to the truth when it is an unpleasant aspect of reality. In the Harvard *Crimson* one youth recounts his own reaction to a nude encounter in the sulphur baths at Esalen. The group leader had asked them to let their eyes roam over each other's bodies and tell the group what they liked and disliked about their own bodies. One of the women (Jessica) said she did not like her breasts because they were big and flabby. The youth looked at her breasts and decided she was right. They *were* big and flabby. But to his surprise he heard the other members of the group assuring her that she had lovely breasts. The woman blushed and thanked her admirers, but the young man was disconcerted. He had mixed feelings. It was very good that they were all looking at their bodies. A person cannot love and be loved until he loves himself ... that was fine—but it was too easy. The boy honestly did not like Jessica's body and could not quite believe it when everyone else professed to. What kind of honesty was this they were discovering? When the stage is set for something good to happen most persons do not want to spoil the act. A few may be willing to dip their toes into the horror of their lives, but most of them do not really want to plunge in all the way—nor do they want to push anyone else who is already standing too close to the edge. If the way to bliss lies through the route of terror there are many who will not take the trip.

There seems to be little doubt that the phenomenon of superheightened awareness actually occurs. In 1901, Richard Bucke published his *Cosmic Consciousness*, a report on such experiences as they have been described throughout history. Since Bucke's early work, heightened awareness as it is emerging in the Western world today has been subject to considerable interpretation and experiment. The names that are used to designate the experience vary, but all of them refer to a moment of consciousness different from normal or usual perception and characterized by dazzling insight or intellectual illumination, and often accompanied by intense feelings of elevation, ecstasy or bliss. Abraham Maslow, who has

studied instances of heightened awareness, has noted that they are relatively infrequent, that they are difficult to produce or deliberately pursue, and that they often alter the life of the individual.

But in the typical group, the pressure to experience awareness is enormous, and the urge to fake it is almost irresistible. Most group members have been coached by friends and by promotional brochures: they believe that a peak experience is not only desirable but necessary if one is to have fullest happiness and mental health. They are programmed for peaks. Further, elation or perceptual strangeness induced by mildly hypnotic or hallucinogenic techniques can easily provide the outward and visible signs of an inner awareness.

In a society like our own, in which sensuality has long been suppressed, sensory awareness—an intense, guiltless concentration upon the sights, sounds, feels and smells of the human and natural world—can represent a revelatory experience and be almost deliriously pleasant. Unfortunately, such sensory awareness tends to occur precisely within a context that reinforces an already well-rooted reaction against mind or thought. Public education has deprived the intellectual experience of significance and emotional excitement, and intricate newfound pleasures of sensory awareness compound the tendency to regard the intellect as the great enemy of all that is natural and human and fun.

While some professors of psychology play pattycake, smear each other with fingerpaints and smash toy castles, other humanistic psychologists have become concerned at the increasing anti-intellectualism in the humanistic movement. They ask whether the rejection of reason is leading us toward cultural disintegration.

The various centers and schools for awareness rarely emphasize intellectual awareness and the powerful passions of scholarship. In many weekend revelations intellectual awareness fails to emerge. Participants never discover that full liberation of the human potential requires a unification of the intellect and the senses, and ecstasy of the mind as well as the body.

Great scientific insights as well as other forms of inspired problem-solving are often moments of intense intellectual awareness in which the individual participates in an experience of knowing what seems essentially passive. It appears to be an experience in which his ego, personality or character, as we commonly use these terms, are not operative. Later, however, when he interprets such an experience, a man's own personal style may become manifest. He may proceed to express or utilize his experience mathematically, in stone, in words, or in wonderful action. The interesting thing is that true and insightful awareness seems always to stimulate belief in and commitment to something that can only be called an *idea*. Dogged concentration and study and persistent refusal to accept failure usually precede and almost invariably follow this transient but very *now* glimpse into pattern or relationship.

The history of science and art is replete with examples of a strong sense of plain old *belief*. Johann Kepler, who provided convincing mathematical evidence to support the heliocentric theory of Copernicus, speaks of the inner conviction in his "deepest soul" that the Copernician ideas represented truth.

> I certainly know that I owe it [the theory] this duty, that I have attested it is true in my deepest soul, and as I contemplate its beauty with incredible and ravishing delight, I should also publicly defend it to my readers with all the force at my command.

Scientists are generally less explicit than religious leaders in reporting their own subjective experiences of awareness, but the pleasure associated with Kepler's experience is unmistakable. In a letter he remarked, "The intense pleasure I have received from this discovery can never be told in words."

It is a convention in the scientific world to report the emergence of a new theory as though it emerged slowly and inevitably from the analytical throttling of data. The scientist is pictured as plodding through his method, discovering some discrepancy in experiment results and myopically tracking this discrepancy until he stumbles over the doorstep of theory. Actually, far more often than not the theory springs into the scientist's vision as a wild surmise, and he spends most of his time searching for facts to fit it. The notion of relativity became intuitively clear to Einstein at the age of 16, in the form of a paradox; he reflected on this phenomenon for 10 years before he was able to support it by mathematical and experimental evidence.

There may be something about the act of knowing that makes it necessary for us to see things all at once and together as a whole if we are to arrive at genuine realization or insight. I believe that real peak awareness represents such a radical, instantaneous, global reorganization within the individual. It is the moment of awareness of creative possibilities, and as such it may be both exhilarating and frightening. It involves a change in the person's conception of himself as well as the form of universe he sees. This change may be particularly striking in terms of his willingness to go along with accepted beliefs and conventions, whether in his discipline, his art, or his society.

Great and moving experiences that cause major shifts in a person's life are unlikely to be served up at a growth center. Such an experience generally occurs whimsically, after a long period of seeking and preparation that may include everything *but* ecstasy. This is particularly true for the individual who is hunting for a way of looking at the problems of modern society: if it is difficult for a physical scientist to escape his frame of reference, it may be more difficult for the social scientist, whose frames are likely to be half-grasped metaphors. An experience close to psychosis may be required to take one outside the collective pressures of our culture. Indeed, some of the most provocative insights have emerged from the experience of terror or torment, and we may be in need of a heightened awareness, not of joy but of medieval horror. For a black man, full awareness of one's blackness in a white man's world may be an agonizing experience, but it may also make him angry enough to do something about it. In short, ecstasy without agony is baloney.

If awareness is really deep or comprehensive the perceiver may discover much that is horrible in himself and in his world. He will find it more difficult to keep his distance from injustice and to pretend that he has no power to change things. Awareness will mean, among other things, an acute sense of his capacity to influence others, an inescapable involvement and a painful recognition of his unity with the rest of mankind. When peasants and GIs bleed in Vietnam, he will bleed with them. When blacks cry out in rage and despair he will join their cry. He will be sucked into the vortex of experience and he may not be able to come back even marginally to the world of private capital, family responsibilities and Blue Cross payments.

In *Gestalt Therapy*, Frederick Perls and his colleagues provide techniques for expanding awareness of one's own body and making contact with the environment. One of these is the technique of tasting and learning to assimilate one's food instead of swallowing it whole. The object is to help the person become more aware and selective about food and about all life experiences. But, suppose that I try the Perls taste experiment during lunchtime at the factory. I buy a pre-packaged beef sandwich and a cup of coffee at the snack bar. I chew it thoroughly and savor the taste. The beef is cold, overcooked, dry; the bread tastes and smells like soft plastic. This awareness of taste, in accordance with the prescribed techniques, stimulates a larger awareness of my surroundings. The sandwich makes me more aware of the factory itself. The dry beef sandwich is a characteristic part of the total environment. I notice that the work I do is dull, meaningless and repetitive. The people who work around me behave like colorless automatons who exchange occasional forced smiles in the hall. And I am one of them! I continue the day in the full agony of awareness of who I am, where I am and what I am doing. When I leave work I notice the faces on the subway. Is this what the world is really like? For a moment, I consider getting another job, but all those other dead bodies on the subway come from other jobs. Our society is filled with meaningless other jobs, and people spend the best and most useful moments of their waking hours performing these tasks. The awareness experiment has placed me in a painful and frightening dilemma, for I now realize that I do not want to go on living in this kind of world. The intensity with which I experience my surroundings increases my sense of urgency to the point of suicide or revolution. This is known as a bad trip and it all started because I was willing to let myself go when I tasted that sandwich. In that one sandwich was wrapped the futility and drudgery of our modern civilization.

Many growth centers do not know what they are getting into: they expect merely to escape boredom and futility. There have been a few psychotic episodes during or directly after weekends of awareness, which means that growth centers have not taken a really close look at their goals and at the orientation of their programs in relation to the applicants they are willing to accept. They have not faced—or do not want to face—the difficult decision as to whether they will offer a therapeutic program for the maladjusted or an experience in expanded consciousness in which the individual puts his psyche on the line to risk the possibility of growth or personal disaster. If they offer the first they have an obligation to protect their patients from overly threatening or disruptive experiences. If they offer the second they should prepare those who seek out the experience of awareness to face a higher level of personal risk than the present participants seem to be willing to take.

The crucial problem that must be faced by the moderate center for awareness is that one does not go in search of the holy grail of personal fulfillment with full immunity from the dragons along the way. If the individual is really in search of awareness, he must be prepared for an ego-shattering experience in which there is genuine danger. One does not achieve great rewards without taking great risks. Perhaps this problem could be solved simply by honest advertising. If a center were more explicit about the purpose of a group, it could induce more adequate preparation in the participants. Anyone in psychotherapy could be advised to discuss commitment to an encounter group with his therapist before attending. However, all these suggestions depend on the standards set by the center and the *intent* of the group leader. If one's goal is salesmanship rather than self-understanding, anything can be used as part of the come-on. One can easily imagine a superficial encounter group in which the leader decided to beef up his image by appearing dangerous. He might paraphrase the billboards of the old Frankenstein movies with a warning challenge to the participant: "If you have a weak ego, don't attend!"

In the last analysis there does not appear to be any way around the old-fashioned problem of ethics. It is clear that a group leader, whether he calls himself a therapist or a philosopher, has a professional responsibility to learn about the people in his group before he attempts to lead them into an experience designed to expose all their nerve endings—to both pleasure and pain. An experience of awareness can be profound and deeply moving if it is approached with proper preparation, but the preparation is precisely that aspect of the experience that is most frequently slighted in the indiscriminate urge to reach everyone.

28

Can They
Go Home Again?

Richard W. Brislin and
H. Van Buren, IV

Benjamin Franklin once related an experience he had with people moving from one culture to another:

> At the treaty of Lancaster, in Pennsylvania, anno 1744, between the Government of Virginia and the Six Nations, the commissioners from Virginia acquainted the Indians by a speech, that there was at Williamsburg a college with a fund for educating Indian youth; and that if the chiefs of the Six Nations would send down half a dozen of their sons to that college, the government would take care that they be well provided for, and instructed in all the learning of the white people.

The Indians' spokesman replied:

> . . . We are convinced . . . that you mean to do us good by your proposal and we thank you heartily. But you, who are wise, must know that different nations have different conceptions of things; and you will not therefore take it amiss, if our ideas of this kind of education happen not to be the same with yours. We have had some experience of it; several of our young people were formerly brought up at the colleges of northern provinces; they were instructed in all your sciences; but, when they came back to us, they were bad runners, ignorant of every means of living in the woods,

unable to bear either cold or hunger, knew neither how to build a cabin, take a deer, nor kill an enemy, spoke our language imperfectly, were therefore neither fit for hunters, warriors, nor counsellors; they were totally good for nothing.

> We are however not the less obligated by your kind offer, though we decline accepting it; and, to show our grateful sense of it, if the gentlemen of Virginia will send us a dozen of their sons, we will take care of their education, instruct them in all we know, and make men of them.[1]

Cleveland et al. tell of an experience shared by many people who live temporarily outside the United States and then go back to their home towns. They quote one of their interviewees:

> In my home town there are probably many people who still don't realize that the world is round. I remember when we got home from Moscow people asked me how it was there, but before I could open my mouth, they would begin telling me how Uncle Charlie had broken his arm. They profess interest in things abroad, but they really aren't interested.[2]

These stories are a good introduction to the experiences of East-West Center grantees as well as to our program designed to lessen their potential difficulties. The East-West Center is an international educational institution located on the main campus of the University of Hawaii. Over 1,000 participants each year come from the United States and 40 countries and territories from Asia and the Pacific area. There are three types of participants (degree students, professional development students, and fellows), but this presentation is concerned mostly with degree students.

These participants almost always have the equivalent of a bachelor's degree from a school in their home countries, and they come to the East-West Center both to participate in its programs and to earn master's (sometimes Ph.D.) degrees at the University of Hawaii. The participants, then, are away from their homes for an average of two years. Certainly there are advantages to the rich experience of living and working with many types of people

Reprinted from *International Educational and Cultural Exchange*, 9, 19–24. Copyright © 1974, United States Advisory Committee on International and Cultural Affairs.

one meets at the Center, but it is not all a bed of Plumeria petals.

When a person lives in a culture other than his own for a significant length of time, his attitudes and outlook change.[3] Many aspects of his home country will also have changed, for instance, the attitudes of his friends and family and the physical elements of the environment that he remembers. An interesting and important fact that has emerged from research in recent years is that a person who is most successful at adjusting to a new culture is often the worst at readjusting to his old culture.[4]

Perhaps the explanation is that a person who adjusts readily is one who can accept new ideas, meet and talk intelligently with people from many countries, and be happy with the stimulation that he finds every day. This same person may readjust poorly when he goes home since his new ideas conflict with tradition. He can find no internationally minded people, and he finds no stimulation in the country he already knows so well. Training to prepare people for such *reverse* culture shock problems has been uncommon. For these reasons, we have been involved in research on reorientation cross-cultural seminars, and we sometimes call it our "Can you go home again?" program.

The seminars involve East-West Center grantees who are about to return home after a two-year stay in Hawaii. The seminars include U.S. participants since few of them will return to home towns in which they will have daily contact with friends from Asia and the Pacific. Actually, we have found that the readjustment-to-home can be most severe for U.S. participants because they do not expect any problems. Instead, they maintain that "I'm not going back to another country!" We argue that in many ways they *are* going from one culture (the State of Hawaii and the East-West Center) to another (somewhere on the mainland U.S.A.).

We are now building a file of specific, critical incidents that students encounter back home, such as jealousy on the part of colleagues, friends' indifference to their intercultural experience (we call this the "Uncle Charlie" syndrome, referring to the anecdote

related previously), and return to close supervision by parents as opposed to their relative independence at the East-West Center. These critical incidents are based on letters and reports from participants who have returned home. Many will be given as examples throughout this presentation.

We do not suggest that students will have these problems, but rather we present these and other conflicts as potential problems and encourage students to think them through. The assumption is that if students work through these issues before going home and prepare for potential conflicts, they will have fewer problems after they actually return home. During these seminars at the East-West Center, of course, the students have social support from staff and friends which they might not find at home.

WORRYING HELPS

The theoretical basis for the seminar is that of Janis (see also the summary presentation by Elms), who wrote about preparation for stressful events.[5] Using the concept, "the work of worrying," he argued that worrying about potentially stressful events is helpful. Such work can force the person to learn as much as possible about the event, to prepare for its negative effects so as not to be surprised by them, and to envisage what he might do if any of the negative effects indeed occur.

The principle has widespread application, and Janis made one specific recommendation for its use with surgical patients.[6] He suggested that if patients were told basic facts about their upcoming operations and were able to work through in their minds exactly how they might feel, they might be less affected by post-operational pain. The goal is to have people *not taken by surprise* when they feel the inevitable post-operational pain.

Egbert et al. found in a study that such "worry-prepared" patients felt less emotional stress, were given less pain-killing medication, and were released from the hospital an average of three days sooner than control patients who did not undergo such preparation.[7]

Based on this work, we have asked East-West Center grantees, just before they return home, to work out potential difficulties in their minds. We present them with stories like that told by Ben Franklin to stimulate thinking. We also talk about the beneficial aspects of such thinking by explaining the medical research by Janis and Egbert and by sharing humorous stories with them. We suggest only that the possibility of such problems exists. The charge has been made that we tell people what *will* happen, and that this is paternalistic. Our response is simple: we don't.

CONTENT OF THE PROGRAM

We have held four reorientation seminars at the East-West Center (May 1972, December 1972, May 1973, December 1973), all run over a two-day period. Improvements, based on staff and participant feedback from the earlier seminars, have been incorporated into the later ones. The following summary describes the content of the May 1973 seminar. Each session is begun by a "kickoff" speaker who brings up different issues to stimulate thinking, and then participants have open discussion. Kickoff speakers always present specific difficulties *they* and others have faced, and we include these here since they both give an idea of a session's content and the issues brought up in free discussion. The participants do almost all the talking for 75–80 percent of any given session.

Friends and Relations

The first session of a seminar deals with family and personal aspects of returning home. Emphasis is on relations with one's mother, father, siblings, and friends. At every seminar, at least one person was about to return home (Asia) and be faced with an arranged marriage, and these people had been dating freely in Hawaii. At the last seminar, the kick-off speaker was an American who told about his own stress in returning from Japan to Akron, Ohio. If speakers relate their own experiences (as they have done at every seminar), participants see that the readjustment is a normal process and that they are not "kooks" if they are faced with a problem.

The following is from a former participant's letter, and it is typical of the examples given by the speakers:

> One of the most difficult things to adjust to was living at home with my family. The forced independence being away from home became something I grew accustomed to; living in a dorm or apartment, not having to tell my whereabouts all the time [etc.]. Things such as these which were considered of positive survival value (independence) are not acceptable at one's own home. Even among friends, I felt there was more need to conform. It was hard to change from home-living to apartment-living abroad, but it is perhaps even harder to change back again.

Some participant comments during discussion of the general topic of relations with friends and family are as follows:

> I think the expectations, mine and my friends and relatives, might have undergone a change. There will be an initial period of adjustment when failure to meet up with the expectations might result in frustration and tension.
>
> I am afraid to go back to my old self. It is so easy to return to your old shell and adjust yourself to other people's expectations. The hardest thing is to keep and develop what I have learned here.
>
> Be aware of "too" Westernized behavior and attitudes picked up in U.S.A. which might offend relatives and friends back home.

Short-Term Adjustments

The emphasis in this session is on the issues that would be problematic over a *short* period of time as contrasted to a longer period of time. We recommend that a person not be overwhelmed by short-term problems and should not feel that "I'm making a poor readjustment" if small problems are immediately troublesome.

For instance, adjusting to the custom concerning which sex walks through doors first is a short-term problem, advancing on the job is a long-term issue. Another recommendation is for participants who want to change their old culture. We suggest that they try to change smaller, more manageable aspects rather than the culture as a whole. From a letter:

> Now that I am back, I realize how difficult it will be for me to use my East-West Center studies to change the curriculum in my department. I want to put the "new math" into my school. . . .
>
> But before I can even plan any new curriculum, I must convince my principal and the staff of the school that this is a worthwhile change. There is strong resistance, especially from older teachers. . . .
>
> I believe it may take me two years before I can convince the staff to let me try my new ideas. But I think it is very important that I not give up, but keep trying. . . .

Professional Relations

The third part focuses on the problems involved in returning to a job and professional colleagues.

Speakers have given especially vivid examples. A staff member from Japan has reported that Japanese often *hide* the fact that they have an American college degree since it is not so useful in job advancement as an in-country degree. A staff member from the Philippines emphasized that she is especially careful about interpersonal relations there, because such relations are much more sensitive and can interfere with work to a greater degree than in the United States. The following is a letter that we use, and was written by a person whose colleague had received an East-West Center grant. Incidentally, this is the first author's favorite discussion starter.

> Please pardon me for writing suddenly to you to ask a favor of you. My name is . . . I am a teacher of English at Senior High School in Kyoto, Japan. I am 39 years old, so I'm not qualified to the admission to your university. However I want to study English at your university by all means. It is quite impossible

for you to lift the age limit from 35 to about 45? You might think that it is troublesome to teach a 40-year-old student, but I hope you'll teach a student who is very eager to study though he may be rather old.

> To tell the truth, one of my fellow teachers is going to enter your university. He and I live in the same small town, and I am his superior at our school. In this situation, it is impossible for me to continue staying at the present school, he will be greatly respected as an English teacher by all the teachers and students at our school and the inhabitants of our small town. On the other hand it is easy to guess what will happen to me. I have been worried for the past several months.

From participant discussions:

> I might look forward to a different job where I can put into use the knowledge that I gained here. I might find that this cannot be done in my present job.
>
> The employment problem is the major problem. I am worried about the prospect of going home and doing nothing.
>
> Feelings of frustration on the job for not being able to do what I think I can do due to insufficient funds, facilities, etc.
>
> Communication with current happenings in my academic field will be cut off.

Non-Western Perspective

This session on the non-Western perspective did not exist at our first seminar (May 1972). Its addition is an example of our desire to improve based on evaluative feedback. After the first seminar, an Asian participant wrote on her evaluation form that it was clear that the seminar had been "structured by American scholars" and that the staff should be more aware of the Asian psychology.

This comment struck us as quite reasonable, and so we asked the Asian students at later seminars to design their own session. We asked a Japanese female graduate student in psychology, who had read all the evaluation forms from the first seminar, to provide as much direction as necessary. At one of the later seminars, the participants decided to have an open discussion of what others back home will *expect* of the returnees. While, as American outsiders to this session, we would have to say that the group seemed quiet and that the ideas expressed seemed repetitious of those brought out in other sessions, the participants rated it highly. We realize the value of a session designed by the group as a whole, so we will retain such a session for future seminars.

Playing the Role

In one session participants were asked to prepare short skits, acting out what might happen after they return home. Participants were given the option of writing a script or simply writing down a few ideas that they would develop as the role play or skits continued. The skits were videotaped and played back to the staff and participants immediately on a TV monitor. The videotaping increases the impact,[8] and adds to the popularity of the session since everyone enjoys seeing himself on television. The tapes are available for examination by visitors to the East-West Center.

In the seminars, almost all participants have chosen to be somewhat humorous in their skits, reinforcing our recommendation to keep a light heart concerning readjustment. All roles such as "father," "mother," and "boss" are played by participants. Some of the skits went as follows:

1. A returning son shows slides of the East-West Center to his parents, and they comment on the scanty clothing of the girls and talk about an arranged marriage for their son.

2. A returnee comes home to a party arranged by her family, relatives, and old friends. She is shocked to see how *they* have changed because they are wearing the latest fashions, doing the latest dances, and using the most current slang.

3. A Pacific Islander returns home and is faced with an ultimatum from his fa-

ther: either he cuts his hair or he leaves the house.

4. Former participants are at a party with people who know little or nothing about Asia and the East-West Center. The chatter is filled with embarrassing pauses, non sequiturs, ridiculous generalizations about Asians, and so forth. Finally, the participants and the other people break a previously arranged engagement with, "Well, I just remembered we have to do something else."

5. A female participant is being interviewed for a job by the boss of a small company. It becomes clear during the interview that the boss is interested in typing speed, not experiences with living and working with people from 40 countries; job experience, not ability to translate into Thai; and shorthand, not abstract knowledge of generative grammatical theory's generalizations to English language teaching.

Nonverbal Behavior

The session on attribution and nonverbal behavior draws material from the social psychological literature. We explain general notions of attribution theory,[9] especially two major findings: (1) People judge actions of others as due to traits, but that they are more likely to judge the same actions in themselves as due to situational pressures; (2) People use extremely limited and sometimes faulty information in making trait inferences about others.

This leads to a question for discussion: Will people back home make trait judgments based on the behavior that they see in returnees, even though this information is limited? Will the trait inferences be negative (uppity, too-Americanized, snobbish, know-it-all, etc.)? Our approach is similar to the culture assimilator work of Fiedler et al., who also use specific and critical incidents of this type to generate understanding of the attribution process.[10]

The emphasis on attributions made by others leads into nonverbal behavior since participants have often learned gestures common to other nationalities. We show a videotape that we have made on American gestures, and then ask, "Are you bringing any back, and will there be problems because of it?" For instance, Americans scratch the side of their head when thinking about the answer to a difficult question, and Japanese scratch the top of their heads. The question for discussion: What will people think if they see a Japanese returnee making the quick American version of this nonverbal behavior? We have already presented the principle that there will be a trait inference from this inadequate piece of data, so the important point is that there *will* be an inference. Other examples center around the greater amount of bodily movement involved in American as contrasted with Asian gestures, the differing distances people use in ordinary conversation across different cultures,[11] and the fact of returnee-as-oddity and thus the subject of much discussion by people back home.

Keeping in Touch

Finally, we have a session on maintaining cross-cultural relations. This session has the largest number of specific recommendations and is most unique to the special nature of the East-West Center. It is led by the alumni officer who tells about what East-West Center publications the participants will continue to receive, different associations organized by former participants in various countries, the alumni directory, occupations now held by former participants, names of volunteers in various countries who will help the new returnee join the alumni organizations, and so forth.

Generally, recommendations deal with maintaining ties with people in the different countries and how to meet others with similar international orientations. We always schedule this session last because it is uplifting, positive, and a relief after the analysis of potential negative aspects of returning home.

RATING THE PROGRAM

A treatment of the reorientation seminar's evaluation is especially difficult because one of the authors has published perhaps the most severe criticisms of cross-cultural training evaluation in general.[12] In those publications, he recommended the following among many others: (1) gathering behavioral measures related to recommended program outcome, such as the types of interpersonal interactions occurring *outside* of program hours; (2) comparing people who have gone through a seminar with those who have not; (3) gathering data long after a program ends, since the goal of the seminar is to affect future behavior; (4) being evaluated by people not associated with the original program.

EVALUATION DATA FROM PARTICIPANTS IN VARIOUS SEMINARS FOR FOUR SESSIONS
Name of Session

Various Seminars	Role Relations	Short/ Long-term Adjustments	Role Playing and Videotaping	Maintaining Cultural Ties
Seminar 1 (5/72) (N=22)	22.8	34.8	34.6	33.9
Seminar 2 (12/72) (N=12)	deleted	34.6	38.3	36.1
Future Seminars	will not be used	Design includes gathering feedback from future seminar participants		

N-Number of participants
Note: Cell entries are averages for responses to 6 seven-point evaluative scales (see text). A perfect score would be 42.

We recognize that these standards are desirable and, therefore, are least satisfied with the evaluation aspect of the reorientation seminars. Our efforts will continue and will include follow-ups of seminar participants long after they have returned home (number 3, above), by people not associated with the original seminars (number 4, above). To date, we have three major sources of information, mostly aimed at showing "how we are doing." The data gathered tell (1) if participants are enthusiastic or if they are bored, (2) if they are learning anything, and (3) their suggestions for future programs.

Measures of both single session and total program acceptance are determined by standard attitude scales, specifically semantic-differential adjectives. After each session, participants completed a questionnaire containing these seven-point scales: useful-useless; boring-interesting; unimportant-important; bad-good; intelligent-unintelligent; unstimulating-stimulating. The participants also completed scales measuring their feelings about having learned anything new, their thinking about the future, and their insights into themselves as returnees. This method is admittedly not innovative or exciting, but it gives us valuable information and "keeps us on our toes" because we gather it for every program.

In the table we use examples from two programs, and show how the evaluation design extends into the future. Note that ratings of the sessions have been maintained or have increased across the two programs, and that the same ratings will be gathered in the future. One session from the first seminar was rated so low that it was deleted from the next seminar. The second program's ratings are very high, perhaps because we took many of the first-program's participant comments into account, as mentioned below. Complacency is a luxury we cannot enjoy.

The measure of learning is simply the participants' answers to this question, completed before and after the program: "What problems do you think you might have after you return to your country? These might be any type of problem such as personal, family, job-related, and so forth."

The results from answers to this question are likewise encouraging. The average number of answers (summarized for all programs to date) increased from one before the seminar to four after the seminar. This shows that participants are indeed learning and are becoming more cognitively complex in their thinking about the future.

One reason that the ratings improved from earlier to later sessions is probably because of the excellent participant comments for the first (especially) and second programs. For instance, during the first seminar, we tried a session devoted to role relations in marriage and in the family; but it was not completely successful; and so we did not have such a seminar again (see table). The participants' answers in response to the open question, "Do you have any other comments?" tell why.

> Not well enough focused.
>
> Too short. No substantial development in the discussion.
>
> Not enough time given for explanation of the sociological terms involved.

We presented another comment that led to improvement earlier in describing the genesis of the "Non-Western Perspective" session. As a final example, one participant felt that students would be able to contribute more if they knew in advance what the seminar was about. Following up, we prepared reading material and circulated information to potential participants before the next program, letting them know when we were available to talk with them about the upcoming seminar.

PLACE AND PLANNING IMPORTANT

The physical setting of the reorientation seminar is very important. If we have learned anything from our experience with the programs, it is that the seminar must be held at a good distance from the East-West Center, preferably at a camp or retreat over 20 miles away. Without this removal from the Center, the situational pressures of invitations from nonreturnee friends, need to go to the drugstore for a tube of toothpaste, and competition from television take their toll on session attendance. Consequently, when the faithful see that attendance at sessions has decreased, their morale declines. Our recommendation is that seminars be held away from a familiar environment that has a well-established schedule attached to it.

In general, the planning, administering, follow-up, and evaluation of transportation, housing, food, and service are a very important job. These details can often make or break participants' favorable response to a program. We recommend one person be assigned the responsibility for all the mechanics of a program so that the details do not interfere with the program. Allow time for planning and carrying out these comparatively insignificant and annoying details lest you find yourself in the position of man who, for want of a nail, loses the battle.

It would be easy to argue, using exactly the data presented in this paper, that we are causing returnees needless worry. Critics could point to the respondent who gave only one potential problem prior to the seminar but seven after, and they could say that ethical concerns come into question. Our response is that the worry will be beneficial for many returnees if problems actually do arise.

Even if problems *do not* occur, the returnees who participate in the seminar will learn what *does* happen to a large number of people. One of the implicit assumptions of the East-West Center is that Asian, Pacific, and U.S. grantees will learn about the nature of people who have a multicultural orientation. One aspect of such people, of course, is the nature of the issues faced when they move from their "home" culture to another and back.

Because of our seminar, participants have an opportunity (for the most part, their only formal opportunity) to learn about this process. This point became clear to us when a participant congratulated us on the seminar and said, "I've learned so much. I never dreamed that there were all these things that can happen when people move from culture to culture."

ENDNOTES

[1] B. Franklin, "Remarks concerning the savages of North America," pamphlet (1784), in *The works of Benjamin Franklin, Vol. II* (Boston: Tappan and Dennet, 1844).

[2] H. Cleveland, G. J. Mangone and J. C. Adams, *The Overseas Americans* (New York: McGraw-Hill, 1960): 25.

[3] *Ibid.*; S. Bochner, "The Mediating Man and Cultural Diversity," in R. Brislin, ed., *Topics in Culture Learning* (Honolulu: East-West Culture Learning Institute, 1973): 23–37; J. Useem and R. Useem, *The Western-Educated Man in India* (New York: Dryden Press, 1955); "American-Educated Indians and Americans in India: A Comparison of Two Modernizing Roles," *Journal of Social Issues, 24* (4), 1968: 143–158.

[4] Bochner, *op. cit.*

[5] I. Janis, *Psychological Stress* (New York: Wiley, 1958); A. Elms, *Social Psychology and Social Relevance* (Boston: Little, Brown, 1972).

[6] Janis, *op. cit.*

[7] L. Egbert et al. "Reduction of Postoperative Pain by Encouragement and Instruction," *New England Journal of Medicine, 270*, 1964: 825–827.

[8] K. Bailey and W. Sowder, "Audiotape and Videotape Self-Confrontation in Psychotherapy," *Psychological Bulletin, 74*, 1970:127–137.

[9] E. Jones et al., *Attribution: Perceiving the Causes of Behavior* (Morristown, NJ: General Learning Press, 1971).

[10] F. Fiedler, T. Mitchell and H. Triandis, "The Culture Assimilator: An Approach to Cross-Cultural Training," *Journal of Applied Psychology, 55,* 1971:95–102.

[11] R. Sommer, *Personal space.* New York: Prentice-Hall, 1969.

[12] R. Brislin, "The Content and Evaluation of Cross-Cultural Training Programs," in D. Hoopes, ed., *Readings in Intercultural Communication,* Vol. III (Pittsburgh: Regional Council for International Education, 1973): 79–122.

29

The Process of Reentry

Gary R. Weaver

GOOD NEWS—BAD NEWS

Everyone who has adapted to another culture has gone through culture shock. Those who claim they did not may not have recognized the signs, or perhaps they never really adjusted to the other culture. Tourists seldom experience culture shock because they are short-term sojourners who never actually enter another culture. Many diplomats do not experience culture shock because of their isolation within the diplomatic community and their insulation from the local society.

Almost all students, business people, development workers, and others who must actually live within a new culture and interact with host nationals do experience some form of culture shock. The good news is that the vast majority handle this stress successfully, with some reliable evidence indicating that they grow from the experience. Reactions to the stress of cross-cultural adjustment are simply necessary "growing pains" that eventually lead to greater emotional and intellectual maturity, a more flexible personality, and a wider global perspective. Increased confidence in one's own ability to solve problems creatively is another benefit.

Another piece of good news is that, contrary to popular opinion, long-term sojourners seldom "lose" their native culture while overseas. Ironically, they instead usually find their culture by leaving it. The world-renowned Nigerian jazz artist Fela once said that he discovered what it really meant to be an African when he left Africa.

Reprinted from *The Advising Quarterly,* 27 (Winter 1994), 1–8, AMIDEAST, 1730 M Street, NW, Suite 1100, Washington, D.C., 20036-4505.

In a new culture, sojourners become more aware of what makes them different and consciously examine culturally embedded values, beliefs, and thought patterns. They gain both greater awareness of their home culture and greater awareness of the individual "self" and of what is important to them.

Now the bad news. On the return home the sojourner passes through another adjustment period often termed "reverse culture shock" or "reentry-transition stress." The limited evidence suggests that this experience is even more severe and protracted than culture shock and that it sets in much more quickly. Furthermore, those who have adapted best to life overseas tend to have the most difficulty reentering their home culture.

The space shuttle can provide one useful metaphor of these adjustment periods. Extreme stress occurs as the shuttle leaves the earth's atmosphere and *enters* outer space. Once in space, far less stress is exerted on the vehicle. However, *reentry* to the earth's atmosphere is another very stressful period. In fact, the stress of returning to the earth may be even greater than that of leaving it.

THE CONTINUUM OF ADJUSTMENT

Most scholars agree that cross-cultural adjustment can be graphed as a U-curve. Travelers initially experience a short period of excitement and exhilaration when entering another culture. They are fascinated with the newness of everything and are meeting people who want them to feel welcome. This period is often referred to as the "tourist" or "honeymoon" phase because sojourners are not yet fully involved in the host culture.

Disillusionment soon develops as sojourners face the real difficulties of using public transportation, shopping, attending classes, and working with host nationals. Such disillusionment marks the beginning of culture shock. Interpersonal communication begins to appear ineffective and breaks down. Sojourners long for familiar things from home—the weather, food, language—doubting their ability to solve problems and function in the new environment. Cut off from others, they feel disoriented and out of control.

The severity and duration of culture shock depend upon the individual and on the type of culture to which the individual must adapt. Although Americans experience some degree of culture shock when adapting to England, generally the greater the difference between cultures, the more severe the adjustment difficulties. Some individuals can tolerate more stress than others and quickly develop coping strategies, new ways of perceiving the world, and alternatives for solving problems.

Most sojourners do eventually snap out of this uncomfortable stage as they develop new friendships and begin to feel comfortable with the social and physical environment. They begin to develop a more adequate, flexible, somewhat bicultural personality. This recovery period completes the U-curve, though sojourners may experience a few other "down" periods before returning home.

Adaptation to one's home culture follows a similar pattern, although the stress sets in much more quickly, is more severe, and lasts longer. The so-called U-curve thus becomes a W-curve or continuum of adjustment. If one leaves home again and enters another culture, in all likelihood the pattern will continue and culture shock will recur.

These transitional periods of stress are somewhat analogous to the common cold. Culture shock and reverse culture shock are not terminal, yet there is no "cure." The "symptoms" are similar for each person but also vary with the individual, as does the severity and duration. Recovery does not provide immunity; one can suffer the experience many times.

Individuals develop their own techniques for dealing with the symptoms of a cold—get plenty of rest, drink liquids, eat chicken soup, and so forth. As people experience culture shock, they develop coping strategies to help them minimize its severity and duration. Many of these strategies are just as useful for dealing with reverse culture shock.

WHY IS REVERSE CULTURE SHOCK WORSE THAN CULTURE SHOCK?

Surveys of sojourners preparing to return home show that most anticipate little or no difficulty in readapting to their native culture. However, most will actually experience more stress during reentry than during their entry into another culture. Those who adjusted best and were the most successful overseas usually experience the greatest amount of difficulty with reverse culture shock.

A host of factors help explain this phenomenon. The most significant is that few returnees anticipate reverse culture shock. When we expect a stressful event, we cope with it much better. We rehearse our reactions, think through the course of adjustment, and consider alternative ways to deal with the stressful event. We are prepared both physically and emotionally for the worst that could happen.

Most sojourners are already expecting stress before they leave home. They know they will miss family and friends, and they are anxious about adjusting to new food, a different language, public transportation, and so forth. On the other hand, few sojourners worry about returning home.

Those who adjust best overseas and are the most successful have probably changed the most during their sojourn. They have more confidence in their abilities to adapt and succeed and thus are the least likely to be anxious about returning home. For example, adolescent children usually adjust very quickly and easily to a new culture, yet they tend to experience much greater reentry stress than their parents.

In an overseas culture, host nationals expect newcomers to make mistakes and be different. Most intuitively understand that the sojourner will experience stress adapting to the new physical and social environment and will long for friends and family back home.

At home, everyone expects the returnee to fit in quickly. They are much less tolerant of mistakes and have little empathy for the difficulties of reverse culture shock—such problems are not expected or accepted. The honeymoon period may last only a few days or hours.

THE BREAKDOWN OF INTERPERSONAL COMMUNICATION

The causes of reverse culture shock are quite similar to those of culture shock. A breakdown of interpersonal communication again occurs, resulting in enormous frustration and pain. Most returnees do not realize that this breakdown is the cause of their distress. Consequently, they are unaware of what provokes the reactions commonly labeled as symptoms of reverse culture shock.

When people communicate, they send messages, not meanings. The meanings are in their heads, and the messages merely try to express them. If two people experience the world in a similar way, their messages will elicit similar or parallel meanings. If they experience the world differently, their messages usually elicit different meaning. And, what would be a message to one person may have no meaning whatsoever to another. Even which messages are noticed may be different in different cultures. Of course, most people assume everyone else pays attention to the same messages they do and that everyone gives the messages the same meaning.

Americans are primarily verbally oriented people. When they communicate face-to-face, they pay attention to what is said and tend to be less consciously aware of nonverbal messages—tone of voice, posture, gestures, facial expressions, social distance, touch, eye contact, and so forth. On the other hand, non-Western people often pay much greater attention to nonverbal messages and consciously send them more frequently in interpersonal communication.

If an African spends a great deal of time in the United States, he becomes much more conscious of verbal messages and decreases his awareness of nonverbal messages. In the United States, his verbal abilities are highly rewarded and reinforced while his nonverbal subtlety only leads to confusion. Conversely, an American having spent time in Africa returns home adept at sending and receiving nonverbal messages yet perhaps less conscious of direct verbal messages.

One learns what nonverbal messages mean and how and when to use them simply by growing up in a particular culture. To a large extent, their meanings and usage are not explicitly taught but are learned tacitly and are understood at a subconscious level. For example, the American social distance is about

an arm's length while it is perhaps only ten to twelve inches for an African. Americans seldom use touch to communicate, especially between individuals of the same sex.

While in the United States, the African sojourner tacitly learns to maintain an arm's length when talking and to offer a brisk handshake, almost immediately released. Upon his return to Africa, he is met by family and friends at the airport. His cousin rushes to shake his hand and continues greeting him without releasing his grip. Others crowd around him as they welcome him home. He tries to pull away from his cousin's grip and backs away from those who are talking to him. The returnee suddenly feels as if everyone is very pushy and intruding on his personal space.

His friends and family suddenly realize how he has changed. He seems cold and standoffish. They consciously notice how he will not hold hands and how he steps back when they try to talk to him. The returnee may be quite oblivious to the nonverbal messages he is sending or why he feels uncomfortable.

While in the United States, the African student learned that Americans are often very rushed and thus it is perfectly polite to greet others with a quick "hi." At home, people expect him to engage in more personal conversation, asking "How are you?" "How is your family?" "How are you feeling?" and so forth. Of course, a polite person would respond with a great deal more than "fine." The returnee finds that others perceive him as rude or abrupt because he no longer is comfortable engaging in lengthy greetings. If he "properly" greeted everyone, he would never get to work on time.

In the United States, frankness and fairly direct feedback are appreciated. Americans do not want to guess at one's response to a question and they feel uncomfortable with ambiguous or nonverbal answers. A clearly stated "yes" or "no" is usually very polite to an American while indirection, subtlety, or "maybes" are often experienced as inscrutable or deceptive.

In non-Western, rural cultures, a high premium is placed on social harmony. Thus, if one cannot comply with another's wishes, a flat "no" remains discourteous. Such a response is considered abrasive, abrupt, and overly negative. Because everyone wants to say "yes" to maintain good feelings, the absence of an affirmative response is sufficient to communicate "no." In such cultures, people tend to respond negatively with some nonverbal sign or such phrases as "maybe," "it is difficult," or "God willing." While perhaps circuitous and ambiguous to an American, such a response is quite clear and polite for many non-Westerners.

An American returning home from a non-Western culture has picked up these subtleties. Overseas he was highly regarded for his graciousness and efforts to maintain good social relations. To American friends, he seems evasive and indecisive, while to him they appear downright rude.

THE "UNCLE CHARLIE SYNDROME"

Cleveland et al. describe a common experience of returnees. In the words of an interviewee:

> In my hometown, there are probably many people who still don't realize the world is round. I remember when we got home from Moscow people asked me how it was there, but before I could open my mouth, they would begin telling me how Uncle Charlie had broken his arm. They profess interest in things abroad, but they really aren't interested. [1]

Sojourners want to share their overseas experiences, yet trying to do so is a painfully difficult task. After a few days of listening to anecdotes, viewing photos, and receiving gifts, most friends and family members lose interest. Very often the most meaningful experiences really cannot be communicated. These messages have little meaning to those who have never actually lived overseas. It is somewhat like trying to fully share the wonder of a sunset with a blind person.

The parochialism of the home society becomes more obvious than ever before to these sojourners, especially in contrast with the more global perspective acquired while away. Although they have discovered many hidden aspects of their own culture by going overseas and have broadened their view of the world, they have also returned more critical of their own society. To adapt overseas, sojourners had to be more tolerant of other points of views, change many of their attitudes, and open their minds to new ways of perceiving reality. Interestingly, this tolerance and open-mindedness is not always extended to those back home.

While Uncle Charlie's broken arm may seem insignificant to the returnee, it was probably a traumatic event for the family. The returnee's lack of interest in Uncle Charlie's broken arm may be very unsettling to those back home.

OTHER COMMUNICATION BARRIERS

Students returning from the United States to poorer countries are sometimes faced with envy and resentment from those who did not have the opportunity to travel abroad. Often, the image of America held by those at home is based upon an assumption that everyone there has great wealth, and it may be anticipated that returnees will carry back expensive gifts for all.

These students may have written glowing letters home describing their experiences. Sometimes they have failed to describe their financial struggles, thereby reinforcing the perception that they have ample funds. Perceived to be carrying home the "golden fleece," the students may be faced with a host of new obligations—paying school fees for younger siblings, living in a style that becomes a college graduate, providing loans to older family members, and so forth. They cannot hope to fill these new and unexpected roles or to match the new identity ascribed to them by friends and family.

Students who have remained overseas for a long period face a barrier of time separating them from family and friends. To get on with life, some loved ones left at home may have needed to go through a cycle of grief for the departed sojourner. They have experienced the anger and depression that often characterize grief, and have psychologically "buried" the sojourner. Upon the sojourner's return, it is as if a ghost had appeared. Intimate relationships cannot simply continue from where they were at departure. They must be evaluated and developed again, taking into account the change that has occurred because of the sojourn.

REACTIONS OR "SYMPTOMS"

Most returnees take for granted their ability to effectively communicate with friends and family. The breakdown of communication causes frustration and pain, which, in turn, lead to the physical and psychological reactions associated with stress. Because this stress is not expected, reactions are usually much more severe than those of entry culture shock.

Initially, many returnees engage in "flight" behavior. They may withdraw from others, fantasize about returning overseas, or sleep a great deal. The returnee is often perplexed by these subconscious reactions to the breakdown of communication.

A sense of being out of control is very common. Gregarious sojourners may find themselves avoiding others at home. Fantasies begin to preoccupy them, and returnees may suspect that they acquired some illness overseas accounting for excessive sleeping. Reactions to the situation begin to control returnees and, being unaware of the cause of these reactions, they may not consider alternative ways to cope with the original breakdown of communication.

Returnees to non-Western cultures often find this period especially difficult because they cannot flee or avoid others. While there is great respect for privacy in the United States, this attitude is rare in cultures that emphasize kinship and friendship ties over the individual. Americans might not find it strange for someone to avoid others for a few days. In many cultures of Africa, Latin America, and Asia, to do so is almost impossible and would be viewed as bizarre behavior.

Flight is untenable for returnees. They cannot escape others permanently, sleep away their days, or go back overseas again. They remain trapped in a painful situation that appears hopeless. At this point, a second reaction usually develops—"fight" behavior or aggression. While perfectly normal under the circumstances, many returnees are confused by their own aggressive behavior. Some even feel guilty, especially returnees to the United States, where anger is often equated with irrationality.

Anger is often displaced onto those lower in the social hierarchy, somewhat like the boy who is spanked by his mother and walks out the front door and kicks the cat. Or anger may be directed toward loved ones who are simply convenient scapegoats. For no apparent reason, a minor disagreement with a taxi driver becomes an emotional blowup or a small marital spat explodes into rage.

Because of the value placed on rationality and the overwhelming sense of guilt and loss of control caused by such reactions, some returnees internalize or deny their anger. This denial actually makes matters worse—depression is often attributed to internalized anger. Adding to the problem, hopelessness and lack of control cause some returnees to feel helpless. They can perceive no way of coping with their feelings and are unaware of what is causing them to behave in such irrational ways. Their sense of hopelessness, helplessness, and lack of control causes them to simply give up trying to control the situation. They learn to be helpless, and learned helplessness is also often considered a major factor in depression.

Many other reactions occur to the breakdown of communication. For example, returnees may neurotically distort and deny the complexity of reentry. Some behave as if they have never been abroad, much like a soldier who refuses to accept the reality of battlefield experiences once at home. Such a person denies the impact of the experience and refuses to even try discussing it with others.

Other sojourners go to the opposite extreme. They never actually return home, or they deny they are at home. The Nigerian returnee who studied in London wears three-piece tweed suits, smokes a pipe, and drinks tea every afternoon and scotch in the evening. He speaks in an exaggerated British accent and drones on constantly about how wonderful everything was in London and how terrible everything is in Lagos. Of course, he forgets the bad times he had while abroad and ignores the many positive aspects of his homeland.

An interesting modification of these distortions and denials is illustrated by a group of young men in The Gambia who are referred to as the "Been-Tos." They gather nightly in a small bar and unconsciously exclude those who have never sojourned overseas. Conversation is almost entirely about where they have been to—some have been to London, others to New York, and so forth. They constantly relive their overseas adventures, much like many Peace Corps volunteers who have formed their own "Been-To" cliques in the United States.

COPING STRATEGIES

The most effective way to minimize the severity and duration of reverse culture shock is to anticipate its occurrence. If returnees are aware of the pattern of cross-cultural adjustment, including the reentry phase, they can fairly easily recognize symptoms and develop specific coping strategies. Many of these coping skills can be drawn from those developed overseas in going through culture shock.

"Decompression"

When the American hostages were first released from captivity in the American Embassy in Iran, they were taken to Germany for a few days. The State Department explained that their brief stay there was not simply for the purposes of debriefing and medical examination, but also for "decompression." This amounted to allowing time for the former hostages to consider how the United States had changed during their captivity. They were encouraged to anticipate reentry difficulties. In light of the very good adjustment the hostages made after their return to the United States, this stay seems to have served its purpose.

Most returnees do not have the opportunity to "decompress." They usually must begin functioning in their society immediately upon arrival. Perhaps it would be better if only the sojourner could return via boat or train instead of by airplane, allowing time to think through the process of reentry.

Communication Outlets

While one should avoid the exclusivity of "Been-To" cliques, spending time with others who can empathize and suggest ways to cope with reentry stress is very helpful. Fellow returnees often want to hear about overseas adventures, with an interest born from their own multicultural, international experience. They may also serve as mentors for newly returned sojourners, and can assure these returnees that their reactions are normal and only transitional. Returnees may feel that their adjustment difficulties are the result of personal inadequacies. It is good news indeed to learn that almost all returnees share these difficulties and manage to complete the cycle of adjustment successfully.

Another coping strategy is often naturally used by those adjusting to culture shock. During their first few weeks overseas, many sojourners write numerous lengthy letters home. While friends and family may greatly appreciate these letters, the real beneficiary is the sojourner, who may be subconsciously compensating for the communication breakdown experienced in entering this new culture by frantically communicating with people at home. As friendships overseas develop, the letter writing decreases because the need to communicate intimately is now satisfied in the host culture.

Maintaining contact with friends overseas, whether by letter, telephone, or electronic mail, is a very good way to cope with the breakdown of communication during reverse culture shock. Of course, the ultimate goal is to develop good relationships and intimate communication with friends and family rather than to rely on compensatory communication.

Stress Management

While overseas, most sojourners develop ways of coping with the physical and psychological stress of adaptation through various so-called "stress management" techniques such as exercising, maintaining a healthy diet, and developing daily routines that allow for some escape from the bombardment of stimuli and demands placed on them. These same techniques can be used to cope with the stress of reentry. Such basic strategies can be especially important because returnees are often quickly immersed in their social and work milieu before they have a chance to "catch their breath."

Cues or Reinforcers

As sojourners adapt overseas, they become comfortable with the new physical and social environment—the food, weather, buildings, people, music, and ways of interacting. Life becomes more predictable as they learn what to expect from others and what is expected of them. They learn how to get things done, solve problems, greet people, accept gifts, give tips, negotiate and bargain over prices, and determine appropriate social roles. All these environmental elements may be termed "cues" or "reinforcers." The absence of home-culture cues makes sojourners feel like "fish out of water" until they adjust to new cues in the overseas culture. Returnees in turn miss the cues and reinforcers to which they adapted overseas.

Generally, those who go overseas and insist on starting fresh without any reminders of home have a much more difficult task adjusting than those who take along potent cues such as a favorite photograph or tape of music. One way to cope with loss of cues is to *transfer* cues from one's home environment to the overseas culture. The same idea holds true for returnees. That is, transferring cues from overseas to home is an effective way to cope with the stress caused by loss of overseas cues.

Many sojourners consciously consider which cues they want to take home—articles of clothing, recipes, a musical instrument, or photographs. Others transfer cues without knowing it and only realize a cue's real value in easing reentry transition stress when it is lost. Some returnees would rather have their stereo stolen than the cheap tribal mask they have hanging on their living room wall.

While sojourners cannot bring people home from overseas, they can join together with nationals from the overseas culture through organizations in their local community. Thus the social interactions to which they became accustomed overseas can take place at home. Other coping strategies that involve the transfer of cues might include subscribing to publications from the host culture, dining at restaurants that feature host culture food, or listening to shortwave broadcasts from the host country.

Returnees can also *modify* cues in their home culture, making them similar to overseas cues. For example, one can create something similar to the West African *fufu* out of Bisquick. An African returning from the United States can prepare local food that resembles a McDonald's Big Mac and fries. A party might include some music from overseas and, with some creativity, one could mix home and host culture clothing.

When going overseas, it helps a great deal to develop opportunities to bid farewell and "let go of" the most important social cues— family and close friends. Such rituals provide significant psychological comfort when one is overseas, cut off from loved ones.

The same is true for those who are leaving close friends overseas to return home. Prior to departure, one should be certain to take part in events that allow for farewells to happen. Those who depart abruptly without having allowed plenty of time for the ritual of saying goodbye often find it more difficult to readjust at home.

IDENTITY AND CULTURAL TRANSITION

When adapting to another culture, sojourners necessarily go through an "identity crisis," growing into new roles and ways of looking at the world and themselves. Values and behaviors that were reinforced at home often go unrewarded in a new culture. Ways of perceiving reality and solving problems that allowed one to function effectively at home become dysfunctional overseas. The sojourner may also be ascribed entirely different roles and status in the new culture.

Giving up inappropriate behaviors, adjusting one's hierarchy of values, developing new ways of solving problems, and adapting to new roles involves passing through a period of self-doubt, disorientation, and personal examination of one's values and beliefs. From this perspective, the so-called "symptoms" of culture shock are simply "growing pains" that lead to the development of new skills and ways of perceiving the world, greater flexibility in dealing with life's problems, enhanced self-awareness, and increased self-confidence.

In her book *Passages*, Gail Sheehy suggests that human beings as they go through identity crises might be compared to hardy crustaceans. "The lobster grows by developing a series of hard protective shells. Each time it expands from within, the confining shell must be sloughed off. It is left exposed and vulnerable until, in time, a new covering grows to replace the old."[2] Going through culture shock, the sojourner sheds a protective structure and is left exposed and vulnerable—"but also yeasty and embryonic again, capable of stretching in ways . . . [unknown] before."[3]

The lobster shedding its shell is still fundamentally the same, except more mature. Similarly, the sojourner passing through culture shock is still basically the same except for having new ways of seeing the world and a host of new alternatives for solving problems and considering reality.

As with any other identity crisis, culture shock involves giving up an inadequate perceptual and problem-solving system to allow a more adequate, expanded system to be created. It is a sort of death-rebirth cycle. Unfortunately, many returnees are not aware of how much they have grown overseas, and friends and family expect them to return as they were when they left.

For those leaving a wealthy country and returning to a poorer country, the situation may be even more difficult because of new roles and status ascribed to the returnee. Such returnees are often expected to return home and assume new financial responsibilities, live in greater style, and perhaps act as intermediary between foreign visitors and home country nationals in the workplace. These new responsibilities are often overwhelming and usually quite unexpected.

The increased global-mindedness of returnees is sometimes accompanied by increased intolerance of parochialism on the part of those at home. While returnees bring with them an enhanced awareness of their home culture, they have also seen it as an outsider while abroad and thus are often more critical of the inconsistencies inherent in any cultural system. In addition, many returnees have highly romanticized their own countries while overseas and are amazed to find that the streets are not as clean as they imagined, the people not as warm and friendly, and the efficiency not as great as seemed the case while out of the country.

Disillusionment sets in quickly for those who glorified their homeland while overseas, and again the returnees must go through a death-rebirth cycle—giving up the identity that worked so well overseas to take on a new one at home. While no one can regress to the predeparture "self," many will try to deny the impact of their overseas experience. Others may attempt to hang onto the identity acquired while overseas, but this obviously will not work at home. Another identity must be developed and new "growing pains" will accompany its birth.

CONCLUDING THOUGHTS

Cross-cultural adjustment should be considered a continuum with at least two low periods—entry to another culture and reentry to one's home culture. With awareness of the process of adjustment and recognition of the "symptoms" of stress, individuals can develop their own special coping strategies. Thus, the severity and duration of these stressful periods can be minimized and the entire process can become one of great personal growth.

During culture shock, one's effectiveness is inhibited. The stress produces a great distraction from work or study, and the more quickly one comes out of the down period, the sooner one becomes more effective. The stress of reentry similarly affects effectiveness and is perhaps even more of a problem because returnees are expected to perform well almost immediately upon arrival. The evidence is also fairly clear that reentry stress is much more severe and longer lasting than culture shock.

Students returning home are expected to be agents for the so-called "transfer of technology." In many cases, their governments sent them specifically to gain knowledge and skills that would enhance national development. Reverse culture shock, however, can interfere with this transfer and sometimes prevent it from occurring.

While most sponsored programs for studying or working abroad include orientation to prepare sojourners for the difficulties of culture shock, few include orientation for reentry. In fact, both sojourners and their sponsors often assume that the journey ends when one arrives home. In truth, the psychological sojourn does not end until one has successfully overcome reverse culture shock. Perhaps greater attention should be given to reentry transition orientation. If not, the stress of this passage may actually defeat the purpose of the sojourn and turn a potentially maturing experience into needlessly prolonged stress and pain.

ENDNOTES

[1] H. Cleveland, G. Mangone, and J. Adams, *The Overseas Americans* (New York: McGraw-Hill, 1960), 26.

[2] Gail Sheehy, *Passages: Predictable Crises of Adult Life* (New York: Bantam, 1977), 235.

[3] *Ibid.*, 235.

REFERENCES

Adler, Nancy J. *International Dimensions of Organizational Behavior.* 2d ed. Boston, MA: PWS-Kent Publishing Co., 1991.

Austin, Clyde N., ed. *Cross-Cultural Reentry: A Book of Readings,* Abilene, TX: Abilene Christian University Press, 1986.

Brislin, Richard W., and H. Van Buren IV. "Can They Go Home Again?" *Cultural Exchange* 9 (1974):19–24.

Cleveland, H., G. Mangone, and J. Adams. *The Overseas Americans.* New York: McGraw-Hill, 1960.

Paige, R. Michael, ed. *Cross-Cultural Orientation: New Conceptualization and Applications.* Lanham, MD: University Press of America, 1986.

Sheehy, Gail. *Passages: Predictable Crises of Adult Life.* New York: Bantam, 1977.

30

World-Wise Kids

Nina Killham

He's blond-haired, blue-eyed, and Timothy Mechem still thinks of himself as East African. He was born 21 years ago to American missionary parents in Zambia and never stepped off the continent until 1985. He speaks Chichewa, understands Swahili and, to this day, his accent is as thick as honey.

Mechem is a Global Nomad—someone having spent his formative years living outside his passport country—U.S. or otherwise—with parents sponsored by various institutions, namely the Foreign Service, government or international agencies, the military, church missions, international corporations or businesses.

On the average, a Global Nomad has lived in six different countries by the time he is 18 years old—his cultural identity becoming gradually unglued from that of his monocultural parents and forming into a new sensibility. Global Nomads include the Kennedy children, George Bush's children, John Denver and Brook Astor.

Though no one has counted all the Global Nomads living in the Washington area, it's probably safe to say that with sponsors like the Pentagon, State Department and World Bank, this city must have the highest percentage in the country. In 1988, the number of Americans living abroad reached 2,054,148, with an estimated 230,000 of them American students attending overseas schools. About 10,000 students graduate from such schools each year.

A silent minority, Global Nomads now are being touted across the country by such groups as Global Nomads International, Mu Kappa (especially for missionary youths) and Interaction, Inc. (for the care of youth and families in the expatriate community) as possessing unique characteristics—distinct from those who grew up in their native culture.

These include superior diplomacy, flexibility, linguistic ability, patience and sophistication. On the down side, there's insecurity in relationships, unresolved grief stemming from constantly leaving friends throughout childhood, and rootlessness.

One of the most difficult questions Global Nomads can be asked is where they are from. The common response will be, "when?" Says David Pollock, director of Intercultural Inc., "I know a girl who said, 'I'm from Egypt.' I asked, 'How long did you live in Egypt?' and she answered, 'Well, I actually never lived in Egypt. The last time I lived at home we lived in Mozambique, but my parents are in Egypt.'" Home becomes not a geographic notion, but an emotional one.

Anna Maripuu, the daughter of a Swedish United Nations official, who has just finished her masters degree in international affairs and economics at George Washington University, was born in Sweden, lived in the United States from ages 6 to 12 and then lived in developing countries before returning to the United States for her college studies.

It's a life, she says, that produces misunderstandings—"I'll mention home in a conversation three times and it can mean three different places." In her mind, the differences are clear, she says, but her friends do not understand how her loyalties can be so neatly split.

And often after several years abroad, American Global Nomads return to find that "home" in the United States is yet another unknown culture to learn. This is the time, says Norma McCaig, founder of Global Nomads International in Washington, when the flexibility, patience and diplomacy they have acquired through the years need to be at full tilt.

Stephanie Turco, 24, the daughter of a Foreign Service officer, who lived in India, Pakistan and Afghanistan from the time she was 2, came back to the States with a gold ring in her nose. "People thought I didn't speak English. They would talk about me in the elevator. 'What's that thing in her nose, how ugly.' I didn't say anything. I was so embar-

Reprinted from *The Washington Post*, 15 February 1990, B5. Copyright © 1990 by Nina Kilham.

rassed, but it made me feel very alienated for a long time. I didn't trust people for a long time."

For these dependents, assimilation does not necessarily end their odyssey. Many Global Nomads speak of an internal clock that continues to ring every few years, prodding them to pack up and move. Some call it itchy feet, some call it ants-in-the-pants. "I call it having sand in their shoe," says Ruth Hill Useem, professor emeritus of sociology, education and anthropology at Michigan State University, who coined the phrase Third-Cultured-Kid (TCK).

According to Useem, the average TCK changes colleges twice. This rootlessness not only has a strong negative effect on careers, it sabotages relationships, too. Marriages between TCKs and others often are strained by the TCK's perpetual craving for a change of scene.

Jim Bradford, an independent radio producer who recognizes the destructive pattern in his love life, says: "I am not staying long enough to see a relationship through." Bradford followed his father to Japan, Paraguay, Peru and Honduras until his 18th birthday and then continued his nomadic life on his own by working in Ecuador, the Dominican Republic, Guatemala and Nicaragua. His internal clock, he says, rings loud and clear. "I feel the urge every two or three years. In fact, I'm trying to go back to Latin America right now."

And even if they do settle down, there is a tendency to remain unattached. It's not uncommon to run into a Global Nomad who has lived in the same apartment for more than 10 years, but still has a portable TV, unbreakable dishes, folding furniture and unpacked boxes in the basement.

Anthony Bates, also the dependent of a Foreign Service officer, who lived in London, Paris, Hong Kong and Berlin by the time he was 12, says he tends to feel unattached emotionally. "There are times when I don't want to but I am; I can't help it. Other times it's useful." Like the other day when a fight broke out in front of him at the line to buy Metro fare cards and he stood back and watched as if it were a movie. "In some ways I'm always the foreigner, separate and apart, but in some ways I'm always at home. It's strange. The two things can coexist."

Most characteristics of a multicultural upbringing, however, are positive and are the focus of groups like TCK Student Services, Tim Mechem's fledgling support group for TCKs at American University. "The TCKs don't realize that they are special," says Mechem. "I want to tell them it's okay that they're weird."

Mechem remembers feeling weird himself when he realized his Sub-Saharan African mentality set him apart from other American students. "We tend to talk slower, we tend to take things in and think about them before responding. We like to take one task at a time and finish, rather than doing a million things at once. And we tend to be very fatalistic. What happens, happens."

Mechem says he feels comfortable with the atmosphere at American University, where it is not unusual to walk into a common area, he says, "and run into a Chinese girl and a Mali student cracking jokes with a Swiss, all in Russian."

Some Global Nomads find that even their English needs translation. Says Anthony Bates, "I'll say I'm mad about my flat and Americans will think I'm angry about my flat tire, when I'm really saying I love my apartment."

According to Ruth Useem, 90 percent of TCKs are conversant in at least one other language. Also, Global Nomads, through studies, have shown to be good observers, less judgmental and less prejudicial.

"I feel that I can easily deal with different personalities, different nationalities," says Stephanie Turco. "I'm used to juggling. I sort of slide into uptight or different situations. I'm not made nervous by wondering whether or not I'm doing the right thing."

Most important, says Intercultural Inc.'s David Pollock, a Global Nomad tends to have a three-dimensional view of the world. "A TCK will read a headline in a newspaper, and can often smell the smells, hear the sounds, and identify with the pain and disaster a half a world away," says Pollock. "Their world view is the expanded world view."

Jim McCaffrey, vice president of Training Resources Group, a managing and developmental consulting firm in Alexandria, has a different perception. Global Nomads, he says, have not necessarily cornered the market on intercultural skills. "I don't make the a priori assumption that a Global Nomad is a better multiculturalist. I've seen people who lived all over the world who've been as insensitive as a brick."

In McCaffrey's opinion, the ideal candidate for an intercultural job is a Global Nomad with the double experience of living in a foreign country as a child and again as an adult. "I want someone who has lived there and made something out of it, who has thought about it—one doesn't necessarily lead to the other."

Says Pollock: "We have to recognize that part of the role of the third-cultured people of today is to be the culture bridge and culture brokers for the whole generation." The Global Nomad of today, he says, is the prototype of the citizen of the twenty-first century.

31

Third Culture Persons

Kathleen A. Finn Jordan

Ask someone where they are from, and the answer you will expect to receive may be, "Chicago," "New York," "California," or "Kansas." Even when dealing internationally, expected answers can be "Paris, "Milan, or "Tokyo." But increasingly there is another answer being given, "When?" This answer often comes from those who honestly need to know a time frame before they can give you a geographic reference. They might answer something like "Well, I've lived in the Netherlands, France, and Germany, and Mom and Dad are in South Africa right now, but I'm an American." These people are the children of parents who have been assigned to positions overseas, or who have taken jobs overseas. The positions they take can be in any variety of capacities, from government-related postings, military, or international business assignments to missionary work. The positions they hold may be diplomats, teachers, military personnel, artists, oil-riggers, United Nations' staff, bilingual stenographers, reporters, bankers, technical consultants, or multinational corporation executives, but they all have something in common.[1] The children they raise will live in a variety of cultures and places, and none of them will necessarily be the culture or place that the parents call home.

Geoff, a child of missionary parents, lived abroad for fifteen years, moving between Cameroon, England, Zaire, and Taiwan. When he tried to return to the United States after his sojourn, he began to realize just how much his overseas experience set him apart from his peers in the United States.

> Academics would have been the easiest transition and social life would have been the most difficult. I had no idea, even after I had come back to the States and left again after the seventh grade, about what Americans in general or American High School students did, how they acted, or what they were instructed in, so it was in essence coming to a new culture because it had been 5 years since I had been in the states, and, even in the seventh grade, I didn't enjoy that year . . . subconsciously I am an American and I readjusted myself to my new home. My home now, always my home on paper.[2]

Geoff and others who have shared his experience of growing up as children of sponsored adults overseas are "third culture kids" (TCKs).[3] These people have had to develop ways of relating the many cultures of which they are a part. In so doing, they create a composite set of values, norms, and social structures for themselves that contains some of all the cultures to which they relate.[4] But, in creating a composite of these cultures, they are actually creating another, distinct "third culture" which is a part of, yet apart from, the other cultures. These third culture persons are not truly members of any of the cultures in which they have lived, but have developed their own separate and distinct culture that exists between those cultures.

There are many things that distinguish the third culture person from those we term monocultural. Monocultural individuals are those who, like the vast majority of the people in the world, were primarily raised in a single culture. They learned the language, norms, behavior patterns and culture that were inherent to the land where they were raised, and this land was most often the land of their ancestors. Throughout their developing years, monocultural people might have changed physical locations within a country or culture, but the culture and country within which they operated remained in large part the same.[5]

This article is first published here. Dr. Jordan is a Consulting Educational Counselor in Washington, D.C. and a Research Associate at Michigan State University.

A third culture person, specifically a third culture kid (TCK), was raised in more than one country and culture. TCKs were often raised in four, five, or even six or more countries over the course of their development, and rarely were any of these countries or cultures those which their parent's called home. For the TCK, this home identification may be nothing more than a name on his/her parents' passports. A third culture kid may never have seen, or been a part of, this place until they return to the "home" country for a post-secondary education. But growing up and developing in so many environments has, in many cases, led these individuals to develop an understanding not only of those cultures in which they have been raised, but also an understanding and set of skills for dealing with *any* other culture.

CHARACTERISTICS OF THIRD CULTURE PERSONS

Wayne, a TCK of missionary sponsorship, lived abroad for 13 years, and moved through six countries. When he returned to the United States, he noted that for a long time he was an observer.

> By observation it was easier than learning by mistakes 'cause I didn't have to suffer. I began to analyze people. . . . I found that I am adaptable and I can go and live anywhere, but to find out why I live in a certain way takes at least a year. I'm interested in people and because of that I first observe them and try to learn fundamental things about civilization and integrate those things. After that I go into other things.[6]

Wayne knows that he has the skills to live almost anywhere in the world. He can go into a country and adapt to life in that country, but he won't necessarily understand why he does certain things. This is often a problem that TCKs have when entering a new environment, or even returning to a relatively familiar one. They feel both a part of the culture, and apart from it. Their "third cultureness" actually prevents them from being completely a part of any particular culture. They have adapted to

moving, to changing relationships and locales, but being adapted to change may preclude any feeling of having roots in a single culture. This is possibly the most common perception among TCKs: that they are part of all of their respective cultures, yet also apart from all of them. Their experiences make them different by changing the way TCKs attribute value and meaning, thus orienting them to a broader, more multicultural context.[7] Their culture is the third culture.

Researchers observing TCKs as they return to the home country for post-secondary education have also been able to identify other common traits in the third culture personality. TCKs seem to develop an identity management that differs from those who grow up in their own countries, including an exceedingly complex sense of identity. This sense of their identity reflects their overseas experience, and affects their social relationships with individuals and groups. When asked about their initial life plans, TCKs almost always include an ambition to return to a mobile, international lifestyle.[8] As a group, they are more comfortable intrapersonally than interpersonally, they function as perceptive observers: slow to jump in, mapping the territory, collecting information and processing it, and, while doing all of that, feeling marginal at the outset of their exposure to any new environment, though constructively so. Their academic skills stand by them as they seek to acquire appropriate social skills. These characteristics are most often seen by researchers when the TCKs return to the home country to attend post-secondary institutions (colleges and universities).

The following is a list of general characteristics and observations pulled from an ongoing study of 696 adult third culture kids (ATCKs) who are between the ages of 24 and 90.[9] All participants have spent at least a year abroad as the minor dependent of an American parent in the Third Culture role, are currently residing in the United States, and were willing to fill in a twenty-four page self-administered questionnaire. It must be noted that third culture kids can come from any country, and their parents from any culture. This study is based on those with United States citizenship solely because of their accessibility to the researchers. Similar results have been noticed among TCKs with other citizenships.

- As children, the TCKs in the study lived in four to six countries by the age of 18–19. They attended private non-profit or profit-making schools primarily set up for the education of foreigners. Some schools were set up by their parents' sponsor (DoD schools, Joint Embassy Schools, missionary boarding schools) and others by private, not-for-profit or profit-making groups.

- Approximately 82% of this group speak foreign languages regularly, or occasionally, and these languages often reflect their own personal, mobile history, rather than their own ethnicity.

- On the point of reentry for many, and the coincidence of that point with the commencement of post-secondary school, their academic transitions are more facile than their emotional and affective transitions; TCKs experience prolonged adolescence.

- TCKs' college behavior seems consistent with mobility patterns experienced during their childhood years. Seldom do they graduate in four years from the same college in which they enrolled as freshman, and even more infrequently in the major they first declare. Continuing a pattern of mobility and change, 38% did not graduate from the first college they attended; 45% attended three or more colleges; and 44% of those who earned a bachelor's degree finished after age 22. Over 80% now function as professionals, semi-professionals, executives, or managers/officials. TCKs are four times more likely to earn bachelor's degrees than their United States counterparts.

- TCKs, though their behavior is adaptive to the settings they inhabit, never fully adapt to American life; they are somewhat out-of-sync in aspects of their lives outside of education.

- Two-thirds of the sample feel that it is important to have an international dimension in their lives, though they perceive they have more transnational knowledge and skills than they have the opportunity to use; three-fourths of them feel "different" from those who have not had an overseas experience, but they do not feel isolated.

- ATCKs have problems relating to their own ethnic groups. However, they are internationally experienced and continue their international involvement; they are adaptable and relate easily to diversity, they are helpers and problem-solvers.

- Over 40% have completed a graduate degree and some others are close to completion of one. Most report an excellent education in overseas schools; third culture childhood experiences affected 43% greatly (27% somewhat) in their choice of college and experience; 25% chose international majors and many others pursued interests inspired by their overseas posts.

- 25% work in educational settings; 17% in medical or legal fields. An equal number are self-employed—one third are presidents of their own companies. Over 75% participate in volunteer work in their communities, and about half (47%) report those volunteer activities are related to the international area.

DEVELOPMENT OF THE TCK PERSONALITY

The development of the TCK personality is reflective of a series of adjustments and a never-quite-completed process of adaptation. These individuals have extraordinary demands placed on them to adapt to new environments, new places, new people, and new cultures. It is the same type of adaptation which is required of those going through culture shock, but without necessarily having the benefit, or baggage, of a culture which they can call home. While this sometimes leads to a very unsettled life, it can also produce an individual who is not easily influenced by the prejudices of others, and who may be extremely open-minded when encountering anything new.

Adaptation involves interaction between an individual's perception of self and perceptions of the environment. TCKs' management of the process of adaptation reflects the complex identities they have developed from their overseas experiences and their patterns of mobility. Their adaptive pattern involves a series of transactions, including: internalizing the fact of change of place, or return to the 'home' country; maintaining extensive networks; managing an intense process of grieving; experiencing a purposeful lack of goals and realistic expectations; maintaining the third culture identity; making integrative adjustments; and the experience of culture shock.[10]

In addition to this process of adaptation, some commonalities among TCKs have been observed in both self and perceptions of the environment. They see themselves as:

- unique
- connected with global reality
- enhanced and enriched by their overseas experience
- superior and/or elite
- mobile
- a part of, yet apart from
- open and enjoying diversity
- ambivalent, independent yet dependent, mature in some ways, yet immature in others
- knowledgeable in a world sense, but naive on return to the country of their citizenship.

In the case of the environment, TCKs offered perceptions of both their overseas environments and the U.S. environment. Impressions of their overseas environments were:

- intense appreciation of the third culture
- love of travel
- value of mobility as a lifestyle
- intense interaction in the family
- strong family ties
- enjoyment of a small, enhanced environment with the benefits of a high standard of living
- close personal relationships with teachers and friends

- a deep sense of connectedness with world events
- creativity in the use of leisure time.

Their perceptions of the U.S. environment were a sense of shock at:

- the largeness of scale
- the importance of the media
- the dynamics of the peer social scene
- the materialism and ethnocentrism of most peers they encountered
- the lack of interest in their personal experiences as students who lived abroad, and
- the overall informality and friendliness of the peer environment as they observed it.

For TCKs, the process of adaptation has been facilitated by the role of a sponsoring organization. In many of the studies that have been done on TCKs, their development appears more influenced by the sponsorship role than by the host country or any individual post. The sponsor provides a continuity of structure and roles, and from this structure TCKs develop modes of being and becoming. The importance of parents' roles are communicated as a fixed and significant point in the TCK's life. The loss of meanings and references which are encountered with each new assignment or move may be mediated by this structure. It provides a stability of meaning and value for objects and roles within the sponsoring organization. For the military dependent, this means that the command structure, and his/her place in it, will be the same at any base to which he/she may be transferred. For the Foreign Service dependent, the embassy will always provide a sense of security and continuity with its structure and its support of the family while abroad. This can be very comforting for the TCK, and the whole family, when they are undergoing an instantaneous defamiliarization.[11] During a time when meaning is being stripped from almost all other aspects of their lives, the sponsor remains constant. Life structures, tasks, geographical address and travels all flow from the sponsor. The sponsor ascribes a certain status to both the individual and the family living abroad.

It is the loss of this "ascribed status" of the sponsoring organization that many TCKs lament upon return to the home culture. That status provides a role which is instantly recognized within the sponsorship group, as well as within the greater third culture environment. This status helps to facilitate transition and provide meaning by acting as an anchor point from which to rebuild the lives of the expatriates and their families. It can also contribute to a sense of elitism.

Cheryl, the dependent of a Foreign Service officer, lived abroad in Denmark, Italy, France, and Germany. Because her father was well-respected in the Foreign Service community, and a high ranking Foreign Service Officer, Cheryl grew up accustomed to living in larger homes, meeting important people, and feeling important because of her father's status in the community. Upon return to her "home" in Washington, D.C., Cheryl felt out of place. She spent her 8th grade year in the United States, and couldn't wait to leave. She made no friends at school, was annoyed by how loud Americans appeared to be, and could not understand what seemed to be the more provincial attitudes and prejudices of her classmates. She also missed being special.[12]

Living abroad, she had been special because of both her nationality as an American, and her father's position with the Foreign Service. "It was like being the big fish in a small pond. You feel special." But when she returned to America, she was "just one of many" at her junior high school. She missed living in fine homes, meeting important people, and being connected to the world. She admits now that she was "probably kind of stuck-up," but the sponsorship role that her father's position placed her in gave her an ascribed status that was simply much higher than what was recognized when she was back in the United States. It fostered a sense of elitism. Living in Washington, D.C., particularly, her ascribed status was lost as she became just another child of a Foreign Service Officer.[13]

TCKs AND REENTRY

Describing reentry with TCKs can be a particularly difficult task. This is mainly due to the fact that reentry is associated with a return to a culture which an individual knew as home prior to a sojourn overseas. The TCK's return to the "home" country may not be a return at all, but just another move to the latest in the series of cultures and countries which comprise their background. A legitimate question can be asked about whether in fact what the TCK experiences on return to the home country is culture shock rather than reentry. For now, however, we will continue to refer to a return to the home country as reentry. It is during the process of reentry that researchers have been able to gain the most information about the ways in which TCKs adapt and react to their new environment.

George, a business dependent, was overseas nine years and reports moves through three countries. He recalls,

> Upon entering college I had trouble getting back into the American style of life. Overseas I played mostly soccer, rugby, and swimming. The first year I just wanted to leave. I had played a lot of soccer in Iran. The whole general malaise I felt bothered me. I just didn't fit in. I had one good friend who lived in my dorm. I had the expectation that it would be great back in the States. I expected some difficulties, but not as many as I had.[14]

George perceives himself as a mobile person, a traveler, and did not identify at all with being in school. He had troubles with the social ambiance, though he notes that his studies were easy for him. Although he enjoyed his time overseas, he feels reentry and entry to college were not experiences he enjoyed or opportunities for growth. He says,

> I experienced a lot of alienation. I was alienated by attitudes people had about things that were different, the group mentality, expressions and ways of doing things. I was only seventeen when I returned and I was just waking up to a lot of things. It was a stage in my life that was passing. Moving all the time you don't have a firm base to set growth in or to look back on. You don't have future goals or an idea for a set job. I

did have an interest in the political aspects of things. I just read a lot.[15]

Cheryl, the dependent of a Foreign Service Officer, could not find a place where she felt she belonged in the United States. She started college attending McGill University in Canada, transferred to the University of New Hampshire, back to McGill, and finally ended up at the Catholic University in Washington, D.C. She reports having trouble with finding her place, never feeling like she belonged anywhere. Now at Catholic University, Cheryl still has almost two years left in her studies, at the end of which she knows she will want to leave Washington, because "it'll be time to move on."[16]

Thomas, a business dependent overseas approximately seven years, really enjoyed his overseas experiences. "I liked my experiences," he states. "As a younger adult you do not have as many restrictions and rules as young adults seem to have in the States. I could do pretty much whatever I pleased." Upon entering the college environment, Thomas was first of all impressed with the large size of the place. Secondly, he noted the friendliness of the people. He shared the fact that he had a "wait and see attitude." According to Thomas, "I'm not that open a kind of person. I usually wait for things to happen to me."[17]

Hans, a TCK with a business sponsorship background, lived overseas for approximately five years. Upon his return, he found that his peer group was far more socially outgoing than he, but also very immature. It was his biggest difficulty in returning to the U.S.

> I knew things that people had no idea about. I had seen places that other people had never seen. I thought I had a real good background in terms of what the world was about and how different people view things. I felt I had more culture but I confronted totally different norms and patterns here and I felt unprepared for it.[18]

As with Hans and Cheryl, TCKs often find that on their return they have no ready reference group. Having become accustomed to dealing with adults, they have not developed the appropriate skills to interact socially with their own peer group in the home country. Because of this, many TCKs continue to relate to the past third culture reference group, or imagine a reference group for the future, usually intellectually or career-related. This is just one of the many internal mechanisms which TCKs develop to deal with the difficulties of entering a new culture. These resources serve them well during the reentry process, but as with any other change, it may take them some time to adjust. In many cases, this process may take up to a year, and the TCK will likely never feel fully a part of the home culture.

Another major contributor to the stress felt by TCKs in their initial reentry period is the loss of the ascribed status provided by the sponsoring organization. When the young adult returns to the States at college age, this ascribed status is no longer operative, and the individual must act for him/herself in yet another new world of meanings and roles. But this time they must do it without the benefit of the continuity provided either by the sponsoring organization, or by their family. The time for return for the TCK does not necessarily coincide with the return of the parents, particularly at college age. Thus, the family that has been so close, and the support the family has offered the TCK through their ongoing transitions, may be on the other side of the globe. All of the issues of separation, loss, reentry/culture shock, confrontation with new and novel patterns of behavior in the "home" country combine with ties loss of both ascribed status and the family support in creating a crisis of independent identity in the TCK.

This crisis of identity that occurs during reentry may cause the TCK to have a delayed commitment process. Some have referred to this delayed development of intimacy and commitment as a prolonged adolescence. This delay of commitment is not relegated solely to interpersonal or intimate relationships, but may extend to basic ideology and choice of occupation. The TCK has to play catch up with his/her peer group, never having developed the social skills that are in operation among this group. During the early reentry period, the "observer" role mentioned earlier by several of the TCKs becomes very important as they work to assimilate and apply the skills that have worked for them in the past when entering new environments. They will observe, map out the local environment and its social dynamics, then begin to assimilate that information into their behavior and interactions. Sometimes, unfortunately, even this observer role can have drawbacks as participation, more than observation, is often the valued trait among American youth. Reentry almost always requires a setting aside of the overseas experience in order to assimilate into the home culture, which only increases the intense grieving period which TCKs must manage when they enter a new culture.

A major part of what can be done for returning TCKs, then, is to help them with this intense period of grieving. Many TCKs don't necessarily get the opportunity to grieve, or to acknowledge the fact that they are grieving. There are too many people, family and friends, demanding that the TCK feel happy about returning home, without realizing that "home" for the TCK may have nothing whatsoever to do with the home their parents recognize. One of the ways to help the TCKs with reentry, then, is to give them a time to both recognize the fact that they are grieving, and to grieve for the loss of friends, family, and a familiar environment. They need to go through a period of accepting the most recent loss, and then they can continue to adapt to the new environment. Many TCKs have developed for themselves a way to manage this grief, but the experience of reentry has also combined the loss of the few stable factors in the TCK's life: the family, the third culture environment, and the sponsorship role and status. Thus, reentry may well be the most intense period of adaptation the TCK experiences.

Elizabeth, a missionary dependent who lived overseas for approximately 10 years, relates, "I've adapted but I still have culture shock when I return to the United States after being out of the country . . . people are very persistent. They have to get things done and tend to rush and push. Overseas, if it doesn't get done, we'll do it tomorrow." Elizabeth feels that people in the United States are insulated from news and events in the rest of the world, and therefore disconnected and uninformed.[19]

Joy Salmons asked early adult TCKs retrospectively to look at their periods of reentry and identify some of the key stresses they encountered during this period. The responses mirrored the results of earlier studies and indicated that the higher the meaningful life, the lower the present stress; the more years since reentry and the higher the intimacy level, the higher the mental health. However, in the area of intimacy, it was found that the level of intimacy was significant in the mental health of men, but did not necessarily contribute to higher mental health in women. Early adult task achievement was affected by the perception of timing, amount of time since reentry, and the degree of intimacy present in their lives.[20]

CONCLUSION

In an ever-shrinking world, the TCK will play an expanding role. As more links are forged, and as communication among members of different cultures becomes more and more common, the skills of adaptation and understanding which are developed by TCKs become invaluable. As the population becomes more mobile, more and more individuals will experience challenges to their self/identity, the need for a concept of home and roots, and the need for strategies for simple adjustment. In order to be able to help these people, we must understand and nurture the TCKs. Having developed between cultures, TCKs are positioned to become the mediators between cultures. Though they may never feel fully a part of a culture, they can be the bridge through which monocultural people learn to appreciate other cultures. These individuals have the resources which are needed to facilitate understanding between cultures with distinct value systems, histories, and norms. With their ability to perceive similarities and differences that might escape the notice of someone not accustomed to looking for cultural cues, TCKs have the potential to bring these groups together to find a common ground. We need the TCKs.

The skills and resources TCKs have developed are not only applicable to the cultures in which they were raised, but can be used across all cultures. As technological society grows, and brings together global society, these skills will be more and more in demand. It will also become increasingly important to understand the TCKs and their needs as their numbers continue to grow.

The greater the interaction among countries and cultures, the greater the instances of families who will live in many other countries and cultures. They could be the facilitators of a global process of "becoming" as global society continues to evolve and needs facilitators who can move through the various cultures. TCKs bring their own unique problems to the international stage, but they also bring skills and an understanding that may be essential for the twenty-first century.

ENDNOTES

[1]Ruth Hill Useem and John Useem, "The Job: Stress and Resources of Americans at Work in the Third Culture." Paper presented for the Twenty-Second Annual Meeting of the Society for Applied Anthropology at Albany, New York (1963.)

[2]Kathleen A. Finn Jordan, "The Adaptation Process of Third Culture Dependent Youth as They Re-enter the United States and Enter College: An Exploratory Study." (Ph.D. dissertation, Michigan State University, 1981), 95.

[3]John Unseem and Ruth Hill Useem, and John Donoghue, "Men in the Middle of the Third Culture: The Roles of American and Non-Western Peoples in Cross-Cultural Administration," *Human Organization* 22 (1963):169–179.

"Third culture" persons, as defined by some researchers, are individuals who find themselves living abroad in certain specific, sponsored roles. These roles include sponsorship by private business, federal agencies, the military, missionary groups, and other categories where the individual assumes a representative, rather than solely individual, role. "Third culture" itself is a generic term used to describe the styles of life created, shared and learned by persons who are in the process of relating their multiple societies. The term "third culture" itself came out of studies done by John Useem in India of Americans participating in various missionary, diplomatic and business programs, and the cross-cultural problems and opportunities that arose from the interaction.

[4]John Useem, "The Community of Man: A Study in the Third Culture," *The Centennial Review* 7 (1962):481–498.

[5]As we approach the century's end, there are fewer and fewer people in the world uninfluenced in some way by another culture. The use of the term "monocultural" should be understood as merely a matter of the conscious degree of influence other cultures have brought to bear. It is difficult to imagine a completely "monocultural" person and that is not what we wish to convey by use of this term.

[6]Kathleen A. Finn Jordan, "The Adaptation Process," 101.

[7]Ongoing study of Adult Third Culture Kids undertaken by sociologists/anthropologists Drs. Ann Baker Cottrel of San Diego University; Ruth and John Useem, professors emeritus of Michigan State University, and Counselor/Therapist Kathleen A. Finn Jordan of Washington, D.C.

[8]Richard Downie, "Re-entry Experiences and Identity Formation of Third Culture Experienced Dependent American Youth: An Exploratory Study," (Ph.D. dissertation, Michigan State University, 1976).

[9]Kathleen A. Finn Jordan, "The Adaptation Process."

[10]*Ibid.*

[11]I.D. Yalom, *Existential Psychotherapy* (New York: Basic Books, 1980).

[12]Cheryl O'Rourke [pseud.], interviewed by Shawn Bates, School of International Service, American University, Washington, D.C., 2 April 1997.

[13]*Ibid.*

[14]Kathleen A. Finn Jordan, "The Adaptation Process," 115.

[15]*Ibid.*

[16]Cheryl O'Rourke, interview.

[17]Kathleen A. Finn Jordan, "The Adaptation Process," 129.

[18]*Ibid.*, 119.

[19]*Ibid.*

[20]Joy Salmon, "The Relationship of Stress and Mobility to the Psychosocial Development and Well-Being of Third-Culture-Reared Early Adults." (Ph.D. dissertation, The Florida State University, 1987.)

32

Beyond Cultural Identity: Reflections on Cultural and Multicultural Man

Peter S. Adler

INTRODUCTION

The idea of a multicultural man[1] is an attractive and persuasive notion. It suggests a human being whose identifications and loyalties transcend the boundaries of nationalism and whose commitments are pinned to a vision of the world as a global community. To be a citizen of the world, an international person, has long been a dream of man. History is rich with examples of societies and individuals who took it upon themselves to shape everyone else to the mold of their planetary dream. Less common are examples of men and women who have striven to sustain a self process that is international in attitude and behavior. For good reason, nation, culture, and society exert tremendous influence on each of our lives, structuring our values, engineering our view of the world, and patterning our responses to experience. No human being can hold himself apart from some form of cultural influence. No one is culture free. Yet, the conditions of contemporary history are such that we may now be on the threshold of a new kind of person, a person who is socially and psychologically a product of the interweaving of cultures in the twentieth century.

Reprinted from *Topics in Cultural Learning*, vol. 2, ed. Richard W. Brislin (Honolulu: East-West Center), August 1974, 23–40, Institute of Cultural Learning.

We are reminded daily of this phenomenon. In the corner of a traditional Japanese home sits a television set tuned to a baseball game in which the visitors, an American team, are losing. A Canadian family, meanwhile, decorates their home with sculptures and paintings imported from Pakistan, India, and Sri Lanka. Teenagers in Singapore and Hong Kong pay unheard of prices for American blue-jeans while high school students in England and France take courses on the making of traditional Indonesian batik. A team of Malaysian physicians inoculates a remote village against typhus while their Western counterparts study Ayurvedic medicine and acupuncture. Around the planet the streams of the world's cultures merge together to form new currents of human interaction. Though superficial and only a manifestation of the shrinking of the globe, each such vignette is a symbol of the mingling and melding of human cultures. Communication and cultural exchange are the pre-eminent conditions of the twentieth century.

For the first time in the history of the world, a patch of technology and organization has made possible simultaneous interpersonal and intercultural communication. Innovations and refinements of innovations, including mass mail systems, publishing syndicates, film industries, television networks, and newswire services have brought people everywhere into potential contact. Barely a city or village exists that is more than a day or two from anyplace else; almost no town or community is without a radio. Buslines, railroads, highways, and airports have created linkages within and between local, regional, national, and international levels of human organization. The impact is enormous. Human connections through communications have made possible the interaction of goods, products, and services as well as the more significant exchange of thoughts and ideas. Accompanying the growth of human communication has been the erosion of barriers that have, throughout history, geographically, linguistically, and culturally separated man from man. As Harold Lasswell[2] has recently suggested, "The technological revolution as it affects mass media has reached a limit that is subject only to innovations that would substantially modify our basic perspectives of one another and of man's place in the cosmos." It is possible that the emergence of multicultural man is just such an innovation.

A NEW KIND OF MAN

A new type of person whose orientation and view of the world profoundly transcends his indigenous culture is developing from the complex of social, political, economic, and educational interactions of our time. The various conceptions of an "international," "transcultural," or "interculture" person have all been used with varying degrees of explanative or descriptive utility. Essentially, they all define a type of person whose horizons extend significantly beyond his or her own culture. An "internationalist," for example, has been defined as a person who trusts other nations, is willing to cooperate with other countries, perceives international agencies as potential deterrents of war, and who considers international tensions reducible by mediation.[3] Others have researched the internationality of groups by measuring their attitudes towards international issues, i.e., the role of the U.N., economic versus military aid, international alliances, etc.[4] And at least several attempts have been made to measure the world-mindedness of individuals by exploring the degree to which persons have an international frame of reference rather than specific knowledge or interest in global affairs.[5]

Whatever the terminology, the definitions and metaphors allude to a person whose essential identity is inclusive of life patterns different from his own and who has psychologically and socially come to grips with a multiplicity of realities. We can call this new type of person multicultural because he embodies a core process of self verification that is grounded in both the universality of the human condition and in the diversity of man's cultural forms. We are speaking, then, of a social-psychological style of self process that differs from others. Multicultural man is the person who is intellectually and emotionally committed to the fundamental unity of all human beings while at the same time he recognizes, legitimizes, accepts, and appreciates the fundamental differences that lie between people of different cultures. This new kind of man cannot be defined by the languages he speaks, the countries he has visited, or the number of international contacts he has made. Nor is he defined by his profession, his place of residence, or his cognitive sophistication. Instead, multicultural man is recognized by the configuration of his outlooks and world view, by the way he incorporates the universe as a dynamically moving process, by the way he reflects the interconnectedness of life in his thoughts and his actions, and by the way he remains open to the imminence of experience.

Multicultural man is, at once, both old and new. He is very much the timeless "universal" person described again and again by philosophers through the ages. He approaches, in the attributions we make about him, the classical ideal of a person whose lifestyle is one of knowledge and wisdom, integrity and direction, principle and fulfillment, balance and proportion. "To be a universal man," writes John Walsh, "means not how much a man knows but what intellectual depth and breadth he has and how he relates it to other central and universally important problems."[6] What is universal about the multicultural person is his abiding commitment to essential similarities between people everywhere, while paradoxically maintaining an equally strong commitment to their differences. The universal person, suggests Walsh, "does not at all eliminate culture differences." Rather, he "seeks to preserve whatever is most valid, significant, and valuable in each culture as a way of enriching and helping to form the whole." In his embodiment of the universal and the particular, multicultural man is a descendant of the great philosophers in both the East and the West.

What is new about this type of person and unique to our time is a fundamental change in the structure and process of his identity. His identity, far from being frozen in a social character, is more fluid and mobile, more susceptible to change and open to variation. The identity of multicultural man is based, not on a "belongingness" which implies either owning or being owned by culture, but on a style of self consciousness that is capable of negotiating ever new formations of reality. In this sense multicultural man is a radical departure from the kinds of identities found in both traditional and mass societies. He is neither totally *a part of* nor totally *apart from* his culture; he lives, instead, on the boundary. To live on the edge of one's thinking, one's culture, or one's ego, suggests Paul Tillich, is to live with tension and movement. "It is in truth not standing still, but rather a crossing and return, a repetition of return and crossing, back-and-forth—the aim of which is to create a third area beyond the bounded territories, an area where one can stand for a time without being enclosed in something tightly bounded."[7] Multicultural man, then, is an outgrowth of the complexities of the twentieth century. Yet unique as he may be, the style of identity embodied by multicultural man arises from the myriad of forms that are present in this day and age. An understanding of this new kind of person, then, must be predicated on a clear understanding of cultural identity.

THE CONCEPT OF CULTURAL IDENTITY: A PSYCHOCULTURAL FRAMEWORK

The concept of cultural identity can be used in two different ways. First, it can be employed as a reference to the collective self awareness that a given group embodies and reflects. This is the most prevalent use of the term. "Generally," writes Stephen Bochner, "the cultural identity of a society is defined by its majority group, and this group is usually quite distinguishable from the minority sub-groups with whom they share the physical environment and the territory that they inhabit."[8] With the emphasis upon the group, the concept is akin to the idea of a national or social character which describes a set of traits that members of a given community share with one another above and beyond their individual differences. Such traits most always include a constellation of values and attitudes towards life, death, birth, family, children, god, and nature. Used in its collective sense, the concept of cultural identity includes typologies of cultural behavior, such behaviors being the appropriate and inappropriate ways of solving life's essential

dilemmas and problems. Used in its collective sense, the concept of cultural identity incorporates the shared premises, values, definitions, and beliefs and the day-to-day, largely unconscious, patterning of activities.

A second, more specific use of the concept revolves around the identity of the individual in relation to his or her culture. Cultural identity, in the sense that it is a functioning aspect of individual personality, is a fundamental symbol of a person's existence. It is in reference to the individual that the concept is used in this paper. In psychoanalytic literature, most notably in the writings of Erik Erikson, identity is an elemental form of psychic organization which develops in successive psycho-sexual phases throughout life. Erikson, who has focused the greater portion of his analytic studies on identity conflicts, has long recognized the anchoring of the ego in a larger cultural context. Identity, he suggests, takes a variety of forms in the individual. "At one time," he writes, "it will appear to refer to a conscious sense of *individual identity;* at another to an unconscious striving for a *continuity of personal character;* at a third, as a criterion for the silent doings of *ego synthesis;* and, finally, as a maintenance of an inner *solidarity* with a group's ideals and identity."[9] The analytic perspective, as voiced by Erikson, is only one of a variety of definitions. Most always, however, the concept of identity is meant to imply a coherent sense of self that depends on a stability of values and a sense of wholeness and integration.

How, then, can we conceptualize the interplay of culture and personality? Culture and personality are inextricably woven together in the *gestalt* of each person's identity. Culture, the mass of life patterns that human beings in a given society learn from their elders and pass upon the younger generation, is imprinted upon the individual as a pattern of perceptions that is accepted and expected by others in a society.[10] Cultural identity is the symbol of one's essential experience of oneself as it incorporates the world view, value system, attitudes, and beliefs of a group with whom such elements are shared. In its most manifest form, cultural identity takes the shape of names which both locate and differentiate the person. When an individual calls himself an American, a Christian, a Democrat, a male, and John Jones, he is symbolizing parts of the complex of images he has of himself and that are likewise recognizable by others. The deeper structure of cultural identity is a fabric of such images and perceptions embedded in the psychological posture of the individual. At the center of this matrix of images is a psychocultural fusion of biological, social, and philosophical motivations; this fusion, a synthesis of culture and personality, is the operant person.

The center, or core, of cultural identity is an image of the self and the culture intertwined in the individual's total conception of reality. This image, a patchwork of internalized roles, rules, and norms, functions as the coordinating mechanism in personal and interpersonal situations. The "mazeway," as Anthony Wallace calls it, is made up of human, non-human, material and abstract elements of the culture. It is the "stuff" of both personality and culture. The mazeway, suggests Wallace, is the patterned image of society and culture, personality and nature all of which is ingrained in the person's symbolization of himself. A system of culture, he writes, "depends relatively more on the ability of constituent units autonomously to perceive the system of which they are a part, to receive and transmit information, and to act in accordance with the necessities of the system. . . ."[11] The image, or mazeway, of cultural identity is the gyroscope of the functioning individual. It mediates, arbitrates, and negotiates the life of the individual. It is within the context of this central, navigating image that the fusion of biological, social, and philosophical realities, then, form units of integration that are important to a comparative analysis of cultural identity. The way in which these units are knit together and contoured by the culture at large determines the parameters of the individual. This boundary of cultural identity plays a large part in determining the individual's ability to relate to other cultural systems.

All human beings share a similar biology, universally limited by the rhythms of life. All individuals in all races and cultures must move through life's phases on a similar schedule:

birth, infancy, adolescence, middle age, old age, and death. Similarly, humans everywhere embody the same physiological functions of ingestion, irritability, metabolic equilibrium, sexuality, growth, and decay. Yet the ultimate interpretation of human biology is a cultural phenomenon; that is, the meanings of human biological patterns are culturally derived. Though all healthy human beings are born, reproduce, and die, it is culture which dictates the meanings of sexuality, the ceremonials of birth, the transitions of life, and the rituals of death. The capacity for language, for example, is universally accepted as a biological given. Any child, given unimpaired apparatus for hearing, vocalizing, and thinking, can learn to speak and understand any human language. Yet the language that is learned by a child depends solely upon the place and the manner of rearing. Kluckhohn and Leighton,[12] in outlining the grammatical and phonetic systems of the Navajo Indians, have argued that patterns of language affect the expression of ideas and very possibly more fundamental processes of thinking. As Benjamin Whorf has suggested,[13] language may not be merely an inventory of linguistic items but rather "itself the shaper of ideas, the program and guide for the individual's mental activity."[14]

The interaction of culture and biology provides one cornerstone for an understanding of cultural identity. How each individual's biological situation is given meaning becomes, then, a psychobiological unit of integration and analysis. Man's essential physiological needs, hunger, sex, activity, and avoidance of pain, are one part of the reality pattern of cultural identity; similarly with those drives that reach out to the social order. At this, the psychosocial level of integration, generic needs are channeled and organized by culture. Man's needs for affection, acceptance, recognition, affiliation, status, belonging, and interaction with other human beings are enlivened and given recognizable form by culture. We can, for example, see clearly the intersection of culture and the psychosocial level of integration in comparative status responses. In America economic status is demonstrated by the conspicuous consumption of products; among the Kwakiutl Indians, status is gained by giving all possessions away in the "potlatch"; and contempt or disrespect for the status of old people in many Asian societies represents a serious breach of conduct demanding face-saving measures.

It is the unwritten task of every culture to organize, integrate, and maintain the psychosocial patterns of the individual, especially in the formative years of childhood. Each culture instruments such patterns in ways that are unique, coherent, and logical to the premises and predispositions that underlie the culture. This imprinting of the forms of interconnection that are needed by the individual for psychosocial survival, acceptance, and enrichment is a significant part of the socialization and enculturation process. Yet of equal importance in the imprinting is the structuring of higher forms of individual consciousness. Culture gives meaning and form to those drives and motivations that extend towards an understanding of the cosmological ordering of the universe. All cultures, in one manner or another, invoke the great philosophical questions of life: the origin and destiny of existence, the nature of knowledge, the meaning of reality, the significance of the human experience. As Murdock has suggested in "Universals of Culture,"[15] some form of cosmology, ethics, mythology, supernatural propitiation, religious rituals, and soul concept appears in every culture known to history or ethnography. How an individual raises and searches for ultimate answers is a function of the psychophilosophical patterning of cultural identity. Ultimately it is the task of every individual to relate to his god, to deal with the supernatural, and to incorporate for himself the mystery of life itself. The ways in which individuals do this, the relationships and connections that are formed, are a function of the psychophilosophical component of cultural identity.

A conceptualization of cultural identity, then, must include three interrelated levels of integration and analysis. While the cultural identity of an individual is comprised of symbols and images that signify aspects of these levels, the psychobiological, psychosocial, and psychophilosophical realities of an individual are knit together by the culture which operates through sanctions and rewards, totems and taboos, prohibitions and myths. The unity and integration of society, nature, and the cosmos is reflected in the total image of the self and in the day-to-day awareness and consciousness of the individual. This synthesis is modulated by the larger dynamics of the culture itself. In the concept of cultural identity, then, we see a synthesis of the operant culture reflected by the deepest images held by the individual. These images, in turn, are based on universally human motivations.

Implicit in any analysis of cultural identity is a configuration of motivational needs. As the late Abraham Maslow suggested,[16] human drives form a hierarchy in which the most prepotent motivations will monopolize consciousness and will tend, of themselves, to organize the various capacities and capabilities of the organism. In the sequence of development, the needs of infancy and childhood revolve primarily around physiological and biological necessities, i.e., nourishment by food, water, and warmth. Correspondingly, the psychosocial needs of the individual are most profound in adolescence and young adulthood when the individual is engaged in establishing himself through marriage, occupation, and social and economic status. Finally, psychophilosophical drives are most manifest in middle and old age when the individual can occupy himself with creativity, philosophic actualization, and with transcendental relationships. As Cofer and Appley rightly point out, Maslow's hierarchy of needs is not an explicit, empirical, verifiable theory of human motivation.[17] It is useful, however, in postulating a universally recognized but differently named process of individual motivation that carries the individual through the stages of life. Each level of integration and analysis in cultural identity, then, can be viewed as both a part of the gridwork of the self image as well as a developmental road map imprinted by the culture.

The gyroscope of cultural identity functions to orchestrate the allegiances, loyalties, and commitments of the individual by giving them direction and meaning. Every human being, however, differentiates himself to some degree from his culture. Just as no one is totally free of cultural influence, no one is totally a reflection of his culture. The cultural identity of an individual, therefore, must be viewed as an integrated synthesis of identifications that are idiosyncratic within the parameters of culturally influenced biological, social, and philosophical motivations. Whether, in fact, such unity ever achieves sufficient integration to provide for consistency between individuals within a given culture is an empirical matter that deals with normalcy and modal personality. The concept of cultural identity, then, can at best be a schema for comparative research between (rather than with) cultures. This schema of cultural identity is illustrated in Figure 1. Though admittedly a fundamental rule of social science must be human variation and the unpredictability of models and theories, a schema of cultural identity and the interplay of psychological and cultural dynamics may lay a groundwork for future research and conceptualization. Particularly useful may be the "eiconic" approach proposed by Kenneth Boulding.[18] His typology of images which include the spatial, temporal, relational, personal, value, affectional, conscious-unconscious, certainty-uncertainty, reality-unreality, and public-private dimensions, may add important perspectives to the comparative study of cultural identity.

THE MULTICULTURAL IDENTITY

The rise of multicultural man is a significant phenomenon because it represents a new psychocultural style of self process. He arises amidst the metamorphosis of both traditional and mass societies, in a transitional time in which man is redefining himself politically, socially and economically. Multicultural man is a radically different sort of human being. Three characteristics distinguish his style of personality from the traditional structure of cultural identity. First, the multicultural person is psychoculturally adaptive; that is, he is situational in his relationships to others and his connections to culture. He maintains no clear boundaries between himself and the varieties of personal and cultural contexts in which he may find himself. The multicultural identity is premised, not on the hierarchical structuring of a single mental image but rather on the intentional and accidental shifts that life's experiences involve. His values and attitudes, world view and beliefs, are always in

Psychophilosophical

(old age)

(middle age)

Psychosocial

(young adulthood)

(adolescence)

Psychobiological

(childhood)

(infancy)

FIGURE 1

reformation, dependent more on the necessities of experience than on the predispositions of a given culture. For multicultural man, attitudes, values, beliefs, and a world view are relevant only to a given context (as is usually learned as a result of the culture shock process) and cannot be translated from context to context. Multicultural man does not judge one situation by the terms of another and is therefore ever evolving new systems of evaluations that are relative to the context and situation.

Second, the multicultural person is ever undergoing personal transitions. He is always in a state of "becoming" or "un-becoming" something different than before while yet mindful of the grounding he has in his own cultural reality. Stated differently, multicultural man is propelled from identity to identity through a process of both cultural learning and cultural un-learning. Multicultural man, like Robert J. Lifton's concept of "protean man,"[19] is always recreating his identity. He moves through one experience of self to another, incorporating here, discarding there, responding dynamically and situationally. This style of self process, suggests Lifton, "is characterized by an interminable series of experiments and explorations, some shallow, some profound, each of which can readily be abandoned in favor of still new, psychological quests." The multicultural man is always in flux, the configuration of his loyalties and identifications changing, his overall image of himself perpetually being reformulated through experience and contact with the world. Stated differently, his life is an on-going process of psychic death and rebirth.

Third, multicultural man maintains indefinite boundaries of the self. The parameters of his identity are neither fixed nor predictable, being responsive, instead, to both temporary form and openness to change. Multicultural man is capable of major shifts in his frame of reference and embodies the ability to disavow a permanent character and change in his social-psychological style. The multicultural person, in the words of Peter Berger is a "homeless mind,"[20] a condition which, though allowing great flexibility, also allows for nothing permanent and unchanging to develop. This homelessness is at the heart of his motivational needs. He is, suggests Lifton, "starved for ideas and feelings that give coherence to his world . . . ," that give structure and form to his search for the universal and absolute, that give definition to his perpetual quest. The multicultural man, like great philosophers in any age, can never accept totally the demands of any one culture nor is he free from the conditioning of his culture. His psychocultural style, then, must always be relational and in movement. He is able, however, to look at his own original culture from an outsider's perspective. This tension gives rise to a dynamic, passionate, and critical posture in the face of totalistic ideologies, systems, and movements.

Like culture-bound man, multicultural man bears within him a simultaneous image of societies, nature, personality, and culture. Yet in contrast to the structure of cultural identity, multicultural man is perpetually re-defining his mazeway. No culture is capable of imprinting or ingraining the identity of multicultural man indelibly; yet, likewise, multicultural man must rely heavily on cultures to maintain his own relativity. Like human beings in any period of time, multicultural man is driven by psychobiological, psychosocial, and psychophilosophical motivations that impel him through life. Yet the configuration of these drives is perpetually in flux and situational. The maturational hierarchy, implicit in the central image of cultural identity, is less structured and cohesive in the multicultural identity. For that reason, his needs and his drives, his motivations and expectations are constantly being aligned and realigned to fit the context he is in.

The flexibility of multicultural man allows great variation in adaptability and adjustment. Adjustment and adaptation, however, must always be dependent on some constant, on something stable and unchanging in the fabric of life. We can attribute to multicultural man three fundamental postulates that are incorporated and reflected in his thinking and behavior. Such postulates are fundamental to success in cross-cultural adaptation.

1. Every culture or system has its own internal coherence, integrity, and logic. Every culture is an intertwined system of values and attitudes, beliefs and

norms that give meaning and significance to both individual and collective identity.

2. No one culture is inherently better or worse than another. All cultural systems are equally valid as variations on the human experience.

3. All persons are, to some extent, culturally bound. Every culture provides the individual with some sense of identity, some regulation of behavior, and some sense of personal place in the scheme of things.

The multicultural person embodies these propositions in the living expressions of his life. They are fundamentally a part of his interior image of himself and the world and as much a part of his behavior.

What is uniquely new about this emerging human being is a psychocultural style of self process that transcends the structured image a given culture may impress upon the individual in his or her youth. The navigating image at the core of the multicultural image is premised on an assumption of many cultural realities. The multicultural person, therefore, is not simply the person who is sensitive to many different cultures. Rather, he is a person who is always in the process of becoming *a part of* and *apart from* a given cultural context. He is very much a formative being, resilient, changing, and evolutionary. He has no permanent cultural character but neither is he free from the influences of culture. In the shifts and movements of his identity process, multicultural man is continually recreating the symbol of himself. The concept of a multicultural identity is illustrated and differentiated from the schema of cultural identity in Figure 2.

The indefinite boundaries and the constantly realigning relationships that are generated by the psychobiological, psychosocial and psychophilosophical motivations make possible sophisticated and complex responses on the part of the individual to cultural and subcultural systems. Moreover, this psychocultural flexibility necessitates sequential changes in identity. Intentionally or accidentally, multicultural persons undergo shifts in their total psychocultural posture; their religion, personality, behavior, occupation, nationality, outlook, political persuasion, and values may, in part or completely, reformulate in the face of new experiences. "It is becoming increasingly possible," writes Michael Novak, "for men to live through several profound conversions, calling forth in themselves significantly different personalities. . . ."[21] The relationship of multicultural man to cultural systems is fragile and tenuous. "A man's cultural and social milieu," continues Novak, "conditions his personality, values, and actions; yet the same man is able, within limits, to choose the milieus whose conditioning will affect him."

Who, then, is multicultural man? Four different variations of the multicultural identity process can be seen in the following case studies. While two of these individuals have been interviewed extensively by the author,[22] the other two are figures of contemporary importance. Each of these persons, in their own unique way, represents the essential characteristics of multicultural man in a vivid and dramatic manner.

1. *C.K.* is a talented musician, an excellent student, a deeply spiritual disciple of an Indian mystic, and at once, both a teacher and a friend to a number of other students. Though outgoing, humorous, and articulate he is likewise a private, almost quiet person who appears to exert a high degree of control over his life. Coming from a large family in which his

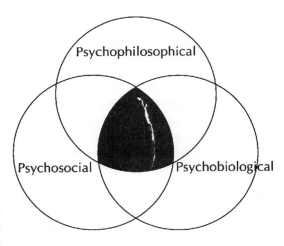

FIGURE 2

father, an engineer, spent a good deal of time abroad, C.K. had an early opportunity to both live and study in a foreign culture. Following high school C.K. spent his college years in the Middle East where he purposely stayed away from other Americans in order to facilitate both contacts with the local people and language learning. His first years in the Middle East were significant: "It was at this point that I began to *see* where I grew up and not just *know* that I had been raised in America." In high school, C.K. had been intensely interested in mathematics and physics; his college career, however, brought about a shift. Increasingly, he found himself interested in music, an interest that would later carry him East both academically and spiritually. It was during his college years that C.K. also became aware of American policy abroad; though never entirely a political activist, C.K. was outspoken and critical of American foreign policy and critical of the Vietnam war. After completing his B.A., C.K. enrolled in graduate studies in ethnomusicology, concentrating his work on the Indian flute. With his wife he then spent a year and a half in India studying under an Indian teacher. His Indian experiences were important. Living and studying in a traditional setting, C.K. became progressively more involved with the philosophic traditions of the country and eventually met a well-known Indian mystic. His encounters with the meditations of this teacher influenced him profoundly. After months of study, meditation, and living with this religious leader and his other disciples, C.K. himself became a disciple. The dissolution of his marriage which he calls "an amicable and agreeable parting" came at roughly the same time. After returning to America to continue his graduate studies in music, C.K., still very much a disciple of his teacher, has continued to both practice and teach meditation. C.K. is very warm and articulate in discussion. He describes life as a series of peaks and valleys, what he calls the "mountain climbing" model of existence. "Life is a series of mountains in which you must go down one mountain in order to go up yet another. Each ascent and descent is difficult but one must be able to experience both the top and the bottom if one is to grow." C.K. is

an exceptional person. His friends to whom he taught meditation come from a variety of disciplines and countries, including some from India and Japan. In his day-to-day experiences, C.K. seems to react situationally. In his own words, he makes every attempt to "be in the here and now" to relate to people individually, and to live as simple and uncomplicated an existence as possible. Though he rejects much talk about mysticism, C.K. lives an ascetic and "feeling" style of life in which he aspires to bring himself in contact with the largest rhythms of nature and of the universe.

2. *Y.N.* is Japanese, an expatriate now residing in Hawaii, and a quiet, intelligent individual. Though he initially is shy with strangers, Y.N. likes very much to play host for his friends. In conversation he will demonstrate techniques of *ju-jitsu,* in which he holds a high ranking belt, and talk about the incidents that have occurred to him in his travels throughout Asia and America. Brought up in a middle-class, relatively traditional home, Y.N. finished high school and taught *ikebana,* the art of flower arrangement. Qualified as a teacher in this and several other aesthetic and martial arts, Y.N. came to America. In high school and his first years in college, Y.N. had become a member of a splinter faction of the *Zengakuren,* the militant student movement in Japan, and had participated actively in numerous demonstrations and student revolts. He describes this time in his life "both a high and low for myself." Though his commitment to the radical movement was deep, he felt strongly the urge to live contemplatively and reflectively as his various masteries had taught him to do. In the tension that surrounded the late 1960s in Japan, and amidst conflicts with his father who was opposed to his radical leanings, he "escaped" to America where he has every intention of remaining until he "finds another place to live." Having disavowed himself from both the aesthetic arts and radical political causes, Y.N. is today employed in a hotel as a means of supporting himself through school. Since coming to the United States, Y.N. has undergone, in his words, a "transformation." He is completely different and realizes that he is no longer able to return to Japan to become reconciled with his family and culture. Nor is he totally at

home in the U.S. Instead, he sees the U.S. as a temporary place for himself and considers the world to be his home. At one point, several years after being in the U.S., Y.N. returned to Japan, but his anxieties rapidly cascaded into a nervous breakdown. Returning to the U.S., he underwent intensive psychotherapy and again resumed his studies, and with an undergraduate degree in history, may move to Australia. Though unsure of his future, he hopes to utilize his studies of history in teaching and writing and seems confident that his inner struggles have prepared him for further changes which he sees as inevitable.

3. *Carlos Castaneda*, familiar through his writings about don Juan, the Yaqui Indian sorcerer, is an anthropologist by training, a Brazilian by birth, and an elusive, intensely private individual. He is known solely through his books and the articles about him that have appeared in popular literature.[23] Castaneda spent most of his life in Argentina and came to the United States to do graduate work in anthropology. Interested in the cultural uses of psychotropic drugs, he began field work with don Juan Mateus, a Yaqui Indian reputed to be a medicine man of great power. After a year of studying with don Juan, Castaneda entered an apprenticeship under the sorcerer and spent the next twelve years working, living, and studying under the old man. His first books documented his experiences with mescalin, peyote, and jimson weed and his progressively deeper involvement with the cultural context in which such drugs are used. In attempting to understand their use, Castaneda had to struggle with a "non-ordinary reality." His writings, taken in series, document his struggles to understand another way of life, his resistances, his failures, and his occasional successes. A trained Western scientist, Castaneda's apprenticeship led him deeper and deeper into the world of the *brujo,* a reality which is as much comprised of phantoms and spirits as it is rattlesnakes and cactus. Progressively more jolted by the extraordinary things he encountered in the world of don Juan, Castaneda documented his experiences, which read like the dream-logs of Jungian psychologists. Throughout his twelve years of apprenticeship, don Juan has progressively brought Castaneda deeper into the "becoming of a man of power and knowledge." At least one of the on-going lessons of don Juan has been responsibility, to personally be accountable for every movement and thought, every behavior and action. To pick the leaves of a plant, to disturb pebbles in the desert, or to shiver in the cold are all ultimate acts of the man who has control of himself. Nothing is chance, yet nothing can be explained logically or rationally. Castaneda, who is somewhat publicity shy, is known only through his writings, and these are quite controversial. Studying, writing, and existing on the far fringe of academic respectability, Castaneda seems comfortable in his relationships to several different cultures.

4. *Norman O. Brown*, born in Mexico of American parents, educated in both England and America, at one time a researcher for the Office of Strategic Services (forerunner of the CIA) is presently a professor of comparative literature and a prominent left-wing thinker. Brown is a fiercely intentional, highly provocative writer whose major contributions have been in fields where he had limited academic training. At one time an obscure teacher of literature, Brown became immersed in a penetrating study of Freud in the late 1950s. Out of his encounters with the psychoanalytic school of psychology, Brown wrote his first book, *Life Against Death*,[24] which sought nothing less than a total overhaul of psychological, social, economic, and political thinking. Using his thoughts on the Freudian concept of repression as a departure point, Brown has attempted to formulate a social theory that is determined to remove all barriers to human liberation. Having jumped freely into the domain of psychologists, sociologists, and political scientists, Brown has come to see hope in madness and in the Dionysian model. His apocalyptic vision encompasses, in his own words, "a shaking of the foundations" which bind man to repetitious, self destructive behavior. Brown is a visionary in the school of Nietzsche and, like Nietzsche, finds liberation in the ultimate destruction of all boundaries. Brown and his writings cannot be encapsulated in a discipline. He overlaps, expands, and bursts areas of study and purposely seeks to shock his intellectual peers with thinking

that is often bizarre, usually outrageous, and always rigorous. He draws from the sources of metaphor: myths, dreams, religion, symbols, and the undercurrents of the unconscious; in drawing together sources from philosophy, theology, psychology, and history he weaves together a theoretical perspective that is both analytic and polemic. Brown is a spokesman for liberation, his enemy the "politics of sin, cynicism, and despair," his goal the ultimate unification of man and nature. Far from being a gadfly, Brown is accepted as a deep and penetrating thinker whose writings have thrust him in the role of both counter-culture hero and enemy of the academic establishment. More than anything else, however, Brown has jumped across disciplines, theories, and traditions in an effort to free the human mind from its blinders. His ultimate vision comes to rest in poetry and in the sublime, if unchallengeable, processes of dialectical confrontation with the barriers of his time.

Each of these individuals, C.K., Y.N., Castaneda, and Brown, share significant elements of the multicultural identity. Each, in their own way, can be understood only contextually, that is, only in relation to the particular time, place, and system we choose to focus on. Each of these individuals has undergone shifts in identity, in some cases quite radical breaks with their previous "selves." C.K. and Castaneda, for example, have followed a course that involves a search for heightened personal consciousness. Y.N. and Brown, on the other hand, have pursued a series of identity changes that have carried them into and through a radical political posture. But in all four of these individuals it is possible to see that there have been fracture points in which the constellation of values, attitudes, world view, and outlook that we call identity has changed. Each of these individuals, different as they are, have embraced, only to let go, one frame of reference in favor of yet another.

Neither C.K., Y.N., Castaneda or Brown are "usual" persons. All of them have perched themselves precariously close to the boundaries of the system. In the case of Y.N., this has involved self exile from his native country; for Brown, this has meant a departure from the perimeters of his training and expertise; for C.K., the experience of self has meant embracing a religious order that is antipodal to the Western tradition; and for Castaneda, it has involved an agonizing indoctrination into an order of experience that carries him far from the careful, methodical schooling of anthropology. Each of these persons is in some sense or another an outsider, intentionally or accidentally dislocated from one frame of reference to another, from one environment of experience to a different one. Though they differ drastically in their personalities, orientations, political values, and personal objectives, they share a similar process of identity change. And though they share a similar process of identity style, they differ greatly in their handling of the stresses and strains, the tensions and problems that ensue from such a fluidity of self. Y.N. has obviously been severely disturbed by the demands placed on him through conflicts in loyalty. Brown has glorified the infantile ego and taken refuge in an intellectual process that necessitates the smashing of all boundaries without regard for the functions such boundaries may perform. Castaneda has removed himself totally from the public view while C.K. has submitted himself to what one might call a dogmatic totalism.

STRESSES AND TENSIONS

The unprecedented dynamism of multicultural man makes it possible to live many different lives, in sequence or simultaneously. But such psychocultural pliability gives rise to tensions and stresses unique to the conditions which allow such dynamism in the first place. Multicultural man, by virtue of the fact that his boundaries are indefinite, his experience more intense, and his lifetime telescoped into modules of congruency, is subject to stresses and strains that are equally unique. At least five of these stresses bear mentioning.

First, multicultural man is vulnerable. In maintaining no clear boundary and form multicultural man is susceptible to confusing the profound and the insignificant, the important and the unimportant, the visionary and the reactionary. "Boundaries can be viewed," suggests Lifton, "as neither permanent nor by definition false, but rather as essential. . . . We require images of limit and restraint, if only to help us grasp what we are transcending. We need distinctions between our biology and our history, all the more so as we seek to bring these together in a sense of ourselves. . . ."[25] Without some form of boundary, experience itself has no shape or contour, no meaning and importance; where the individual maintains no critical edge to his existence everything can become confusion. Experience, in order to be a particular experience, must take place amidst some essential polarity in which there is tension between two opposing forces. Where there is no sense of evil, there can be no sense of the good; where nothing is profane, nothing can be sacred. Boundaries, however indefinite, give shape and meaning to the experience of experience; they allow us to differentiate, define, and determine who we are in relation to someone or something else.

Second, multicultural man can easily become multiphrenic, that is, to use Erikson's terminology, a "diffused identity." Where the configuration of loyalties and identifications is constantly in flux and where boundaries are never secure, multicultural man lays himself open to any and all kind of stimuli. In the face of messages which are confusing, contradictory, or overwhelming, the individual is thrown back on himself and his own subjectivity, with which he must integrate and sort out what he allows himself to take in. Where the multicultural man is incapable of doing this he is pulled and pushed by the winds of communication, a victim of what everyone else claims he is or should be. It is the task of every social and cultural group to organize messages, images, and symbols into terms that the individual can translate into his own existence. But where the messages and stimuli of all groups are given equal importance and validity, the individual can easily be overwhelmed by the demands of everyone else.

Third, multicultural man can easily suffer from a loss of the sense of his own authenticity. That is, multicultural man, by virtue of the fact that he is psychoculturally adaptive, can potentially be reduced to a variety of roles that bear little or no relationship to one another. Multicultural man can lose the sense of congruence and integrity that is implicit in the definition of identity itself. Roles, suggest psychologists, are constellations of behaviors that are expected of an individual because of his place in particular social or cultural arrangements. Behind roles are the deeper threads of continuity, the processes of affect, perception, cognition, and value, that make a whole of the parts. Multicultural man can easily disintegrate into a fragmented splinter who is unable to experience life along any dimension other than institutionalized, routinized expectations placed on him by family, friends, and society.

Fourth, and related to this, is the risk of being a gadfly and a dilettante. Multicultural man can very easily move from identity experience to identity experience without committing himself or his values to real-life situations. The energy and enthusiasm he brings to bear on new situations can easily disintegrate into superficial fads and fancies in which the multicultural person simply avoids any deeper responsibilities and involvements. Flexibility can easily disguise a manner of self process in which real human problems are avoided or in which they are given only superficial importance. Especially in the Western societies, where youth is vulnerable to the fabricated fads of contemporary culture, the multicultural identity process can give way to a dilettantism in which the individual flows, unimpaired, uncommitted, and unaffected, through social, political, and economic manipulations of elites.

Fifth, and finally, the multicultural person may take ultimate psychological and philosophical refuge in an attitude of existential absurdity, mocking the patterns and lifestyles of others who are different from himself, reacting, at best in a detached and aloof way, and at worst as a nihilist who sees negation as a salvation for himself and others. Where the breakdown of boundaries creates a gulf that separates the individual from meaningful relationships with others, the individual may hide behind a screen of barbed cynicisms that harbors apathy and insecurity. In such a condition nothing within and nothing outside of the individual is of serious consequence; the individual, in such a position, must ultimately scorn that which he cannot understand and incorporate into his own existence.

These stresses and strains should not be confused with the tensions and anxieties that are encountered in the process of cross-cultural adjustment. Culture shock is a more superficial constellation of problems that results from the misreading of commonly perceived and understood signs of social interaction. Nor is the delineation of these tensions meant to suggest that the multicultural person must necessarily harbor these various difficulties. The multicultural style of identity is premised on a fluid, dynamic movement of the self, an ability to move in and out of contexts, and an ability to maintain some inner coherence through varieties of situations. As a psychocultural style, multicultural man may just as easily be a great artist or neurotic; he is equally as susceptible, if not more so, to the fundamental forces of our time. Any list of multicultural individuals must automatically include individuals who have achieved a high degree of accomplishment, i.e., writers, musicians, diplomats, etc., as well as those whose lives have, for one reason or another, been fractured by the circumstances they failed to negotiate. The artist and the neurotic lie close together in each of us suggests Rollo May. "The neurotic," he writes, "and the artist—since both live out the unconscious of the race—reveal to us what is going to emerge endemically in the society later on . . . the neurotic is the 'artiste Manque,' the artist who cannot transmute his conflicts into art. . . ."[26]

The identity process of multicultural man represents a new kind of person unfettered by the constricting limitations of culture as a "totalistic" entity. Yet, like men in any age, multicultural man must negotiate the difficulties of cross-cultural contacts. The literature of cross-cultural psychology is rich with examples of the kinds of problems encountered when people are intensely exposed to other cultures. Integration and assimilation, for example, represent two different responses to a dominant culture, integration suggesting the retention of subcultural differences and assimilation implying absorption into a larger cultural system. The relationship between assimilation, integration, and identification, writes Sommerlad and Berry, "suggests that if an individual identifies with his own group, he will hold favourable attitudes towards integration; on the other hand, if he identifies with the host society, he should favour assimilation."[27] Related to this are the various negative attitudes, psychosomatic stresses, and deviant behaviors that are expressed by individuals in psychologically marginal situations. "Contrary to predictions stemming from the theory of Marginal Man," writes J. W. Berry, "it tends to be those persons more traditionally oriented who suffer the most psychological marginality, rather than those who wish to move on and cannot."[28] Multicultural man is, in many ways, a stranger. The degree to which he can continually modify his frame of reference and become aware of the structures and functions of a group while at the same time maintain a clear understanding of his own personal, ethnic, and cultural identifications may very well be the degree to which the multicultural person can truly function successfully between cultures. . . .

Although it is difficult to pinpoint the conditions under which cultural identities will evolve into multicultural identities, such changes in psychocultural style are most likely to occur where the foundations of collective cultural identity have been shaken. "Communities that have been exposed too long to exceptional stresses from ecological or economic hardships," writes J. W. Cawte, "or from natural or man-made disasters are apt to have a high proportion of their members subject to mental disorders."[29] Cawte's studies of the Aboriginal societies of Australia and Turnbull's studies of the Ik in Africa document how major threats to collective cultural identity produce social and psychological breakdown in individuals.[30] Yet, potentially, multicultural attitudes and values may develop where cultural interchange takes place between cultures that are not totally disparate or where the rate of change is evolutionary rather than immediate. The reorganization of a culture, suggests J. L. M. Dawson, "results in the formation of in between attitudes" which Dawson considers "to be more appropriate for the satisfactory adjustment of individuals in transitional situations."[31] The multicultural style, then, may be born and initially expressed in any society or culture that is faced with new exposures to other ways of life.

Conceptualization of a multicultural identity style in terms of personality types, behavior patterns, traits, and cultural background is at best impressionistic and anecdotal. Yet, the investigations of cross-cultural psychologists and anthropologists give increasing credence to the idea of a multicultural man who is shaped and contoured by the stresses and strains which result from cultural interweaving at both the macro and microcultural levels. Seemingly, a multicultural style is able to evolve when the individual is capable of negotiating the conflicts and tensions inherent in cross-cultural contacts. The multicultural person, then, may very well represent an affirmation of individual identity at a higher level of social, psychological, and cultural integration.

Just as the cultures of the world, if they are to merit survival amidst the onslaught of Western technologies, must be responsive to both tradition and change, so too must the individual identity be psychoculturally adaptive to the encounters of an imploding world. There is every reason to think that such human beings are emerging. Multicultural man, embodying, as he does, sequential identities, is open to the continuous cycle of birth and death as it takes place within the framework of his own psyche. The lifestyle of multicultural man is a continual process of dissolution and reformation of identity; yet implicit in such a process is a sequence of growth. Psychological movements into new dimensions of perception and experience tend very often to produce forms of personality disintegration. But disintegration, suggests Kazimierez Dabrowski, "is the basis for developmental thrusts upward, the creation of new evolutionary dynamics, and the movement of personality to a higher level. . . ."[32] The seeds of each new identity of multicultural man lie within the disintegration of previous identities. "When the human being," writes Erikson, "because of accidental or developmental shifts, loses an essential wholeness, he restructures himself and the world by taking recourse to what we may call 'totalism.'"[33] Such totalism, above and beyond being a mechanism of coping and ad-justment, is a part of the growth of a new kind of wholeness at a higher level of integration.

CONCLUSIONS AND SUMMARY

This paper does not suggest that multicultural man is now the predominant character style of our time. Nor is it meant to suggest that multicultural persons, by virtue of their uninhibited way of relating to other cultures, are in any way "better" than those who are mono- or bicultural. Rather, this paper argues that multicultural persons are not simply individuals who are sensitive to other cultures or knowledgeable about international affairs, but instead can be defined by a psychocultural pattern of identity that differs radically from the relatively stable forms of self process found in the cultural identity pattern. This paper argues that both cultural and multicultural identity processes can be conceptualized by the constellation and configuration of biological, social, and philosophical motivations and by the relative degrees of rigidity maintained in personal boundaries and that such conceptualization lays the basis for comparative research.

Two final points might be noted about the multicultural man. First, the multicultural person embodies attributes and characteristics that prepare him to serve as a facilitator and catalyst for contacts between cultures. The variations and flexibility of his identity allows the multicultural person to relate to a variety of contexts and environments without being totally encapsulated or totally alienated from the particular situation. As Stephen Bochner suggests, a major problem of cultural preservation in Asia and the Pacific "is the lack of sufficient people who can act as links between diverse cultural systems."[34] These "mediating" individuals incorporate the essential characteristics of multicultural man. "Genuine multicultural individuals are very rare," he writes, "which is unfortunate because it is these people who are uniquely equipped to mediate the cultures of the world."[35] The multicultural person, then, embodies a pattern of self process that potentially allows him to help others negotiate the cultural realities of a different system. With a self process that is adaptational, multicultural man is in a unique position to understand, facilitate, and research the psychocultural dynamics of other systems.

Second, multicultural man is himself a significant psychological and cultural phenomenon, enough so as to merit further conceptualization and research. It is neither easy nor necessarily useful to reconcile the approaches of psychology and anthropology; nor is there any guarantee that interdisciplinary approaches bring us closer to an intelligent understanding of the human being as he exists in relation to his culture. Yet, the multicultural man may prove to be a significant enough problem in culture learning (and culture unlearning) to force an integrated approach to studies of the individual and the group. "Psychologists," write Richard Brislin, et al., "have the goal of incorporating the behavior of many cultures into one theory (etic approach), but they must also understand the behavior within each culture (emic approach)."[36] Empirical research based on strategies that can accurately observe, measure, and test behavior, and that incorporate the "emic versus etic" distinction will be a natural next step. Such studies may very well be a springboard into the more fundamental dynamics of cross-cultural relationships.

We live in a transitional period of history, a time that of necessity demands transitional forms of psychocultural self process. That a true international community of nations is coming into existence is still a debatable issue; but that individuals with a self consciousness that is larger than the mental territory of their culture are emerging is no longer arguable. The psychocultural pattern of identity that is called for to allow such self consciousness, adaptability, and variation opens such individuals to both benefits and pathologies. The interlinking of cultures and persons in the twentieth century is not always a pleasant process; modernization and economic development have taken heavy psychological tolls in both developed and third world countries. The changes brought on in our time have invoked revitalistic needs for the preservation of collective, cultural identities. Yet, along with the disorientation and alienation which have char-

acterized much of this century comes new possibility in the way human beings conceive of their individual identities and the identity of man as a species. No one has better stated this possibility than Harold Taylor, himself an excellent example of multicultural man:[37]

> There is a new kind of man in the world, and there are more of that kind than is commonly recognized. He is a national citizen with international intuitions, conscious of the age that is past and aware of the one now in being, aware of the radical difference between the two, willing to accept the lack of precedents, willing to work on the problems of the future as a labor of love, unrewarded by governments, academies, prizes, and position. He forms part of an invisible world community of poets, writers, dancers, scientists, teachers, lawyers, scholars, philosophers, students, citizens who see the world whole and feel at one with all its parts.

ENDNOTES

[1]Despite the fact that men and women share an equal investment in psychological developments of our time, it is virtually impossible to express certain concepts in language that is sexually neutral. The idea of a multicultural "man" and other references to the masculine gender are to be considered inclusive of men and women alike.

[2]H. Lasswell, *The Future of World Communication: Quality and Style of Life* (Honolulu: East-West Center Communication Institute, 1972).

[3]D. Lutzker, "Internationalism as a Predictor of Cooperative Behavior," *Journal of Conflict Resolution*, 4 (4), 1960: 426–430.

[4]A. Campbell, G. Gurin and W. E. Miller, *The Voter Decides* (Evanston: Row, Peterson and Co., 1954).

[5]K. Garrison, "Worldminded Attitudes of College Students in a Southern University," *Journal of Social Psychology*, 54, 1961: 147–153; S. Paul, "Worldminded Attitudes of Parijab University Students," *Journal of Social Psychology*, 69, 1966: 33–37; D. Sampson and H. Smith, "A Scale to Measure Worldminded Attitudes," *Journal of Social Psychology*, 45, 1957: 99–106.

[6]J. Walsh, *Intercultural Education in the Community of Man* (Honolulu: The University of Hawaii Press, 1973).

[7]P. Tillich, *The Future of Religions* (New York: Harper and Row, 1966).

[8]S. Bochner, "The Mediating Man and Cultural Diversity," *Topics in Culture Learning*, 1, 1973: 23–37.

[9]E. Erikson, "The Problem of Ego Identity," *Psychological Issues*, 1, no. 1, 1959: 101–164.

[10]M. Singer, "Culture: A Perceptual Approach," in D. Hoopes, ed., *Readings in Intercultural Communication* (Pittsburgh: RCIE, 1971): 6–20.

[11]A. Wallace, "Revitalization Movements: Some Theoretical Considerations for their Comparative Study," *American Anthropologist*, 58, 1956: 264–281.

[12]C. Kluckhohn and D. Leighton, "The Language of the Navajo Indians," in P. Bock, ed., *Culture Shock* (New York: Alfred A. Knopf, 1970): 29–49.

[13]B. Whorf, "Selected Writings of Benjamin Lee Whorf," in J. B. Carroll, ed., *Language, Thought, and Reality* (Massachusetts: Technology Press of MIT, 1957).

[14]A technical reference to the controversial literature examining the "Sapir-Whorf Hypothesis" can be found in "Psycholinguistics" by G. Miller and D. McNeill in Volume 3 of the *Handbook of Social Psychology* ed. G. Lindzey and E. Aronson (Reading: Addison-Wesley Publishing Company, 1968).

[15]G. Murdock, "Universals of Culture," in J. Jennings and E. A. Hoebel, eds., *Readings in Anthropology* (New York: McGraw-Hill Book Company, 1955): 13–14.

[16]A. Maslow, *Toward a Psychology of Being* (Princeton: D. Van Nostrand Company, Inc., 1962).

[17]C. Cofer and M. Appley, *Motivation: Theory and Research* (New York: John Wiley & Sons, Inc., 1964).

[18]K. Boulding, *The Image* (Ann Arbor: The University of Michigan Press, 1956).

[19]R. Lifton, *History and Human Survival* (New York: Vintage Books, 1961).

[20]P. Berger and B. Berger, *The Homeless Mind* (New York: Random House, 1973).

[21]M. Novak, *The Experience of Nothingness* (New York: Harper & Row, 1970).

[22]The examples of both C.K. and Y.N. are condensed from a number of longer case studies done by the author as part of his research on identity changes that result from cross cultural experiences. The full case studies are included in his Ph.D. thesis titled *The Boundary Experience*.

[23]C. Castaneda, *The Techniques of Don Juan* (New York: Ballantine Books, 1969); *A Separate Reality* (New York: Pocket Books, 1971); *Journey to Ixlan* (New York: Simon & Schuster, 1972).

[24]N. Brown, *Life Against Death* (Middletown: Wesleyan University Press, 1959).

[25]R. Lifton, *Boundaries* (New York: Vintage Books, 1967).

[26]R. May, *Love and Will* (New York: Dell Publishing Co., Inc., 1969).

[27]E. Sommerlad and J. W. Berry, "The Role of Ethnic Identification," in G. E. Kearney, P. R. deLacey and G. R. Davidson, eds., *The Psychology of Aboriginal Australians* (Sydney: John Wiley & Sons Australasia Pty Ltd., 1973): 236–243.

[28]J. W. Berry, "Marginality, Stress and Ethnic Identification," *Journal of Cross Cultural Psychology*, 1, 1970: 239–252.

[29]J. E. Cawte, "A Sick Society," in G. E. Kerney, P. R. deLacey and G. R. Davidson, eds., *The Psychology of Aboriginal Australians* (Sydney: John Wiley & Sons Australasia Pty Ltd., 1973): 365–379.

[30]C. Turnbull, *The Mountain People* (New York: Simon & Schuster, 1972).

[31]J. L. M. Dawson, "Attitude Change and Conflict," *Australian Journal of Psychology*, 21, 1969: 101–116.

[32]K. Dabrowski, *Positive Disintegration* (Boston: Little, Brown, & Co., 1964).

[33]E. Erikson, *Insight and Responsibility* (New York: W. W. Norton and Company, 1964).

[34]Bochner, *op.cit.*

[35]*Ibid.*

[36]R. Brislin, W. Lonner and R. Thorndike, *Cross Cultural Research Methods* (New York: John Wiley & Sons, 1973).

[37]H. Taylor, "Toward a World University," *Saturday Review*, 1969: 24, 52.

IV

Education and Counseling

The family is the primary source of enculturation. Through the family we learn our basic values, attitudes, beliefs, and world views. Our primary values and culture are acquired informally simply by growing up in a particular society. The more homogeneous the society, the more homogeneous the child-raising practices.

Schools are the second most important vehicle for enculturation. In most societies, teachers reinforce or more fully develop the primary cultural values imparted by parents. Students gain knowledge and also learn how to better fit into the dominant culture.

At the turn of the century, when there were large numbers of immigrant children,[1] the public school system was the major institution for Americanization. Teachers were expected not only to impart knowledge, but also the appropriate values and behaviors to excel in the New World. In 1896, New York City's Commissioner of Common Schools issued a statement that expressed the view of many American[2] educators. It was the paramount duty of public schools to obliterate "all the distinguishing foreign characteristics and traits . . . as obstructive and warring, and irritating elements."[3]

Evening classes were offered in many neighborhoods for adults who were also expected to learn English and American culture. Henry Ford began an Americanization program at his Detroit automobile plant, where citizenship classes were mandatory for foreign employees. The first sentence they learned to say was "I am a good American."[4]

EDUCATION AND CULTURE

Although some might assume there is such a thing as a value-free education, this is actually quite impossible. Teachers are value-carriers. Most come from the mainstream and/or graduated from colleges and universities which reflect mainstream thought patterns and values. Consequently, they tend to reinforce those values.

Education is both culturally-determined and culture-specific—not just *what* we learn, but also *how* we learn. Facts never speak for themselves. They are placed in a context and arranged according to a hierarchy of importance dictated by the dominant society's values.

Some cultures emphasize rote memorization as the initial and primary way of learning while others begin with "creativity." In cultures where rote memorization is predominant, creativity is also important. However, the argument would be that we cannot be creative until we have mastered basic skills and knowledge. How can one be mathematically creative until he or she learns how to add, subtract, divide, and multiply?

Americans are enraptured with experiential or participatory learning, where students participate in learning through demonstration and various exercises. Most of the rest of the world learns more didactically, with teachers imparting information to the students. And, students do not demonstrate knowledge of skills immediately after it is imparted. They must practice first.

An American teacher might explain long division and then ask students to volunteer to come forward and demonstrate their mastery of long division on the chalkboard. Most mainstream American children will frantically wave their hands to get the teacher's attention. Not only are these students comfortable immediately demonstrating their skills and knowledge, they are competing as individuals for the teacher's attention. And, it really is *individual* competition, because if these are average American school children, they love it when the smart kid on the other side of the classroom gives the wrong answer. There are winners and losers, and it's "me against the group."[5]

Most American Indian children do not raise their hands because in most tribes you do not compete against your peers. Further, you cannot demonstrate a skill until it is fully mastered. What if you fail when you go to the chalkboard? Not only do you lose face, but you also show your arrogance. Indian children will practice their skills alone or within a group of close friends, after which they may demonstrate them to the entire class.[6]

Even the way we think and pose our arguments is culturally influenced. In northern European and mainstream American cultures, children are taught to gather together a vast array of "facts" and then select out those facts which are relevant to making their case. This way of thinking and form of rhetoric might be labeled factual-inductive, abstractive, or analytical. In other cultures, one might start with the conclusions and weave together various "facts." Everything is relevant. This might be called affective-intuitive, associative, or relational thinking.

The factual-inductive way of thinking is typical of good memo writers or lawyers. They state relevant facts in a well-organized manner. The affective-intuitive way is typical of poets and artists—everything is associated with or related to everything else. In some societies, memo writers and lawyers are well-regarded; in others, statues are erected of poets and artists.

Teaching techniques must take into account how students from different cultures learn. Ways of thinking in one culture may not be well-regarded in another, and yet all ways may be useful. And, teachers should consider exactly what values they are consciously and unconsciously communicating—are the values appropriate to a multicultural society in today's increasingly interdependent world?

GENERATIONAL CULTURES

There is little evidence that dominant cultural values in America have changed over the past hundred years, in spite of all the technological and social changes in the society.[7] Dominant or basic cultural values are amazingly resilient, and yet each generation carries with it social change and a reordering of these basic values. This is particularly evident in the United States as young people leave home to enter the workforce, join the military or attend college.

A generation might be thought of as a *cohort*. In its original meaning, a cohort was one-tenth of a 5000-man Roman military legion. Today it means a group of people sharing a common experience over time, often defined by year of birth or year of entry into a group such as the workforce or university.

There is no agreement as to when a generation begins or ends, and there is overlap between generations. Many demographers identify three generations in each century, or spans of about thirty years. And, some social observers believe there are generational cycles. Often they are defined by significant historical events such as the end of a war, a period of economic crisis or a dramatic increase in population. Each generation has a collective self-identity or culture and is a carrier of social change, especially during the period when its members are adolescents or young adults.

The generation of Americans born between 1946 and 1964 is often referred to as the baby boom generation ("boomers").[8] They are the post-World War II generation. However, they are not a monolith. Youth in the mid-1950s until mid-1960s were the Silent Generation who tried to advance in the mainstream culture. Boomers were also members of the activist youth culture or counterculture of the mid-1960s to mid-1970s, and the Me Decade of the mid-1970s to mid-1980s.

The "busters" were born after 1964, and became members of Generation X in the mid-1980s to mid-1990s.[9] They are also members of youth culture today. If it is true that generations cover a thirty-year span and there are historical cycles, there may be parallels that can be drawn between the youth generation at the end of the 1960s and the youth generation at the end of this millennium.

COUNSELING AND CULTURE

Educators impart culture as they impart knowledge and skills. Counselors also impart culture but they focus on emotions and behaviors that may be inappropriate in the mainstream culture. School and job counselors, clergy, mental health experts, and psychologists and psychiatrists are all professionals who help others to fit in to the society, achieve their personal and professional goals, and/or achieve their full potential in life.

Normality and abnormality are both culturally defined and culture-specific. Except for such severe mental health problems as psychosis, what might be normal in one culture could be deemed abnormal in another. Bizarre sexual behavior could be considered criminal behavior requiring incarceration in one culture while in another culture it would be an emotional problem requiring psychiatric counseling or hospitalization. Or, it might not even be considered noteworthy or a "problem."

Counseling or therapeutic approaches and methodologies depend upon one's culture. Emotionally disturbed individuals might be removed from their families in the United States and yet placed within other families in Nigeria. Spiritualism in a Washington, D.C., Latino community might involve a "healer" who assumes the persona or spirit of a person you hate. You can then vent your anger toward this person. This therapeutic technique is comparable to psychodrama at a major mental hospital.

ARTICLES

This section begins with a provocative article by Sarah J. McCarthy, "Why Johnny Can't Disobey." This experienced teacher argues that some of the greatest atrocities in recent history have been committed by followers of malevolent authority figures such as Adolph Hitler, Jim Jones, and Charles Manson. American education teaches children to conform and obey, whereas we actually need children who are nonconformists and who can question authority. We ought to teach children how to disobey if we are to prevent them from becoming mindless followers.

This tendency for young people to obey and conform is also described in "This Cutthroat College Generation." This piece was written about college students in the mid-1970s until the mid-1980s for the op-ed section of a major newspaper—a generation sometimes referred to as the Me Decade or the age of narcissism. It is followed by the article "Whatever!" describing the youth culture of the mid-1980s until the mid-1990s—Generation X. Contemporary youth culture is not yet fully identified nor labeled, but it seems to be different from the Me Decade or Generation X. It may resemble youth during the mid-1960s.

Sociolinguist Deborah Tannen argues that "Teachers' Classroom Strategies Should Recognize That Men and Women Use Language Differently." Her bestselling book, *You Just Don't Understand*, is about conversational styles of men and women, and this article applies her findings to the classroom situation. Speaking in a classroom is more congenial to the language experience of boys than girls, yet "participation" is often considered part of a grade in college.

Another sociolinguist, Thomas Kochman, claims that black and white styles of rhetoric and interaction in the classroom lead to conflict and misunderstanding. His article, "Black and White Cultural Styles in Pluralistic Perspective," is an elaboration of many of his findings described in *Black and White Styles in Conflict*, certainly one of the very best studies of black and white styles of rhetoric.

Both Tannen and Kochman explain differences in communication styles between two identity groups or co-cultures within the United States—women and blacks. They also show how these differences impact learning and interaction in the classroom. Columnist William Raspberry ("Two Styles, One Purpose: Education") goes even further by suggesting that there is a black "learning style" which may be significantly different from that of whites.

Is black or African American English a distinct dialect or just a form of "bad" English?[10] This question has been raised by numerous linguists for well over thirty years, and the vast majority of linguists agree that Ebonics[11] is a distinct social dialect of English. It is systematic, it has a vocabulary or lexicon, a phonology or sound system, and a grammar—a set of rules. It is *not* bad English.

The debate regarding Ebonics is really political and educational, not linguistic. Over two decades ago in Ann Arbor, Michigan, a court ruled that the school system could require teachers whose classes are majority black learn about black dialect. There was never an intent to teach black English to students, but rather to help teachers more effectively teach standard English.

In the fall of 1996, the Oakland school system also passed a resolution recognizing Ebonics as a legitimate language and sought to have teachers learn Ebonics. But, there was no one who wanted children to be taught Ebonics. In the last week of December 1996, the executive committee of the Linguistics Society of America passed a resolution at the association's annual meeting in Chicago validating Ebonics as acceptable derivation of English. These linguists said that using black English as a bridge to standard English might be effective in classrooms. The Linguistics Society supported the Oakland school system's intention to use it to help students learn standard English.

Rick Weiss's article, "Among Linguists, Black English Gets Respect," summarizes the current thinking of most linguists. There are hundreds of books, newspaper, magazine and journal articles written on this heated issue. Many make the erroneous assumptions that black English is bad English and that there is a movement to teach it to students instead of standard English.

"On all sides of the issue, public figures have made statements that are very linguistically uninformed," said Walt Wolfram, an English professor at North Carolina State University who has devoted most of his professional life to the study of black English and is chairman of the Society's Linguistics in Schools Committee. "The whole point is to get children from the language they have been using to standard American language. It is not to keep them using the same language."[12] There are studies that show that once students understand the structural differences between Ebonics and standard English, they begin to demonstrate a greater proficiency in standard English and to minimize their use of Ebonics.[13]

Of course, command of English is essential to advance economically in the U.S. In 1916, one educator believed that it was not only desirable but necessary to offer courses to immigrant adults. He wrote:

> Today the majority of immigrants come to better their economic condition. Therefore it is our first business to teach him English—the colloquial English that will enable him to get on in life; to get a job, to keep it and then to get a better one; to find his way about the streets and to familiarize himself with American life.[14]

Almost all immigrants want their children to learn English in order to advance economically and move about the country. They may not want to give up their native language, but few would restrict their children to that language. Thus, there is no need to pass a law to protect the English language or to make English the "official" and/or "only" language of the U.S.

This English-Only movement is often based on false analogies between French-speaking Canadians and Hispanic Americans. Mark Falcoff's article, "Our Language Needs No Law," describes the irrational fear many Americans have of Spanish. While it is true that many French Canadians do not want their children to learn English, almost all Spanish-speaking immigrants to the U.S. want their children to learn English. They came seeking a better life, not to widen the territory of Spanish-speakers. And, as they integrate economically and culturally and move outside their Spanish-speaking enclaves, they will likely lose their Spanish.

We then turn to the enculturation of children in other countries. Perry Garfinkel's "The Best 'Jewish Mother' in the World" describes how primary Japanese cultural values are taught by the Japanese mother and, in turn, help to explain the enormous academic success of Japanese students. The "education-mama" pushes her children to excel academically in a way very similar to the stereotypical "Jewish Mother" pattern.

The learning style of Chinese is determined by their traditional values. Howard Gardner ("Learning, Chinese-Style") demonstrates how the Chinese style is to teach children exactly how to do things rather than allowing them to learn a task through experimentation. For example, in China when a child is learning a skill requiring dexterity of the hand, the teacher often physically holds the hand of the student and guides it. The child does not try numerous alternative ways of performing the skill until a better way is discovered. This means that creativity in China is evolutionary rather than revolutionary, but nevertheless, it does occur—after the student has mastered the basics.

From the mid-1960s until the mid-1970s, race, ethnicity, culture, gender, and sexual orientation were considered important to an individual's self-esteem. In both education and mental health, it was assumed that if we strengthen one's pride in his or her identity, it would allow for greater learning and better mental health. "Black is beautiful," feminism, the Chicano Movement, Gay Liberation, and so forth, all became slogans of this period. But, this came to an end with the use of such phrases as "genderblind" and "colorblind." These words reflect a backlash to various identity movements.

Gerald Gregory Jackson describes this backlash in his article "The Roots of the Backlash Theory in Mental Health." He begins by providing evidence that there is indeed a black culture in the United States with its own particular set of values. While many of these values appear to be in opposition to dominant white values, they are actually complementary. In fact, they create a form of "diunitality," where not only is there a "union of opposites," but even more, a synergy. The whole is greater than the sum of its parts. That is, blacks can learn a great deal from whites and vice-versa.

In Nigeria, Thomas Adeoye Lambo has been bringing together Western medicine with the African world view to allow psychiatrists and traditional healers to work as a team. Lambo explains how religion, medicine, and traditional values and roles are all blended together in Africa. One cannot separate the mind from the body as in the West.

Sudhir Kakar ("Western Science, Eastern Minds") argues further that the individual, including both mind and body, cannot be separated from society in Eastern cultures. That is, the "self" does not end with the skin but instead has many layers, such as family, friends, and the community. While Western psychotherapy emphasizes empowering the individual or strengthening the so-called ego, the Eastern world view emphasizes individuals blending in harmoniously with others.

These two views appear to be in total opposition and yet they are a part of psychotherapy in each culture. An American therapist might encourage a client to assert his or her independence by pulling away or separating from a dominating parent. On the other hand, a Japanese therapist could urge a client to become even closer to his or her parents to fulfill the need for dependency (or interdependency) and belonging.

We then turn to the area of cross-cultural counseling in the United States. What happens to troubled minority youth in America who are institutionalized in centers for emotionally disturbed children? My two articles in this section apply many of the concepts from various articles in this anthology to explain how emotionally troubled minority children and youth may not be helped therapeutically in residential treatment centers. In fact, in some cases the therapy may be counterproductive, because it does not take into account cultural differences in values, thought patterns, and ways of communicating.

Minority children go through culture shock when they enter institutions based upon mainstream (white) cultural norms of appropriate behavior. Furthermore, if they adapt to the institution, they go through a form of reverse culture shock when returning to their communities. In fact, those who adapted best to the institution often experience the greatest difficulties returning home.

These are traumatic experiences which white middle-class children usually do not experience because in the institution they are adapting to an idealized version of their own culture. When they return home, they may find that the behaviors they acquired in the institution make them even more acceptable in their community.

The last two articles are written by those who have experienced cross-cultural conflict in American schools. Rogelio R. Gomez's "Foul Shots" describes the shame he felt when his high school Hispanic basketball team from one of the *barrios* met with a white team from the wealthy north side of San Antonio. This incident, which happened over twenty years ago, still brings back painful memories for Gomez.

Brian Jarvis, a white high school junior from St. Louis, feels that "schools should teach black and white teens how to be friends." His article, "Against the Great Divide," describes the experience of many young people who find that students informally segregate themselves according to race.

Fortunately, in the past few years many colleges and universities have instituted courses to help students learn about cultural differences and how to bridge the ethnic, gender, class, and racial divides that exist not only in the U.S., but around the globe.

This is not simply a matter of educating young people to become more cross-culturally aware and interculturally adept. As a society becomes more diverse and as intercultural interaction increases around the globe, educators and counselors must also consider the impact of culture on themselves and their professions. To be more effective and helpful with students and clients, they may have to expand their repertoire of techniques and approaches and develop new competencies in intercultural communication.

ENDNOTES

[1]The largest number of immigrants came to the U.S. between 1880 and 1924 and in the record breaking year of 1907, over 75 percent were *not* from northern European countries. Ivan Chermayeff, Fred Wasserman and Mary J. Shapiro, *Ellis Island: An Illustrated History of the Immigrant Experience* (New York: Macmillan Publishing Company, 1991), 23.

[2]I realize that anyone living on the continent of America is an "American." "North American" describes anyone living in the northern hemisphere—Mexicans, Canadians and residents of the U.S. There is no term such as "United Statesian." Thus, with apologies to the rest of the hemisphere, I will use the term "American" to describe residents of the USA.

[3]Chermayeff, Wasserman, and Shapiro, 88.

[4]*Ibid.,* 93.

[5]An excellent discussion of how the classroom is used to teach basic American values is found in Jules Henry, "Golden Rule Days: American Schoolrooms," in *Culture Against Man* (New York: Random House, 1963), 283–301. He describes the emphasis on individual competition and how this behavior is an anathema in many American Indian tribes.

[6]The reluctance of many American Indian children to speak in the classroom or demonstrate knowledge that is not fully mastered is described in Susan U. Philips, "Participant Structures and Communicative Competence: Warm Springs Children in Community and Classroom," in C.B. Cazden, V.P. John, and D. Hymes, eds., *Functions of Language in the Classroom* (New York: Teachers' College Press, 1972), 370–394.

[7]In perhaps the most comprehensive study of American values, Daniel Yankelovich found that the only basic American value he found had changed by the beginning of the 1980s was that of self-denial and deferred gratification. He found that 80 percent of Americans in 1980 were committed to one degree or another to the search for self-fulfillment, at the expense of the older, self-denying ethic of earlier years. Daniel Yankelovich, *New Rules: Searching for Self-Fulfillment in a World Turned Upside Down* (New York: Random House, 1981).

[8]The "boomers" are those 76 million Americans born between 1946–1964—the biggest generation ever. See Landon Y. Jones, *Great Expectations: America and the Baby Boom Generation* (New York: Ballantine Books, 1980).

[9]The countercultural youth movements and identity movements of the mid-1960s are discussed in "American Identity Movements" in Section I, 60–65.

The Me Decade is discussed in this section in "This Cutthroat College Generation" (280–281). Also see Christopher Lasch, *The Culture of Narcissism,* (New York: Warner, 1979).

Generation X and the contemporary youth generation are examined in this section in "Whatever!" (282–286).

[10]Black English is discussed in Section I, "American Identity Movements" (60–65).

[11]Ebonics is formed by combining the words ebony and phonics. It was coined in 1973 by Robert Williams, a black professor of psychology at Washington University, in St. Louis. Black Dialect, Black English, African American English and nonstandard English are other terms used to describe a dialect spoken by many African Americans.

[12]Walt Wolfram quoted by Rene Sanchez, "Ebonics: A Way to Close the Learning Gap?" *The Washington Post,* 6 January 1997, 1 (A).

[13]Courtland Milloy, "Nothing's Funny About Ebonics," *The Washington Post,* 29 December 1996, 1 (B).

[14]Chermayeff, Wasserman, and Shapiro, 93.

33

Why Johnny Can't Disobey

Sarah J. McCarthy

Few people are too concerned about whether Johnny can disobey. There is no furor or frantic calls to the PTA, as when it is discovered that he can't read or does poorly on his S.A.T. scores. Even to consider the question is at first laughable. Parents and teachers, after all, are systematically working at developing the virtue of obedience. To my knowledge, no one as yet has opened a remedial disobedience school for overly compliant children, and probably no one ever will. And that in itself is a major problem.

Patricia Hearst recently said that the mindless state of obedience which enveloped her at the hands of the Symbionese Liberation Army could happen to anyone. Jumping to a tentative conclusion from a tip-of-the-iceberg perspective, it looks as though it already has happened to many, and that it has required nothing so dramatic as a kidnapping to bring it about.

Given our experience with various malevolent authority figures such as Adolph Hitler, Charles Manson, Lieutenant Calley, and Jim Jones, it is unfortunately no longer surprising that there are leaders who are capable of wholesale cruelty to the point of directing mass killings. What remains shocking, however, is that they are so often successful in recruiting followers. There seems to be no shortage of individuals who will offer their hearts and minds on a silver platter to feed the egos of the power-hungry. This becomes even more disturbing when one ponders the truism that society's neurotics are often its cultural caricatures, display-ing exaggerated manifestations of its collective neuroses. There are enough examples of obedience to horrendous commands for us to ask if and how a particular culture sows the seeds of dangerous conformity.

Political platitudes and lip service to the contrary, obedience is highly encouraged in matters petty as well as profound. Linda Eton, an Iowa firefighter, was suspended from her job and catapulted to national fame for the radical act of breast-feeding at work. A dehumanized, compartmentalized society finds little room for spontaneity, and a blatantly natural act like breast-feeding is viewed as a preposterous interruption of the status quo.

Pettiness abounds in our social relationships, ensuring compliance through peer pressure and disapproval, and enforced by economic sanctions at the workplace. A friend of mine, a construction worker, reported to his job one rainy day carrying an umbrella. The foreman was outraged by his break from the norm, and demanded that the guy never again carry an umbrella to the construction site, even if the umbrella *was* black, since it "caused his whole crew to look like a bunch of faggots."

Another friend, though less scandalizing visibly in his job as a security guard during the wee hours for a multinational corporation, was caught redhanded playing a harmonica. Mercifully, he was given another chance, only to be later fired for not wearing regulation shoes.

Ostensibly, such firings and threats are deemed necessary to prevent inefficiency and rampant chaos at the workplace. But if employers were merely concerned about productivity and efficiency, it certainly is disputable that "yes-people" are more productive and beneficial than "no-people." Harmonicas may even increase efficiency by keeping security guards sane, alert, and awake by staving off sensory deprivation. A dripping-wet construction worker could conceivably be less productive than a dry one. And the Adidas being worn by the errant security guard could certainly have contributed to his fleetness and agility as opposed to the cumbersome regulation shoes. The *real* issues here have nothing to do with productivity. What is really involved is an irrational fear of the mildly un-

Reprinted from *The Humanist* (September/October 1979): 5, by permission of Sarah J. McCarthy.

usual, a pervasive attitude held by authorities that their subordinates are about to run amok and need constant control.

These little assaults on our freedom prepare us for the big ones. Having long suspected that a huge iceberg of mindless obedience existed beneath our cultural surface, I was not particularly surprised when I heard that nine hundred people followed their leader to mass suicide. For some time we have lived with the realization that people are capable of killing six million of their fellow citizens on command. Jonestown took us one step further. People will kill themselves on command.

In matters ridiculous and sublime, this culture and the world at large clearly exhibit symptoms of pathological obedience. Each time one of the more sensational incidents occurs—Jonestown, the Mai Lai massacre, Nazi Germany, the Manson murders—we attribute its occurrence to factors unique to it, trying to deny any similarities to anything close to us, tossing it about like a philosophical hot potato. We prefer to view such events as anomalies, isolated in time and space, associated with faraway jungles, exotic cults, drugged hippies, and outside agitators. However, as the frequency of such happenings increases, there is the realization that it is relatively easy to seduce some people into brainwashed states of obedience.

Too much energy and time have been spent on trying to understand the alleged compelling traits and mystical powers of charismatic leaders, and not enough in an attempt to understand their fellow travelers—the obedient ones. We need to look deeper into those who *elected* Hitler, and all those followers of Jim Jones who went to Guyana *voluntarily*. We must ask how many of us are also inclined toward hyperobedience. Are we significantly different, capable of resisting malevolent authority, or have we simply had the good fortune never to have met a Jim Jones of our own?

Social psychologist Stanley Milgram, in his book *Obedience to Authority,* is convinced that:

> In growing up, the normal individual has learned to check the expression of

aggressive impulses. But the culture has failed, almost entirely, in inculcating internal controls on actions that have their origin in authority. For this reason, the latter constitutes a far greater danger to human survival.

Vince Bugliosi, prosecutor of Charles Manson and author of *Helter Skelter,* comments on the Jonestown suicides:

> Education of the public is the only answer. If young people could be taught what can happen to them—that they may be zombies a year after talking to that smiling person who stops them on a city street—they may be prepared.

Presumably, most young cult converts have spent most of their days in our educational system, yet are vulnerable to the beguiling smile or evil eye of a Charles Manson. If there is any lesson to be learned from the obedience-related holocausts, it must be that we can never underestimate the power of education and the socialization process.

Contrary to our belief that the survival instinct is predominant over all other drives, the Jonestown suicides offer testimony to the power of cultural indoctrination. Significantly, the greatest life force at the People's Temple came from the children. Acting on their survival instincts, they went kicking and screaming to their deaths in an "immature" display of disobedience. The adults, civilized and educated people that they were, lined up with "stiff upper lips" and took their medicine like the followers they were trained to be—a training that didn't begin at Jonestown.

When something so horrible as Jonestown happens, people draw metaphors about the nearness of the jungle and the beast that lurks within us. It seems that a more appropriate metaphor would be our proximity to an Orwellian civilization with its antiseptic removal of our human rough edges and "animal" instincts. On close scrutiny, the beast within us looks suspiciously like a sheep.

Despite our rich literature of freedom, a pervasive value installed in our society is obedience to authority. Unquestioning obedience is perceived to be in the best interest of the schools, churches, families, and political institutions. Nationalism, patriotism, and religious ardor are its psychological vehicles.

Disobedience is the original sin, as all of the religions have stated in one way or another. Given the obedience training in organized religions that claim to possess mystical powers and extrarational knowledge and extoll the glories of self-sacrifice, what is so bizarre about the teachings of Jim Jones? If we arm our children with the rationality and independent thought necessary to resist the cultist, can we be sure that our own creeds and proclamations will meet the criteria of reason? The spotlight of reason which exposes the charlatan may next shine on some glaring inconsistencies in the "legitimate" religions. Religions, which are often nothing more than cults that grew, set the stage for the credulity and gullibility required for membership in cults.

A witch hunt is now brewing to exorcise the exotic cults, but what is the dividing line between a cult and a legitimate religion? Is there a qualitative difference between the actions of some venerated Biblical saints and martyrs and the martyrs of Jonestown? If the Bible contained a Parable of Guyana, the churches would regularly extoll it as a courageous act of self-sacrifice. Evidently saints and martyrs are only palatable when separated by the chasm of a few centuries. To enforce their belief, the major religions use nothing so crass as automatic weapons, of course, but instead fall back on automatic sentences to eternal damnation.

Certainly there must be an optimal level of obedience and cooperation in a reasonable society, but obedience, as any other virtue that is carried to an extreme, may become a vice. It is obvious that Nazi Germany and Jonestown went too far on the obedience continuum. In more mundane times and places the appropriate level of obedience is more difficult to discover.

We must ask if our society is part of the problem, part of the solution, or wholly irrelevant to the incidents of over-obedience exhibited at Jonestown and Mai Lai. Reviewing social psychologists' attempts to take our psychic temperatures through empirical measurements of our conformity and obedience behavior in experimental situations, our vital signs do not look good.

In 1951 Solomon Asch conducted an experiment on conformity, which is similar to obedience behavior in that it subverts one's will to that of peers or an authority. This study, as reported in the textbook *Social Psychology* by Freedman, Sears, and Carlsmith, involved college students who were asked to estimate lines of equal and different lengths. Some of the lines were obviously equal, but if subjects heard others before them unanimously give the wrong answer, they would also answer incorrectly. Asch had reasoned that people would be rational enough to choose the evidence of their own eyes over the disagreeing "perceptions" of others. He found that he was wrong.

When subjects were asked to estimate the length of a line after confederates of the experimenter had given obviously wrong answers, the subjects gave wrong answers about 35 percent of the time. Authors Freedman, Sears, and Carlsmith stress:

> It is important to keep the unambiguousness of the situations in mind if we are to understand this phenomenon. There is a tendency to think that the conforming subjects are uncertain of the correct choice therefore are swayed by the majority. This is not always the case. In many instances subjects are quite certain of the correct choice and, in the absence of group pressure, would choose correctly 100 percent of the time. When they conform, they are conforming despite that fact they know the correct answer.

If 35 percent of those students conformed to group opinion in unambiguous matters and in direct contradiction of the evidence of their own eyes, how much more must we fear blind following in *ambiguous* circumstances or in circumstances where there exists a legitimate authority?

In the early sixties, Yale social psychologist Stanley Milgram devised an experiment to put acts of obedience and disobedience under close scrutiny. Milgram attempted to understand why thousands of "civilized" people had engaged in an extreme and immoral act—that of the wholesale extermination of Jews—in the name of obedience. He devised a learning task in which subjects of the experiment were instructed to act as teachers. They were told to "shock" learners for their mistakes. The learners were actually confederates of the experimenter and were feigning their reactions. When a mistake was made, the experimenter would instruct the teacher to administer an ever-increasing voltage from a shock machine which read "Extreme Danger," "Severe Shock," and "XXX." Although the machine was unconnected, the subject-teachers believed that they were actually giving shocks. They were themselves given a real sample shock before the experiment began.

Milgram asked his Yale colleagues to make a guess as to what proportion of subjects would proceed to shock all the way to the presumed lethal end of the shockboard. Their estimates hovered around 1 or 2 percent. No one was prepared for what happened. All were amazed that twenty-six out of forty subjects obeyed the experimenter's instruction to press levers that supposedly administered severely dangerous levels of shock. After this, Milgram regularly obtained results showing that 62 to 65 percent of people would shock to the end of the board. He tried several variations on the experiment, one of which was to set it up outside of Yale University so that the prestige of the University would not be an overriding factor in causing the subjects to obey. He found that people were just as likely to administer severe shock, whether the experiments occurred within the hallowed halls of Yale or in a three-room walk-up storefront in which the experimenters spoke of themselves as "scientific researchers."

In another variation of the experiment, Milgram found that aggression—latent or otherwise—was not a significant factor in causing the teacher-subjects to shock the learners. When the experimenter left the room, thus permitting the subjects to choose the level of shock themselves, almost none administered more than the lowest voltage. Milgram concluded that obedience, not aggression, was the problem. He states:

> I must conclude that [Hannah] Arendt's conception of the *banality of evil* comes closer to the truth than one might dare imagine. The ordinary person who

shocked the victim did so out of a sense of obligation—a conception of his duties as a subject—and not from any peculiarly aggressive tendencies.

This is, perhaps, the most fundamental lesson of our study: ordinary people, simply doing their jobs, and without any particular hostility on their part, can become agents in a terrible destructive process. Moreover, even when the destructive effects of their work become patently clear, and they are asked to carry out actions incompatible with fundamental standards of morality, relatively few people have the resources needed to resist authority. A variety of inhibitions against disobeying authority come into play and successfully keep the person in his place.

A lack of compassion was not a particularly salient personality factor in the acts of obedience performed by the followers of Hitler, Jim Jones, and the subjects in the Milgram experiments. Nazi soldiers were capable of decent human behavior toward their friends and family. Some, too, see an irony in that Hitler himself was a vegetarian. The People's Temple members seemed more compassionate and humanitarian than many, and yet they forced their own children to partake of a drink laced with cyanide. Those shocking the victims in the Milgram experiments exhibited signs of compassion both toward the experimenter and to the persons that they thought were receiving the shocks. In fact, Milgram finds that:

> It is a curious thing that a measure of compassion on the part of the subject, an unwillingness to "hurt" the experimenter's feelings, are part of those binding forces inhibiting disobedience . . . only obedience can preserve the experimenter's status and dignity.

Milgram's subjects showed signs of severe physiological tension and internal conflict when instructed to shock. Presumably, these signs of psychic pain and tortured indecision were manifestation of an underlying attitude of compassion for the victim, but it was not sufficient to impel them to openly break with, and therefore embarrass, the experimenter, even though this experimenter had no real authority over them. One of Milgram's subjects expressed this dilemma succinctly:

> I'll go through with anything they tell me to do. . . . They know more than I do. . . . I know when I was in the service (if I was told) "You go over the hill and we're going to attack," we attacked. So I think it's all based on the way a man was brought up . . . in his background. Well, I faithfully believed the man [whom he thought he had shocked] was dead until we opened the door. When I saw him, I said: "Great, this is great!" But it didn't bother me even to find that he was dead. I did a job.

The experiments continued with thousands of people—students and nonstudents, here and abroad—often demonstrating obedience behavior in 60 to 65 percent of the subjects. When the experiments were done in Munich, obedience often reached 85 percent. Incidentally, Milgram found no sex differences in obedience behavior. Though his sample of women shockers was small, their level of obedience was identical to that of the men. But they did exhibit more symptoms of internal conflict. Milgram concluded that "there is probably nothing the victim can say that will uniformly generate disobedience," since it is not the victim who is controlling the shocker's behavior. Even when one of the experimental variations included a victim who cried out that he had a heart condition, this did not lead to significantly greater disobedience. In such situations, the experimenter-authority figure dominates the subject's social field, while the pleading cries of the victim are for the most part ignored.

Milgram found that the authority's power had to be somehow undermined before there was widespread disobedience, as when the experimenter was not physically present, when his orders came over the telephone, or when his orders were challenged by another authority. Most importantly, subjects became disobedient in large numbers only when others rebelled, dissented, or argued with the experimenter. When a subject witnessed another subject defying or arguing with the experimenter, thirty-six out of forty also rebelled, demonstrating that peer rebellion was the most effective experimental variation in undercutting authority.

This social orientation in which the authority dominates one's psyche is attributed by Milgram to a state of mind which he terms "the agentic state." A person makes a critical shift from a relatively autonomous state into this agentic state when she or he enters a situation in which "he defines himself in a manner that renders him open to regulation by a person of higher status."

An extreme agentic state is a likely explanation for the scenario at Jonestown, where even the cries of their own children were not sufficient to dissuade parents from serving cyanide. Despite some ambiguity as to how many Jonestown residents were murdered and how many committed suicide, there remains the fact that these victims had participated in previous suicide rehearsals. Jim Jones, assured of their loyalty and their critical shift into an agentic state, then had the power to orchestrate the real thing. The supreme irony, the likes of which could only be imagined as appearing in the *Tralfamadore Tribune* with a byline by Kurt Vonnegut, was the picture of the Guyana death scene. Bodies were strewn about beneath the throne of Jones and a banner which proclaimed that those who failed to learn from the lessons of history were doomed to repeat them.

How many of us have made the critical shift into an agentic state regarding international relations, assuming that our leaders know best, even though they have repeatedly demonstrated that they do not? Stanley Milgram predicts that "for the man who sits in front of the button that will release Armageddon, depressing it will have about the same emotional force as calling for an elevator . . . evolution has not had a chance to build inhibitors against such remote forms of aggression."

We should recognize that our human nature renders us somewhat vulnerable. For one thing, our own mortality and that of our loved ones is an unavoidable fact underlying our lives. In the face of it, we are powerless; and in our insecurity, many reach out for sure answers. Few choose to believe, along with Clarence Darrow, that not only are we not the captains of our fate, but that we are not even "deckhands on a rudderless dinghy." Or, as someone else has stated: "There are no answers. Be brave and face up to it." Most of us won't face up to it. We want our answers, solutions to our plight, and we want them now. Too often truth and rational thought are the first casualties of this desperate reach for security. We embrace answers from charlatans, false prophets, charismatic leaders, and assorted demagogues. Given these realities of our nature, how can we avoid these authority traps to which we are so prone? By what criteria do we teach our children to distinguish between the charlatan and the prophet?

It seems that the best armor is the rational mind. We must insist that all authorities account for themselves, and we need to be as wary of false prophets as we are of false advertising. Leaders, political and spiritual, must be subjected to intense scrutiny, and we must insist that their thought processes and proclamations measure up to reasonable standards of rational thought. Above all, we must become skilled in activating our inner resources toward rebellion and disobedience, when this seems reasonable.

The power of socialization can conceivably be harnessed so as to develop individuals who are rational and skeptical, capable of independent thought, and who can disobey or disagree at the critical moment. Our society, however, continues systematically to instill exactly the opposite. The educational system pays considerable lip service to the development of self-reliance, and places huge emphasis on lofty concepts of individual differences. Little notice is taken of the legions of overly obedient children in the schools; yet, for every overly disobedient child, there are probably twenty who are obeying too much. There is little motivation to encourage the unsqueaky wheels to develop as noisy, creative, independent thinkers who may become bold enough to disagree. Conceivably, we could administer modified Milgram obedience tests in the schools which detect hyper-obedience, just as we test for intelligence, visual function, vocational attributes and tuberculosis. When a child is found to be too obedient, the schools should mobilize against this psychological cripple with the zeal by which they would react to an epidemic of smallpox. In alcoholism and other mental disturbances, the first major step toward a reversal of the pathology is recognition of the severity of the problem. Obedience should be added to the list of emotional disturbances requiring therapy. Disobedience schools should be at least as common as military schools and reform schools.

The chains on us are not legal or political, but the invisible chains of the agentic state. We have all gotten the message that it is dangerous and requires exceptional courage to be different.

If we are to gain control of our lives and minds, we must first acknowledge the degree to which we are not now in control. We must become reasonable and skeptical. Reason is no panacea, but, at the moment, it is all that we have. Yet many in our society seem to have the same attitude about rationality and reason that they do about the poverty program—that is, we've tried it and it doesn't work.

Along with worrying about the S.A.T. scores and whether or not Johnny can read, we must begin to seriously question whether Johnny is capable of disobedience. The churches and cults, while retaining their constitutional right to free expression, must be more regularly criticized. The legitimate religions have been treated as sacred cows. Too often, criticism of them is met with accusations of religious bigotry, or the implication that one is taking candy from a baby or a crutch from a cripple. The concept of religious tolerance has been stretched to its outer limits, implying freedom from criticism and the nonpayment of taxes. Neither patriotism nor religion should be justification for the suspension of reason.

And, on a personal level, we must stop equating sanity with conformity, eccentricity with craziness, and normalcy with numbers. We must get in touch with our own liberating ludicrousness and practice being harmlessly deviant. We must, in fact, cease to use props or other people to affirm our normalcy. With sufficient practice, perhaps, when the need arises, we may have the strength to force a moment to its crisis.

34

This Cutthroat College Generation

Gary R. Weaver

Although many college students suspect that something is wrong with the "system"—unemployment, inflation, and the rest—they don't take the trouble to question the values which have led us where we are.

They have seen racial tension erupt into violence. They know that the gap between white and black incomes is wider than it was 10 years ago. They are perplexed that America's divorce rate is number one in the world.

But few discuss problems like these, and most blame them not on some fault in the country's social or political fabric, but on individual weakness. With a Connecticut Yankee mentality, they assert that individuals simply must try harder, get into the mainstream, beat the "system," and achieve their self-centered ends.

THROATIES IN CONTROL

The "throaties" have taken control of the campus. They are the rosy-cheeked kids joining fraternities and sororities, taking est seminars, and selling Amway products—all to beat the system. They join groups not to change the system, or out of altruistic concern for others, but rather to promote their own self-interest.

Many didn't have time to get involved in the recent election, have never read a book written by a black author, and resent taking such "non-career" courses as philosophy, history, sociology, and anthropology. They are affectionately referred to as "throaties" because it is suspected they would cut another student's throat for answers to an exam.

Reprinted from *The Washington Star,* 2 February 1981), 11 (A).

This isn't simply old-fashioned Yankee Doodle competition. It is the individual achievement motive gone haywire. These students resist cooperation, and even sabotage others who might do better.

For many years I have broken a large class into "group projects" where students earn a quarter of their course grade as a small group writing a paper. While this practice was enthusiastically welcomed in the 1960s, it is bitterly resisted and resented today.

Many students cannot tolerate the idea that they may have to cooperate to get a good grade—or that the work of others might lower their grade. Some have even threatened to file a grievance against me because of this "unfair" course requirement.

Students sometimes sabotage each other even when there is no competition for a grade. Theodore I. Rubin, author of *Reconciliations* notes that when his pre-med son was taking a microbiology examination, most of the students made certain that the microscopes they had used were out of focus before passing them on to other students—to make it more difficult for their "colleagues" taking the exam.

It is not unusual to have one student come to my office complaining that another "borrowed" his notes and "accidentally" lost them, or that no one will share notes. I've been threatened with suit, not because a student failed a course, but because a student earned a 'B+' instead of an 'A.'

All this stands in sharp contrast to the pass/fail movement and cooperative attitudes of students in the 1960s, who by all measures could read, write, and think better than today's students.

I'm convinced that many students are in college not to learn, but to earn. The diploma has become simply a union card to get into the mainstream of society. Take the easy course, get a copy of last year's exam, harass the prof.

CHARITY ENDS WITH ME

These are grown-up little leaguers still viciously competing in order to give vicarious satisfaction to their obsessive parents. They have overlearned the lesson that the world is a hostile, dog-eat-dog place, that concern for others only inhibits one's rise to individual success. Charity doesn't begin in the home; it begins and ends with me.

For many of them, as their drive for success meets economic reality, the American dream has become a nightmare. They learn that street cleaners start at higher salaries and have greater job security than new college professors. They discover that it is as difficult to gain admission to law or business school as it is to medical school.

But like any garden-variety neurotic unable to cope with a painful truth, they continue to distort reality—working still harder to make their fantasy world conform with their needs. They also flood our counseling centers. And their suicide rate is climbing.

MORAL DIRECTION

It is often assumed that universities failed in the '60s, but they did not. In fact the university became a beacon for society, stressing the responsibility of the educated to contribute to the moral direction of the country. Universities acknowledged the adulthood of students by allowing them to participate in the decision-making process of the institution. And as for academic achievement, the leaders of student activism were often among the best on campus.

As budgets drop and inflation rises, I don't foresee great efforts to restore creative courses,

hire fresh blood for the faculty, teach students to question authority, or reward them for studying social science, the humanities, or the arts. The percentage of blacks attending college has decreased in the past 10 years—and this trend is likely to increase as pressure is taken off colleges to engage in affirmative action recruiting, and minority scholarships begin to dwindle.

TOO MUCH CALVINISTIC ETHIC

But what alarms me most is the character of our students. The Calvinist work ethic and individualism may once have had important survival value during our history, but today they may prove destructive.

Cooperating, sharing, building a sense of community, and reconciling differences are all vital for solving the problems confronting us.

What we really need for survival is not training, but education—education that encourages young people to stop and ask why. The celebrated violence of the last decade did not come from young activists questioning authority; it came from the *over*conformists— those following tradition in Iran, or a leader in Jonestown, or "the American way" in Greensboro.

Unfortunately, I see few signs that our next generation is prepared to disobey or question their society in a way that could make it a better one.

35

Whatever!

Gary R. Weaver

GENERATIONAL CULTURES

There are cultures or subcultures that are formed by the youth of all societies. Significant events that occur during the formative and adolescent years shape the social character, worldview, and beliefs of each generation.[1] These shared events also give an identity or sense of belonging. Thus, we can speak of generational cultures.

While descriptions of youth cultures are generalizations and perhaps even stereotypes, we can contrast and compare generational cultures to better understand the behavior of youth during a particular period of time. Furthermore, these cultures overlap, influence and conflict with each other. Thus, we can even speak of "countercultures."

This is especially important because we acquire our basic culture, including our primary values, during childhood. While we share primary cultural values with most people in our culture, the hierarchy or ranking of those values may differ depending upon our age, gender, religion, and other cultural groups to which we belong. People who share similar childhood and adolescent experiences during a particular historical period are likely to have a similar hierarchy of values, similar attitudes and similar ways of perceiving the world.

Americans who grew up during the Great Depression of the 1930s or World War II in the 1940s view the world differently than those who grew up during the post-Vietnam War era. If we grew up during a period of scarce resources, unemployment and external threat

we surely are predisposed to have different attitudes than those who grew up in an age of abundance, full employment and no external threats.

YOUTH CULTURES IN AMERICA

American youth in the 1950s were labeled the "ungeneration" or the "silent generation." They were considered conformists who worked hard to get into the dominant or mainstream culture. This was the era of thriving fraternities and sororities, Ivy League clothes, and panty raids. It was also the era of the Korean War, the Cold War, an economic recession, and racial incidents.

Towards the end of the 1950s, there were some who rejected the dominant culture. They were part of the so-called "Beat Generation" who were seen as nihilists by the mainstream society. These "Beatniks" seemed to believe that the culture would somehow self-destruct in materialism, violence, or atomic war. They were existential Bohemians who were often portrayed in the popular press as poets and guitar players hanging out in Greenwich Village. They really did not try to change the society or make it better. They simply dropped out of the society.

The 1960s' youth culture was a counter-culture because many tried to change the dominant culture or what they referred to as "the system."[2] They were called "the prophetic minority" by *Village Voice* writer Jack Newfield[3] because he believed that they would lead the society into a better future. And they will long be remembered as civil rights marchers, anti-war demonstrators and hippies.

The youth activists of the mid-1960s and early 1970s were optimistic idealists—civil rights advocates and peaceniks—who believed they could bring about dramatic change in the society and the world.[4] The economy was strong, unemployment was at an all-time low and record numbers of students were attending colleges and universities.

White and black students came together in various groups to champion the cause of desegregation and integration. In the early 1960s there were sit-ins to desegregate restaurants and public facilities, marches to provide

---

This article is first published here. It follows chronologically "American Identity Movements" and "This Cutthroat College Generation" which are also in this anthology.

equal opportunities for jobs and education, and black voter registration drives. These were all led by young people. In 1968, the most popular book on college campuses was Alex Haley's *Autobiography of Malcolm X*.

John F. Kennedy symbolized this youthful idealism by supporting activist causes that young people overwhelmingly supported. He started the Peace Corps and welcomed Civil Rights marchers into the White House during the 1963 March on Washington. And, it appeared that the U.S. and U.S.S.R. had agreed to avoid direct military conflict. For many young people, when Kennedy stopped the Bay of Pigs invasion of Cuba and Khruschev withdrew the Soviet missiles during the Cuban Missile Crisis, the Cold War seemed to be ending. When the Berlin Wall was erected, the U.S. made no effort to dismantle the wall. Indeed, in the spring of 1963, Kennedy spoke of "making the world safe for diversity."[5]

At the end of the 1960s there were great social and political changes. Affirmative action and desegregation laws were enacted and 18-year-olds could vote. However, the country went through a period of incredible conflict and violence, both domestically and internationally. There were assassinations . . . John Kennedy in 1963, Malcolm X in 1965, and Martin Luther King, Jr., and Robert Kennedy in 1968. This was a decade when there were racial riots and student demonstrations and a war in Southeast Asia. The Vietnam War lasted over ten years, and was the longest and most costly war in American history. It cost over 1.5 million dollars an hour to fight and resulted in more than 50,000 American casualties.

By the mid-1970s, the Vietnam War was over and the Civil Rights Act had been passed. Americans, including young people, were exhausted by the turmoil of the 1960s. Cynicism, skepticism, and disillusionment developed with the lack of a clear victory in Vietnam, the worsening of the economy, and Watergate. Those who were the most cynical were perhaps preadolescents during the 1960s who entered college in the mid-1970s and early 1980s.

Lyndon Johnson's "war on poverty" and the Vietnam War had created economic havoc, especially for young people. According to Abraham Maslow's theory of "Hierarchy of Needs," such basic needs as food, shelter, and security must be met before we can satisfy higher order needs such as self-actualization or altruism.[6] During the 1960s, the basic needs of most students were met and there were ample jobs available for graduates. Thus, they could concern themselves with higher order needs.

In the mid-1970s, there was soaring inflation accompanied by unemployment. Many students believed they would graduate and be unable to find jobs. Thus, they became more concerned with their own economic survival and turned back to the traditional values of individual achievement and competition. As in the 1950s, many young people joined groups to advance their careers or status, but not to improve the lot of others. This was the "culture of narcissism,"[7] with youth trying to enter or beat, but not to change, the dominant culture.

College youth of the mid-1970s through the mid-1980s were part of the "me decade" of self-centeredness and individual competition. They were often seen as the generation who returned to the 1950s, before there were demonstrations, riots and hippies. The percentages of 18–24-year-olds who voted for Ronald Reagan in 1980 was greater than any other age group in the society. Many joined self-improvement groups, such as EST, to learn how to gain everything they wanted, aspiring to become millionaires on Wall Street.

GenX

The youth of the mid-1980s through the early 1990s were portrayed by the popular media as remarkably similar to the Beat Generation of the late 1950s in terms of their nihilistic rejection of the dominant culture. They grew up watching MTV during the "me decade" and became cynical of mainstream institutions and popular culture. Many wore black or tattered clothing and listened to rap music lyrics which attacked women, politicians, and police. This generation became young adults when there were no "causes" to rally around and they were bombarded by the mass media and commercialism.

During this period, the Cold War ended and the Berlin Wall came down. President

Reagan had described the Soviet Union as the "evil empire." But, the empire collapsed. The U.S. won the Persian Gulf War, a war that President Bush depicted as a matter of "good against evil." He also claimed that Saddam Hussein was even worse than Adolph Hitler.

These twentysomethings of today are sometimes referred to as baby "busters," in contrast with the baby "boomers" of the 1960s. Toward the latter part of the 1980s and early 1990s, they also became known as members of "Generation X."[9]

While many youth claimed that the phenomenon of "Generation X" (often known as simply "GenX") was a creation of the mass media, there were others who embraced the label. According to Douglas Rushkoff, a self-proclaimed member of Generation X,

> Most people from outside Generation X condemn the twentysomethings as illiterate, unmotivated, and apathetic couch potatoes: We appear, apparently, to have no career goals, no cultural pride, no political ideology, no family values, and no discernible ambitions.[10]

On the other hand, members of Generation X may view their apathy as a realistic acceptance of underemployment and unemployment as a way of life, a rejection of consumerism, and a result of the struggles of the 1960s generation.

> To most of us, concepts like racial equality, women's rights, sexual freedom, and respect for basic humanity are givens. We realize that we are the first generation to enter a society where, at least on paper and in the classroom, the ideas that Boomers fought for are recognized as indisputable facts. Without the Civil Rights, Environmental, and Women's movements, there would be no GenX now.[11]

Generation X members may not fight for causes or even need causes to rally behind. They are liberated from the restraints of moral correctness and ethical systems and thus seem to be adrift with few absolutes. While others might view this as nihilism, members of Busters may see it as an acceptance of reality without the cushioning platitudes or political correctness of their boomer predecessors.

This flippancy or general apathy is reflected in Generation X terminology: *whatever.*[12]

YOUTH TODAY

It seems as if the 1960s generation was a reaction to the 1950s—it was a countercultural movement against the dominant society. Rather than individual competition, communalism was emphasized. The 1970s and early 1980s were a reaction to the 1960s. The "me decade" could be seen as a reversion to the 1950s. Individual achievement became the norm on college campuses and fraternities and sororities that had almost died in the 1960s were again revitalized.

The late 1980s and early 1990s were a rejection of both prior generations. The idealism of the 1960s was abandoned as well as the Connecticut Yankee individual competitiveness of the first half of the 1980s. If there is any parallel to GenX, it is perhaps the Beat Generation of the late 1950s and early 1960s. Busters and beatniks were both nihilistic and cynical, but GenX members were more heavily influenced by the mass media and commercialism. Some might also argue that the Beat Generation was more intellectually and philosophically grounded in pop-existentialism.

Beatniks were the precursors of the so-called hippies and "flower children." Are busters precursors of a new generation comparable to the 1960s? How might the youth culture of today—the late 1990s—be described? In a pendulum fashion, some would claim that youth are reverting to the 1960s with a certain amount of idealism.[13] Others would perceive them as still part of the Me Decade with an overlay of conservative, traditional American values. They certainly are *not* typified by GenX, and yet there are elements of the buster's culture found among 18–22 year olds.

While Bill Clinton is no John Kennedy, they both won elections against much older opponents after years of Republican rule and they were both overwhelmingly supported by youth. During their years in the White House, the economy expanded and unemployment reached record lows. The economic future looked bright and the possibility of a major war remote. Both symbolized change. However, Clinton is more of a centrist than Kennedy was during his term of office.

The nation's largest annual survey of college freshmen found that youth in the fall of 1996 were more civic-minded and more supportive of many conservative social values than students have been in decades.[14] They appear to want to serve others and improve the overall society—stereotypical characteristics of the activist generation of the 1960s. Record numbers of freshmen are doing volunteer work, and interest in law or business has hit a new low. Interest in teaching careers has reached its highest point in 23 years.

About 72 percent of freshmen reported they had performed volunteer work in the past year, which is 10 points higher than it was in 1989. About 38 percent said they volunteer once a week. Both figures are the highest the survey has ever recorded since it began in the 1960s. This is not the nihilistic cynicism of GenX.

On social and personal issues, the results were mixed. In many ways they resembled conservative positions of the overall society in the early 1980s. Although strong majorities wanted more gun control and tougher environmental laws and supported gay rights, they also endorsed many conservative views. For example, support for abortion rights continued to decline after peaking at 65 percent in 1990. In 1996, 56 percent of students favored it, one of the lowest levels since the survey began in the 1960s. Seventy-two percent said society shows "too much concern for criminals" and about 80 percent wanted to keep the death penalty.

Perhaps as a result of fear of sexually transmitted diseases, students seemed more conservative in their sexual mores. Support for casual sex reached a new low. And, much like the "cutthroat college generation" of the early 1980s, they still seem determined to succeed at the university, so much so that some continually harass professors to raise their grades.[15]

Characteristic of GenX, students also showed apathy toward government and poli-tics. Only about 30 percent said they considered keeping up with current events "very important." But supporters did not decline, as they have for most of this decade. Student rallies or protests have become rare on college campuses.[16]

For many students, cultural, racial, and ethnic diversity is a fact of life and not a social issue. Universities and colleges continue to include American students from diverse backgrounds, and foreign student enrollments are at an all-time high. There also seems to be increasing diversity of knowledge on many campuses where such courses as cross-cultural communication, intercultural relations, and ethnic studies are part of the basic curriculum.

Edgar F. Beckham, Dean of the College Emeritus of Wesleyan University, notes that students can avoid diversity in higher education, just as it is possible to stay out of the library. But, most are "taught to handle difficult dialogues about race, gender and sexual orientation. Exposure to human and cultural diversity is preparing them better for civic participation and the work force of the next century."[17]

It is difficult to categorize any generation. However, there may be historical cycles with youth at the end of this millennium resembling youth at the end of the 1960s. Both generations share many basic cultural values and beliefs. Their skepticism about politics reflects a traditional attitude Americans have held about government and its role in people's lives and the economy. Modern technology and telecommunications certainly has had a dramatic impact on the current generation, but it has also been met with a healthy youthful skepticism and critical attitude.

The current generation is not cynically nihilistic. Rather, they are activists who optimistically believe that each individual can make a difference in changing the world to make it better. Volunteerism and individual action has always been a vital aspect of the American culture. Pioneers helped each other to build their barns and plow their fields.

American youth are living in a world of incredible diversity. And, modern telecommunications, travel and commerce are creating a global society. Eliminating discrimination and desegregation may have been goals of the prophetic minority, today they are taken as givens.

Young people are learning how to interact with those who are culturally different on both the domestic and global level. Intercultural communication is a way of life for many. More importantly, they are faced with the challenge of creating a truly pluralistic or culturally synergistic society where individual and cultural differences are valued and yet the whole—America—is even greater than the sum of these multicultural parts.

ENDNOTES

[1]David Reisman's *The Lonely Crowd: A Study of the Changing American Character* is a good example of study of the social character of different generations in America (Garden City, NY: Doubleday & Company, Inc., 1953. Originally published by Yale University Press in 1950).

[2]See Gary R. Weaver, "American Identity Movements," in Section I, 60–65, and "All Is Not Quiet on the Academic Front," *Connecticut Law Review,* 3(3), Spring 1971: 466–478.

[3]Jack Newfield, *A Prophetic Minority* (New York: The New American Library, 1966).

[4]Gary R. Weaver, "Introduction" to *The University and Revolution,* eds. Gary R. Weaver and James H. Weaver (Englewood Cliffs, NJ: Prentice-Hall, Inc., 1969), 1–17.

[5]John F. Kennedy, Commencement Address at American University, Spring 1963.

[6]Abraham Maslow, *Toward a Psychology of Being* (Princeton: D. Van Nostrand Company, Inc., 1962).

[7]Christopher Lasch, *The Culture of Narcissism: American Life in An Age of Diminishing Expecta-* tions (New York: W. W. Norton & Company, Inc., 1978).

[8]See Gary R. Weaver, "This Cutthroat College Generation," in this section, 280–281.

[9]The term "Generation X" was the name of a 1980s punkish Billy Idol band. However, Douglas Coupland's novel *Generation X: Tales for an Accelerated Culture* was the first to use it as a way of categorizing the post-boomer culture.

[10]Douglas Rushkoff, *The GenX Reader* (New York: Ballantine Books, 1994), 3–4.

[11]*Ibid.,* 6.

[12]"So—what is GenX? There's no answer, because that's an ignorant boomer question. Who knows? Who cares? Whatever." Mark Salveit, "Whatever," in *ibid.,* 53. He is a Harvard graduate who claims to have held over forty jobs. He believes that any attempts to categorize Generation X are doomed to failure.

[13]Arthur M. Schlesinger, Jr., *The Cycles of American History* (Boston: Houghton Mifflin Company, 1986).

[14]Rene Sanchez, "Survey of College Freshmen Finds Rise in Volunteerism," *The Washington Post* (January 13, 1997), 6 (A). More than 250,000 freshmen at nearly 500 universities nationwide took part in the survey conducted by UCLA's Higher Education Research Institute.

[15]Kurt Wiesenfeld, "Making the Grade," *Newsweek* (June 17, 1996), 16. This physicist, who teaches at Georgia Tech in Atlanta, claims that "many students wheedle for a degree as if it were a freebie T shirt."

[16]Diane Kockler, "Has Protesting Gone Out of Style?" *Cityview* (independent weekly in central Iowa), April 16, 1997.

[17]Edgar F. Beckham, "Diversity Opens Doors to All," *New York Times,* Education Life, section 4A (5 January 1997), 58.

36

Teachers' Classroom Strategies Should Recognize That Men and Women Use Language Differently

Deborah Tannen

When I researched and wrote my latest book, *You Just Don't Understand: Women and Men in Conversation*, the furthest thing from my mind was reevaluating my teaching strategies. But that has been one of the direct benefits of having written the book.

The primary focus of my linguistic research always has been the language of everyday conversation. One facet of this is conversational style: how different regional, ethnic, and class backgrounds, as well as age and gender, result in different ways of using language to communicate. *You Just Don't Understand* is about the conversational styles of women and men. As I gained more insight into typically male and female ways of using language, I began to suspect some of the causes of the troubling facts that women who go to single-sex schools do better in later life, and that when young women sit next to young men in classrooms, the males talk more. This

Reprinted from *The Chronicle of Higher Education*, 37, no. 40 (19 June 1991): B1, B3. Copyright © 1991 by Dr. Deborah Tannen.

is not to say that all men talk in class, nor that no women do. It is simply that a greater percentage of discussion time is taken by men's voices.

The research of sociologists and anthropologists such as Janet Lever, Marjorie Harness Goodwin, and Donna Eder has shown that girls and boys learn to use language differently in their sex-separate peer groups. Typically, a girl has a best friend with whom she sits and talks, frequently telling secrets. It's the telling of secrets, the fact and the way that they talk to each other, that makes them best friends. For boys, activities are central: their best friends are the ones with whom they do things. Boys also tend to play in larger groups that are hierarchical. High-status boys give orders and push low-status boys around. So boys are expected to use language to seize center stage: by exhibiting their skill, displaying their knowledge, and challenging and resisting challenges.

These patterns have stunning implications for classroom interaction. Most faculty members assume that participating in class discussion is a necessary part of successful performance. Yet speaking in a classroom is more congenial to boys' language experience than to girls', since it entails putting oneself forward in front of a large group of people, many of whom are strangers and at least one of whom is sure to judge the speakers' knowledge and intelligence by their verbal display.

Another aspect of many classrooms that makes them more hospitable to most men than to most women is the use of debate-like formats as a learning tool. Our educational system, as Walter Ong argues persuasively in his book *Fighting for Life*,[1] is fundamentally male in that the pursuit of knowledge is believed to be achieved by ritual opposition: public display followed by argument and challenge. Father Ong demonstrates that ritual opposition—what he calls "adversativeness" or "agonism"—is fundamental to the way most males approach almost any activity. (Consider, for example, the little boy who shows he likes a little girl by pulling her braids and shoving her.) But ritual opposition is antithetical to the way most females learn and like to interact. It is not that females don't fight, but they don't fight for fun. They don't *ritualize* opposition.

Anthropologists working in widely disparate parts of the world have found contrasting verbal rituals for women and men. Women in completely unrelated cultures (for example, Greece and Bali) engage in ritual laments: spontaneously produced rhyming couplets that express their pain, for example, over the loss of loved ones. Men do not take part in laments. They have their own, very different verbal ritual: a contest, a war of words in which they vie with each other to devise clever insults.

When discussing these phenomena with a colleague, I commented that I see these two styles in American conversation: many women bond by talking about troubles, and many men bond by exchanging playful insults and put-downs, and other sorts of verbal sparring. He exclaimed: "I never thought of this, but that's the way I teach: I have students read an article, and then I invite them to tear it apart. After we've torn it to shreds, we talk about how to build a better model."

This contrasts sharply with the way I teach: I open the discussion of readings by asking, "What did you find useful in this? What can we use in our own theory building and our own methods?" I note what I see as weaknesses in the author's approach, but I also point out that the writer's discipline and purposes might be different from ours. Finally, I offer personal anecdotes illustrating the phenomena under discussion and praise students' anecdotes as well as their critical acumen.

These different teaching styles must make our classrooms wildly different places and hospitable to different students. Male students are more likely to be comfortable attacking the readings and might find the inclusion of personal anecdotes irrelevant and "soft." Women are more likely to resist discussion they perceive as hostile, and, indeed, it is women in my classes who are most likely to offer personal anecdotes.

A colleague who read my book commented that he had always taken for granted that the best way to deal with students' comments is to challenge them; this, he felt, was self-evident, sharpens their minds and helps them develop debating skills. But he had noticed that women were relatively silent in his classes, so he decided to try beginning discussion with relatively open-ended questions and letting comments go unchallenged. He found, to his amazement and satisfaction, that more women began to speak up.

Though some of the women in his class clearly liked this better, perhaps some of the men liked it less. One young man in my class wrote in a questionnaire about a history professor who gave students questions to think about and called on people to answer them: "He would then play devil's advocate . . . *i.e.*, he debated us. . . . That class *really* sharpened me intellectually. . . . We as students do need to know how to defend ourselves." This young man valued the experience of being attacked and challenged publicly. Many, if not most, women would shrink from such "challenge," experiencing it as public humiliation.

A professor at Hamilton College told me of a young man who was upset because he felt his class presentation had been a failure. The professor was puzzled because he had observed that class members had listened attentively and agreed with the student's observations. It turned out that it was this very agreement that the student interpreted as failure. Since no one had engaged his ideas by arguing with him, he felt they had found them unworthy of attention.

So one reason men speak in class more than women is that many of them find the "public" classroom setting more conducive to speaking, whereas most women are more comfortable speaking in private to a small group of people they know well. A second reason is that men are more likely to be comfortable with the debate-like form that discussion may take. Yet another reason is the different attitudes toward speaking in class that typify women and men.

Students who speak frequently in class, many of whom are men, assume that it is their job to think of contributions and try to get the floor to express them. But many women monitor their participation not only to get the floor but to avoid getting it. Women students in my class tell me that if they have spoken up once or twice, they hold back for the rest of the class because they don't want to dominate. If they have spoken a lot one week, they will remain silent the next. These different ethics of participation are, of course, unstated, so those who speak freely assume that those who remain silent have nothing to say, and those who are reining themselves in assume that the big talkers are selfish and hoggish.

When I looked around my classes, I could see these differing ethics and habits at work. For example, my graduate class in analyzing conversation had 20 students, 11 women and 9 men. Of the men, four were foreign students: two Japanese, one Chinese, and one Syrian. With the exception of the three Asian men, all the men spoke in class at least occasionally. The biggest talker in the class was a woman, but there were also five women who never spoke at all, only one of whom was Japanese. I decided to try something different.

I broke the class into small groups to discuss the issues raised in the readings and to analyze their own conversational transcripts. I devised three ways of dividing the students into groups: one by the degree program they were in, one by gender, and one by conversational style, as closely as I could guess it. This meant that when the class was grouped according to conversational style, I put Asian students together, fast talkers together, and quiet students together. The class split into groups six times during the semester, so they met in each grouping twice. I told students to regard the groups as examples of interactional data and to note the different ways they participated in the different groups. Toward the end of the term, I gave them a questionnaire asking about their class and group participation.

I could see plainly from my observation of the groups at work that women who never opened their mouths in class were talking away in the small groups. In fact, the Japanese woman commented that she found it particularly hard to contribute to the all-woman group she was in because "I was overwhelmed by how talkative the female students were in the female-only group." This is particularly revealing because it highlights that the same person who can be "oppressed" into silence in one context can become the talkative "oppressor" in another. No one's conversational style is absolute; everyone's style changes in response to the context and others' styles.

Some of the students (seven) said they preferred the same-gender groups; others preferred the same-style groups. In answer to the question "Would you have liked to speak in class more than you did?" six of the seven who said Yes were women; the one man was Japanese. Most startlingly, this response did not come only from quiet women; it came from women who had indicated they had spoken in class never, rarely, sometimes, and often. Of the 11 students who said the amount they had spoken was fine, 7 were men. Of the four women who checked "fine," two added qualifications indicating it wasn't completely fine: One wrote in "maybe more," and one wrote, "I have an urge to participate but often feel I should have something more interesting/relevant/wonderful/intelligent to say!!"

I counted my experiment a success. Everyone in the class found the small groups interesting, and no one indicated he or she would have preferred that the class not break into groups. Perhaps most instructive, however, was the fact that the experience of breaking into groups, and of talking about participation in class, raised everyone's awareness about class participation. After we had talked about it, some of the quietest women in the class made a few voluntary contributions, though sometimes I had to insure their participation by interrupting the students who were exuberantly speaking out.

Americans are often proud that they discount the significance of cultural differences: "We are all individuals," many people boast. Ignoring such issues as gender and ethnicity becomes a source of pride: "I treat everyone the same." But treating people the same is not equal treatment if they are not the same.

The classroom is a different environment for those who feel comfortable putting themselves forward in a group than it is for those who find the prospect of doing so chastening, or even terrifying. When a professor asks, "Are there any questions?" students who can formulate statements the fastest have the greatest opportunity to respond. Those who need significant time to do so have not really been given a chance at all, since by the time they are ready to speak, someone else has the floor.

In a class where some students speak out without raising hands, those who feel they must raise their hands and wait to be recognized do not have equal opportunity to speak. Telling them to feel free to jump in will not make them feel free; one's sense of timing, of one's rights and obligations in a classroom, are automatic, learned over years of interaction. They may be changed over time, with motivation and effort, but they cannot be changed on the spot. And everyone assumes his or her own way is best. When I asked my students how the class could be changed to make it easier for them to speak more, the most talkative woman said she would prefer it if no one had to raise hands, and a foreign student said he wished people would raise their hands and wait to be recognized.

My experience in this class has convinced me that small-group interaction should be part of any class that is not a small seminar. I also am convinced that having the students become observers of their own interaction is a crucial part of their education. Talking about ways of talking in class makes students aware that their ways of talking affect other students, that the motivations they impute to others may not truly reflect others' motives, and that the behaviors they assume to be self-evidently right are not universal norms.

The goal of complete equal opportunity in class may not be attainable, but realizing that one monolithic classroom-participation structure is not equal opportunity is itself a powerful motivation to find more diverse methods to serve diverse students—and every classroom is diverse.

ENDNOTE

[1]Walter Ong, *Fighting for Life* (New York: Cornell University Press, 1981).

37

Black and White Cultural Styles in Pluralistic Perspective

Thomas Kochman

I. INTRODUCTION

American society is presently in a period of social transition from a structurally pluralistic society to a culturally pluralistic one. The difference between the two kinds of pluralism is in the political arrangement of their culturally heterogeneous parts. Within structural pluralism the socially subordinate cultural person or group unilaterally accommodates the dominant (Anglo-American male) cultural group on the latter's terms. This pattern of accommodation can be said to have constituted an American policy orientation regarding the integration of immigrants and (with further important qualification) indigenous and other minorities into the larger American society. As Theodore Roosevelt said in 1919: "If the immigrant who comes here in good faith becomes an American and assimilates himself to us he shall be treated on an exact equality with everyone else."[1]

The "us" or "American" in Roosevelt's statement represents the socially dominant Anglo-American male, only recently (within the framework of cultural pluralism) identified as a "hyphenated" American too, alongside Afro-American, Irish-American, Polish-American, Italian-American, Jewish-American, et al., but having (within the framework of

Reprinted from *Test Policy and Performance: Education, Language, and Culture*, ed. Bernard R. Gifford (Boston: Kluwer Academic Publishers, 1989): 259–296.

structural pluralism) effectively pre-empted the unhyphenated term "American" for themselves, with others being less "American" to the extent that they were "hyphenated." As Roosevelt said in the same speech: "But this [equality] is predicated on the man's becoming in very fact an American and nothing but an American. . . . There can be no divided allegiance here. Any man who says he is an American but something else also, isn't an American at all."

Presumably to the extent that other groups regarded themselves (or were made to regard themselves by others) as "something else also," they were also less entitled to social equality. Thus we have the condition established here of "cultural assimilation (to the dominant Anglo male group) as a prerequisite to social incorporation," or perhaps, more accurately, as a first step, cultural dissimilation with regard to one's original non-Anglo ethnic group (and, especially, repudiation of it in terms of political allegiance). Of course, to the extent that non-white racial groups were generally regarded as "unassimilable"—a view that kept them from participating in and benefiting from the white ethnic labor movement[2]—they could not achieve the racial/cultural identity that, within the dominant group's integrationist policy, was theoretically prerequisite to achieving social equality.

Practically speaking, structural pluralism exerted its political influence within the public sector through the schools and other official Americanizing agencies, such as for Native Americans, the Bureau of Indian Affairs.[3] But except for the neighborhood public school there were few other Americanizing forces working directly at the local community level to overcome the competing influence of non-Anglo ethnoculturalism operating through and within the local religious institution and family. In this pattern, the dominant group controls the process of social incorporation into and the patterns of behavior within the public sector, but leaves the local community sector relatively free to culturally define itself. In effect, this pattern constitutes the definition of and limits to the "melting pot," the dominant metaphor used to characterize the "Americanization" process (and one fitting within a structurally pluralistic conception of "integration"). As Roosevelt again put it:

> We have room for but one language here, and that is the English language, for we want to see that the crucible turns our people out as Americans, of American nationality, and not as dwellers in a polygot boarding house.

Equity within structural pluralism is seen as treating everyone the same. This serves both the social interest of cultural assimilation to Anglo-American male norms—to benefit equally from the same treatment one has to become like the (Anglo-American) person for whom that treatment was designed—and the social interest of economy and efficiency: officials need only to choose the one "best" way, with individuals held responsible for adapting themselves as best they can to that same "best" treatment. The fact that the same treatment might produce unequal effects, a point emphasized in the Bilingual Education Act of 1968 (*United States Statutes at Large*, Vol. 81, p. 817, taken from Hakuta), was indifferently accepted as the unavoidable "fallout" of this form of equity:

> There is no equality of treatment merely by providing students with the same facilities, textbooks, teachers, and curriculum; for students who do not understand English are effectively foreclosed from any meaningful education.[4]

The structural arrangement within cultural pluralism reflects greater political equality among the culturally heterogeneous units. "Anglo-Americans" are one group among other "hyphenated" Americans, and the accommodation process among different culturally distinctive groups is reciprocal rather than unilateral. As with structural pluralism, the public arena again provides the stage within which culturally pluralist issues are developed and negotiated (as for example, with regard to what would constitute intergroup "reciprocity"). The dominant metaphor within cultural pluralism is the "salad bowl," not the "melting pot," in which the identity and integrity of the culturally distinctive units remain intact while contributing to the overall quality, effect, and purpose of the whole.

II. CULTURAL PLURALISM AND BLACK AND WHITE CULTURAL DIFFERENCES

Insofar as present mainstream American attitudes towards cultural diversity by and large have been those generated by structural pluralism, differences in Black and White mainstream linguistic and cultural patterns, perspectives, and values are likely to be seen through a mindset that attaches greater social respectability, if not conceptual validity, to the White mainstream cultural style. The ubiquity of such a mindset becomes obvious when we realize that Black and White cultural and linguistic differences are manifested in approaches to assessing others and being assessed oneself in terms of ability and performance in school, college, and the workplace (for example, consider judgments and inferences which follow emotionally heated confrontation as an instance of Black functional "truth-seeking" style, described below). Indeed, through its school system and other social agencies, the dominant social group still insists upon "linguistic and cultural assimilation as a prerequisite to social incorporation," thereby instituting a policy and program whereby pressures are brought to bear upon Blacks and members of other minority groups to accommodate the dominant social group exclusively on the latter's terms. And in fact, when interest has been shown in American minority languages and cultures in the past it has generally been geared to understanding them *for the purpose of easing their social and cultural transition into the American mainstream,*[5] an attitudinal stance consistent with the "melting pot" concept within structural pluralism.

What disturbs me about this accommodation process is its unidirectional and nonreciprocal character. Those members of minority cultures who wish to become socially incorporated into the American mainstream do need to learn about mainstream American linguistic and cultural patterns. In some instances, it might even benefit them to use and embrace such patterns as necessity or desire might dictate.

But what about the needs of the American mainstream? The nonreciprocal nature of the process of cultural assimilation of minorities does not permit the mainstream American culture to learn about minority cultural traditions nor benefit from their official social incorporation. It also suggests an unwarranted social arrogance: that mainstream American society has already reached a state of perfection and cannot benefit from being exposed to and learning from other (minority) cultural traditions. I reject that assumption, and I demonstrate that in the stance I take here by promoting a view of the culturally different patterns and perspectives of Blacks and mainstream Whites from a social standpoint that regards them as equally respectable and valid (of course, therefore, also equally accountable to criticism, as on functional grounds, when such may be warranted).[6]

Styles of Work and Play

The following sections will detail the contents of some of the culturally different patterns as they appear in the domains of work and play. An overview is presented in Figure 1 below.

Being and Doing

In American mainstream culture Whites (especially males) are taught to see themselves as individuals rather than as members of a group. Yet when they become members of an organization or team they are frequently called upon to subordinate their individuality to fit the hierarchy and role-requirements established by the group. The nature of the subordination process takes the form of seeing the group as more important than oneself ("There is no letter 'I' in the word 'team'"). This process often leads to a fused self or identity (organized around what mainstream individuals do professionally) such as when White males talk about themselves in terms of a corporate "we" rather than as an individual "I."

Organizational culture also qualifies individuality in other respects. White mainstream American cultural style in the areas of organized work and play is serious, methodical, and systematic, characterized by what Harrison has called "mental set": a stance or attitude in which action or activity (doing) is seen to evolve out of a tightly structured plan, schedule, or procedure.[7] The conception and implementation of the plan is comprehensive (attempts are made beforehand to take all relevant variables into account and control for them), prescribed (from top management on down), and systematized (through standard operating procedures). The purpose of mental set is to render processes and outcomes orderly and predictable.

Within this role-oriented structure, individuals operating within and through mental sets are taught to see themselves in essentially instrumental terms ("You are what you do!"). Those parts of the self that are drawn upon are those mental and physical skills that functionally contribute (in some direct way) to organizational objectives. Aspects of the self that cannot be justified as directly contributing to the established task are disallowed as not only non-functional but as subversive. They are seen to promote and sustain individual allegiance to non-work-related values which, among other things, White mainstreamers believe, threaten undivided attention to the task necessary to do work well. Individuals with similar skills, roles, and tasks are seen within the team or organizational framework as "interchangeable" parts. As a result of these social pressures within the organization, the more distinctive aspects of White male individuality (self and identity) within mainstream American culture are more often realized in isolation: outside the context of a work group, rather than within it.

The relationship between the individual and the plan within the framework of "mental set" is analogous to that between the per-

FIGURE 1
Styles of Work and Play

Black	White
Patterns	
Mental "Reflex"	Mental "Set"
Spontaneous	Methodical
Improvisational	Systematic
Exaggerated	Understated
Expressive	Restrained
Personalized	Role-Oriented

Issues

Being/Doing: Individuality
Team Work/Play: Individuality; Functionality

former and the text within the "compositional" tradition in the performing arts. The principal interaction there is between the performer and the text or composition.[8] The role and responsibility of the performer is with regard to the text: the revelation of its "embodied meaning," and consequently, with a sense of fidelity to the author's or composer's original conception. Thus, performers are constrained in their interpretation and rendition of the text so as not to take "undue liberties." Chicago symphony oboist Ray Still makes this point in the context of objecting to the tradition (apparently as a result of his having been influenced by jazz music values):

> It's almost an unwritten law that we're not supposed to glissando—sliding from one note to another, as jazz musicians do so often—on a wind instrument. Only string instruments and the voice are supposed to do it. When I do it—I like my glisses—some eyebrows are raised. They say, "Oh, Ray is bending his instrument, now, trying to show his jazz technique." But that tradition burns me up. Why shouldn't we do it?[9]

Black cultural style in work and play evolves out of a conception that sees "change" rather than "set" as the constant aspect of cosmic and social order. Consequently, the Black cultural psyche operates out of "mental reflex,"[10] one oriented to "move through changes" as changing modes or circumstances determine. In conjunction with the Black penchant for generating powerful imagery, change becomes that aspect of order that "revitalizes an event."[11] The cultural style that Blacks have developed that serves "going through changes" is improvisation. And the force within the individual that motivates and complements improvisation is spontaneity ("I'm not a prize fighter, I'm a *surprise* fighter").

Consistent with this view of cosmic and social order, Black cultural style evolves out of a performance (as opposed to compositional) tradition;[12] consequently, the principal interaction is between the performer and the audience (the goal there being "engendered feeling."[13] Within this tradition, performers are granted great license to improvise with regard to the text—in effect to generate new "text" as

they go along—and, through the simultaneous and direct demonstration of the individual performer's virtuoso ability and powers of evocation, to produce "engendered feeling" in the audience.[14]

There is, of course, a performance dimension within the Western compositional tradition, too, that aims at "engendered feeling," but, as Keil argues, with "music composed for repetition, 'engendered feeling' has less chance" than when "music is left in the hands of the performer (improvised)."[15]

Critical differences between the compositional and performance traditions, then, are those of substance, principal focus, and direction. As Keil says, "a good composer gives some spontaneity to his form and, conversely, a good improviser tries to give some form to his spontaneity."[16] Likewise, as Harrison notes, actors in the White American theater aim at generating *affective memory*, which allows them to repeat the same emotion night after night.[17] In the Black theater, on the other hand, actors try to generate *effective memory*, which allows them to produce real, spontaneously conceived emotions, so as to produce (as the *context* rather than the *text* demands) the truest emotional response capable of galvanizing the (audience's) collective unconscious.[18] Thus, where White mainstream cultural style is oriented to shape the context to fit the text, Black cultural style is oriented, rather, to shape the text to fit the context.

Black individuality is realized within the framework of strong interpersonal connectedness, but, as Young states "not with absorption or acceptance of group identity as higher than individual identity."[19] Moreover, while there is emphasis on instrumental forms of doing, focus is also on individual character and style ("doing one's *own* thing"), leading to more personalized and idiosyncratic expressions of doing (as opposed to the more routine, uniform, and impersonal [role-oriented] forms of doing characteristic of self-presentation within White mainstream organizational culture).

Stylistic Self-Expression
Stylistic self-expression within White mainstream culture is minimalist in character: "a style of no style";[20] thus, characterized by

economy and efficiency ("the shortest distance between two points," "no wasted moves"), and modest (self-effacing) understatement and restraint ("If you've got it, you don't need to flaunt it").

Stylistic self-expression within Black culture is characterized by dramatic self-conscious flair. A nice descriptive example comes from Milhomme's portrait of Felix Toya, Ghana's dancing traffic policeman:

> Dubbed "Toyota" or "Life Boy" by city's taxi drivers, Constable Toya attracts as much pedestrian traffic as he directs vehicles. Lookers applaud and cheer, drivers toot their horns, and sometimes take an extra turn on the roundabout as Felix oscillates and gyrates, lifts, bends and pirouettes, making an art form out of his assigned task, never missing a step or a signal-change. Few Ghanians own Walkmans, but in the privacy of his own mind, Constable Toya creates a symphony of sounds and rhythms to which he moves with grace and precision. He is the ultimate street performer, taking cues from his environment and entertaining a diverse audience of fleeting yet appreciative fans.[21]

Black stylistic self-expression is also characterized by inventive (humorously ironic) exaggeration as in the self-promotion of demonstrably capable aspects of self ("If you've got it, flaunt it") or even by less demonstrably positive capabilities ("If you don't have it, flaunt it, anyway"), which is all part of Afro-American boasting: the "making of one's noise."[22] As "Hollywood" Henderson said, "I put a lot of pressure on myself to see if I can play up to my mouth."[23] But exaggeration also serves to characterize (and neutralize the impact of) negative situations, such as poverty. ("The soles on my shoes are so thin, I can step on a dime and tell you whether it's heads or tails.")

Conflict and Confluence

Individuality/Functionality

The functional rule for getting things done follows the norms for appropriate stylistic self-presentation and expression within the two cultures. The White mainstream cultural rule is governed by the principles of economy and efficiency, which serve to promote the uniform, impersonal, minimalist, and instrumental (role-oriented) style considered standard within mainstream White organized work and play. Thus the rule here is "make only moves that are necessary to getting the job done."

The Black cultural rule serves to promote the standards within the Black performance tradition, which is, as Abrahams has said for individual performers to bring about an experience in which their creative energies and the vitality of others may find expression.[24] Blacks accomplish this by executing tasks with bold originality and dramatic flair. Insofar as it is in "how" things get done that the energetic involvement of others and stylistic self-expression occur, rather than in "what" gets done, Blacks say (to protect the individual right of original self-expression), "Tell me what to do but not how to do it." Consonant with this purpose, the functional rule for Blacks is "so long as the moves that are made do not interfere with getting the job done, they should be allowed."

These two different cultural rules clash in the workplace and in the playground with great regularity.[25] One example of this clash is in the restrictions set forth in the professional football rules governing "spiking" the football (throwing it forcefully to the ground): a self-celebrating expression of personal accomplishment (resembling an exclamation point [!]) by which Black players punctuate their achievement. Were a player to "spike" the football after scoring an important first down, he would be penalized. The official reason given for assessing the penalty is "delay of game." In actuality there is no real "delay of game" because after a team scores a first down the line markers have to be moved, and a new football is thrown in from the sidelines; there may even be a TV commercial. At issue is the different aesthetic standard governing stylistic self-expression within Black and White mainstream culture. "Spiking" the football is permitted in the end zone after a touchdown, but only by the player who actually scores the touchdown. So when the White quarterback of the Chicago Bears, Jim McMahon, scored a touchdown and gave the football to one of the linemen to spike (in recognition of his cooperative and instrumental role in the touchdown) the officials assessed a penalty on the ensuing kickoff. As a measure of the acceptance of the Black cultural view on such matters in professional sports, it is significant that the reaction of both White announcers at the time of its occurrence, and of Bear quarterback Jim McMahon, when interviewed afterward, was to regard the assessment as "stupid."

Other aspects of cultural conflict center around the issue of individual entitlement for stylistic self-expression and authorization for making changes in how a task is to be done. In White mainstream organizational culture, stylistic self-expression, when it occurs at all, tends to be a function of rank. Consequently, it is often the chief executive male officer in the organization who in manner or dress, "shows-off," or otherwise demonstrates a more individually expressive (non-instrumental?!) style (for example, Lee Iacocca, Ray Kroc, Douglas MacArthur, and so forth).

In Black culture, however, stylistic self-expression is an individual entitlement. Consequently, one does not have to be the president of the company to drive an expensive top-of-the-line car or wear fashionable clothes. However, this cultural pattern often gets Blacks into trouble in White mainstream organizations since the latter interpret such individual stylistic self-expression as a presumption: a laying claim to a greater rank or title in the organization than the Black person actually holds.

As to authorization for how a task is to be accomplished, the Black dictum "Tell me what to do, but not how to do it," while establishing a protection for the individual right to self-expression, also asserts that the final authority for the implementation of a task rests with the doer/performer. However, White mainstream organizational culture, through the framework of "mental set" sees the authorization of a standard protocol or procedure to rest with the designer of the plan: the manager/composer. This difference also gets Blacks into trouble in the organization because they get accused here once again either of arrogating to themselves authority to which their rank or role in the organization does not entitle them,

or of being insubordinate or uncooperative, even when they do the task differently in the interests of getting the job done, when doing it in the way it was officially prescribed would have failed.

The Role and Function of Competition

In organized work and play within White mainstream culture, the role and function of competition is to provide a climate and context to determine which pair of adversaries (individual or group) can dominate the other. The role and function of competition in organized work and play within Black culture is twofold. It is not only to set the stage for determining which opponent can dominate the other, though it is also that (and intensely so), but also for each individual or group to use their opponent (as a foil is used in theater), to show off their skill in the process of doing so. The cultural difference is one of focus and emphasis. For Blacks, as Abrahams has said, competition provides the atmosphere in which performers can best perform.[26] The Black goal therefore is divided between winning (dominating one's opponent), and showboating (displaying one's ability vis-à-vis one's opposition so as to show it off at its highest level of accomplishment). This display function sets competition within Black culture apart from its counterpart in White mainstream culture. As basketball player Lloyd Free said:

> The fans have the right idea about pro basketball's regular season. . . . They know there are too many games and it's silly to play all that time to eliminate so few teams from the playoffs.
>
> So why do they even come to our games? . . . They come to see a show and that's why guys like myself and Dr. J and David Thompson are so popular. We make the fun and the excitement. Man, you just don't get serious in this business until the playoffs.[27]

This divided function of competition (winning and showboating) together with another cultural pattern, that of individual identity not being subordinate to group identity (the individual can succeed even if the team does not) leads to a more diffused focus in competitive play. This diminishes somewhat the singular importance attached to team winning that exists within White mainstream culture, represented by the assertion attributed to Vince Lombardi: "Winning may not be everything. But losing isn't anything." It especially takes the hard edge off losing. (As Blacks say, "The best you can do is the best you can do.") In the following passage, Red Holzman responds to a question about frequent reports that today's players don't take defeat as hard as yesterday's heroes. Without attributing this different attitude directly to Black cultural influence, he nonetheless supports the culturally dichotomous view presented here (albeit within the framework of differences in "older" and "newer" player attitudes towards losing):

> When I first started to coach in the pros, guys would come into the locker room after a tough loss and break up the furniture or brood or act like there was no tomorrow. It was like they had committed a crime by losing.
>
> Now as a coach, I certainly don't want my players to take any defeat lightly. But when you're part of an 82 game schedule, you're playing five times in the next six nights, and you're rushing to catch an airplane. I don't think it's too smart to carry those kinds of feelings with you. In that respect, I think today's players handle things a lot better emotionally.[28]

Also, Blacks attach some importance to "having fun" in organized play, which also translates into winning and losing not being taken as seriously as in White mainstream culture, as Lloyd Free's comments above also suggest. The different Black cultural view on the nature and function of competition, combined with attitudes towards individual display and showmanship, and losing and "having fun" in organized play, have no doubt helped shape the more general public attitude often expressed today that tends to regard baseball and basketball as being as much "entertainment" as "sport."

The element of "fun" and "showboating" that Blacks bring into organized competitive play is negatively valued by Whites, except perhaps where it has commercial value (cf. the "Harlem Globetrotters"), especially insofar as Whites tends to see organized or competitive play as more like work: serious (even somber) and important, and therefore, prescriptive, patient, methodical, systematic, role-oriented, and so on. It is as though Whites are bringing work-related values into organized competitive play, thereby making "play" resemble "work," while Blacks are bringing play-related values (such as spontaneity, improvisation, and fun) into organized competitive play, thereby making "work" resemble "play." Also, insofar as Blacks introduce these values alongside stylistic self-expression also regarded as "extra-curricular" within the strictly functional White cultural mind-set—Blacks would be regarded by Whites as not sufficiently "serious" or "interested" in getting the job or task accomplished.

Concentration

This interpretation is reinforced by the different meaning that Blacks and Whites give to "concentration to task." For White mainstreamers "concentration" means undivided attention: focusing upon one thing and one thing only. For Blacks, "concentration" means divided attention: attending to task accomplishment while simultaneously concentrating on doing it with flair or expressive style. Because Black attention is divided here, Whites believe that the focus on style is *at the expense of* focus on task to the ultimate detriment of task accomplishment. But this view misrepresents the Black cultural pattern which inherently protects against that happenstance by giving no credit for stylistic self-expression *if the person does not succeed in accomplishing the task.* Thus, in the above description of the "dancing policeman" Felix Toya, it was very important that he never missed a signal change even as he never missed a step. As Holt said with regard to Black (functionally) expressive performance, "everything must come together"[29]

Of course, the White view that sees Black divided attention to task as dysfunctional with regard to task accomplishment may in some instances simply be a pretext for discrediting Black preoccupation with stylistic self-expression. This view is based upon the value-orientation within White mainstream culture that sees allegiance to non-work-related values (as it defines "work") as corrosive of the American commitment to the work ethic. There is no question that Black preoccupation with stylistic self-expression does express an allegiance to values other than those promoted by and within White mainstream American culture. But so far, that allegiance has not sacrificed task accomplishment, nor is there any indication to lead one to suppose that it will. Moreover, the Black introduction of these other "play" values (such as "fun") into the workplace may ultimately have a revitalizing effect and in the end constitute a real contribution to mainstream American organized work and play culture.

Expenditure of Energy

Another difference in work style within Black and White mainstream culture centers around expenditure of energy. The White mainstream concept of "hustle" describes a work or play pattern of high energy expenditure often greater than is actually needed to perform a given task. The message being communicated with this "energy to spare" approach is, directly, worker zeal for the task at hand, and, more generally, from the organizational standpoint, a cooperative "ready, willing, and able" worker attitude. The Black approach is based upon a "conservation of energy" principle: to expend only as much (or little) energy as it takes to accomplish effectively the task at hand. One Black woman said that that pattern came about as a result of Blacks "picking cotton" all day long where the goal was to make only those moves that were absolutely necessary. But whether the "conservation of energy" principle originated with cotton picking or simply was applied to that and/or other oppressive and exploitative "colonial" work situations is not clear.

Regardless of the origin of the pattern— the application of the conservation of energy principle to work and play situations—expenditure of excess energy is seen by Blacks as "wasteful," and "stupid" ("definitely 'uncool'") and, when directed by others, still carries with it strong connotations of "being exploited." Yet to Whites, the conservation of energy principle, as the antithesis of "hustling," often

communicates lack of dedication to task or of motivation or interest in the job. This is so even when Blacks actually accomplish the same amount of work with their "energy-efficient" method that White workers accomplish with and through "hustling."[30]

Styles of Discourse

Truth-creating processes

Argument versus discussion. Black and White "truth-creating processes" are those protocols and procedures that each cultural group has established as appropriate for the working through of disagreements and disputes or for otherwise "getting at the truth." For Blacks, the appropriate truth-creating process is "sincere" argument (as opposed to the form of argument that is quarreling, which Blacks also have). For White mainstream people, discussion rather than argument is the idealized (if not always realized) truth-creating process. Thus, a White middle-class couple will say that they had a "discussion that 'deteriorated' into an argument," therein showing that argument is more like quarreling than a sincere attempt at truth-seeking. Notwithstanding the occasional failures by those in the American mainstream to realize discussion norms, the cultural standards are there nonetheless to structure attitudes and otherwise serve as a social barometer for evaluating verbal behavior or discourse style, either that of oneself or others. The same holds true for Blacks in those social contexts where sincere argument rather than discussion is the cultural standard for expressing disagreement and resolving disputes.

Black argument as a cultural style is (as for other ethnic groups), confronting, personal, advocating, and issue-oriented. White discussion style is non-confronting, impersonal, representing, and peace- or process-oriented, the latter expressed by such concepts as "compromise," and "agreeing to disagree." An overview of these differences is shown in Figure 2.

The issues that divide Blacks and Whites culturally and account for how they assess each other's behavior—Blacks regard Whites here as "insincere" and "devious"; Whites see Blacks as "argumentative" and "threatening"—

revolve around the value of contentiousness or struggle, the separation (or fusion) of reason and emotion, the separation (or fusion) of truth and belief, and finally, self-control. I will briefly consider each of these in turn.[31]

Struggle. In the context of truth-seeking, struggle or contentiousness is unifying for Blacks, polarizing for Whites. Blacks view struggle or contentiousness as positive, while Whites view it as negative. A metaphor to describe the difference would be individuals holding opposite ends of a rope while pulling against each other. Whites essentially see only the opposition: individuals pulling in opposite directions. Blacks see individuals pulling in opposite directions, to be sure, but more tellingly, also being held together by the same rope (that is, the individuals are cooperating in their opposition, and cooperating more than they are opposing).

Black and White attitudes towards the value of struggle stem from these different positions. Thus, if disagreement at a meeting were likely to generate heat and strong emotions, Whites would say it was better not to contend than to contend ("I can't talk to you now. You're too emotional!"); on the other hand, Blacks would say it was better to contend than not to contend. This is because Whites see the prevention of potential damage to the harmony of social relationships as tak-ing precedence over the expression of their individual views. If they were to threaten such harmony (however contrived or artificial), Whites would see this as "selfish," "self-indul-gent," or "impolite." For Blacks, on the other hand, the powerful expression of one's personal views takes precedence over sustaining a surface harmony that may have no real (sincere) foundation, which Blacks would see as "hypocritical" or a "charade."

The attitudes of Whites and Blacks are also based in part on their respectively different (culturally determined) capacities to manage emotionally charged disagreements. Both attitudes and capacities are directly linked in turn to systems of etiquette within the two cultures.[32]

For example, the etiquette system governing social interaction in the public arena within White mainstream culture declares that (except under certain socially "marked" occasions, like a "talk" or "lecture") the social rights of the receiver deserve greater consideration than the rights of the assertor. As a consequence, mainstream Americans are socialized to regard the protection of their own and other people's sensibilities (when they are in the receiver role) as deserving principal consideration, even when that may be at the expense of their own or others' feelings (emotions) when they or others are in the assertor

---

FIGURE 2
Truth-Creating Processes

Black	White
Argument	Discussion

Patterns

Black	White
Confronting	Non-confronting
Personal	Impersonal
Advocating	Representing
Truth- or issue-oriented	Peace- or process-oriented

Issues

Struggle
Reason/Emotion
Truth/Belief
Self-control

Behavioral Meanings

Black	White
"Whites are insincere and devious"	"Blacks are argumentative and threatening"

role. This pattern within the mainstream American etiquette system generates (relative to Black culture) a low offense/low defense pattern of public social interaction. This is because protecting the sensibilities of themselves and others requires mainstreamers to moderate the intensity level of their self-assertion to the level that "others" (that is, receivers) can comfortably manage. And insofar as the intensity level that mainstream receivers can comfortably manage is culturally programmed to be low ("sensitive"), the level of self-assertion must also be commensurately low. Thus, low defense generates low offense. In turn, low offense (under the rubric of *protecting* sensibilities) maintains low defense because it withholds from mainstreamers regular exposure to the more potent stimuli that would enable them to learn how to manage intense interactions more effectively (at least so as not to be overwhelmed by them).

By way of contrast, Black culture generates a (relatively) high offense/high defense pattern of public social interaction. This comes about as a result of the culture granting the assertor rights that are at least equal to, and often greater than (especially when aroused), the rights of the receiver. As Harrison said:

> Blacks are not known . . . to ever be totally desensitized, defused, or repressed in their emotions when dealing with definable antagonisms. A black person would not pussyfoot with an insult from a white—or a black—if rendered with the slightest edge of an acerbity that might threaten one's security: the response would be fully acted out, regardless of the name of the game which deems it necessary to be sensitive to the other feller.[33]

Thus, where the process of accommodation in White mainstream culture is for assertors to consider the sensibilities of receivers first, even at the expense of their own feelings (emotions), the process of accommodation in Black culture is the reverse: for receivers to accommodate assertors' feelings (emotions) especially when they are charged (as when following the "impulse towards truth" in sincere argument).

And it is the greater priority given to feelings (emotions) over sensibilities within Black culture that produces the high offense/high defense pattern. The receivers' orientation to accommodate self-presentation of high emotional intensity exposes them to such presentations on a regular basis, which, in turn, improves their capacity to manage them effectively. In such a way does high offense generate high defense. Reciprocally, the greater capacity of receivers to manage emotionally charged self-presentations allows individuals to assert their feelings (emotions) more freely with the confidence that others can receive them without becoming overwhelmed by them. In such a way does high defense sustain and promote high offense.

Comparatively, then, the psychological consequences of these different sociocultural orientations is that for Whites it hurts them more to hear something unfavorable than it hurts them not to express their feelings (as in abandoning themselves to the "impulse towards truth"). For Blacks, it hurts them more not to express their feelings than to hear something unfavorable.

These different attitudes and capacities generate different levels of comfort and tolerance among Blacks and Whites when meetings become emotionally charged and lead to directly opposite evaluations of such proceedings. Thus, at one such meeting among Black and White staff at a local psychological clinic in Chicago, Blacks left saying that was the "best" staff meeting that they had ever had. Whites left saying it was the "worst" staff meeting that they had ever had.

Another way of characterizing Black and White attitudes towards struggle is that Blacks put truth before peace whereas Whites put peace before truth. In the mainstream American political arena, to be "peace"-oriented ultimately means to accommodate established political arrangements, before which truth is sacrificed in the form of compromise. The Black orientation in the political arena is, as with interpersonal disagreements and disputes, again to put truth before peace, which is to say, to keep the truth intact and politicize on its behalf.

These different cultural orientations account for the way Blacks and Whites assess each other's public self-presentation style, as for example the cultural style of public officials. For example, those who admired Chicago Mayor Harold Washington (mostly Blacks), did so partly, as the *Chicago Sun-Times* said for "sticking to his guns."[34] In Washington's case this meant not compromising his reformist platform despite the fact that politically, for the first three years of his office (and during the time that the above *Sun-Times* editorial was written) he was opposed by a majority bloc of aldermen, who prevented him from getting any of his administrative appointments passed through the city council (to push for his reformist programs). His critics, mostly Whites, such as the culturally mainstream editorial writers of the *Sun-Times* believed he was "too stubborn [prideful?!] to be [politically?!] effective." Thus, the *Chicago Sun-Times* editorial said, "We believe an accommodation [between the Mayor's administration and his political opposition] should have been reached, and could have been reached, without terrible violence to principle."[35] The orientation that principle (truth) should be bent to accommodate political realities reflects the White mainstream cultural view. However, the Black cultural view (such as, to change the political realities to accommodate the truth) was the one that prevailed in this instance. Washington refused to compromise his reformist agenda by seeking an accommodation with the leader of the political opposition, Ed Vrdolyak, whom he viewed as the "incarnation of corruption." Instead, he pushed for a redistricting of the city ward map which forced new aldermanic elections that gave Washington the majority voice in the city council and enabled him for the first time since his election to put his own administrative team in office to push forward his reformist program.

It is also possible to look at the White mainstream and Black cultural styles as situationally (as well as ethnoculturally) determined. In this view, the priorities within the White mainstream cultural pattern (that sacrifices truth to accommodate political realities) are consistent with an establishment ("inpower") social orientation. Thus, when the Equal Rights Amendment became an issue for White middle-class women, they reversed their usual socially mainstream priorities of placing peace before truth by putting truth before peace, and also by replacing their customary discussion mode with sincere argument.

Reason and Emotion/Truth and Belief. Mainstream American culture believes that truth is objective, which is to say, external to the self; consequently, it is something to be discovered rather than possessed. This assumption has led mainstream Americans to view themselves instrumentally as objective truth seekers following the model and method of cognitive science in getting at (scientific) truth. In that instrumental view the means must be consistent with the end: one needs a rational means to produce a rational (reliable) result, one that also would be replicable from person to person insofar as individuals applied the same (rational/scientific) method to the truth-seeking process. Replicability of method would also ensure a standard or uniform mental process leading to a predictable outcome (see the discussion under "mental set" above).

The emphasis on replication and standardization of method produces a generalized focus and concern with process, also leading individuals to come to see themselves in process terms and to regard as intrusive those aspects of self that would interfere with the instrumentalization of themselves as neutrally objective (rational) truth seekers. Emotion and belief are especially suspect: those elements of self that were part of an earlier traditional view that saw truth as subjective, as something internal, to be possessed, as in belief (and defended through argument,[36] as opposed to something objective, external, and discoverable. This has led mainstream Americans to see emotion and belief as contaminants, that undermine their neutrally objective self/stance that defines and regulates rational (scientific) engagement and inquiry. The effort to free reason and truth from the contaminating influence of emotion and belief has led people to define reason and objective truth seeking *in terms* of the other category: not by virtue of what rationality is (a mental process characterized by a clear, accurate, and logical progression of thought), but by what it is not. So practically speaking, people now consider themselves and others "rational" to the extent that they are *not* emotional. And insofar as "rationality" is promoted at the expense of emotionality, people socialized to realize "rational" self-presentations are often, in reality, becoming socialized to realize unemotional self-presentations instead.

The above mainstream American cultural attitude and practice ultimately lead to the separation of reason and emotion. Likewise, the following line of reasoning on the relationship of objective truth seeking and belief leads to the cultural separation of truth and belief. Mainstream Americans say "no one person has a monopoly on the truth," and "the more strongly individuals believe that they do own the truth, the less likely it is to be the truth." The first of these statements asserts that individuals vary in their points of view, that the best that individuals can have is a point of view, and that any individual point of view can only be part of the truth (the more complete or "whole" truth theoretically constituting a sum of all of the different points of view that are or can be brought to bear upon the overall topic or situation). Expressed in mathematical terms a truth that contains the perspectives of individuals A and B is more complete (and therefore "better") than a truth that contains only the point of view of individual A or individual B. This view ultimately leads mainstreamers, such as new journalists, to define appropriate truth seeking as a balance of opposing viewpoints.[37]

The second statement ("the more strongly individuals believe that they do own the truth, the less likely it is to be the truth") incorporates the views expressed in the first and also says something about the nature of the self as objective truth seeker. In addition to being rational, individuals are obliged to be sufficiently open-minded to receive and reflect upon points of view other than their own. Implicit in this view is the implication that to the extent that individuals believe that their point of view is *the* truth, they will be less likely to be so receptive or considerate. So strongly held beliefs in themselves have also come to be seen as polarizing and defeating of the kind of in-

teractional cooperation individuals need to realize for the objective truth-seeking process to work. This is in spite of the fact that it may be other attributes—those that accompany the assertion of owned truths (beliefs/convictions)—that more directly account for such "closed-minded" resistance, not the fact of having strong convictions, per se, or expressing them in a certain (as opposed to tentative) manner. Nonetheless, the public presumption that strongly held views disable the objective truth-seeking process has led individuals to view positively those who do not hold or express strong views whether those individuals are actually engaged in objective truth-seeking or not—their stance evokes the "open-minded" attitude of the objective ("scientific") truth seeker. So personnel forms test for mental "rigidity" or its converse, "flexibility," by asking recommenders to rate individuals on whether they are "respectful and accepting of others," insofar as they adapt their thinking "to allow for other persons' points of view." Individuals who are less able to adapt their thinking to allow for other points of view are presumably rated as *less* respectful of others.[38]

Some Functions of Neutrality

The equation of the absence of emotion/strong convictions with the neutrality necessary for "rational deliberation" within the framework of objective truth seeking has served to legitimize and promote neutrality (often characterized as impersonal involvement or detachment) as a *general* mainstream cultural style, which is to say, as the preferred manner of public self-presentation even when individuals are not engaged in the process of objective truth seeking. Neutrality that was conceived and employed as a means to an end has thus been taken out of context to become instead a socially authorized end product of mainstream American acculturation. And as such it takes on a new social character and works to serve mainstream American social and political interests in other ways.

For example, neutrality as a generalized public posture easily translates into indifference, thereby enabling mainstream Americans to serve goals and interests that they might be less able or willing to serve were they socialized into another kind of public cultural style, as for example, the more contentious (agonistic) style that defines the Black (or for that matter Jewish) public presentation of self and engagement of others in truth seeking and other forms of social discourse.[39]

Neutrality also does not compel ownership of a point of view. And that allows for the production of *representatives* (as opposed to *advocates*) and generates the characteristic impersonal public participation style of mainstream Americans. I call it involvement without commitment (that is, conviction). Thus individuals can engage in "discussion" without having a point of view or predisposition to an outcome, but not in sincere "argument."

The process of developing spokespersons rather than advocates—those whose role and function is to represent other people's views rather than their own—begins early in school. Students, by and large, are essentially given "credit" for representing the "authoritative" points of view of others, as on exams and papers, but not for cultivating or developing their own view of things, even when such an explicit formulation might be very helpful and relevant to what they ultimately do for a living (such as a "philosophy of education" for a teacher).

Later on, when individuals are asked to become "team" players in organizations, they are also asked to represent the authorized "official" point of view. To the extent that they have strong personal convictions, they are likely to be less able or willing to represent points of view with which they do not agree, and especially those with which they personally disagree.

The socialization into a neutral (representational!) style may also facilitate disaffiliation with one's original roots/loyalties, thereby setting the stage for subsequent reaffiliation to mainstream organizational norms and values ("One needs to move out [in order] to move up"). Ultimately, it helps to promote an identity in terms of what an individual does (one that commits being to doing) as opposed to one that commits doing to being.

In generating indifference, neutrality also facilitates a greater acceptance of authority.[40] It allows individuals to sacrifice truth in the interests of truce (peace) and regard "compromise" as the morally sanctioned "solution" to ideological or political conflict (the mainstream American notion of "compromise" requires that individuals accept as the new truth that which is defined within the framework of the new political reality)[41] and to rationalize the accommodation to established political interests as simply being "realistic."[42]

Blacks do not separate reason and emotion or truth and belief. The goal of Black representation is not "rationality," *per se,* if by "rationality" one means exclusively a linear processing and presentation of information, but "consciousness," which simultaneously attends to what is going on inside one's gut as well as one's head: a mind/body fusion instead of a mind/body dichotomy. Similarly, truth is not separated from belief, but rather, expressed in terms of belief, and processed (in truth seeking) through the crucible of argument.

Evaluations of Behavioral Meanings

The separation of reason and emotion and truth and belief by Whites when they engage in disagreements and disputes produces the more detached and impersonal style of self-presentation characteristic of discussion, which, in conjunction with the avoidance of direct confrontation, Blacks personally characterize as "insincere," and generally consider to be dysfunctional of the truth-creating process. The Black characterization of Whites as "insincere" refers both to their impersonal self-presentation style when engaging in disagreement ("It seems as though Whites do not believe what they are saying themselves"), as well as Whites' unwillingness to engage in direct confrontation, or any kind of dialogue at all, as when things begin to get emotionally charged.

Blacks also have characterized the White discussion style as "devious," perhaps a more severe indictment even than "insincere." This characterization stems from Whites frequently not owning the position they are representing, nor seeing such ownership as a requirement when engaging in disagreement or debate. The basis for the White style and attitude has its roots in the mainstream culture that (as discussed above) gives credit for "authoritative" views, not the individual's own view (often discredited as simply "opinion"). Such "authoritative views" have become established with White mainstream culture as making one's self-presentations more persuasive. From the Black standpoint, however, only those views that an individual takes ownership of are admissible when engaging in disagreement or debate. This is because Blacks believe that all points have to be processed through the crucible of argument, even those of established "authority." Whites often see such authoritative views as above challenge (at least by non-experts). Moreover, in not accepting them as their own, they also do not accept responsibility for the validity of the view that they are representing, on whose contents they are being challenged. (White student: "It wasn't me that said it." Black student: "But you introduced it.") Blacks see the White behavior here as "cheating," as attempting to get credit for a particular view without allowing such a view to be processed through the crucible of argument. Thus, when White students would say, "Well, Marshall McLuhan said . . . ," Black students would interrupt, "Wait a minute! Marshall McLuhan's not here. If he were here I'd be arguing with him. Are you willing to accept his view that you are representing as your own [to allow it to be processed through argument]?" The White student is then caught up short, saying, "I haven't thought enough about it to have a personal position on it." Blacks tend to view such comments with great suspicion.

In some instances, Blacks do not believe that Whites do not have a position on what they are (re)presenting, but rather, believe that Whites are trying to avoid the anticipated challenge to the position by claiming not to own the position that they, in fact, do have. And *that*, Blacks would allege, is "cowardly" and "devious."

Finally, the Black characterization of the non-confronting, impersonal, representational, "peace" (process)-oriented White presentation style here as "devious" derives from its similarity to the pattern of self-presentation that Blacks adopt when they are "lying," as one Black woman put it. The White style for Blacks is the opposite of the "for real" style (which for Blacks is confronting, personal, advocating, and truth (issue)-oriented). Thus, the White "discussion" style here is the one that Blacks adopt when "they do not care enough about the person or issue to want to waste the energy on it" or, when "it is too dangerous to say what they truly feel and believe." This often occurs for Blacks in those situations where they cannot be "for real" and have to "front" (that is, hide their true feelings and opinions).

Whites characterize the Black style as "argumentative." This characterization stems from the personal approach that Blacks use when engaging in argument. Blacks do not just debate the idea, as Whites do. They debate the person debating the idea. Thus, in such a context, your idea is only as good as your personal ability to argue it.[43]

The White view of Black style as "argumentative" also stems from the Black view that insists that Whites own and defend the position that they may only be representing, which Whites may be unwilling or unable to do, for reasons given above.

More seriously, Whites also characterize the Black argumentative style as "threatening," as when meetings get emotionally charged. This view has its origin in differences in White and Black cultural views of "self-control" as well as what constitutes "threatening" behavior.

Briefly, emotional *self-control* in White mainstream culture is characterized and practiced as self-restraint: containing or reining in emotional impulses. Consequently, when emotions are "out" they are perceived by Whites (as they function for Whites) as "out of control." For Blacks, self-control is characterized and practiced as control over emotions, not only at the level of containment, but also at the level of emotionally intense self-expression. The Black cultural concept for controlling one's emotions is "being 'cool.'" And the caveat "to be cool" is often invoked in situations that are "hot."[44] But "being cool" in such situations does not mean realizing a state of emotional self-denial or restrained emotional expression, but rather being in control of one's emotional heat and intensity (whether laughter, joy, or anger). So in Black culture it is possible for individuals to be "hot" and "cool" at the same time (instigating performers who try to heat up the scene while "proclaiming [their] own cool").[45] So what constitutes a state of "out of control" for Whites constitutes an "in-control" state for Blacks.

The White view of Black emotional behavior as "threatening" also stems from Blacks and Whites having different conceptions of what constitutes a "threat," which is linked in turn to different cultural conceptions about when a "fight" begins. For Whites a "fight" begins when emotional confrontation gets intense (as when opponents raise angry voices, get insulting, and utter threats). For Blacks a "fight" begins, when, in the context of such an angry confrontation, *someone makes a provocative move*. Were neither of the opponents to "make [such] a move," notwithstanding the loud, angry, confrontive, insulting, intimidating talk, from the Black standpoint, they are still only "talking."[46] A "threat" for Whites then, begins when a person *says* they are going to do something. A "threat" for Blacks begins when a person actually *makes a move* to do something. Verbal threats, from the Black standpoint, are still "only talk."

ENDNOTES

[1]Theodore Roosevelt, in *El Grito: A Journal of Mexican American Thought.* "Editorial: Keep Up the Fight for Americanism," Berkeley, CA: Quinto Sol Publications, vol. 1 (2), 1968: 5.

[2]Herbert Hill, "Anti-Oriental Agitation and the Rise of Working-Class Racism," *Society* 10 (2), 1973: 43–54.

[3]A. D. Fisher, "White Rites versus Indian Rights," *Transaction* 7 (1), 1969: 29–33.

[4]Kenū Hakuta, *The Mirror of Language: The Debate on Bilingualism* (New York: Basic Books, 1986).

[5]Alfred A. Aarons, Barbara Y. Gordon and William A. Stewart, eds., "Linguistic-Cultural Differences and American Education," *Florida FL Reporter* 7 (1), 1969; Courtney B. Cazden, Vera P. John and Dell Hymes, eds., *Functions of Language in the Classroom,* New York: Teachers College Press, 1972; Miles V. Zintz, *Education Across Cultures* (Des Moines: Wm. C. Brown, 1963).

[6]Thomas Kochman, *Black and White Styles in Conflict* (Chicago: University of Chicago Press, 1981): 34–35, 151.

[7]Paul C. Harrison, *The Drama of Nommo* (New York: Grove, 1972).

[8]Charles Keil, "Motion and Feeling in Music," in *Rappin' and Stylin' Out,* in Thomas Kochman, ed.(Urbana: University of Illinois Press, 1972): 83ff.

[9]Florence H. Levinsohn, "Still the Oboist," *Reader [Chicago's Free Weekly]* 16 (3), 1986: 20.

[10]Harrison, 35.

[11]*Ibid.*, 7.

[12]Keil, 84–85.

[13]*Ibid.*, 86.

[14]*Ibid.*

[15]*Ibid.*, n. 6.

[16]*Ibid.*, 85–86.

[17]Harrison, *op. cit.*

[18]*Ibid.*, 157.

[19]Virginia H. Young, "Family and Childhood in a Southern Negro Community," *American Anthropologist* 72, 1970: 269–288; see also Diane K. Lewis, "The Black Family: Socialization and Sex Roles," *Phylon* 36 (3), 1975: 221–237.

[20]Roger D. Abrahams, *Talking Back,* Rowley, MA: Newbury, 1976, 8–9, 90–91.

[21]Janet Milhomme, "Brake Dancing in Accra," *LA Extra*, May 16–22, 1986, 37.

[22]Thomas Kochman, *Black and White Styles in Conflict* (Chicago: University of Chicago Press, 1981): 65; Karl Reisman, "Noise and Order," in *Language in its Social Setting*, William W. Gage, ed. (Washington, DC: Anthropological Society of Washington, 1974): 60.

[23]Atkin Ross, "'Hollywood Henderson' at Super Bowl," *Christian Science Monitor*, January 18, 1979, 16.

[24]Roger D. Abrahams, *Talking Back* (Rowley, MA: Newbury, 1976): 9.

[25]Thomas Kochman, *Black and White Styles in Conflict*, 145–152.

[26]Roger D. Abrahams, *Positively Black* (Englewood Cliffs, NJ: Prentice-Hall, 1970): 42.

[27]Phil Elderkin, "The Serious Side of a Super-Showman," *Christian Science Monitor*, April 4, 1979, 17.

[28]Phil Elderkin, "Red Holzman—the Marco Polo of Pro Basketball," *Christian Science Monitor*, March 5, 1981: 16.

[29]Grace Sims Holt, "Communication in Black Culture: The Other Side of Silence," *Language Research Reports* 6, 1972: 60; see also Kochman, *Black and White Styles in Conflict*, 138ff.

[30]Kochman, *op. cit.*, 157–159.

[31]*Ibid.*, 16–42.

[32]*Ibid.*, 106–129; "The Politics of Politeness," in *Meaning, Form and Use in Context: Linguistic Applications*, Deborah Schiffrin, ed., Georgetown University Roundtable on Languages and Linguistics (Washington, DC: Georgetown University Press, 1984): 200–209.

[33]Harrison, 150.

[34]*Chicago Sun-Times*, August 21, 1984, 35.

[35]*Ibid.*, April 23, 1986, 2.

[36]Walter J. Ong, S.J. *Orality and Literacy: The Technologizing of the Word* (New York: Methuen, 1982).

[37]The positions are assumed *a priori* to have an equal claim on the truth regardless of the respective merits of the position. The moral goal is to realize a fair and equitable process rather than to proselytize on behalf of one or another particular position.

[38]Note that being "objective" is equated here with being open to other people's viewpoints *regardless of how those other viewpoints were arrived at*. The effect of only one individual being "open-minded" and/or "neutrally objective" does not necessarily promote *objective* truth. It may simply weaken the self by allowing for a unilateral *adaptation to another person's* "closed mind," non-negotiable assertions.

[39]Thomas Kochman, *Black and White Styles in Conflict*; Deborah Schiffrin, "Jewish Argument as Sociability," *Language in Society, 13* (3), 1984: 311–335; see also Ong, *op. cit.*, for a discussion of the agonistic style of teaching in "oral" cultures.

[40]Chester L. Barnhard [1938], *The Functions of the Executive* (Cambridge: Harvard University Press, 1954).

[41]Compare Cooper's review and summary of Caplan's Arab and Jew in Jerusalem.

> One difference is in the concept of compromise. The Arabic term nearest to the English word "compromise" is *Teswiyeh,* which to Jerusalem Arabs means suspending rather than ending an active dispute. "The meaning of *Teswiyeh* seems to be based upon an ethical imperative to continue fighting forever for what is right, although it might be expedient to interrupt the struggle or to hide it for a time because it interferes unduly with practical aspects of life." (quoting Caplan and Caplan, p. 114). Western negotiators, in contrast, view a compromise as involving each side's giving up a little of what it regards as a just claim and finding a middle ground which each side can agree is relatively just. They admit that each side's notion of what is right may not be absolute. Thus the settlement implies that each party has modified its original demands *as well as the principle on which it is based* [italics added].

Robert L. Cooper, "Review of *Arab and Jew in Jerusalem: Explorations in Community Mental Health*" by Gerald Caplan and Ruth B. Caplan (Cambridge, MA: Harvard University Press), *Language in Society* 15 (1), 1980: 111–115.

[42]Thomas Kochman, "Crosscultural Communication: Contrasting Perspectives, Conflicting Sensibilities," *Florida FL Reporter* 9, 1971: 53–54.

[43]This also means that it would be inappropriate for others to jump in to support the person who, because of personal inadequacy, cannot marshall enough support for their own position themselves. Such attempts are rebuffed, usually by the person who is winning the argument, by "Wait a minute. I am arguing with *him* [that person being the one who has been temporarily caught shorthanded in coming back with a reply]. When I'm through arguing with *him*, I'll argue with *you*."

[44]Roger D. Abrahams, *Talking Back*, 84–85.

[45]*Ibid.*, 84.

[46]See Kochman, *Black and White Styles in Conflict*, 43ff for a complete discussion.

38

Two Styles, One Purpose: Education

William Raspberry

A number of school systems, reluctantly conceding a consistent achievement gap between black and white students, have committed themselves (and, in some cases, significant dollars) to closing the gap.

It is a commendable attitude, an example of America's can-do spirit. But is it likely to produce results?

A good deal depends on the nature of the racial gap. Is it really a socioeconomic gap revealing only the unsurprising fact that children of the middle class do better in school than the children of the poor? Is it the result of home or societal factors that predispose white children toward academic exertion? Or are there really "learning style" differences between black and white children that can be productively exploited?

Janice E. Hale-Benson thinks that learning style is the key, a theory she explores in her book, "Black Children: Their Roots, Culture, and Learning Styles." And although she freely acknowledges that she has not discovered final answers, she believes that enough is known to warrant serious research into the question.

"I have written a book," she says, "to stimulate a different conversation and, I hope, a different research orientation toward the education of black children."

She begins with two assumptions, one unarguable and one certain to prove contro-

versial. The first is that black children, whatever their cultural differences, "must achieve competency in mastering the tools of this culture if they are to survive." The second is that there survives in melting-pot America a distinct Africa-rooted black culture whose neglect by educators steeped in the European traditions predisposes black youngsters to academic underachievement.

Hale-Benson, an associate professor of early childhood education at Cleveland State University, contends (she cites the work of Rosalie Cohen) that the African tradition, with its stress on family and other personal relationships, produces a "relational" style of processing information, a style that features approximation, contextual meaning and focuses on people. The European style tends to be analytic, emphasizing precision, universal meaning and focuses on things.

Schools, and the standardized tests on which they rely for measurement, require the analytic approach, which means that the intelligence of black children frequently goes unrecognized and unrewarded—even on the so-called culture-free tests. She quotes Cohen:

"The most intelligent relational pupils score the worst of all. Their ability to reach higher levels of abstraction through relational pathways takes them farther away from the higher levels of abstraction reached through analytic pathways. . . .

"Highly intelligent high-relational pupils were found, in fact, to communicate best with the demands of the school on the concrete level. . . . It appears, therefore, that given concrete settings with intelligence held constant, high-relational pupils can compete with analytic ones. It is only when high levels of analytic abstraction are required that their ability to compete is inhibited."

Nor is it only in learning and testing that the cultural differences work to the disadvantage of blacks, Hale-Benson believes. Black children, boys in particular, are more likely than whites to be labeled "hyperactive" or "aggressive" because white teachers don't understand the difference between verbal "fighting" and "woofing," a verbal ritual that may actually reduce the likelihood of a fight.

In addition, teachers may underestimate the need for young black children to be touched and held and given frequent compliments and praise, all features of the African child-rearing style.

Hale-Benson, who is black, argues that since black children grow up in a distinct culture, they require "an educational system that recognizes their strengths, their abilities and their culture, and that incorporates them into the learning process." It all sounds reasonable.

But even if the research she urges proves her correct, prodigious problems will remain. Surely a white-dominant society (or school system) cannot be expected to shift to a teaching style that favors black children at the expense of whites. Is it possible for a teacher to employ both styles in a single classroom? Should black children—at least underachieving black children—be assigned to separate classrooms, perhaps with black teachers?

In short, is the logical outcome of her theory a return to separate-but-equal education?

39

Among Linguists, Black English Gets Respect

Rick Weiss

The heated debate over whether Ebonics should be used in the classroom comes as no surprise to sociolinguists, who study how people mold language to their needs and how language molds people's views of one another.

So crucial is a common language to people's sense of security, experts say, that the smallest difference—whether it's a foreign accent or a non-standard grammar, as occurs in Ebonics—can quickly bring to the surface deep-seated, ethnic fears.

"As soon as someone opens his mouth, we make judgments," said Stanford University linguist Merritt Ruhlen. "It's almost as visible as skin color."

Compared with skin color, language offers far more opportunities to discriminate. People speak approximately 5,000 different languages around the world, 1,000 of them in Africa alone. Countless dialects—or variants of mother tongues—enrich the linguistic spectrum further.

Yet from a linguistic point of view, linguists say, there is no such thing as a good language or a bad one. Nor are dialects subject to judgment, so long as they meet the basic requirement of having clearly defined rules. In that regard, Ebonics—which most linguists call black or African American English—passes the test.

That conclusion was formalized [the first week of January, 1997] by the executive com-

mittee of the Linguistic Society of America, which passed a resolution at the association's annual meeting in Chicago validating Ebonics as an acceptable derivation of English and supporting the Oakland school system's recently stated intention to use it to help students learn standard English.

"People used to believe that African American English was illogical, poorly constructed and inadequate for any cognitive or linguistic growth," said John R. Rickford, a Stanford University professor who serves on the society's governing board. "This is the same view we're hearing now from some white people who are upset that this should get any quarter in the schools. But while it is certainly different from standard English, it is not inferior.

"The important question is, 'Is it systematic, regular and complex insofar as it involves a vocabulary or lexicon, a phonology or sound system, and a grammar—a set of rules?'" Rickford said. Black English meets those requirements, he said, and as such it deserves respect even as students are encouraged to learn the standard English they will need to advance in American society.

The public controversy over how schools ought to deal with black English has been exacerbated, some linguists said, because some people believed that the Oakland school system was endorsing black English as a separate language. The linguistic society resolution sidestepped this question, noting the distinction between a language and a dialect is often more political than linguistic. But experts tend to agree that black English is not a language.

Language is a spoken form of communication with rules of pronunciation and grammar that make it unintelligible to people who speak only other languages. That is not the case with Ebonics. Although standard English speakers unfamiliar with Ebonics may have trouble understanding some black English words or phrases, the similarities far outweigh the differences. Speakers of standard English generally are able to understand 80 percent or more of black English, the level of intelligibility that many linguists say indicates a shared language.

Many linguists call black English an English dialect that is as unique and well-defined

---

Reprinted from *The Washington Post*, 6 January 1997, 10 (A).

as Australian English, Irish English or any of the dozens of other English dialects spoken around the world.

There are four types of dialects, said Harold C. Fleming, a retired Boston University linguist and founder of the Association for the Study of Language in Prehistory.

Regional dialects, such as American Southern English, are geographically based. Occupational dialects are pegged to jobs. (Among television news reporters, for example, "almost everyone sounds like Diane Sawyer—even the men," Fleming said).

Ideolects are personal dialects. William Buckley's hallmark English is an excellent example, Fleming said, consisting of a unique blend of mostly New England and Long Island English.

Social dialects, of which black English is representative, are specific to a cultural or social group and often a target of discrimination.

Remember the plight of Eliza Doolittle in "My Fair Lady," as the Cockney speaker struggled to say where in Spain the rain mainly falls, to break free of society's biases? "The situation with black English is so much like Cockney it's amazing," Fleming said.

George Bernard Shaw, who wrote the play "Pygmalion" upon which "My Fair Lady" was based, was well aware of how quick society is to judge people by their dialects. "It is impossible for an Englishman to open his mouth," he wrote in the introduction to Pygmalion, "without making some other Englishman despise him."

Linguists, however, say such judgments are arbitrary.

"If history had gone differently and Africans had come over and founded America and raided Europe and brought white slaves over, and this country ended up with a 10 percent white minority that was kept in ghettos and spoke white English, you'd find the same problems in reverse," Ruhlen said. "People would be saying, 'Why can't the whites learn good black English?' We spend all our time in school learning 'good' and 'bad' grammar and can't see that it's an historical accident that white English is called the best."

That doesn't mean they are equally profitable in American society, and the linguistic society resolution encourages efforts to help speakers of black English learn standard English. Ironically, several experts said, the battle to keep Ebonics out of the schools may slow that linguistic integration. Some researchers have found that classes incorporating Ebonics can help some students make the transition to standard English.

40

Our Language Needs No Law

Mark Falcoff

THE IRRATIONAL FEAR OF SPANISH

The United States, the most successful country in history, manages to be kept awake at night by imaginary perils. The latest threat to our well-being seems to be the prospect of losing our national language. Apparently you and I won't be speaking English much longer if something isn't done to prevent it.

But not to fear! Congress is riding to the rescue, with English-only legislation that would forbid the use of foreign languages on ballots and other federal documents. The House has passed a bill that would make English the official language, and Bob Dole favors the idea. The object, we are told, is to accelerate the adoption of English by immigrants and discourage the persistence of linguistic ghettos.

Though 150 or so languages are spoken in this country, the supporters of the bill aren't worried about Urdu or Mandarin. They are concerned about the 14 million people whose native language is Spanish.

The United States is one of the world's major Spanish-speaking countries. It produces some of the most important Spanish-language television and radio programs. It has a vigorous Spanish-language press, and even mainstream publishers are beginning to print Spanish-language novels, essays and other nonfiction.

Mark Falcoff is a resident scholar at the American Enterprise Institute.

Reprinted from Op-Ed section of *The New York Times*, 5 August 1966, 17 (A).

Should this worry us? House Speaker Newt Gingrich thinks so, and as an example of the perils of linguistic pluralism he cites the movement in French-speaking Quebec to secede from English-speaking Canada.

Outside of Washington, particularly in the West and Southwest, the response to the Spanish peril has bordered on the hysterical, fed by small groups of populist xenophobes. They are often driven to this position by the incendiary rhetoric of Hispanic activists who threaten to "take back" the West.

Let's look at the facts, not emotions. Most Spanish-speaking immigrants come to the United States seeking a better life, not to widen the territorial arc of their language. Most regard learning English as fundamental to economic and social advancement. The persistence of Spanish reflects not so much resistance to linguistic integration as it does the uninterrupted flow of newcomers. If there were no new immigrants from Spanish-speaking countries for 20 years, the percentage of Spanish speakers would diminish. If that is what most Americans want, let us revise the immigration laws.

Those who think English requires special protective legislation should look at what is going on in our society and elsewhere. English is the international language of finance, commerce, diplomacy, science and education, particularly higher and technical education. As the *lingua franca* of popular culture, it is spreading across the globe, particularly among young people, who consider English the key to all things modern, prosperous and hip. Why should teen-agers of Latin origin be any different?

The United States is not vulnerable to the traps of linguistic separatism exemplified by countries with more evolved bilingual cultures. Unlike Canada, Belgium or Switzerland, America has no literary intellectual class dedicated to maintaining a consistent level of quality in a second language. (Indeed, the quality of spoken Spanish in the United States is often poor; some bilingual advertisements in New York subway cars are full of grammatical howlers.)

As Hispanics integrate economically and culturally into our society, they will likely lose their linguistic distinctiveness. Though the presence of a large Spanish-speaking population is a reality, we will never become a linguistically bifurcated country.

There are many divisive forces in American society, but language is not one of them. The United States is not a Balkan principality; there is no point in it acting as if it were.

41

The Best "Jewish Mother" in the World

Perry Garfinkel

Ten-year-old Seiji Hashimoto is not doing well in school. Despite his family's high expectations, he is about to flunk out. His mother, who is particularly upset with his scholastic performance, falls ill. Seiji blames himself for his mother's sickness and redoubles his efforts at school. His grades improve, and his mother's illness suddenly disappears.

The Naganos' only son does no chores. "Why?" asks a researcher. "Because," Mrs. Nagano replies, "it would break my heart to take him away from his studies."

Except for the names, these anecdotes sound like those told by many Jewish sons and daughters. The doting Jewish mother may have finally met her match. The Japanese mother is, according to researchers in the vanguard of cross-cultural studies of scholastic effectiveness, a key factor in the Japanese education advantage. Says George De Vos, a University of California–Berkeley anthropologist who has been studying Japanese culture for 25 years, "She is the best 'Jewish mother' in the world."

Harvard University psychologist Jerome Kagan concurs with this analogy. "Until her child goes to school," says Kagan, "the Japanese mother devotes herself to the rearing of the child. In verbal and nonverbal ways, she reminds the child of her deep, deep, warm feelings and that the child is the most important thing in the world to her. Then she says, 'After all I've done for you, don't disappoint me.' She's like the Jewish mother who says,

Reprinted from *Psychology Today* 17, no. 19 (September 1983): 56–60, Sussex Publishers, Inc.

'What do you mean you're not hungry—after I've slaved all day over a hot stove for you.'"

The decline of education in the United States has been front-page news for years and may well develop into a prime political issue in the next Presidential election. To cite just one statistic, Scholastic Aptitude Test scores have fallen 49 points in verbal aptitude and 31 points in math in the past 20 years. But while politicians search for ways to redress this shortcoming and educators argue the merits of traditional versus progressive education, a few researchers are looking to the Orient for an answer, and at least one is alarmed at the East-West gap. "Americans just don't understand that they are truly behind," says Harold Stevenson, a psychologist at the University of Michigan. "You talk about Sputnik," Stevenson says, referring to the 1957 Soviet orbital launch that jolted Americans into a frenzied effort to catch up in the space race. "Well, there's a similar message in the Japanese advantage in education."

Since 1971, Stevenson has made nine trips to the Far East to determine how the Japanese and Chinese cultures have won this advantage. The answer is complex, but one factor seems paramount. "The Japanese mother is a very important influence on the education of her children," says De Vos. "She takes it upon herself to be the responsible agent, reinforcing the educational process instituted in the schools."

The most single-minded Japanese "Jewish" mother is known as *kyoiku-mama*, which translates roughly as "education-mama." She approaches the responsibility for her children's education with unrelenting fervor. She pushes her children to excel academically and sends them to ubiquitous after-school classes, known as *juku*, or to private tutors to assure good grades. Mothers are also so highly vocal in the influential Japanese PTAs that some Japanese half-jokingly suggest that the organization be renamed the MTA.

Cross-cultural research conducted by Stevenson and others during the past decade has only begun to document the education gap—particularly in the areas of science and math. For example: First and fifth-graders in the United States scored significantly lower in math achievement than Japanese or Taiwanese: 10 percent of American fifth-graders couldn't divide 42 by 6, 9 percent couldn't divide 24 by 3, and 91 percent failed to compute the perimeter of a four-sided figure. The corresponding percentages for Japanese were 6, 5, and 56; for Taiwanese they were 4, 4, and 67.

In science achievement tests, given by the International Association for the Evaluation of Educational Achievement to children in 15 industrialized countries, 10-year-old Japanese children scored 5 points and 14-year-olds 9 points above the average for all countries combined. American children at these ages achieved scores almost identical to the average.

A study comparing fifth-graders in an American Midwestern city to those in a city several hours north of Tokyo found that not one of the 20 American classrooms did as well in math as any of the Japanese classes. In other words, the average score of the highest-achieving American class was below the worst-performing Japanese class. Only one of the 100 top-scoring fifth-grade math students was American.

Two current hypotheses explaining Japanese supremacy in school math and science achievement can be dispensed with. One is that the Japanese are inherently smarter than Americans. This theory, which appeared in *Nature* (May, 1982), used national samples that were not comparable, says Stevenson, who dismisses the notion that there are any national differences in intellectual functioning. The other explanation, that the Japanese have fewer students per classroom, is inaccurate. All available data indicate that American classes are smaller.

Another factor that may warrant further study is the status of teachers in Japan and the United States. While a society's regard is not easy to quantify, starting salaries for Japanese teachers are higher than for any other government employee. And in Japan the term for teacher, *sensei*, is one of the highest forms of address that can be bestowed on a person.

How much time children spend in school is easy to quantify. Stevenson and a group from the Center for Human Growth and Development at the University of Michigan found

that Japanese children attend school on average of 240 days a year, compared to 178 for Americans. Actual instruction time is 25 percent greater in Japan. What's more, Japanese students spend more time on their homework. According to estimates Stevenson gathered from parents, Japanese first-graders put in an average of 233 minutes a week on their lesson after school, fifth-graders 368 minutes. In the United States, the times are 79 minutes and 256 minutes respectively.

Stevenson also asked American and Japanese mothers how much time someone in the family spent helping their first-graders with homework. The Japanese mothers reported an average of 24 minutes a night, the American mothers, 14.

This is only one small indication of how deeply mothers are involved in Japanese education. A more profound influence is the intensely close relationship between mother and child. She carries from generation to generation some of the most pervasive values of Japanese society: the work ethic, selflessness, and group endeavor.

"To a Japanese," points out Hideo Kojima of Nagoya University in Japan, "the training of children is not simply a technical matter but one that involves the deepest mutual and reciprocal relationships between parent and child." It's not surprising, then, that the Japanese mother, as one researcher wrote, "views her baby much more than do Western mothers as an extension of herself, and psychological boundaries between the two of them are blurred."

When it comes to disciplining her child, the Japanese mother is more inclined than the American mother to appeal to feelings as a coercive tool. Where an American mother might demand that a child stop doing something of which she disapproved, the Japanese mother is more likely simply to express displeasure. Kojima cites the "many Japanese writers (on child rearing) who recommend mildness in the direct verbal teaching of children. They say that children should be admonished in a firm but calm manner, and that adults not use abusive language or show anger and impatience. Such behavior leads children to resent and eventually disobey the urgings of the older authority . . . thus ceasing their development of wisdom and abilities."

"The Japanese," De Vos adds, "are extremely conscious in their child-rearing of a need to satisfy the feeling of dependency developed within an intense mother-child relationship in order to maintain compliance and obedience. Good will must be maintained so that the child willingly undertakes the increasingly heavy requirements and obligations placed upon him in school and at home."

Using obligation to assure compliancy, the Japanese mother sets a style that is reflected in the interdependent fabric of society as a whole. It is seen most clearly in the strong group orientation of the Japanese. They are trained to agree from a very early age. "Harmonious human relationships," Kojima writes, "may be a basic Japanese value orientation."

One further indication of this difference is that certain key Japanese values lose meaning in translation. For example, the translation of *gaman, nintai,* or *shimbo* as perseverance or forbearance fails to convey the positive sense of self-sacrifice and suffering in the words. "There is a strong positive value inherent in these terms," says Harumi Befu, a Stanford University anthropologist of Japanese background. They have the effect of exhorting the Japanese to endure experiences with a Spartan attitude.

One example of how these values are carried into the classroom is Stevenson's observation that Japanese students stay at a task longer than do Americans. In his comparative studies of first- and fifth-graders, American children were away from their desks 25 percent more than Japanese. Similarly, Japanese mothers credit "effort" as the key determinant of a child's achievement in school, says Stevenson, while American mothers name "ability" as the more important factor.

Befu describes this Japanese tendency towards perseverance as "role perfectionism," the desire to meet the precise requirements of a given role. Role perfectionism, says Befu, is one of the prime motivators of Japanese children and mothers.

If the Japanese mother-child relationship could be summarized in a word, that word would be *amae.* Again, it is a term that resists English translation, and attempts to define it get verbose. Hiroshi Azuma, professor of education at the University of Tokyo, defines it as "an attitude toward people characterized by affection, feelings of dependency, and the expectation of an emotionally satisfying response." More succinctly, *amae* is love combined with a strong sense of reciprocal obligation and dependence.

Amae is at the foundation of Japanese teaching, according to Azuma. It is the bond between mother and child, and, later, child and teacher, that makes the child "more attentive to what others say, think and feel, more willing to accept the intrusion of significant others into his or her learning, thinking, and feeling; more likely to model after them; better ready to work together; more responsive to recognition from them; and more willing to strive for a common goal."

The Japanese approach to education is not without costs. The stress suffered by students vying for coveted acceptances to universities is one of them. *Juku,* the after-hours school, is an unwanted by-product of this competition, as is the practice of lavishing gifts on teachers in an attempt to gain special attention for their children. In one city, the gift-giving escalated so sharply that the teachers themselves tried to put a stop to it.

Another drawback is the discouragement of intellectual creativity. De Vos tells of the plight of a Japanese graduate student studying in America. "He could quote everyone," De Vos says, "but when someone asked him what he thought, he went into a depression. He realized he had never asked himself that question."

This April, Japanese and American educators, psychologists, sociologists, anthropologists, and linguists met at Stanford's Center for Advanced Study in the Behavioral Sciences to discuss child development in Japan and the United States. While discussions were sometimes generalistic and unwieldy, studies in both countries seemed to zero in on correlations between the mother-child relationship and school achievement. "We're throwing seeds into the wind," said conferee Joseph Campos, a psychologist from the University of Denver, who left for the Far East following the conference to conduct cross-cultural studies on the development of emotions.

Stevenson plans a tenth trip to the Orient for follow-up studies on preschoolers. Future research should yield more definitive distinctions between American and Japanese approaches to education. For now, it appears that a "Japanese advantage" indeed exists. It may be time to ask ourselves whether the Japanese approach can be transplanted to American soil. Or, to put it another way, should we, too, become a nation of Japanese Jewish mothers?

42

Learning, Chinese-Style

Howard Gardner

For a month in the spring of 1987, my wife Ellen and I lived in the bustling eastern Chinese city of Nanjing with our 1-1/2-year-old son Benjamin while studying arts education in Chinese kindergartens and elementary schools. But one of the most telling lessons Ellen and I got in the difference between Chinese and American ideas of education came not in the classroom but in the lobby of the Jinling Hotel where we stayed in Nanjing.

The key to our room was attached to a large plastic block with the room number embossed on it. When leaving the hotel, a guest was encouraged to turn in the key, either by handing it to an attendant or by dropping it through a slot into a receptacle. Because the key slot was narrow and rectangular, the key had to be aligned carefully to fit snugly into the slot.

Benjamin loved to carry the key around, shaking it vigorously. He also liked to try to place it into the slot. Because of his tender age, lack of manual dexterity and incomplete understanding of the need to orient the key just so, he would usually fail. Benjamin was not bothered in the least. He probably got as much pleasure out of the sounds the key made as he did those few times when the key actually found its way into the slot.

Now both Ellen and I were perfectly happy to allow Benjamin to bang the key near the key slot. His exploratory behavior seemed harmless enough. But I soon observed an intriguing

Reprinted from *Psychology Today,* 23, no. 12 (December 1989): 54–56. Copyright © 1989, Sussex Publishers, Inc.

phenomenon. Any Chinese attendant nearby would come over to watch Benjamin and, noting his lack of initial success, attempt to intervene. He or she would hold onto Benjamin's hand and, gently but firmly, guide it directly toward the slot, reorient it as necessary, and help him to insert it. The "teacher" would then smile somewhat expectantly at Ellen or me, as if awaiting a thank you—and on occasion would frown slightly, as if to admonish the negligent parent.

I soon realized that this incident was directly relevant to our assigned tasks in China: to investigate the ways of early childhood education (especially in the arts), and to illuminate Chinese attitudes toward creativity. And so before long I began to incorporate this key-slot anecdote into my talks to Chinese educators.

TWO DIFFERENT WAYS TO LEARN

With a few exceptions my Chinese colleagues displayed the same attitude as the attendants at the Jinling Hotel. Since adults know how to place the key in the key slot, which is the ultimate purpose of approaching the slot, and since the toddler is neither old enough nor clever enough to realize the desired action on his own, what possible gain is achieved by having the child flail about? He may well get frustrated and angry—certainly not a desirable outcome. Why not show him what to do? He will be happy, he will learn how to accomplish the task sooner, and then he can proceed to more complex activities, like opening the door or asking for the key—both of which accomplishments can (and should) in due course be modeled for him as well.

We listened to such explanations sympathetically and explained that, first of all, we did not much care whether Benjamin succeeded in inserting the key into the slot. He was having a good time and was exploring, two activities that *did* matter to us. But the critical point was that, in the process, we were trying to teach Benjamin that one can solve a problem effectively by oneself. Such self-reliance is a principal value of child rearing in middle-class America. So long as the child is shown exactly how to do something—whether it be placing a key in a key slot, drawing a rooster or making amends for a misdeed—he is less likely to figure out himself how to accomplish such a task. And, more generally, he is less likely to view life—as Americans do—as a series of situations in which one has to learn to think for oneself, to solve problems on one's own and even to discover new problems for which creative solutions are wanted.

TEACHING BY HOLDING HIS HAND

In retrospect, it became clear to me that this incident was indeed key—and key in more than one sense. It pointed to important differences in the educational and artistic practices in our two countries.

When our well-intentioned Chinese observers came to Benjamin's rescue, they did not simply push his hand down clumsily, hesitantly or abruptly, as I might have done. Instead, they guided him with extreme facility and gentleness in precisely the desired direction. I came to realize that these Chinese were not just molding and shaping Benjamin's performance in any old manner: In the best Chinese tradition, they were *ba zhe shou jiao*— "teaching by holding his hand"—so much so that he would happily come back for more.

The idea that learning should take place by continual careful shaping and molding applies equally to the arts. Watching children at work in a classroom setting, we were stunned at their facility. Children as young as 5 or 6 were painting flowers, fish and animals with the dexterity and panache of an adult; calligraphers 9 and 10 years old were producing works that could have been displayed in a museum. In a visit to the homes of two of the young artists, we learned from their parents that they worked on perfecting their craft for several hours a day.

Interested as I was in the facility of the young artists, I wondered whether they could draw any object or only something they had been taught to portray. After all, in the practice of calligraphy, the ordinary method involves painstaking tracing of the same characters over and over. Suddenly I had a minor inspiration. I decided to ask three 10-year-olds to draw my face. The assignment at first nonplussed my three guinea pigs, but soon they undertook it with gusto, and each produced a credible job. To be sure, one picture had me looking like one of the Beatles, the second like a Chinese schoolboy, the third as Charlie's aunt is usually portrayed, but each of them bore at least a family resemblance to its subject. I had found out what I wanted: Chinese children are not simply tied to schemata; they can depart to some extent from a formula when so requested.

CREATIVITY: EVOLUTIONARY OR REVOLUTIONARY?

If I had to indicate the typical Chinese view of creativity, it would run as follows: In every realm, there are accepted means for achieving competence—prescribed and approved performances. There is really no good reason for attempting to bypass a long-established route, although a modest degree of latitude can be tolerated as the traditional form is acquired. Though the point of acquisition may never be totally reached (Zen Buddhist masters ask their charges to create the same sound or form or movement thousands of times), competent performers are sanctioned to introduce increasing departures from the approved forms. By this distinctively evolutionary path, the products of the master eventually come to be reasonably deviant from the canon. This is "approved creativity." Even so, the relationship to the canon continues to be evident, and critical discussion of an adult master may center on fruitful as opposed to idiosyncratic deviations.

While these views of the creative realm are not the modern Western ones, they seem entirely viable to me. We might contrast the Western, more "revolutionary" view, with a more "evolutionary" view espoused by the Chinese. There is a virtual reversal of priorities: the young Westerner making her boldest departures first and then gradually reintegrating herself into the tradition; and the young Chinese being almost inseparable from the tradition, but, over time, possibly evolving to a point as deviant as the one initially staked out by the innovative Westerner.

One way of summarizing the American position is to state that we value originality and independence more than the Chinese do. The contrast between our two cultures can also be conceptualized in terms of the fears we both harbor. Chinese teachers are fearful that if skills are not acquired early, they may never be acquired; there is, on the other hand, no comparable hurry to inculcate creativity. American educators fear that unless creativity has been acquired early, it may never emerge; on the other hand, skills can be picked up later.

However, I do not want to overstate my case. There is certainly creativity in China: creativity by groups, by selected individuals in the past and by numerous Chinese living in diverse societies around the world today. Indeed, as a society, China compares favorably with nearly every other in terms of the scientific, technological and aesthetic innovations that have emerged over the centuries.

There is also the risk of overdramatizing creative breakthroughs in the West. When any innovation is examined closely, its reliance on previous achievements is all too apparent (the "standing on the shoulder of giants" phenomenon). Perhaps as Claude Levi-Strauss has argued, it is misleading to speak of creativity as though it ever occurs from scratch; every symbolic breakthrough simply represents a certain combination of choices from within a particular symbolic code.

But assuming that the antithesis I have developed is valid, and that the fostering of skills and creativity are both worthwhile goals, the important question becomes this: Can we glean, from the Chinese and American extremes, a superior way to approach education, perhaps striking an optimal balance between the poles of creativity and basic skills?

43

The Roots of the Backlash Theory in Mental Health

Gerald Gregory Jackson

The cultural basis of mental health research conducted on Afro-Americans has been frequently discussed and debated.[1] Given relatively less attention in such discussions are the theoretical underpinnings of the debates and the contradictory interpretations of the assessed behaviors of Afro-Americans. For example, a number of writers have stated that much of the research involving Afro-Americans is either predicated upon or the consequence of the "deficit hypothesis." Very few, however, have provided a theoretical framework for conceptualizing a deficit hypothesis in research methodology. The application of the deficit hypothesis to research findings, therefore, is frequently an arbitrary decision.

The pitfalls of this approach to mental health research on Afro-Americans are part of the focus of this paper. In general, this paper is a step toward establishing a framework for interpreting mental health research on or about Afro-Americans. It is the corollary of earlier publications by this author on the subject of Afro-centric works in the field of mental health.[2] It is, in part, an extension of the thesis that a traditional West African cultural perspective is necessary to the understanding of contemporary Afro-American behaviors, needs, and problems.[3] It examines in greater depth the idea that the schism between Afro-American and

Reprinted from *The Journal of Black Psychology* 6, no. 1 (August 1979): 17–45, by permission of Sage Publications.

Euro-American mental health professionals is the result of their historically divergent cultures and experiences.[4] Where this paper departs appreciably from earlier works is in its focus on the theoretical base of the observable difference between Afro-American and Euro-American modes of thought.[5]

Research in cerebral dominance suggests that the dominance of one sphere is related to specific views of the universe.[6] It has also been affirmed that the behaviors of entire civilizations can be understood as a consequence of the dominance of a specific sphere of the brain.[7] Rarely, however, has the model been applied to conflicts between Afro-Americans and Euro-Americans, even though some have affirmed the possibility of this nexus.[8] Carried a step farther, it is proposed that the inclusion of the area dubbed "the psychology of consciousness"[9] will deepen our understanding of the cognitive and physiological basis of racial conflicts and serve as a source for predicting future obstacles and successes in the area of mental health research and practice. To date, there have been a number of allusions in the field of mental health to the existence of a White and Black backlash.[10] As a consequence of not postulating a theoretical base for the backlash hypothesis, works intended to introduce Afro-American culture into interpretations of child-rearing practices,[11] of adolescence[12] and adulthood,[13] of family therapy,[14] and of culturally specific counseling and psychotherapy techniques[15] have been interpreted as defensive rhetoric[16] rather than as attempts to introduce changes in the administration of mental health services to conform to the environmental and psychological circumstances of Afro-Americans.[17]

Evidence in the form of a backlash theory will serve as a reference point in explaining the increase since the 1960s in the literature on the conflicts between Afro- and Euro-American mental health professionals. A description of the White and Black backlash will consider the effect of the backlash phenomenon on the interpretation of the variable of race in the selection of therapists, research subjects, and program development. Examples will be given of its influence on mental health concepts and research trends, followed by a recommendation that the concept of diunitality be included in mental health research and practice.

THE THEORETICAL BASE OF THE BACKLASH PARADIGM

One model[18] used to explain the racial clash in the field of mental health is based upon Rapoport's[19] classification of descriptive and predictive models. According to Berry, "The descriptive model is an empirical description of extant relationships and is employed to gain insight into multiple relationships among sets of data. The predictive model, on the other hand, employs some empirical description to predict other empirical relations and approximates the traditional use of the hypothesis."[20] Consistent with the diunital approach advanced by Dixon and Foster,[21] the model used in this instance is both descriptive and predictive; that is, the backlash formulation is established upon known relationships, and on this basis behavioral consequences are predicted.

Cobbs termed the "White backlash" the climate of retaliation.[22] It is predicated, he observed, on Afro-American assertiveness during the 1960s. For example, Comer cited a number of responses to Afro-American assertion in the field of mental health that will be seen as variants of a White backlash.[23] He indicated that a number of researchers viewed the charges against Euro-American researchers in the Afro-American community as unjust and as part of a scheme by avaricious Afro-Americans to gain control of research and intervention program money. He thought that other individuals viewed the negative attitude toward testing and research as an understandable but excessive and self-defeating reaction to the historical Black-White relationship. Still other individuals acknowledged that the response of the Afro-American community was healthy, and in some cases just, but one that would pass in time as the members of the community gained more success in all phases of American life. In contrast, Cobbs affirmed that psychiatrists and other professionals deny their culpability in the existence of White racism by assuming that they are exempt.[24] In his opinion, though, it is precisely because so many rationalize their "exempt" role that the

climate of reprisal is present in the United States today. Comer attempted to provide some insight into the "Black backlash."[25] Its justification, he stated, lay in the failure of traditional researchers to go beyond the deficit hypothesis or to press for societal changes based upon the implications of their research.

The assessments by Cobbs and Comer overlooked the possibility that the basis of the differences in these perspectives is the divergent cultures of Afro- and Euro-Americans. The racial climate today is not appreciably different from that of the past; contemporary race relations in the United States only appear to be different. During the 1960s, Afro-Americans, to a more noticeable degree, divested themselves of their appearance of acquiescence and vocalized their dissatisfaction with the functioning of most institutions in America, particularly mental health ones. The resultant "climate of retaliation" that was suggested by Cobbs as a new conceptual development may be understood as merely a cultural system's attempt to maintain its integrity against a different type of intellectual structure.[26] This idea can be amplified through a sociogenic and psychogenic perspective of Afro- and Euro-American differences.

The Sociogenic Approach

Weaver conceptualized cultural systems as abstractive and associative.[27] Although his theory is incomplete in terms of the role of economics and the physical environment in the creation of cultural enclaves,[28] it does provide one broad framework for comprehending how Afro- and Euro-Americans may idiosyncratically perceive reality, and it highlights the difference between a reliance upon the left versus the right hemispheres of the brain. In Weaver's view, an abstractive culture would have certain characteristic ingredients. First, the language used is technical and provides a common means for performing tasks without considering who said what to whom. Such a language is easily written, but conveys little feeling because it is the message, not the communicator, that is important. Abstractive societies are typically large and technologically complex systems; individual differences, or subgroup differences, are leveled to provide a common mode of communication. In general, this form of society is composed of groups of people who do not know each other well enough to trust one another spontaneously. As a consequence, what a person is becomes irrelevant to the system because only what a person does is important. In the final analysis, "the abstractive society is very logical, achievement oriented and humane, but it also leads to alienation, lack of whole self-identity, a schizoid personality and, consequently, is very inhuman."[29] Ironically, this form of society is more humane because it is less in-group oriented than what will be defined as an associative culture. However, this less rigid frame of reference also contributes to an inability to grant the wholeness of people and to take note of such supposedly irrelevant criteria as ethnic identity, personal feelings, and individual thoughts.[30]

In contrast, the language used in the associative culture is the by-product of a much smaller society or of one composed of small, intimate groups who share kindred experiences. The language in its spoken form, according to Weaver, is more sophisticated than the standard language of the abstractive culture. In the same vein, it is seldom written, a quality that apparently encourages the exchange of information through dyadic communication. In this process, communicators share more than words; they share also their physical presence. Body language and tone of voice become interrelated parts of a whole exchange. An element that reinforces the language pattern is the structure of the society. As implied earlier, it is a homogeneous community, or one where everyone shares the same childhood experiences, values, and perceptions. In such a milieu, written rules become less essential because there exists a commonality of experience among all members, and one can therefore infer the behavior of others from one's own behavior. In comparison with an abstractive culture, the community of the associative culture is more human because it gives a sense of spontaneity, predictability, in-group identity, wholeness, and belonging; however, it is more inhumane and can even be turned into a fascistic political order because it

excludes outsiders and is often very rigid, ascriptive, and illogical (behavior is determined by custom rather than reason, and numerous implicit factors are associated with specific behavior).

In partial support of Weaver's conceptualization, research has found that groups of Afro-American children, compared with Euro-Americans, are more cooperative than competitive,[31] and that the extended family structure is more viable for Afro-Americans than for Euro-Americans.[32] This same family has been found to be more social than its Euro-American counterpart,[33] and as a community, Afro-Americans have been found to be more involved in social action groups than have other visible minorities.[34] The "affective" or "feeling" approach to life is nurtured by the Afro-American family. This approach not only reinforces a positive attitude towards others,[35] but emphasizes an affective symbolic imagery mode of thought process,[36] frequently interpreted as an intuitive mode.[37]

In summary, although the sociogenic approach is helpful in broadly defining differences between Afro- and Euro-Americans, it provides little insight into the role of the "brain" in guiding the actions of individuals. Hall felt that "the manner in which people are sensorially involved and how they conceptualize the use of time, determines not only at what point they are crowded but the methods of relieving crowding as well."[38] He classified Afro-Americans as "high contact" people and observed that such people required higher densities than low contact people and may require more protection or screening from outsiders.[39] Relative to this, he hypothesized that "low contact" people adhered to a monochronic time system, wherein time is compartmentalized and one thing is scheduled at a time, whereas high contact people are polychronic and, as a consequence, keep several operations going at once. Monochronic people become disoriented when faced with competing activities and often, therefore, find it easier to function if they can separate activities in space, whereas their counterparts tend to collect activities.

As an impetus, then, the notion of time as a variable, coupled with Mbiti's description of how Africans viewed time[40] and Ornstein's treatise on the mediation of the brain in the experience of temporality,[41] pointed to the need to incorporate a psychogenic approach into the study of the backlash phenomenon.

The Psychogenic Approach

The other support for Weaver's thesis can be seen through a psychogenic perspective in general, and the inventive and innovative components of Black psychology in particular.[42] For example, Nichols termed what Weaver called the abstractive culture "the Euro" approach.[43] In his estimation, the latter emphasizes a cognitive approach to life, is a man-to-object orientation, and is individually focused, whereas the "Afro" approach is affective, man-to-man, and group focused. Nichols asserted that adherents of the Euro-approach code events more easily when they can be counted and quantitatively measured. Events that cannot be interpreted according to this rule, he reasoned, would be seen as being in opposition to reality, and therefore viewed less favorably. From another point of view, it has been observed that a human being is distinct from other forms of life in that he is not born with an innate prescription of reality[44] or, as Gorman and Wessman observed:

> Compared with other animals, humans live not merely in a broader "reality" but in a new and transformed dimension of "reality." Rather than fairly direct, automatic and immediate responses to external stimuli, there are delays and interruptions through central cognitive processing involving complex and flexible systems of symbolic representation and meaning. Humans do not exist simply in a physical world; they experience and inhabit a symbolically transformed universe. The implication of these ideas is that there is not a single objective reality and a uniform, universal temporality. [45]

Benedict asserted that no definable human group could place equal emphasis on contrary forms of reality,[46] and she suggested, therefore, that different cultural groups will select one or more aspects to the exclusion of others.[47] What can be deduced from this para-

dox is that while man's sense organs play a critical part in determining reality, the specific interpretation made of it is also based upon his culturally grounded perceptual sets.[48] As one empirical base for this supposition, research and expositions on the psychology of consciousness[49] shed some light on the psychological origin of group differences in the interpretation of mental health research and practice, and illuminate the need to examine traditional West African society more closely.[50] To elaborate, the "psyche" of the Western world has been suggested as being dominated by the left hemisphere of the brain,[51] and this mode coincides with Weaver's description of the abstractive culture. Accordingly, it has been reported that the left hemisphere is (a) rational or takes information bit by bit and processes it in a linear, logical manner; (b) verbal and carries on mathematical reasoning; (c) accessible to scientific investigation; (d) aggressive; and (e) troubled by the process of associating names with faces.[52] In contrast, the right hemisphere has been said to represent the mental life of the Eastern world and has been characterized as (a) intuitive and abstractive; (b) nonverbal and creative; (c) less accessible to scientific investigation; (d) passive; and (e) not troubled by the process of associating names with faces. What this line of research has not explicitly noted is that the characteristic division of "consciousness" into dichotomous poles and the negative interpretation of right hemisphere functions stem from a decidedly Western (left hemisphere) mode of reasoning.[53] This is the seedbed of many mental health conflicts and of the inability to conceptualize a third view of the area of cerebral dominance in cultural orientation.[54]

Suggestive of this third line of inquiry into cerebral functioning and Afro-American culture, Toldson and Pasteur stated:

> The Western world is horribly uncomfortable with the expression of feeling or affective energy. Accordingly, its constituents and advocates have sought to suppress those aspects of the human personality that are emotional, intuitive, creative, holistic, meditative, instinctual, and sensuous and to elevate those aspects that are logical, analytical, sequential, propo-

sitional, causal, or, collectively, cognitive. The oneness of being concept in the African way of life promotes the elevation of the total person or all that of which a human is capable. Moreover, the expression of emotional energy is the cornerstone to achieving and sustaining optimal mental health. Such expressions free the soul, render the heart and mind accessible to new learning experiences, and exalt humanness.[55]

Confirming Toldson and Pasteur's portrayal of Western thought, Bateson observed:

> We as Westerners, think in transitive terms, something acts on, or is like, something else. These are only parts of a whole system. But our language and so our thinking only lets us construct it in a lineal fashion, and not as a whole circuit. ... The Western world begins by making splits, then drawing boundaries, then solidifying those boundaries. Then we fool ourselves into believing what we have made ourselves see. Solidifying boundaries is very comfortable, because it allows us to deny our experience.[56]

Consistent with the hypothesis of a Western reliance upon left hemispheric thought, Americans have been reported to honor and elevate "rational" thought, a linear-progressive concept of time, verbal and mathematical skills, and individualistic and competitive behavior, or in summary, a nuclear family model.[57] Many research studies give evidence that Afro-Americans are viewed in the United States as genetically inferior, superstitious, lazy, happy-go-lucky, ignorant, musical, very religious, stupid, physically dirty, naive, and criminal,[58] or the opposite of Euro-Americans, who are portrayed as intelligent, virtuous, sexually controlled, rational, ambitious, and law-abiding.[59] What, therefore, is typically seen as racial differences may be the interpretation of behaviors by the left hemisphere of the brain.[60] Hunt's typology of racial perspectives suggests a different way of viewing the operation of the human brain.[61] The White perspective is characterized by an elevation of the cognitive and a subordination of the affective, whereas the Black perspective entails neither the elevation of the cognitive nor the affective. Hunt views

the Black perspective as allowing one or the other domain to take primacy depending upon the situation. This view is similar to Dixon's construct of the affective-symbolic imagery mode of thought that explains the way Afro-Americans conceptualize reality.[62] To fathom, however, the emergence of an Afro-American psyche and the implications of this unique mode of thought for mental health research and treatment, one may have to include an African referent. For example, Senghor advanced the idea that the African impulse is not to dominate the object through its dissection and analysis by "discursive" reason but to install itself in an intuitive manner through emotion.[63] Conceptually, his definition of an African ethos is akin to Weaver's description of an associative culture and symbolizes current descriptions of the manner in which Afro-Americans process information.[64] As a corollary, Senghor hoped to create a new humanism that combined European rationality with African intuitiveness,[65] or (as Tempels noted in 1945) the African had a direct, intuitive, harmonious relation to life and the cosmos that was different from the cold conceptual logic of European civilization.[66] His hope has been partially fulfilled in the development of an Afro-American "psyche"[67] and is typified in Dixon and Foster's concept of diunitality.[68] According to the authors, the concept was advanced as a means of ameliorating racial polarization and conflicts in America. In their review of previous research on the subject of race relations, for example, they found an implicit assumption in such works that "everything falls into one category at the same time."[69] As a result of this philosophical orientation, they concluded, it is generally believed that Afro-Americans represent one exclusive racial cultural category and Euro-Americans another, and the inference drawn is that they are "mutually exclusive, contradictory and antagonistic."[70] As a paradigmatic alternative, they suggested the use of the diunital approach, i.e., the idea of a harmonious uniting of "opposites." They proposed that since the original cultures of Afro- and Euro-Americans have been influenced by one another, in reality neither group is totally free to perceive itself as all African or European. They speculated that the state of diunitality would be attained when "black and white Americans accept the contradictions endemic in their cultural environments as mutually rewarding and mutually relevant."[71] Critics, however, have charged that the concept is not a panacea because of the imbalance in the distribution of power between Afro- and Euro-Americans.[72] The barrier, it is affirmed, is not that the imbalance in power or that the concept is illogical (based upon Plato's concept of one);[73] the barrier is the absence of a presentation of an alternative system of thought. To illustrate, many years ago, Whorf advanced the hypothesis that language determines behavior and that Indo-European languages represented only one set of perceptions of reality.[74] He even postulated that Indo-European languages may actually hamper a clear perception of what actually occurs in the universe. In his words, and in line with Bateson's criticism of the manner in which Americans have become accustomed to reasoning, Whorf stated:

> The metaphysics underlying our own language, thinking and modern culture (I speak not of the recent and quite different relativity metaphysics of modern science) imposes upon the universe two grand COSMIC FORMS, space and time; static three-dimensional infinite space, and kinetic one-dimensional uniformity and perpetually, flowing time—two utterly separate and unconnected aspects of reality (according to this familiar way of thinking). The flowing realm of time is, in turn, the subject of a threefold division: past, present, and future.[75]

One example of a limitation resulting from the structure of Indo-European languages, and one that is germane to research on Afro-Americans, is the use of the constant, "the sum of causality," approach in research. Conceptually, Caplan and Nelson noted a heavy reliance on this approach in psychological research and pointed out that "in its most extreme form, this model would assume that person-centered and situational-centered factors are dichotomous and mutually exclusive (i.e., if one type of factor is shown to be causally operative, it is assumed that the other type of factor does not operate at all)."[76] They re-

ported that the chief focus of interest for psychologists, especially when dealing with real world problems, is on person-centered variables. What is particularly relevant here is Caplan and Nelson's study of the 1970 *Psychological Abstracts* on research dealing with Afro-Americans, who, they noted, "represent the largest, most visible, and most frequently studied group in a problematic relationship to the rest of society."[77] They found that psychologists had invested a disproportionate amount of time, funds, and energy in studies that lent themselves to interpreting the difficulties of Afro-Americans in terms of personal shortcomings, had overlooked the importance of other kinds of forces that operate on Afro-Americans, and had thereby reinforced the negative labeling of a group already politically and socially vulnerable.

BEYOND THE BLACK BACKLASH

Shifting from a reliance upon a deficit hypothesis, it will be shown, is more more complex than the Black backlash pattern of reacting to Euro-American scholarship would suggest. A major reason for the inertia in this realm is that what Afro-Americans are really demanding is a movement away from a Euro-American cultural approach, or specifically, a competitive economic system, reductionistic reasoning (e.g., social class vs. race), linear progressive view of time (e.g., future vs. past), nuclear family model and a constricted expression of emotions (e.g., predictable vs. spontaneous behavior), and language.[78] This different approach between Euro- and Afro-Americans to the concept of family, time, behavior, and social institutions has also been suggested by G. Jackson.[79] What needs to be reiterated, however, is the link between the concept of diunitality as a racial perspective and African languages and notions of "science." Wobogo reported a number of African terms that reflect the concept of diunitality.[80] For example, "Anokwalei Enyo" means "Two relative truths," and it is used to define "the components of duality in a manner which stresses their interrelationship without implying whether that relationship is harmonious or antagonistic."[81] In his words, "The word opposite derives from oppose! As such it is biased because it emphasizes conflict to the exclusion of other modes of interaction. Anokwalei Enyo expresses the association of two entities whose interaction mode can be cooperative, antagonistic or neutral. Only an analysis can determine which is true, even in a potential sense."[82]

Determining the truth in mental health research is the focus of the following discussion. Before beginning this discussion, it may be beneficial to recapitulate the overt workings of the White and the Black backlash and to indicate their possible origin in right and left hemispheric modes of thought. In this regard, Comer reported that Afro-Americans did not view traditional approaches to research as helpful and that their concerns were interpreted as a screen to control the conduct of research in Afro-American communities. As a rationale for their response it was suggested that Afro-Americans merely wanted to gain access to research monies. Such an interpretation is valid within a hedonistic and competitive view of society; however, it collides with the African concept of the group and care syndrome.[83] Similarly, Comer revealed that Afro-American concerns over testing were viewed as stemming from a preoccupation with race relations. This reductionistic view of the subject is consistent with the use of logical positivism as a mode of thought, but overlooks a perspective that conceptualizes intelligence in nonquantitative and moral terms,[84] and a perspective that incorporates a view of the past use of assessment instruments on Afro-Americans into its reasoning pattern. This kind of historical view is in contrast to the traditional cultural approach of Americans to history. In the words of Hall:

> The American's view of the future is linked to a view of the past, for tradition plays an equally limited part in American culture. As a whole, we push it aside or leave it to a few souls who are interested in the past for very special reasons. . . .[85]

Relative to this point of view, the idea that the reaction of Afro-Americans will change as they gain more success in American society is based also on a culturally biased view of time. In this instance, it is the notion that time is linear, and that Afro-Americans, being akin to immigrants, will eventually make progress. This point of view, however, does not dovetail with the perennial concerns of Afro-Americans,[86] and negates other meaningful perceptions of time. A time frame that has greater explanatory power for an interpretation of the Afro-American experience is the African view of time as spiral.[87] Such a time frame reflects the barriers Afro-Americans encounter in the form of institutional and individual racism.

What remains at this juncture is to give evidence of the operations of the backlash phenomenon and to show how it correlates with the theoretical postulates on the psychology of consciousness and Black psychology.

THE CULTURAL BIAS OF PROFESSIONAL LITERATURE REVIEWS

The relevance of the race of the professional person in assisting Afro-American clients is ingrained in the annals of the mental health movement in the United States. As early as 1919 Jones advocated the employment of Afro-American welfare workers in large industrial plants, and Atwell, a year later, asserted that they should be used to deal with Afro-American groups.[88] Indicative of the depth of concern surrounding this issue, during the 1940s a number of papers were published that either centered on the issue of the race of the professionals who deal with Afro-American clients[89] or that gave at least partial attention to this matter.[90] A more important source of insight into the workings of distinct cultures and modes of thought is the articles that reviewed the literature on the factor of race in therapeutic relationships. They came into prominence during the early part of the 1970s and reflect, to a degree, the maturity of the mental health professions and the assertiveness of the Afro-American community during the 1960s. The most frequently cited reference in this category is a review by Sattler, who concluded from his research that a more positive outcome appeared to result from racially congruent relationships.[91] Of note was his recommendation that future studies should be more experimentally rigorous with the variable of race. A year later, Gardner published a review of "The Therapeutic Relationship under Varying Conditions of Race."[92] Differing somewhat from Sattler, Gardner ended his account with this statement: "Once these barriers to effective psychotherapy have been dealt with and overcome, the contents and efficacy of therapeutic communication should differ in no important way from that which characterizes psychotherapy where issues of race do not exist."[93] In contrast, McGrew asserted that Afro-American clients should have Afro-American counselors[94] and G. Banks added that it was important for an Afro-American professional to work with Afro-American clients because it conveyed to the group that its members are desirous of helping one another.[95] On the other hand, Mizio concluded, from her review of the literature on the "White worker and minority client," that special training could help compensate for differences between worker and client.[96] Similarly, Kadushin attempted to level out the variable of race with the conclusion from his review that discussions in racial terms dichotomized a variegated situation. Illustrative of his own encapsulation in a dichotomous mode of thought, however, he pointed out that "interview interaction with a lower-class black male militant is quite different from interview interaction with a middle-class female black integrationist";[97] and elsewhere he stated that ". . . although race is important, the nature of the interpersonal relationship established between two people is more important than skin color, and although there are disadvantages to racially mixed worker-client contacts, there are special advantages."[98] Sager, Brayboy, and Waxenburg concluded also that a White therapist could assist a Black client. They added, however, that "It is clear that the alleviation of the mental ills of a population rests first on the remedying of the social ills of the nation. Similarly, the treatment of the psychic pains of an individual or family cannot be divorced from treatment of the conditions in which they live."[99] In another review on the same subject, J. Jackson expanded upon the role of the Euro-American psychiatrist with Afro-American clients. In her estimation, "some can function in 'stop-gap' roles; others can function adequately where both the psychiatrist and the patient can handle adequately race issues; still others can function indirectly by enlarging the goal of black clinicians. All can help stop racial oppression, thereby reducing black mental illnesses directly attributable to race."[100]

Since 1972, review articles have exemplified not only ideological differences but the inappropriateness of a Western or linear concept of time. A linear progressive model of time would suggest that the review articles would advance thinking on the subject. However, in going with an African concept of spiral time, A. Jackson published a review article that is comparable in content to the review by Gardner.[101] Denmark and Trachtman published a review with an assertion parallel to that of Banks,[102] and Carkhuff published one with a conclusion similar to Kadushin's.[103] Jerome Siegel published a review in which he supposedly found little clear information on the primary relevance of race and suggested, as Sattler declared four years earlier, that more research needed to be conducted.[104] In the same vein, Higgins and Warner concluded from their review that race was not paramount;[105] however, Harrison conducted a review of similar research and echoed sentiments in his conclusion that are similar to those of Banks.[106] The crux of the debate is revealed in the concluding remarks of an overview of the same literature by Bryson and Bardo, who wrote:

> The general conclusion seems to be that although counselor race as a single variable is insufficient qualification for predicting effectiveness, it is a factor that must be considered. Consequently, it is imperative that those involved in training counselors or others in helping roles design and implement programs that will correct or modify the negative aspects of counselors' attitudes and behaviors.[107]

The debate outlined above, it should be stressed, was never really over skin color per se but the ramification of skin color in the United States. For instance, research has found that skin color connotes differences in ability and behavior.[108] To counteract, therefore, the negative appraisal given to Afro-American attributes, the doctrine of color-blindness emerged; however, since it rested upon a system of thought that dichotomizes, it, too, it will be seen, is a form of the White backlash.

THE BACKLASH THEORY APPLIED TO THE DOCTRINE OF COLOR-BLINDNESS

Seward cautioned researchers against judging Afro-Americans by Euro-American norms and asserted that "color is inherent in the concept of self."[109] Similarly, Adams wrote: "Were it not for distinctions based upon color, Whites and Negroes of the same class would find that their modes of living and thinking and acting were very similar, and that they possessed much more in common than one of their own race far removed in the social scale."[110] Rather than deal with the variable of race, Wylie in a subsequent review and evaluation of research in the area of self-concept omitted studies focusing on race,[111] and Edwards in a study of the relevance of the variable in personality research purportedly found that it was irrelevant.[112] In contrast, had certain investigators included the factor of racial perspective, they might have discovered among Afro-Americans the cultural link to an African identity that Noble's discussion of self-concept research articulated.[113] Such an analysis could have provided one basis for a consideration of why some research suggests that Afro-Americans interpret the concept of being "Black" in a more positive light,[114] that is, a sense of self jointly derived from the dominant culture and the embedded Afro-American subculture.[115]

The doctrine of color-blindness, or the notion that a failure to acknowledge skin color is the best approach to the delivery of mental health services,[116] a derivative of the melting pot concept, has had a detrimental impact on epidemiological and clinical research on the race of the therapist and of the client. Epidemiological research is the foundation for clarifying the need for, and the planning of, treatment and prevention programs.[117] Yet, the prevalence of the doctrine of color-blindness

has accounted for the paucity of epidemiological investigations that take into account the variable of race.[118] Though it is not obvious to some, a number of flaws are inherent in an approach of this kind to the delivery of mental health services, and these faults partially confirm the validity of the backlash model. Crawford attributed his failure in answering questions regarding the prevalence and incidence of mental illness in Afro-Americans to the failure of professionals to collect the necessary data.[119] Within the many epidemiological studies published,[120] Fischer has detected methodological errors that are consistent with a Euro-American cultural orientation.[121] The implications of his findings are clear. It has been charged that such errors in epidemiological research are the consequence of institutional racism and that psychiatrists pay greater attention to extending mythical definitions of Afro-American psychopathology than to providing psychiatric services for actual Afro-American clients.[122] This is accomplished by defining certain behaviors as criminal in Afro-Americans, but as sickness in Euro-Americans, and by defining Afro-Americans as untreatable.[123] Even when services are delivered, an ignorance of the factor of race in research on effectiveness leaves similar questions unanswered. Yamamato, James, and Palley found a substantial body of literature on the general problems of meeting the expectations of the lower-class client.[124] However, none of the data discussed the racial groups among the lower class, and there is evidence of a difference.[125] The critical point is made more forcefully by Krebs, who reported that if race had not been included in an examination based upon class, the manifestations that he found of inadequate treatment of Afro-American clients in comparison with Euro-American clients would have been overlooked.[126] Darryl Smith found that White students in general viewed the variable of race as relatively trivial, but that minority group members in his study ascribed importance to the factor of racial similarity in the relationship between the professional and client.[127]

THE BACKLASH THEORY APPLIED TO THE CONCEPT OF SOCIAL CLASS

Consistent with the backlash theory in general, Lorion conducted a review of the literature on the lower-class client in therapy, but gave only minor attention to minority groups.[128] To him, the problem was a matter of reintroducing the reader to the plight of low-income patients seeking mental health treatment; however, according to the backlash theory, his study may be considered as an offshoot of the doctrine of color-blindness and a propensity to dichotomize the variable of social class and race. The "blindness" aspect of his study is illustrated in the history of studies that suggested a similar class interpretation of the factor of race. In 1945 Myra Stevens credited Afro-American professionals with a comparatively greater ability to establish rapport with Afro-American clients and implied, therefore, a cultural bond between them.[129] She did not, however, stop at this point. Negating her initial credit, she subsequently added that the Afro-American professionals, nevertheless, experienced resistance like that of their Euro-American colleagues although the problems that Afro-Americans experienced were related to class distinctions and frictions within the race. The net result of her reasoning was the establishment of social class as a more salient variable than subculture in such interactions, and a reversal in the etiology of the problem Afro-Americans encounter in gaining assistance. In a slightly different vein, Kahn, Buchmueller, and Gildea conducted a case study of the variable of race and concluded that it was unimportant in the conduct of therapy.[130] They had found that an Afro-American female social worker, who had subsequently replaced a Euro-American in an Afro-American school, was not more successful in employing techniques found suitable in Euro-American schools. Thematically, those publications that allegedly demonstrated that a Euro-American professional could successfully treat an Afro-American client[131] can be interpreted as a part of the thrust to downplay factors attendant to race in the United States. For example, in a study of why Afro-Americans were not included in clinical studies, Weiss and Kupfer reported that Afro-American culture and racial stereotypes governed the rejection of Afro-American clients, and they argued that Afro-Americans should be included to insure the representativeness of clinical theories and practices.[132] Despite their recommendations, the backlash type of research has continued to the present. The race of the professional is still shown not to be a primary determinant of successful counseling or psychotherapy.[133] There have also been studies that suggest that the race of the psychometrist is inconsequential in explaining why Afro-Americans, as a whole, tend to score lower on intelligence tests than Euro-Americans.[134] With reference to the backlash theory, both kinds of investigations can be interpreted as a reaction to the proliferation of articles during this period that focused exclusively on the problems of Euro-American professionals in assisting Afro-American clients[135] or as a response to the assertion that even an untrained Afro-American was more competent than a trained Euro-American professional in counseling or psychotherapy with Afro-American clients.[136] In short, the doctrine of color-blindness is an analogue to what Slater defined as the "toilet assumption," a notion that he advanced to explain the relationship between technological advancement in America and its pattern of thought. The idea is that "unwanted matter, unwanted difficulties, unwanted complexities and obstacles will disappear if they are removed from our immediate field of vision."[137] It is a by-product of affluence, and as an American characteristic pattern of thought, Slater asserted, it guided efforts to remove the underlying problems of society further and further from daily experience and daily consciousness. In the end, he observed, among the masses it decreased the knowledge, skill, resources, and motivation necessary to deal with profound matters. For example, the subtle aspect of this relationship is exemplified in a study of the "radical therapy" movement. Talbott reported that its advocates criticized traditionalists for serving only White, middle-class clients, but that their own primary organ of communication revealed that radical therapists treated "White" middle-class dropouts in free clinics.[138] He found little in their journal about treating the poor, the working class, or the Afro-Americans, and little concerning methods for coping with obstructive bureaucracies. In general, he found little information on providing services to the non-middle-class, non-White, non-rebelling population, and this practice is allowed to continue because of the polemic over the variable of race in research.

THE BACKLASH THEORY APPLIED TO CLINICAL RESEARCH

Another way of presenting the backlash theory is through a study of the factors in clinical research that are frequently overlooked. First, it has been indicated in clinical reports that the presence of Afro-American staff members is a crucial determinant of the successful outcome of a therapeutic relationship between Afro-American clients and Euro-American professionals.[139] Second, it has been pointed out that the nature of the problem (i.e., practical task vs. personal problem), in contrast to the diagnostic label placed on the client, can determine whether a Euro-American professional will be able to assist an Afro-American client.[140] Third, a low rate of utilization of the facility has been acknowledged as an indication of the effectiveness of the treatment administered as well as the length of time Afro-Americans continue in therapy.[141] Fourth, the presumption of skin color differences (Black vs. White) as the sole variable to control for in such investigations, or the addition of socioeconomic class, defies the findings of intragroup differences based upon racial self-designation,[142] obviates the finding that traditional indices of social position are inapplicable in judging Afro-American social-class standing,[143] and incorrectly presumes that the traditional indices of scientific inquiry are applicable when there is sound empirical and theoretical evidence to the contrary.[144] Fifth, most studies do not manipulate the variable of therapeutic modality used even though a number of writers have made the point that the use of culturally specific techniques is imperative with Afro-American clients.[145] Sixth, most studies do not control for the influence of training and the Afro-American experience on the effectiveness of the Afro-American professional, variables which are cited as causing their failure to func-

tion maximally with Afro-American clients.[146] In short, these reproofs patently overlook the more philosophical questions of whether Afro-American clients view the delivery of mental health services and the role of subjects in experiments in ways similar to Euro-Americans.[147]

Carried a step farther, one does not have to use skin color in order to deny Afro-Americans mental health services. In this regard, Vontress noted that while color of skin, curl of hair, and slave heritage could be seen as serving within American society as primary exclusionary variables, they could also be seen as stimulating the development of secondary exclusionary variables.[148] In his view, the secondary exclusionary variables would be differences in language, values, education, income, housing, and culture in general. Within the framework of his theory, it was hypothesized that these secondary exclusionary factors would be the rationalizations given by individuals for conforming to the practices established to exclude Afro-Americans from the benefits of American society, including such human services as those offered by the mental health professions. To elaborate, in a case study designed to show how psychologists can assist in legal problems, it showed how the psychologist was instrumental in disproving the charge that school systems were employing tests to bar or minimize the number of Afro-American students entering selective schools in Boston.[149] In such a situation, the professional is less apt to be condemned for excluding persons for this secondary reason than for excluding persons because of skin color. Relatedly, research conducted on the relationship between Afro-Americans and the law enforcement system in the United States is another example of the use of the White backlash strategy in research. In one study, it was reported that the common complaint of gross and widespread discrimination in their practices did not hold up,[150] and in another that the police are no more prejudiced against Afro-Americans than the average American.[151] These interpretations not only conflict with other opinions on the same subject,[152] but they also are in contrast to empirical evidence.[153] Yet they illustrate the erroneous conclusions that can result when the attitude of Afro-Americans toward their "Blackness" is omitted from examination.[154] Dillingham, for example, in studying the attitudes of Afro-Americans toward the courts and the police, found that the Black-consciousness, defined in terms of preference to be termed "Black or Afro-American" rather than "colored or Negro," was a more salient factor than either sex or education in determining the individual's attitude about treatment within the criminal justice system.[155] He pointed out that the factors of alienation and Black consciousness, omitted in previous studies, proved to be two of the most important factors in shaping the attitudes and beliefs of Afro-Americans.

The pivotal source of the problem is the use of a dichotomous as opposed to a diunital approach because, in a system that has relied upon the former approach, a pro-Afro-American finding is conceptualized as being implicitly and explicitly anti-Euro-American. In support of this contention, in response to a report of a study that found that Afro-American children had an increase in their self-concept,[156] the suggestion was made that it would be interesting to learn if such children also had an increase in their anti-White feelings.[157] Although research has shown that this concern is unfounded,[158] the only genuine means of discounting such ideas theoretically is via the use of the diunital concept. Anything short of this fundamental step of analysis results in various reassertions, rebuttals, or collectively, a backlash. It should be added that implicit in the diunital interpretation of Euro-American culture as a source of values is equal consideration of the ethos of traditional West African society.[159] The concept of "oneness," for example, not only antedates the current notion of holistic health; it gives substance to the actions of Afro-Americans on behalf of the Afro-American community and provides a conceptual base for contemporary expositions on the Afro-American family, the church, and the approach to mental health problems.[160] For example, the ideal client in a Euro-American cultural system, in contrast to the Afro-American perspective,[161] is pictured as one who relies upon thinking rather than feeling and who is introspective, verbal, and relatively successful economically. In this regard, Kennedy suggested than an Afro-American client may not achieve total success because the ego ideal in treatment was "White,"[162] whereas Cross postulated that the highest level of Afro-American self-actualization entailed an identification with Afro-Americans.[163] Furthermore, a study on schizophrenia among Afro-Americans found that the key difference between schizophrenics and non-schizophrenics with comparable economic backgrounds was the former's identification with "White" society.[164]

Time, in this Western philosophical frame, is interpreted as something that has to be compartmentalized, and clients therefore are expected to present their problems at some arbitrarily established point and place and to restrict the expression of their concerns to this contrived time and place.[165] Relatedly, the propensity toward the cognitive over the affective functioning is an integral part of the criteria for acceptance into, and success in, graduate and professional training. Pinderhughes, for example, charged that this process is based upon academic grades and test scores rather than humanitarian services, and may be one reason why training programs have resisted requests to recruit and graduate more Afro-American professionals.[166] To those professionals who undertake careers at such institutions, the option is given either to conform to traditional standards of performance or be denied recognition, advancement, and tenure.[167] Coincidentally, curricula have continued to reflect little of the Afro-American experience, and training sites continue to remain in Euro-American middle-class settings.[168] Reinforcing the errors of training institutions, professional associations have neither elevated Afro-American professionals to influential positions nor responded to their requests for attention and change. A further insurance of professional impotence consists of the fact that funding sources for the control of research support for the study of Afro-Americans have remained in Euro-American control.[169]

In short, a key to an alternative to the backlash phenomenon is the concept of diunitality. It suggests that such concepts as time, aesthetics, and race could be viewed as possessing both positive and negative valences, rather than as constituting dichotomous poles.

It would seem, therefore, that the use of the concept would not only enhance mental health services to Afro-Americans but would also provide a more universal framework from which to establish research models and practices.[170]

ENDNOTES

[1]G. G. Jackson, "Cultural Seedbeds of the Black Backlash in Mental Health," *Journal of Afro-American Issues*, 4 (1), 1976: 70–91.

[2]G. G. Jackson, "The African Genesis of the Black Perspective in Helping," *Professional Psychology*, 7 (3), 1976: 363–367; "The Emergence of a Black Perspective in Counseling," *Journal of Negro Education*, 46 (3), 1977: 230–253; "Community Mental Health, Behavior Therapy and the Afro-American Community," *Research in Education* (ERIC Document Reproduction Service No. ED 159 501), February 1979.

[3]G. G. Jackson, "The African Genesis of the Black Perspective in Helping."

[4]G. G. Jackson, "Cultural Seedbeds of the Black Backlash in Mental Health"; "Community Mental Health, Behavior Therapy and the Afro-American Community."

[5]G. G. Jackson, "Black Psychology as an Avenue to the Study of Afro-American Behavior," *Journal of Black Studies*, 1979; "The Origin and Development of Black Psychology: Implications for Black Studies and Human Behavior," *Studia Africana*, 1979.

[6]R. Ornstein, "The Split and Whole Brain," *Human Nature*, 1 (5), 1978: 76–83.

[7]R. Ornstein, *The Psychology of Consciousness* (New York: Harcourt, Brace and Jovanovich, 1977).

[8]Compare G. G. Jackson "Community Mental Health, Behavior Therapy and the Afro-American Community"; "The Origin and Development of Black Psychology: Implications for Black Studies and Human Behavior"; M. Pines, "We Are Left-Brained or Right-Brained," *New York Times Magazine*, 9 September 1973: 32–33, 121, 123, 132–134.

[9]R. Ornstein, *The Psychology of Consciousness.*

[10]P. M. Cobbs, "White Mis-education of the Black Experience," *Counseling Psychologist*,1970, 2: 23–27; J. P. Comer, "Research and the Black Backlash," *American Journal of Orthopsychiatry*, 40, 1970: 8–11.

[11]J. P. Comer and A. F. Poussaint, *Black Child Care* (New York: Simon & Schuster, 1975);

C. McLaughlin, *The Black Parents' Handbook* (New York: Harcourt, Brace and Jovanovich, 1976); P. Ross and B. Wyden, *The Black Child— A Parents' Guide"* (New York: Peter H. Wyden, 1973); A. Wilson, "The Developmental Psychology of the Black Child" (New York: *United Brothers Communications Systems*, 1978).

[12]R. L. Taylor, "Psychosocial Development Among Black Children and Youth: A Reexamination," *American Journal of Orthopsychiatry*, 46, 1976: 4–19.

[13]W. E. Cross, Jr. "The Thomas and Cross Models of Psychological Nigrescence: A Literature Review," *The Journal of Black Psychology*, 5 (1), 1978: 13–32.

[14]H. McAdoo, "Family Therapy in the Black Community," *American Journal of Orthopsychiatry*, 47 (1), 1977: 75–79.

[15]G. G. Jackson, "Is Behavior Therapy a Threat to Black Clients?" *Journal of the National Medical Association*, 68 (5), 1976: 362–367; "Community Mental Health, Behavior Therapy and the Afro-American Community."

[16]G. G. Jackson, "Cultural Seedbeds of the Black Backlash in Mental Health."

[17]G. G. Jackson, "The African Genesis of the Black Perspective in Helping."

[18]J. Berry, *Human Ecology and Cognitive Style* (New York: John Wiley & Sons, 1976).

[19]A. Rapoport, "Mathematical Models of Social Interaction," in R. Luce, R. Bush, and E. Galanter, eds., *Handbook of Mathematical Psychology,* vol. 2 (New York: Wiley, 1963): 493–579.

[20]Berry, 38–39.

[21]V. Dixon and B. Foster, eds., *Beyond Black or White* (Boston, MA: Little, Brown & Company, 1971).

[22]Cobbs, *op. cit.*

[23]Comer, *op. cit.*

[24]Cobbs, *op. cit.*

[25]Comer, *op. cit.*

[26]P. Slater, *The Pursuit of Loneliness* (Boston: Beacon Press, 1970).

[27]G. Weaver, "American Identity Movements: A Cross Cultural Confrontation," *Intellect*, March 1975: 377–380.

[28]Compare G. Albee, "The Protestant Ethic, Sex, and Psychotherapy," *American Psychologist*, 32 (2), 1977: 150–161.

[29]Weaver, 380.

[30]W. Bromberg, "Delinquency Among Minorities—Afro-Americans," *Corrective Psychiatry and Journal of Social Therapy*, 14 (4), 1968: 209–212;

J. Hodge, D. Struckman and L. Frost, eds., *Cultural Bases of Racism and Group Oppression* (Berkeley, CA: Two Riders Press, 1975).

[31]B. Richmond and G. Weiner, "Cooperation and Competition Among Young Children as a Function of Ethnic Grouping, Grade, Sex, and Reward Condition," *Journal of Educational Psychology*, 64, 1973: 329–334.

[32]W. Hayus and C. Mindel, "Extended Kinship Relations in Black and White Families," *Journal of Marriage and the Family*, 35, 1973: 51–57.

[33]F. Stultz, "Intra-Urban Social Visiting and Leisure Behavior," *Journal of Leisure Research*, 5 (1), 1973: 6–14.

[34]S. Martin and R. Kapsis, "Participation of Blacks, Puerto Ricans, and Whites in Voluntary Associations: A Test of Current Theories," *Social Forces*, 56, 1978: 1053–1071.

[35]N. Coppock, "Liberation and Struggle: Concepts for the African Family," *Journal of Black Psychology*, 2 (2), 1975: 44–52; R. Hill, *The Strengths of Black Families* (New York: Emerson Hall, 1971).

[36]V. Dixon, "World Views and Research Methodology," in L. King, V. Dixon, and W. Nobles, eds., *African Philosophy: Assumption and Paradigms for Research on Black Persons* (Los Angeles, CA: Fanon Research & Development Center, 1976).

[37]J. Rychlak, "Affective Assessment, Intelligence, Social Class and Racial Learning Style," *Journal of Personality and Social Psychology*, 32, 1975: 989–995.

[38]E. T. Hall, *The Hidden Dimension* (New York: Anchor Books, 1969).

[39]G. G. Jackson, "Black Psychology as an Avenue to the Study of Afro-American Behavior."

[40]J. S. Mbiti, *African Religions and Philosophy* (New York: Anchor Books, 1971).

[41]R. Ornstein, *On the Experience of Time* (New York: Penguin Books, 1969).

[42]G. G. Jackson, "The Origin and Development of Black Psychology: Implications for Black Studies and Human Behavior."

[43]E. Nichols, "Culture Affects Thought Process," *Guidepost*, 16, 1974: 7.

[44]J. Conner, "The Social and Psychological Reality of European Witchcraft Beliefs," *Psychiatry*, 38, 1975: 366–381.

[45]B. Gorman and A. Wessman, eds., *The Personal Experience of Time* (New York: Plenum Press, 1977).

[46]R. Benedict, *Patterns of Culture* (New York: Mentor Books, 1946): 6.

[47]M. Cole, J. Gay, J. Glick and D. Sharpe, *The Cultural Context of Learning and Thinking* (New York: Basic Books, 1971); J. Hodge, D. Struckman and L. Frost, eds., *Cultural Bases of Racism and Group Oppression*.

[48]U. Neisser, *Cognitive Psychology* (New York: Appleton-Century-Crofts, 1967).

[49]R. Ornstein, "The Split and Whole Brain," *The Psychology of Consciousness;*

[50]G. G. Jackson, "Community Mental Health, Behavior Therapy and the Afro-American Community."

[51]R. Ornstein, *The Psychology of Consciousness.*

[52]C. Buck, "Knowing the Left from the Right," *Human Behavior*, June 1976: 29–35; E. Kiester and D. Cudhea, "Robert Ornstein: A Mind for Metaphor," *Human Behavior*, June 1976: 16–23; W. Sage, "The Split Brain Lab," *Human Behavior*, June 1976: 25–28.

[53]R. Ornstein, "The Split and Whole Brain."

[54]G. G. Jackson, "The Origin and Development of Black Psychology: Implications for Black Studies and Human Behavior."

[55]I. Toldson and A. Pasteur, "Therapeutic Dimensions of the Black Aesthetic," *Journal of Non-White Concerns*, 4 (3), 1976: 105–117.

[56]D. Goleman, "Breaking Out of the Double Bind," *Psychology Today*, August 1978: 42–51.

[57]G. Albee, "The Protestant Ethic, Sex, and Psychotherapy"; P. Slater, *The Pursuit of Loneliness* (Boston: Beacon Press, 1970); M. Wallace, "The Uses of Violence in American History," *American Scholar*, 40 (1), 1970: 81–102.

[58]J. A. Banks, "Racial Prejudice and the Black Self-Concept," in J. A. Banks and J. D. Gramb, eds., *Black Self-Concept—Implications for Education and Social Science* (New York: McGraw-Hill, 1972); J. A. Bayton, "The Racial Stereotypes of Negro College Students," *Journal of Abnormal and Social Psychology*, 36, 1941: 99–102; J. A. Bayton, L. Austin and K. Burke, "Negro Perception of Negro and White Personality Traits," *Journal of Personality and Social Psychology*, 1, 1965: 250–253.

[59]K. B. Clark, "Black and White: The Ghetto Inside," in R. Gutherie, ed., *Being Black* (San Francisco: Canfield Press, 1970).

[60]A. W. Boykin, "Black Psychology and the Research Process: Keeping the Baby but Throwing Out the Bath Water," *Journal of Black Psychology*, 4 (1 & 2), 1977–1978: 43–64; "Psychological/Behavioral Verve in Academic/Task Performance: Pretheoretical Considerations," *Journal of Negro Education*, 4 (67), 1978: 343–354.

[61]D. Hunt, "Reflections on Racial Perspectives," *Journal of Afro-American Issues*, 2, 1974: 361–370.

[62]Dixon, *op. cit.*

[63]S. Allen, "The African Heritage," *Black World*, 20 (3), 1971: 14–18.

[64]Bromberg, *op. cit.*; Dixon, *op. cit.*; S. D. Mayers, "Intuitive Synthesis in Ebonics: Implications for a Developing African Science," in L. M. King, V. Dixon and W. W. Nobles, eds., *African Philosophy: Assumption and Paradigms for Research on Black Persons* (Los Angeles, CA: Fanon Center Publications, 1976); B. Matthews, "Voices of Africa in the Diaspora," *New Directions*, 4 (2), 1977: 16–19.

[65]L. Senghor, "The Problematics of Negritude," *Black World*, 20 (1), 1971: 4–24.

[66]B. King and K. Ogungbesan, *A Celebration of Black and African Writing* (London: Oxford University Press, 1975).

[67]G. G. Jackson, "The Origin and Development of Black Psychology: Implications for Black Studies and Human Behavior."

[68]Dixon and Foster, *op. cit.*

[69]*Ibid.*, 25.

[70]W. Nelson, "A review of *Beyond Black or White: An Alternative America* by V. Dixon and B. Foster," *Contemporary Black Issues in Social Psychology* (Washington, D.C.: ECCA Publication, 1975).

[71]*Ibid.*, 26.

[72]*Ibid.*; W. Van Horne, "Concerning the Shortcomings of the Diunital Approach to Race Relations: And Some Thoughts on Black Power," *Contemporary Black Issues in Social Psychology*, (Washington, D.C.: ECCA Publications, 1975).

[73]*Ibid.*

[74]B. Whorf, "An American Indian Model of the Universe," in J. Carroll, ed., *Language, Thought and Reality* (Cambridge, MA: Massachusetts Institute of Technology Press, 1976); J. Carroll, ed., *Language, Thought, and Reality. Selected Writings of Benjamin Lee Whorf* (Cambridge, MA: M.I.T. Press, 1976).

[75]*Ibid.*, 59.

[76]N. Caplan and S. Nelson, "On Being Useful: The Nature and Consequences of Psychological Research on Social Problems," *American Psychologist*, 28, 1973: 199–211.

[77]*Ibid.*, 203.

[78]G. G. Jackson, "Community Mental Health, Behavior Therapy and the Afro-American Community."

[79]G. G. Jackson, "The Origin and Development of Black Psychology: Implications for Black Studies and Human Behavior."

[80]V. Wobogo, "Anokwalei Enyo (two truths story)," *Black Books Bulletin*, 5 (3), 1977: 18–23.

[81]*Ibid.*, 18.

[82]*Ibid.*, 18–19.

[83]G. G. Jackson, "Cultural Seedbeds of the Black Backlash in Mental Health."

[84]K. B. Clark, *Pathos of Power* (New York: Harper & Row, 1974).

[85]E. T. Hall, *The Silent Language* (Greenwich, CN.: Fawcett, 1959): 21.

[86]J. Carpenter, "Black Actions and Reactions to White Racism in American Education," *Journal of Black Psychology*, 1 (2), 1974: 65–83.

[87]J. Daniels and G. Smitherman, "How I Got Over: Communication Dynamics in the Black Community," *Quarterly Journal of Speech*, 62 (1), 1976: 26–39.

[88]P. Lide, "The National Conference on Social Welfare and the Black Historical Perspective," *Social Service Review*, 47, 1973: 171–203.

[89]L. Brown, "Race as a Factor in Establishing a Casework Relationship," *Casework*, 31 (3), 1950: 91–97; I. Lindsay, "Race as a Factor in the Caseworker's Role," *Social Casework*, 27, 1947: 101–107.

[90]H. G. Canady, "The Effect of 'Rapport' on the I.Q.: A New Approach to the Problem of Racial Psychology," *Journal of Negro Education*, 5, 1936: 209–219; M. Stevens, "Meeting the Needs of Dependent Negro Children," *The Family*, 26, 1945: 176–181; C. Williams, "Special Considerations in Counseling," *Journal of Educational Sociology*, 22, 1949: 608–613.

[91]J. M. Sattler, "Racial Experimenter Effects in Experimentation, Testing, Interviewing, and Psychotherapy," *Psychological Bulletin*, 72, 1970: 127–160.

[92]W. Gardner, "The Differential Effects of Race, Education, and Experience," *Journal of Clinical Psychology*, 28, 1972: 87–89.

[93]*Ibid.*, 86.

[94]J. McGrew, "Counseling the Disadvantaged Child: A Practice in Search of a Rationale," *School Counselor*, 18, 1971: 165–176.

[95]G. Banks, "The Effects of Race on One-to-One Helping Interviews," *Social Service Review*, 45, 1971: 137–146.

[96]E. Mizio, "White Worker—Minority Client," *Social Work*, 17, 1972: 82–86.

[97]A. Kadushin, "The Racial Factor in the Interview," *Social Work*, 17, 1972: 88–98.

[98]*Ibid.*, 98.

[99]C. Sager, T. Brayboy and B. Waxenburg, "Black Patient—White Therapist," *American Journal of Orthopsychiatry*, 42, 1972: 415–423.

[100]J. Jackson, "Face to Face, Mind to Mind, It Sho' Nuff Ain't No Zombie Jamboree," *Journal of the National Medical Association*, 64, 1972: 145–150.

[101]A. Jackson, "Psychotherapy: Factors Associated with the Race of the Therapist," *Psychotherapy: Theory, Research and Practice*, 10, 1973: 271–277.

[102]F. Denmark and J. Trachtman, " The Psychologist as Counselor in College 'High Risk' Programs," *Counseling Psychologist*, 4 (2), 1973: 87–92.

[103]R. Carkhuff, "Black and White in Helping," *Professional Psychology*, 3, 1972: 18–22.

[104]J. Siegel, "A Brief Review of the Effects of Race in Clinical Service Interactions," *American Journal of Orthopsychiatry*, 44, 1974: 555–562.

[105]E. Higgins and R. Warner, "Counseling Blacks," *Personnel and Guidance Journal*, 53, 1975: 382–386.

[106]D. Harrison, "Race as a Counselor-Client Variable in Counseling and Psychotherapy: A Review of the Research," *Counseling Psychologist*, 5, 1975: 124–133.

[107]S. Bryson and H. Bardo, "Race and the Counseling Process: An Overview," *Journal of Non-White Concerns*, 4 (1), 1975: 5–15.

[108]J. Williams and J. K. Morland, *Race and Color and the Young Child* (Durham, NC: University of North Carolina Press, 1976); J. Williams and J. Stabler, "If White Means Good, then Black . . .," *Psychology Today*, July 1973: 50–54.

[109]G. Seward, *Psychotherapy and Culture Conflict* (New York: Ronald Press, 1956): 129.

[110]W. Adams, "The Negro Patient in Psychiatric Treatment," *American Journal of Orthopsychiatry*, 20, 1951: 305–310.

[111]R. Wylie, *The Self-Concept* (Lincoln, NE: University of Nebraska, 1961).

[112]D. Edwards, "Black versus Whites: When Is Race a Relevant Variable?" *Journal of Personality and Social Psychology*, 29, 1974: 139–149.

[113]W. W. Nobles, "Psychological Research and the Black Self-Concept: A Critical Review," *Journal of Social Issues*, 29, 1973: 11–31.

[114]W. M. Banks, "The Changing Attitudes of Black Students," *Personnel and Guidance Journal*, 48, 1970: 739–745; J. Fish and C. Larr, "A Decade of Change in Drawings by Black Children," *American Journal of Psychiatry*, 129, 1972: 421–425; J. Holtzman, "Color Caste Changes Among Black College Students," *Journal of Black Studies*, 4, 1973: 92–101; S. Ward and J. Braum, "Self-Esteem and Racial Preference in Black Children," *American Journal of Orthopsychiatry*, 42, 1972: 644–647.

[115]J. Cole, "Culture: Negro, Black, and Nigger," *Black Scholar*, 1, 1970: 40–44; J. Heiss and S. Owens, "Self-Evaluation of Blacks and Whites," *American Journal of Sociology*, 78, 1972: 360–369; J. D. McCarthy and W. L. Yancey, "Black is Proud," *Human Behavior*, March 1973: 45.

[116]J. Hubert, *Report Writing in Psychology and Psychiatry* (New York: Harper and Row, 1961); B. Siegel, "Counseling the Color-Conscious," *School Counselor*, 17, 1970: 168–170.

[117]M. Sabshin, H. Diesenhaus and R. Wilkerson, "Dimensions of Institutional Racism in Psychiatry," *American Journal of Psychiatry*, 127, 1970: 787–793.

[118]Comer, *op. cit.*

[119]F. R. Crawford, "Variations Between Negroes and Whites in Concepts of Mental Illness, Its Treatment," in S. Plog and R. Edgerton, eds., *Changing Perspectives in Mental Illness* (New York: Holt, Rinehart and Winston, 1969).

[120]R. M. Frumkin, "Race and Major Mental Disorders," *Journal of Negro Education*, 23, 1954: 97–98; B. Malsberg, "Mental Disease Among Negroes: An Analysis of First Admissions in New York State, 1949–1951," *Mental Hygiene*, 43, 1959: 422–459; B. Pasamanick, "Some Misconceptions Concerning Differences in the Racial Prevalence of Mental Disease," *American Journal of Orthopsychiatry*, 33, 1963: 72–86.

[121]J. Fischer, "Negroes and Whites and Rates of Mental Illness: Reconsideration of a Myth," *Psychiatry*, 32, 1969: 428–446.

[122]Sabshin, Diesenhaus and Wilkerson, *op. cit.*

[123]G. Lowe and H. Hodges, "Race and the Treatment of Alcoholism in a Southern State," *Social Problems*, 20, 1972: 240–252; A. F. Poussaint, "A Negro Psychiatrist Explains the Negro Psyche," in R. Gutherie, ed., *Being Black* (San Francisco: Canfield Press, 1970).

[124]J. Yamamoto, Q. James and N. Palley, "Cultural Problems in Psychiatric Therapy," *Archives of General Psychiatry*, 19, 1968: 45–49.

[125]H. Graff, L. Kenig and G. Radoff, "Prejudice of Upper Class Therapist Against Lower Class Patients," *Psychiatric Quarterly*, 45, 1971: 475–487; H. Gross, M. Herbert, G. Knatternud and L.

Donner, "The Effect of Race and Sex on the Variation of Diagnoses and Disposition in a Psychiatric Emergency Room," *Journal of Nervous and Mental Disease, 148,* 1969: 638–642; A. Jackson, H. Berkowitz and G. Farley, "Race as a Variable Affecting the Treatment Involvement of Children," *Journal of Child Psychiatry, 13* (1), 1974: 20–31; R. Stevens, "Interracial Practices in Mental Hospitals," *Mental Hygiene, 36,* 1952: 56–65; S. Sue, "Clients' Demographic Characteristics and Therapeutic Treatment: Differences That Make a Difference," *Journal of Consulting and Clinical Psychology, 44,* 1976: 864; S. Sue, H. McKinney, D. Allen and J. Hall, "Delivery of Community Mental Health Services to Black and White Clients," *Journal of Consulting and Clinical Psychology, 42,* 1974: 794–801.

[126]R. Krebs, "Some Effects of a White Institution on Black Psychiatric Patients," *American Journal of Orthopsychiatry, 41,* 1971: 589–596.

[127]D. Smith, "Preferences of University Students for Counselors and Counseling Settings," *College Student Personnel Journal, 15,* 1974: 53–57.

[128]R. Lorion, "Patient and Therapist Variables in the Treatment of Low-Income Patients," *Psychological Bulletin, 81,* 1974: 344–354.

[129]M. Stevens, "Meeting the Needs of Dependent Negro Children."

[130]J. Kahn, A. Buchmueller and M. Gildea, "Group Therapy for Parents of Behavior Problem Children in Public Schools," *American Journal of Psychiatry, 108,* 1951: 351–357.

[131]W. Adams, "The Negro Patient in Psychiatric Treatment"; J. Kennedy, "Problems Posed in the Analysis of Negro Patients," *Psychiatry, 15,* 1952: 313–327; M. Shane, "Some Subcultural Considerations in the Psychotherapy of a Negro Patient," *Psychiatric Quarterly, 34,* 1960: 9–27; U. Sommers, "An Experiment in Group Psychotherapy with Members of Mixed Minority Groups," *International Journal of Group Psychotherapy, 3,* 1953: 254–269; H. St. Clair, "Psychiatric Interview Experience with Negroes," *American Journal of Psychiatry, 108,* 1951: 113–119.

[132]B. Weiss and D. Kupfer, "The Black Patient and Research in a Community Mental Health Center: Where Have All the Subjects Gone?" *American Journal of Psychiatry, 4* (131), 1974: 415–418.

[133]B. Backner, "Counseling Black Students: Any Place for Whitey," *Journal of Higher Education, 41,* 1970: 630–637; F. Barrett and F. Perlmutter, "Black Clients and White Worker—A Report from the Field," *Child Welfare, 51,* 1972: 19–24; D. Brieland, "Black Identity and the Helping Person," *Children, 16,* 1969: 171–176; P. Cimbolic, "Counselor Race and Experience Efforts on Black Clients," *Journal of Consulting and Clinical Psychology, 39,* 1972: 328–333; "T Group Efforts on Black Clients' Perceptions of Counselors," *Journal of College Student Personnel, 14,* 1973: 296–302; E. Dorfman and R. Kleiner, "Race of Examiner and Patient in Psychiatric Diagnosis and Recommendations," *Journal of Consulting Psychology, 26,* 1962: 393; T. Ewing, "Racial Similarity of Client and Counselor Satisfaction with Counseling," *Journal of Counseling Psychology, 21,* 1974: 446–447; E. Higgins and R. Warner, "Counseling Blacks;" J. Siegel, "A Brief Review of the Effects of Race in Clinical Service Interactions."

[134]A. Jensen, "The Effects of Race of Examiner on the Mental Test Scores of White and Black Pupils," *Journal of Educational Measurement, 2,* 1974: 1–14; L. McClelland, "Effects of Interviewer—Respondent Race Interactions on Household Interview Measures of Motivation and Intelligence," *Journal of Personality and Social Psychology, 29,* 1974: 392–397; W. Pryzwanski, C. Nicholson and N. Uhl, "The Influence of Examiner Race on the Cognitive Functioning of Urban and Rural Children of Different Races," *Journal of School Psychology, 12,* 1974: 2–7.

[135]G. Ayers, "The White Counselor in the Black Community: Strategies for Effecting Attitude Change," *Journal of Rehabilitation, 36,* 1969: 20–22; J. Bloch, "The White Worker and the Negro Client in Psychotherapy," *Social Casework, 13,* 1968: 36–42; A. Gitterman and A. Schaeffer, "The White Professional and the Black Client," *Social Casework, 53,* 1972: 280–291; Mizio, *op. cit.;* D. Smith, "The White Counselor in the Negro Slum School," *School Counselor, 14,* 1967: 268–272; R. Williams and J. Kirkland, "The White Counselor and the Black Client," *Counseling Psychologist, 4,* 1971: 114–116.

[136]R. Lindberg and C. Wrenn, "Minority Teachers Become Minority Counselors," *Personnel and Guidance Journal, 50,* 1972: 219–222; L. Tyler, "Reflections on Counseling Psychology," *Counseling Psychologist, 3,* 1973: 6–11.

[137]Slater, *The Pursuit of Loneliness,* p. 15.

[138]J. Talbott, "Radical Psychiatry: An Examination of the Issues," *American Journal of Psychiatry, 22,* 1974: 121–127.

[139]C. Burns, "White Staff, Black Children: Is There a Problem?" *Child Welfare, 50,* 1971: 90–96; E. Fibush, "The White Worker and the Ne-

gro Client," *Social Casework*, 36, 1965: 271–277; F. Reissman, *The Culturally Deprived Child* (New York: Harper & Row, 1962); J. Winer, A. Pasca, F. Dinello and S. Weingarten, "Non-White Student Usage of University Mental Health Services," *Journal of College Student Personnel*, 15, 1974: 410–412.

[140]Gitterman and Schaeffer, *op. cit.*; G. Gurin, *Inner-City Negro Youth in Job Training Project: A Study of Factors Related to Attrition and Job Success* (Ann Arbor, MI: University of Michigan, Institute of Social Research, 1958).

[141]Krebs, *op. cit.*; D. Warren, A. Jackson, J. Nugaris and G. Farley, "Differential Attitudes of Black and White Patients Toward Treatment in a Child Guidance Clinic," *American Journal of Orthopsychiatry*, 43, 1973: 384–393.

[142]G. Dillingham, "Black Attitudes Toward Police and the Courts," *Black World*, 24, 1974: 4–13; G. G. Jackson and S. Kirschner, "Racial Self-Designation and Preference for a Counselor," *Journal of Counseling Psychology*, 20, 1973: 560–564; O. Kerner, *Report of the National Advisory Commission on Civil Disorders* (New York: Bantam Books, 1968); D. Rafky, "Are Cops Prejudiced?" *Human Behavior*, August 1973: 38.

[143]C. Thorpe, "Black Social Structure and White Indices of Measurement," *Pacific Sociological Review*, 15, 1972: 495–506.

[144]R. Green, "The Social Responsibility of Psychology," *The Journal of Black Psychology*, 1, 1974: 25–29; R. A. Schermerhorn, "Psychiatric Disorders Among Negroes: A Sociological Note," *American Journal of Psychiatry*, 112, 1956: 878–882.

[145]G. G. Jackson, "The African Genesis of the Black Perspective in Helping," "The Emergence of a Black Perspective in Counseling"; "The Origin and Development of Black Psychology: Implications for Black Studies and Human Behavior".

[146]R. Bell, "The Culturally Deprived Psychologist," *Counseling Psychologist*, 2, 1971: 104–107; M. Calnek, "Racial Factors in the Counter-Transference: The Black Therapist and the Black Patient," *American Journal of Orthopsychiatry*, 40, 1970: 39–46; G. Fooks, "Dilemmas of Black Therapists," *Journal of Non-White Concerns*, I, 1973: 181–191; C. Funnye, "The Militant Black Social Worker and the Urban Hustle," *Social Work*, 15, 1970: 5–13; W. H. Grier and P. M. Cobbs, *Jesus Bag*, (New York: McGraw-Hill, 1971); P. Smith, "Counselors for Ghetto Youth," *Personnel and Guidance Journal*, 47, 1968: 279–281.

[147]A. J. Franklin, "White Clinicians Should Know About Testing Black Students," *Journal of Negro Educational Review*, 28 (3 and 4), 1978: 202–218; L. Rivers, "The Influence of Auditory-, Visual-, and Language-Discrimination Skills on the Standardized Test Performance of Black Children," *Journal of Non-White Concerns in Personnel and Guidance*, 6 (3), 1978: 134–140; O. L. Taylor, "Language issues and testing," *Journal of Non-White Concerns*, 6 (3), 1978: 125–133; R. Williams and H. Mitchell, "The Testing Game," *Negro Educational Review*, 28 (3 and 4), 1977: 172–182.

[148]C. Vontress, "Counseling the Racial and Ethnic Minorities," *Focus on Guidance*, 5, 1973: 1–12.

[149]L. Paul, "The Psychologist's Role in Litigation Concerning Test Discrimination," *Professional Psychology*, 5, 1974: 32–36.

[150]T. Monohan, "The Disposition of Juvenile Offenders by Race and Sex in Relation to the Race and Sex of Police Officers," *International Review of Modern Sociology*, 2, 1972: 1–11.

[151]D. Rafky, "The Attitudes of Black Scholars Toward the Black Colleges," *Journal of Negro Education*, 41, 1972; 320–330.

[152]A. Aswadu, "Black View of Prison," *Black Scholar*, 2, 1971: 28–31; R. Chrisman, "Black Prisoners, White Law," *Black Scholar*, 2, 1971: 44–46; A. F. Poussaint, "The Plight of the Black Prisoner"; W. Wade, "The Politics of Prison," *Black Scholar*, 2, 1971: 12–18.

[153]H. Burns, "Black People and the Tyranny of American Law," *Annals*, 407, 1973: 156–166; L. Cargan and M. Coates, "The Indeterminate Sentence and Judicial Bias," *Crime and Delinquency*, 20, 1974: 144–156; G. Johnson, "The Negro and Crime," *Annals of the American Academy of Political and Social Sciences*, 1941: 93–104; S. Nagel, *The Legal Process from a Behavioral Perspective* (Homewood, IL: Dorsey, 1969); K. Parker and B. Stebman, "Legal Education for Blacks," *Annals of The American Academy of Political and Social Sciences*, 407, 1973: 144–155; M. Wolfgang and M. Reidel, "Race, Judicial Discretion and the Death Penalty," *Annals of the American Academy of Political and Social Science*, 407, 1973: 119–133; D. Warren, Jackson, Nugaris, and Farley, *op. cit.*; D. Warren, *Justice in Recorders' Court. An Analysis of Misdemeanor Cases in Detroit.* Paper presented at the 65th annual meeting of the American Sociological Association, Denver, Colorado, 1971.

[154]Compare Cross, *The Thomas and Cross Models of Psychological Nigrescence.*

[155]Dillingham, *op. cit.*

[156]Ward and Braum, *op. cit.*

[157]"Black Children's Drawings," *Human Behavior,* May 1974: 46.

[158]J. Toomer, "Beyond Being Black: Identification Alone Is Not Enough," *Journal of Negro Education, 44* (2), 1975: 189–199.

[159]G. G. Jackson, "The Origin and Development of Black Psychology: Implications for Black Studies and Human Behavior."

[160]*Ibid.*; "Community Mental Health, Behavior Therapy and the Afro-American Community,"

[161]G. G. Jackson, "The African Genesis of the Black Perspective in Helping"; "Community Mental Health, Behavior Therapy and the Afro-American Community"; "The Emergence of a Black Perspective in Counseling."

[162]Kennedy, *op. cit.*

[163]W. E. Cross, Jr. "The Negro-to-Black Conversion Experience," *Black World, 20* (9), 1971: 13–27.

[164]H. Goldenberg, "The Role of Group Identification in the Personality Organization of Schizophrenic and Normal Negroes." Unpublished doctoral dissertation, University of California at Los Angeles, 1969.

[165]Dixon, *op. cit.*

[166]C. Pinderhughes, "Cleavage and Conflict in the Black Middle Class," *Ebony*, August 1973: 174–179.

[167]G. Kennard, "Stanford U Denies Tenure to Muslim Psychology Prof," *Muhammad Speaks, 14,* 1975: 7–8; P. Wilcox, "A Letter to Black Educators in Higher Education," *Annals of the American Academy of Political and Social Science, 404,* 1972: 101–117.

[168]Bell, *op. cit.*; B. Jones, O. Lightfoot, D. Palmer, R. Wilkerson and D. Williams, "Problems of Black Psychiatric Residents in White Training Institutes," *American Journal of Psychiatry, 127,* 1970: 798–803; P. Smith, *op. cit.*

[169]L. Gary, "A Mental Health Research Agenda for the Black Community," *Journal of Afro-American Issues, 4* (1), 1976: 50–60; C. Pierce, "The Formation of the Black Psychiatrists of America," in C. Willie, B. Kramer, and B. Brown, eds., *Racism and Mental Health* (Pittsburgh, PA: University of Pittsburgh Press, 1973).

[170]G. G. Jackson, "The Cultural Gap in the Cultural Therapy Approach to Drug Abuse," *Drug Forum,* 1979.

44

Psychotherapy in Africa

Thomas Adeoye Lambo

Some years ago, a Nigerian patient came to me in a state of extreme anxiety. He had been educated at Cambridge University and was, to all intents and purposes, thoroughly "Westernized." He had recently been promoted to a top-level position in the administrative service, bypassing many of his able peers. A few weeks after his promotion, however, he had had an unusual accident from which he barely escaped with his life. He suddenly became terrified that his colleagues had formed a conspiracy and were trying to kill him.

His paranoia resisted the usual methods of Western psychiatry, and he had to be sedated to relieve his anxiety. But one day he came to see me, obviously feeling much better. A few nights before, he said, his grandfather had appeared to him in a dream and had assured him of a long and healthy life. He had been promised relief from fear and anxiety if he would sacrifice a goat. My patient bought a goat the following day, carried out all of the detailed instructions of his grandfather, and quickly recovered. The young man does not like to discuss this experience because he feels it conflicts with his educational background, but occasionally, in confidence, he says: "There is something in these native things, you know."

To the Western eye, such lingering beliefs in ritual and magic seem antiquated and possibly harmful—obstacles in the path of modern medicine. But the fact is that African cultures have developed indigenous forms of psychotherapy that are highly effective because they are woven into the social fabric. Although Western therapeutic methods are being adopted by many African therapists, few Africans are simply substituting new methods for traditional modes of treatment. Instead, they have attempted to combine the two for maximum effectiveness.

The character and effectiveness of medicine for the mind and the body always and everywhere depend on the culture in which the medicine is practiced. In the West, healing is often considered to be a private matter between patient and therapist. In Africa, healing is an integral part of society and religion, a matter in which the whole community is involved. To understand African psychotherapy one must understand African thought and its social roots.

It seems impossible to speak of a single African viewpoint because the continent contains a broad range of cultures. The Ga, the Masai, and the Kikuyu, for example, are as different in their specific ceremonies and customs as are the Bantus and the Belgians. Yet in sub-Saharan black Africa the different cultures do share a consciousness of the world. They have in common a characteristic perception of life and death that makes it possible to describe their overriding philosophy. (In the United States, Southern Baptists and Episcopalians are far apart in many of their rituals and beliefs, yet one could legitimately say that both share a Christian concept of life.)

The basis of most African value systems is the concept of the unity of life and time. Phenomena that are regarded as opposites in the West exist on a single continuum in Africa. African thought draws no sharp distinction between animate and inanimate, natural and supernatural, material and mental, conscious and unconscious. All things exist in dynamic correspondence, whether they are visible or not. Past, present, and future blend in harmony; the world does not change between one's dreams and the daylight.

Essential to this view of the world is the belief that there is continuous communion between the dead and the living. Most African cultures share the idea that the strength and influence of every clan is anchored by the spirits of its deceased heroes. These heroes are omnipotent and indestructible, and their importance is comparable to that of the Catholic

Reprinted from *Human Nature* 1, no. 3 (March 1978): 32–39.

saints. But to Africans, spirits and deities are ever present in human affairs; they are the guardians of the established social order.

The common element in rituals throughout the continent—ancestor cults, deity cults, funeral rites, agricultural rites—is the unity of the people with the world of spirits, the mystical and emotional bond between the natural and supernatural worlds.

Because of the African belief in deities and ancestral spirits, many Westerners think that African thought is more concerned with the supernatural causes of events than with their natural causes. On one level this is true. Africans attribute nearly all forms of illness and disease, as well as personal and communal catastrophes, accidents, and deaths to the magical machinations of their enemies and to the intervention of gods and ghosts. As a result there is a deep faith in the power of symbols to produce the effects that are desired. If a man finds a hair, or a piece of material, or a bit of a fingernail belonging to his enemy, he believes he has only to use the object ritualistically in order to bring about the enemy's injury or death.

As my educated Nigerian patient revealed by sacrificing a goat, the belief in the power of the supernatural is not confined to uneducated Africans. In a survey of African students in British universities conducted some years ago, I found that the majority of them firmly believed that their emotional problems had their origin in, or could at least be influenced by, charms and diabolical activities of other African students or of people who were still in Africa. I recently interviewed the student officers at the Nigeria House in London and found no change in attitude.

The belief in the power of symbols and magic is inculcated at an early age. I surveyed 1,300 elementary-school children over a four-year period and found that 85 percent used native medicine of some sort—incantations, charms, magic—to help them pass exams, to be liked by teachers, or to ward off the evil effects of other student "medicines." More than half of these children came from Westernized homes, yet they held firmly to the power of magic ritual.

Although most Africans believe in supernatural forces and seem to deny natural causality, their belief system is internally consistent. In the Western world, reality rests on the human ability to master things, to conquer objects, to subordinate the outer world to human will. In the African world, reality is found in the soul, in a religious acquiescence to life, not in its mastery. Reality rests on the relations between one human being and another, and between all people and spirits.

The practice of medicine in Africa is consistent with African philosophy. Across the African continent, sick people go to acknowledged diviners and healers—they are often called witch doctors in the West—in order to discover the nature of their illness. In almost every instance, the explanation involves a deity or an ancestral spirit. But this is only one aspect of the diagnosis, because the explanation given by the diviner is also grounded in natural phenomena. As anthropologist Robin Horton observes: "The diviner who diagnoses the intervention of a spiritual agency is also expected to give some acceptable account of what moved the agency in question to intervene. And this account very commonly involves reference to some event in the world of visible, tangible happenings. Thus if a diviner diagnoses the action of witchcraft influence or lethal medicine spirits, it is usual for him to add something about the human hatreds, jealousies, and misdeeds that have brought such agencies into play. Or, if he diagnoses the wrath of an ancestor, it is usual for him to point to the human breach of kinship morality which has called down this wrath."[1]

The causes of illness are not simply attributed to the unknown or dropped into the laps of the gods. Causes are always linked to the patient's immediate world of social events. As Victor Turner's study of the Ndembu people of central Africa revealed, diviners believe a patient will not get better until all the tensions and aggressions in the group's interrelations have been brought to light and exposed in ritual treatment.[2] In my work with the Yoruba culture, I too found that supernatural forces are regarded as the agents and consequences of human will. Sickness is the natural effect of some social mistake—breaching a taboo or breaking a kinship rule.

African concepts of health and illness, like those of life and death, are intertwined. Health is not regarded as an isolated phenomenon but reflects the integration of the community. It is not the mere absence of disease but a sign that a person is living in peace and harmony with his neighbors, that he is keeping the laws of the gods and the tribe. The practice of medicine is more than the administration of drugs and potions. It encompasses all activities—personal and communal—that are directed toward the promotion of human well-being. As S. R. Burstein wrote, to be healthy requires "averting the wrath of gods or spirits, making rain, purifying streams or habitations, improving sex potency or fecundity or the fertility of fields and crops—in short, it is bound up with the whole interpretation of life."[3]

Native healers are called upon to treat a wide range of psychiatric disorders, from schizophrenia to neurotic syndromes. Their labels may not be the same, but they recognize the difference between an incapacitating psychosis and a temporary neurosis, and between a problem that can be cured (anxiety) and one that cannot (congenital retardation or idiocy). In many tribes a person is defined as mad when he talks nonsense, acts foolishly and irresponsibly, and is unable to look after himself.

It is often assumed that tribal societies are a psychological paradise and that mental illness is the offspring of modern civilization and its myriad stresses. The African scenes in Alex Haley's *Roots* tend to portray a Garden of Eden, full of healthy tribesmen. But all gardens have snakes. Small societies have their own peculiar and powerful sources of mental stress. Robin Horton notes that tribal societies have a limited number of roles to be filled, and that there are limited choices for individuals. As a result each tribe usually has a substantial number of social misfits. Traditional communities also have a built-in set of conflicting values: aggressive ambition versus a reluctance to rise above one's neighbor; ruthless individualism versus acceptance of one's place in the lineage system. Inconsistencies such as these, Horton believes, "are often as sharp as those so well known in modern industrial societies.... One may even suspect that some of the young Africans currently rushing from the country to the towns are in fact escaping from a more oppressive to a less oppressive psychological environment."[4]

Under typical tribal conditions, traditional methods are perfectly effective in the diagnosis and treatment of mental illness. The patient goes to the tribal diviner, who follows a complex procedure. First the diviner (who may be a man or a woman) determines the "immediate" cause of the illness—that is, whether it comes from physical devitalization or from spiritual possession. Next he or she diagnoses the "remote" cause of the ailment: Had the patient offended one of his ancestor spirits or gods? Had a taboo been violated? Was some human agent in the village using magic or invoking the help of evil spirits to take revenge for an offense?

The African diviner makes a diagnosis much as a Western psychoanalyst does: through the analysis of dreams, projective techniques, trances and hypnotic states (undergone by patient and healer alike), and the potent power of words. With these methods, the diviner defines the psychodynamics of the patient and gains insight into the complete life situation of the sick person.

One projective technique of diagnosis—which has much in common with the Rorschach test—occurs in *Ifa* divination, a procedure used by Yoruba healers. There are 256 *Odus* (incantations) that are poetically structured; each is a dramatic series of words that evoke the patient's emotions. Sometimes the power of the *Odus* lies in the way the words are used, the order in which they are arranged, or the starkness with which they express a deep feeling. The incantations are used to gain insight into the patient's problem. Their main therapeutic value, as is the case with the Rorschach ink blots, is to interpret omens, bring up unconscious motives, and make unknown desires and fears explicit.

Once the immediate and remote causes are established, the diagnosis is complete and the healer decides on the course of therapy. Usually this involves an expiatory sacrifice meant to restore the unity between man and deity. Everyone takes part in the treatment; the ritual involves the healer, the patient, his family, and the community at large. The group rituals—singing and dancing, confessions, trances, storytelling, and the like—that follow are powerful therapeutic measures for the patient. They release tensions and pressures and promote positive mental health by tying all individuals to the larger group. Group rituals are effective because they are the basis of African social life, an essential part of the lives of "healthy" Africans.

Some cultures, such as the N'jayei society of the Mende in Sierra Leone and the Yassi society of the Sherbro, have always had formal group therapy for their mentally ill. When one person falls ill, the whole tribe attends to his physical and spiritual needs.

Presiding over all forms of treatment is the healer or *nganga*. My colleagues and I have studied and worked with these men and women for many years, and we are consistently impressed by their abilities. Many of those we observed are extraordinary individuals of great common sense, eloquence, boldness, and charisma. They are highly respected within their communities as people who through self-denial, dedication, and prolonged meditation and training have discovered the secrets of the healing art and its magic (a description of Western healers as well, one might say).

The traditional *nganga* has supreme self-confidence, which he or she transmits to the patient. By professing an ability to commune with supernatural beings—and therefore to control or influence them—the healer holds boundless power over members of the tribe. Africans regard the *nganga*'s mystical qualities and eccentricities fondly, and with awe. So strongly do people believe in the *nganga*'s ability to find out which ancestral spirit is responsible for the psychological distress of the patient, that pure suggestion alone can be very effective.

For centuries the tribal practice of communal psychotherapy served African society well. Little social stigma was attached to mental illness; even chronic psychotics were tolerated in their communities and were able to function at a minimal level. (Such tolerance is true of many rural cultures.) But as the British,

Germans, French, Belgians, and Portuguese colonized many African countries, they brought a European concept of mental illness along with their religious, economic, and educational systems.

They built prisons with special sections set aside for "lunatics"—usually vagrant psychotics and criminals with demonstrable mental disorders—who were restricted with handcuffs and ankle shackles. The African healers had always drawn a distinction between mental illness and criminality, but the European colonizers did not.

In many African cultures today, the traditional beliefs in magic and religion are dying. Their remaining influence serves only to create anxiety and ambivalence among Africans who are living through a period of rapid social and economic change. With the disruption and disorganization of family units, we have begun to see clinical problems that once were rare: severe depression, obsessional neurosis, and emotional incapacity. Western medicine has come a long way from the shackle solution, but it is not the best kind of therapy for people under such stress. In spite of its high technological and material advancement, modern science does not satisfy the basic metaphysical and social needs of many people, no matter how sophisticated they are.

In 1954 my colleagues and I established a therapeutic program designed to wed the best practices of traditional and contemporary psychology. Our guiding premise was to make use of the therapeutic practices that already existed in the indigenous culture, and to recognize the power of the group in healing.

We began our experiment at Aro, a rural suburb of the ancient town of Abeokuta, in western Nigeria. Aro consists of four villages that lie in close proximity in the beautiful rolling countryside. The villages are home to Yoruba tribesmen and their relatives, most of whom are peasant farmers, fishermen, and craftsmen.

Near these four villages we built a day hospital that could accommodate up to 300 patients, and then we set up a village care system for their treatment. Our plan was to preserve the fundamental structure of African culture: closely knit groups, well-defined kin networks, an interlocking system of mutual obligations and traditional roles.

Patients came to the hospital every morning for treatment and spent their afternoons in occupational therapy, but they were not confined to the hospital. Patients lived in homes in the four villages or, if necessary, with hospital staff members who lived on hospital grounds—ambulance drivers, clerks, dispensary attendants, and gardeners. (This boarding-out procedure resembles a system that has been practiced for several hundred years in Gheel, a town in Belgium, where the mentally ill live in local households surrounding a central institution.)

We required the patients, who came from all over Nigeria, to arrive at the village hospital with at least one relative—a mother, sister, brother, or aunt—who would be able to cook for them, wash their clothes, take them to the hospital in the morning, and pick them up in the afternoon.

These relatives, along with the patients, took part in all the social activities of the villages: parties, plays, dances, storytelling. Family participation was successful from the beginning. We were able to learn about the family influences and stresses on the patient, and the family members learned how to adjust to the sick relative and deal with his or her emotional needs.

The hospital staff was drawn from the four villages, which meant that the hospital employees were the "landlords" of most of the patients, in constant contact with them at home and at work. After a while, the distinction between the two therapeutic arenas blurred and the villages became extensions of the hospital wards.

Doctors, nurses, and superintendents visited the villages every day and set up "therapy" groups—often for dancing, storytelling, and other rituals—as well as occupational programs that taught patients traditional African crafts.

It is not enough to treat patients on a boarding-out or outpatient basis. If services are not offered to them outside of the hospital, an undue burden is placed on their families and neighbors. This increases the tension to which patients are exposed. An essential feature of our plan was to regard the villages as an extension of the hospital, subject to equally close supervision and control.

But we neither imposed the system on the local people nor asked them to give their time and involvement without giving them something in return. We were determined to inflict no hardships. The hospital staff took full responsibility for the administration of the villages and for the health of the local people. They held regular monthly meetings with the village elders and their councils to give the villagers a say in the system. The hospital also arranged loans to the villagers to expand, repair, or build new houses to take care of the patients; it paid for the installation of water pipes and latrines; it paid for a mosquito eradication squad; it offered jobs to many local people and paid the "landlords" a small stipend.

Although these economic benefits aided the community, no attempt was ever made to structure the villages in any way, or to tell the villagers what to do with the patients or how to treat them. As a result of economic benefits, hospital guidance, and a voice in their own management, village members supported the experiment.

In a study made after the program began, we learned that patients who were boarded out under this system adapted more quickly and responded more readily to treatment than patients who lived in the hospital. Although the facilities available in the hospital were extensive—drug medication, group therapy sessions, modified insulin therapy, electroconvulsive shock treatments—we found that the most important therapeutic factor was the patient's social contacts, especially with people who were healthier than the patient. The village groups, unlike the hospital group, were unrehearsed, unexpected, and voluntary. Patients could choose their friends and activities; they were not thrown together arbitrarily and asked to "work things out." We believe that the boarded-out patients improved so quickly because of their daily contact with settled, tolerant, healthy people. They learned to function in society again without overwhelming anxiety.

One of the more effective and controversial methods we used was to collaborate with native healers. Just as New Yorkers have faith in their psychoanalysts, the pilgrims have faith in their priests, the Yoruba have faith in the *nganga*; and faith, as we are learning, is half the battle toward a cure.

Our unorthodox alliance proved to be highly successful. The local diviners and religious leaders helped many of the patients recover, sometimes through a simple ceremony at a village shrine, sometimes in elaborate forms of ritual sacrifice, sometimes by interpreting the spiritual or magical causes of their dreams and illnesses.

At the beginning of the program patients were carefully selected for admission, but now patients of every sort are accepted: violent persons, catatonics, schizophrenics, and others whose symptoms make them socially unacceptable or emotionally withdrawn. The system is particularly effective with emotionally disturbed and psychotic children, who always come to the hospital with a great number of concerned relatives. Children who have minor neurotic disorders are kept out of the hospital entirely and treated exclusively and successfully in village homes.

The village care system was designed primarily for the acutely ill and for those whose illness was manageable, and the average stay for patients at Aro was, and is, about six months. But patients who were chronically ill and could not recover in a relatively short time posed a problem. For one thing, their relatives could not stay with them in the villages because of family and financial obligations in their home communities. We are working out solutions for such people on a trial-and-error basis. Some of the incapacitated psychotic patients now live on special farms; others live in Aro villages near the hospital and earn their keep while receiving regular supervision. The traditional healers keep watch over these individuals and maintain follow-up treatment.

We have found many economic, medical, and social advantages to our program. The cost has been low because we have concentrated on using human resources in the most effective and strategic manner. Medically and therapeutically, the program provides a posi-tive environment for the treatment of character disorders, sociopathy, alcoholism, neuroses, and anxiety. Follow-up studies show that the program fosters a relatively quick recovery for these problems and that the recidivism rate and the need for aftercare are significantly reduced. The length of stay at Aro, and speed of recovery, is roughly one third of the average stay in other hospitals, especially for all forms of schizophrenia. Patients with neurotic disorders respond most rapidly. Because of its effectiveness, the Aro system has been extended to four states in Nigeria and to five countries in Africa, including Kenya, Ghana, and Zambia. At each new hospital the program is modified to fit local conditions.

Some observers of the Aro system argue that it can operate only in nonindustrial agrarian communities, like those in Africa and Asia, where families and villages are tightly knit. They say that countries marked by high alienation and individualism could not import such a program. Part of this argument is correct. The Aro approach to mental health rests on particularly African traditions, such as the *nganga*, and on the belief in the continuum of life and death, sickness and health, the natural and the supernatural.

But some lessons of the Aro plan have already found their way into Western psychotherapy. Many therapists recognize the need to place the sick person in a social context; a therapist cannot heal the patient without attending to his beliefs, family, work, and environment. Various forms of group therapy are being developed in an attempt to counteract the Western emphasis on curing the individual in isolation. Lately, family therapy has been expanded into a new procedure called network therapy in which the patient's entire network of relatives, coworkers, and friends become involved in the treatment.

Another lesson of Aro is less obvious than the benefits of group support. It is the understanding that treatment begins with a people's indigenous beliefs and their world view, which underlie psychological functioning and provide the basis for healing. Religious values that give meaning and coherence to life can be the healthiest route for many people. As Jung observed years ago, religious factors are inherent in the path toward healing, and the native therapies of Africa support his view.

A supernatural belief system, Western or Eastern, is not a sphere of arbitrary dreams but a sphere of laws that dictate the rules of kinship, the order of the universe, the route to happiness. The Westerner sees only part of the African belief system, such as the witch doctor, and wonders how wild fictions can take root in a reasonable mind. (His own fictions seem perfectly reasonable, of course.) But to the African, the religious-magical system is a great poem, allegorical of human experience, wise in its portrayal of the world and its creatures. There is more method, more reason, in such madness than in the sanity of most people today.

ENDNOTES

[1] Robin Horton, "African Traditional Thought and Western Science," *Africa* 37 (1967): 50–71.

[2] Victor Turner, *Revelation and Divination in Ndembu Ritual* (New York: Cornell University Press, 1975).

[3] S. R. Burstein, "Public Health and Prevention of Disease in Primitive Communities," *The Advancement of Science* 9 (1952): 75–81.

[4] Robin Horton, *The Traditional Background of Medical Practice in Nigeria,* Institute of African Studies, 1966.

REFERENCES

Lambo, T. A., "A World View of Mental Health: Recent Developments and Future Trends," *American Journal of Orthopsychiatry* 43, (1973): 706–716.

Lambo, T. A., "Psychotherapy in Africa," *Psychotherapy and Psychosomatics* 24 (1974): 311–326.

45

Western Science, Eastern Minds

Sudhir Kakar

Ramnath is a 51-year-old man who owns a grocery shop in the oldest part of the city of Delhi. When he took the unusual step of coming to see me, a Western-trained psychoanalyst, he was suffering from an unspecified anxiety which became especially acute in the company of his father. He did not call it anxiety, of course, but a "sinking of the heart." This condition was less than three years old, a relatively new development.

Ramnath had, on the other hand, long suffered from a number of other complaints, in particular a nervous stomach. It is now never quite as bad as it was in the months following his marriage some 30 years ago, when it was accompanied by severe stomach cramps and an alarming weight loss. His father had taken him to the hospital, where he was X-rayed and tested. Finding nothing wrong with him, the doctors had prescribed a variety of vitamins and tonics which were not of much help. Older family members and friends had then recommended a nearby *ojha*—"sorcerer" is too fierce a translation for this mild-mannered professional of ritual exorcism—who diagnosed his condition as the result of magic practiced by an enemy, namely his newly acquired father-in-law. The rituals to counteract the enemy magic were expensive, as was the yellowish liquid emetic prescribed by the *ojha*, which periodically forced Ramnath to empty his stomach with gasping heaves. In any event, he was fully cured within two months of the *ojha*'s treatment and the cramps and weight loss have not recurred.

Reprinted from *The Wilson Quarterly* 15 (Winter 1991): 109–116, Woodrow Wilson International Center for Studies.

Before coming to see me about his more recent anxiety, Ramnath had been treated with drugs by various doctors: by allopaths (as Western-style doctors are called in India) as well as homeopaths, by the *vaids* of Hindu medicine as well as the *hakims* of Islamic tradition. He had gone through the rituals of two *ojhas* and was thinking of consulting a third who was highly recommended.

His only relief came through the weekly gathering of the local chapter of the *Brahmakumari* (literally "Virgins of Brahma") sect which he had recently joined. The communal meditations and singing gave him a feeling of peace and his nights were no longer so restless. Ramnath was naturally puzzled by the persistence of his anxious state and its various symptoms. He had tried to be a good man, he said, according to his *dharma*, which is both the "right conduct" of his caste and the limits imposed by his own character and predispositions. He had worshipped the gods and attended services in the temple with regularity, even contributing generously toward the consecration of a Krishna idol in his native village in Rajasthan. He did not have any bad habits, he asserted. Tea and cigarettes, yes, but for a couple of years he had abjured even these minor though pleasurable addictions. Yet the anxiety persisted, unremitting and unrelenting.

At first glance, Ramnath's understanding of illness and well-being seems incredibly cluttered. Gods and spirits, community and family, food and drink, personal habits and character, all seem to be somehow intimately involved in the maintenance of health. Yet these and other factors such as biological infection, social pollution, and cosmic displeasure—which most Asians would also acknowledge as causes of ill health—only point to the recognition of a person's simultaneous existence in different orders of being. To use Western categories, from the first birth cry to the last breath, an individual exists in his or her *soma, psyche,* and *polis.* In other words, a person is simultaneously a body, a self, and a social being. Ramnath's experience of his illness may appear alien to Westerners only because the body, the self, and the *polis* do not possess fixed, immutable meanings across cultures.

The concept of the body and the understanding of its processes are not quite the same in India as they are in the West. The self—the Hindu "subtle body"—is not primarily a psychological category in India, though it does include something of what Westerners mean by "psyche." Similarly, for most Indians, the *polis* consists not only of living members of the family and community but of ancestral spirits, other "spirit helpers," and the gods and goddesses who populate the Indian cosmos.

An Indian is inclined to believe that his or her illness can reflect a disturbance in any of these orders of being. If a treatment, say, in the bodily order fails, one is quite prepared to reassign the cause of the illness to a different order and undergo its particular curing regimen—prayers or exorcisms, for instance—without losing regard for other methods of treatment.

The involvement of all orders of being in health and illness means that an Indian—and this holds true for the Chinese and Japanese too—is generally inclined to seek more than one cause for illness in especially intractable cases. An Indian tends to view these causes as complementary rather than exclusive and arranges them in a hierarchical order by identifying an immediate cause and then more peripheral and remote causes.

To continue with our example: Ramnath had suffered from migraine headaches since his adolescence. Doctors of traditional Indian medicine, *Ayurveda*, had diagnosed the cause as a humoral disequilibrium—an excess of "wind" in the stomach which periodically rose up and pressed against the veins in his head—and prescribed *Ayurvedic* drugs, dietary restrictions, as well as liberal doses of aspirin. Such a disequilibrium is usually felt to be compounded by personal conduct—bad thoughts or habits which, in turn, demand changes at the level of the self. When a disease like Ramnath's persists, its stubborn intensity may be linked with his unfavorable astrological conditions, requiring palliative measures such as a round of prayers. The astrological "fault" probably will be further traced back to the bad *karma* of a previous birth about which, finally, nothing can be done—except, perhaps, the cultivation of a stoic endurance with the

help of the weekly meetings of the "Virgins of Brahma" sect.

Ramnath had turned to me, a representative of Western psychological medicine in an Asian country, not knowing what to expect but willing and in fact eager to carry out all my instructions. He was at first puzzled and then increasingly dismayed that a psychoanalyst did not dispense wise counsel but expected the "client" to talk, that I wanted to follow his lead rather than impose my own views or directions on the course of our sessions.

In the universe of healers, Ramnath had slotted me into a place normally reserved for a personal guru. From the beginning, he envisioned not a contractual doctor-patient relationship but a more intimate guru-disciple bond that would allow him to abdicate responsibility for his welfare. This is, of course, not uncommon in modern psychotherapeutic practice in other Asian countries. In Japan, for instance, the therapist is often considered the personification of the wise old sage—like an old Zen master—benevolently directing sincere, hardworking patients toward happiness, in the tradition of the Buddha who rewards devotion with mercy.

We can understand Ramnath's dismay better if we remember that the guru model also demands that the therapist demonstrate his compassion, interest, warmth, and responsiveness much more openly than is usual or even possible in the normal model governing Western psychotherapeutic relationships. Furthermore, the emphasis on therapeutic communication through words runs counter to the dominant Indian idiom in which words are only a small part of a vast store of signs and symbols. The pitch and intonations of voice, facial expressions, hand gestures, and bodily movements are expected to play a large role in any close interpersonal encounter. From Ramnath's viewpoint—and I tend to agree with him—my clinical detachment (though leavened with a subversive Indianness we both shared) was inconsistent with the way a guru ought to behave.

As Ramnath discussed his illness, there was a striking absence of the psychological terms which roll so easily off the lips of most Western middle-class patients. Ramnath, as I mentioned, complained of a "sinking of the heart" rather than anxiety. He would talk of a burning of the liver rather than rage. Here he is similar to the Chinese patient who talks of his *shen-qui* or "waning of the kidneys" and his *qi-ji* or "frustrated breathing." The absence of psychological language has led some Western psychiatrists to conclude that the Chinese or, for that matter, Indians tend to make psychological symptoms somatic. This may be a hasty conclusion. One reason for the physical presentation of symptoms by Asians is the greater shame associated with purely psychological complaints. Even more importantly, both the Chinese and the Indians do not distinguish as sharply between psyche and *soma* as Westerners do. M. L. Ng, a Hong Kong-based psychiatrist, remarks, "When a Chinese complains of *sinn i*, which literally means a pressing discomfort over the chest or heart, a fellow Chinese immediately understands that he is not just complaining about a heart or chest discomfort but also about a feeling of depression, worry, or loss." Similarly, in India if one tries to determine whether a patient who says "my heart does not feel up to it" or "my liver is not doing its work" actually means the physical organ or some emotional disturbance, it often evokes puzzlement, for the patient has never distinguished between the two aspects (body and emotion)—that is, if he or she is not Westernized.

The very word for health in Hindi—*swastha*, from the root *swa* (I) and *astha* (stable)—implies something which is present or stable in the "I": not in the body, not in the mind, not in the various organs, but in the underlying self.

As an analyst, one of my chief concerns is the personal, life-historical dimensions of Ramnath's symptoms, especially of the anxiety which gets worse in his father's presence. Ideally, I would like him to be biographically introspective, which I know is not a natural process in Indian or, for that matter, Chinese or Japanese culture. It is rarely recognized that such introspection—a *sine qua non* for psychoanalytically oriented therapies—is a peculiarly Western trait, deeply rooted in Western philosophical and literary traditions. It can be traced back to later Greek thought where the defini-

tions of the self and of identity became contingent upon an active process of examining, sorting out, and scrutinizing the "events" and "adventures" of one's own life. This kind of introspection is simply not a feature of most Asian cultures and their literary traditions. Indian autobiographies, for instance, with rare exceptions, are evocations of places and accounts of careers—records of events from which the self has been excised. The meditative procedures involved in Indian "self-realization," to which introspective activity might conceivably be compared, are of a different nature altogether and aim at radically different goals. The Indian injunction "Know thy Self" (*atmanam vidhi*) refers to a self very different from the one referred to by Socrates. It is a self uncontaminated by time and space and thus without the life-historical dimension which is the focus of psychoanalysis and of Western romantic literature.

An Indian analyst knows that his patients who are not highly Westernized will usually not recognize their emotional problems as having a genesis in a "psyche" or in their personal histories. If not attributed to possession by malevolent or unsatisfied spirits who definitely lie *outside* the individual, the disorders and conflicts are often seen as the product of the *karma* of a previous life. A woman in her early thirties, becoming aware of her rage against her husband as revealed in a dream, spontaneously exclaimed to me, "Ah, these are due to my *samskaras* [the karmic traces from a past life]. However hard I try to be a good wife, my bad *samskaras* prevent me." Introspection in the Western sense may have to be taught, so that an Indian analyst is often more didactic than his Western colleague, skirting perilously close to the analytical sin of suggestion. Yet heightened didactic activity on the part of the Indian or Asian analyst need not be *ipso facto* suggestive, which would be to go against his professional identity. The analyst can exhort, encourage, and interact, so long as he refrains from suggesting the content of an unconscious conflict and lets the patient discover it for himself.

The conflicting demands of an Asian culture and of Western psychotherapy, however, are not always so easy to reconcile. The reconciliation becomes much more difficult if the therapist and the patient do not share—as they often do not in Asian countries—fundamental culture assumptions about human nature, human experience, and the fulfilled human life. For psychotherapy depends upon how health and maturity are defined in a particular culture. Even Sigmund Freud conceded this point when he wrote, "In an individual neurosis we take as our starting point the contrast that distinguishes the patient from his environment, which is assumed to be 'normal.'" In other words, psychotherapy is the practical application of cultural myth that is normally shared by both the patient and the therapist.

The model of man underlying most Western types of psychotherapy is uniquely a product of the post-Enlightenment period in Western history. In the psychological revolution that occurred during this period, the older ideas about the metaphysical scope of the mind narrowed and the mind came to be viewed as an isolated island of individual consciousness, profoundly aware of its nearly limitless subjectivity. The perspective of almost all varieties of modern psychotherapy is thus informed by a vision of human experience that emphasizes man's individuality and his self-contained psyche. Each of us lives in his own subjective world, pursuing personal pleasures and private fantasies, constructing a life and a fate which will vanish when our time is over. Together with other value-laden beliefs of the Enlightenment—in individual autonomy and individual worth, in the existence of an objective reality that can be known, in the possibility of real choice—the individualist model of man has pervaded contemporary psychotherapy.

The goals of Western forms of psychotherapy are then very much related to the individual even in those instances where the therapy, in its techniques, addresses the group. All Western therapies talk, in some fashion or other, about the growth, development, and self-actualization of the individual. They talk of increasing the individual's environmental mastery, his positive attitudes toward himself, and his sense of autonomy.

By contrast, in India I had the case of a 28-year-old engineer who came to the initial interview accompanied by his father and sister. Both relatives described his central problem as one of "unnatural" autonomy. As one said: "He is very stubborn in pursuing what he wants without taking our wishes into account. He thinks he knows what is best for himself and does not listen to us. He thinks his own life and career more important than the concerns of the rest of the family."

Indian patients, like Chinese and Japanese, have in their minds what might be called a *relational model* of the self, which is quite different from the individual model of the post-Enlightenment West. In Asia, the person derives his nature or character interpersonally. He is constituted of relationships. His distresses are thus disorders of relationships not only within his human—and this is important—but also his natural and cosmic orders. The need for attachment, connection, and integration with others and with his natural and supernatural worlds represents the pre-eminent motivational thrust of the person, rather than the press or expression of any biological individuality.

The tendency to look at a person in transpersonal or relational terms is reflected in all aspects of Indian culture, from astrology to medicine to classical poetry. The Indian image of the body, for instance, emphasizes its intimate connection with nature and the cosmos. It stresses an unremitting interchange taking place all the time between the person and the environment, in which the location of the self, so to speak, is not circumscribed by the boundaries of the skin. This is in marked contrast to the typical individualistic Western image of a clearly etched body, sharply differentiated from the rest of the objects in the universe, with the self "inside" the body. Similarly, traditional Chinese culture conceptualizes man as an integral part of nature, as a microcosm of the universe, with his functioning dependent on the smooth circulation of the Yin and Yang forces which are part of the universe.

The Asian psychotherapist is acutely aware of this conflict between two sets of psychotherapeutic assumptions. The Western assumptions—stemming from an individualistic model of man and crucial in the formation of the therapist's professional identity—are epitomized in classical psychoanalysis. These include, in the words of psychologist Kenneth Kenniston, a "limitless respect for the individual, faith that understanding is better than illusion, insistence that our psyches harbor darker secrets than we care to confess, refusal to promise too much, and a sense of the complexity, tragedy, and wonder of human life." The other set of assumptions, which derives from the relational model and is absorbed in the therapist's very bones from his culture, stresses that surrender to powers greater than the self is better than individual effort. The source of human strength, in the Asian view, lies in a harmonious integration with one's group, in entering into the living stream, naturally and unselfconsciously, of the community life, and in cherishing the community's gods and traditions.

Fortunately for the Asian psychotherapist and his patients, the conflict between the two models of man is not, in practice, a simple dichotomy. Both visions of human experience are present in all the major cultures, though a particular culture may, at times, emphasize one at the expense of the other. Relational values, which were submerged during the nineteenth and first half of the twentieth century in the West, now increasingly inform Western modes of psychotherapy. Similarly, stirrings of individualism have not been completely absent from the history of Asian societies.

The Asian psychoanalyst has a choice, for instance, whether to orient his practice more toward the newer "object-relations" therapy which concerns the internalization of early family relationships—an approach which does not run counter to the dominant cultural orientation of his patients. Or he can resolutely stick to Freud's classical individualistic model, confident that, because of modernization throughout the world, he will find enough patients who will see him as their best ally in the realization of their full individuality.

In his more helpless moments, though, when confronted with the cultural incomprehension of his patients—an incomprehension

the Asian analyst is often tempted to confuse with personal obduracy—he can always console himself with the thought that Freud himself called psychoanalysis one of the impossible professions. Unfortunately, it is impossible for the Indian, Chinese, or Japanese analyst to repeat Freud's words with the same saving sense of irony.

ASIA'S HIDDEN HEALTH PROBLEM

For health conditions, the twentieth century has been the proverbial best of times and worst of times in Asia. Infectious diseases, such as tuberculosis and typhoid fever, which once swept in mortal plagues across the Asian continent, have dramatically declined. Today, in industrialized East Asia, the death rate from infectious disease is among the lowest in the world. Even in India and in China, where the rate remains high, it has nonetheless dropped to less than half of what it was earlier this century.

But because of "modernization," and the changes in behavior and diet it has brought, Asian death rates from chronic disease have risen alarmingly. Consider only the "small matter" of cigarette smoking. In China, nicotine consumption increases by 10 percent each year; more than 60 percent of adult men now smoke. From 1957 to 1984, deaths from cardiovascular diseases rose by 250 percent, while deaths from cancer and stroke registered similar increases.

Yet it is in the realm of mental health and behavioral problems that modernization has had the gravest consequences. A "just-say-no" American politician could scarcely envision in his worst nightmare the increase in drug use—and drug-related violence—in the past few years in Asia. Fifteen years ago Pakistan had fewer than 50,000 heroin addicts; today it has more than one million. More than 10 percent of all adults in Thailand are addicted to some form of opium. As with drugs, so with drink: Alcohol consumption is rising, even in Japan and China, whose populations were once considered almost immune to alcoholism. The rise in drug and alcohol abuse is accompanied by increasing juvenile delinquency, family breakdown, abandonment of children, suicides, and widespread mental illness.

There is a fallacy or myth that mental illness is a "luxury" of advanced societies. In Asia, depression and anxiety account for more visits to primary-care providers than do infectious diseases. From 10 to 20 percent of all outpatient visits in Asian countries are for depression and anxiety, which, however, are usually neither diagnosed nor treated effectively. Even when a mental illness is no more common than in the past—as with schizophrenia—the sheer numbers of cases in the populous Asian nations are daunting. There are six million schizophrenic patients in China, and one million in Pakistan. To treat them, Pakistan has perhaps 100 psychiatrists—one for every 10,000 schizophrenics. China may have, all told, 3,000 mental health experts and fewer than 80,000 hospital beds for the mentally ill. One fact is thus indisputable: Asia cannot follow the Western model for treating mental health problems.

And often what could be done is not done, so powerful is the stigma attached to mental illness. In Taiwan a $70-billion trade surplus has financed the creation of outstanding medical facilities for all disorders—except mental illness. The mentally ill in Taiwan, as in mainland China, are simply locked up in appalling institutions. For patients seeking help on an outpatient basis, the prospects are hardly brighter. The length of the first visit to a health-care provider averages less than five minutes; the length of the typical return visit is only two minutes. In many Asian societies, the biomedical care system is thus as much the problem as it is the solution.

Economists tend to see modernization as an unalloyed good, but the psychologist must acknowledge that, in Asia at least, modernization has been accompanied by a grave worsening of mental health. What is to be done? Individual psychotherapy can help somewhat but is hardly available except to a narrow group of affluent Westernized elites. Beyond that, what good does it do when psychology or psychiatry defines problems but has nowhere near the resources needed to treat them? Does it help to label the victims of ethnic violence in India or in Sri Lanka as sufferers of "posttraumatic stress disorder?" Such medicalization trivializes the social and political sources and moral consequences of suffering, while it offers no health benefits to the millions who suffer.

—*Arthur Kleinman, Professor of Anthropology and Psychiatry of Harvard, has conducted research in East Asia since 1968. He is the author of* Patients and Healers in the Context of Culture (1980), Social Origins of Distress and Disease (1986), *and* Rethinking Psychiatry (1988).

PSYCHOTHERAPY IN JAPAN: *HAMLET* WITHOUT GERTRUDE

Can psychotherapy, laden with its "Western" assumptions about the individual, be directly imported into Asia? Japan would seem the ideal country to test this question.

Psychotherapy works best in a secular culture, and the Japanese are at least as secular as Europeans and Americans. Individual psychotherapy is also an expensive proposition, but Japan is the one Asian nation sufficiently affluent to support psychotherapy on a wide scale. Even in the West, many intellectuals, from D. H. Lawrence to Jean-Paul Sartre, opposed the psychoanalytic understanding of the unconscious, but Japanese writers and novelists have explored the workings of an inner mind as irrational and perverse as anything in Freud. And the Japanese have certainly integrated every other Western social science—anthropology, political science, sociology—wholeheartedly into their culture.

The supposed affinity of the Japanese for psychotherapy proves, at first glance, justified: Graduates of Buddhist seminaries talk about Freud, and the popular "new religions" hire psychologists to conduct group-therapy sessions. Yet when it comes to individual psychotherapy, there seems to be a resistance to many basics of Freudian psychology. The reasons for this, according to George De Vos, a psychologist in the anthropology department at Berkeley, are not hard to find.

The Japanese may have largely dispensed with a religion of the gods, De Vos observes, but they still have a religion—that of the family. Because of the family's sacrosanct character, Freudian investigations into its workings—such as ambivalence toward a parent or a parent's role in a patient's neurosis or, especially, the ways in which a maternal figure may not be all-loving and good—are practically taboo. "Such concepts," De Vos writes, "cannot be pursued by a Japanese who wishes to remain Japanese."

A Japanese, instead of investigating his past, romanticizes it: Instead of analyzing his early childhood, he creates fictions about it. The Japanese, De Vos says, learn to control their thoughts hypnotically: "One comes to reinterpret past behavior of parents as possible expressions of love, perhaps previously ignored or misinterpreted because of one's immature selfishness."

Even for adults, expressions of individuality are often considered signs of selfish immaturity. Freud's definition of psychological health described an autonomous individual. But for most people in Japan, De Vos writes, "autonomy is anomie—a vertigo of unconscionable alienation leaving life bereft of purpose." Consequently, the Westernized understanding of mental illness and healing is, in Japan, often stood on its head: A neurosis, for example, is not the person's inability to achieve "individuation" but his incapacity to fulfill role expectations.

Alan Roland, the author of *In Search of Self in India and Japan* (1988), agrees with many of De Vos's conclusions, but he nonetheless finds that psychotherapy is slowly taking hold in Japan. The Japanese Psycho-

analytic Association alone has over 1,000 members, 80 percent of them psychiatrists. Roland says that Japan was never burdened by a colonial legacy which denigrated its indigenous culture. Japanese psychotherapists have thus found it easy to maintain the uniqueness of the Japanese psyche, and they have re-written classical psychoanalytic theory with an unFreudian lack of inhibition.

The all-important Oedipus complex, for example, has been transformed into nearly its opposite—the Ajase complex (named after a Buddhist myth). The Oedipus complex tells of an irreconcilable conflict among father, mother, and son; in the Ajase complex, the father is absent from the picture—and so is the irreconcilability. Although in adolescence the son may rage over the "loss" of his mother's unqualified love, he finally repents after realizing her great sacrifices for him. Japan's most famous psychoanalytic theorist, Takeo Doi, has gone even further and challenged the entire Freudian framework, in order to justify dependency. In *The Anatomy of Dependence* (1973), Doi argued that Western vocabularies lack even the terms to understand, much less to appreciate *amae*—the healthy Japanese "need" for psychological dependency. Indeed a pathological condition, *hinikureta* (warping), is produced when one's sense of dependency is frustrated. Concepts like *amae* undercut traditional psychotherapeutic goals, but, as Roland points out, "a psychoanalytic world view that guides the person in a world of crumbling cultural and social supports is not at this point very appropriate to the Japanese."

Japan—when and if it experiences the individualism and family strains of other advanced societies—could well revert to more traditional Freudian therapy. Now, however, Japan is in the unusual position of welcoming Western psychotherapy but, because of its inability to scrutinize family life changing it into something else. Psychotherapy in Japan resembles, if not quite *Hamlet* without the Prince of Denmark, then *Hamlet* without Gertrude, the suspect mother.

46

Facing the Cultural Crisis in Child Care

Gary R. Weaver

There is a crisis in child care today which will only get worse unless we begin to consider the cross-cultural dynamics of child care and try to redress the racial and ethnic imbalance between child care workers and children in group care. The implications of increasing minority children and decreasing minority staff are grave indeed, given the current lack of concern for affirmative action and the worsening economic and social situation for minority children. At the very least it is imperative that we acknowledge the existence of different cultures and ask ourselves if we are really helping troubled children to become better adjusted or engaging in a form of cultural imperialism which is ultimately destructive to the minority child.

Nonwhite youth are rapidly increasing as a percentage of the overall population and they tend to come from families that are disproportionately confronted with severe economic and social stress. While they are most likely to need professional child care, the institutions they enter are predominantly and increasingly white, both in terms of staff and therapeutic milieu.

According to a 1987 study, 77 percent of child care workers are white and yet over half of all youth in group care are minorities.[1] All available demographic data suggests that this gap will dramatically widen in the near future and there are no indications that child care

Reprinted from *Journal of Child and Youth Care Work* 4 (Summer 1988): 5–27. Copyright © 1988 by the National Organization of Child Care Work in cooperation with the Child and Youth Care Learning Center, University of Wisconsin, Madison.

agencies are attempting to narrow it. In fact, child care workers themselves seem to be relatively unconcerned. Among the hundreds of workshops and presentations given at various child care conferences and as part of in-service training, certainly no more than a half dozen even mentioned this critical issue.

Imagine these figures and trends reversed. That is, what if child care agencies had 77 percent minority staff and more than 50 percent white, middle class children? Let us further suppose that the difference were increasing—in four or five years, 80 percent of all child care workers are nonwhite and 80 percent of all youth in group care are white. There would be an uproar over the cultural discrepancy. Some might assert that there are too few white role models and claim that the staff could not fully empathize with the social and behavioral culture of white children. There would be concern that white children might go through some sort of "culture shock" as they adapt to the nonwhite environment and certainly they would have difficulties readapting to their white communities.

The 1980s have been a period of individual self-centeredness and a lack of concern for the plight of others. Issues of race and ethnicity certainly are not priority concerns of most Americans. The current popular cliché guiding agencies offering social services is *colorblindness*. This appears fair and egalitarian but it actually amounts to denying that racial and ethnic differences exist and conveniently allows us to ignore the imposition of mainstream (white) norms for appropriate behavior, values, and thought patterns. Colorblindness causes us to view culturally different behavior as pathological and results in cultural homogenization to a white, middle class mold, all under the guise of good child care.

PREVENTION TO DETENTION

The economic, social and educational gaps that impact minority children are much greater today than they were at the beginning of the tumultuous 1960s. When urban ghettos erupted in rage during the 1960s, the government developed numerous public programs to prevent such explosions from ever occurring again. There was a national effort to *cure* the diseases of racism, discrimination and poverty among the disadvantaged and *prevent* such symptoms as school drop-outs, crime, and riots.

Programs that would prevent delinquency and crime, provide greater educational opportunities, and increase employment of minorities, are today being weakened or dismantled. The trend is toward *controlling the symptoms* of such socio-economic diseases as racism, discrimination and poverty, rather than treating the causes. Crime prevention is being replaced by criminal detention; troubled youth are being removed from schools; the federal government has become an enemy of affirmative action; and bigger jails, courts, and police forces are now fashionable.

During the turmoil of the 1960s, great efforts were made to allow minorities to compete fairly in the socio-economic and political system and to compensate for previous discriminatory practices and injustices. Especially after the murder of Martin Luther King in 1968 and the resultant urban riots, it was acknowledged by most that it was the responsibility of government to deal with racism, unemployment, educational and economic inequality, and poverty. The goal of creating a "Great Society" without racism and discrimination was shared by many who joined together to fight a "War on Poverty."

The primary target of these programs was minority youth and their families in the form of affirmative action, community development, and educational enhancement programs. While many of these efforts were far too expensive and wasteful, the economic and educational gap between whites and nonwhites was narrowed. Headstart and other such childhood enrichment programs raised both grades and opportunities for nonwhite youth. Many minorities who today live in upper middle class suburban communities are evidence of the success of these programs.

Minority youth took pride in their ethnic and racial backgrounds as various identity movements arose, which, in turn, raised their confidence and self-esteem. Black Power, Indian Power, Hispanic Power, and other such affirmations of the worth of ethnic identity all served to encourage youth to attain their highest economic and educational levels. And the doors seemed to be opening to allow them to reach these aspirations.

However, by the early 1970s it was obvious that the economy could not simultaneously tolerate a War on Poverty and a war in Vietnam. The Vietnam War cost over a million and a half dollars an hour to fight for over ten years and, at its conclusion, unemployment and inflation began to increase. The economic drain of the Vietnam War, domestic programs, and the oil crises of the 1970s led to the worst recession in over twenty years, which caused many to turn inward and concern themselves with their own personal economic future. The altruism and optimism of the 1960s gave way to self-centeredness and pessimism in the 1970s.

Our defeat in Vietnam, the Watergate affair, the oil crisis, and the Iran hostage humiliation all contributed to a spirit of cynicism and disillusionment with government. Charles Reich's *Greening of America* of the 1960s[2] became Christopher Lasch's *Culture of Narcissism* in the mid-1970s.[3] Politicians began to campaign against government to get elected and advocated the abolition of programs designed to remedy economic, social and political inequality.

A cynical, individualistic, competitive spirit was promoted by various groups and cults which applied a bizarre combination of group relations techniques with a philosophy of Connecticut Yankee individualism. Individual materialistic self-fulfillment could be attained by joining *est* or selling Amway products, and college students no longer sought to "change the system" but, rather, to "beat the system" by joining the "right" fraternity or sorority. Preppies were only Yuppie larvae who dreamt of excelling in a laissez-faire system which was built on me-ism and socio-economic Darwinism.

The vast majority of white Americans believe things have gotten better for minorities and no longer perceive them as disadvantaged. Some even suggest that the blame for America's economic problems rests on the shoulders of the poor—"welfare queens" who are ripping off solid, tax-paying citizens and "bums" who are too lazy to work and, instead, live off the sweat of hardworking Americans. Most perceive these "cheats" and "loafers" to be nonwhites who number into the hundreds of thousands and are creating a "culture of poverty" which only spawns more of their kind.

Actually, most people on welfare or below the poverty level are white; well over 90 percent of those on welfare could not work if jobs were available, and the "cheating" is certainly much less than cost overruns for the military. There is little evidence that a "culture of poverty" is developing or has ever existed in this country.[4] This perception really amounts to nothing more than scapegoatism or "blaming the victim." Yet, it does help to justify neglect of the disadvantaged and implies that the poor are responsible for their own fate.

In the early 1980s, unemployment was nearly 25 percent in Detroit. When asked what the government was going to do about this high unemployment, a government official responded that if people were unemployed in Detroit, they should move to Texas. This was the responsibility of the unemployed, not the federal government. And, when there was an outcry over the many homeless people freezing to death on the streets of the nation's capital, it was suggested by a member of the Administration that these street people actually preferred to be homeless.

While those who are homeless, poor or on welfare are predominantly white, politicians and the media tend to portray them as nonwhite. And, the proportion or percentage of nonwhites who are homeless, poor or on welfare is much greater than whites. Nonwhites are much more likely to be unemployed and suffer from other forms of socio-economic malaise than whites. Programs which were designed to eliminate these social ills benefited whites in greater numbers than nonwhites, yet the popular perception is that they were simply handouts for nonwhites who were solely responsible for their own misfortunes and the drain on the pocketbook of hardworking, middle class, white Americans.

"Blaming the victim," "benign neglect," "scapegoatism," and "culture of poverty" are phrases that aptly reflect the current mood of mainstream Americans toward the greatly dis-proportionately poor, unemployed, undereducated, and urbanized minority Americans. Fewer jobs exist for the unskilled today than at any time in the past twenty years; unemployment among minorities is well over twice the rate of whites; the education gap between nonwhites and whites is wider than at the end of the 1960s; each year a smaller percentage of minorities attend college; bilingual education is being cut; and there are strong political backlashes against government programs designed to help minorities and immigrants. To assert that "they" are responsible for their own fate or that they can "pull themselves up by their bootstraps" is callous and cynical.

The anti-civil rights, anti-affirmative action posture taken by the Reagan administration has emboldened racists, and the social climate in America today suggests that racism is tolerable again, and even fashionable in some neighborhoods. The moderate, black columnist Carl R. Rowan asserts that "naked, violent racism is on the upsurge in America."[5] In 1986, New York Mayor Edward I. Koch asked for a national commission on racism and a local conference to address the issue of racial problems in New York City. In a December 28, 1986 appearance on CBS' "Face the Nation," Koch said he believes "that since the Kerner Commission of 1968, that racism has decreased in this country." However, he noted that "we still have the cancer of racism. Anyone who says the country . . . is free of racism is not telling the truth or is simply an ostrich whose head is buried in the sand." Certainly, racism plays a part in the current attitude toward the disadvantaged who comprise a greater percentage of minority populations.

Educational enhancement and enrichment programs, community development efforts, and job placement training are daily being weakened or eliminated, yet these programs might well prevent unemployment, crime, poverty and much of the social and political malaise confronting many Americans. In child care, preventive programs and early treatment approaches are no longer fashionable. The current trend is toward punishment as a deterrent, building larger detention facilities, preadjudication centers to hold youth, and treating minors as adults. We are perhaps the only country on earth that has adolescents on death row.

Hardline panaceas such as "tough love" and the "scared straight" Rahway prison project are cheap, appear efficient, and relieve everyone of considering the root causes of juvenile crime. However, these approaches only control the symptoms and, as serious investigation of the Rahway project showed, they do not work. They provide simplistic approaches to very complex problems and at the same time punish those who do not fit the mainstream norms of success or behavior.

The logic of free market, competitive individualism leads to the inescapable conclusion that the disadvantaged and deviant, including troubled youth, are responsible for their own plight. Just as each individual is responsible for taking the opportunity of the abundance of America and to achieve individual success, each is responsible for failure. If one accepts this "psychology of abundance," there can be no explanation for deviance or failure except a lack of commitment or will to succeed.

To suggest that minority youth can freely transcend their socio-economic and familial environment if they really want to, or that they alone are to blame for their failure and difficulties with the dominant society, is unrealistic and cruel. Worse, it narrows the approaches for helping them to punishment as deterrence, isolation from society to prevent their transgression against others, and rehabilitation after they are already in trouble. They often cannot "pull themselves up by their bootstraps" because they have no boots.

CULTURE-AND-PERSONALITY

When minorities are in conflict with dominant society, most assume it is a matter of "economics" or "politics"—the distribution of scarce resources or power. While both are very important, there is a more fundamental, unconscious clash occurring at the cultural and psychological level.[6] For example, during the youth and civil rights movements of the 1960s, many resorted to political and economic labels to explain the phenomena. Blacks were economically disadvantaged and, therefore, once they could have their fair share of

the socio-economic pie, the conflict would be resolved. Youth were malcontents who were influenced by radical political philosophies such as Communism. Once they left the ivory towers of academia and entered the "real world," they would grow up and settle down.

While there are political and economic factors involved in these confrontations, it could be argued that they were secondary to the cross-cultural clashes. Blacks were concerned about cultural oppression as much as political and economic oppression. In Mead and Reich, youth were identified as being part of a counterculture with values, beliefs, and behaviors that were in stark opposition to those of the mainstream culture.[7] The primary battle was between cultures with concurrent political and economic implications. Most participants were not the poor or the politically inspired. They were American with a different cultural perspective than that of the dominant culture.

Like a rubberband, the countercultural movements of the late 1960s went into the opposite direction of the mainstream culture. Today, the rubberband has snapped back to the dominant culture in terms of values, beliefs and behaviors. Many of the current approaches to child care that are impacting minority youth are a direct result of this backlash and, to understand them fully, we must take a culture-and-personality perspective, after which the focus can move to the economic and political. This is a much more complete approach but it best helps explain the dramatic reversals in child care, especially in terms of the minority child.

The concept of culture is often misunderstood because there are thousands of definitions for "culture." Almost all include the notion that culture is acquired or learned by growing up in a particular society. We know it exists because people in the same society have roughly the same values, beliefs, thought patterns, ways of perceiving the world, and behavior. Something causes this to happen which we may label *culture*.

Culture is somewhat like the term "personality" and, in fact, it is difficult to separate personality from culture. A teacher may help all children to write in a similar way but each will have his or her own particular handwriting. Culture causes all members of a society to share ways of thinking, perceiving, and behaving but each person will differ somewhat from the norm.

Personality is always a generalization or stereotype. When we describe someone's personality, we are speaking of his or her *characteristic* ways of behaving which were learned during the formative years and carried into adulthood. Fred might be described as an "extravert" because he usually behaves in an outgoing, gregarious manner and enjoys interacting with others. This generalization is very useful for explaining his behavior and predicting what he is likely to do in certain social situations. However, at times, perhaps when he is alone, he is rather withdrawn and shy or an "introvert."

Culture is also a generalization and stereotype. We can describe some cultures as "secular" and others as "religious," while there are elements of both in all cultures. It is really a matter of degree. Asian cultures are generally more passive than Western cultures and harmony may be more important than change in most non-Western cultures. These adjectives are useful generalizations because they help us to explain the behavior of most people in the society and allow us to predict behavior under certain circumstances.

Sigmund Freud divided the mind into two interrelated parts with the subconscious controlling the conscious. Further, he suggested the mind is like an iceberg with the conscious comprising only the small tip above the water level of awareness. The greater part is hidden or unconscious, yet it often controls our conscious thoughts and behaviors.

This same metaphor can be applied to culture which can be divided into "internal" and "external" culture. External culture is the small tip of the iceberg and would include such overt manifestation as customs, behavior, language, and the artifacts of culture such as art, music and literature. The greatest part of culture is hidden below the water level of awareness. Internal culture includes implicitly learned thought patterns, values, beliefs, and perceptions. To understand external cul-

ture, we must raise internal culture to conscious awareness perhaps through the trauma of leaving our own culture and entering another.[8]

Just as we acquire our basic personality during the formative years as we interact with others, we learn our culture. We come into this world somewhat like brand new computers, and culture is the program given to us by our society. Out of the vast array of stimuli and information that bombards us, our culture teaches us which information or "input" gets into our heads and via which sensory channels. Like a lens, it selects out what we will attend to. This information is then organized according to priorities or values which are ranked by the society. Our "input" or behavior cannot be understood unless we know how we are programmed.

To be human is to have a culture. In 1800 there was a 12-year-old boy who ran naked in the fields of the French countryside. He ate raw meat and howled at the moon at night. When he was captured he was seen around wolves and it was assumed that he must have been raised by wolves. This was the only logical explanation of his animalistic behavior.

Today we know that Itard's wolf-boy was not raised by wolves.[9] He was simply abandoned by his parents as an infant and, by some miracle, managed to survive outside a human culture. Thus, he took on none of the characteristics we would call "human." Very little, if any, human behavior is instinctual. We have the longest maturation period of any species and must learn or be programmed by our society to become human. The analogy between infants and unprogrammed computers is really not that farfetched.

Culture and personality are interrelated and mutually interdependent systems. You touch a culture at one point and it reverberates through the entire system and, in turn, affects personalities within the society. Consider the impact of the auto on the American culture— including the family, courting behavior, values, the subculture of youth, and so forth.

An economic or political change will obviously have repercussions throughout a culture. Over a period of time, there will be an impact on internal culture—values, beliefs, perceptions, and thought patterns. However, the initial impact will be on external culture: behavior. The internal part of culture is slow to change because it is primarily unconscious. When there is a conflict or dissonance between behavior and beliefs, beliefs will change to bring about consonance.[10] One cannot deny the behavior and, in our striving for consonance between beliefs and behavior (internal and external culture), only the beliefs may change.

On the other hand, if we can change values, thought patterns, beliefs, or perceptions, we can change behavior.[11] But, this is much more difficult. Take an elderly Italian in Philadelphia who has been there since the age of 15. He is now 85 years old and has little accent to his speech and appears to be an average, mainstream American. However, have a few glasses of wine and some pasta with him, and it becomes apparent that he is still very Italian, especially in terms of his ways of thinking, beliefs, values, and perceptions of the world. His behavior has changed, but there are still strong elements of the culture he brought with him from Italy buried in his unconscious mind.

Surely, there are differences between minority and mainstream Americans that are culturally based. With Hispanics and Asians, this is obvious. While the black American experience is much further removed from African cultural roots, the isolation and insulation of blacks from the mainstream through racism certainly caused them to share a cultural experience unlike that of white Americans. The ghetto walls not only kept blacks inside, they kept whites out.

True pluralistic integration has not taken place and even the modest desegregation that exists today is not more than a few decades old. Furthermore, child-raising practices which instill internal culture are passed down from generation to generation and change very little.[12] Many of us will raise our children as our grandparents raised our parents. Thus, the black American culture or subculture which existed 100 years ago is still learned unconsciously by black American youth today.

This acceptance of differences between minority and mainstream culture was openly acknowledged and celebrated during the various identity movements of the late 1960s, yet today it is denied under the rubric of "colorblindness" and "equality." In fewer than 20 years culture has become irrelevant to child care. Nonmainstream children are not only denied their cultural differences, they are forced to fit the norms of the mainstream society.

MELTING POTS AND CULTURAL COOKIE CUTTERS

Most Americans are unaware of their own culture and take it for granted. In fact, some might argue that there is no such thing as the American culture in the sense that there are French, British, Asian, African, and Latin American cultures. "Melting pots," "salad bowls," and "soups" are often used as metaphors which illustrate the apparent mixture of many cultures rather than any distinct American culture. Not only is the concept of culture misunderstood or ignored, the average American does not even believe he or she has a culture.

Americans do not systematically study their own culture. In anthropology departments, scholars write papers on Africans, Asians, and sometimes subcultural groups within the United States, but little is written about the mainstream or dominant culture. Some of the best studies of the American culture have been written by foreigners such as Alexis de Tocqueville or Gunnar Myrdal.[13]

America's formative years were unlike those of European states. There was no drawn-out developmental phase during which the nation-state and nationalism emerged from a feudal period, evolving from villages and city-states. The American nation began abruptly with the immigration of northern Europeans from the Old World who left their homes, extended families, titles and cultures behind to enter the New World.

During this period, they were isolated and insulated from the rest of the world by the two oceans. This was not simply a matter of geography. Settlers preferred to be removed from the rigid class system, political and religious oppression, corruption, and violence of the Old World. This was articulated clearly in George Washington's Farewell Address when he asserted that the U.S. wanted to remain uninvolved in the wars going on in Europe. In the 1820s, the Monroe Doctrine further warned that European nations should stay out of the Western hemisphere. Isolationism was a matter of public policy.

Early in the national psyche the habit of not examining the American culture was the accepted practice. There was primarily a one-way flow from the Old to the New World. As immigrant children entered the public education system, with the encouragement of their parents, they gave up the culture of the Old World including its languages, class assumptions, perceptions, and ways of dealing with the social and physical environment. Indeed, immigrant parents often learned better how to cope with the new environment by observing their children who were free of the Old World cultures.[14]

Studies of Peace Corps volunteers, businessmen, and other overseas sojourners find that a principal result of their experience is that they become more conscious of their own culture. As long as we are surrounded by people who share our values, perceptions, ways of thinking, beliefs, and behaviors, we take them for granted. Ironically, by leaving our culture and being immersed in another, we become more aware of our own culture. Even Fela, the highest paid jazz artist in the world, who comes from Nigeria, once claimed that he did not know what it meant to be an African until he left Africa. During the formative years of the U.S., Americans did not have this experience. In fact, they wanted to be isolated from other cultures.

It is very difficult for Americans to understand how the personalities of others are shaped by their culture because so few Americans are aware of the impact of their own culture on their personalities. Just as Western psychology assumed that the individual exists outside the context of a community or culture,[15] Americans often fail to appreciate how one is affected by cultural experiences. This fits nicely with a philosophy of political and economic liberalism, individualism, self-reliance and independence.

An unquestioned metaphor which perpetuates a cultureless self-image is the so-called American "melting pot." It describes a process of assimilation and an assumption of a truly pluralistic society whereby immigrants threw their respective cultures into a pot. The mixture was stirred and heated until it melted down into a harmonious blend of cultures from all over the world with no distinct or dominant culture.

While there is some truth to this, the melting pot is mostly a myth. One would have to search diligently to find equal contributions from all the cultures brought to these shores. Immigrants from Latin America, Asia, Africa, and even southern Mediterranean cultures do not find the richness of their cultures melted evenly into this pot. They melted no further than tacos, chop suey, shish kebab, and pizza— two of which were invented in this country.

Rather than a melting pot, there has been a cultural "cookie cutter" with a white, male, Protestant, Anglo-Saxon mold. The price one paid to enter the mainstream or dominant culture was to give up those cultural characteristics which did not fit this mold. This is not a process of "cultural pluralism" but, instead, "cultural homogenization" or, in political terms, "cultural imperialism."

While all might be free to *acculturate* or learn the norms and behaviors of the mainstream, the ability to enter was controlled by the dominant culture. Acculturation is a process of learning or acquiring another culture while *assimilation* is a matter of being accepted as a member of another culture. Assimilation was determined by those with political, social and economic power as in many colonial societies.[16] To be accepted, one had to discard all cultural characteristics which did not fit the cookie-cutter mold of Anglo-America.

Mainstream folk often self-righteously affirm the melting pot myth with statements such as: "My Grampa Stripinski came to this country at the turn of the century—an illiterate Polish Jew who couldn't even speak English. He worked hard as a laborer in the streets of Milwaukee, and look at his family today! Every grandchild has a college education! Now, why-in-the-hell can't blacks and Puerto Ricans do the same thing?"

This is a perfectly reasonable and legitimate question, if we had a melting pot. It suggests that if Grampa Stripinski could move his family into the middle class, all others could do likewise, unless they simply did not have the determination, fortitude, and character to do so. Those who could not enter the mainstream really did not want to and were therefore responsible for their own plight in the American society.

But, did Grampa Stripinski and his immigrant family simply melt into the pot? If he was typical of many Jews coming at the turn of the century, he may have temporarily suspended the public practice of his Jewish faith to blend into the Protestant community. Also, there was a great deal of overt anti-Semitism during those days, especially in the Midwest. This is a well-documented pattern of assimilation described by such eminent researchers as Harvard's Will Herberg in his classic study, *Protestant, Catholic, Jew*.

If he was typical of many immigrants coming at the turn of the century, he probably did not allow his children to speak Polish. The better they learned English without an identifiable accent, the quicker they moved into the mainstream culture. He may have even changed his name to make it a bit more Anglo. Today, the Stripinskis might be the Stevens or the Stevensons. Even Ronald Reagan's grandfather changed his name.

Obviously, Grampa Stripinski did not simply throw his culture into the pot. He gave up those cultural characteristics that did not fit the cookie-cutter mold. The reason blacks and Puerto Ricans could not easily enter the mainstream is not that they chose to remain isolated from the dominant culture or lacked the character typical of white immigrants. They could not change their skin color or hair texture to fit the mold. They were identifiably different and thus were not allowed to assimilate. While this may have been true of first generation white immigrants who could not hide their accents, their English-speaking children quickly assimilated. Regardless of the quality of English or the mastery of mainstream values and behaviors, non-whites and their offspring were not permitted to assimilate.

The cookie-cutter mold still exists today. Over 70 percent of all Americans could be classified as Protestant and the Episcopalians (Church of England) are the richest in terms of per capita income. In 1960 there was a tremendous reaction against a Catholic running for President. Quarters were circulated with red caps painted atop George Washington's head with finger nail polish. With a red skullcap, Washington takes on an uncanny appearance to (then) Pope John XXIII. The message was that if Kennedy were elected President, the Pope would run the country. He was elected, and the Pope did not run the country. But, why was this an issue if Americans believed in a melting pot? Surely there were many other Catholics who could have been elected President before 1960.

The greatest number of Americans can trace their ancestry back to the British, followed by Germans and Irish. There is no official national language in the U.S. and yet English usage has predominated. The Continental Congress once met to discuss what language ought to be used when conducting business. In those days, most delegates spoke German. The journalist, Benjamin Franklin, even published his first newspaper in German. Rumor has it that the British delegates to the Continental Congress bribed a few of the Germans, and English won out. In spite of the common use of German and even the Prussian Horace Mann's impact on education, the cookie-cutter mold of Anglo-America determined the unofficial language of government.

Today, there is a very emotional backlash against bilingual education and the use of Spanish. Seven states have voted to make English their official language and there is a strong movement afoot to legislate English the official language of the nation. Why in the 1980s is this an issue, if we believe in the melting pot?

In 1980, voters in Dade County, Florida, passed a referendum outlawing the use of Spanish on street signs. If the object of a stop sign is to prevent a motorist from hitting another, who cares about the language in which it is written? On the other hand, if the object of the stop sign is to force one to read English—to fit the cookie-cutter mold—then it ought to be in English.

There have been many times and places in America when the majority of a population did not speak English, yet we did not have images of a separatist Montreal in mind. It was primarily transitory because they wanted their children to learn English. Hispanics today also want their children to learn English. Otherwise, they will be trapped forever in Miami or Los Angeles. These families want to melt, but they also may prefer to retain Spanish with their English. This is not a threat to the idea of a melting pot, pluralistic society. It does undermine the cookie-cutter mold.

WHAT IS "THE AMERICAN CULTURE"?

The dominant or mainstream American culture is still Anglo-American in terms of socioeconomic and political power, accepted norms of behavior, values, beliefs, and ways of thinking. The average American is white, middle class and urban. And, the behavior which is deemed normal is that of the mainstream. Institutions, such as schools and child care centers, both consciously and unconsciously accept and enforce the norms of the dominant culture regardless of the impact on the nonmainstream child. Indeed, the cookie-cutter operates daily in these institutions.

We can accept this definition of *the* American culture without denying the great diversity which exists in the U.S. and the changes that have taken place over the past two decades. Certainly, there is more ethnic diversity in America than in any other country on the globe except the Soviet Union. In the 1984 Presidential election, a black ran for President and a female Italian Catholic ran for Vice President. Nevertheless, the *average* American fits the cookie-cutter mold. Identifiable ethnic minorities might be considered *subcultures*, not because they lack the richness or depth of the mainstream, but because they are dominated by the mainstream culture.

It is asserted that Americans are basically watered-down or underdeveloped northern Europeans because the early settlers were primarily from the north of Europe. Large waves of southern European immigrants really did not come until the nineteenth century. However, this is as erroneous as the melting pot assumption. The first settlers were hardly "typical" northern Europeans. They were highly mobile, willing to travel to the New World

knowing that over 20 percent would die en route. The average European was living in a small house, as did his parents and grandparents, and one would have to be a bit unusual to start a journey knowing there was a good chance of dying along the way. These were high-risk takers.

Most were Calvinists and Puritans who had a fundamental religious belief that God rewards those who work hard and it is up to each individual to earn status in society based upon personal effort, not family background. Socioeconomic mobility was anticipated in a society without titles or nobility, monarchs, a rigid class system, extended families, or gross disparities in wealth and opportunity. This was a bizarre belief given the reality that the likelihood of rising above one's social or economic station at birth was almost nil in Europe in those days.

Early American colonists were really outcasts, fleeing religious and political oppression and persecution in Europe. Some others left to avoid fighting the endless wars. Today, they would be considered draft-dodgers. And, some were criminals who were exiled to the New World. To view these settlers as simply typical northern Europeans would be a gross distortion of reality.

Many of their behaviors and customs—external culture—resembled typical northern Europeans, but in terms of internal culture, they were atypical. The mainstream American values and beliefs found today date back to these formative years and most have remained unconscious and unquestioned until the turmoil of the 1960s. When these values and beliefs were planted in the American soil, they flourished and became even more significant than anywhere in Europe.

Colonial America was isolated from the wars of Europe. The land had unlimited natural resources, a coastline with hundreds of natural harbors, and a continually expanding economy. There was a small population and a desperate need for manpower. A psychology of abundance developed based upon the abundance of opportunity to succeed in the New World. If one was willing to work hard, there was a strong probability of economic advancement. Given the abundance of resources and opportunities, only those who were unwilling to work would fail. If God rewarded those who worked hard, those who failed were obviously responsible for their own fate. The slogan might have been, "cursed are the poor" with this combination of physical environment and the Protestant Work Ethic.

The values and beliefs that are most important in any culture are those that are rewarded. The Work Ethic was highly reinforced in this environment. Had colonists landed in Antarctica, it is unlikely that individual achievement, earned status, competition and hard work would have been important values and beliefs. Not only would they have gone unrewarded, they might have inhibited survival. Affiliations with others, an extended family to depend upon, and cooperation would have been higher on their hit parade of values.

Furthermore, had the first settlers not shared the Work Ethic, it is unlikely that an American culture, as we know it today, would have developed. It was the combination of values and physical environment that allowed for the formation of a culture we may term "American," as distinguished from most other cultures around the globe.

It was no accident that the Bible of capitalism, Adam Smith's *Wealth of Nations*, was published in 1776. Free enterprise, market capitalism and political liberalism were built upon assumptions of individual achievement, social mobility within a class system, and an anti-government philosophy. They also grew in the greenhouse environment of America with an abundance of natural resources, limited population, and continually expanded economy. Americans had to extend themselves into the rest of the world to export their agricultural products and insure their economic growth. Thus, Freedom of the Seas was added by Thomas Jefferson to the foreign policy of isolationism. It was clear that only to guarantee continued domestic growth would Americans involve themselves beyond their own shores.

A self-righteousness developed based upon the tremendous success of these early colonists. In the minds of many, it was obvious that the New World was chosen by God. The evidence was the political, economic and social success of these Americans who were not mired in corruption, war, despotism, and a riding class system which imprisoned most in poverty. The disposition to be unconcerned about the rest of the world and to perceive it as evil was established during these formative years. A melodramatic good-guys versus bad-guys perception—the morally strong American against the immoral world—emerged with its dualist absolutes of Heavens and Hells, Angels and Devils, and later the Free World and the Communist World.

When opportunities became more limited on the East Coast, there was a movement to the West. Nuclear families in covered wagons survived on the frontier with their "cowboy values"—self-reliance, rugged individualism, and independence. The romantic heroes of this period were pioneer families and lone adventurers such as Daniel Boone, Davey Crockett, and Paul Bunyan. Americans have always admired men of action who have achieved success through their own individual efforts. Statues throughout the country which are erected to commemorate historical events usually depict individuals in action or ready for action. We remember the War of Independence with a Minuteman carrying his rifle, rather than a group of old men sitting around a table signing a Declaration of Independence. In many other countries, statues of thinkers, artists, poets, and writers abound.

True success is individual success. No politician today will stand before the masses and acknowledge all those who helped him achieve his victories. Rather, he will portray himself as Abe Lincoln raised in a log cabin. Horatio Alger, Rudolph the Red-Nosed Reindeer, and Rambo all perpetuate the myth of the one hero. Even the beloved Jonathan Livingston Seagull is a happy seagull who separates himself from his flock. He becomes the Charles Atlas of the seagull world, practicing his swoops and his dives until he surpasses all other seagulls. He then returns to his flock to teach all the others how to really fly. Is this not the American Dream?

When a grade school teacher asks her children, "Who knows the answer to this problem" the children frantically wave their arms to get her attention. Consciously, she is teaching math, but unconsciously she is programming their little cultural computers. Each time the child waves an arm, the child is learning competition. It is not simply competition, it is *individual* competition because each child loves it when the smart child on the other side of the room gives the wrong answer. Even team sports, such as football, celebrate the myth of individualism. On Monday morning, we discuss Sunday's game in terms of the quarterback or the player who scored a touchdown, totally ignoring the rest who dance in victory or spike their ball. And, the crowd goes wild as if he made the touchdown all by himself, totally ignoring a half dozen other players with cleat marks up their backs.

Of course, the corollary to the myth of individual success and achievement is the belief that one is individually or personally responsible for failure. This is the only logical explanation given the melting pot myth, the psychology of abundance, and the assumption that all could be individually successful. When unemployment peaked in the early 1980s, American laborers did not organize to change their government. In fact, they overwhelmingly supported President Reagan in his 1984 re-election bid. In Europe and many other areas of the world, workers would blame their leaders for their unemployment and try to change their government, but in the U.S. workers apparently blamed themselves for their plight. Alcoholism, impotency, and suicide increased among newly unemployed laborers. Americans feel individually responsible for their failures.

Certainly the poor and disadvantaged are not solely responsible for their lack of success, yet Americans often do blame them and they blame themselves.[17] During periods of overall prosperity, as during the 1960s, Americans may become more understanding and benevolent towards those who are less fortunate. But, during periods of a restrictive economy, such as the 1970s, a self-centeredness sets in to supersede the altruism.

The current mood is one of individualist dog-eat-dogism. The assumption is that everyone has an equal opportunity to succeed and no special advantages ought to be given to those who fail. The families of children who fail are held accountable, not the schools or other institutions of the society. And, in some cases, the children alone are blamed for their failure. Rather than being helped to overcome their socio-economic misfortunes, they are treated as contaminants to be isolated, punished and sometimes modified so that they may fit back into the overall society.

"COLOR BLINDNESS" AND CULTURAL HOMOGENIZATION

Americans believe in the melting pot but, in practice, they apply the cookie cutter. For those who could fit the mold, socio-economic advancement in a class society was possible based upon one's individual efforts. Status was earned or determined by what one did. Being male or female, black or white, Protestant or Catholic, is theoretically irrelevant to one's position in the society if, and only if, one could fit the cookie-cutter mold.

The most common verb in standard American English is "to do," perhaps because doing is so important in a society without ascribed status or roles. What one does even determines identity. Each semester at The American University I ask students to tell me who they are in a few sentences. Almost all tell me what they do—"I'm a biology major" or "I'm completing my masters in communications." Ask people at a cocktail party, "Who are you?" Most will tell you what they do and then ask, "What do you do?" as if what you do is who you are.

Certainly, lack of respect for the elderly and the unemployed is related to their diminished status and identity when they no longer "do" anything. These nonproductive people often find their own self-esteem dramatically lowered when they stop doing. Because of the myth of individual responsibility for success or failure, they sometimes feel guilty for their own plight. Some feel worthless and may even give up on life. This perhaps explains why suicide and alcoholism increased among the newly unemployed during the recession of the early 1980s. And there was an upsurge of impotency among these former workers. Even "manhood" is earned and is affected by no longer being able to do.

Unlike laborers in Europe, American workers did not blame their government for their dire situation. They did not organize to change the government but instead strongly supported the Administration. Suicide, alcoholism, and impotency all suggest these victims blamed themselves. Retirement is almost a vulgar word in America while in other cultures it is welcomed. The average lifespan of a Boeing Aircraft retiree is 18 months. Is it any wonder that there is a very strong push to eliminate retirement in the United States?

Identifiable minorities, those who could not fit the mold, were treated as *castes within the class system*. Nonwhites were ascribed status and identity based upon who they *were*, not what they *did*. It was not a matter of individual achievement or the acquisition of wealth. Less than 25 years ago, a black millionaire could not sit next to an illiterate white laborer in a southern diner.

While this apartheid-like system no longer exists, we have moved to the opposite extreme and forced minorities to deny who they are, including their own cultural and racial differences. In many ways, "color blindness" is as oppressive to identifiable minorities as the overt racism of the pre-1960s. This is especially true for children in child care facilities today.

To explain this apparent contradiction between color blindness and ethnic or racial oppression, we must go back to the 1960s. When we think of the changes of that period, many consider the Civil Rights Act, the 18-year-old right to vote, and other such political accomplishments. However, the most sweeping changes were primarily cultural. Assumptions held by Americans for hundreds of years were questioned by the vast majority. At the top of the list would be the melting pot assumption of how one enters the mainstream of the American society.

The first sit-ins were actually efforts to get into the melting pot and in no way challenged the myth or the process. This was a *quantitative* protest similar to the labor movement. Laborers and blacks wanted their fair share or quantity of the socioeconomic pie. After workers established the right to organize for fair salaries, benefits, and practices, they blended into the middle class of America and proved

that, given an equal opportunity, they could be successful. Blacks wanted the same right of entrance. However, they could not give up their differences to fit the cookie-cutter mold as white laborers did. The price of entry was exorbitant and impossible to pay.

No one really challenged the reality of the cookie-cutter process or questioned the price of entry until the mid-1960s when "Black Powerism" arose. With the assertion of black identity the civil rights movement became *qualitative*. Blacks not only established the right to maintain their cultural and racial identities and still enter the mainstream; they also questioned the worth of the American pie if it meant continually earning identity and self-esteem in a dog-eat-dog society.

This was surely the first existential movement in American history and is the basis of all identity movements since then. Women's Liberation, Chicano Liberation, Gay Liberation, and all other such movements assert the right to be different and still have their fair share of the American pie. They refuse to pay the price of giving up or denying their cultural and group identities. Who they *are* is as important as what they *do*.

Up to the time of the Black Power movement, racists and liberals perceived themselves as opposites. Racists believed that those who are genetically different are therefore inferior. Liberals assumed that all are equal and there are no differences between people. On the surface, this appears just and fair to everyone, including minorities. But, there was an unspoken corollary which might be stated this way: "There are no differences between whites and blacks. *Given an equal opportunity, they would be just like us.*" The norm is "us" or the white, Anglo-Saxon, Protestant male. This is again the cookie-cutter assumption, not a melting pot. Identifiable minorities are perceived as pathological or underdeveloped white people.

The liberal position is roughly akin to color blindness in that it denies the reality and right of people to be different than the cookie-cutter mold. From a cultural standpoint, it argues for homogenization of cultures. From a political standpoint, it is a form of cultural imperialism.

Black Powerism posted a third perspective which asserted the right to be different and still have an equal opportunity to enter the mainstream. It was not anti-white, but instead pro-black, and advocated genuine pluralism in the United States. If we truly practice the melting pot, why can't one be black and still have equal access to the socioeconomic and political system? Why do successful women have to behave like men or deny their femininity? And, why can't Hispanics retain their rich cultural heritage and Spanish while working within the dominant society where they would necessarily communicate in English?

This third position acknowledges that there are cultural, racial, and sexual differences among Americans, yet these differences do not imply inferiority or superiority. True pluralism accepts differences whereas liberalism and color blindness denies them. The richness of a melting pot is its diversity and the union of a variety of cultures and identity groups. The cookie cutter forces individuals to cast off those cultural characteristics which do not fit the mainstream mold to produce a homogeneous society.

This approach has been described as "realistic humanism"[18] or "diunitalism"[19] in contrast to the deficit approach of the color blind. Some would argue that the current perspective in mental health is actually a "backlash" against this third perspective. The deficit hypothesis in mental health is based on the assumption that minorities, and especially blacks, are simply deficient in opportunities, their families are pathological, and their communities are unlike those populated by mainstream white Americans. Given these assumptions, the society ought to remedy the deficiencies and minorities will then be "the same as" (equal to) whites.

The diunital model would accept the difference between minority and mainstream cultures. To be helpful to minority clients and communities, assistance should be offered within the context of their cultures. Further, the differences between minority and mainstream cultures produce a variety of approaches which strengthen the overall society. Carried to a somewhat romantic extreme, the heterogeneous mix becomes a union of opposites and the whole is greater than the sum of the parts. Diunitalism provides an alternative to the backlash of color blindness and replaces homogeneity as a goal with heterogeneity. In effect, it simply asserts that Americans should practice what they preach: melting pot pluralism.

The culture of group child care is overwhelmingly white. Most child care professionals are white, the values determining appropriate behavior and therapy are white, and child care work often amounts to forcing all children to fit a white, middle-class cultural mold. The population of children needing group care is steadily turning nonwhite and the impact of the white group child care culture is devastating in terms of its impact on their self-esteem, self-image, and ethnic or racial pride. It is downright destructive to their mental well-being.

Behavioral psychology with its emphasis on overt behavior, quantification, and a preoccupation with manipulating "appropriate" behavior, leads child care workers to ignore the impact of culture on personality. In fact, behaviorists never have actually developed a theory of personality. They typically draw analogies between human behavior and animal behavior in controlled social environments, totally disregarding the impact of culture on behavior. On the other hand, behaviorism provides an Apollonian approach to child care management and funding which lends itself nicely to observable and measurable studies.

The behavioral approach to child care abets the cultural shaping to the white mold. Instead of focusing on who the child *is* in the context of his or her personal and cultural experiences, the child care worker is expected to observe, record, and control what the child *does*, as if children grow up removed from the influences of race and ethnicity. Of course, the institution and staff have a culture which is taken for granted and unconsciously imposed upon all children. They are compelled to accept and understand the institution's white culture and, in turn, nonwhite children are expected to give up or repress their culturally different behavior and values. The minority child's culture is not simply viewed as "different." Rather, his or her culturally determined behavior is often perceived as abnormal, inappropriate, and an impediment to good therapy. This child's culture is not simply ignored, it must be denied.

Central to good child care is an assumption that the child's self-esteem and self-image ought to be enhanced. The minority child's self-esteem and self-image is already low when entering the institution. A repeat of Kenneth Clark's famous 1940s study of children's self-image demonstrated that feelings of racial inferiority among black children are as strong now as forty years ago.[20] Preschool black children were again given black and white dolls which were identical except for color. They were asked which doll they wanted to be, which was "bad" or "nice," which was a "nice color," and which they would like to have. Two-thirds of the black children preferred the white dolls, the same percentage as in the 1940s study.

Surely entering a white institution where the rules and expectations for appropriate behavior are white only serves to further undermine the self-image of the minority child. If a large percentage of children are culturally different than the staff, the burden of cross-cultural understanding ought to be the burden of the staff, not the children. The staff needs to be aware of the repercussions of cultural domination, of cross-cultural adaptation, and of ways to use cultural differences to enhance the psychological well-being of the child. However, anthropology, sociology, and even social psychology are often considered extraneous to staff discussions and professional conferences.

Lastly, child care professionals seldom are encouraged or rewarded for posting philosophical questions regarding their work. These questions must be raised if we want to effectively help all children and avoid harming the minority child. Are we forcing nonwhite children to fit white norms of behavior? What do we really mean by "appropriate behavior" and might it actually amount to white, mainstream behavior? Can we really "empathize" with the child who is culturally different? Are role models provided for minority children and are nonwhite role models important for mainstream children? These are much more than tangential, philosophical issues. They are indeed *ethical* questions which ought to be uppermost in the minds of everyone involved in child care, but especially for those on the "front line."

ENDNOTES

[1] M. Krueger, R. Lauerman, et al., "Professional Child and Youth Care Work in the United States and Canada: A Report of the NOCCWA Research and Study Committee," *Journal of Child and Youth Care Work*, 3, 1987: 17–31.

[2] C. A. Reich, *The Greening of America* (New York: Random House, 1970).

[3] C. Lasch, *The Cultural of Narcissism: American Life in an Age of Diminishing Expectations* (New York: W. W. Norton & Company, Inc., 1978).

[4] W. Ryan, *Blaming the Victim* (New York: Collier Books, 1971).

[5] C. Rowan, "Behind the Resurgence of Racism," *The Washington Post*, December 23, 1986: A23.

[6] G. Weaver, "Police and the Enemy Image in Black Literature," in E. C. Viano and J. H. Reiman, eds., *Police and Society* (Lexington, MA: Lexington Books, 1975): 139–147.

[7] M. Mead, *Culture and Commitment: A Study of the Generation Gap* (Garden City, NY: Natural History Press/Doubleday & Company, Inc., 1970).

[8] E. T. Hall, *Beyond Culture* (New York: Doubleday, 1976).

[9] L. Malson, *Wolf Children and the Problem of Human Nature* (New York: Monthly Review Press, 1972).

[10] L. Festinger, *A Theory of Cognitive Dissonance* (Stanford, CA: Stanford University Press, 1957).

[11] D. C. McClelland, *The Achieving Society* (New York: The Free Press, 1967).

[12] P. M. Cobbs and W. H. Grier, *Black Rage* (New York: Basic Books, Inc., 1968).

[13] A. de Tocqueville, *The Recollections of Alexis de Tocqueville* (London: The Harvill Press, 1948); K. G. Myrdal, *An American Dilemma: The Negro Problem and Modern Democracy*, 1944.

[14] Mead, *op. cit.*

[15] T. Doi, *The Anatomy of Dependence* (Tokyo: Kodansha International, Ltd., 1971).

[16] A. L. Rich and D. M. Ogawa, "Intercultural and Interracial Communication: An Analytical Approach," in L. A. Samovar and R. E. Porter, eds., *Intercultural Communication: A Reader*

(Belmont, CA: Wadsworth Publishing Co., 1982): 43–49.

[17]Weaver, *op. cit.*

[18]G. Weaver, "This Cutthroat College Generation," *The Washington Star*, February 2, 1981: A11.

[19]G. G. Jackson, "The Roots of the Backlash Theory in Mental Health," *The Journal of Black Psychology,* 6 (1), August 1979: 17–45. Also, in this section, 320–338.

[20]M. Forster, "The Random Sample," *Child Care Work,* 5 (4), Winter 1987: 3.

47

The Crisis of Cross-Cultural Child and Youth Care

Gary R. Weaver

TIM: THERAPY OR BRAINWASHING?

On my way to a humanistic psychology conference in Honolulu, I landed in San Francisco to change planes. I had caught the red-eye out of Washington, D.C. and stayed awake throughout the flight. Flying at night always panics me.

Waiting for my plane to the tropics during the early morning hours was an exercise in endless tedium. This was the era of hippies, war protesters, "black militants," and somehow I expected San Francisco's airport to be different from Washington's National or Chicago's O'Hare. I looked forward to ponytails, headbands, peace buttons, and Afros, but instead found polyester leisure suits, nondescript business attire, and beehive hair styles.

Drowsy, bored, and disappointed with the universality of airport crowds, I slumped down in a chair with my carry-on bag securely locked between my ankles. It was time to catch up on some much-needed shut-eye.

"Got a dollar?" Someone was tapping on my knee. "Sir, could I have a dollar?"

I pulled myself up while checking with one hand to be certain my bag was still tucked

Reprinted from *The Crisis of Cross-Cultural Child and Youth Care Choices in Caring: Contemporary Approaches to Child and Youth Care Work*, eds. Mark A. Krueger and Norman W. Powell, Washington, D.C.: 65–103. Copyright © 1990 by the Child Welfare League of America.

between my feet. About ten inches from my face was a teenage boy with dark complexion, well-worn light blue Levi shirt and trousers, a red headband, and jet black hair that flowed over his collar. Somehow his thick, wire-rimmed glasses didn't complement this fashion statement, but then, these were the days before cheap contact lenses.

"Do–you–have–a–dollar?" This time he said each word carefully and distinctly as if I didn't speak English.

"For what?" Having flown all night in total terror to save money on airfare, I wasn't about to part with a dollar without some explanation. Humanistic psychologists are both human and frugal.

A grin crept over his face as he struggled for an answer to this complex, and somewhat convoluted, question. For a moment, he looked like one of my graduate students who had just received the questions for his comprehensive examination.

"To eat," he blurted out, obviously delighted that he had found the right answer.

The ball was back in my court. I was faced with continuing a conversation of two- and three-word sentences or giving him a dollar. The thought of bargaining him down to a smaller sum never entered my mind.

For hours I had carefully avoided beginning a conversation with another human being. Long ago, I discovered how dangerous it is to lean over to a neighbor on an airplane and ask, "How are you today?"

Now, however, I was ready for a conversation and this young man was the most interesting person I had seen at the airport. Perhaps I could lead him into four- or five-word sentences.

"Why should I give you money?"

"Because."

Not a bad response if this were a philosophy course. This young fellow would be comfortable at the humanistic psychology conference. He speaks Zen.

"Because of what?"

"Because I don't have any money. I'm a runaway from Indian school. My mother is an invalid. I have no place to live, no job, and I'm hungry. Please give me a dollar."

I should have stopped while I was ahead. The "let-me-tell-you-my-life-story" conversation I had so carefully avoided on the plane had just begun, but the challenge of trying to carry on a conversation with him could be the most stimulating thing at San Francisco International Airport. Humans are social animals and must communicate, which is probably why some of us talk to ourselves when there's no one else to talk to. I had at least two hours before my plane took off, and it was worth a dollar to hear this young panhandler's pitch.

"Who are you?" This question usually elicits a job description—people tell you what they do—but Tim actually told me who he was. He claimed to have grown up on a reservation on the West Coast where his grandfather was a tribal chief. Like many young American Indians, he was shipped out-of-state to a federal Indian school where he mixed with boys from dozens of different tribes from around the United States. He hated school and ran away. His mother couldn't care for him because she had been struck with polio and could move about only with the aid of crutches and leg braces. His father had abandoned his mother before he was born.

Tim had been in San Francisco for nearly a year and was able to survive with handouts from strangers. The best hustling was at the airport where tourists were fascinated with his appearance. They were not at all reluctant to give a dollar to an Indian boy. And it was obvious that he had great verbal skills with which to pry money out of even the most hardened skinflint.

It seemed Tim was as eager to talk to someone as I was. Most travelers either ignored him or handed over their money, but few engaged in conversation. He asked who I was and where I was going. I explained that I taught psychology (a knee-jerk response—I told him what I did) and was on my way to a conference.

It was actually an enjoyable encounter, although I was fairly sure that much of what he told me was pure fabrication. Nevertheless, it was entertaining and certainly worth a dollar. After my flight was announced, I stood up and pulled a business card and two dollars out of my wallet. I will hand a business card to almost anyone—drunks in bars, obnoxious salesmen, lonely old ladies on airplanes. It is perhaps an overreaction to my labor-class family background.

"If you get to D.C., give me a call! Okay?" Fat chance, but it is the customary thing to say. Tim tucked the bills and card in his breast pocket, smiled broadly, and gave me a curt wave of his hand. "Have a good trip, Doc!"

A few months later, I was awakened by the phone at three in the morning. I tried to avoid answering the phone in the hope that my wife would pick it up and I could drift back to sleep, but she can usually hold out longer than I in this game.

"Collect call for Dr. Weaver from Tim." Tim! Tim who? I have no relative named Tim. Of course, no student who actually expects to graduate would call me collect at three in the morning. I accepted the call.

"Doc, I need your help. Remember, I'm the escapee from Indian school." When will I ever learn to stop handing out business cards?

Tim was in a detention facility in San Francisco after having attempted suicide by taking a variety of drugs. In California, it is apparently against the law to attempt suicide. He was placed in a hospital because he was found unconscious with his nose broken from his attempt to bash his head against a brick wall. The life history he gave me at the airport was entirely true. As a juvenile without a parent who could care for him, he was a ward of the court. The judge decided to commit him to a state hospital for therapy and counseling and he would soon be transferred. He could leave the mental hospital when he was deemed "normal" or when he was an adult and no longer considered a threat to himself.

Tim phoned me because he knew no other psychologist who might be able to convince the judge that he was emotionally stable and should be released. It was amazing how rationally and persuasively Tim presented his case to me. Nevertheless, attempted suicide calls for help. I suggested he cooperate with the court. He could then get good treatment, three meals a day, and a place to sleep. I assured him that, in my opinion, he would probably be out of the hospital and on the streets within a few months.

He pleaded that he actually did not intend to commit suicide. It was simply a matter of accidently mixing too many different drugs at one time. But I held firm and asked him to write and let me know how things were at the mental hospital. After about a half hour, he was somewhat convinced that going along with the court was the best alternative. He really didn't have any choice in the matter. He was transferred the next day.

Over the next month, I received two or three lengthy letters from Tim describing his experiences in the hospital. He was an excellent writer and intelligent. He felt that he was being held prisoner and the only way he could get out of the hospital was to allow himself to be "brainwashed." At first I dismissed his arguments as typical resistance to therapy, but gradually his position began to make sense.

The hospital used a form of milieu therapy whereby the peer group helps to determine the wellness and progress of a patient. Everyone was assigned to a particular group of boys who would, by consensus, rate each other somewhere along a continuum from severely disturbed to normal. The criteria were based upon behavior within the group.

If a boy is perceived as withdrawn, uncooperative, given to explosions of rage, and so forth, he might be ranked a Level Five. At Level Four, he relates to others, but he is extremely closed emotionally, shows little concern for others, and is still prone to bouts of anger. Self-disclosive interactive behavior takes place at Level Three. On this level, the youth also displays authentic emotions such as breaking down in tears while relating a traumatic event in his life. At Level Two, self-disclosure continues, accompanied by affective communication, and the patient demonstrates self-control, insight, and altruism. Still, there is some uncertainty as to whether he can make it outside the institution. At Level One the boy is certified sane or normal and is allowed to exit the institution and return to society again.

This all sounds reasonable and fair. Yet the very behavior that the facility considered normal was quite abnormal for an American Indian. Being self-disclosive, breaking down emotionally in front of others, and relating traumatic experiences are all equated with losing face, shame, and humiliation. Tim would never display this behavior before other boys in his tribe, and he certainly could never behave this way in front of Anglos.

In Tim's mind, this was brainwashing. He was being forced to give up his culture and adopt the Anglo culture. He had failed at everything—school, finding a job, even committing suicide. The only shred of self-esteem and pride he had left was his identity as an American Indian. How would other boys in his tribe interpret this behavior? What would his grandfather think of him?

Tim was right. To gain release, he had to display the behavior appropriate for mainstream children in therapy. He had to act like a white youth. And, deep down, he knew he was expected to think and feel like a white boy. Indeed, this *was* a form of brainwashing or cultural oppression.

If a white youth were placed in an American Indian group, it would be obvious that the expected and accepted norms of appropriate behavior would be inappropriate for the single white child. Tim was the only Indian in an all-white group, and the standards of normality were equally inappropriate. Furthermore, there were no American Indians on the staff, and the entire institution dictated that mainstream behavior was the criterion of normality.

I phoned the hospital and explained to his floor supervisor who I was and how I had met Tim. I told him of Tim's concerns and stressed the importance of his culture to his psychological well-being. His worldview, values, beliefs, and perceptions determined a great deal of his behavior. The price he paid to be considered normal—to give up his culture—was a price no white child had to pay. Surely, the hospital could adjust its therapeutic model for these cultural differences. Perhaps some sort of one-on-one therapy would be more effective and less threatening for Tim.

"I've studied anthropology in college. Don't give me all this Indian crap!" The supervisor was unswayed and claimed he had already heard all this from Tim. All the boys were treated in the same manner and the therapeutic model was standard for everyone. There would be no exceptions.

I was then faced with a dilemma—should I advise Tim to give in and perhaps risk losing his self-esteem and ethnic pride? Or should I encourage him to fight to his last breath to maintain his ethnic integrity? A great deal of his anger was a result of his inability to adapt to the social group in the institution and his feeling of aloneness in a white world. Should he stop fighting the mold he was being forced into, or struggle to keep his self intact, including his American Indian culture? He had already spent a great deal of time in "isolation" because of his acting-out behavior, which of course was a reaction to the environment and pressures of the institution.

I compromised. I suggested he "scope"—observe the so-called normal white youths, mimic their behavior, and realize that this is a strategy to gain release. This was not a retreat or cowardice, but instead, a strategic withdrawal. It had certainly worked for many prisoners of war and allowed them to survive and keep their sanity.

To this day, I think of the ethical implication of my advice. Was I undermining sound therapy? Or was the therapeutic model actually doing more harm than good for Tim? Was I being professional or was I simply caught up in the warped logic of a severely disturbed adolescent? Does one child's pride and cultural identity supersede the years of experience and research that must have gone into the creation of this therapeutic model?

Within a year, Tim was released. Had he not played the role of a white youth, there was a good likelihood he would have remained institutionalized until he reached the age of 18. In the struggle to maintain his cultural identity, he was probably strengthened and grew a great deal. He had found a way to keep his culture when faced with the overwhelming power that tried to take it away.

He eventually hitchhiked across the continent and lived with our family. There was no drug use or emotional outburst or depression, and no denying his American Indian identity. He spent endless hours reading books on American Indians and even worked at the Bureau of Indian Affairs. He was never brainwashed.

THE DEMOGRAPHICS OF CHILD CARE

In the next decade the numbers of white youths in institutions for troubled youths will steadily decrease while the number of minority youths will inevitably increase. The demographic trends clearly show that these institutions will be filled with a grossly disproportionate number of black, Hispanic, and other nonmainstream residents. At the same time, child care workers will probably remain predominantly white.

The birthrate in the United States, which has declined almost steadily since the first census in 1790, fell to an all-time low about 10 years ago and has remained there, below replacement level, ever since.[1] The overall national birthrate is approximately 15.5 per 1,000. For whites, however, it is 14.6 and for blacks, 20.9. The black population is increasing at a much faster rate than the white or overall population.

Were it not for immigration, the low level of reproduction would cause the population of the United States to begin shrinking before the middle of the next century. Over a quarter of the increase in population for the past few years has been the result of immigration, with most coming from Hispanic and Asian nations. Their birthrates are far higher and median ages far lower than the national average of white Americans.

The average age of whites is well over 32, yet the median age of blacks is about 26 and the median age of Hispanics is 25. The percentage of youths among minority populations is much greater than among white Americans. This steadily widening gap between white and minority median ages and birthrates will result in a disproportionate number and percentage of youths within minority groups.

Young men are responsible for most crime, and because of the sharp drop in birthrates, the number of young men is declining.[2] Minority birthrates, however, are not declining as rapidly. If the vast majority of felonies continue to be committed by juveniles, we can anticipate that programs dealing with these troubled youths will be drawing from a population that is increasingly disproportionately nonwhite.

It is not simply a matter of birthrates and median ages that accounts for the impending demographic shifts in institutions dealing with troubled youths. Black youths are often clustered in urban areas, come from low-income and single-parent families, and are exposed daily to social and physical deprivation. The pressures on their families are much greater than those on white Americans. They are more likely to come from broken homes, twice as likely to come from unemployed families, twice as likely to lie below the poverty level, and at least three times as likely as white youths to be unemployed.

Hispanic families are also overwhelmingly centered in urban areas with even higher rates of unemployment and poverty than blacks. Their educational attainments are lower and they are burdened with distinct language and cultural differences that only serve to enhance their distance from the mainstream of America.

Thirty years ago most immigrants were fairly well educated and came from the middle or upper class of their own countries, especially if they came from non-European nations. The majority were professionals fleeing political oppression. Today, they are undereducated, lower class, and fleeing economic oppression. They tend to cluster in urban areas rife with poverty and crime. In spite of their traditional extended families, immigrant youths are also faced with enormous socio-economic difficulties that tear apart the fabric of the family. They are often trapped between cultures, marginal to both the traditional culture of their parents and that of their host country peers.

Is it any wonder that minority youths may have more behavioral problems than mainstream youths? Even without the demographic shifts, we would expect that they would be disproportionately poor, unemployed, living in urban areas, and would come from families overwhelmed by socioeconomic stress. Regardless of their rising numbers and percentage in the population, these youths obviously are more likely to have difficulties coping with modern society. In the near future they may swamp courts, schools, and institutions that deal with maladjusted young people.

The staff members of these institutions, however, will continue to be mainly mainstream or white. The percentage of minority child care workers and other professonals dealing with troubled youths is certainly less than 10%. Fewer than 1% of all professionals in the field of mental health are Hispanic. Approximately 60% of all children in group care facilities are minority children, and yet the staff members of these programs are over 77% white.[3]

WHAT IS NORMAL BEHAVIOR?

Except for such extremes as psychosis and physiological disorders, normality is usually culturally defined as being like others in the dominant society. It is exceedingly difficult to quantify and observe values, beliefs, thought patterns, and perceptions. Thus, normality rests overwhelmingly on behavior. Those not behaving according to the norms of white, middle-class, mainstream America often are perceived as engaging in pathological or abnormal behavior. Yet true pathological behavior is socially and psychologically destructive, not merely different from the dominant group.

Most people unconsciously place negative value judgments on that which is culturally different. What "they" do is bad, inappropriate, wrong, or abnormal, not simply different. An American might say that "the British drive on the wrong side of the road," when, in fact, they drive on the left side of the road. Or a foreign visitor might tell co-nationals that "Americans eat bad food," when he really means that Americans eat different food than people in his country. This tendency to perceive culturally different behavior negatively is most likely to occur when people are unaware of the concept of culture and the lens of their own culture.

It is almost impossible to describe culturally different behavior objectively because we view it through the lens of our own cultural experiences. This causes us not only to select out that which our culture has deemed significant and ignore evidence that might contradict or confuse our simple perspective, but also adds an evaluative dimension where our behavior becomes normal, and their different behavior becomes abnormal. If we cannot describe the behavior of others objectively, how can we possibly understand or empathize with that behavior?

Sometimes that which is culturally different is not even given attention. It is ignored or denied, and other people and the artifacts of their culture are treated as invisible or marginal. This is somewhat like the tourist in Mexico who asks a vendor the price of a serape. "Three hundred pesos," the vendor replies. "No, how much is it in real money?"

Children who are culturally different are not simply viewed as different. Their culture is ignored or denied and the children feel marginal. And their behavior is often perceived as abnormal, when in fact it may be only culturally different. To illustrate, consider the following scenario:

> Gloria, a six-year-old, inner-city black child has been having difficulty in school. Her teacher, a white, middle-class woman in her mid-thirties, tells Gloria to ask her mother to come to school to see her after class. Gloria responds, "No ma'am, she be sick." What might the teacher think of this response: Gloria is not very bright—she is speaking bad English. The teacher then suggests that Gloria ask her mother to come to school next week, after class. Gloria again responds, only more emphatically this time, "No, ma'am. She *be* sick." Now, what does the teacher think? Not only is Gloria speaking bad English, she is probably lying. How does Gloria know that her mother will be sick next week?

All of the teacher's assumptions are wrong. Gloria is neither dumb nor is she lying. Gloria is using the tense of the verb "to be" to mean an ongoing process. Her mother is chronically ill. This tense no longer exists in standard American English, but it is found in most non-Western languages and even Shakespearean English. Ironically, one could conclude that Gloria is much brighter than her teacher because she is quite properly using a verb tense that her teacher doesn't know.

The verb "to be" is the most common verb in so-called Black English, a reflection of the cultural emphasis placed on who you are—family background, age, relationships with others, and so forth. Gloria's form of English is a vital part of her culture and reflects a value system and thought pattern typical of many non-Western cultures. To survive and excel in a standard English world, she must of course use standard English in the classroom; black dialect is necessary to communicate with her peers in the community. It offers a sense of belonging and in-group membership so paramount for the development of self-esteem. It is totally appropriate for Gloria to speak Black English with her friends on the playground or in the community.

The teacher is engaging in a subtle form of unconscious racism. Had Gloria grown up in Scotland and spoken a Scottish dialect with her peers on the playground, she might be perceived as very intelligent, especially if she then spoke the King's English in her classroom. Gloria has mastered one language—Black English. Her problem is learning another language—Standard English—and knowing when it is appropriate to use one or the other. An outstanding example is Dr. Martin Luther King, who would often give the same speech to a black audience in Black English and to a white audience in Standard English.

Gloria's teacher views her as deficient in language skills, while she communicates quite well with her friends. Instead of considering her speech as a bilingual problem, the teacher is unconsciously viewing Gloria as an underdeveloped white child. This denies Gloria the right to be different, it treats her culture as an inferior version of mainstream America, and the burden of cross-cultural understanding and communication rests on her shoulders, not the teacher's.[4]

Unfortunately, although the teacher may never voice her assumptions, Gloria is more likely than a white child to receive the negative nonverbal messages "you are dumb" and "you are lying." Some researchers claim that nonmainstream children are the most adept at receiving nonverbal cues.[5] If we treat people as if they are unintelligent, we may well create a self-fulfilling prophecy. Children, in particular, are likely to believe they are not very bright and, in turn, perform at levels far below their capabilities.

When asked a question, white American school children enthusiastically compete with each other for the teacher's attention by frantically waving their arms in the air. Not only do these children want the opportunity to be first to give the correct answer, they love it when the "smart" child on the other side of the room gives the wrong answer. It is literally a matter of each individual student in competition with the entire class, and there is only one winner.

American Indian children seldom wave their arms, which may indicate to the teacher that they are uninvolved or don't know the right answer. Compared to the Anglo children, the American Indian children may appear slow in the teacher's eyes. Among American Indians, however, learning does not take place by observation of a skill immediately followed by a demonstration of the skill before others. In their group-oriented culture, one does not publicly compete against peers. Social harmony and cooperation are much more important values than individual competition.

The learning style and ways of demonstrating knowledge are different for American Indian children, yet the teacher attributes uninvolvement and lack of intelligence to their behavior. Within their culture, their behavior is expected, accepted, and appropriate. Waving one's arm for attention, trying to demonstrate publicly a newly learned skill, and competing with classmates, would be quite abnormal.[6] Who one is—a friend, a member of the in-group, a person who values social harmony and cooperation—is much more important than what one does as an individual. The ascribed status of group member supersedes earned status as an individual.

CONFLICTING LEARNING STYLES AND THOUGHT PATTERNS

What one learns and how one learns is culturally determined,[7] yet most people assume everyone learns the same things in the same ways as they do. Each culture teaches its members to solve problems and think in similar patterns that are specific to that particular culture. Nevertheless, most people assume everyone thinks the same way. If people do not think the way you do, they are often viewed as pathological thinkers. They are "immature," "ignorant," "unintelligent," and "uneducated." Not only is normal behavior primarily culturally defined, but so too are the ways in which we learn and think.

Abstractive, inductive, and analytical thinking and problem solving are typical of mainstream Americans. Learning is usually done individually, with an emphasis on precision, quantification, and the selection of relevant data to solve a problem. Most intelligence, aptitude, and achievement tests measure this type of learning.

There is strong evidence that American Indians, black Americans, and even many white females think associatively, deductively, and relationally. The preferred learning style involves others, and there is an emphasis on generalizations, qualification, and bringing together all data to solve a problem. The mainstream style focuses on universalistic meanings and things, whereas the relational style features approximation, contextual meaning, and people.[8]

These are simply two different ways of thinking and learning; neither is better than the other. Most intelligence tests measure only "abstractive" knowledge and thought, yet many great intellectuals think contextually or in images. Einstein was a terrible mathematician and conceived his theories in terms of whole images. He had to translate his theories into the "abstractive" mathematical language and learning style of Euro-Americans.[9]

Children who think in terms of associations, relationships, or images are often labeled unintelligent or immature. Piaget believed that "abstractive thinking" was more qualitatively mature than "complexive" or relational thought. If we apply his model to Einstein, he would be categorized as a preadolescent thinker. Of course, most nonmainstream children would also fail to reach Piaget's highest level of intellectual development.

When these culturally different children enter the educational system, they are confronted with a cross-cultural clash of learning styles, especially around the sixth grade, when we notice a sharp fall-off of their performance.

Often the family is blamed for not providing support or educational enhancement. The only significant change in their relationships with others, however, is their interaction with teachers and the school system. It is at about the sixth grade that "abstractive," rather than associative, skills become emphasized. Decline in academic performance begins to occur at this time for American Indian and black children.

As these children begin to be perceived as stupid or immature, their self-esteem and confidence start to wane, and they may even begin to unconsciously doubt their own intellectual abilities. Is it any wonder that they might engage in acting-out behavior, given this assault on their self-image and the frustrations of trying to cope with a foreign culture?

Differences in thought patterns and learning styles are highly significant in cross-cultural education and child care; this is an extremely complex and unconscious manifestation of cross-cultural conflict. Attention is primarily given to behavior—to what a child does—not how the child thinks or learns. Who the child is—his or her internal culture—is hidden and ignored. And yet, who the child is determines behavior. The conflict of cultures often creates the "abnormal" behavior of the nonmainstream child. When two cultural icebergs collide, the greatest impact occurs below the water level of awareness at the base where we find internal culture.

To illustrate these differences in thought patterns, let us consider a history teacher who asks students to write an essay examination on the following topic: "Discuss the American Civil War between 1861 and 1862." As the teacher reads through the essays she finds a paper filled with lengthy run-on paragraphs. In the middle of this essay, James, the student who wrote it, has included discussion of his father and the neighborhood in which he grew up.

The teacher confronts him. "James, you cannot write three-page paragraphs. You must organize your writing into a series of distinct paragraphs with a lead or topic sentence, subsentences, and a transitionary sentence that leads into the next paragraph. And your father

and neighborhood are really irrelevant to the American Civil War."

James is a black child who thinks associatively or relationally. He ties thoughts together almost poetically and, in his mind, everything that is associated with the topic is relevant. His father is very much like General Lee in his demeanor, and a fire in his father's neighborhood created the kind of havoc and remorse that occurred as the North moved through the South. In a poetic fashion, James wrote of the "sad buildings" and "grieving animals." He was engaging in what Piaget would term anthropomorphic thought by giving human traits and feelings to nonhuman things, a clear indication of immature intellectual development in Piaget's model.

James flunked his examination, not because of lack of intelligence or understanding, but because he failed to think in an "abstractive" manner. What the teacher actually wanted was for James to consider all the lectures she had given and all the books that were read and select out or abstract that which the teacher felt was pertinent to the topic. James' problem was that he related everything to the topic and communicated in an associative style. He wrote his essay as a whole image, a poem, rather than a series of precise and distinct paragraphs. Perhaps this helps explain why poetry is so much admired in his black community. The teacher wanted an office memo, not a poem.

The style of learning that excites James the most is highly participatory in the context of a group. If he is excited about an idea, he wants to share his enthusiasm, and sitting alone before an open book does not allow for interaction with others. In church, when the preacher moves the congregation, they verbally participate by shouting "Amen" and "all right." Contrast this with the behavior of white Episcopalians in a suburban community.

The teacher perceived the behavior of his black children as disruptive and a sign that they are not learning, when in fact, had they quietly sat taking notes, little learning would be taking place. If the teacher understood James' culture, including his typical style of learning, thought patterns, and associative communication, he would not make these negative attributions to James' behavior. Furthermore, he would know that James' real problem is learning another culture that has a different way of gaining knowledge, thinking, and communicating. James is abnormal only to the degree that he has not internalized the norms of the teacher's culture regarding education. In his own community or culture, he is perfectly normal.

Here is another example of where the burden of understanding and adjustment rests on the child, not the adult. A bicultural approach would lessen the probability that James would feel inferior, unintelligent, and academically incapable. James must, of course, learn to think and communicate in a mainstream fashion, given the nature of American society. He certainly does not want to remain encapsulated in his neighborhood community, and he does want to excel academically. But he is not verbally and intellectually underdeveloped or deprived, he is not unintelligent, and he is not intellectually immature. He is simply culturally different from the mainstream.

CROSS-CULTURAL PERCEPTION

Picture yourself as a young, white policeman patrolling the inner city of a large metropolitan area on a hot summer evening. Gang muggings and break-ins have taken place in the area and most of the residents are black. You come upon a group of about a dozen black male youths on a street corner gesturing violently and shouting obscenities at each other. You overhear one young man shout at another, "Yo muther, she like a railroad track cause she bin laid all over the land!" This insult is accompanied by a menacing finger pointed at another youth who is rocking back and forth as if to prepare for an assault.

The situation presents itself as a potential explosion of rage and you step in to break up the group. Obviously a fight is brewing or the young men wouldn't be standing in the streets shouting insults at each other with menacing gestures. But is this the reality or only your image of reality? In effect, it makes no difference once you've acted, because you have the power and authority of being an enforcer of the law.

These inner-city youths were merely engaging in a friendly form of interaction called "Joning," "the numbers," or "the dozens." Each one tries to out-insult the other, often very poetically, until the opponent cannot come back with a clever insult that is more sophisticated and poetic than the one given. The street corner was a meeting place, especially on hot evenings when the lack of air conditioning makes the tenements unbearable. And although there was little real hostility present during the exchanges, your intrusion would definitely provoke hostility from the group.

Lack of cultural understanding and the element of tension caused you to react with your rule of thumb, to judge the situation only in terms of your own experience and perceptions. Certainly a group of young white men standing on a street corner in suburbia and insulting each other would connote anger and hostility. But this is a different cultural milieu, and careful observation would have contradicted that assumption in the inner city. For example, had you quietly observed for a few minutes you would have heard laughter after each insult from the other members of the group and the menacing gestures would have soon appeared as almost choreographed, teasing nonverbal expressions and not actually spontaneously hostile movements.[10]

The average white policeman can draw on his own behavior to predict the behavior of other whites; he cannot necessarily do so with blacks. A group of black juveniles standing on a street corner shouting insults at each other regarding their respective mothers might appear as a disturbance to the white policeman, while to the average black it is an acceptable way of interacting that has little potential for violence. The white policeman has no way of predicting the behavior of blacks from his own experience, and he consequently turns to the rules (the system) to judge what is proper or improper. There is ambiguity—the normal cues to aid in judging the situation are no longer present—that consequently produces anxiety. Thus, he is tempted to oversimplify, distort, and perhaps even project his own frustrations and hostility into the scenario. He uses his rule of thumb, but his thumb carries much more force than that of the average citizen. The net effect is prejudice enforced with the threat or actuality of violence.

Cross-cultural misunderstanding is inevitable when two different cultures are interacting during conflict or high-anxiety situations, and most of the interaction is nonverbal. A gesture, the symbol of a gun, a shout—all can be misinterpreted and usually are.[11] During a period of conflict, the need to act and react is most likely to cause us to fail to consider all possible causes and variables of situations.

It is much easier to generalize negative characteristics of another's behavior when we lack experience with and knowledge of his or her culture. The psychologist Adorno once defined prejudice as "being down on that which you are not up on." If you know the culture of others, you know their motives and you can place their behavior in the context of their culture. If you are ignorant of their culture, however, they become dehumanized, and are judged only by the standards of your own culture-specific experiences.

On one hand, when "we" do something negative, we often attribute the behavior to the situation. We do not normally engage in this bad or inappropriate behavior. On the other hand, when "they" do something negative, it is because it is their typical behavior. It is a trait of those people. "I cheated on that examination because the professor was unfair, but Hispanic kids are always cheating." This tendency to make situational attributes to our bad behavior and trait attributions to their behavior is a fundamental error in cross-cultural perception.[12] It is most likely to happen if we know little of another's culture and crisis or conflict is taking place.

To be fair, let us reverse our hypothetical illustration and imagine yourself as a black policeman who has grown up in the inner city of Washington, D.C. You have joined the police force of a small midwestern town that is predominantly white. As you pull up to an intersection, you glance out your car window and see a group of white teenagers jammed into a small car. To your amazement, one young man has dropped his trousers and has his bottom hanging out the car window.

This could only be indecent exposure and you arrest the young man. In white communi-

ties, however, this might be a fairly normal form of adolescent play called "mooning." Although it is unlikely you would ever see a black teenager engaging in this behavior, it is rather common among white adolescents. As a black policeman, your rule of thumb leads to the conclusion that this is indecent and, in fact, a criminal act. Rather than seeing it as a part of normal, albeit strange, white male teenage behavior, you might attribute it to the sexual perversion of these boys. It is possible that you could perceive it as an intentional affront to you—a form of racism intended to embarrass or humiliate the observer.

Here, "possibilistic" thinking is added to "rule of thumb" thinking. It is indeed possible that this white youth went out of his way to expose his posterior to you because you are black, but it is highly improbable.[13] Chances are that the youth was quite shocked to be caught in this awkward situation by a policeman, regardless of race. When we assume the possible as probable, we are engaging in a form of paranoia that causes us to become even more ethnocentric and self-centered. We cannot develop empathy for the other person or put ourselves in his or her shoes to understand the motivation for a particular behavior. We cannot put the behavior in the context of the situation or culture of the other person.

In child and youth care, days are filled with conflict and crisis. How often do child care workers perceive behavior of culturally different children in the context of their culture or the situation? Do we make trait attributions instead of situational attributions to inappropriate behavior? Do we apply our rule of thumb when we should be considering all variables to account for that behavior? Do we sometimes engage in possibilistic rather than probabilistic thinking?

CROSS-CULTURAL INTERACTION

Each of us has a particular worldview or image of reality. When we interact with others, we often assume that they share our perceptions and give the same meaning to messages as we do. If we have few similar experiences, however, we do not perceive reality in similar ways, and consequently our messages have quite different meanings.

Our perceptions influence our thought patterns, values, and beliefs, which, in turn, influence our perceptions.[14] We act and react according to our image of reality. To this extent, our perception or image of reality, not reality itself, is what determines behavior, including our interactions with others. While some might view all human interactions as an opportunity for competition, others might view them as opportunities for cooperation. Sitting alone in a cafeteria because we seek privacy might be perceived by others as being aloof, hostile, or arrogant.

The meaning we give to messages is determined by our experiences or culture. We do not send meaning, we send messages. If we have experienced the world in similar ways, then our messages will elicit similar meanings. Meanings are in our head. If I sit facing an old Arab with my ankle on my knee and the bottom of my shoe exposed to his view, he would be highly insulted. The sole of my shoe touches the earth, which is filthy and, in his culture, I am exposing my filthy shoe to his face. In the United States, this is a typically macho way of sitting, and the bottom of one's shoe has no particular meaning.

If I am speaking to the Arab gentleman, it is highly unlikely he is paying attention to a word I am saying, because he has been programmed by his culture to attend to this shocking message—"bottom of shoe in my face." The verbal messages I am sending are not getting through because they are overwhelmed by my strong nonverbal message. Further, in his culture, people are generally more aware of nonverbal messages than in the mainstream American culture. Imagine yourself talking to someone who has his finger in his nose and is speaking to you; chances are you would not pay much attention to what he is saying.

Our culture teaches us what messages to attend to and what those messages mean. This is especially true of nonverbal messages, because their meanings are almost entirely culture-specific. Moreover, we learn how to communicate nonverbally simply by growing up and participating with others in the culture. Verbal communication is learned formally,

explicitly, in the classroom, while nonverbal communication is learned informally, implicitly, through interaction with others. Because nonverbal communication skills are unconsciously acquired, most of us are unaware that we are constantly sending and receiving these messages and giving them meanings.

One researcher found that in face-to-face interaction perhaps 90% of the messages we send that communicate feelings are sent nonverbally—by our facial expression, tone of voice, posture, gesture, and spatial distance.[15] The meanings we unconsciously give to these messages are almost entirely based upon our experiences in our own culture. If simultaneous verbal and nonverbal messages are contradictory, the nonverbal messages have greater credibility. For example, most of us have left an interview feeling that we know we will not get the job, although the interviewer may have given rather positive assurances we might have the job. In all likelihood, the interviewer's face, tone of voice, or gestures told us that we were not going to be hired and these messages were much more powerful than the verbal assurances.

Nonverbal messages have such unconsciously attributed culture-specific affective meaning that they are a major source of communications breakdown between people of different cultures. When Jesse Jackson chants "I AM SOMEBODY!" and involves the audience in repeating the chant, many whites are repulsed and equate this emotionalism and audience participation with loss of control, demagoguery, and manipulation. Blacks tend to perceive Jackson as a powerful speaker whose sincerity is demonstrated by his emotional style. Audience participation is an indication that he is in tune with all present, as when a black minister's moving sermon elicits shouts of "AMEN!" from the congregation.

According to linguist Thomas Kochman, "blacks treasure boldness and audacity as signs of leadership ability, while in 'mainstream American politics,' boldness and audacity are taken to mean an individual is not stable, not a team player."[16] Blacks also make a distinction between arguing and fighting that whites do not. For blacks, verbal confrontation can go a long way before physical confrontation is threatened. Arguing with emotive boldness is a way of truth seeking. A person who will not confront another about a problem is not concerned and does not attach importance to either the problem or the other person involved. Thus, in an argument, whites think "fight" long before blacks do.

In child and youth care, how often do white workers give the meaning "fight" to a message sent by a black coworker or child that was intended to mean "I care," "I feel strongly about this," or "I sincerely want to resolve this matter?" Child care workers often seek to keep a lid on situations, yet how many times do they use preemptive force to stop a "fight" that may be merely a verbal confrontation? Is a child or coworker perceived as unstable or out of control simply because he or she uses a different style of communication?

Conversely, how are white child care workers perceived by their black coworkers and children when they respond to a bold, emotional statement with cool, unemotional words? Is it any wonder that some whites are viewed as inhuman or insincere when they may feel they are only being professional, rational, and in control?

If a conflict does take place, when do we begin to negotiate? Among Hispanics, disputes follow steps or chains that are different from those of Anglos.[17] Because of the high premium placed upon social harmony, Hispanics may not speak out when they are first offended. After many such slights, however, they seem to explode uncontrollably. This indicates "I can't take it anymore. I'm upset. Let's talk about it." The emotional outburst may be the first verbalization that something is wrong. Furthermore, it sets the stage for negotiation because all the cards are on the table.

To an Anglo-American, the outburst is equated with loss of control, irrationality, and fight. He may feel the Hispanic ought to have spoken up when the first offense occurred rather than waiting until there is no possibility of rational discussion. At the very moment when the Hispanic wants to discuss a problem, the Anglo-American thinks the dispute has gone well beyond the discussion stage. During the Malvinas or Falkland Island War between Britain and Argentina, the Argentines were genuinely perplexed when the British refused to negotiate once the fighting had begun. From Argentina's perspective, the British were being totally unreasonable.[18]

In a child care facility, white counselors may appear unreasonable to Hispanic children when they refuse to negotiate once a lively and emotional verbal exchange has taken place. Black children might not even see a need to negotiate because the situation is not actually a fight, it is only an impassioned discussion.

How one resolves a conflict is also culture-specific. For example, among Asians, Arabs, Hispanics, and Africans, great store is placed in not losing face or being shamed. If a conflict is actually taking place before others, it is very difficult for either party to back off. Thus, third party intermediaries are often essential, and it is assumed that members of one's in-group will step in to mediate, thereby preventing the disputants from losing face. These intermediaries must be perceived as connected or related to the combatants. In a family dispute, another member of the family might play this role, but not a stranger.

Anglo-Americans rather believe that it is the responsibility of the disputants to settle matters among themselves. Third parties ought not to get involved and are not really responsible for what happens. This is somewhat like the old Spencer Tracy movies where the juveniles punch each other out as the good father or priest stands by to be sure no other children get involved.

A child who comes from a culture where the community and family act as intermediaries may assume that he can allow the dispute to escalate verbally because an intermediary will step in before blows are thrown. A child who comes from a culture where intermediaries do not play a part in conflict, however, may feel the intermediaries are interfering. Even when intermediaries are expected to play a part, how they play that part and in what relationship they are to the disputants are all important variables.

Generally, nonmainstream children are much more adept at reading nonverbal cues than mainstream children and their verbal and nonverbal messages can be fully understood only if one knows their cultural background.

Mainstream children rely much more on direct verbal communication where the meanings of messages are not so embedded in the context of the culture. Unless we understand the culture of another person, it is extremely difficult to send and receive messages that have parallel meanings. During a conflict situation, we are most likely to give meaning to messages based upon our own cultural understandings. Thus, we often exacerbate a conflict rather than help to resolve it.

Because attitudes and feelings are primarily communicated nonverbally and the meanings we give to nonverbal messages are mostly unconscious and culture-specific, a great deal of attention must be given to how and what we communicate without using words. Consider the following illustration:

> Jose is an 11-year-old Puerto Rican child who is constantly chatting with the female student sitting next to him in his classroom. Almost daily his Anglo female teacher must remind him to stop talking during class. One morning, however, she is upset by a personal problem before entering the classroom, and she has grown annoyed by having to constantly remind Jose to stop talking to the girl. As the class begins, Jose leans over to whisper something to his friend and the teacher decides it is time to stop this behavior once and for all. She yells out, "Jose! How many times do I have to tell you to be quiet when I'm speaking?" As she is admonishing Jose, Jose looks down at the floor and mutters, "Yes, ma'am." The teacher approaches Jose, grabs him by the chin, and pulls his face toward hers. "Look at me when I'm talking to you," she shouts, and continues to lecture him on how rude and distracting his behavior has been over the past school year.[19]

Jose will probably hate this teacher for the rest of his life, yet she may have no idea that he feels this way. Although she may regret losing her temper, the incident was rather straightforward and Jose was the offending party, not she. As she spoke to him, he looked away to avoid her reprimand. She, in turn, grabbed his chin to force him to look at her for a few seconds so that he fully understood and paid attention to what she was saying.

Jose was sorry to have provoked her outburst and he did what many Puerto Rican children are expected to do when being reprimanded by an adult—he looked down at the floor. This is polite behavior in his culture and demonstrates that he knows he is wrong. To look an adult in the eye while being reprimanded is to assume defiance. This is also true in many other parts of the world including sections of Asia and Africa. The behavior that the teacher viewed as avoidance of wrongdoing and a deserved reprimand was, in Jose's culture, an acceptance of the wrongdoing and reprimand.

The teacher then grabbed his chin. At the age of 11, Jose perceived himself not as a child, but rather, a young man. To grab a man's face is a serious violation of his sense of masculinity, especially when done by a female who is not a member of the family or who is quite old. The teacher humiliated Jose in front of his peers and the girl with whom he was so fond of talking. Of course, had he done something very bad at home, his mother might grab his chin. But in this case he did not burn down the school, he had just tried to communicate politeness and accept his responsibility for what had happened, and the teacher not only rejected his efforts, she escalated the incident by treating him like a child and offending his sense of machismo.

It is understandable that a child would not comprehend the breakdown of communication that has occurred in this illustration. Note, however, that the burden of understanding is placed on Jose, not his teacher. If the teacher had a class with large numbers of Puerto Rican children, it would be reasonable to expect her to know something of their culture, including their ways of communicating. The same would be true of a white teacher with a majority of black, American Indian, or Asian children.

If the misunderstandings have not completely alienated these children, they are eventually expected to fit into the mold of appropriate behavior dictated by the teacher's culture. As they grow older, they learn what meanings the teacher intended, and they learn his or her verbal and nonverbal language. The anger and hurt probably were caused when they were very young and, over time, they may forget what incidents caused these feelings. Nevertheless, as young adults they still resent Anglo teachers and think of school as something painful. They may not know why their white teachers aroused hostile feelings, but those feelings do not simply go away with time. Rather, they seem to build up and fester, ready to explode at any moment of confrontation with a white authority figure.[20]

CHILD AND YOUTH CARE INSTITUTIONS AS COOKIE CUTTERS

How often do child care professionals view behavior that is simply culturally different from the mainstream as abnormal, or even worse, pathological? Do child care workers verbally or nonverbally communicate negative judgments to children, thereby creating a self-fulfilling prophecy? Are children getting "better" by behaving like mainstream children? Are we controlling, manipulating, and shaping minority behavior to fit our own conception of the mainstream world without regard to the price children must pay to become "normal" by giving up their own culture? If so, we are engaging in cultural oppression, or trying to bring about cultural homogenization—all in the name of caring and helping.

Does the average child care worker really understand who the nonmainstream children are—their culture, values, beliefs, thought patterns, and worldview? Certainly in child and youth care the emphasis is more on doing than being, and the deficit hypothesis is the underlying principle in dealing with minority children. What children do is all important and the child care worker is often paid to observe, control, manipulate, and shape behavior. Of course, fairness means that behavior ought to be regulated with consistency and standardization. All should behave in the same way, and all should be treated equally—but by whose standards?

Today there is a backlash against cultural diversity in education and child and youth care. Affirmative action, cultural identity programs, bilingual and bicultural education, and most community programs that accentuate cultural differences have been cut back or abandoned. "Colorblindness" and the deficit hypothesis have a special impact on child and youth care because of their overemphasis on behavior at the expense of identity or internal culture.

Since children may end up in a center because of nonmainstream behavior, and normality depends on their behaving in a mainstream manner, therapy becomes nothing more than getting them to fit the dominant mold. And this is all done "for the good of the child." The process is not one of throwing their culture into the melting pot of a pluralistic child care institution. It is one of forcing the child to fit into the cookie cutter mold with a white, Protestant, male, Anglo-Saxon shape.

> An 11-year-old Guatemalan boy by the name of Jesus was admitted to an institution for emotionally disturbed children because of his inability to control his temper in his suburban school and his acting-out behavior. His command of English was good, although he had a heavy accent. Before joining the other children on the athletic field, he met with the center's secretary to be certain all his papers were in order. She felt that Jesus was a strange name that would cause him to be teased. Thus, from that moment on he was known as Jess, a name he couldn't pronounce and that did not sound similar to Jesus in Spanish. As he walked onto the athletic field, he had a new name. How quickly one loses identity in the United States! In Guatemala one's name is seldom altered and, in fact, one usually has a name that includes both the father and mother's family name.
>
> Jesus didn't just walk onto the athletic field—he strutted onto the field. He knew he was the oldest boy in the center, and he was the eldest son in his family. His age gave him an ascribed status and role and he had to carry himself in accordance with that role. He was not simply one of the children, he was the young man of the institution. He would not allow other children to beat him in any sport and he took no guff from

them. Even the college students who were his counselors were treated as equals, in that he looked them directly in the eye when they spoke to him, and he would not tolerate being spoken to as a child.

His behavior was interpreted by many of the staff members as arrogant, cocky, and defiant. Some felt that he needed to have this taken out of him, for his own good. When he got into a fight with two or more boys, some counselors would briefly turn their heads in hopes that Jesus would get the "wind knocked out of his sails": what he needed was some humility.

Of course, Jesus was behaving in a fairly normal way for a Guatemalan, and other children would have accepted and expected this behavior in Guatemala. Jesus was acting like a responsible young man upholding the ascribed status given by age and sex. To allow other children to beat him in sports would cause him to lose face. To let the counselors speak to him as a child would cause him to be shamed. And his swagger would be in sync with that of other 11-year-old Guatemalan males.

Within a few weeks Jesus was given another label—"sex pervert." No one actually used these words, but he was discovered masturbating, and he seemed to be preoccupied with sexual talk. Further, he was caught in bed with another boy, and was placed in a private room as if he had to be isolated from the other children so as not to contaminate the institution. He openly bragged about his sexual exploits with girls in his suburban community, to the delight of the other children and the consternation of the staff. If his accounts were true, Jesus had more sexual experience than most of the male staff members.

One counselor was a devout Roman Catholic who felt it was his responsibility to remind Jesus that masturbation was a sin. With that admonition, Jesus got the message—he was a pervert. This self-image was reinforced by his having been isolated from the other children at night. Not only was the institution punishing him, God would soon join in!

It would be normal for a boy his age in Guatemala to be concerned with sex and to boast of imaginary sexual exploits. This is all part of machismo and would be understood as such in Latin America. And while his introduction of masturbation to the institution was a novelty for most of the younger boys, it was a skill many precocious 11-year-olds would have acquired. He was certainly no pervert.

As the children were lining up to take showers one evening, a staff member noticed that Jesus was not circumcised. For supposed health reasons, his mother was urged to have him circumcised. The meaning of all this was very clear to Jesus—he was having a portion of his penis removed because of his behavior. It was a Freudian nightmare for this young man.

His mother decided to return to Guatemala and notified the institution that Jesus would be leaving. During a subsequent staff meeting, the issue of Jesus' departure was raised and it was generally agreed that his progress would be undermined by the return to his homeland. One counselor blurted out, "Jess is American!"

Jesus had been in the country only three or four years. Certainly, he had not lost his native culture and he spoke fluent Spanish. Perhaps what this counselor really meant was that Jesus was almost broken—he was almost forced into the cookie cutter mold. Indeed, to survive emotionally, Jesus had become more withdrawn and less "arrogant," he had stopped talking about sex, and he even stopped wincing when others called him Jess. He learned to obey the commands of the staff and accept his punishment with proper humility. He was almost normal. He was almost mainstream American.

MINORITY CHILDREN EXPERIENCE CULTURE SHOCK

Nonmainstream children go through genuine culture shock when they enter the institution's culture. The stress of entering this new culture is certainly as great as that of anyone adjusting overseas, maybe even greater, because it is not anticipated, the lack of control is more apparent, and children are neither emotionally nor intellectually as well prepared to deal with culture shock.

The assumptions regarding normality are mainstream, and most of the staff members are mainstream. Thus, the children get little support from others, especially the staff members, because the latter are culturally different and they themselves have never experienced culture shock. Children are not oriented to the dynamics of cross-cultural adjustment, they do not anticipate the difficulties, they already have emotional problems or they wouldn't be in the facility, and the cultural differences are extreme.

People who live overseas usually go through an initial period of stress that is related to the problems of adjusting to another culture. The most common characteristic is a sense of helplessness or lack of control. This malady is primarily a result of the breakdown of communication between people from different cultures; a loss of home-cultural cues as to what is appropriate behavior; the absence of that which is familiar, such as the physical and social environment; and the identity crisis we all go through when we are immersed in a new social situation.

Nonmainstream children experience pain upon entering the child care facility—the pain of being unable to communicate effectively; the pain of lost cultural cues that make life predictable and provide psychological security; the pain of struggling to maintain an identity in the face of overwhelming powers that not only fail to acknowledge their cultural identity but demand that they give up the identity and take on another.

Without role models to relate to, or others who can empathize with their feelings, the children often irrationally vent their frustration with aggression. Little attention is paid to who the nonmainstream children are, only what they do. And they are indeed trapped, with no control over their environment. They feel helpless, and the situation is hopeless.

When an animal is placed in a cage with an electric grid on the floor, it wanders about aimlessly. When the grid is electrified, its first reaction is to try to escape from the cage—avoidance, escape, or flight behavior. This is the most common initial reaction of anyone who experiences the pain of culture shock.

Flight behavior manifests itself in many ways. The children may be perpetually sleepy. Much of the pain is a result of the breakdown of communication, especially nonverbal communication that unconsciously transmits feelings and is overwhelmingly culture-specific. Children take the ability to communicate for granted because they have been communicating effectively and spontaneously with others since they were two or three years old. Now everything is confused, messages are ambiguous, contradictory, or have no meaning whatsoever. They feel cut off from others. Sleeping allows them to avoid interacting with those who are the source of this pain.

The children may withdraw into their own world or interact only with those who are culturally similar. The withdrawal may be misperceived as hostility, and the banding together with others from their culture as an attempt to avoid blending into the dominant institutional culture. Teachers may describe them as slow or lethargic and counselors might view them as uncooperative or even severely disturbed. The staff members do not understand why the children are behaving as they do. Instead of attributing their behavior to the situation, they often give trait attributions—"He's got a chip on his shoulder." "Hispanic kids are always moody and into being macho." Or, "Black kids stick together and won't mix with the other kids." Sometimes the trait attributions are even more negative—"He's lazy." Or, "He's really a sick kid."

Of course, the children cannot totally withdraw from others for long. They live in a social environment in the institution. Let us place another animal into our hypothetical cage and turn on the electric grid. This time, close all doors to prevent any escape from the painful environment. Within minutes the animals will attack each other and eventually one will die. When any animal is trapped in a painful situation from which there is no escape or avoidance of pain, flight turns into fight behavior or aggression.

This is obviously irrational. Logically, the animals should attack the cage or the sadistic social scientist pressing the button, but instead they attack each other. Similarly, nonmainstream children are trapped in an institutonal setting that creates pain. They cannot totally withdraw from others, and they cannot escape the institution, although they will certainly try their best. They feel helpless, everything seems hopeless, and they have no control over the environment or their feelings and behavior. The anger may be directed toward anyone in the institution. Certainly, children who are committed to lockup facilities leave those facilities more aggressive and angry than when they entered. The social and physical environment causes that behavior.

Sometimes the anger is internalized and the children become self-destructive. And, at times, the sense of hopelessness leads to learned helplessness and its consequent depression. Freud believed that one of the primary causes of suicide was anger that could not be externalized for social reasons and was then turned upon oneself. Studies of old people trapped in institutions where they have no control over their environment, contrasted with those who have a sense of control, show that their life spans are much shorter.[21] Those who could not influence decisions about when to go to bed, when and what to eat, or recreational activities seemed to give up on life and felt helpless. They were much more severely depressed and saw no alternative but to give in to death.

The autistic hostility[22] and learned helplessness of the children may be interpreted as a sign of improved behavior—the children appear cooperative and calmed down. But from a psychological perspective, the children are in worse shape than before they entered the facility. Many staff members are simply relieved that the children are no longer exploding in rage, and fail to recognize the severe depression.

The pain caused by the breakdown of interpersonal communication is not relieved by withdrawal or aggression. If the cause of the pain is the ineffectiveness of communication, cutting out others only makes it worse. In an institutional setting, aggression can lead only to further restrictions limiting interaction with others. Again, the source of the pain is the inability to communicate. Because we are social animals, we must communicate; old

people who live alone may invent others to communicate with because of this need.

That the breakdown of communication produces pain is evident when we lose a loved one with whom we have shared intimate communication. Or, as a teenager, perhaps we fell in love with someone who, when angry, showed it in a passive-aggressive way by not answering our phone calls or letters. We may have found ourselves acting a bit crazy or uncontrolled—pounding on his or her door at two in the morning, or even instigating a dispute to get some emotive communication out of the other person.

When we do something over and over again that gets rewarded, we perpetuate that behavior. When this behavior is no longer rewarded, we experience pain. The children we have been talking about have their lives—they know how to greet people, communicate displeasure, and begin a friendship. In the child and youth care facility, this message system doesn't work. Perhaps thousands of times we have dropped coins in a soda machine and received the reward for our behavior—a can of soda. Then, one day, we drop coins and no can appears. What do we do? I know many who would begin to kick the machine. It is illogical, irrational, and even childish. Although it does not get us the soda, we feel a lot better after kicking the machine.

When flight and fight behavior fail to alleviate the pain, children may become increasingly neurotic. This is a complex situation, and they may unconsciously distort and deny reality in an effort to remove ambiguity. This reaction might be termed filter behavior.

They might withdraw to those from their own culture and try to create a little "inner city," "San Juan," "Chinatown," or "tribe" within the institution. The avoidance of other children is often justified with dualistic thinking—"my friends are good" and "the white kids and staff are bad." The opposite also sometimes occurs. Nonmainstream children may reject those from their own culture and band together with whites. They try to deny their own culture and justify this behavior by thinking, "the white culture is great," while their own culture is "terrible." In both cases, the children are simplifying a painful and complex reality by opting for one culture over the other. They see the two as mutually exclusive and find no area of overlap or compromise.

When we enter another culture, we feel like fish out of water. Cues that made us feel comfortable are absent. Faces are different, people communicate differently, the food is different, and there is a genuine object loss. Problem-solving approaches that worked all our lives no longer seem to work, and we begin to doubt our ability to function in this new social environment. Our resultant confusion, anger, and depression are reactions to the stress of cross-cultural adjustment—it is situational, not chronic. Yet it appears as if the misery will never end, and even worse, nobody seems to be concerned about us.

As nonmainstream children go through the various stages of culture shock, staff members not only fail to understand the situational nature of the children's behavior, they compound the stress by reacting to the children's reactions, creating a "conflict cycle"[23] and power struggle. The dominant culture will eventually win out and as the children's behavior changes, their values and beliefs may slowly begin to change. The dissonance between their newly imposed behavior and their old values and beliefs will only add to their frustrations. They cannot deny the behavioral changes. The only thing that can change to bring about consonance is their belief and value system.[24] Like Winston Smith in *1984*, they may even begin to love "Big Brother" and hate themselves.

HIGH RECIDIVISM OF MINORITY YOUTH

After the children are released from the child care facility to reenter their community, in theory it's all uphill. They are deemed normal or well adjusted. Minority children, however, are much more likely than the mainstream child to return soon to the facility. The recidivism rate of minority children is much higher than that of mainstream children.

When they return, the debate within the facility often revolves around two basic positions. Some argue that the children were released too early. Others just as vehemently bemoan how the bad community ruined all of their good work. At times, a mixture of these two positions is taken. The children and/or their community are to blame. Seldom does one question whether the child care facility itself bears some responsibility.

In all probability, the children went through reentry/transition stress or reverse culture shock[25] when they tried to readjust to their home culture. They learned the behaviors, values, and beliefs of the mainstream culture. That is, they acculturated to the facility or would have never been released and considered normal. If they were returning to a mainstream community, indeed they were better prepared to function and cope with the world than before they entered the facility, but the very behavior that was appropriate in the institution may be totally inappropriate or counterproductive in their nonmainstream community.

The process of readjustment to their home culture is remarkably similar to the process they went through in the institution. Again, a breakdown of communication occurs. Their family and friends cannot empathize with the experiences they have had in the facility, the communicative style they acquired is strange, and even some of their nonverbal patterns are no longer similar to the others. They are out of sync with their own culture.

Again, there is a loss of cues. They grew accustomed to institutonal life—its food, surroundings, ways of solving problems and interacting. The identity that emerged in their struggle between cultures in the facility is different from the one they took with them when they entered the facility. The various reactions to the stress of their community set in and, before long, they are in trouble again.

People in their community are unlikely to understand what they are going through and react to their reactions, creating another conflict cycle. Distortion and denial or filter behavior are again present. They may deny the experience they went through in the facility, somewhat like the war veteran who refuses to accept the reality of his traumatic experiences on the battlefront. They pretend they never left home and were unaffected by their institutionalization. People who have not shared their experiences are not interested in hearing their stories and they are unable to understand them anyway. It is like describing and sharing the experience of a sunset with a blind person.

The opposite sometimes occurs. That is, the children might deny that they have returned to their home culture. An American sojourner who returns from a stay in England may speak with an exaggerated British accent, wear three-piece suits, and smoke a pipe while continually extolling the virtues of England and putting down the United States. These children refuse to give up the behavior of the institution and disparage that of their community. To justify this reaction, they actually believe that everything in the institution was good and everything in their own community is bad.

Minority children may join together with those who have shared their institutional experience and avoid those who have not. In Gambia, West Africa, there is a bar where the "Been To's" hang out nightly. They are not members of a particular tribe. They have all studied overseas, however, and spend most of their time talking about where they have been to—some have been to London, others to Paris or New York, and so on. They constantly relive their experiences and avoid socializing with those who have not left the community. The "been-to" minority children can share, romanticize, and relive their experiences in the institution, and the group becomes an exclusive gang that cuts out the rest of the community. In some cases, the experience may be viewed as some sort of manhood or puberty ritual—"been to" a juvenile detention center.

As with culture shock, almost all of these behaviors are unconscious reactions to the stress of adaptation and the breakdown of communication, loss of cues, and the consequent identity crisis. When these youngsters go through flight, they may try to withdraw from their family and friends. In the extended family and in-group community, however, privacy cannot be won. It is unlikely that most minority children could find a place to be alone. Fight behavior is more probable, and it may be channeled to those who are lower on the social hierarchy or who present little retaliatory threat, such as members of the family or

younger children. The returning children may be as confused by their own strange behavior as their family and friends.

Reverse culture shock may be even more stressful and severe than culture shock. One study of Americans returning from overseas found that over 70% felt that they had greater difficulty readjusting to the United States than adjusting to overseas.[26] Perhaps the reason it is more stressful is that it is almost completely unanticipated. When we anticipate a stressful event, we are much better able to cope with it.[27] When people go overseas, they worry about different food, new language, transportation difficulties, loss of friends, and so forth. People do not worry about going home and do not anticipate stress. Returning minority children do not anticipate the stress of reentering their own community, the loss of familiar institutional physical and social cues, or the new identity they bring.

We know of techniques for minimizing reentry/transition stress and helping individuals to develop coping strategies that allow them to control their reactions.[28] Primarily it is a matter of convincing returnees that they may go through reverse culture shock so that they can rehearse or anticipate the difficulties. For mainstream children, this is not a great problem because they are returning from a mainstream institution to a mainstream culture. For minority children, it is almost essential that the institution provide some sort of reentry training. Without this training the children have a very slim chance of avoiding conflict with others and returning to an institutional setting. It is unreasonable and almost cruel to expect the children to understand the process of reentry, and it is cynical to blame them or their community for their failure to readjust to the community. The responsibility rests firmly on the shoulders of child and youth care professionals.

Those children who are most successful at adjusting to the institutional culture are often the least successful at readjusting to their home culture.[29] They may have adopted new rules that are not entirely welcome in their community. And their intense identification with the mainstream culture that helped them adapt interferes with their home culture identity.

Often these children do not realize how much they have really changed until they have returned home. Thus, from the view of both the staff and the children themselves, there is little expectation of difficulty.

Both culture shock and reverse culture shock must be considered as processes that can be understood, and coping strategies can be developed that will minimize the severity and duration of symptoms. If the staff and the minority children can understand the process and anticipate the stress, there will automatically be a sense of greater self-control on the part of the children and an increased possibility of considering alternative behaviors to cope with stress. Without this awareness, the children become victims of their own reactions and lose control.

There is no cure for culture shock but there are ways of minimizing its effects and using the experiences in a positive way. For example, children who successfully go through culture shock have a greater sense of self-control, a broader range of perceptions and coping strategies, and experience freedom from their cultural prison. Successful adaptation should cause the children to be more multicultural[30] and flexible in their responses to various social environments. However, this type of growth does not come about without some pain—in this case, the pain of cross-cultural adjustment and readjustment.

Only if staff members understand the dynamics of cross-cultural adjustment can they help to make this a positive experience for the children. Without their understanding, it is almost inevitable that they will make it a negative experience that may seriously damage the children's sense of identity and self-confidence. Furthermore, the staff will necessarily bear an overwhelming amount of responsibility for the recidivism of the minority child.

THE NEED FOR CROSS-CULTURAL EDUCATION OF CHILD AND YOUTH CARE WORKERS

Child care workers must understand the impact of culture on behavior and the dynamics of cross-cultural adjustment and communication to better serve the nonmainstream child.

To be an effective child care worker, it may be as important to study anthropology and cross-cultural communication as to study psychology. This is especially so if the demographic trend of increasingly greater numbers of minority children entering child care facilities continues.

We desperately need more minority child and youth care workers. The number has actually decreased in the past five years. Minority children need adult models to serve as ego ideals, to model cross-cultural interactive behavior, and to empathize with their experiences. White staff members and children also need these nonmainstream child care worker to break stereotypes they might have. Observing minority group members in the high-status role child care worker makes preconceptions untenable and leads to the formation of more positive attitudes.[31]

All child care workers ought to understand the concept of culture and appreciate the reality that they have been conditioned by their own culture to perceive and think in particular ways. The first step in understanding how the culture of others affects one's thinking, values, beliefs, perceptions, and behaviors is to understand one's own culture.

Culture is like an iceberg; only the tip is exposed. Behavior—or external culture—is the smallest part. To truly understand the child, we must go below the level of awareness and find out what is inside the child's mind. Internal culture, including values, beliefs, thought patterns, perceptions, and worldview, determines external culture, or what the child does. Unless we can understand the internal culture, we will mistakenly evaluate behavior based on our own cultural expectations. Further, we may make trait, rather than situational, attributions to the child's negative behavior.

The unspoken ideal is to be whitelike, yet the nonmainstream child is not, and never will be, white. Various studies of black children who had an increase in their positive self-concept and ethnic identity showed no increase in their antiwhite feelings. Moreover, a study of severely disturbed black patients found that those most severely disturbed identified with white society, as opposed to their own ethnic culture.[32] Strengthening a child's cultural identity is absolutely no threat to the white institution, and it may be essential to providing the type of therapy most appropriate to the nonmainsteam child.

It is equally important for mainstream child and youth care workers to appreciate the richness of nonmainstream cultures. If the child care worker views nonmainstream children as deficient, the children will pick up the message, even if it is not verbally expressed. Nonmainstream children are exceedingly sensitive to nonverbal messages and are the ones most likely to pick up the message that they are inferior. This, in turn, may create a self-fulfilling prophecy—the children will meet our expectations.

We know that the international sojourner must understand the process of cross-cultural adjustment to overcome his or her reactions and develop effective coping strategies that may minimize the stress of culture shock. Nonmainstream children should also have some understanding of how and why they react as they do. Only then are the children free to act, instead of reacting, in relation to the institutional environment. Only then do the children maintain a sense of control and understand that their feelings are normal and shared by others who have gone through this experience.

Certainly every child and youth care worker ought to understand the dynamics of culture shock so that he or she does not become part of the conflict cycle by reacting to the child's reactions. The burden of responsibility for cross-cultural understanding and communication should be moved from the shoulders of the child to the professional child and youth care worker. Only the child and youth care worker can effectively break the conflict cycle and prevent it from leading to a power struggle.

Simply helping children anticipate the stress of reentry to their own culture may be enough to greatly cut down the severity of reverse culture shock. They have already gone through the process of adaptation once, and the process of readaptation to their own culture is similar. We can draw from experiences they had in the institution to help them better cope with those they will encounter in their community. Many of the coping strategies they already know can be used again, but they must be prepared to use them.

The child and youth care worker ought to avoid confusing sympathy and identification with empathy. Sympathy may be appropriate in many instances, but it is not very helpful and gives no understanding of the child's world. Identification assumes the child care worker can be like the child. At times, this may also be appropriate, but it will not help us understand the child or meet the child's need. Instead, we must develop cultural empathy—trying to understand the way the child views the world and feels about it. Only then can we truly understand the child's behavior and free ourselves from our own cultural biases.

Children from different cultures have different worldviews, values, beliefs, ways of interacting, and behaviors. To understand their behavior we must place it in the context of their culture. In the process, inevitably we will begin to understand our own culture and its impact on our perceptions, values, beliefs, and behavior. Awareness of our own internal culture is a fortunate by-product of cross-cultural interaction and awareness of the culture of others. At this point, not only will we be more helpful to troubled minority children, we will achieve the freedom to transcend our own culture.

ENDNOTES

[1] B. Rensberger and P. Hilts, "Birthrate in U.S. Remains Below Replacement Level," *The Washington Post,* 27 October 1986: 6 (A).

[2] S. Rich, "Sharp Decline in Crime Rates Forecast for Rest of Century," *The Washington Post,* 26 October 1986: 4 (A).

[3] M. Krueger, R. Lauerman, J. Beker, V. Savicki, P. Parry and N. Powell, "Professional Child and Youth Care Work in the United States and Canada: A Report of the NOCCWA Research and Study Committee," *Journal of Child and Youth Care Work,* 3, 1987.

[4] W. Raspberry, "Black Kids Need Standard English," *The Washington Post,* 1 October 1986: 19 (A).

[5] A. Mehrabian, "Communication Without Words," *Psychology Today,* 2 (4), 1968: 53–55.

[6]S. U. Philips, "Participant Structures and Communicative Competence: Warm Springs Children in Community and Classroom," in *Functions of Language in the Classroom,* C. B. Cazden, V. P. John, and D. Hymes, eds. (New York: Teachers College Press, 1972): 370–394.

[7]E. T. Hall, *Beyond Culture* (New York: Doubleday, 1976).

[8]R. A. Cohen, "Conceptual Styles, Culture Conflict, and Nonverbal Tests of Intelligence," *American Anthropologist,* 71, 1969: 828–856.

[9]Hall, *op. cit.*

[10]J. Williams, "Missing the Message: Thomas Kochman on Cultural Crossed Signals," *The Washington Post,* 9 February 1985: B1, B8.

[11]G. Weaver, "American Identity Movements: A Cross-Cultural Confrontation," *Intellect,* March 1975: 377–380; *see also* "Understanding and Coping with Cross-Cultural Adjustment Stress," in *Cross-Cultural Orientation: New Conceptualizations and Applications,* R. M. Paige, ed. (Lanham, MD: University Press of America, 1986): 111–145.

[12]R. W. Brislin, *Cross-Cultural Encounters* (New York: Pergamon Press, 1981).

[13]E. Fromm, *May Man Prevail?* (Garden City, NY: Anchor Books, 1961).

[14]M. R. Singer, *Intercultural Communication: A Perceptual Approach* (Upper Saddle River, NJ: Prentice-Hall, Inc., 1987).

[15]Mehrabian, *op. cit.*

[16]J. Williams, *op. cit.*

[17]Hall, *op. cit.; see also Psychology Today: An Introduction,* 5th ed. (New York: Random House, 1983).

[18]C. Travis, "Interview with Edward Hall. Edward T. Hall: A Social Scientist with a Gift for Solving Human Problems," *GEO,* 5, March 1985: 13–14.

[19]T. Kochman, "Cross-Cultural Communication: Contrasting Perspectives, Conflicting Sensibilities," *The Florida FL Reporter,* Spring/Fall 1971: 53–54.

[20]T. I. Rubin, *The Angry Book* (New York: Collier Books, 1969).

[21]E. J. Langer and J. Rodin, "The Effects of Choice and Enhanced Personal Responsibility for the Aged. A Field Experiment in an Institutional Setting," *Journal of Personality and Social Psychology,* 34, 1976: 191–198.

[22]T. Newcomb, "Autistic Hostility and Social Reality," *Human Relations,* 1, 1947: 69–86.

[23]N. J. Long and B. Duffner, "The Stress Cycle or the Coping Cycle? The Impact of Home and School Stresses on Pupils' Classroom Behavior," in *Conflict in the Classroom: The Education of Emotionally Disturbed Children,* 4th ed., N. J. Long, W. C. Morse, and R. G. Newman, eds. (Belmont, CA: Wadsworth Publishing Company, 1980): 218–228.

[24]L. Festinger, *A Theory of Cognitive Dissonance* (Stanford, CA: Stanford University Press, 1957).

[25]G. Weaver, "The Process of Reentry," *The Advising Quarterly,* 2, Fall 1987: 1, 3–7.

[26]M. C. Mercil, "Planning and Conducting Reentry Transitional Workshops," Washington, D.C.: Youth for Understanding, International Student Exchange (updated).

[27]L. Egbert, G. Battit, C. Welsh and M. Bartless, "Reduction in Postoperative Pain by Encouragement and Instruction of Patients," *New England Journal of Medicine,* 270, 1964: 825–827.

[28]G. Weaver and P. Uncapher, "The Nigerian Experience: Overseas Living and Value Changes," paper presented at 7th Annual SIETAR Conference, Vancouver, B.C., Canada, March 11, 1981.

[29]S. Bochner, *The Mediating Man: Cultural Interchange and Transitional Education* (Honolulu, HI: East-West Center, 1973).

[30]P. S. Adler, "Beyond Cultural Identity: Reflections on Cultural and Multicultural Man," in *Topics in Cultural Learning,* Vol. 2, R. W. Brislin, ed. (Honolulu, HI: East-West Center, 1984): 168–183.

[31]Brislin, *op. cit.*

[32]G. G. Jackson, "The Roots of the Backlash Theory in Mental Health," *The Journal of Black Psychology,* 6 (1), August, 1979: 17–45.

48

Foul Shots

Rogelio R. Gomez

Now and then I can still see their faces, snickering and laughing, their eyes mocking me. And it bothers me that I should remember. Time and maturity should have diminished the pain, because the incident happened more than 20 years ago. Occasionally, however, a smug smile triggers the memory, and I think, "I should have done something." Some act of defiance could have killed and buried the memory of the incident. Now it's too late.

In 1969, I was a senior on the Luther Burbank High School basketball team. The school is on the south side of San Antonio, in one of the city's many barrios. After practice one day our coach announced that we were going to spend the following Saturday scrimmaging with the ball club from Winston Churchill High, located in the city's rich, white north side. After the basketball game, we were to select someone from the opposing team and "buddy up"—talk with him, have lunch with him and generally spend the day attempting friendship. By telling us that this experience would do both teams some good, I suspect our well-intentioned coach was thinking about the possible benefits of integration and of learning to appreciate the differences of other people. By integrating us with this more prosperous group, I think he was also trying to inspire us.

But my teammates and I smiled sardonically at one another, and our sneakers squeaked as we nervously rubbed them against the waxed hardwood floor of our gym. The prospect of a full day of unfavorable comparisons drew us from a collective groan. As "barrio boys," we

were already acutely aware of the differences between us and them. Churchill meant "white" to us: It meant shiny new cars, two-story homes with fireplaces, pedigreed dogs and manicured hedges. In other words, everything that we did not have. Worse, traveling north meant putting up a front, to ourselves as well as to the Churchill team. We felt we had to pretend that we were cavalier about it all, tough guys who didn't care about "nothin'."

It's clear now that we entered the contest with negative images of ourselves. From childhood, we must have suspected something was inherently wrong with us. The evidence wrapped itself around our collective psyche like a noose. In elementary school, we were not allowed to speak Spanish. The bladed edge of a wooden ruler once came crashing down on my knuckles for violating this dictum. By high school, however, policies had changed, and we could speak Spanish without fear of physical reprisal. Still, speaking our language before whites brought on spasms of shame—for the supposed inferiority of our language and culture—and guilt at feeling shame. That mixture of emotions fueled our burning sense of inferiority.

After all, our mothers in no way resembled the glamorized models of American TV mothers—Donna Reed baking cookies in high heels. My mother's hands were rough and chafed, her wardrobe drab and worn. And my father was preoccupied with making ends meet. His silence starkly contrasted with the glib counsel Jim Anderson offered in "Father Knows Best." And where the Beaver worried about trying to understand some difficult homework assignment, for me it was an altogether different horror, when I was told by my elementary school principal that I did not have the ability to learn.

After I failed to pass the first grade, my report card read that I had a "learning disability." What shame and disillusion it brought my parents! To have carried their dream of a better life from Mexico to America, only to have their hopes quashed by having their only son branded inadequate. And so somewhere during my schooling I assumed that saying I had a "learning disability" was just another way of saying that I was "retarded." School

Rogelio R. Gomez is a fiction writer living in San Antonio.

Reprinted from *The New York Times Magazine,* 13 October 1991, 24, 69.

administrators didn't care that I could not speak English.

As teen-agers, of course, my Mexican-American friends and I did not consciously understand why we felt inferior. But we might have understood if we had fathomed our desperate need to trounce Churchill. We viewed the prospect of besting a white, north-side squad as a particularly fine coup. The match was clearly racial, our need to succeed born of a defiance against prejudice. I see now that we used the basketball court to prove our "blood." And who better to confirm us, if not those whom we considered better? In retrospect, I realize the only thing confirmed that day was that we saw ourselves as negatively as they did.

After we won the morning scrimmage, both teams were led from the gym into an empty room where everyone sat on a shiny linoleum floor. We were supposed to mingle—rub the colors together. But the teams sat separately, our backs against concrete walls. We faced one another like enemies, the empty floor between us a no man's land. As the coaches walked away, one reminded us to share lunch. God! The mere thought of offering them a taco from our brown bags when they had refrigerated deli lunches horrified us.

Then one of their players tossed a bag of Fritos at us. It slid across the slippery floor and stopped in the center of the room. With hearts beating anxiously, we Chicanos stared at the bag as the boy said with a sneer, "Y'all prob-ably like 'em"—the "Frito Bandito" commercial being popular then. And we could see them smiling at each other, giggling, jabbing their elbows into one another's ribs at the joke. The bag seemed to grow before our eyes like a monstrous symbol of inferiority.

We won the afternoon basketball game as well. But winning had accomplished nothing. Though we had wanted to, we couldn't change their perception of us. It seems, in fact, that defeating them made them meaner. Looking back, I feel these young men needed to put us "in our place," to reaffirm the power they felt we had threatened. I think, moreover, that they felt justified, not only because of their inherent sense of superiority, but because our failure to respond to their insult underscored our worthlessness in their eyes.

Two decades later, the memory of their gloating lives on in me. When a white person is discourteous, I find myself wondering what I should do, and afterward, if I've done the right thing. Sometimes I argue when a deft comment would suffice. Then I reprimand myself, for I am no longer a boy. But my impulse to argue bears witness to my ghosts. For, invariably, whenever I feel insulted I'm reminded of that day at Churchill High. And whenever the past encroaches upon the present, I see myself rising boldly, stepping proudly across the years and crushing, underfoot, a silly bag of Fritos.

49

Against the Great Divide

Brian Jarvis

I always notice one thing when I walk through the commons at my high school: the whites are on one side of the room and the blacks are on the other. When I enter the room, I think I'm at an African nationalist meeting. The atmosphere is lively, the clothes are colorful, the voices are loud, the students are up and about, the language is different and there's not a white face to be seen. But the moment I cross the invisible line to the other side, I feel I've moved to another country. There are three times as many people, the voices are softer, the clothes more subdued. Everyone's sitting or lying down, and one has as much chance of seeing a black student as a Martian.

The commons is a gathering spot where students relax on benches and talk with friends. They also buy candy and soda, watch TV and make phone calls. It's a place where all sorts of things happen. But you'll never find a white student and a black student talking to each other.

After three years, I still feel uncomfortable when I have to walk through the "black" side to get to class. It's not that any black students threaten or harass me. They just quietly ignore me and look into the other direction, and I do the same. But there's one who sometimes catches my eye, and I can't help feeling awkward when I see him. He was a close friend from childhood.

Ten years ago, we played catch in our backyards, went bike riding and slept over at one another's house. By the fifth grade, we

Brian Jarvis was 16 and a high-school junior in St. Louis when this was written.

Reprinted from *Newsweek*, 3 May 1995, 14.

went to movies and amusement parks, and bunked together at the same summer camps. We met while playing on the same Little League team, though we attended different grade schools. We're both juniors now at the same high school. We usually don't say anything when we see each other, except maybe a polite "Hi" or "Hey." I can't remember the last time we talked on the phone, much less got together outside of high school.

Since entering high school, we haven't shared a single class or sport. He plays football, a black-dominated sport, while I play tennis, which is, with rare exception, an all-white team. It's as if fate has kept us apart; though, more likely, it's peer pressure.

In the lunchroom, I sit with my white friends and my childhood friend sits with his black ones. It's the same when we walk through the hallways or sit in the library. If Michael Jackson thinks, "It don't matter if you're black or white," he should visit my high school.

I wonder if proponents of desegregation realized that even if schools were integrated, students would choose to remain apart. It wasn't until 1983 that St. Louis's voluntary city-suburban desegregation program was approved. Today, my school has 25 percent black students. While this has given many young people the chance for a better education, it hasn't brought the two races closer together.

In high school, I've become friends with Vietnamese-Americans, Korean-Americans, Iranian-Americans, Indian-Americans, Russian-Americans and exchange students from France and Sweden. The only group that remains at a distance is the African-Americans. I've had only a handful of black students in all my classes and only one black teacher (from Haiti).

CRUCIAL COURSE

In its effort to put students through as many academic classes as possible and prepare them for college, my school seems to have overlooked one crucial course: teaching black and white students how to get along, which in my opinion, would be more valuable than all the others. It's not that there haven't been efforts to improve race relations. Last fall, a group of black and white students established a program called Students Organized Against Racism. But at a recent meeting, SOAR members decided that the separation of blacks and whites was largely voluntary and there was little they could do about it. Another youth group tried to help by moving the soda machine from the "white" side of the commons to the "black" side, so that white students would have to cross the line to get a Coke. But all that's happened is that the students buy their sodas, then return to their own territory.

Last summer, at a youth camp called Miniwanca in Michigan, I did see black and white teens get along. I don't mean just tolerate one another. I mean play sports together, dance together, walk on the beach together and become friends. The students came from all races and backgrounds, as well as from overseas. Camp organizers purposely placed me in a cabin and activity group that included whites, blacks, Southerners, Northerners and foreigners, none of whom I'd met before.

For 10 days, I became great friends with a group of strangers, at least half of whom were black. One wouldn't know that racism existed at that idyllic place, where we told stories around campfires, acted in plays and shared our deepest thoughts about AIDS, parents, abortion and dating. Everyone got along so well there that it was depressing for me to return to high school. But at the same time, it made me hopeful. If black and white teenagers could be friends at leadership camp, couldn't they mix in school as well?

Schools need to make it a real priority to involve whites and blacks together as much as possible. This would mean more multicultural activities, mandatory classes that teach black history and discussion of today's racial controversies. Teachers should mix whites and blacks more in study groups so they *have* to work together in and out of school. (Students won't do it on their own.) And most important, all students should get a chance to attend a camp like Miniwanca. Maybe the Clinton administration could find a way to help finance other camps like it.

As it is now, black and white teenagers just don't know one another. I think a lot about my friend from childhood—what he does on weekends, what he thinks about college, what he wants to do with his life. I have no answers, and it saddens me.

V

The Mass Media, Conflict, and National Images

The ways in which we are entertained and informed by the mass media both reflect and shape the way we view ourselves, others and the world at large. For example, surveys consistently show that most Americans believe that the majority of poor people are black, yet most are white.[1] This is because the face of poverty on TV news and in news magazines is overwhelmingly black.

The popular media can dehumanize groups and perpetuate stereotypes. On American TV, people from the rural South in the U.S. are often characterized as hillbillies with funny accents. The men are lanky and unkempt with a taste for moonshine and an aversion for honest work while hillbilly women are either the Granny—a gaunt woman with straight, unkempt hair—or the oversexed and under-dressed hillbilly babe.[2] These stereotypes affect not only the way in which others view people from the South, but the way in which people in the South view themselves.

In American movies, blacks are disproportionately cast in roles as criminals, Latin Americans as drug runners, and Arabs as terrorists. The characters of the "good guys" are usually well developed while these "bad guys" are portrayed as caricatures, not whole human beings. Thus, when they are eventually killed, no one really cares.

The media may determine how you perceive conflict on the national and international level. Is your image of the world one of conflict between good and evil with good winning out (a melodrama)? Or, is it tragedy where good people sometimes do bad things and bad people sometimes do good things and evil may win out? Can you compromise with your opponent to find a peaceful solution to your differences?

The dominant American culture has traditionally valued action, not talk. Furthermore, if you see the world as a melodrama and perceive yourself as moral or good and your enemies as less than human and absolutely demonic, it is almost impossible to resolve conflict peacefully.

INTERNATIONAL CONFLICT

International conflict is often caused by a genuine clash of interests between nations which cannot be resolved through peaceful means. For example, a nation may attempt to expand its borders or increase its economic and political power at the expense of another nation. Negotiation, arbitration and adjudication fail to help it achieve these objectives. After weighing such factors as economic and military capability, the resolve of citizens to support armed aggression, and the strengths and weaknesses of the enemy, a realistic decision is made to engage in war.

However, the primary causes of war may have little to do with such realistic or rational considerations. Perceptions or images of reality may be more important than reality itself when it comes to explaining the dynamics of international conflict. And, subjective and irrational drives, such as power, pride and fear, may be the strongest reasons for conflict.

Psychological and cultural factors also cause, exacerbate and prolong conflicts between nations. Some nations may be genuinely hegemonic and have a drive for power over others. Aggression thus becomes a tool for promoting national interests. World War II Germany may be the most outstanding example of such a nation.

However, most nations engage in war for defensive reasons—they are motivated by fear, not aggression. Fear is a psychological phenomenon based upon our *perception* of reality, not reality itself. How we imagine the world to be motivates our behavior. Fear can be both rational and irrational. If we believe that another person intends to do us harm, we defend ourselves even if there is no real threat.

Both American involvement in Vietnam in the 1960s and Soviet involvement in Afghanistan in the 1970s were motivated more by fear than by any hegemonic, aggressive drive. Both countries asserted that their aggression was defensive—the U.S. claimed it was protecting South Vietnam from North Vietnamese aggression and the Soviet Union claimed it was supporting the government of Afghanistan from a CIA-led takeover. Whether these threats were real or imagined is largely irrelevant. The consequence was the same—war.

NATIONAL IMAGES

Perceptions of ourselves and others are part of our culture-and-personality system. They are a result of our beliefs and experiences. When perceptions are shared and passed down from one generation to another within a country they are often referred to as "national images." The history of a nation is a vital part of this image because it is based upon events which are selected, highlighted and organized in a way that makes the country special when compared with others.

To understand and predict the behavior of an individual, we must consider that person's history. While we must be cautious in drawing parallels between individual and national behavior, it seems reasonable that if we are to understand and predict national behavior, we must also consider the history that people share in a nation.

Someone who experienced a traumatic childhood with an authoritarian father who exercised strict discipline based upon severe punishment or the threat of punishment, may be exceedingly fearful as an adult. He or she might even be somewhat paranoid. In the paranoid's world view, everyone else is seen as a threat. Paranoids may engage in irrational *possibilistic* thought rather than realistic or *probabilistic* thought.[3] While it is possible that the world is intent on doing one harm, it is not very probable.

In a homogeneous nation where most share the same childhood raising practices, if the role of the typical father is authoritarian, we might speak of an "authoritarian society." In this type of society the divisions between superiors and subordinates are clearly drawn and there are fairly rigid social hierarchies. A somewhat paranoid outlook is prevalent on both personal and national level.

These people have a fearful perception of the world. Their *image* of others is that they are threats and their self-image is that of people who are threatened. This national paranoid image may be reinforced by actual threats or attacks from other nations.

Sometimes paranoids engage in preemptive attacks and strike-out at others before they are assaulted. They do not see this as offensive behavior. Instead, it is consistent with their image of the world as hostile; they are simply defending themselves from the potential aggression of others. To understand and predict the behavior of paranoids we must get inside their heads to know how they perceive reality. This does not mean we agree with their motives, accept their behavior, or share their reality world.

I am describing *empathy,* which is not sympathy for or identification with another person. *Sympathy* is an outsider's perspective—we don't know what motivated a behavior, we simply react to it by "feeling sorry" for the other person. It is primarily a matter of feeling with others and is affective. *Identification with* a person means sharing the perceptions, feelings, and thoughts of another so much so that we become like the other person. Empathy, on the other hand, means understanding how another views the world and organizes information to fit that image. It is primarily cognitive.

People from the same culture or nation share historical experiences and have common ways of perceiving the world. Thus, just as we can speak of individual images and empathy for individuals, we can also speak of *cultural or national images* and the ability to develop *cultural or national empathy.*

Our national image becomes more important during a war because our ingroup membership gives us a sense of ego support. The ingroup/outgroup distinction between "us" and "them" becomes clearer as we try to eliminate ambiguities. We become good and peaceful as they become increasingly more evil and aggressive. We perceive our aggression as defensive, while their aggression is offensive. This dualistic oversimplification is found in most major international conflicts.

MELODRAMA AND TRAGEDY

An *enemy image* develops to give a sense of belonging and to clarify a complex reality. This melodramatic perspective is somewhat like the old American cowboy movies, where the "good guys" are clearly identifiable because they wear white hats and are absolutely angelic, while the "bad guys" wear black hats and are completely demonic. Of course, the good guys always win.

The American people may be more susceptible to melodramatic imagery than Europeans or others because it is a young country that did not go through a feudal period or fight numerous lengthy wars on its own soil. The dualistic thinking of fundamentalist Protestantism (good and evil, heaven and hell, angels and devils, etc.) and the impact of melodramatic themes and images in the mass media both reflect and reinforce the traditional tendency to perceive the world as a melodrama.

The most popular movie in the U.S. during the summer of 1996 was "Independence Day." It was a classic example of melodrama. Aliens from outer space were trying to conquer earth and the President flew the plane that led the attack against them. Americans loved this modern day science fiction cowboy movie.

In 1996, Americans were glued to their television sets watching the O.J. Simpson trial. Viewership of CNN increased over 600 percent when it broadcast this murder trial, perhaps because it was presented as a melodrama or entertainment. At the end of the day, legal experts were featured in news shows to give their opinions as to who lost and who won—the prosecutor or the defense—somewhat like a football game. But, this was not a melodrama, it was a tragedy. Innocent people had been murdered.[4]

In reality, international conflict is much more of a tragedy than a melodrama. Neither party is completely good or bad, fear may be a much more powerful cause of aggression than hostility, and the tragic reality is that in war all combatants may lose.

Aspects of an image include experience or history, education and the influence of the mass media. A nation with a history of actual continued aggression from others, or the perception of ongoing external threat, is predisposed to view the world as hostile. Because the nation has survived in this hostile and threatening world, the national self-image may be one of noble endurance. Delusions of persecution and grandeur may coexist. The educational system stresses past wars and the heroism of one's own people, while the mass media often reinforce the melodramatic enemy image.

Enemy soldiers are often dehumanized and portrayed as ignoble animals. Their violent deaths are sometimes abstract or removed from reality. We talk of tonnage dropped, sorties, or tanks killed without considering bodies torn apart and grieving families. The 1991 Persian Gulf War was viewed somewhat like a video game for some Americans, who saw few dead bodies of Iraqi soldiers or civilians on television, yet were entranced by the high-tech precision of American missiles.

ARTICLES

Journalist Ellen Goodman believes that the only way to change melodramatic imagery is to allow the mass media to show war for what it really is—violent, tragic death and destruction. Her article, "In Defense of Casualty Pictures on TV," was written as a reaction to the tendency of the mass media to dehumanize modern warfare and our enemies. She believes that TV ought to make war more human and personal.

Meg Greenfield also supports portraying **authentic**, tragic violence on television ("TV's True Violence"). In fact, she believes that real violence ought to be shown because it has traditionally been a part of classic literature and drama. The problem with television is the **fictional** portrayal of violence, which may, "in time, render us incapable of recognizing and responding to the real thing."

Bloody violence can be found in fairy tales, mythology, Shakespeare, and operas, but it is part of a cultural expression that helps us to understand the tragedy of deadly conflicts. George Gerbner ("Marketing Global Mayhem") shares Meg Greenfield's viewpoint on romanticized, escapist and gratuitous violence in contemporary mass media. He favors the realistic portrayal of death and violence without the "happy endings produced on the dramatic assembly-line."

Gerbner found that overexposure to violence-laden media "cultivates an exaggerated sense of insecurity and mistrust, and anxiety about the mean world seen on television." This sense of vulnerability and fear is greatest for women, minorities, and older people who are heavy viewers and more often depicted as victims of violence.[5]

Although the most highly-rated television programs in the U.S. are not violent, violence sells well around the globe. Melodramatic violence is characterized by dramatic, simplistic, dualistic imagery that needs no translation. It is especially appealing to young viewers who are a greater proportion of the population in most non-European countries. With the overwhelming edge America has had on the worldwide mass media market,[6] its violent yet unrealistic images may have an even greater impact outside the U.S.

Goodman, Greenfield, and Gerbner are opposed to romanticized, melodramatic violence and support the realistic portrayal of violence in entertainment and news media. On the other hand, Robert Jay Lifton and Richard A. Falk find that humans often deny and distort a painful reality so that they can get on with their lives. "On Numbing and Feeling" describes the phenomenon of "psychic numbing," which occurs when we are overwhelmed by tragic reality. If we are bombarded by casualty pictures on TV every night, we may simply filter out these images and numb ourselves to the psychological pain they produce.

Sam Keen's "Faces of the Enemy" argues that "our problem lies not in our technology, but in our minds, in our ancient tendency to create our enemies in our own imagination." He describes the many images we have seen throughout human history to dehumanize others, such as depicting them as barbarians, rapists, beasts, and even as enemies of God.

Of course, the enemy image is a distortion. Jack G. Shaheen, author of *The TV Arab*,[7] blames most of the distortion on the mass media for portraying Arabs as less than human. In his article, "The Face of Arabs in American Mass Media," he claims that because of this dehumanized image, it is difficult for Americans to empathize with Arabs as full human beings.

Enemies often see in others the very characteristics they deny in themselves. While we perceive our enemy to be hostile, aggressive, and demonic, our enemy perceives us in the same way. That is, we have a *mirror image* of each other.

Social psychologist Urie Bronfenbrenner's article, "The Mirror Image in Soviet-American Relations," is perhaps the first description of this phenomenon. In the summer of 1960, during a trip to the USSR, he discovered that Soviets and Americans had roughly the same self-image and enemy image.

This was at the height of the Cold War and for over thirty years most of the writing on enemy images helped to explain the dynamics of Soviet-American hostility. While the Cold War has ended, these findings and theories would apply to almost any war, including the Vietnam War,[8] the Arab-Israeli conflict,[9] the Persian Gulf War,[10] or even the war between ethnic and religious groups in the former Yugoslavia.

Psychologist Ralph K. White has written extensively on the cognitive psychological aspects of the enemy image. His article provides case studies of Soviet behavior during the Cold War. "Empathizing with the Rulers of the USSR" explains White's definition of empathy and provides strong evidence that much of Soviet behavior during the Cold War was indeed defensive.[11]

In "The Face of the Enemy," psychiatrist Jerome Frank takes a much more psychoanalytic approach to explaining why enemies are dehumanized. He explains how we often project onto others the very aggressive and hostile tendencies we deny in ourselves, and then attack others for being hostile. Hence, we also produce a self-fulfilling prophecy. If we treat others as if they are hostile, they will often become hostile.

Robert Jervis's book *Perception and Misperception in International Politics*[12] has become a classic in the psychology of war and the field of political psychology. In the brief excerpt in this section, he discusses how Leon Festinger's theory of cognitive dissonance helps us understand why decision-makers often alter their perceptions of reality to conform with decisions they have made. These cognitive distortions help them to justify their behavior and produce consonance between their actions and beliefs.

Lastly, economist Kenneth E. Boulding takes a systems approach to image theory in his article "National Images and International Systems." He views a people's national image as a result of history and suggests that it changes with time and experience in the international system.

New nations often have unsophisticated images of themselves and the world. They are somewhat narcissistic or self-centered and are unable to compromise or understand how other nations view the world. In White's terms, they lack realistic empathy.

As nations evolve, citizens realize they are part of an international system. Gradually, their national image becomes more sophisticated and they see themselves as one actor in a collection of interrelated nations. In addition, they understand how other nations might view them and the world.

Boulding also discusses the entire system of nations and develops a grid which allows us to measure the amount of hostility or friendliness in a particular region of the world or the international system as a whole. This economic systems approach offers an interesting macro-level analysis of the role of image in international relations. Boulding suggests we might even be able to predict conflict by understanding and quantifying national images around the world.

War clearly begins in the minds of human beings. It is often caused by our perception of reality, not necessarily reality itself. The psychological and cultural bases of international affairs may be much more important than actual military capability when it comes to international conflict. If we want to prevent or stop wars, we must understand how people from other nations or cultures think and how they view themselves and others. We need to develop realistic national or cultural empathy.

But, we should begin by becoming more consciously aware of our own national and cultural images. How has our history, educational system, and mass media shaped our perception of the world? Only by understanding our own perceptions or images and our motivations can we explain and predict our nation's actions and reactions in the increasingly interdependent world.

ENDNOTES

[1]Martin Gilens, a Yale political scientist, analyzed the race of people pictured as poor in TV news stories and in photos in *Time, Newsweek* and *U.S. News & World Report* between 1988 and 1992 and reported his findings in the spring 1997 issue of *Public Opinion Quarterly.* Blacks comprised about 29 percent of the nation's poor during this period, but made up 62 percent of the people pictured in news magazine stories about poverty. He found the same pattern on the three major television networks, where 65 percent of the people featured in stories about poverty were black. (Proportionately, poverty affects a higher percentage of the black population. About 29 percent of all blacks live in poverty, compared with about 11 percent of all whites.) Reported in "Unconventional Wisdom: Poverty in Black and White" by Richard Morin, *The Washington Post,* 18 May 1997: (C5).

[2]Based upon a study written by sociologists Gary Foster and Richard Hummel in the spring 1997 issue of *Sociological Spectrum* and reported in "Needed: A Hillbilly Anti-Defamation League" by Richard Morin, *The Washington Post,* 4 May 1997, p. C5. Examples of television shows featuring stereotypical hillbillies are "Dukes of Hazzard," "The Beverly Hillbillies," "Green Acres," "Hee-Haw," or more recently, animated cartoons such as "The Simpsons" and "King of the Hill."

[3]Erich Fromm, *May Man Prevail?* (Garden City, NY: Doubleday & Company, Inc./ Anchor, 1961), 19–21.

[4]Meg Greenfield suggests that real-life sagas are replacing fictionalized dramas on television. The O. J. Simpson and Menendez brothers trials, the prolonged Clarence Thomas—Anita Hill confrontation in the Senate hearing, and the case of Air Force Lieutenant Kelly Flinn's adultery and insubordination are preferred forms of national entertainment. Many of the characters in these incidents, such as lawyers, have become celebrities in their own right and have made fortunes writing books and appearing in the mass media. "Real-Life Miniseries," *The Washington Post,* 26 May 1997: 19 (A).

[5]In earlier research, Gerbner found that the elderly are exposed to more television than other age groups in America. Because old people are often portrayed as feeble and victims of crime, their expectation far exceeds the probability that they will, in fact, be victims. See Harry Waters, "Life According to TV," *Newsweek,* 6 December 1982: 136–140.

[6]See Herbert I. Schiller, *Mass Communications and American Empire* (Boston: Beacon Press, 1969).

[7]Jack G. Shaheen, *The TV Arab* (Bowling Green, OH: Bowling Green State University Popular Press, 1984).

[8]Ralph K. White, *Nobody Wanted War: Misperception in Vietnam and Other Wars* (rev. ed.), (New York: Doubleday/Anchor, 1970).

[9]Ralph White, "Misperception in the Arab-Israeli Conflict," *Journal of Social Issues 33* (1), 1977: 190–220.

[10]Hamid Mowlana, George Gerbner, and Herbert I. Schiller, eds., *Triumph of the Image: The Media's War in the Persian Gulf—A Global Perspective* (Boulder: Westview Press, 1992).

[11]Ralph White's article "Soviet Security: Malignant obsession" goes one step further—it asserts that the Soviets were almost paranoid in their concern for security. In fact, White claims that the 1983 shooting down of the Korean passenger plane KAL 007 was a consequence of misperceptions motivated by paranoid fear. In *Psychology Today*, November 1983: 6, 9.

[12]Robert Jervis, *Perception and Misperception in International Politics* (Princeton: Princeton University Press, 1976).

50

In Defense of Casualty Pictures on TV

Ellen Goodman

Now that the heavy fighting in Beirut is over and the PLO has been shipped off to live in assorted nations, I am left with one lingering image of this war. No, for once, it's not an image I saw on television. It's an image I saw *of* television.

In my lifetime, I've watched a lot of wars in prime time. Usually there are good guys and bad guys. Usually, those wars are resolved before the commercial.

But in the news, it's different. In the news, wars go on and on. In the news, we see less glory and more gore. In the news, the sides are not divided into good guys and bad guys, but aggressors and victims.

It was true in Vietnam, it was true in Iran and Iraq, Afghanistan and El Salvador, and now in Lebanon. We beam home the pictures of the wounded, the innocent bystanders, the casualties. And the war lovers don't like that.

Ever since Vietnam, we've heard complaints that television news was somehow biased. There were angry accusations that the nightly news fomented the protest movement in the '70s. Now we hear that the camera, simply by filming the uprooted of Beirut, the refuse of war, made a statement against the Israeli artillery.

There were suggestions that it wasn't quite cricket to offer up "features" on the effects of the war on a family, a street, a building, a neighborhood. I even heard that there was

something unfair about "human interest" stories on the wounded of the militarized zone stories giving them names and faces and titles: aunt, son, father.

Well, I agree that television is biased. To the degree that TV does its job well, tells us the facts of life in a conflict, it is intrinsically anti-war.

It's anti-war because the average person sitting in the living room responds to another human being. However immunized by years of war movies, we know, as Eliot said in "E.T.": "This is reality." War may be impersonal. But introduce us to a single person, tell us what she thinks, tell us what he feels, tell us what happened to his or her life—and we will care. It is our saving grace.

In our war-sophisticated world, we have learned that before we can kill people, we have to dehumanize them. They are no longer human beings but gooks or kikes or animals. The Japanese who experimented on human guinea pigs in World War II called them *maruta*: logs of wood.

It is even easier when we lob missiles from an invisible distance or drop bombs from 15,000 feet at "targets." It's more like an Atari game than a murder. Conversely, the more we humanize people, the more we personalize war, the harder it is to commit.

Our ability to make war impersonal is scariest when we think of nuclear war games. Some years ago, Roger Fisher, a Harvard Law School professor, made a radical proposal for bringing nuclear war home to the man who could actually wage it. We would implant the code needed to fire the first missiles in a capsule near the heart of a volunteer. The president would have to kill one human being before he could kill millions.

"I made suggestions," says Fisher now, "to demonstrate the difference between the abstract question of saying that I am prepared to kill 20 million people in the defense of freedom and the personal human question saying I am prepared to kill somebody I know, in order to do this.

"There's a difference between saying, we'll exercise Plan A, Option 6B and saying, 'Uh, George, I'm afraid I have to kill you in order to exercise the nuclear option. Shall we do it right here on the White House carpet or in the bathroom?' It brings home what it's about."

In conventional warfare, television does that same sort of thing. It brings home what war is all about: killing, wounding, destroying. It doesn't film ideas, but realities. TV isn't in the war room or the computer room, but the hospital room.

This is not unabashed praise of TV. There are enormous risks in slanted war coverage. It's easy to make yesterday's villain into today's victim. It's easy to portray self-defense as aggression, and be manipulated into sympathy for terrorists.

But if we can't solve problems in confrontations that are resolved before the commercial, if war usually produces victims, not answers, then we have to see this in human terms and witness the personal edge of devastation.

There are people who worry that humanizing war will undermine our resolve to wage it. I say, that is our greatest hope.

51

TV's True Violence

Meg Greenfield

Television violence is up for discussion again as yet another argument rages over whether and how much to curb it. I believe no subject in our society generates more hypocrisy and confusion, and that is saying something. Is there too much wanton, even obscene violence on TV, day in and day out? Of course there is, and it is disgusting, unless you are partial to the vivid, colorful sight of exploding heads and strung-out guts and guys endlessly careering around shooting other guys as a matter of mindless, pointless habit. Most of this stuff has long since abandoned any pretense to what the Supreme Court once called, in the context of an obscenity ruling, "redeeming social value." It's gore for gore's sake, drama based on violence as a first and only resort in conflict. Should the TV people who produce, market and broadcast this junk exercise restraint? Of course they should; I am not talking about the imposition of government codes or statutes here, of which I am eternally leery, but rather about the purveyors of this escalating mayhem having the taste and public spiritedness to do some necessary cutting back and toning down themselves.

When I say the subject has been a source of world-class hypocrisy I am referring in part to the fact that, although this is now changing, over the years it has generally been the liberals who objected to excessive violence on the tube and the conservatives who objected to the raw sexual stuff and that the two tended often to switch positions and use each other's arguments either pro or anti violence and pro or anti explicit sex. (Where sex and violence increasingly mix on the screen and in fact become a single phenomenon each chooses to see only what it wants to.) One side will tell you that the violence has a terrible seductive effect on the viewers who are coarsened by it and inspired to emulate the carefree aggression that they see. The same will be said of all the panting, pawing sex you witness on the tube—that it is corrupting viewers—only it will often be said this time by the same people who deny that violence has any effect on subsequent viewer behavior; it will, correspondingly, also tend to be denied by those who argue that violence does affect viewers' behavior.

Again, I think it's obvious that this bombardment has a coarsening impact on those people who watch faithfully, and especially where children are concerned, it is surely giving many the idea that what they see portrayed on the screen as a matter of course is what they and others are expected to do in real life. Or, at a minimum, this coarsening involves making the unthinkable just a little less unthinkable, a little more OK.

My own objections, however, which are twofold, are somewhat different. First it is not the violence or shocking gore itself to which I object in TV fiction, but rather the volume, profligacy and undiscriminating nature of their presentation. You may read in the classics or observe in the theatrical production of Shakespeare, among others, episodes every bit as shaking and horrible as whatever it is that caused you to turn away from the TV screen the other night. I once saw one of Shakespeare's occasional but memorable onstage eye-gougings enacted in Cambridge, England, with the aid of suddenly popping out peeled grapes. It's the sort of thing you tend to remember long after you have forgotten the names of the characters in the play. Moreover, much Elizabethan theater and other works to which we now defer as classics had plenty of bloody hacking, slashing and related butchery to them designed to amuse an audience given to the enjoyment of bear-baiting, public hangings and assorted other fun.

But in the better of this literature anyway, the violence in the story meant something; it was singular; it was committed by a particularly cruel character; it had some purpose beyond its mere power to titillate, frighten and repel. Nor do I think any age has seen anything comparable to our own unending, daily inundation of the home by filmed, super-realistic closeup portrayals of human violence, of maiming and mutilation and slaughter. And although I also suspect that viewers, including kids, are probably better at keeping in mind the difference between art (if that's what it is) and life than some suppose, I do think there's a danger that a continuous diet of this sort of thing can eventually make us insensitive and impervious to the genuine article when we see it.

Here I come out for the only kind of TV violence I favor: the real stuff. This is my second worry about all the fictional violence on TV: that it will dull our reactions to the kind that is filmed not on a set but from Bosnia or Liberia or places in this country. I am not talking here of the kind of depiction of horrors that should be treated gingerly in the press, such as shockingly gruesome photographs of stricken or dead people whose living friends and relatives will be needlessly hurt all over again by the reproduction of this image. I am talking about those truly jarring, unsettling, very hard not to turn from images of the wounded kids in Sarajevo, murder victims in a dozen other massacres and wars, or screaming, limbless ones who committed no crime and caused no grievance but were merely unlucky enough to be in there when the terrorist group struck.

DIFFERENT CRITICS

There is, you understand, a whole school, different from the ordinary critics of TV violence, that thinks *this* kind of violent or bloody or just plain scary TV representation should go, but for policy reasons. These are the people who maintain that such a large dose of ugly reality and pain will get us all riled up as individuals or as a society or a government and cause us to take some kind of a position or think we have to do something or otherwise act in a way that they find troubling. There are people who say the filming of war scenes in Vietnam was wrong because of its impact on so much of the public, who believe that the horrors shown in Somalia or Sarajevo or Tiananmen are also something with which we cannot be trusted, that they tend to make us emotional and lead us away from the rigorous, coldhearted intellectual discipline required for policymaking. I grant that such sights on TV can be partial as to truth and in some ways misleading. But I think in an age of excessive governmental memoranda, autointoxication and blather, they are worth a thousand staged pictures of violence and a million political words. If we can't be trusted with the sight of violent reality or required to deal with it, we ought to go out of business. My main worry about TV violence of the senseless, mindless made-up kind is that it may, in time, render us incapable of recognizing and responding to the real thing.

52

Marketing Global Mayhem

George Gerbner

INTRODUCTION

Humankind may have had more bloodthirsty eras, but none as filled with images of violence as the present. We are awash in a tide of violent representations the world has never seen. There is no escape from the massive invasion of colourful mayhem into the homes and cultural life of ever larger areas of the world.

Of course, there was blood in fairy tales, gore in mythology, murder in Shakespeare. Violence is a legitimate and even necessary feature of cultural expression, balancing deadly conflicts and compulsions against tragic costs. But the historically limited, individually crafted and, selectively, used symbolic mayhem has been swamped by violence with happy endings produced on the dramatic assembly-line.

The violence and terror we see on television bear little or no relationship to their actual occurrence. Neither their frequency nor their nature resembles trends in crime statistics. Rather, they follow marketing formulas that call for injecting "action" into dramatic programs and news. Our recent study found that crime and violence news doubled while actual violence declined, precluding the possibility of balanced reporting.

Our long-standing research project called Cultural Indicators[1] has found that children

Dr. Gerbner is Professor and Dean Emeritus of the Annenberg School of Communication, University of Pennsylvania and as Adjunct Professor in the School of International Service at American University.

Reprinted from *The Public* 2, no. 2 (1995): 71–76.

are born into a cultural environment of five violent acts per prime-time hour, four times as many in presumably humorous children's programs, and two to three entertaining murders a night. Contrary to the hype that promoted them, most actual uses of cable, video, cassettes, and other new technologies make the dominant patterns penetrate even more deeply (but not more cheaply) into everyday life.

Our analysis has found that exposure to violence-laden media cultivates an exaggerated sense of insecurity and mistrust, and anxiety about the mean world seen on television. Furthermore, the sense of vulnerability and dependence imposes its heaviest burdens on women and minorities.

Media violence demonstrates power and paves the way for repression. It is an integral part of an increasingly centralised, conglomerated and globalised media production and distribution system that has drifted out of democratic reach. That system creates the cultural environment in which we all live, with television its mainstream.

A child today is born into a home in which television is on an average of more than seven hours a day. For the first time in human history, most of the stories about people, life and values are told not by parents, schools, churches, or others in the community who have something to tell, but by a group of distant conglomerates that have something to sell.

This is a radical change in the way we employ creative talent and the way we cast the cultural environment. The roles we grow into and the ways others see us are no longer home-made, hand-crafted, community-inspired. They are products of a complex manufacturing and marketing process. Television is the mainstream of the process. Our Cultural Indicators research project has built a cumulative database describing many thousands of characters, programs, and items that map key features of the new cultural environment.

Fewer sources fill more outlets more of the time with ever more standardised fare designed for global markets. Global marketing streamlines production, homogenises content, sweeps alternative perspectives from the mainstream, and moves cultural policy beyond democratic, or even national, reach. There is no historical precedent, constitutional provision, or legislative blueprint to confront the challenge of the new consolidated controls that really count—global conglomerate controls over the design, production, promotion and distribution of media content and the power relationships embedded in it.

The casting and fate of characters in television drama set the stage for violence and other power-plays to follow. Women play one out of three roles in prime time television, one out of four in children's programs, and one out of five of those who make news. They fall short of majority even in daytime serials. They age faster than men, and as they age, they are more likely to be portrayed evil and to be victimised.

People of colour, the vast majority of humankind, are less than 11 per cent of prime-time and 3 per cent of children's program casts. When Americans, they are mostly middle-class, making the race issue virtually invisible. Latino/Hispanics, over nine per cent of the US population, are about one per cent of prime time and half of that of children's program casts. A child viewer sees the fewest minorities.

In the overwhelmingly middle-class consumer world of television, poor people play a negligible role. The low-income 13 per cent of the US (and much larger percentage of minorities) is reduced to 1.3 per cent or less on television. A disproportionate number of ill-fated characters come from the ranks of poor, Latino and foreign men, and African-American and poor women.

Programs designed specifically for children's favourite viewing time, Saturday morning, present a world that is even harsher than prime time. The inequities of prime time are magnified Saturday morning. A child will see about 123 characters each Saturday morning, but rarely, if ever, a mature female as leader. Married and parent images are curiously rare and gloomy in children's programs. Mid-life and older women in Saturday morning children's programs are the least visible but most evil and, consequently most highly victimised group; this is where the witches are.

Casting and fate also affect those who deliver the news, who are referred to and cited in the news, and who are news. In most essential characteristics, news deals with the exercise of power: who has it, who uses it, who seeks it, and, most of all, who threatens it.

Women decline in representation from 35 per cent as newscasters to 20 per cent as authorities cited and 17 per cent as newsmakers. Other minorities are also most visible delivering and least visible making news. When they do, they are most likely to appear as criminals. African-Americans make news as criminals at least twice as often as other groups do, despite the fact that 62 per cent of criminals are white.

THE MEAN WORLD SYNDROME

Our analysis based on large national probability sample surveys indicates that long-term regular exposure to television tends to make an independent contribution to the feeling of living in a mean and gloomy world. The "lessons" range from aggression to desensitization and to a sense of vulnerability and dependence.

Heavy viewers are more likely than comparable groups of light viewers to overestimate one's chances of involvement in violence; to believe that one's neighborhood is unsafe; to state that fear of crime is a very serious personal problem; and to assume that crime is rising, regardless of the facts of the case. Heavier viewers in every subgroup (defined by education, age, income, gender, newspaper reading, neighbourhood, etc.) express a greater sense of insecurity and mistrust than do light viewers in the same groups. Other results show that heavy viewers are also more likely to have bought new rocks, watchdogs, and guns "for protection." Finally, viewers who see members of their own group have a higher calculus of risk than those of other groups feel the most vulnerable and dependent.

This unequal sense of danger, vulnerability and general unease, combined with reduced sensitivity, invites not only aggression but also exploitation and repression. Bombarding viewers by violent images of a mean and dangerous world remains, in the last analysis, an instrument of intimidation and terror.

That is the deeper problem of violence-laden television.

IS THIS WHAT THE VIEWERS WANT?

Television violence is an overkill of "happy violence"—swift, cool, effective, without tragic consequences and in other ways divorced from real life and crime statistics. "Happy violence" is the by-product of a manufacturing and marketing process that defies popular taste and imposes uniformity on creative people and viewers.

There is no evidence that, other factors being equal, violence *per se* is giving most viewers "what they want." The most highly rated programs are usually not violent. A test of the relationship between violence and ratings refutes the standard rationalization for violent programming.

Our study compared the average Nielsen ratings of two samples of over 100 programs each to test the popularity of the violence formula. The samples were drawn from the Cultural Indicators Data Archive for the past five seasons. In one sample all programs have high levels of violence; in the other sample no programs contain violence. Average Nielsen ratings and shares for the two samples were then compared.

The Table 1 gives the results. It shows that violence *per se* consistently receives lower ratings.

The overall average rating of the violent sample is 11.1; the same for the non-violent sample is 13.8. The share of the violent and non-violent samples is 18.9 and 22.5, respectively. Furthermore, the non-violent sample was more highly rated than the violent sample for each of the four seasons.

The evidence also shows that most people suffer the violence inflicted on them with diminishing tolerance. A March 1985 Harris survey showed that 78 per cent disapprove of violence they see on television. A Gallup poll of October 1990 found 79 per cent in favour of "regulating" objectionable content in television. A Times-Mirror national poll in 1993 showed that Americans who said they were "personally bothered" by violence in entertainment shows jumped to 59 per cent from 44 per cent in 1983. Furthermore, 80 per cent said entertainment violence was "harmful" to society, compared with 64 per cent in 1983, and almost twice as many people—58 per cent compared with 31 per cent—said entertainment violence bothered them more than news violence.

Local broadcasters, legally responsible for what goes on the air, also oppose the overkill and complain about loss of control. The trade paper, *Electronic Media,* reported in August 1993 the results of its own survey of 100 general managers across all US regions and in all market sizes. Three out of four said there is too much needless violence on television; 57 per cent would like to have more input on program content decisions.

WHAT DRIVES "HAPPY VIOLENCE"?

Why, then, does a public relations-conscious and politically sophisticated industry persist in risking domestic backlash and international embarrassment for its perennially violent fare? The answer is that violence "travels well" on

TABLE 1
Comparison of Nielsen ratings of violent and non-violent network prime-time dramatic programs aired 1988–93

Years aired	Violent Programs N = 104		Non-violent programs N = 103	
	Rating	Share	Rating	Share
1988–89	12.8	21	4.5	24
1989–90	12.0	20	14.8	24
1990–91	8.4	17	10.5	21
1991–92	11.3	19	14.8	23
1992–93	10.0	16	13.0	20
Overall means	11.1	18.9	13.8	22.5

the global market. Rapid concentration, conglomeratisation, and globalisation in the media industry bring streamlining of production, economies of scale, and emphasis on dramatic ingredients most suitable for aggressive international promotion.

Most program producers barely break even on the domestic market. They are forced onto the world market and into all forms of syndication, including cable and video sales, to make a profit. Program production and distribution systems are merging, reversing prior antitrust restraints on monopolization, and moving toward total control of the world market by a handful of conglomerates.

Global marketing needs a dramatic ingredient that requires no translation, is primarily image-driven, "speaks" action in any language, and fits into a conventional pattern in many cultures. That ingredient is violence. (Graphic sex is second, but, ironically, that runs into more inhibitions and restrictions than violence.)

Syndicates demand "action" because it "travels well around the world," said the producer of "Die Hard 2" (which killed 264 compared to 18 in "Die Hard 1," produced in 1988). "Everyone understands an action movie. If I tell a joke, you may not get it but if a bullet goes through the window, we all know how to hit the floor, no matter the language."[2]

Bruce Gordon, President of Paramount International TV Group, explained that "The international demand rarely changes. . . . Action-adventure series and movies continue to be the genre in demand, primarily because those projects lose less in translation to other languages. . . . Comedy series are never easy because in most of the world most of the comedies have to be dubbed and wind up losing their humour in the dubbing."[3]

An analysis of international data in the Cultural Indicators database compared a sample of 250 US programs exported to 10 countries with 111 programs shown in the US only during the same year. Violence was the main theme of 40 per cent of home-shown and 49 per cent of exported programs. Crime/action series comprised 17 per cent of home-shown and 46 per cent of exported programs. What violent programs lose on ratings, they more than make up by grabbing the attention of younger viewers whom advertisers want to reach and by extending their reach globally.

THE LIBERATING ALTERNATIVE

Far from reflecting creative freedom, the global strategy wastes talent, chills originality, and fails to serve the tastes and needs of any country. The Hollywood Caucus of Producers, Writers and Directors, speaking for the creative community, said in a statement issued on the eve of the August 1993 "summit" conference on television violence: "We stand today at a point in time when the country's dissatisfaction with the quality of television is at an all-time high, while our own feelings of helplessness and lack of power, in not only choosing material that seeks to enrich, but also in our ability to execute to the best of our ability, is at an all-time low."

There is an alternative. It is not the "electronic superhighway." Given the convergence of communication technologies, the concentration of ownership, and the shrinking of independent creative opportunities, the notion that the new convergence will provide more jobs and greater choice is a technocratic fantasy. The same (or fewer) programs now being mass-produced for the largest possible markets will run on more channels more of the time, while informercial hustle, direct marketing, gambling, and videogames (billed as interactive multimedia democracy) will fill the rest. Cross-media synergy, and the global consolidation of electronic marketing is more likely to reduce than to increase the creation of new cultural resources unless provision is made to loosen the noose of global formulas from around the necks of creative people.

More freedom, not more censorship, is the effective and acceptable way to increase diversity and reduce television violence to its legitimate role and proportion. The role of government, if any, is to turn its anti-trust and civil rights oversight on the centralised and globalised industrial structures and marketing strategies that impose violent stereotypes on creative people and foist it on the children of the world. The role of citizens is to offer a liberating alternative to the repressive movements and proposals in the field.

That liberating alternative exists in the Cultural Environment Movement. CEM is a new international coalition of media, professional, labour, religious, health-related, women's and minority groups opposed to private corporate as well as government censorship.[4] CEM is working for freedom from stereotyped formulas; for respecting the integrity of cultures and opposing the homogenisation; for investing in a freer and more diverse cultural environment; and for citizen participation in cultural decisions that shape our lives and the lives of our children.[5]

ENDNOTES

[1]The "Cultural Indicators" project is an ongoing research project, started in 1967, tracking the world of network television and the long-range consequences of viewing.

[2]Ken Auletta, "What Won't They Do," *The New Yorker*, 17 May 1993: 45–46.

[3]Bruce Gordon, News Story. *Broadcasting & Cable,* 15 June 1992: 19.

[4]CEM is preparing for its "founding convention" in March 1996 in St. Louis, hosted by the Webster University. For more information write to: CEM, P.O. Box 31847, Philadelphia, PA 19104, USA.

[5]George Gerbner, "Television Violence: The Power and the Peril," *Gender, Race, and Class in Media: A Critical Text-Reader,* eds. G. Dines and J. M. Humez (New York: Sage, 1995).

53

On Numbing and Feeling

Robert Jay Lifton and
Richard A. Falk

We are always much less than we could be. We have moments of high intellect or of passionate emotion, but seem limited in our capacity to sustain optimal combinations of two.

Diminished feeling, in one sense, begins with the structure and function of the human brain. Neurophysiologists make clear that the brain serves as much to keep out stimuli as it does to receive them. In other words, our brain is so constructed as to limit what we can eventually feel, lest it be so overwhelmed as to lose its capacity to organize or to respond at all.

For as human beings we must do considerable psychic work in connection with anything we take in. That is, we perceive nothing nakedly but must re-create anything we encounter by means of our marvelous and vulnerable cerebral cortex. If we can speak of anything as *human* nature, it is this symbolizing principle as such. Hence I speak of a "formative process," the constant creation and re-creation of images and forms that constitutes human mentation. Much of this process takes place outside of awareness, or is what we call "unconscious." But it is the existence of this formative-symbolizing tendency that makes possible the wonders of our imagination on the one hand, and our psychological disturbances and destructive impulses on the other.

Here too psychic and physical survival require a balance between feeling and not feel-

ing. And that balance can readily go out of kilter, causing us to feel either too much or too little. Indeed, our contemporary nuclear threat not only contributes to upsetting that balance but raises questions about just what kind of balance between feeling and numbing is desirable or possible.

In Hiroshima, people I interviewed told me how, when the bomb fell, they were aware of people dying around them in horrible ways but that, within minutes or even seconds, they simply ceased to feel. They said such things as "I simply became insensitive to human death," or referred to a "paralysis of the mind." I came to call this general process psychic numbing and, in its most acute form, psychic closing-off. For survivors it was a necessary defense mechanism, since they could not have experienced full emotions in response to such scenes and remained sane. The numbing entailed de-realization of what was actually happening along such inner psychological sequences as: "If I feel nothing, then death is not taking place," or "then I cannot be threatened by the death all around me," or "then I am not responsible for you or your death."

As useful to them as it was at the time, the numbing process did not necessarily end when the immediate danger was over. It would continue over weeks, months, or even years, and become associated with apathy, withdrawal, depression, despair, or a kind of survivor half-life with highly diminished capacity for pleasure, joy, or intense feelings in general.

Observing victims, I began to wonder about the numbing that must take place in those who make, test, or anticipate the use of nuclear weapons. For potential perpetrators simply cannot afford to imagine what really happens to people at the other end of the weapon.

This was true of American scientists constructing the first atomic bombs at Los Alamos in New Mexico. Responding to the call to win the race against an evil enemy to construct a decisive weapon, then after the defeat of Germany still seeing themselves as contributing to their country's wartime military struggle and intent upon succeeding in what had been an extraordinarily dedicated collective effort and on confirming that the thing would really *work,* "they were frantically busy and extremely security conscious and . . . there was even some half-conscious closing of the mind to anything but the fact that they were trying desperately to produce a device which would end the war. . . ."[1] And so powerful was their scientific leadership that almost everyone else at Los Alamos "let Oppenheimer take protective custody of their emotion."

Moral questions were raised only by a few scientists from the Chicago group when they had essentially completed their work on the project. But their reflections were informed precisely by a beginning capacity to imagine and feel what might occur at the other end of the weapon. Eugene Rabinowitch, five years later, recalled how, "In the summer of 1945, some of us walked the streets of Chicago vividly imagining the sky suddenly lit by a giant fireball, the steel skeletons of skyscrapers bending into grotesque shapes and their masonry raining into the streets below, until a great cloud of dust arose and settled over the crumbling city."[2] And he goes on to say that, "From this vision arose the weak and inadequate attempts that groups of scientists made to stop the hands of the clock before it struck the first hour of the atomic age."[3]

Nuclear scientists had experienced such images long before that.

> Standing around the first nuclear fire lit under the West Stands of the athletic field of the University of Chicago in December 1942 and, two-and-a-half years later in July 1945, watching the flash of the first atomic bomb explosion at Alamogordo, the scientists had a vision of terrible clarity. They saw the cities of the world, including their own, going up in flames and falling into dust.[4]

But once they embarked on making the bomb, once the numbing had set in, that kind of vision was in most cases suppressed. And subsequently, over decades, there was the psychological process of "learning to live with the bomb," which scientists came to share with political and military leaders along with the rest of us; specific forms of numbing evolved that blocked out what happened at the other end of nuclear weapons and enabled one to get on with things.

What I am calling psychic numbing includes a number of classical psychoanalytic defense mechanisms: repression, suppression, isolation, denial, undoing, reaction formation, and projection, among others. But these defense mechanisms overlap greatly around the issue of feeling and not feeling. With that issue so central to our time, we do well to devote to it a single overall category, which we can observe operating in different ways and under different conditions in virtually any individual mind.

Psychic numbing has to do with exclusion, most specifically exclusion of feeling. That exclusion can occur in two ways. There is first the blocking of images, or of feelings associated with certain images, because they are too painful or unacceptable. The second is absence of images, the lack of prior experience in relation to an event. We have difficulty imagining nuclear holocaust or responding with feeling to the idea of it happening, because we have virtually no prior images that readily connect with it. In either case—and the two patterns are likely to coexist—the formative process is affected. Indeed, just as the defense mechanisms are part of Freud's model of instinct and defense, so may we view the concept of psychic numbing as a part of the model of symbolization of life and death. When numbing occurs, the symbolizing process—the flow and recreation of images and forms—is interrupted. And in its extreme varieties, numbing itself becomes a symbolic death: One freezes in the manner of certain animals facing danger, becomes as if dead in order to prevent actual physical or psychic death. But all too frequently the inner death of numbing has dubious value to the organism. And it may itself become a source of grave danger.

We may thus speak, very generally, of three levels of numbing: the numbing of massive death immersion; the numbing of enhancement; and the numbing of everyday life. The first, the numbing of massive death immersion, is epitomized by Hiroshima and Nagasaki. The "paralysis of the mind" already mentioned involves a radical dissociation of the mind from its own earlier modes of response—from constellations of pain and pleasure, love and loss, and general capacity for fellow feeling built up over a human lifetime. We may, indeed, speak of the mind being severed from its own forms. When that happens, psychic action—mental process in general—more or less shuts down. There are in-between states in which limited forms of planning and action (flight or rescue of family members) can occur, even though feelings are largely blunted.

The numbing of enhancement is of the opposite variety. Here feeling is diminished in some spheres of the mind in order to make possible more accomplished behavior or more intense feeling in other spheres. One can point to the selective professional numbing of the surgeon, who cannot afford to feel the consequences of failure. Or to that of the painter or musician, who block out a great variety of influences in order to enhance and intensify the image or the musical phrase.

Finally, there is the problematic category of the numbing of everyday life. Here we may say that the ordinary brain function of keeping out stimuli becomes strained by the image overload characteristic of our time. Apart from nuclear weapons, the mass-media revolution creates the unique situation in which virtually any image from anywhere on the globe, and indeed from any point in our historical or cultural past, becomes available to any individual at any moment. This historically new situation contributes to a contemporary psychological style of perpetual experimentation and increasing capacity for shifts from one kind of involvement (with people, ideas, ways of living) to another. I speak of this as the Protean style, after the talented but unsteady Greek sea god who was a notorious shapeshifter and could readily change into virtually any natural, animal, or human form, but who had great difficulty holding on to a functional form of his own. . . .

More personally, I referred earlier to my discovery in Hiroshima that, seventeen years after the event, no one had studied its general human effects, but I must note here my own previous resistance to the city. Although I had first gone to Japan in 1952 (as an air force psychiatrist in response to the medical draft of that time) and had spent more than two-and-

one-half years in Japan (about half in the military and half in connection with a study of Japanese youth), it was not until my second long stay was drawing to a close in 1962 that I first visited Hiroshima. And I did so then because I thought I should take a look at the city, having begun to be concerned about nuclear dangers through participating in the early academic peace movement at Harvard during the late 1950s. (I suspect now that a part of me anticipated the possibility of doing a psychological study there, but even then I seemed to have to complete the other, less threatening work first.) When I began to talk to various people in Hiroshima about working there, I felt encouraged by their responses and enthusiastic about proceeding. But from the first moment I began to conduct actual interviews with survivors, everything was different. Now the bomb seemed right there with us, virtually in the room. I felt myself overwhelmed and frightened by the detailed, grotesque descriptions of specific atomic bomb experiences, by the very descriptions I sought from the people I talked to. I was staying in a Japanese inn alone at the time, my wife and infant son not having yet joined me from Kyoto where we had been living. For a few days I felt anxious, and at night slept fitfully and had disturbing dreams. I began to ask myself whether I should abandon the study and leave Hiroshima.

But then, quite suddenly, my anxiety seemed to recede as I found myself listening carefully during the interviews for psychological patterns in survivors' descriptions. In other words, I had begun to carry out my professional task, with the aid of the selective professional numbing I have mentioned in connection with surgeons. Without some such numbing I would have been incapable to feel the pain altogether in what I was hearing. Nonetheless, it was a form of numbing, and I go back to that experience whenever I try to sort out the never fully resolvable struggles of professionals and others around how much to feel. Since then I have frequently become aware of situations in which I used various psychological maneuvers to distance myself from precisely the nuclear weapons threat with which I have been so consistently concerned.

In response to nuclear weapons, numbing is all too easy, widespread, and "natural" for just about everyone. But in saying that, and in depicting these various forms of numbing—indeed, in exploring our mind's dilemmas around nuclear weapons—we are doing something that only human beings can do. We are reflecting on ourselves and our situation in the service of greater awareness. And in that awareness, even just its beginning, lies our hope.

ENDNOTES

[1]A. K. Smith, "Behind the Decision to Use the Atomic Bomb: Chicago 1944–45," *Bulletin of the Atomic Scientists* 1 (October 1958): 3–10.

[2]E. Rabinowitch, "Five Years After," in *The Atomic Age* (New York: Basic Books, 1963).

[3]*Ibid.*

[4]*Ibid.*

54

Faces of the Enemy

Sam Keen

The world, as always, is debating the issues of war and peace. Conservatives believe safety lies in more arms and increased firepower. Liberals place their trust in disarmament and nuclear freeze. I suggest we will be saved by neither fire nor ice, that the solutions being offered by the political right and left miss the mark. Our problem lies not in our technology, but in our minds, in our ancient tendency to create our enemies in our own imagination.

Our best hope for avoiding war is to understand the psychology of this enmity, the ways in which our mind works to produce our habits of paranoia, projection, and the making of propaganda. How do we create our enemies and turn the world into a killing ground?

We first need to answer some inevitable objections, raised by the advocates of power politics, who say: "You can't psychologize political conflict. You can't solve the problem of war by studying perception. We don't *create* enemies. There are real aggressors—Hitler, Stalin, Qaddafi."

True: There are always political, economic, and territorial causes of war. Wars come and go; the images we use to dehumanize our enemies remain strangely the same. The unchanging projection of the hostile imagination are continually imposed onto changing historical circumstances. Not that the enemy is innocent of these projections—as popular wisdom has it, paranoids sometimes have *real* enemies.

Nevertheless, to understand the hostile imagination we need to temporarily ignore the question of guilt and innocence. Our quest is for an understanding of the unchanging images we place on the enemy.

Reprinted from *Esquire*, vol. 101, February 1984, 67–72. Copyright © 1984 by The Hearst Corporation.

THE ENEMY AS CREATED BY PARANOIA

Paranoia is not an occasional individual pathology, but rather it is the human condition. History shows us that, with few exceptions, social cohesion within tribes is maintained by paranoia: when we do not have enemies, we invent them. The group identity of a people depends on division between insiders and outsiders, us and them, the tribe and the enemy.

The first meaning of *the enemy* is simply the stranger, the alien. The bond of tribal membership is maintained by projecting hostile and divisive emotions upon the outsider. Paranoia forms the mold from which we create enemies.

In the paranoid imagination, *alien* means the same as *evil*, while the tribe itself is defined as good: a single network of malevolent intent stretches over the rest of the world. "They" are out to get "us." All occurrences prove the basic assumption that an outside power is conspiring against the community.

THE ENEMY AS ENEMY OF GOD

In the language of rhetoric, every war is a crusade, a "just" war, a battle between good and evil. Warfare is a ritual in which the sacred blood of our heroes is sacrificed to destroy the enemies of God.

We like to think that theocracies and holy wars ended with the coming of the Industrial Revolution and the emergence of secular cultures in the West. Yet in World War I the Kaiser was pictured as the devil; in World War II both Germany and the U.S. proclaimed *Gulf mit uns*, "In God We Trust"; each accused the other of being Christ-killers. Sophisticated politicians may insist that the conflict between the U.S. and the U.S.S.R. is a matter of pragmatic power politics, but theological dimensions have not disappeared. President Reagan warns us against "the aggressive impulses of an evil empire" and asks us to "pray for the salvation of all those who live in totalitarian darkness, pray they will discover the joy of knowing God."

By picturing the enemy as the enemy of God we convert the guilt associated with murder into pride. A warrior who kills such an enemy strikes a blow for truth and goodness. Remorse isn't necessary. The warrior engaged in righteous battle against the enemies of God may even see himself as a priest, saving his enemy from the grip of evil by killing him.

THE ENEMY AS BARBARIAN

The enemy not only is a demon but is also a destroyer of culture. If he is human at all, he is brutish, dumb, and cruel, lower on the scale of evolution than The People. To the Greeks he was a barbarian. To the Americans he was, most recently, a "gook" or "slant." To the South African he is a black or "colored."

The barbarian theme was used widely in World War II propaganda by all participants. Nazi anti-semitic tracts contrasted the sunny, healthy Aryan with the inferior, dark, and contaminated races—Jews, Gypsies, Eastern Europeans. American soldiers were pictured as Chicago-style gangsters. Blacks were portrayed as quasi-gorillas despoiling the artistic achievements of European civilization. One poster used in Holland warned the Dutch that their supposed "liberators" were a melange of KKK, jazz-crazed blacks, convicts, hangmen, and mad bombers. In turn, the U.S. frequently pictured the Germans as a Nazi horde of dark monsters on a mindless rampage.

The image of the barbarian represents a force to be feared: power without intelligence, matter without mind, an enemy who must be conquered by culture. The warrior who defeats the barbarian is a culture hero, keeping the dark powers in abeyance.

THE ENEMY AS RAPIST

Associated with the enemy as barbarian is the image of the enemy as rapist, the destroyer of motherhood.

As rapist, the enemy is lust defiling innocence. He is according to Nazi propaganda the Jew who lurks in the shadows waiting to seduce Aryan girls. Or in the propaganda of the Ku Klux Klan he is the black man with an insatiable lust for white women. In American war posters he is the Jap carrying away the naked Occidental woman.

The portrait of the enemy as rapist, destroyer of the madonna, warns us of danger and awakens our pornographic imagination by reminding us of the enticement of rape. The appeal to sexual adventure is a *sine qua non* in motivating men to go to war: To the warrior belong the spoils, and chief among the spoils are the enemy's women.

THE ENEMY AS BEAST, INSECT, REPTILE

The power of bestial images to degrade is rooted in the neurotic structure of the hostile imagination. Karen Horney has shown that neurosis always involves a movement between glorified and degraded images of the self. In warfare we act out a mass neurosis whereby we glorify ourselves as agents of God and project our feelings of degradation and impotence upon the enemy. We are superhuman; therefore they must be subhuman. By destroying the bestial and contaminated enemy we can gain immortality, escape evil, transcend decay and death.

THE ENEMY AS DEATH

In the iconography of propaganda, the enemy is the bringer of death. He is Death riding on a bomb, the Grim Reaper cutting down youth in its prime. His face is stripped of flesh, his body a dangling skeleton.

War is an irrational ritual. Generation after generation we sacrifice our substance in a vain effort to kill some essential enemy. Now he wears an American or Soviet face. A moment ago he was a Nazi, a Jew, a Moslem, a Christian, a pagan. But the true face of the enemy, as Saint Paul said, is Death itself. The unconscious power that motivates us to fight for peace, kill for Life, is the magical assumption that if we can destroy this particular enemy we can defeat Death.

Lying within each of us is the desire for immortality. And because this near-instinctive desire for immortality is balanced by the precariously repressed fear that death might really eradicate all traces of our existence, we will go to any extreme to reassure ourselves. By submitting to the divine ordeal of war, in which we are willing to die or kill the enemy who *is* Death, we affirm our own deathlessness.

THE RELUCTANT KILLERS

It is easy to despair when we look at the human genius for creating enemies in the image of our own disowned vices. When we add our mass paranoia and projection to our constantly progressing weapons technology, it seems we are doomed to destroy ourselves.

But the persistent archetypal images of the enemy may point in a more hopeful direction. We demean our enemies not because we are instinctively sadistic, but because it is difficult for us to kill others whom we fully recognize as human beings. Our natural empathy, our instinct for compassion, is strong: society does what it must to attempt to overcome the moral imperative that forbids us from killing.

Even so, the effort is successful only for a minority. In spite of our best propaganda, few men and women will actually try to kill an enemy. In his book *Men Against Fire*, Brigadier General S.L.A. Marshall presents the results of his study of American soldiers under fire during World War II. He discovered that *in combat* the percentage of men who would fire their rifle at the enemy *even once* did not rise above 25 percent, and the more usual figure was 15 percent. He further discovered that the fear of killing was every bit as strong as the fear of dying.

If it is difficult to mold men into killers, we may still hope to transform our efforts from fighting an outward enemy to doing battle with our own paranoia. Our true war is our struggle against the antagonistic mind. Our true enemy is our propensity to make enemies. The highest form of moral courage requires us to look at ourselves from another perspective, to repent, and to reown our own shadows. True self-knowledge introduces self-doubt into our minds. And self-doubt is a healthy counterbalance to the dogmatic, self-righteous certainty that governs political rhetoric and behavior; it is, therefore, the beginning of compassion.

55

The Face of Arabs in American Mass Media

Jack G. Shaheen

During the 1991 Persian Gulf War more than 200,000 American troops were transported to Saudi Arabia. Americans at home were captivated by television images of the military engagement as Desert Shield became Desert Storm. Thousands of armed forces from Egypt, Morocco, Syria and other Arab countries were stationed and fought alongside American military men and women in the Saudi Desert. In spite of this shared wartime experience with Arab allies, most Americans today have little understanding of Arab peoples.

Massive media coverage of the Gulf War provided a unique opportunity for American journalists and scholars to promote more accurate and human portraits of Arabs by presenting Arabs as complex human beings with all the passions, intellect, strengths and frailties found among all peoples.[1] They might have challenged Americans to look beyond the myths—the distortions, stereotypes and caricatures perpetuated in the mass media. As President Kennedy said: "The great enemy of truth is very often not the lie, deliberate, contrived and dishonest, but the myth, persistent, persuasive, and realistic."

Even today the myth of Arabs as demonic and less-than-human still exists, perpetuated largely by both the entertainment and news media. Unfortunately, the constant live televi-

This essay appears here in print for the first time. Jack G. Shaheen is Professor Emeritus of Mass Communication at Southern Illinois University and a CBS news consultant on Middle East affairs. He is the author of *The TV Arab*.

sion coverage of the Gulf War neither changed nor challenged old stereotypes—they are as strong, and as harmful, as they were before the War.

THE IMAGE OF ARABS IN FAMILY ENTERTAINMENT

As an Arab-American, I have found that ugly caricatures have had an enduring impact on my family.[2] I was sheltered from prejudicial portraits at first. My parents came from Lebanon in the 1920s; they met and married in America. Our home in the steel city of Clairton, Pa., was a center for ethnic sharing—black, white, Jew and Gentile. There was only one major source of media images then, at the State movie theater where I was lucky enough to get a part-time job as an usher. But in the late 1940s, Westerns and war movies were popular, not Middle Eastern dramas. Memories of World War II were fresh, and the screen heavies were the Japanese and the Germans. True to the cliché of the times, the only good Indian was a dead Indian. But when I mimicked or mocked the bad guys, my mother cautioned me. She explained that stereotypes blur our vision, corrupt the imagination and hurt others.

She was right. I remember the Saturday afternoon when my son, Michael, who was seven, and my daughter, Michele, six, suddenly called out: "Daddy, Daddy, they've got some bad Arabs on TV." They were watching the great American morality play, TV wrestling. Akbar the Great, who liked to hear the cracking of bones, and Abdullah the Butcher, a dirty fighter who liked to inflict pain, were pinning their foes with "camel locks." From that day on, I knew I had to try to neutralize the media caricatures.

It hasn't been easy. With my children, I have watched animated heroes Heckle and Jeckle pull the rug from under "Ali Boo-Boo, the Desert Rat," and Laverne and Shirley stop "Sheik Ha-Mean-Ie" from conquering "the U.S. and the world." I have read comic books like the *Fantastic Four* and *G.I. Combat* whose characters have sketched Arabs as "lowlifes" and "human hyenas." Negative stereotypes are everywhere. A dictionary informed my youngsters that an Arab is a "vagabond, drifter, hobo and vagrant." Whatever happened, my wife wondered, to Aladdin's good genie? She questioned why Arabs were not defined as they once were in the 1947 edition of *Webster's New International Dictionary,* as "one of the oldest and purest of peoples, and along with the Jews, constitute the best representatives of the Semitic race."

To a child, the world is simple: good versus evil. But my children and others with Arab roots grew up without ever having seen an Arab, or an American of Arab heritage, on the silver screen after which to pattern their lives. It seems that it is easier for a camel to go through the eye of a needle than for a screen Arab to appear as a genuine human being.

Hollywood producers must have an instant Ali Baba kit that contains scimitars, veils, sunglasses, and such Arab clothing as *chadors* and *kufiyahs.* In mythical "Ay-rabland" an endless desert with oil wells, tents, twelfth-century palaces, mosques, goats, camels, and shepherds prevails. Between the sand dunes, the camera focuses on a mock-up of a palace from *Arabian Nights*—or a military base.

Emotions are primitive, with greed and lust dominant; compassion and sensitivity are virtually nonexistent. Walt Disney's *Aladdin* (1992), the second-most successful animated picture ever, is a good example of the abhorrent Arab stereotype presented as fantasy for both children and adults. The problems begin with the film's defamatory opening number, belted out by a shady-looking storyteller crossing the desert atop a camel. The song goes like this:

> *Oh, I come from a land*
> *From a faraway place*
> *Where the caravan camels roam.*
> *Where they cut off your ear*
> *If they don't like your face.*
> *It's barbaric, but hey, it's home.*

To say a distinct culture is "barbaric" is to show prejudice and accept stereotypes. The song slanders an entire people, setting the tone of the movie. The lyrics and successive scenes inform viewers that Arabs are not like us: *they* are uncouth and cruel.

What impressions of Arabia can small children have when hearing *Arabian Nights,* a song whose main enticing theme is uncivilized folk advocating ear-chopping? What do they make of hideous Arabian guards chasing Aladdin throughout the film, scabbards flying, just because the famished youth stole a loaf of bread?

What do youngsters think of dialogue enhancing the "barbarian Arab" theme, as when a brutal guard screams at Aladdin, "I'll have your head for a trophy, you street rat"? What do children assume about Islam, a religion embraced by more than one billion people, on hearing a street vendor insist that the standard penalty for stealing is chopping off the thief's hand? One telling scene in the movie shows a grotesque Arab, scabbard poised, about to remove Princess Jasmine's hand, simply because she took an apple to feed a starving child. Finally, what do children think of Jafar, a hissably vain vizier, determined to "slice a few throats"?

The negative images keep flowing into family films. Disney trounced Arabs again in 1994 by displaying hook-nosed, buck-toothed "desert skunks" in the animated movie *The Return of Jafar.* In 1995, Touchtone Pictures, a subsidiary of Walt Disney Co., released *Father of the Bride, Part II,* its rendition of a feel-good family. Consider the plot: George Banks is an upper middle-class, happily married, suburban white male. He has everything a father could hope for: a well-mannered son and a married daughter living only one mile from his 24 Maple Drive home.

However, Banks is shocked to learn he will soon be a grandfather, and doubly shocked when his wife tells him that she also is pregnant. Pending the babies' arrival, George and his wife decide to sell the family's longtime home. Buyers surface quickly: the crass Habibs.

Mr. Habib smokes, needs a shave, and speaks with a thick accent. "When can you move?" blurts out the sleazy Habib, thrusting a handful of thousand dollar bills at George. When his wife attempts to speak, Habib barks mumbo-jumbo phrases at her. Mrs. Habib heels, perpetuating Hollywood's stale image of the Arab woman as a mute, submissive nonentity.

When George and his daughter go to their Maple Drive residence for one last look, mushy music underscores past sentiments. The two recall carving initials on a tree, playing basketball, etc. The music changes abruptly as Habib enters the scene, tossing his cigarette and crushing it on the immaculate walkway. There goes the neighborhood.

The next day, the evil Habib steers a wrecking ball toward George's home, asserting, "See, I demolish house, put two in its place." George pleads: "Don't bulldoze my memories, man! I'm begging you." Habib becomes Shakespeare's Shylock; he returns the house only after extorting $100,000 from poor George.

The impact of family and children's movies—especially animated films—is particularly profound because the negative images of Arabs are planted in developing psyches. Even cartoons and comic books feature the Arabs as the enemy: Arabs versus Donald Duck, Batman, Sergeant Rock, and Hawkman. In a study of 218 Arab types appearing in 215 comic books, I found 149 characters portrayed as "evil," 30 characters portrayed as "good," and 39 characters portrayed as "common people." Hence, the comic book reader sees three villainous Arabs for every heroic one.[3]

Nearly all Arab villains in the comic books fall into one of three categories: the repulsive terrorist, the sinister sheik, or the rapacious bandit. And all of them, Arab men and women, come with their own distorted gender roles. At least fifty instances of Arab terrorist activity were recorded in this study of comic books.

In his *Calvin and Hobbes' Tenth Anniversary Book*, Bill Watterson writes that, like films, "Comic strips have historically been full of ugly stereotypes, the hallmark of writers too lazy to honestly observe the world." Declared Watterson, "The cartoonist who resorts to stereotypes reveals his [or her] bigotry."[4]

Sadly, repetitious and negative Arab images sustain dehumanized portraits across generations. There is a commanding link between make-believe aberrations and the real world. It has been said that "stereotypes have the longest half-life in the history of the globe. They will not go away."[5]

MASS MEDIA IMAGES OF ARABS OVER THE YEARS

Prior to the Gulf War, many Americans probably had never met an Egyptian, a Saudi, or a Syrian; most never visited an Arab country. For many, their knowledge of Arabs came from the mass media, which provide virtually all images average Americans have of the peoples of the world.[6]

Yet the media's Arab lacks a human face. Images on movie screens and television present the Arab as a bogeyman, the quintessential Other. Almost nothing is shown of the Arab world's tradition of hospitality, its rich culture and history, or the value of its principal religion, Islam, a faith embraced by some 180 million Arabs in 21 nations.

Plato recognized the power of myths when he said that those who tell the stories also rule society. More recently, Professor George Gerbner of the Annenberg School of Communication has said, "If you can write a nation's stories, you needn't worry about who makes the laws. Today television tells most of the stories to most of the people most of the time."[7]

For nearly two decades, I have studied how Arab peoples are depicted in the United States, giving special emphasis to the "entertaining" images of television programs and motion pictures. My research has produced convincing evidence that lurid and insidious portraits are the media's staple fare.

In the more than 800 feature films and hundreds of television programs I studied, producers bombard audiences with rigid and repulsive depictions that demonize and delegitimize the Arab. These images do not just entertain; they narrow our vision and blur reality. Most Arabs are poor, not rich; they are farmers, not desert nomads; they have never mounted a camel, lived in a tent, or seen an oil well.[8]

ARAB WOMEN

Arab women fare little better than men in the entertainment media. They are portrayed as mute, uneducated, unattractive, enslaved beings who exist solely to serve men. Appearing as obese belly dancers, or as chattel—mindless harem maidens, or silent bundles of black cloth who carry jugs on their heads, they are seen trekking across the desert behind camels.

Print journalists help perpetuate the stereotype. Meg Greenfield, the editorial page editor of the *Washington Post,* wrote in a *Newsweek* column that Muslim women are slavish, submissive, and forced to stay at home. She emphasizes "the contempt with which the Saudis treat women."[9] One wonders where she obtained this information and how extensive her contacts with Saudis actually have been.

It is true that in Western eyes there are problematic aspects to the status of Arab women, just as there are problematic aspects to the status of Western women from an Arab perspective. Although there are nearly 500 million Muslim women—the Muslim world ranges from Guinea on the west coast of Africa to Borneo in the South China Sea—the most distorted and misunderstood aspect of Islam concerns the status of women. For centuries Muslim women had property and legal rights greater than those afforded to women in Europe and North America.

In the United States and in the 14 Arab nations I have visited, I have come to know women, Muslim and Christian, who are protected, loved, honored, and respected for being physicians, teachers, journalists, architects, and/or homemakers. We almost never see Arab women portrayed in those roles in the entertainment media, much less modeled after Anwar Sadat's widow, Jihan, whose life as an intellectual and outstanding Egyptian spokeswoman is clearly the antithesis of the prevailing stereotype. Another of the many distinguished Arab women overlooked by the Western media is Dr. Hanan Ashrawi who was one of the most prominent members of the Jordanian-Palestinian delegation at the Madrid Peace conference in 1991.[10]

AMERICA'S BOGEYMAN IS THE ARAB

Almost all images of Arabs in American popular culture are dangerously threatening. They surface as either oily billionaires or bombers, rarely are they portrayed as average human beings or as victims. For example, the 1994 box office hit *True Lies* (1994) depicts *kufiyah*-clad Arab Muslim terrorists igniting an A-bomb off the Florida Keys. Audiences cheered when Arnold Schwarzenneger mowed them down. They are hardly ever seen ordinary people practicing law, driving taxies, singing lullabies, or healing the sick. The absence of positive, fully human media images nurtures suspicion and stereotypes.[11] Movies in the 1980s and 1990s suggest that Americans are at war with Arabs, forgetting the fact that out of 21 Arabs nations, America is friendly with 19 of them.

The Arab image parallels the image of the Jew in Nazi-inspired German films. Just as the Jew was made the scapegoat for Germany's problems in such movies as *Jud Suss* (1940) and *The Eternal Jew* (1940), the Arab has become the demon of today. We deplore the false portrait of Jews as a swarthy menace. Yet a similar portrait has been accepted and transferred to another group of Semites—the Arabs.

The Arab-as-terrorist stereotype has evolved over a period of four decades. There are numerous similarities between the savage American Indian depicted in early Westerns and the dehumanized Palestinian portrayed in recent movie dramas such as *Executive Decision* (1996), *Navy SEALs* (1990), *Delta Force III: The Killing Game* (1991), *Killing Streets* (1991), *Wanted Dead or Alive* (1987), and *The Delta Force* (1986) which portrayed the Palestinian as Enemy Number One.

Made-for-television movies such as *Hostage Flight* (1985), *Sword of Gideon* (1986), *Terrorist on Trial* (1988), and *Voyage of Terror* (1990), augment the film image. Producers selectively frame the Palestinian as a demonic beast with neither compunction nor compassion, who abducts, abuses, and butchers men, women, and children.

What is forgotten in all this is that the great majority of Palestinians, like all other human beings, seek peace and abhor violence. Yet on silver screens Palestinians adorned in fatigues and *kufiyahs* almost never appear as victims of violence or as displaced persons relegated to refugee camps, or even as normal human beings. When, if ever, has the viewer seen a Palestinian man embracing his wife or children, writing poetry, or attending the sick? As journalist Edward R. Murrow said, what we do not see is often as important, if not more important, as what we do see.

Few Americans have ever talked with Palestinians or heard them speak. Thus, when they are continually dehumanized and demonized in the mass media viewers equate them with cultural Others. Until recently, they were represented as mere numbers killed or injured, or were simply "terrorists." They were not portrayed as people with feelings, names, faces, identities and families.

Some print and broadcast journalists have started to challenge this stereotype. They are now revealing more humane images of Palestinian Arabs, a people who traditionally suffered from the myth that Palestinian equals terrorist.

In the past few years more humanized images have been conveyed in newscasts, including images of families grieving over dead loved ones who have been killed and maimed in mortar or rocket attacks, or images of youngsters beaten by Israeli soldiers. This is the human tragedy of war, and Palestinian men, women and children have been among the many victims.

Yet other print journalists perpetuate the Arab terrorist stereotype. In the summer of 1993, *The New Yorker* ran a cover illustration titled "Castles in the Sand." It showed three normal, all-American children at play on a beach, building sand castles. A fourth child with a crazed expression, wears sunglasses and a *burnoose*. This youth represents an Arab or Arab-American.

His body is isolated in the right corner of the cover, away from the other children. With shovel in hand, he leaps, feet first, toward a sand replica of the World Trade Center. His intentions—to demolish the building. The cover creates a new media myth—even Arab children learn to be terrorists. Recognizing that their illustration injured innocents, the magazine's editors eventually apologized.

Since the February 23, 1993 bombing of the World Trade Center, Arab-Americans have been frightened throughout the country with both verbal and physical assaults.[12] They are being collectively indicted by association for the alleged crimes of a few.

ISLAM PORTRAYED AS A VIOLENT RELIGION

Television not only portrays the Arab people as inherently violent, it also fosters the idea that a particular religion supports violence—a religion that includes over a billion people, the majority of whom are not Arab. On October 3, 1994, CBS-TV's "Eye on America" presented Islam not as a religion but as a political threat. The program asserted that money is being raised by Arabs and Muslims in the U.S. for a "holy war" both here and in the Middle East. This charge has also been made by journalist Steven Emerson, who was featured in November, 1994 on the television program "60 Minutes" and on the November PBS program "Jihad! In America."

Of course there are individuals—Arabs, Irish, Italians, Jews, and others—preaching enmity and financing terror. But they are a small minority. No doubt some of what Emerson says about a tiny minority of Arabs and Muslims spewing hate and advocating violence is true. There are some Muslim extremists in the United States. But when he states that future attacks by "Muslim radicals" in the U.S. "seem inevitable," he not only offers no substantiating evidence but slanders an entire group of people.

Englishman John Buchan declared in his popular 1916 novel, *Greenmantle,* "Islam is a fighting creed, and the mullah still stands in the pulpit with the Koran in one hand and a drawn sword in the other."[13] This image has been enhanced by such contemporary television documentaries as *The Islamic Bomb* and *The Sword of Islam;* books tagged *Inflamed Islam* and *The Fire of Islam;* magazine and newspaper essays titled "The Roots of Muslim Rage," "The Militant Revival," and "Muslim Time Bomb."

In March 1996, for 10 days the film *Executive Decision* was the second highest grossing film in the U.S. market. At the screening I attended the audience whistled and applauded when Americans terminated gun-toting Palestinians. In this movie, Nagi Hassan (David Suchet) and his accomplices hijack a 747 plane en route to Washington, D.C. with 406 passengers aboard. Nagi's Palestinian Muslim terrorists intend to drop enough lethal nerve gas to kill everyone on the Eastern seaboard.

Throughout, violence is equated with the Holy Koran. Holding the Holy Koran in one hand and a bomb in another, a Palestinian enters London's swank Mariott Hotel, blowing up scores of people. And prior to killing passengers, a Muslim prays, then shouts, "It's the sword of Islam . . . sent to deliver a blow to the belly of the infidel!"

Few Americans realize that the word "Islam" comes from the Arabic root, s-l-m, meaning peace. Advocating brotherhood and understanding, Islam is the religion of peace; many Muslims are creating bridges of understanding between Arabs and Israelis, Arabs and Americans. Peace is basic to the tenets of Islam, and yet Muslim efforts to stem violence and develop harmony with others have not been conveyed by the mass media.

"Stories about Muslims often focus on extremists," says Hillary Rodham Clinton; it is "not fair to apply a negative stereotype to all Muslims. . . . The reality is that the vast majority . . . of Muslims in the United States are loyal citizens, whose daily lives revolve around work, family and community. People who found spiritual guidance and substance in Islam represent all walks of life."[14]

CONSEQUENCES OF ARAB/MUSLIM STEREOTYPES

Damaging words and pictures have a telling effect, teaching people whom to hate and fear. Not so long ago, screen images taught viewers that Asians were sneaky, blacks were Sambos, Italians were mafiosi, Irishmen were drunks, Jews were greedy, and Hispanics were greasy. The time is long overdue for image-makers to begin eradicating bigotry of *all* types.

The prejudice projected in popular films creates and perpetuates feelings of insecurity, vulnerability, alienation, and even denial of heritage among America's Arabs and Muslims. These images have an especially devastating impact on the self-esteem of children of Arab ancestry.

Only four days after the 1996 release of the film *Executive Decision,* employees of a Denver radio station burst into a mosque and began harassing worshipers.[15] The station broadcast the incident live. One DJ played the national anthem on a trumpet; another donned a mock turban and a Mahmoud Abdul-Rauf T-shirt.[16]

Continuously repeated, the various stereotypes perpetuated by the mass media have a formidable and enduring impact. Consider the National Conference's 1994 survey on Inter-Group relations. Pollster Louis Harris conducted in-depth interviews with nearly 3,000 people; Asians, Latinos, blacks, and whites were asked about negative stereotypes. Forty-two percent agreed with the statement that "Muslims belong to a religion that condones or supports terrorism." Forty-seven percent concurred with the assertion that Muslims "are anti-Western and anti-American"; and 62 percent agreed with the declaration that Muslims "segregate and suppress women."[17]

In the minds of bigots these stereotypes legitimize and justify their violent acts against Arab-Americans and Muslims. In September 1994, a $1 million mosque in Yuba City, California was burned to the ground. In October of the same year, vandals attempted to torch a mosque in Brooklyn, New York.

Since the 1995 bombing of a federal building in Oklahoma City, more than 300 hate crimes have been committed against Arab Americans and Muslims and eight mosques have been vandalized and burnt to the ground. Why did so many Americans believe the journalists who prematurely reported that the bomber in Oklahoma City was someone who looked "Middle Eastern"?

SUGGESTIONS TO MOVE TOWARD A REALISTIC IMAGE OF ARABS

There are 6 to 8 million Muslims in the United States; by the year 2000, Muslims will constitute 27 percent of the world's population. Because religion is such an emotional and important aspect of the Arab image, it would help to decrease misunderstanding if journalists and educators would write about the commonalities of Christianity, Islam, and Judaism. These religions have mutually compatible aspirations and share a common God, as well as most of the same teachers and prophets. The emphasis in Islam, as in other religions, is on living righteously and justly. Religious leaders also could explain that Islam, like Christianity and Judaism, maintains that all humankind is one family in the care of God.

It would be a step in the right direction if movie and TV producers developed characters modeled after real-life Arab-Americans. We could then see someone like White House correspondent Helen Thomas, whose father came from Lebanon, in a movie like *The American President* (1996), a heart surgeon patterned after the real-life Dr. Michael DeBakey on television shows like "E.R." or "Chicago Hope," a lawyer such as Ralph Nader on "Law and Order," a Palestinian teacher like Columbia University's Edward Said in "Dangerous Minds," or a Syrian-American playing tournament chess on television like Yasser Seirawan, the Seattle grandmaster.

Although producers select scripts, actors can speak out. No one affiliated with Disney's *Father of the Bride, Part II* denounced the stereotypes. Why didn't actor Levy, who plays Habib, complain? Why did noted performers Steve Martin and Diane Keaton remain silent? Why were there no protests from members of the Screen Writers', Actors', or Directors' Guilds of America? With the exception of *Entertainment Weekly*'s Ken Tucker, who wrote, "The caricature of a cold, rich Middle Easterner [Habib] amounts to a glaring ethnic slur,"[18] why are movie critics mum?

Most Americans do not fill movie theaters that show films perpetuating racist and anti-Semitic images. Yet, because producers continue presenting movies denigrating Arabs, viewers are becoming accustomed to seeing stale images of Arabs as "terrorists," "radicals," "militants," and "fanatics," taking them for granted.

Journalists and educators could expose Arab-bashing in the media and in public discourse. Politicians, too, should speak out against cardboard caricatures. They should refer to Arabs as friends, not just as moderates. When all image-makers rightfully begin to treat Arabs and other minorities with respect and dignity, we may begin to unlearn our prejudices.

A positive example of this is filmmaker George Lucas who recently spoke about what artists "teach" with their creations. He even criticized "himself for the scene played for laughs in *Raiders of the Lost Ark* (1981) where Indiana Jones drops his bullwhip and casually guns down an Arab swordsman."[19]

All groups contain some Attila-the-Hun types, but they are the minority. History teaches us that a major obstacle to world peace is the tendency of image-makers to dehumanize others and to enhance myths. As a *New York Times* editorial stated after the Gulf War: "Bigotry thrives on slanderous stereotypes, and the crazed Arab is today's version of the Teutonic hordes and the yellow peril . . . . To hold a diverse Arab world collectively responsible for a single leader's [Saddam Hussein] misdeeds traduces an entire population."[20]

Responsible citizens as well can act to combat prejudicial portraits. For example, in November 1994, a St. Louis evening newscast featured "Terrorism and Money," a story painting resident Muslims as supporters of terrorism. After reading the story, the president of the Jewish Community Relations Council, J. David Levy was so concerned that he wrote to KMOV-TV's news director: "We abhor the violence of terrorism and those who support it. We also abhor the stereotyping of communities. Unfortunately, your presentation did just that to the Islamic community. We ask, that in the future, sensitivity be shown and there be no blanket condemnation, implicit or explicit, of entire groups."[21]

Almost immediately, the station aired an apology and for three consecutive Tuesdays presented a series focusing on Islam. The programs debunked malevolent myths and helped strengthen the bonds among peoples—Christians, Jews, Hindus, and Muslims.

Soon after he launched Operation Desert Shield, President Bush said that the actions of Saddam Hussein went "against the tradition of Arab hospitality, against the tradition of Islam." The President's words help dilute prejudice by debunking prepackaged Arab stereotypes. We need more such high-level declarations to encourage us to examine carefully the realities of the region, both bad and good.

There is a dangerous and cumulative effect when prejudicial messages remain unchallenged. In time, I believe that educators as well as media professionals will eventually define, document and discuss the racism prevalent in the media's image of Arabs. The ultimate result should be an image of the Arab as neither saint nor devil, but as a fellow human being, with all the potential and frailties that condition implies.

Ultimately, I believe we will accept the wisdom of Holocaust survivor and Nobel Prize winner Elie Wiesel who said, "There are good people and bad people in every community. No human race is superior; no religious faith is inferior."[22]

ENDNOTES

[1]See Jack G. Shaheen, "The Persian Gulf Crisis Gives Scholars a Chance to Encourage More Accurate Depictions of Arabs," *The Chronicle of Higher Education,* 37(9), 31 October 1990: B1, B3.

[2]See Jack G. Shaheen, "The Media's Image of Arabs," *Newsweek,* 29 February 1988, p. 10.

[3]Jack G. Shaheen, "The Comic Book Arab," *The Link,* 24(5), November–December 1991: 1–11.

[4]Bill Watterson, *Calvin and Hobbes Tenth Anniversary Book* (Andrews and McMeel: Kansas City, 1995), 202.

[5]Professor Carol Gluck, Columbia University historian, interview with Jack G. Shaheen on January 8, 1997.

[6]An historical review of the cinematic portrayal of Arabs can be found in Jack G. Shaheen's "Cinematic Images of the Arab World," *Arab Journal for the Humanities,* Kuwait University, Issue No. 54,(Winter 1996): 395–416.

[7]George Gerbner quoted in Harry F. Waters, "Live According to TV," *Newsweek,* 6 December 1982, 136.

[8]On television and in motion pictures, the media's sheik is projected as uncultured and ruthless, attempting to buy media conglomerates (*Network,* 1977); destroy the world economy (*Rollover,* 1981); use nuclear weapons against America and Israel (*Wrong is Right,* 1982); influence foreign policies (*Protocol,* 1984); and kidnap Western women (*Jewel of the Nile,* 1985).

[9]Meg Greenfield, "A Glitch in the Talk Machine?" *Newsweek,* 17 September 1990, 76.

[10]See interview between Jack Shaheen and Hanan Ashrawi featured in Jack G. Shaheen, "Commentary: The Face of the Palestinians," *St. Louis Post-Dispatch,* 7 November 1991, 3C.

[11]An historical review of the cinematic portrayal of Arabs can be found in Jack G. Shaheen's "Cinematic Images of the Arab World," *Arab Journal for the Humanities,* Kuwait University, Issue No. 54 (Winter 1996): 395–416.

[12]Many specific examples are given in Jack G. Shaheen's "Commentary: The Arab Stereotype And Prejudice," *St. Louis Post-Dispatch,* 23 November 1993, 11C.

[13]John Buchan, *Greenmantle* (Thomas Nelson & Sons, Ltd: London, 1916), 17.

[14]Hillary Rodham Clinton quoted in "The White House Celebrates *Eid al Fitr,*" *Islamic Horizons,* May/June, 1996, 21.

[15]AP, "Disc Jockeys' Act Called Hate Crime," *Colorado Dispatch,* 22 March 1996, 3a.

[16]Mahmoud Abdul-Rauf, a Denver Nuggets' basketball star, would not stand for the national anthem because of his religious beliefs.

[17]Data from "National Conference Poll: Taking America's Pulse," published by *National Conference,* New York, March 1994.

[18]Ken Tucker, *Entertainment Weekly,* Review of "Executive Decision," 15 December 1995, 50.

[19]Bruce Handy, "The Force is Back," *Time,* 10 February 1997, 73.

[20]Editorial, "It's Racist, but Hey, It's Disney," *New York Times,* 14 July 1993, A18 L.

[21]J. David Levy, letter sent to the *St. Louis Post-Dispatch,* cited by Jack G. Shaheen in "Commentary: Violent Stereotypes of a Peaceful People, *St. Louis Post-Dispatch,* 6 December 1994, 11B.

[22]Elie Wiesel cited in *Ibid.*

56

The Mirror Image in Soviet-American Relations

Urie Bronfenbrenner

I should explain by way of introduction that I was in the Soviet Union during the summer of 1960, about a month after the U-2 incident. The primary purpose of my trip was to become acquainted with scientific developments in my field, which is social psychology. But in addition to visiting laboratories at universities and institutes, I wanted also to become acquainted with *living* social psychology—the Soviet people themselves. It was my good fortune to be able to speak Russian. I was traveling with a tourist visa on a new plan which permitted me to go about alone without a guide. Accordingly, after spending the first two or three days of my visit in a particular city at scientific centers, I would devote the remaining days to walking about the town and striking up conversations with people in public conveyances, parks, stores, restaurants, or just on the street. Since foreigners are a curiosity, and I was obviously a foreigner (though, I quickly learned, not obviously an American), people were eager to talk. But I also went out of my way to strike up conversations with people who weren't taking the initiative—with fellow passengers who were remaining silent, with strollers in the park, with children and old people. Or I would enter a restaurant deciding in advance to sit at the third table on the left with whoever should turn out to be

Excerpted from "The Mirror Image in Soviet-American Relations: A Social Psychologist's Report," *Journal of Social Issues* 16, no. 3 (1961): 45–56, by permission of Society for the Psychological Study of Social Issues.

there. (In Soviet restaurants it is not uncommon to share a table with strangers.)

These conversations convinced me that the great majority of Russians feel a genuine pride in the accomplishments of their system and a conviction that communism is the way of the future not only for themselves but for the rest of the world as well. For several reasons my Soviet journey was a deeply disturbing experience. But what frightened me was not so much the facts of Soviet reality as the discrepancy between the real and the perceived. At first I was troubled only by the strange irrationality of the Soviet view of the world—especially their gross distortion of American society and American foreign policy as I knew them to be. But then, gradually, there came an even more disquieting awareness—an awareness which I resisted and still resist. Slowly and painfully, it forced itself upon me that the *Russian's distorted picture of us was curiously similar to our view of them—a mirror image.* But of course our image was real. Or could it be that our views too were distorted and irrational—a mirror image in a twisted glass?

It was—and is—a frightening prospect. For if such reciprocal distortion exists, it is a psychological phenomenon without parallel in the gravity of its consequences. For this reason, the possibility deserves serious consideration.

THE MIRROR IMAGE MAGNIFIED

Let us then briefly examine the common features in the American and Soviet view of each other's societies. For the Russian's image I drew mainly, not on official government pronouncements, but on what was said to me by Soviet citizens in the course of our conversations. Five major themes stand out.

1. They Are the Aggressors

The American view: Russia is the warmonger bent on imposing its system on the rest of the world. Witness Czechoslovakia, Berlin, Hungary, and now Cuba and the Congo. The Soviet Union consistently blocks Western proposals for disarmament by refusing necessary inspection controls.

The Soviet view: America is the warmonger bent on imposing its power on the rest of the world and on the Soviet Union itself. Witness American intervention in 1918; Western encirclement after World War II with American troops and bases on every border of the USSR (West Germany, Norway, Turkey, Korea, Japan); intransigence over proposals to make Berlin a free city; intervention in Korea, Taiwan, Lebanon, Guatemala, Cuba. America has repeatedly rejected Soviet disarmament proposals while demanding the right to inspect within Soviet territory—finally attempting to take the right by force through deep penetration of Soviet airspace.

2. Their Government Exploits and Deludes the People

The American view: Convinced communists, who form but a small proportion of Russia's population, control the government and exploit the society and its resources in their own interest. To justify their power and expansionist policies they have to perpetuate a war atmosphere and a fear of Western aggression. Russian elections are a travesty, since only one party appears on the ballot. The Russian people are kept from knowing the truth through a controlled radio and press, and conformity is insured through stringent economic and political sanctions against deviant individuals or groups.

The Soviet view: A capitalistic-militaristic clique controls the American government, the nation's economic resources, and its media of communication. The group exploits the society and its resources. It is in their economic and political interest to maintain a war atmosphere and engage in militaristic expansion. Voting in America is a farce, since candidates for both parties are selected by the same powerful interests leaving nothing to choose between. The American people are kept from knowing the truth through a controlled radio and press and through economic and political sanctions against liberal elements.

3. The Mass of Their People Are Not Really Sympathetic to the Regime

The American view: In spite of the propaganda, the Soviet people are not really behind their government. Their praise of the government and the party is largely perfunctory, a necessary concession for getting along. They do not trust their own sources of information and have learned to read between the lines. Most of them would prefer to live under our system of government if they only could.

The Soviet view: Unlike their government, the bulk of the American people want peace. Thus, the majority disapproved of American aggression in Korea, the support of Chiang Kai-shek, and above all, of the sending of U-2. But of course they could do nothing, since their welfare is completely under the control of the ruling financier-militaristic clique. If the American people were allowed to become acquainted with communism as it exists in the USSR, they would unquestionably choose it as their form of government. ("You Americans are such a nice people; it is a pity you have such a terrible government.")

4. They Cannot Be Trusted

The American view: The Soviets do not keep promises and they do not mean what they say. Thus, while they claim to have discontinued all nuclear testing, they are probably carrying out secret underground explosions in order to gain an advantage over us. Their talk of peace is but a propaganda maneuver. Everything they do is to be viewed with suspicion, since it is all part of a single coordinated scheme to further aggressive communist aims.

The Soviet view: The Americans do not keep promises and they do not mean what they say. Thus, they insist on inspection only so that they can look at Soviet defenses; they have no real intention of disarming. Everything the Americans do is to be viewed with suspicion (e.g., they take advantage of Soviet hospitality by sending in spies as tourists).

5. Their Policy Verges on Madness

The American view: Soviet demands on such crucial problems as disarmament, Berlin, and unification are completely unrealistic. Disarmament without adequate inspection is meaningless; a "free Berlin" would be equivalent to a Soviet Berlin; and a united Germany without free elections is an impossibility. In pursuit of their irresponsible policies the Soviets do not hesitate to run the risk of war itself. Thus, it is only due to the restraint and coordinated action of the Western alliance that Soviet provocations over Berlin did not precipitate World War III.

The Soviet view: The American position on such crucial problems as disarmament, East Germany, and China is completely unrealistic. They demand to know our secrets before they disarm; in Germany they insist on a policy which risks the resurgence of a fascist Reich; and as for China, they try to act as if it did not exist while at the same time supporting an aggressive puppet regime just off the Chinese mainland. And, in pursuit of their irresponsible policies, the Americans do not hesitate to run the risk of war itself. Were it not for Soviet prudence and restraint, the sending of a U-2 deep into Russian territory could easily have precipitated World War III.

It is easy to recognize the gross distortions in the Soviet views summarized above. But is our own outlook completely realistic? Are we correct, for example, in thinking that the mass of the Soviet people would really prefer our way of life and are unenthusiastic about their own? Certainly the tone and tenor of my conversations with Soviet citizens hardly support this belief.

But, you may ask, why is it that other Western observers do not report the enthusiasm and commitment which I encountered?

I asked this very question of newspapermen and embassy officials in Moscow. Their answers were revealing. Thus one reporter replied somewhat dryly, "sure, I know, but when a communist acts like a communist, it isn't news. If I want to be sure that it will be printed back home, I have to write about what's wrong with the system, not its successes." Others voiced an opinion expressed most clearly by representatives at our embassy. When I reported to them the gist of my Soviet conversations, they were grateful but skeptical: "Professor, you underestimate the effect of the police state. When these people talk to a stranger, especially an American, they *have* to say the right thing."

The argument is persuasive, and comforting to hear. But perhaps these very features should arouse our critical judgment. Indeed, it is instructive to view this argument against the background of its predecessor voiced by the newspaperman. To put it bluntly, what he was saying was that he could be sure of getting published only the material that the *American people wanted to hear.* But notice that the second argument also fulfills this objective, and it does so in a much more satisfactory and sophisticated way. The realization that "Soviet citizens *have* to say the right thing" enables the Western observer not only to discount most of what he hears but even to interpret it as evidence in direct support of the West's accepted picture of the Soviet Union as a police state.

It should be clear that I am in no sense here suggesting that Western reporters and embassy officials deliberately misrepresent what they know to be the facts. Rather, I am calling attention to the operation, in a specific and critical context, of a phenomenon well known to psychologists—the tendency to assimilate new perceptions to old, and unconsciously to distort what one sees in such a way as to minimize a clash with previous expectations. In recent years, a number of leading social psychologists, notably Heider, Festinger, and Osgood, have emphasized that this "strain toward consistency" is especially powerful in the sphere of social relations—that is, in our perceptions of the motives, attitudes, and actions of other persons or groups.[1] Specifically, we strive to keep our views of other human beings compatible with each other. In the face of complex social reality, such consistency is typically accomplished by obliterating distinctions and organizing the world in terms of artificially simplified frames of reference. One of the simplest of these and hence one of the most inviting, is the dichotomy of good and bad. Hence we often perceive others, be they individuals, groups, or even whole societies as simply "good" or "bad." Once this fateful decision is made, the rest is easy, for the "good" person or group can have only desirable social characteristics and the "bad" can have only reprehensible traits. And once such evaluative stability of social perception is established, it is extremely difficult to alter. Contradictory stimuli arouse only anxiety and resistance. When confronted with a desirable characteristic of something already known to be "bad," the observer will either just not "see" it, or will reorganize his perception of it so that it can be perceived as "bad." Finally, this tendency to regress to simple categories of perception is especially strong under conditions of emotional stress and external threat. Witness our readiness in times of war to exalt the virtues of our own side and to see the enemy as thoroughly evil.

Still one other social-psychological phenomenon has direct relevance for the present discussion. I refer to a process demonstrated most dramatically and comprehensively in the experiments of Solomon Asch, and known thereby as the "Asch phenomenon."[2] In these experiments, the subject finds himself in a group of six or eight of his peers, all of whom are asked to make comparative judgments of certain stimuli presented to them; for example, identifying the longer of two lines. At first the task seems simple enough; the subject hears others make their judgments and then makes his own. In the beginning he is usually in agreement, but then gradually he notices that more and more often his judgments differ from those of the rest of the group. Actually, the experiment is rigged. All the other group members have been instructed to give false responses on a predetermined schedule. In any event, the effect on our subject is dramatic. At first he is puzzled, then upset. Soon he begins to have serious doubts about his judgment, and in an appreciable number of cases, he begins to "see" the stimuli as they are described by his fellows.

What I am suggesting, of course, is that the Asch phenomenon operates even more forcefully outside the laboratory where the game of social perception is being played for keeps. *Specifically, I am proposing that the mechanisms here described contribute substan-* *tially to producing and maintaining serious distortions in the reciprocal images of the Soviet Union and The United States.*

My suggestion springs from more than abstract theoretical inference. I call attention to the possible operation of the Asch phenomenon in the Soviet-American context for a very concrete reason: I had the distressing experience of being its victim. While in the Soviet Union I deliberately sought to minimize association with other westerners and to spend as much time as I could with Soviet citizens. This was not easy to do. It was no pleasant experience to hear one's own country severely criticized and to be constantly outdebated in the bargain. I looked forward to the next chance meeting with a fellow Westerner so that I could get much-needed moral support and enjoy an evening's invective at the expense of Intourist and the "worker's paradise." But though I occasionally yielded to temptation, for the most part I kept true to my resolve and spent many hours in a completely Soviet environment. It was difficult but interesting. I liked many of the people I met. Some of them apparently liked me. Though mistaken, they were obviously sincere. They wanted me to agree with them. The days went on, and strange things began to happen. I remember picking up a Soviet newspaper which featured an account of American activities in the Near East. "Oh, what are they doing now!" I asked myself, and stopped short; for I had thought in terms of "they," and it was my own country. Or I would become aware that I had been nodding to the points being made by my Soviet companion where before I had always taken issue. In short, when all around me saw the world one way, I too found myself wanting to believe and belong.

And once I crossed the Soviet border on my way home, the process began to reverse itself. The more I talked with fellow westerners, especially fellow Americans, the more I began to doubt the validity of my original impressions. "What would you expect them to say to an American?" my friends would ask. "How do you know that the person talking to you was not a trained agitator?" "Did you ever catch sight of them following you?" I never did. Perhaps I was naive. But then, recently I reread a letter written to a friend during the last week of my stay. "I feel it is important," it begins, "to try to write to you in detail while I am still in it, for just as I could never have conceived of what I am now experiencing, so, I suspect, it will seem unreal and intangible once I am back in the West." The rest of the letter, and others like it, contain the record of the experiences reported in this account.

In sum, I take my stand on the view that there *is* a mirror image in Soviet and American perceptions of each other and that this image represents serious distortions by *both* parties of realities on either side.

THE MIRROR IMAGE PROJECTED

And if so, what then? Do not distortions have adaptive functions? Especially in war is it not psychologically necessary to see the enemy as thoroughly evil and to enhance one's self-image? And are we not engaged in a war, albeit a cold war, with the Soviet Union?

But is not our hope to bring an end to the cold war and, above all, to avoid the holocaust of a hot one? And herein lies the terrible danger of the distorted mirror image, for *it is characteristic of such images that they are self-confirming;* that is, each party, often against its own wishes fulfills the expectations of the other. As revealed in social-psychological studies, the mechanism is a simple one: if A expects B to be friendly and acts accordingly, B responds with friendly advances; these in turn evoke additional positive actions from A, and thus a benign circle is set in motion. Conversely, where A's anticipations of B are unfavorable, it is the vicious circle which develops at an accelerating pace. And as tensions rise, perceptions become more primitive and still further removed from reality. Seen from this perspective, the primary danger of the Soviet-American mirror image is that it impels each nation to act in a manner which confirms and enhances the fear of the other to the point that even deliberate efforts to reverse the process are reinterpreted as evidences of confirmation.

Manifestations of this mechanism in Soviet-American relations are not difficult to find. A case in point is our policy of restricting the travel of Soviet nationals in the United States by designating as "closed areas" localities that correspond as closely as possible to those initially selected by Soviet authorities as "off limits" to Americans in the USSR. As was brought home to me in conversations with Soviet scientists who had visited the United States, one of the effects of this policy is to neutralize substantially any favorable impressions the visitor might otherwise get of American freedoms.

To take another example in a more consequential area: in a recent issue of *Atlantic Monthly*, Dr. Hans Bethe, an American physicist who participated in negotiations at the Geneva Conference on nuclear testing, reports that our tendency to export trickery from the Soviets led us into spending considerable time and energy to discover scientific loopholes in their proposals which could have permitted them to continue nuclear tests undetected. As a result, our scientists did succeed in finding a theoretical basis for questioning the effectiveness of the Soviet plan. It seems that if the Soviets could dig a hole big enough, they could detonate underground explosions without being detected. Says Dr. Bethe:

> I had the doubtful honor of presenting the theory of the big hole to the Russians in Geneva in November 1959. I felt deeply embarrassed in so doing, because it implied that we considered the Russians capable of cheating on a massive scale. I think they would have been quite justified if they had considered this an insult and walked out of the negotiations in disgust.
>
> The Russians seemed stunned by the theory of the big hole. In private, they took Americans to task for having spent the last year inventing methods to cheat on a nuclear test cessation agreement. Officially, they spent considerable effort in trying to disprove the theory of the big hole. This is not the reaction of a country that is bent on cheating.[3]

But the most frightful potential consequence of the mirror image lies in the possibility that it may confirm itself out of existence. For if it is possible for either side to interpret concessions as signs of treachery, it should not be difficult to recognize an off-course satellite as a missile on its way. After all, we, or they, would be expecting it.

But it is only in the final catastrophe that the mirror image is impartial in its effects. Short of doomsday, we have even more to lose from the accelerating vicious circle than do the Soviets. Internally, the communist system can justify itself to the Soviet people far more easily in the face of external threat than in times of peace. And in the international arena, the more the United States becomes committed to massive retaliation and preventive intervention abroad, the more difficult it becomes for uncommitted or even friendly nations to perceive a real difference in the foreign policies of East and West.

BREAKING THE MIRROR IMAGE

How can we avoid such awesome consequences? One step seems clearly indicated: we must do everything we can to break down the psychological barrier that prevents both us and the Russians from seeing each other and ourselves as we really are. If we can succeed in dispelling the Soviet Union's bogeyman picture of America, we stand to gain, for to the same degree that militant communism thrives in a context of external threat, it is weakened as this threat is reduced. And as the raison d'être for sacrifice, surveillance, and submission disappears there arises opportunity for the expression of such potential for liberalization as may still exist in Russian society.

ENDNOTES

[1] F. Heider, *The Psychology of Interpersonal Relations* (New York: Wiley, 1958); L. Festinger, *A Theory of Cognitive Dissonance* (Evanston, IL: Row, Peterson, 1957); C. Osgood, *Graduated Reciprocation in Tension-Reduction* (Urbana: University of Illinois, Institute of Communications Research, 1960).

[2] S. E. Asch, "Studies of Independence and Conformity: I. A Minority of One Against a Unanimous Majority," *Psychological Monographs 70,* no. 9 (1956).

[3] Hans A. Bethe, "The Case for Ending Nuclear Tests," *Atlantic Monthly 206,* no. 2 (August 1960): 46.

57

Empathizing with the Rulers of the USSR

Ralph K. White

INTRODUCTION

If we in the West want to survive, by avoiding nuclear war, it behooves us to empathize realistically with the rulers of the Soviet Union.

Two words in that statement, "empathize" and "rulers," call for definition.

A sharp distinction is made here between empathy and sympathy. Although two words are often used almost interchangeably, empathy will be defined for the purposes of this paper as a realistic *understanding* of the thoughts and feelings of others, while sympathy will be defined, in accordance with its derivation, as *feeling with* others. Empathy is cognitive; sympathy is affective.

While the two processes often occur together and are causally related, this distinction between them is important, especially when we are talking about an opponent who is caught, as we are, in what Morton Deutsch calls a "malignant process" of hostile interaction.[1] It is extremely difficult to "feel with" such an opponent, chiefly because his hostility to oneself is so genuine and so genuinely dangerous. A plea for warmhearted sympathy with the Soviet rulers would be psychologically naive. A plea for realistic empathy with them, however, is not naive, and is of crucial importance at this stage in the history of the human race. If we do not clearly recognize their hostility, we will not be tough in the ways we should be tough, and, if we do not clearly recognize their essential humanity, we

Reprinted from *Political Psychology* 4, no. 1, 1983, by permission of Plenum Publishing Corporation.

will not be reasonable and cooperative in the ways we must be in order to survive.

Now the word "rulers." The realistic word is not "leaders"; it is "rulers," with all of the implied condemnation that that word carries with it. As most of us see the Soviet system (and that includes me), it is a terrible system, now proven to be economically inefficient as well as ruthlessly undemocratic. It is still essentially totalitarian, as it was in the days of Stalin's one-man rule and his mammoth Gulag Archipelago, though much less cruelly so, and now oligarchic rather than autocratic. The rulers are still rulers, grimly determined to cling to the essentials of their own power both in the USSR and in the outlying but adjacent areas (East Europe, Afghanistan, Mongolia) that they now control. In this respect the term "mirror-image," made familiar by Urie Bronfenbrenner is by no means fully accurate.[2] There are significant psychological differences between them and our own elected leaders, and in our effort to see their humanity there is no need to lean over backward and ignore those differences. Also, the rulers are the ones we must understand and deal with if we want peace—not the Soviet public.

On the other hand, we need to make a clear distinction between the evil of their domestic policies and the question whether, in their own self-interest, their foreign policies are mainly defensive in motivation.

Their Defensively Motivated Policies

The main thesis of this paper is that their foreign and defense policies *are* mainly defensive in motivation, as ours are. In this respect the mirror-image concept is valid.

If that proposition is true, full acceptance of it by our American leaders would make an enormous difference on the side of peace.

It is far from being accepted now. To be sure, many of President Reagan's critics feel that his budget-busting nuclear buildup is leading to two kinds of disaster: the immediate disaster of economic stagnation and the delayed disaster of an uncontrolled arms race and nuclear war. He and most of his advisers, on the other hand, are quite probably sincere in their apparent belief that the buildup is imperatively needed. They believe it because they take for granted two underlying assumptions that, if they empathized realistically with the Soviet rulers, they would recognize in all probability as false.

They assume, first, that the men in the Kremlin, already well ahead of us in nuclear strength (or likely to forge ahead in the near future) are driving toward a nuclear first-strike capability—a first strike that we will be powerless to deter unless we greatly increase our own nuclear strength to make it comparable to theirs. Second, they assume that the Soviet rulers are bent on attacking Western Europe by conventional means unless deterred by comparable force on our side (conventional or in the form of deployment of tactical nuclear weapons) plus an implied threat that we might be the first to use them. Both assumptions, it should be noted, imply that the Soviet rulers' motives are primarily offensive not defensive. That is the assumption that must be carefully, objectively examined.

The opposite proposition is by no means original. It reflects what I see as the mainstream of thinking among the best of the American scholars whose main concern is understanding Soviet foreign policy—scholars such as George Kennan, Adam Ulam, Robert Tucker at Princeton, Marshall Shulman, Helmut Sonnenfeldt, Robert Kaiser.[3] It is my impression that the interpretations of most of these men, though not all, would be fairly close to those offered here. It is interesting that not one of them is a professional psychologist. However, Urie Bronfenbrenner, whose firsthand knowledge of Soviet thinking is perhaps greater than that of any other Western psychologist, would surely agree with most of it, since it is in line with his own mirror-image idea.[4] This paper attempts to convey to other political psychologists, and interpret in somewhat psychological terms, what scholars of that type—most of them—have been saying for many years.

Let us look specifically at each of the Reagan administration's two assumptions described above:

A Soviet First Strike?

The President contends that we must strenuously expand our nuclear strength in order to deter a Soviet first strike, since the USSR's strategic arsenal now surpasses ours, or soon will. A familiar reply is to deny his premise of strategic inferiority. Critics of it insist that although our own former nuclear superiority has indeed been lost, it has been replaced by a kind of rough equivalence.[5]

That familiar argument is highly controversial and will not be relied on here, though it does seem likely that some of our hardliners have considerably exaggerated the present nuclear superiority of the USSR.

An equally familiar and much less controversial reply is that parity, or even an approach to parity, is not needed as long as each side has a powerful and fairly invulnerable second-strike capability. We have such a capability now, much of the hardware mounted on submarines that would be extremely difficult to find and destroy. Therefore, even if the Soviet Union were capable of a counterforce strike that would totally destroy all the land-based missiles in Western Europe and North America (which seems unlikely), the penalty might well be that blast, firestorms, and radiation would destroy some three-quarters of the Soviet population. It seems extremely unlikely that any sane Soviet decision maker would accept such a prospect.

A less familiar but very strong argument is that the Soviet people and their rulers acquired in World War II an overwhelming fear and horror of war as such. Their searing experience in that war is a fact we all know, but most of us have not been vividly reminded of it for many years and are likely to forget it when thinking of present Soviet attitudes. One Western visitor (a guide at our big exhibit in Moscow) described it in this way:

> They are not allowed to forget *their* war for a day. Their suffering was terrible. Perhaps they could not forget it even if allowed, but officially it is enforced so much that even the young, who didn't know it [at the time], are tremendously

and emotionally aware of it. . . . Often it is strict party-line propaganda even to the words used, but very often it is fervently believed. There were many, many tearful eyes when this subject came up.

The rulers suffered too; Krushchev's son, for instance, was killed in the war. And they know a nuclear war could be much worse.

That is scarcely a picture of a country that would deliberately embark on another big war. For the most convincing of all reasons—self-preservation—the Soviet Union wants peace.

Paul Nitze saw part of the truth when he said, of the Soviet decision makers, "They don't want war; they want the world."[6] It would be more accurate to say: They would *like* to have the world, but they know they can't get it for a long time to come, and their horror of war is so great that they are quite unlikely to take, knowingly, even serious risk of a big war in order to expand their power.

The practical upshot of this line of thinking is greatly reassuring. It is that we do not need to incur the costs and risks of economic stagnation or of an uncontrolled arms race for the sake of nuclear parity. Parity is irrelevant. As long as we have a relatively invulnerable second-strike capability, the Soviet Union is adequately deterred from attempting a nuclear first strike. We can safely have a freeze, and a no-first-use policy, and even the agreed-upon 50% cut in nuclear weapons that George Kennan recommends.

An Invasion of Western Europe?

There are six excellent reasons why the thought of attacking Western Europe is hardly on Soviet minds at all.

First, and most important, is the horror of war that has just been described.

Second, in their desire to expand their influence, the Soviet leaders have for many years turned their attention much more to the Third World than to Europe or the United States. Angola, Ethiopia, South Yemen, Cambodia, Afghanistan—all of them are in the Third World. Attention to the Third World has been predominant approximately since the time of the Bandung Conference: it is predominant in present doctrine ("wars of liberation") and in practice.

Third, they have learned from bitter experience, especially in Hungary, Czechoslovakia, Poland, and Afghanistan, about the costs of domination. Even semidomination, as in Cuba, South Yemen, and Vietnam, has cost them more rubles than they like to think about. Would they want, in West Germany, France, or Britain, the kind of headache they now have in Poland?

Fourth, they know things are going well for them now in Western Europe, without war or conquest. Their trade relations, represented, for instance, by the pipeline, are profitable to both sides, and they have recently learned how useful the economic gains of Western Europe can be in driving a wedge between it and the United States. They know that any serious threats of conquest, in an attempt to "Finlandize" Western Europe, could ruin all of that and drive the West Europeans back into the arms of "American imperialism."

Fifth, they know that it would be a big and costly war even if it remained conventional and they won it. Although they are greatly superior to the United States alone in numbers of troops, tanks, and artillery, that is far less true when our NATO allies are taken into account. The picture presented by hardliners in the United States also often fails to mention several other elements of real Soviet weakness: the Soviet leaders' felt need to keep a large fraction of their forces on the border of China, the obvious unreliability of many of the Warsaw Pact forces, the abundance of anti-tank weapons in Western Europe, the near certainty that France would fight along with NATO if there were a clear Soviet invasion, the better quality of Western weapons, and, probably most important, the traditional advantage of the defense over the offense. Military men variously estimate it as 2 to 1, 3 to 1, or some higher ratio, but regularly with a substantial advantage attributed to the defense as such.[7]

Sixth, the old men in the Politburo are also very cautious men, and have been so at least since the death of Stalin in 1953. They backed down on Berlin and Cuba; they used force in Hungary and Czechoslovakia only to keep what they already had; they swallowed their pride when we mined the harbor of Haiphong; they backed down immediately after our SAC-alert threat; and even in Afghanistan they probably thought beforehand that they were taking very little risk. We Americans sometimes forget that during the period since World War II, we have fought two wars with our own troops on far-away foreign soil, in Korea and Vietnam, and that while one of them, Korea, was unequivocally defensive, the other one, Vietnam, was not. During that time the Soviet Union has never done so. Its caution—not its virtue—made such actions seem too risky.

It should be noted that not one of these six reasons rests on any assumption of Soviet virtue, or good will, or trustworthiness. Not one rests on what they say about themselves. All of them are strictly matters of Soviet national self-interest, as we have reason to think that the Soviet interest is perceived by the men in the Kremlin.

The practical upshot of this line of thinking also is reassuring. It means that we do not need to deploy theater nuclear weapons in Western Europe, including that terrible, uninspectable weapon, the cruise missile. We can with reasonable safety adopt a no-first-use policy, there as elsewhere. And it means that, while it may be desirable to do more than in the past to help Western Europe defend itself with conventional arms, we surely do not need to do much more.[8]

Recent Soviet Aggression?

A critically important question still has to be answered: What about recent Soviet acts of aggression—in Angola, Ethiopia, South Yemen, Cambodia, Afghanistan? And how about the recent Soviet arms buildup, to a point far beyond what seems to us necessary for their self-defense? Don't actions speak louder than words, and don't Soviet actions show that their motivation must be more offensive than defensive?

An attempt to empathize suggests that the last question, phrased as it is in terms of only two kinds of motivation, is misleading in that there is at least one other important motive to be considered: competition for influence in the Third World (felt to be legitimate competition), combined with anger at what is felt to be an American attempt to exclude the Soviet Union—now a superpower comparable to the United States—from that competition. If we take the situational context of each recent Soviet action into account [as Jones and Nisbett would have us do],[9] that motive emerges as probably more important than either offense or defense, strictly defined.

Angola? The Soviet rulers could see their intervention and Cuba's as justified by a desire to help the Angolan people defend themselves against an actual invasion by South Africa, aided by Zaire and by America's CIA. (That invasion did occur.)

Ethiopia? They could see their siding with Ethiopia as justified by Somalia's armed aggression in an attempt to seize the Ogaden province.

Yemen? They could see their aid to South Yemen as on a par with American aid to North Yemen.

Cambodia? They could see their client, Vietnam, as liberating the Cambodian people from the unspeakable wholesale cruelty of Pol Pot.

Afghanistan? The question here is not whether the Soviet action should be called aggression. It should. The psychologically interesting question is whether the motivation behind the action, from the Soviet rulers' own point of view, was mainly defensive—as defensive as, let's say, our own motivation in Vietnam.[10]

That is not a far-fetched comparison. There are a number of intriguing similarities. Of course, there are also differences, some of which (e.g., the fact that Afghanistan is right on the border of the USSR, while Vietnam is about as far from the United States as it could possibly be) are not in our favor. The similarities, though, are striking. The chief one is that we, like the Soviet rulers, used our own troops to shore up a "friendly" government that we had helped to come to power but that had become demonstrably unpopular in the countryside and faced a dangerously increasing popular revolt.

There are also other similarities. Like them, we managed to replace an incompetent leader

(Diem, Amin) whose incompetence seemed likely to lead to disaster. Like them, we covered our intervention with the mostly phony pretext that we were protecting a put-upon nation from a danger originating mainly outside its borders. But we, at least, believed that our fighting and our pretense were justified by a genuine emergency: the danger that an area which had been part of our sphere of interest, the "Free World," would slip away and become part of the other side unless we intervened. We (at least our leaders, and at first most of the interested American public) felt that such a loss would hurt the credibility of our assurances elsewhere, and probably create a domino process that would seriously weaken the Free World itself.[11]

Was there anything comparable to that in the thinking of the Soviet rulers when in December 1979 they sent their troops in? Was their chief motive defensive, in the same sense in which ours was in Vietnam?

Most of us have rejected that possibility out of hand, if in fact it ever occurred to us at all. How could the Bad Guys have any such understandable motive? A few, though, have studied the question with more care, and some of them have taken the question of a defensive motive quite seriously.

Their case does not rest on the phony Soviet assertion that the Americans, Pakistanis, and Chinese were the main culprits. It rests partly on the fact that for many years before the "April Revolution" in 1978, Afghanistan had been friendly to and befriended by the USSR. It was already, before 1978, somewhat within the Soviet sphere of interest. Then in 1978, a coup by a group of left-wing army officers and urban Marxist intellectuals in Kabul put a clearly pro-communist government into power. (How much popular support or acceptance the new group had at that time is not clear.) Probably a Soviet role behind the scenes, and certainly the near presence of Soviet military power, had much to do with the success of the coup, and it may well be that more guilt attaches to the role of the Soviet rulers at that point than to their later use of troops, which was in a sense a natural consequence of what had happened in 1978.

In any case, from a Soviet point of view the April Revolution was a decisive turning point in that it established Afghanistan as a fairly full-fledged member of the "socialist community" which the Soviet Union was now obligated to "protect" from subversive reactionary influences as it was obligated to "protect" Hungary and Czechoslovakia. Psychologically Afghanistan could have become a part of their extended territorial self-image (the "socialist community") in somewhat the same way that after 1954 South Vietnam became for many Americans a part of America's extended territorial self-image (the "Free World"), which it too was obligated to protect.

Already in April 1978, the more informed members of the Politburo must have had doubts as to how democratic, and how socialist, the new Afghanistan was, and after the ensuing popular revolt gathered momentum, their doubts must have grown greatly. But were their doubts before the revolt necessarily greater than the doubts of informed Americans, after 1957 (when Diem first clearly showed his colors as an anti-democratic dictator), as to how democratic and pro-American south Vietnam was?

If they did more or less believe that Afghanistan had voluntarily joined the socialist community, that fact throws quite a different light on the nearly universal American assumption that in 1979 the Soviet rulers were consciously invading the Free World, in a spirit much more aggressive than that in which they had previously used their own troops to keep what they had in Hungary and Czechoslovakia. From their point of view, the men in the Kremlin may have seen it as quite comparable to Hungary and Czechoslovakia, about which they also had doubts as to the pro-Soviet feelings of the people.

That does not make their action less reprehensible. It can be argued that holding down an unwilling people is as evil as conquering them in the first place. But the implications for the future are different. The momentous implications that a great many Americans have seen in the Soviet action—that the Soviet Union had probably now embarked on a career of conquest comparable to that of Hitler, and that the West's access to Persian Gulf oil was now in greater danger—are not necessarily realistic. An alternative reading is at least equally plausible—that in Politburo eyes it was, like Hungary and Czechoslovakia, another example of their old, intense, basic principle: Keep what you have. The alternative might well have seemed to be a long-term domino process of disintegration within their already precarious empire, ultimately endangering the USSR itself. In any case, their prestige was now at stake.

A question remains: If they allowed the revolt to succeed, would the result, in their view, have been merely a neutral country, neutral as it was before 1978, or did they picture the country slipping all the way over to the camp of the Soviet Union's enemies, the United States, Pakistan, and China? Their accusation that the revolt itself was inspired and supported mainly by those alien forces does not need to be taken seriously; it was plainly a cover story, like their claim that "Afghanistan" itself asked for their help. But their anxiety about an ultimate addition of a new country to the ranks of their enemies may have been quite real.

We Americans sometimes forget, when we are attributing motives to the Soviet rulers, how they probably perceive the whole story of what we have done in the Middle East: the initial support and later lavish financial help we gave to the Shah, a pro-American dictator as cruel and ultimately as unpopular as Diem was in Vietnam; our SAC alert in 1973 in which we in effect threatened the USSR with a possible nuclear war if it insisted on sending troops to keep the cease-fire between Egypt and Israel; our consistent support of an Israel they probably perceive as both aggressive and intensely anti-Soviet; our tie-up with the most reactionary Arab rulers; our backing away from the Vance-Gromyko communiqué; and our exclusion of the Soviet Union from the peace process, on the assumption that, though the Middle East is on their border and not on ours, we alone have the right to play a "leading" role there. When faced with the prospect of a disintegrating Afghanistan, might they not have really believed that, if they did not intervene to restore order, and if the country completely

disintegrated, we and the Pakistanis and the Chinese would probably be right there to pick up the pieces?

Finally, there is the question of the steady, formidable Soviet arms buildup, to a level that seems to us unnecessary for their defense. Does it indicate an aggressive purpose?

Perhaps, but again the hypothesis of a primarily defensive motive is plausible. What seems to us unnecessary may not seem so to them.

It should be remembered first that the Soviet Union, like the United States, constitutes only roughly 6% of the world's population. Unlike us, though, they look out on the remaining 94% and see it, not very unrealistically, as mainly hostile to themselves. They remember Hitler's unprovoked attack. They see a Western Europe allied with a hostile United States in NATO and, like the United States, surpassing them in scientific and industrial strength; they see a United States comparable to them in strength and every few years inventing horrible new aggressive weapons; they see a United States that has been increasingly hostile to them, for no reason they regard as remotely adequate, since the heady Nixon-Kissinger detente in the early 1970s; they see a China enormously larger than the USSR in population and irrational in its hostility to them; they see a frighteningly efficient Japan increasingly in rapport with China against them; they see a Moslem Middle East that is ambivalent and potentially friendly but deeply suspicious of "atheistic Communism."

Moreover, they know that nearly all their allies in East Europe are unreliable; they suspect that parts of the USSR itself may be hostile. Their economy is mysteriously stagnating. They have lost Yugoslavia, China, Egypt, Indonesia—each much more important than Angola, Ethiopia, South Yemen, Cambodia, or Afghanistan. Worst of all, they are baffled by the mounting hostility of the United States—*before* Afghanistan—as shown by the SAC alert, the Jackson-Vanik amendment, the rapprochement with China, their exclusion from the Middle East peacemaking, the substantial increase in the American arms budget, the new prospect of deadly cruise missiles and Pershing II missiles in Western Europe, the fading hopes for a SALT II agreement. Their ideology provides them a reason: The rulers of capitalism are implacably, incurably hostile to "socialism" and would destroy it if they dared.

Is it implausible that—however mistakenly—their main motive for arming might be, like ours, long-term self-defense? Especially when, in mirror-image contrast with what American military men are saying, the Soviet military men are saying that they are *not* strategically superior to the United States, but have achieved only a precarious and probably temporary equality?

Naturally, like most human motives, theirs are probably mixed. The word "main" in what has just been said should be noted: "their main motive for arming might be, like ours, long-term self-defense." Most importantly, along with their fear of a hostile world led by us, there may well be a sizable admixture of pride. Wounded pride, and now something else, much more unattractive—a compensatory, arrogant, we'll-show-the-world pride in their newly achieved military strength, plus anger at the arrogant Americans who do not seem to realize that the USSR, the other superpower, must now be treated as an equal.

It will be remembered that a third motive, different from either offense or defense strictly defined, was suggested above: competition for influence in the Third World. They probably think of such influence partly as a defensive counterweight to the West's and China's other forms of strength, but also, and perhaps primarily, as an end in itself. It must be inherently satisfying to their national ego, and all the more satisfying, because their ego has been bruised in so many other ways.

We Americans should understand that motive, since we have it ourselves, and when we feel it in ourselves, we do not see it as reprehensible in any way. We think: Of course, the Good Guys need to gain power and influence compared with the Bad Guys. Our ego too has been bruised in recent years, by the obvious loss of our former preeminent number-one position in the world, and by our baffling inability to handle our own economy. Our new bumptious self-assertion, best described by Yankelovich and Kaagan,[12] may well be a compensatory response to that bruising. When we see a Soviet Union that is similarly

prideful and competitive, in Angola, Afghanistan, and elsewhere, we can perhaps understand them best by looking inward and understanding ourselves.

In this sense they *are* "aggressive." So are we.

THE PSYCHOLOGY OF EMPATHY

The importance of realistic empathy is not limited to the fact that it is a major antidote to war. The need for it extends to every form of human conflict and conflict resolution, between groups on every level of society and also between individuals—e.g., married couples, and parents versus children. As political and social psychologists, we would be wise to give it our best analytical attention.

One generalization that seems to emerge from the examples offered here is that a considerable amount of realistic empathy with a national opponent can be achieved by simply trying, sincerely and persistently, to achieve it. Empathy is not an esoteric gift granted only to highly sensitive, "intuitive" persons, nor does it rest mainly on the kind of erudition that only specialists can hope for. Some methods of cultivating it are obvious: attentive listening to genuine representatives of the other side, reading what they have written (with a combination of open-mindedness and healthy skepticism), reading the news with an intention to be fair, and, probably most important, persistently asking oneself certain obviously relevant questions such as "How would I feel if I were facing the situation they are facing now?" and "How would I feel if I had been through the experiences they have been through?"

Consider, for instance, the fact that the grueling experience of the Russians in World War II is now seldom mentioned by Americans when they talk or write about the feelings of the Soviet people (and their rulers) toward a possible nuclear war. The proposition offered here, that they are vividly aware of the horrors of war as such, is as a rule not refuted; it is simply not thought about, though the historical fact is widely known by educated Americans. They probably would think of it if they merely tried to be fair, and asked themselves "How would I feel about war as such if I had been through the experiences I know the Russians have been through?" It is a clear case of unconsciously motivated selective inattention.

Some Other Examples

We too seldom ask: "How would I feel about starting a nuclear war if I were in the Kremlin confronting a United States that was much inferior in overall nuclear strength but that still had a second-strike capability, mounted on hard-to-destroy submarines, that could in retaliation devastate most of Russia's cities?" In other words: "Is parity really necessary for nuclear deterrence?"

We too seldom ask: "If I were among the 6% or so of the world's population who are Russian, and believed that more than half of the remaining 94% were hostile to my country, would I want at least as much military strength as my worst enemy had?"

We too seldom ask: "If I were a Russian, living next door to the Middle East, would I resent the effort of the United States to exclude my country from the affairs of that area? Suppose the Russians tried to do that to us in the Caribbean area; how would I feel?"

Why do so many people on each side fail to ask such questions sincerely and persistently?

One fairly obvious answer is: Such questions are dissonant with a preexisting diabolical enemy image.[13] If a person's mind is full of the devil image of his opponent—"they are determined to conquer the world, and will do anything to achieve it, lying, cheating, anything; the only language *they* understand is the language of equal or superior force"—he feels satisfied that he knows the answers already and does not need to ask any such questions. In effect, the enemy is not pictured as human, with the result that the question "How would *I* feel if . . ." has no relevance.

It is not necessary to ignore the obvious fact that in some ways the men in the Kremlin are very different from ourselves. The chief thing needed for realistic empathy is simply to recognize that they are at least as greatly concerned about their own self-preservation as we are, and to ask how, if we were in their shoes, we would be trying to preserve our country and ourselves.

When empathy is lacking, what are the thoughts and feelings, in opponents' minds, that are most likely to go unrecognized? What are the typical blind spots in the nonempathizer's picture of his opponent?

Three kinds of things are, as a rule, subject to denial or selective inattention:

1. The opponents' *longing for peace,* which is usually as great as one's own—for instance, that of the Soviet public and its rulers, based largely on the suffering and devastation of World War II.

2. The opponents' *fear* of being the victim of aggression, which is often as great as one's own fear of aggression by them—for instance, the Soviet fear of the non-communist world, and their apparent obliviousness to our fear of them.

3. The opponents' natural, understandable *anger* at things one's own country has done, which have been so thoroughly rationalized by oneself that intense anger on the part of others is not expected—for instance, Soviet anger at our losing interest in SALT II, and at our exclusion of them from the Middle East peace process.

These three blind spots are characteristic of the hardliners on each side. There is also one that is characteristic of many softliners: an underestimation of the power motive on the other side (e.g., competition for influence in the Third World, as an end in itself), as well as the element of active hostility (a desire in enemy minds to hurt or destroy one's own country) that is a natural result of points 2 and 3—fear and anger. An example might be the overly rosy hopes on each side at the time of the Nixon-Kissinger detente. An *under*estimation of the depth and intensity of the hostility on the other side is entirely possible in those who fervently hope for peace and think wishfully, belittling the psychological obstacles, on both sides, that block the paths to peace.

There is a paradox here. On the one hand, there is the diabolical enemy image which regularly imputes to the enemy implacable, aggressive hostility to one's own country. On the other hand, there is the tendency that I have called the "pro-us illusion,"[14] consisting of an underestimate of two kinds of enemy hostility, fear and anger. Can both be true?

A partial resolution of the paradox seems possible, though, if we notice the word "implacable" in what has just been said about the diabolical enemy image, and invoke the familiar psychological mechanisms of rationalization and projection.

The diabolical enemy image, like the moral self-image, which is its constant counterpart (since together they constitute the black-and-white or good-guys-and-bad-guys image of the conflict), means that all of the guilt in the situation is imputed to the enemy and none to oneself. The assumption is: *we* have done nothing that could have aroused in them a rational fear of future aggression by us, or legitimate anger at any of the things we have done. All of the genuine sins of one's own side are denied, rationalized, ignored, or forgotten, and all guilt is projected onto the enemy. The projection part of this process increases the imputing of unjustified, spontaneous, inherent evil and hostility to the opponent, while the rationalization part of the process, denying any guilt in the self, reduces or eliminates any imputing of justified, situationally determined aggressive behavior to the same opponent. "Since we have done nothing wrong, how could anyone honestly fear us or be angry at us?" In brief, unjustified hostility can be perceived in an enemy; justified hostility cannot.

Essentially the same interpretation can be expressed in the terms of attribution theory.[15] The diabolical enemy image in an observer's mind attributes an inherent, "dispositional" characteristic to the "actor": irrational hostility, a craving for unlimited power, or both. At the same time the situational factors determining the actor's behavior (including the real sins of one's own country, usually much exaggerated in the actor's mind) are not seen by the observer at all. Seeing them would require empathy, and empathy is in very short supply.

DETERRENCE AND TENSION REDUCTION

The entire analysis in this article tends to support two conclusions on how nuclear war can be avoided:

1. In recognition of the strong and deeply ingrained hostility on the other side we need to maintain certain prudent types of armed deterrence, including a good second-strike capability and adequate defensive strength in Western Europe—adequate to keep alive in Soviet minds their present intense revulsion from war as such.

2. Much more urgently, in view of their fairly advanced state of the "malignant process" we have been enmeshed in during the past 8 years, and in view of the importance of long-term fear and understandable anger at our own behavior on the Soviet side of that process, we need to reduce in the Soviet rulers' minds that war-promoting, arms-race-accelerating types of fear and anger. In a word, if "tension" is defined as those types of fear and anger, we need to reduce tension.[16] Where we can do it without letting down our guard in any immediately dangerous way, we should take a long fresh look at our own behavior and try to make it more reasonable, more restrained, and more cooperative.

Similarly, we need to reduce the same kinds of exaggerated, unrealistic fear and anger in ourselves. Our education and our mass media have an obligation to humanize, in realistic ways, the present diabolical image of the Soviet enemy.

SUMMARY

1. The foreign and defense policies of the USSR are mainly defensive in motivation, as ours are. In this respect the mirror-image concept is valid, and two assumptions underlying American policy are not valid.

2. The Soviet rulers are deterred from a nuclear first strike by our second-strike capability and by their first-hand knowledge of the horrors of war. Nuclear parity is irrelevant.

3. The Soviet rulers, for six good reasons of national self-interest, are deterred

from an attack on Western Europe with conventional weapons. Here too there is no need for parity.

4. From the Soviet point of view our actions in the Third World have been much more provocative than theirs. Their perception of the danger to them in Afghanistan was probably similar to our perception of the danger to us in Vietnam.

5. Nonemphathizers tend to ignore three strong feelings in the minds of their supposedly diabolic enemies: a longing for peace, a long-term fear (usually excessive) of aggression by one's own country, and anger (usually excessive) at things one's own country has done.

6. The opponents' ingrained hostility requires prudent deterrence by us. At the same time, reversal of the present malignant interactive process requires greater emphasis by us on reducing the war-promoting, arms-race-accelerating types of fear and anger in their minds—i.e., reducing "tension." And on reducing it in ourselves.

ACTION IMPLICATIONS

Although the connections between this psychological analysis and a number of practical issues have been far from adequately covered, those issues are so urgent that it is appropriate to conclude with a simple listing of several of them, with references that may help the reader to explore these issues more fully. The analysis does seem to add weight to the case for the following specific actions and nonactions:

- A nuclear freeze.
- A no-first-use policy, not only in words, but also in all our military planning.[17]
- Keeping a strong second-strike capability, especially on submarines (with a strenuous buildup of the command-control-and-communication structure that is an essential and now vulnerable part of it.[18]

- Keeping an adequate defensive conventional capability in Western Europe.[19]
- A drastic cutback, by at least 50%, in the nuclear arsenals on both sides.[20]
- Negotiating an agreement with the Soviet rulers not to use combat forces in the Third World.[21]

ENDNOTES

[1]M. Deutsch, "The Prevention of World War III: A Psychological Perspective," Presidential address delivered at the annual meeting of the International Society of Political Psychology, Washington, D.C., June 26, 1982.

[2]U. Bronfenbrenner, "The Mirror-Image in Soviet-American Relations," *Social Issues* 17 (3), 1961: 45–56. Compare R. K. White in H. C. Kelman, ed., *International Behavior: A Social-Psychological Analysis* (New York: Holt, Rinehart and Winston, 1965); J. Frank, *Sanity and Survival: Psychological Aspects of War and Peace* (New York: Vintage Books, 1967): 115–136.

[3]G. F. Kennan, "The Reith Lectures," reprinted in Kennan's *Memoirs: 1950–1963* (Boston: Little, Brown, 1972); A. Ulam, *The Rivals: America and Russia Since World War II* (New York: Viking, 1971); R. C. Tucker, "Self-Images and How They Influence Adversary Images," paper read at the annual meeting of the International Society of Political Psychology, Washington, D.C., June 26, 1982; M. D. Shulman, *Stalin's Foreign Policy Reappraised* (New York: Athenaeum, originally published by Harvard University Press, 1963, 1965); R. G. Kaiser, *Russia: The People and the Power* (New York: Pocket Books, 1976); "U.S.–Soviet Relations: Goodbye to Detente. America and the World, 1980," *Foreign Affairs* 59 (3), 1981.

[4]Bronfenbrenner, *op. cit.*

[5]See, for instance, A. M. Cox, *Russian Roulette: The Superpower Game* (New York: Times Books, 1982); R. Barnet, "The Search for National Security," *The New Yorker*, April 27, 1981: 50–140.

[6]P. H. Nitze, "Strategy in the Decade of the 1980s," *Foreign Affairs*, Fall 1980: 90.

[7]Cox, *op.cit.*; Barnet, *op. cit.*

[8]M. Howard, "The Case for Keeping a Strong Conventional Arms Capability," letter to *The Times* (London), November 3, 1981, quoted by Cox, *op. cit.*: 147, 210.

[9]E. Jones and R. Nisbett, *The Actor and the Observer: Divergent Perceptions of the Causes of Behavior* (General Learning Press, 1971).

[10]Sources for the following discussion on Afghanistan include especially J. C. Hurewitz, "The Middle East: A Year of Turmoil. America and the World, 1980," *Foreign Affairs* 59 (3), 1981; Barnet, *op. cit.*, 16–38; V. Petrov, "New dimensions of Soviet foreign policy," in F. D. Margiotta, ed., *Evolving Strategic Realities: Implications for U.S. Policymakers* (Washington, D.C.: National Defense University Press, 1980): 16–38; G. Arbatov, "A Soviet commentary," in A. M. Cox, ed., *Russian Roulette: The Superpower Game* (New York: Times Books, 1982): 173–199. On Vietnam, see R. K. White, *Nobody Wanted War: Misperception in Vietnam and Other Wars,* rev. ed.(New York: Doubleday/Anchor, 1970).

[11]N. Sheehan et al., *Pentagon Papers* (New York: Bantam, 1971).

[12]D. Yankelovich and L. Kaagan, "Asserting America. America and the World, 1980," *Foreign Affairs 59* (3), 1981: 696–713.

[13]R. Jervis, *Perception and Misperception in International Politics* (Princeton: Princeton University Press, 1976): 143–201.

[14]White in Kelman, *op. cit.*, 63–64; "Three Not-So-Obvious Contributions of Psychology to Peace," 34–38.

[15]Jones and Nisbett, *op. cit.*

[16]Compare C. E. Osgood, *An Alternative to War or Surrender* (Urbana, IL: University of Illinois Press, 1962); A. Etzioni, *The Hard Way to Peace* (New York: Collier Books, 1962).

[17]McG. Bundy, G. Kennan, R. McNamara, and G. Smith, "Nuclear Weapons and the Atlantic Alliance," *Foreign Affairs,* Spring 1982: 753–768.

[18]J. D. Steinbruner, "Nuclear Decapitation," *Foreign Policy 45,* Winter 1981/1982: 16–28.

[19]Howard, *op. cit.*

[20]G. F. Kennan, "Address on the Occasion of His Receiving the Albert Einstein Peace Prize," (Washington, D.C., May 19, 1981): 201–202, quoted by Cox, *op. cit.*

[21]*Ibid.*, 156–164.

58

The Face of the Enemy

Jerome D. Frank

An ingenious experiment by J. W. Bagby of New York's Roosevelt Hospital illustrates the phenomenon of perceptual filtering. This psychologist asked American and Mexican school teachers to look into a device that showed simultaneously a different picture to each eye. One eye saw a picture of a baseball player and the other saw a bullfighter.

An overwhelming proportion of the Americans "saw" the baseball player; the overwhelming proportion of Mexicans "saw" the bullfighter. What these teachers saw, of course, *was* mostly determined by their cultural filter.

No psychiatrist or psychologist would be so rash as to claim that one can make solid inferences about the behavior of nations from that of individuals, but it is startling how often similarities between the man and his country emerge when one starts looking carefully.

One psychological principle certainly is highly relevant to international affairs: a person's beliefs and his expectations largely determine how he thinks and how he behaves. Since citizens of a nation tend to share the same beliefs and expectations, this principle is important if we are to understand how nations see each other and behave toward one another.

Characteristic of each nation's self-image is the belief in national sovereignty, territorial rights and national strength. Each nation believes in its right to pursue vital interests regardless of the effects on other nations.

The degree of fear in which one nation holds another nation depends upon perception of adversary ability and intent to harm.

Reprinted from *Psychology Today*, November 1968. Copyright © 1968, Sussex Publishers, Inc.

Whether the people of one nation perceive those of another as enemies depends primarily upon the nature of relations between the two countries. Thus it is when national interests clash and nations are in conflict that the enemy image begins to take its menacing shape. Because of the universal and innate distrust of strangers, a foreign power easily can arouse a sense of threat. Once the opinion-makers have singled out the threatening nation, this innate distrust is focused.

The Russian invasion of Czechoslovakia was portrayed by the American mass media as an unprovoked rape of a country struggling toward freedom; the Russians justified it as necessary to forestall a takeover by anticommunist forces imperiling the security of the Warsaw Pact nations. With the U.S. invasion of the Dominican Republic, the shoe was on the other foot. To us, the action was necessary to remove a Communist threat to our security. To Russia, it was an unprovoked assault on the freedom of that little country.

Enemies create anxiety leading to a progressive simplification of their image in our eyes, and this results in formation of what has been called the mirror image of the enemy. These reciprocal images differ, of course, in the relative prominence of particular features. But to a surprising degree, enemies attribute the same virtues to themselves and the same vices to their opponents.

One excellent study of Russian and American self-images—as expressed in a selection of articles in both mass and elite publications of each nation—shows that virtually 100 percent of the articles described the adversary's goal as international domination or expansion.

Each nation's press portrayed the other nation as aggressive and treacherous, and neither Americans nor Russians accepted the idea that the other was motivated by self-preservation.

Americans tended to be more realistic about their own motives for offering foreign aid, with 42 percent of the articles in American periodicals indicating that the purpose of foreign aid was to strengthen their own side. But in Soviet Union publications, 95 percent of the articles claimed that their own foreign-aid programs were just to be helpful, or else to make it possible for the countries to maintain neutrality. The press on both sides was virtually unanimous in claiming that the *other* side offered foreign aid not to help, but to strengthen a power position and to weaken that of their opponent.

The reciprocal images differed sharply in one respect—foreign policy. Some 69 percent of the Russian items regarded international events as predictable, while only seven percent of the American items took this view. Strangely, this general view was contradicted by the way each side saw the other's specific behavior. The Russians described American foreign policy as a wild and unpredictable response to events, and the Americans tended to see Russian foreign policy as a masterful part of a deep-laid plot. Practically no articles in either American nor Russian publications stated that national military measures would bring about the other's downfall, and so there was reinforcement for the peaceful self-image of each nation.

In addition, the press of both nations indicated belief that internal weaknesses and contradictions in the other's system would lead to its eventual downfall. This finding is supported by Urie Bronfenbrenner of Cornell, a Russian-speaking psychologist, who did some informal but careful interviewing of people from different walks of life during a visit to the Soviet Union.

The Russians he interviewed believed that the people of the United States were being deluded and exploited, that they did not fully support the U.S. Government, that American leaders could not be trusted, and that U.S. foreign policy bordered on madness. (Many Americans reflect the flip side of the coin in their view of the Russians.)

Bronfenbrenner also found that nearly all of the Russians who came up to him and began a conversation expressed considerable discontent with life in the Soviet Union. On the other hand, more than 75 percent of the Russians who did not speak until he had initiated the conversation identified fully with the Soviet way of life and the U.S.S.R. world view.

Another American scientist, Konrad Krauskopf of Stanford University, who visited the Soviet Union about the same time as Bronfenbrenner, had an opportunity for long, informal conversations with his Russian counterparts. He reported: "The Westerner regards the Russians as controlled for the most part without their knowledge, by an oligarchy of rapacious and malevolent men who seek constantly to foment world revolution. The Russian is equally convinced that the West (in Russian eyes, the West *is* the United States, and all other Western countries are American satellites) is victimized by a small group of profit-mad monopolists who pull the strings that control the government and the communications media, and who try to instigate wars in order to sell munitions . . . it was impossible to resolve this difference in viewpoint. Each of us was repeating what he had read in his own newspapers, and each was suspicious of the other's sources."

A striking feature of the enemy mirror which Americans and Russians hold is the perception that it is *leaders* who are the real villains, and that the general population of the other country is either well disposed to one's own nation—or if they are not, it is because their leaders have misled them. Concomitant with this view is the belief that the masses in the other nation are discontented and would overthrow their leaders if only they could.

This combination is wonderfully consoling for citizens of both countries. It creates a positive image of one's own nation as a savior, and it simultaneously provides convenient, visualizable devils—the leaders—on whom to focus hostility and hate. This is illustrated by the Communists' monomania with "capitalists and monopolists" and with their intellectual concern for the "oppressed masses." And it is shown in the American tendency to focus on enemy leaders as targets—the Kaiser in World War I, Hitler in World War II, Stalin in the Cold War and more recently Castro, Mao, and Ho Chi Minh.

Contributing to the formation of the mirror image of the enemy is the need men have to reduce cognitive dissonance. When our perceptions of the enemy do not fit our preconceived image, anxiety is created and builds up. The effort to reduce this anxiety accounts for many phenomena in human thinking and behavior, and as there is continual effort to make our world view emotionally consistent, even if it is not logically consistent.

In order to survive, every person must organize the flood of experiences pouring in on him so that he can predict the effects of his behavior both upon people and upon other things. This organizing process starts as soon as he is born, and it is guided by his experiences with his family and with other people in his society.

In general, we filter and interpret incoming information to fit our preconceptions. Value systems are usually abstract enough so we can interpret events to fit beliefs, and also reinterpret our own behavior to make sure that it is consistent with those beliefs. The strain toward consistency tends, of course, to *reinforce* the enemy image.

But the same process also can help destroy the enemy image when a former enemy becomes a needed ally. This is illustrated by a long series of public opinion polls on how Americans characterize people in other countries. In polls, respondents often are asked to choose from a list of adjectives the ones which best describe the people of another nation. In 1942, the first three adjectives chosen to characterize the Germans and the Japanese were: warlike, treacherous and cruel. Not one of these adjectives was among the top three describing the Russians, but by 1966, all three adjectives had disappeared from American descriptions of the Germans and Japanese, and the Russians were seen as warlike and treacherous. Predictably, the Communist Chinese by 1966 had become "warlike" and "treacherous" and "cruel." (Interestingly, the characterization "hardworking" rates high among descriptions of all these countries, whether friends or foes. A hardworking enemy is more to be feared, and a hardworking ally is a greater source of strength.)

A change in the American view of the Germans and Japanese followed their *total* defeat. The enemy ceased to be dangerous, and our demand for consistency required that the enemy image be altered. A factor supporting the change was the American belief that these former enemy nations were needed to help combat the spread of Communism.

Thus, in the eyes of many Americans the "warlike, treacherous, cruel, slant-eyed, buck-toothed little Japs" of World War II have become a highly cultivated, industrious, charming, and thoroughly attractive people.

The American image of the German people is even more remarkable—it has flipped four times in less than half a century. Americans admired the Germans before World War I for their industry, their culture and their scientific know-how. Then during the war, Germans became the hated "Huns." Next, the Germans of the Weimar Republic, a democracy, were regarded favorably. The Nazis changed that. Today the Germans once more are staunch allies, even though many of the government officials are former Nazis.

By and large, the Germans today are the same people the Americans hated yesterday. Our change from hostility to friendliness has been made easier by the Germans' formal renunciation of Nazism. But, in retrospect, it may be observed that if these individuals were true Nazis, their change is suspect; and if most were not true Nazis, then they did not warrant our earlier hatred.

The strain to develop a consistent world view may lead nations with contrasting ideologies to exaggerate the differences in their behavior, and this raises the hopeful possibility that national value systems need not actually change much in order to permit acceptance of coexistence.

A study of American and Russian value systems by R. K. White of George Washington University shows that the American capitalist system which Soviet citizens have been taught to fear is not actually so very different from the "Good Society" that the Russians themselves would like to see develop in the U.S.S.R. Both systems are relatively modest variations on themes that seem to be among the common great aspirations of the human race.

In stressing how the group to which a person belongs determines his world view, I do not mean to imply that his view cannot be transcended by reflection and self-awareness. Today, human survival may depend on those individuals who can surmount a tribal outlook and appreciate the world views of people of other cultures.

A psychologically crucial part of the world view of any group is its ideology, and ideological differences contribute to the dehumanization of the enemy. Humans differ from other creatures primarily in the power to symbolize, so that we respond not only to physical violence but to psychological threats to our ideology or self-esteem.

Since nations cannot exist without ideologies, periodic "holy wars" may seem to be inevitable. But two factors mitigate this gloomy prospect. It is more satisfying psychologically to convert members of a rival belief system than to kill them. Conversion confirms superiority.

In addition, ideologies do not have to proclaim that they have exclusive possession of the truth. Some religions, such as Hinduism, declare that all religions have tapped some aspect of the Truth, and some secular ideologies, such as the American one, value diversity of viewpoints in many areas. Adherents of world views like these can coexist with others indefinitely without resorting to armed conflict to protect their beliefs.

In the Vietman war, ideological issues have become crucial. The North Vietnamese and the Viet Cong see themselves as fighting neocolonialism, as well as furthering the Communist ideology.

From a strictly materialistic viewpoint, Vietnam is of minor strategic importance to the United States.

The United States Government sees its action in Vietnam as part of a worldwide commitment to prevent the spread of Communism. And the U.S. also is motivated by a determination to show the world that we are steadfast, that we stand by our commitments.

The Vietnam war has assumed the ideological characteristics of a holy war. Throughout history, such holy wars usually end in mutual exhaustion after tremendous carnage, and with the survivors on both sides still clinging to their beliefs. Psychologically speaking, the notion that making people suffer causes them to abandon their beliefs is a hangover from the days of the Crusades.

Nations at war could be said to resemble children for whom punishment brings contrition only under certain conditions. As every parent knows, one can control behavior by punishment, but whether the punishment alters a basic attitude depends mainly on the child's belief that it was deserved.

There are studies that have attempted to relate personality attributes of individuals to their international attitudes, and most of these studies have dealt with an authoritarian character pattern whose dynamic core is the result of repressing strong hostility to parents and to other authority figures. The person with such a character pattern exaggerates the importance of power, of force, and of domination and submission in human affairs. He displaces his hostility to safer targets than the authority figures at home. He projects his internal psychological conflicts onto external enemies, and he expresses his bottled-up aggressive and sexual feelings indirectly by overconcern with the "immoral" behavior of foreigners and of the "out" groups in his own society.

People with authoritarian personalities score high on the "F-Scale," which consists of a series of statements like: "What youth needs most is strict discipline, rugged determination and the will to work and fight for family and country"; "Most of our social problems would be solved if we could somehow get rid of the immoral, crooked and feeble-minded people"; "People can be divided into two classes, the weak and the strong." The greater the number of such statements a person agrees with, the higher his score, and a high F-score correlates positively with extreme nationalism.

Within each country, individuals differ in the degrees that they see foreigners as enemies. At one extreme are those we might call xenophobic, those who hold a morbid dislike of foreigners and the other extreme are the xenophiles, who display an excessive acceptance of protestation of peaceful intent on the part of a foreign power, as well as holding hostility toward the leaders of their own country. Both extremists are likely to be hostile toward authority figures, but the xenophobe displaces his aggression to a foreign group and the xenophile focuses on his own leaders.

Since an enemy is seen as a threat to the survival of one's own nation, to change the enemy's image implies dropping one's guard. And the enemy's image has certain dynamic properties that make it resistant to change. First, an enemy mobilizes a nation's sense of solidarity and strength. He becomes a convenient scapegoat for internal problems. Second, the image that a nation holds of its enemy eventually will bring about behavior from the enemy that makes the image a reality.

The view that the actions of the other nation always are based on hostile motives may create a self-fulfilling prophecy. This term refers to the fact that a person's expectations come true. . . . A classic example of this is the international arms race. Each side anticipates that the other will add to its armament. In response to this expectation each increases its own arms, thereby fulfilling the expectations and convincing the other side that its fears are justified—which leads naturally to another round of arms increases.

Leaders on each side fear that their own people are so naive that they easily can be misled by enemy propaganda. The temptation to break off entirely or to restrict communication with the enemy is a strong one. Since the enemy is untrustworthy, if we communicate with him, he may trick us or learn something about us that we do not want him to know.

Another source of distortion of the enemy's characteristics is what G. Icheiser called the "mote-beam phenomenon." People who harbor unacceptable feelings may try to relieve their anxiety by projecting these traits to others, and then attacking them for possessing those traits. A person who tries to hide his own aggressiveness from himself is usually quick to spot aggression in others. In the same way, some Americans who turn a blind eye to the inequities in civil rights for Blacks are very concerned about the restrictions of freedom in the Soviet Union.

Bronfenbrenner showed some American fifth and sixth graders photographs of Russian roads lined with young trees. When he asked why the Russians had planted trees along the road, two of the answers were: "So that people won't be able to see what is going on beyond the road" and "It's to make work for the prisoners." When he asked why American roads have trees planted along the side, the children said "for shade" and "to keep the dust down."

The distorted image of the enemy acts, finally, to block acceptance of his genuine conciliatory moves. An apparently friendly gesture tends to be seen as either evidence of the enemy's weakening, or an effort to create dis-

sension within one's own ranks. These responses are apparent in the Vietnam war. The Viet Cong interpret American gestures of peace as evidence of a weakening will to fight, while the American government sees the enemy's proposals as propaganda aimed at creating dissension in the United States.

An experiment done in a boy's camp by Muzafer Sherif of Pennsylvania State College some years ago suggests that activities requiring cooperation have a powerful effect in reducing antagonism between two hostile groups. When the boys arrived at camp, they were divided into two groups. Then the groups were made enemies through athletic competitions. In time, they became like two hostile nations. Members in each group chose friends only from among themselves, looked down on boys in the other group, and the two groups fought at every opportunity.

Once when a member of one group tried to act as a peacemaker, he was promptly ostracized by his fellows.

Then the camp director surreptitiously arranged events to force cooperation between the two groups. For example, he secretly arranged to have the camp water supply interrupted, and the whole camp had to work together to make necessary "repairs." A truck carrying food for an overnight hike "unaccountably" ran into a ditch. It took all the boys to pull it out with a tow-rope. A series of such events finally broke down hostility between the two groups, and friendly relations eventually were restored.

I would hesitate to generalize from boys in conflict to nations in conflict were it not for certain obvious parallels. In a sense, the nations of the world are in the same predicament today as the boys in that camp. Nations have to cooperate in order to survive, and the international scene contains many opportunities for cooperative activities, like those in the boys' camp, in yielding mutual benefits which one nation alone cannot attain. The International Geophysical Year is a good example.

The first step in contacting the enemy is psychologically the most difficult, and it takes considerable courage to make contact with a distrusted adversary, because this means exposure to dangers not only from the enemy but from one's own side. Here perhaps we can take advantage of what psychiatrists have learned about establishing communication with a frightened, angry and suspicious person. The first step, we have found, is simply to show persistent willingness to listen and to refuse to be discouraged by rebuffs. While you firmly defend yourself against physical attack, you ignore mere verbal abuse. It does not pay to be too friendly. The hostile person is convinced that you mean him no good, and so he is prone to interpret an overly friendly manner as an effort to deceive him. A firm and reserved, but not unfriendly manner, gets farther in reaching out to him.

Communication is only the first step. From a psychological standpoint, a central long-term task is learning how to foster cooperative projects among nations.

The chief danger of the distorted enemy image is that it makes false perceptions as hard to change as if they were true. Only by becoming highly aware of the psychological process that forms images can we hope to dispel the false aspects of an image. Otherwise, the difficulties in communicating with the enemy progressively harden our image of him. Fantasy fills the gaps left by insufficient information, and the face of the enemy reflects our own fears.

59

Cognitive Dissonance and International Relations

Robert Jervis

The theory of cognitive dissonance can explain a number of puzzling misperceptions. The basic outlines of the theory are not startling, but some of its implications are contrary to common sense and other theories of cognitive consistency. The definition of dissonance is relatively straightforward: "two elements are in a dissonant relation if, considering these two alone, the obverse of one element would follow from the other." For example, the information that a Ford is a better car than a Chevrolet is dissonant with the knowledge that I have bought a Chevy.

The basic hypotheses are: "1. The existence of dissonance, being psychologically uncomfortable, will motivate the person to try to reduce dissonance and achieve consonance. 2. When dissonance is present, in addition to trying to reduce it, the person will actively avoid situations and information which would likely increase the dissonance."[1]

The basis of dissonance theory lies in the postulate that people seek strong justification for their behavior. They are not content to believe merely that they behaved well and chose wisely—if this were the case they would only have to maintain the beliefs that produced their decisions. Instead, people want to minimize their internal conflict. This leads them to

Excerpted from Robert Jervis, *Perception and Misperception in International Politics* (Princeton: Princeton University Press, 1976), Chapter 11, 382–406.

seek to believe that the reasons for acting or deciding as they did were overwhelming. The person will then rearrange his beliefs so that they provide increased support for his actions.

Knowledge of the advantages of rejected courses of action and costs of the chosen one will be a source of uncomfortable dissonance that he will try to reduce. To do this he will alter his earlier opinions, seeing more drawbacks and fewer advantages in the policies he rejected and more good points and fewer bad ones in the policy he adopted. He may, for example, come to believe that the rejected policy would not satisfy certain criteria that he originally thought it would, or that those criteria are less important than he originally believed, or that the chosen policy will not cost as much as he first thought. The person may also search out additional information supporting his decision and find new reasons for acting as he did and will avoid, distort, or derogate new dissonant information.

If doubts nevertheless creep in, he will redouble his efforts to justify his decision. As a result, "Following a decision there is an increase in the confidence in the decision or an increase in the discrepancy in attractiveness between the alternatives involved in the choice, or both."[2] This is known as the "spreading apart of the alternatives" because of the perceived increase in the gap between the net advantages of the chosen policy and those of the rejected ones.

As the last quote implies, the theory has been developed only for post-decision situations. Two further conditions are necessary. First, there must be a "definite commitment resulting from the decision. . . . It seems that a decision carries commitment with it if the decision unequivocally affects subsequent behavior."[3] Second, the person must feel that his decision was a free one, i.e. that he could have chosen otherwise. If he had no real choice, then the disadvantages of the policy will not create dissonance because his lack of freedom provides sufficient justification for his action.

Making such a decision will, according to dissonance theory, greatly alter the way a person thinks. Before reaching his decision the individual will seek conflicting information and make "some compromise judgment between the information and his existing cognitions or between bits of information inconsistent with each other and with his existing cognitions." But once the person has reached a decision, he is committed and "cannot process information and make some compromise judgment."[4] Quite the contrary, the person must minimize the extent to which the evidence pointed in the opposite directions.

An ingenious demonstration, an anecdote, and an international example illustrate the meaning of this phenomenon and show that it occurs outside the laboratory. Immediately after they place their bets, race track bettors become more confident that their horse will win. A few hours after deciding to accept a job offer that he had agonizingly considered for several months, a professor said, "I don't understand how I could have seriously thought about not taking the job." And the doubts of British Liberals about whether to go to war in 1914 were almost totally dissolved after the decision was reached.[5]

Many decision-makers speak of their doubts vanishing after they embarked on a course of action, or they say that a situation seemed much clearer after they reached a decision. Evidence that would have been carefully examined before the decision is rejected at later stages.

The American decision not to intervene in Vietnam in 1954 was followed by a spreading apart of the alternatives. When they were considering the use of force to prevent a communist victory, Dulles and, to a lesser extent, Eisenhower believed that a failure to act would expose the neighboring countries to grave peril. When the lack of Allied and domestic support made intervention prohibitively expensive, American decision-makers altered their perceptions of the consequences of not intervening. Although they still thought that the immediate result would be the fall of some of Indochina, they came to believe that the further spread of communism—fear of which motivated them to consider entering the war—would not necessarily follow.

They altered their views to reject the domino theory, at least in its most deterministic formulation, and held that alternative means could save the rest of Southeast Asia. It was argued—and apparently believed—that collective action, which had initially been sought in order to hold Vietnam, could stabilize the region even though part of Vietnam was lost.[6] By judging that military victory was not necessary, the decision-makers could see the chosen policy of not intervening as greatly preferable to the rejected alternative of unilateral action, thereby reducing the dissonance aroused by the choice of a policy previously believed to entail extremely high costs.

ENDNOTES

[1]Leon Festinger, *A Theory of Cognitive Dissonance* (Stanford: Stanford University Press, 1957): 13, 31; *also see* Jack Brehm and Arthur Cohen, *Explorations in Cognitive Dissonance* (New York: John Wiley & Sons, 1962): 16.

[2]Morton Deutsch, Robert Krauss, and Norah Rosenau, "Dissonance or Defensiveness?" *Journal of Personality*, 30 (1962): 27.

[3]*Ibid.*, 83.

[4]Brehm and Cohen, *Explorations in Cognitive Dissonance*, 106.

[5]Robert Knox and James Inkster, "Postdecision Dissonance at Post Time," *Journal of Personality and Social Psychology*, 8 (1968): 319–323; Cameron Hazlehurst, *Politicians at War*, London: Jonathan Cape (1971): 46–48, 92–117.

[6]Melvin Gurtov, *The First Vietnam Crisis* (New York: Columbia University Press, 1967): 119–122.

60

National Images and International Systems

Kenneth E. Boulding

An international system consists of a group of interacting behavior units called "nations" or "countries," to which may sometimes be added certain supra-national organizations, such as the United Nations.

Each of the behavior units in the system can be described in terms of a set of "relevant variables." Just what is relevant and what is not is a matter of judgment of the system-builder, but we think of such things as states of war or peace, degrees of hostility or friendliness, alliances or enmity, arms budgets, geographic extent, friendly or hostile communications, and so on. Having defined our variables, we can then proceed to postulate certain relationships between them, sufficient to define a path for all the variables through time. Thus we might suppose, with Lewis Richardson,[1] that the rate of change of hostility of one nation toward a second depends on the level of hostility in the second and that the rate of change of hostility of the second toward the first depends on the level of hostility of the first. Then, if we start from given levels of hostility in each nation, these equations are sufficient to spell out what happens to these levels in succeeding time periods. A system of this kind may (or may not) have an *equilibrium* position at which the variables of one period produce an identical set in the next period, and the system exhibits no change through time.

Reprinted from *Journal of Conflict Resolution* 3, no. 2 (June 1959), 120–131. Copyright © 1959 by Sage Publications.

Mechanical systems of this kind, though they are frequently illuminating, can be regarded only as very rough first approximations to the immensely complex truth. At the next level of approximation we must recognize that the people whose decisions determine the policies and actions of nations do not respond to the "objective" facts of the situation, whatever that may mean, but to their "image" of the situation. It is what we think the world is like, not what it is really like, that determines our behavior. If our image of the world is in some sense "wrong," of course, we may be disappointed in our expectations, and we may therefore revise our image; if this revision is in the direction of the "truth" there is presumably a long-run tendency for the "image" and the "truth" to coincide. Whether this is so or not, it is always the image, not the truth, that immediately determines behavior. We act accordingly to the way the world appears to us, not necessarily according to the way it "is." Thus in Richardson's models it is one nation's image of the hostility of another, not the "real" hostility, which determines its reaction. The "Image," then, must be thought of as the total cognitive, affective, and evaluative structure of the behavior unit, or its internal view of itself and its universe.[2]

Generally speaking, the behavior of complex organizations can be regarded as determined by *decisions,* and a decision involves the selection of the most preferred position in a contemplated field of choice. Both the field of choice and the ordering of this field by which the preferred position is identified lie in the image of the decision-maker. Therefore, in a system in which decision-makers are an essential element, the study of the ways in which the image grows and changes, both of the field of choice and of the valuational ordering of this field, is of prime importance. The image is always in some sense a product of messages received in the past. It is not, however, a simple inventory or "pile" of such messages but a highly structured piece of information-capital, developed partly by its inputs and outputs of information and partly by internal messages and its own laws of growth and stability.

The images which are important in international systems are those which a nation has of itself and of those other bodies in the system which constitute its international environment. At once a major complication suggests itself. A nation is some complex of the images of the persons who contemplate it, and as there are many different persons, so there are many different images. The complexity is increased by the necessity for inclusion, in the image of each person or at least of many persons, his image of the image of others. This complexity, however, is a property of the real world, not to be evaded or glossed over. It can be reduced to simpler terms if we distinguish between two types of persons in a nation—the powerful, on the one hand, and the ordinary, on the other. This is not, of course, a sharp distinction. The power of a decision-maker may be measured roughly by the number of people which his decisions potentially affect, weighted by some measure of the effect itself. Thus the head of a state is powerful, meaning that his decisions affect the lives of millions of people; the ordinary person is not powerful, for his decisions affect only himself and the lives of a few people around him. There is usually a continuum of power among the persons of a society: thus in international relations there are usually a few very powerful individuals in a state—the chief executive, the prime minister, the secretary of state or minister of foreign affairs, the chiefs of staff of the armed forces. There will be some who are less powerful but still influential—members of the legislature, of the civil service, even journalists, newspaper owners, prominent businessmen, grading by imperceptible degrees down to the common soldier, who has no power of decision even over his own life. For purposes of the model, however, let us compress this continuum into two boxes, labeled the "powerful" and the "ordinary," and leave the refinements of power and influence for later studies.

We deal, therefore, with two representative images, (1) the image of the small group of powerful people who make the actual decisions which lead to war or peace, the making or breaking of treaties, the invasions or withdrawals, alliances, and enmities which make up the major events of international relations, and (2) the image of the mass of ordinary people who are deeply affected by these deci-sions but who take little or no direct part in making them. The tacit support of the mass, however, is of vital importance to the powerful. The powerful are always under some obligation to represent the mass, even under dictatorial regimes. In democratic societies the aggregate influence of the images of ordinary people is very great; the image of the powerful cannot diverge too greatly from the image of the mass without the powerful losing power. On the other hand, the powerful also have some ability to manipulate the images of the mass toward those of the powerful. This is an important object of instruments as diverse as the public education system, the public relations departments of the armed services, the Russian "agitprop," and the Nazi propaganda ministry.

In the formation of the national images, however, it must be emphasized that impressions of nationality are formed mostly in childhood and usually in the family group. It would be quite fallacious to think of the images as being cleverly imposed on the mass by the powerful. If anything, the reverse is the case: the image is essentially a mass image, or what might be called a "folk image," transmitted through the family and the intimate face-to-face group, both in the case of the powerful and in the case of ordinary persons. Especially in the case of the old, long-established nations, the powerful share the mass image rather than impose it; it is passed on from the value systems of the parents to those of the children, and agencies of public instruction and propaganda merely reinforce the images which derived essentially from the family culture. This is much less in new nations which are striving to achieve nationality, where the family culture frequently does not include strong elements of national allegiance but rather stresses allegiance to religious ideals or to the family as such. Here the powerful are frequently inspired by a national image derived not from family tradition but from a desire to imitate other nations, and here they frequently try to impose their images on the mass of people. Imposed images, however, are fragile by comparison with those which are deeply internalized and transmitted through family and other intimate sources.

Whether transmitted orally and informally through the family or more formally through schooling and the written word, the national image is essentially a *historical* image—that is, an image which extends through time, backward into a supposedly recorded or perhaps mythological past and forward into an imagined future. The more conscious a people is of its history, the stronger the national image is likely to be. To be an Englishman is to be conscious of "1066 and All That" rather than of "Constantine and All That," or "1776 and All That." A nation is the creation of its historians, formal and informal. The written word and public education contribute enormously to the stability and persistence of the national images. The Jews, for instance, are a creation of the Bible and the Talmud, but every nation has its bible, whether formed into a canon or not—noble words like the Declaration of Independence and the Gettysburg Address—which crystallize the national image in a form that can be transmitted almost unchanged from generation to generation. It is no exaggeration to say that the function of the historian is to pervert the truth in directions favorable to the images of his readers or hearers. Both history and geography as taught in national schools are devised to give "perspective" rather than truth: that is to say, they present the world as seen from the vantage point of the nation. The national geography is learned in great detail, and the rest of the world is in fuzzy outline; the national history is emphasized and exalted; the history of the rest of the world is neglected or even falsified to the glory of the national image.

It is this fact that the national image is basically a lie, or at least a perspective distortion of the truth, which perhaps accounts for the ease with which it can be perverted to justify monstrous cruelties and wickednesses. There is much that is noble in the national image. It has lifted man out of the narrow cage of self-centeredness, or even family-centeredness, and has forced him to accept responsibility, in some sense, for people and events far beyond his face-to-face cognizance and immediate experience. It is a window of some sort on both space and time and extends a man's concern far beyond his own little lifetime and petty interests. Nevertheless, it achieves these virtues usually only at the cost of untruth, and this fatal flaw constantly betrays it. Love of country is perverted into hatred of the foreigner, and peace, order, and justice at home are paid for by war, cruelty, and injustice abroad.

In the formation of the national image the consciousness of great *shared* events and experiences is of the utmost importance. A nation is a body of people who are conscious of having "gone through something" together. Without the shared experience, the national image itself would not be shared, and it is of vital importance that the national image be highly similar. The sharing may be quite vicarious; it may be an experience shared long ago but constantly renewed by the ritual observances and historical memory of the people, like the Passover and the Captivity in the case of the Jews. Without the sharing, however, there is no nation. It is for this reason that war has been such a tragically important element in the creation and sustenance of the national image. There is hardly a nation that has not been cradled in violence and nourished by further violence. This is not, I think, a necessary property of war itself. It is rather that, especially in more primitive societies, war is the one experience which is dramatic, obviously important, and shared by everybody. We are now witnessing the almost unique phenomenon of a number of new nations arising without war in circumstances which are extremely rare in history, for example—India, Ghana, and the new West Indian Federation, though even there there are instances of severe violence, such as the disturbances which accompanied partition in India. It will be interesting to see the effect, if any, on their national images.

We now come to the central problem of this paper, which is that of the impact of national images on the relations among states, that is, on the course of events in international relations. The relations among states can be described in terms of a number of different dimensions. There is, first of all, the dimension of simple geographical space. It is perhaps the most striking single characteristic of the national state as an organization, by contrast with organizations such as firms or churches, that it thinks of itself as occupying, in a "dense" and exclusive fashion, a certain area of the globe. The schoolroom maps which divide the world into colored shapes which are identified as nations have a profound effect on the national image. Apart from the very occasional condominium, it is impossible for a given plot of land on the globe to be associated with two nations at the same time. The territories of nations are divided sharply by frontiers carefully surveyed and frequently delineated by a chain of customs houses, immigration stations, and military installations. We are so accustomed to this arrangement that we think of it as "natural" and take it completely for granted. It is by no means the only conceivable arrangement, however. In primitive societies the geographical image is not sharp enough to define clear frontiers; there may be a notion of the rough territory of a tribe, but, especially among nomadic peoples, there is no clear concept of a frontier and no notion of a nation as something that has a shape on a map. In our own society the shape on the map that symbolizes the nation is constantly drilled into the minds of both young and old, both through formal teaching in schools and through constant repetition in newspapers, advertisements, cartoons, and so on. A society is not inconceivable, however, and might even be desirable, in which nations governed people but not territories and claimed jurisdiction over a defined set of citizens, no matter where on the earth's surface they happen to live.

The territorial aspect of the national state is important in the dynamics of international relations because of the *exclusiveness* of territorial occupation. This means that one nation can generally expand only at the expense of another; and increase in the territory of one is achieved only at the expense of a decrease in territory of another. This makes for a potential conflict situation. This characteristic of the nation does not make conflict inevitable, but it does make it likely and is at least one of the reasons why the history of international relations is a history of perpetual conflict.

The territorial aspect of international relations is complicated by the fact that in may cases the territories of nations are not homogeneous but are composed of "empires," in which the populations do not identify themselves with the national image of the dominant group. Thus when one nation conquers another and absorbs the conquered territory into an empire, it does not thereby automatically change the culture and allegiances of the conquered nation. The Poles remained Polish for a hundred and twenty-five years of partition between Germany, Austria, and Russia. The Finns retained their nationality through eight hundred years of foreign rule and the Jews, through nearly two thousand years of dispersion. If a nation loses territory occupied by disaffected people, this is much less damaging than the loss of territory inhabited by a well-disposed and loyal population. Thus Turkey, which was the "sick man of Europe" as long as it retained its heterogeneous empire, enjoyed a substantial renewal of national health when stripped of its empire and pushed back to the relatively homogeneous heartland of Anatolia. In this case the loss of a disaffected empire actually strengthened the national unit.

The image of the map-shape of the nations may be an important factor affecting the general frame of mind of the nation. There is a tendency for nations to be uneasy with strong irregularities, enclaves, detached portions, and protuberances or hollows. The ideal shape is at least a convex set, and there is some tendency for nations to be more satisfied if they have regularly round or rectangular outlines. Thus the detachment of East Prussia from the body of Germany by the Treaty of Versailles was an important factor in creating the fanatical discontent of the Nazis.

A second important dimension of the national image is that of hostility or friendliness. At any one time a particular national image includes a rough scale of the friendliness or hostility of, or toward, other nations. The relationship is not necessarily either consistent or reciprocal—in nation A the prevailing image may be that B is friendly, whereas in nation B itself the prevailing image may be one of hostility toward A; or again in both nations there may be an image of friendliness of A toward B but of hostility of B toward A. On the whole, however, there is a tendency toward both consistency and reciprocation—if nation A pictures itself as hostile toward B, it usually also pictures B as hostile toward it, and the image is likely to be repeated in B. One exception to this rule seems to be observable: most nations seem to feel that their enemies are more hostile toward them than they are toward their enemies. This is a typical paranoid reaction; the nation visualizes itself as surrounded by hostile nations toward which it has only the nicest and friendliest of intentions.

An important subdimension of the hostility-friendliness image is that of the stability or security of the relationship. A friendly relationship is frequently formalized as an alliance. Alliances, however, are shifting; some friendly relations are fairly permanent, others change as the world kaleidoscope changes, as new enemies arise, or as governments change. Thus a bare fifteen or twenty years ago most people in the United States visualized Germany and Japan, even before the outbreak of war, as enemies, and after Hitler's invasion of Russia, Russia was for a while regarded as a valuable friend and ally. Today the picture is quite changed: Germany and Japan are valuable friends and allies; Russia is the great enemy. We can roughly classify the reciprocal relations of nations along some scale of friendliness-hostility. At one extreme we have stable friendliness, such as between Britain and Portugal or between Britain and the Commonwealth countries. At the other extreme we have stable hostility—the "traditional enemies" such as France and Germany. Between these extremes we have a great many pairs characterized by shifting alliances. On the whole, stable, friendly relations seem to exist mainly between strong nations and weaker nations which they have an interest in preserving and stable hostile relations between adjacent nations, each of which has played a large part in the formation of the other.

Another important dimension both of the image and of the "reality" of the nation-state is its strength or weakness. This is, in turn, a structure made up of many elements—economic resources and productivity, political organization and tradition, willingness to incur sacrifice and inflict cruelties, and so on. It still makes some kind of sense to assess nations on a strength-weakness scale at any one time. Strength is frequently thought of in military terms as the ability to hurt an opponent or to prevent one's self from being hurt by him. There are also more subtle elements in terms of symbolic loyalties and affections which are hard to assess but which must be included in any complete picture. Many arrays of bristling armaments have been brought low by the sheer inability of their wielders to attract any lasting respect or affection. No social organization can survive indefinitely unless it can command the support of its members, and a continuing sense of the significance of the organization or group as such is much more durable a source of support than is the fleeting booty of war or monopoly. The Jews have outlasted an impressive succession of conquerors. These questions regarding the ultimate source of continuing strength or weakness are difficult, and we shall neglect them in this paper.

In order to bring together the variables associated with each nation or pair of nations into an international system, we must resort to the device of matrix, as in Figure 1. Here the hostility-friendliness variable is used as an example. Each cell , a_{ij}, indicates the degree of hostility or friendliness of nation I (of the row) toward nation J (of the column). For purposes of illustration, arbitrary figures have been inserted on a scale from 5 to −5, −5 meaning very hostile, 5 very friendly, and 0 neutral.[3] A matrix of this kind has many interesting properties, not all of which can be worked out here but which depend on the kind of restraints that we impose on it. If we suppose, for instance, that the relations of nations are reciprocal, so that I's attitude toward J is the same as J's toward $I,$ the matrix becomes symmetrical about its major diagonal—that is, the lower left-hand triangle is a mirror image of the upper right-hand triangle. This is a very severe restriction and is certainly violated in fact: there are unrequited loves and hates among the nations as there are among individuals. We can recognize a *tendency*, however, for the matrix to become symmetrical. There is a certain instability about an unrequited feeling. If I loves J and J hates I, then either J's constant rebuff of I's affections will turn I's love to hate, or I's persistent wooing will break down J's distaste and transform it into affection. Unfortunately for the history of human relations, the former seems to be the more frequent pattern, but the latter is by no means unknown.[4]

The sum totals of the rows represent the over-all friendliness or hostility of the nation at the head of the row; the sum totals of the columns represent the degree of hostility or friendliness *toward* the nation at the head of the column. The sum of either of these sums (which must be equal, as each represents a way of adding up all the figures of the matrix) is a measure of the over-all friendliness or hostility of the system. In the example of Figure 1, B is evidently a "paranoid" nation, feeling hostile toward everyone and receiving hostility in return; D is a "neutral" nation, with low values for either hostility or friendliness; E is a "friendly" nation, reciprocating B's general hostility but otherwise having positive relations with everyone. In this figure it is evident that A,C and E are likely to be allied against B, and D is likely to be uncommitted.

In the matrix of Figure 1 no account is taken of the relative size or power of the different nations. This dimension of the system can easily be accommodated, however. All that is necessary is to take the power of the smallest nation as a convenient unit and express the power of the others in multiples of this unit. Then in the matrix we simply give each nation a number of places along the axes equal to the measure of its power. Thus in Figure 2 we suppose a system of three nations, where B is twice as powerful as C and A is three times as powerful as C; A is then allotted three spaces along the axes, B two, and C one. The analysis of the matrix proceeds as before, with the additional constraint that all the figures in the larger boxes bounded by the lines which divide the nations should be the same, as in the figure.

The difference between the sum of a nation's column, representing the general degree of support or affection it *receives,* and the

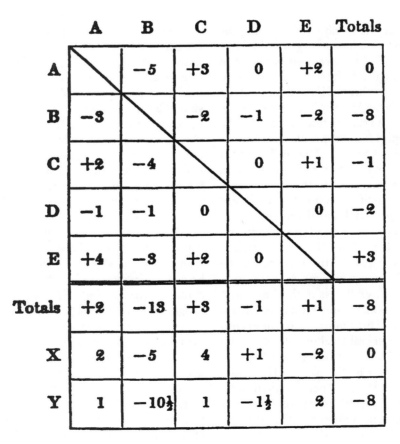

	A	B	C	D	E	Totals
A		−5	+3	0	+2	0
B	−3		−2	−1	−2	−8
C	+2	−4		0	+1	−1
D	−1	−1	0		0	−2
E	+4	−3	+2	0		+3
Totals	+2	−13	+3	−1	+1	−8
X	2	−5	4	+1	−2	0
Y	1	−10½	1	−1½	2	−8

FIGURE 1

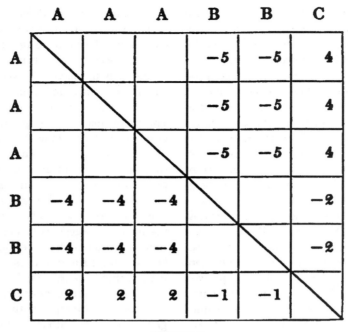

	A	A	A	B	B	C
A				−5	−5	4
A				−5	−5	4
A				−5	−5	4
B	−4	−4	−4			−2
B	−4	−4	−4			−2
C	2	2	2	−1	−1	

FIGURE 2

sum of a nation's row, now representing the sum of support or affection it *gives,* might be called its *affectional balance.* This is shown in the row X in Figure 1. It is a necessary property of a matrix of this kind that the sum of all these balances shall be zero. They measure the relative position of each nation in regard to the degree of support it can expect from the international system as a whole. Thus in Figure 1 it is clear that B is in the worst position, and C in the best position, vis-à-vis the system as a whole. Another figure of some interest might be called the *affectional contribution,* shown in the line Y. This is the mean of the column and row totals for each nation. The total affectional contribution is equal to the total of all the figures of the matrix, which measures the general hostility or friendliness of the whole system. The affectional contribution is then a rough measure of how much each nation contributes to the general level of hostility of the whole system. Thus in the example of Figure 1 we see that nation B (the paranoid) actually contributes more than 100 per cent to the total hostility of the system, its extreme hostility being offset to some extent by other nations' friendliness.

One critical problem of an international system, then, is that of the *dynamics* of the hostility matrix. We can conceive of a succession of such matrices at successive points of time. If there is a system with a "solution," we should be able to predict the matrix at t_1 from the knowledge we have of the matrix at t_0 or at various earlier times. The matrix itself will not, in general, carry enough information to make such predictions possible, even though it is easy to specify theoretical models in which a determinate dynamic system can be derived from the information in the matrix alone.[5]

The difficulty with "simple" systems of this nature is that they are very much more simple than the reality which they symbolize. This is because, in reality, the variables of the system consist of the innumerable dimensions of the images of large numbers of people, and the dynamics of the image are much more complex than the dynamics of mechanical systems. This is because of the structural nature of the image; it cannot be represented simply by a set of quantities or variables. Because of this structural nature, it is capable occasionally of very dramatic changes as a message hits some vital part of the structure and the whole image reorganizes itself. Certain events—like the German invasion of Belgium in 1914, the Japanese attack on Pearl Harbor in 1941, the American use of the atom bomb at Hiroshima and Nagasaki, the merciless destruction of Dresden, and the Russian success with Sputnik I—have profound effects and possibly long-run effects on reorganizing the various national images. The "reorganizing" events are hard both to specify and to predict; they introduce, however, a marked element of uncertainty into any dynamic international system which does not exist, for instance, in the solar system!

In spite of this difficulty, which, oddly enough, is particularly acute in short-term prediction, one gets the impression from the observation of history that we are in the presence of a true system with a real dynamic of its own. We do observe, for instance, cumulative processes of hostility. If we had some measures of the hostility matrix, however crude, it would be possible to identify these processes in more detail, especially the "turning points." There is an analogy here with the business cycle, which also represents a system of cumulative stochastic processes subject to occasional "reorganizations" of its basic equations. Just as we can trace cumulative upward and downward movements in national income, the downward movements often (though not always) culminating in financial crisis and the upward movements often leading to inflation and a subsequent downturn, so we can trace cumulative movements in the hostility matrix. We have "prewar" periods corresponding to downswings, in which things go from bad to worse and hostility constantly increases. The total of all the hostility figures (e.g., –8 on Fig. 1) is a striking analogue of the national-income concept. It might be called the "international temperature." Just as there is a certain critical point in a deflation at which a financial crisis is likely to ensue because of the growing insolvency of heavily indebted businesses, so there is a critical point in the rise of hostility at which war breaks out. This critical point itself depends on a number of different factors and may not be constant. Some nations may be more tolerant of hostility than others; as the cost of war increases, the tolerance of hostility also increases, as we see today in the remark-

able persistence of the "cold war." A deflation or downturn, however, may reverse itself without a crisis, and a "prewar" period may turn into a "postwar" period without a war. Indeed, in the period since 1945 we might identify almost as many small international cycles as there have been business cycles! The "upturn" may be a result of a change of government, the death of certain prominent individuals, or even a change of heart (or image!) on the part of existing rulers. The catharsis of a war usually produces the typical "postwar" period following, though this is often tragically short, as it was after the end of World War II, when a "downturn" began after the revolution in Czechoslovakia. The downturn is often the result of the reassertion of a persistent, long-run character of the system after a brief interlude of increasing friendliness. There seems to be a certain long-run tendency of an international system toward hostility, perhaps because of certain inescapable flaws in the very concept of a national image, just as there also seems to be a long-run tendency of an unregulated and undisturbed market economy toward deflation.

In considering the dynamics of an international system, the essential properties of the image matrix might be summed up in a broad concept of "compatibility." If the change in the system makes for greater compatibility the system may move to an equilibrium. The "balance-of-power" theory postulates the existence of an equilibrium of this nature. The record of history, however, suggests that, in the past at least, international systems have usually been unstable. The incompatibility of various national images has led to changes in the system which have created still greater incompatibility, and the system has moved to less and less stable situations until some crisis, such as war, is reached, which represents a discontinuity in the system. After a war the system is reorganized; some national units may disappear, others change their character, and the system starts off again. The incompatibility may be of many kinds, and it is a virtue of this kind of rather loose model that the historian can fill in the endlessly various details in the special situations which he studies. The model is a mere dress form on which the historian swathes the infinite variations of fashion and fact.

In the model we can distinguish two very different kinds of incompatibility of images. The first might be called "real" incompatibility, where we have two images of the future in which realization of one would prevent the realization of the other. Thus two nations may both claim a certain piece of territory, and each may feel dissatisfied unless the territory is incorporated into it. (One thinks of the innumerable irredenta which have stained the pages of history with so much blood!) Or two nations may both wish to feel stronger than, or superior to, each other. It is possible for two nations to be in a position where each is stronger than the other *at home*, provided that they are far enough apart and that the "loss of power gradient" (which measures the loss of power of each as we remove the point of application farther and farther from the home base) is large enough. It is rarely possible, however, for two nations each to dominate the other, except in the happy situation where each suffers from delusions of grandeur.

The other form of incompatibility might be called "illusory" incompatibility, in which there exists a condition of compatibility which would satisfy the "real" interests of the two parties but in which the dynamics of the situation or the illusions of the parties create a situation of perverse dynamics and misunderstandings, with increasing hostility simply as a result of the reactions of the parties to each other, not as a result of any basic differences of interest. We must be careful about this distinction: even "real" incompatibilities are functions of the national images rather than of physical fact and are therefore subject to change and control. It is hard for an ardent patriot to realize that his country is a mental, rather than a physical, phenomenon, but such indeed is the truth! It is not unreasonable to suppose, however, that "real" incompatibilities are more intractable and less subject to "therapy" than illusory ones.

One final point of interest concerns what might be called the impact of "sophistication" or "self-consciousness" on national images and the international system. The process of so-phistication in the image is a very general one, and we cannot follow all its ramifications here. It occurs in every person in greater or less degree as he grows into adult awareness of himself as part of a larger system. It is akin almost to a Copernican revolution: the unsophisticated image sees the world only from the viewpoint of the viewer; the sophisticated image sees the world from many imagined viewpoints, as a system in which the viewer is only a part. The child sees everything through his own eyes and refers everything to his own immediate comfort. The adult learns to see the world through the eyes of others; his horizon extends to other times, places, and cultures than his own; he learns to distinguish between those elements in his experience which are universal and those which are particular. Many grown people, of course, never become adults in this sense, and it is these who fill our mental hospitals with themselves and their children.

The scientific subculture is an important agency in the sophistication of images. In the physical world we no longer attribute physical phenomena to spirits analogous to our own. In the social sciences we have an agency whereby men reach self-consciousness about their own cultures and institutions and therefore no longer regard these as simply given to them by "nature." In economics, for instance, we have learned to see the system as a whole, to realize that many things which are true of individual behavior are not true of the system and that the system itself is not incapable of a modicum of control. We no longer, for instance, regard depression as "acts of God" but as system made phenomena capable of control through relatively minor system change.

The national image, however, is the last great stronghold of unsophistication. Not even the professional international relations experts have come very far toward seeing the system as a whole, and the ordinary citizen and the powerful statesman alike have naïve, self-centered, and unsophisticated images of the world in which their nation moves. Nations are divided into "good" and "bad"—the enemy is all bad, one's own nation is of spotless virtue. Wars are either acts of God or acts of the other nations, which always catch us completely by surprise. To a student of international systems the national image even of respectable, intellectual, and powerful people seems naïve and untrue. The patriotism of the sophisticated cannot be a simple faith. There is, however, in the course of human history a powerful and probably irreversible movement toward sophistication. We can wise up, but we cannot wise down, except at enormous cost in the breakdown of civilizations, and not even a major breakdown results in much loss of knowledge. This movement must be taken into account in predicting the future of the international system. The present system as we have know it for the past hundred or even thousands of years is based on the widespread acceptance of unsophisticated images, such as, for instance, that a nation can be made more secure *merely* by increasing its armaments. The growth of a systems-attitude toward international relations will have profound consequences for the dynamics of the system itself, just as the growth of a systems-attitude in economics has profound consequences for the dynamics of the economic system.

If, as I myself believe, we live in an international system so unstable that it threatens the very existence of life on earth, our main hope for change may lie in the rapid growth of sophistication, especially at the level of the images of the powerful. Sophistication, of course, has its dangers also. It is usually but a hair's-breadth removed from sophistry, and a false sophistication (of which Marxism in some respects is a good example) can be even more destructive to the stability of a system than a naïve image. Whichever way we move, however, there is danger. We have no secure place to stand where we are, and we live in a time when intellectual investment in developing more adequate international images and theories of international systems may bear an enormous rate of return in human welfare.

ENDNOTES

[1] *See* A. Rapoport, "Lewis F. Richardson's Mathematical Theory of War," *Journal of Conflict Resolution, I,* September, 1957: 249, for an excellent exposition.

[2] *See* K. E. Boulding, *The Image* (Ann Arbor: University of Michigan Press, 1956), for an exposition of the theory on which this paper is based.

[3] The problem of the measurement of hostility (or friendliness) is a very interesting one which we cannot go into extensively here but which is not so hopeless of a solution as might at first sight appear. Possible avenues are as follows: (1) A historical approach. Over a period of years two nations have been at war, threatening war, allied, bound by treaty, and so on. Each relation would be given an arbitrary number, and each year assigned a number accordingly; the average of the years' numbers would be the index. This would always yield a symmetrical matrix—that is, the measure of I's relation to J would be the same as J's relation to I, or $a_{ij} = a_{ji}$. (2) An approach by means of content analysis of public communications (official messages, newspaper editorials, public speeches, cartoons, etc.). This seems likely to be most immediately useful and fruitful, as it would give current information and would also yield very valuable dynamic information about the *changes* in the matrix, which may be much more important than the absolute figures. The fact that any measure of this kind is highly arbitrary is no argument against it, provided that it is qualitatively reliable—that is, moves generally in the same direction as the variable which it purports to measure—and provided also that the limitations of the measure are clearly understood. It would probably be advisable to check the second type of measure against the more objective measures derived from the first method. The difficulty of the first method, however, is the extreme instability of the matrix. The affections of nations are ephemeral!

[4] George F. Kennan once said: "It is an undeniable privilege of every man to prove himself in the right in the thesis that the world is his enemy; for if he reiterates it frequently enough and makes it the background of his conduct, he is bound eventually to be right" ("The Roots of Soviet Conduct," *Foreign Affairs,* July 1947). If for "enemy" we read "friend" in this statement, the proposition seems to be equally true but much less believed.

[5] As a very simple example of such a system, let $(a_{ij})t$ be a cell of the matrix at time t and $(a_{ij})t+1$ be the corresponding value at time $t+1$. Then if for each cell we can postulate a function $(a_{ij})_{t+1} = F(a_{ij})_t$, we can derive the whole $t+1$ ma-

trix from the t matrix. This is essentially the dynamic method of Lewis F. Richardson, and in fairly simple cases it provides an interesting way of formulating certain aspects of the system, especially its tendency toward *cumulative* movements of hostility (armed races) or occasionally of friendliness.

VI

Intercultural Aspects of Conflict and Negotiation

There are similarities and differences among all individuals and cultures. The psychological approach to understanding conflict tends to emphasize *similarities* among people. For example, the dynamics of perception and cognition found in image theory apply to everyone. Or, all humans respond to inescapable pain by engaging in aggression.

Political scientists and international relations experts often assume that there are common factors and causes for international conflict. Political, economic and military power and its distribution and security are the primary concerns of states. War is simply a way of asserting power or preserving security when peaceful means no longer work.

A cultural approach assumes *differences*—each culture is unique and human behavior cannot be explained without understanding the impact of culture. While many psychologists and political scientists believe that the commonly held principles of conflict and negotiation are universal and applicable to all societies, culturalists believe that these principles are often specific to particular cultures. They must always be considered in the context of each culture and the dynamics of intercultural communication and interaction.

INTERNATIONAL CONFLICT

There are intercultural aspects to all human conflicts on the interpersonal, community, national or international level. It is increasingly difficult to separate these levels of conflict because the world is shrinking and the interpersonal and local issues are interrelated with both national and global issues. And, there are more ethnic cultures within countries.

Today many of the civil wars within nations involve ethnic and cultural differences. And, they tend to spill over into other regions of the world and involve other countries. Wars between countries are no longer simply regional but instead involve combatants from very different cultures or even civilizations. Religion and basic cultural values may be replacing traditional issues of political power and economics as causes of international conflict.

INTERCULTURAL MEETINGS

Even intercultural meetings are often frustrating because of differences in communicative styles and assumptions as to how and when to elect leaders, set agendas or get down to business. How we regard conflict and negotiation also varies with culture, yet most people believe everyone deals with conflict in the same way.

Rural Southerners are much more likely to want to develop rapport during the first few minutes of an initial group encounter. They value harmonious group relations, are often indirect and circuitous in their conversation, and they seem to be rather relaxed or "laid back." Time devoted to maintaining and cultivating good relations with others is perhaps more important than simply doing a job and, in fact, it allows business to progress more smoothly when it is time to get down to business.

A good conversation is like a dance where there is a specific tempo or pace. When people of different cultures come together, they are often out-of-sync in conversational style. How people communicate, not simply what they communicate, is determined by culture. And, conversational style may be even more important than the content of conversation in cross-cultural communication.

During discussions, New Yorkers not only cut off conversational loops, they often interrupt sentences of others or even complete them. A sign of rapport among New Yorkers is when someone cuts into your conversation. To a rural Southerner this is aggressive, abrasive, abrupt, and disrespectful.

The tendency of the Southerner to speak slowly and drag out the pronunciation of words may strike New Yorkers as childish or unsophisticated. The rapid, staccato speech pattern of New Yorkers may sound like machine gun fire to the rural Southerner. Differences in rhythm or synchrony of conversation, in and of themselves, create misunderstanding and discomfort.

High-context, associative thinkers or *Be-ers* tend to be much more adept at using and translating nonverbal messages. Mainstream American, low-context, abstractive thinkers or *Do-ers* concentrate on words and even more on written words. Be-ers prefer the physical presence of another person so that they can relate nonverbal messages to verbal messages and use all their senses to know if the other person is honest, sincere, committed, and so on. They feel very uncomfortable with telephone conversations or memos unless they are supplemented with face-to-face encounters.

When should a group get down to business? In "to be" cultures, where group harmony is highly regarded, there is often a premium placed upon developing rapport before discussing business. To begin doing business before getting to know all members would be very rude. It would imply that no one cares who you are and you don't care who they are.

During this get-acquainted phase, it would be impolite to engage in a formal question and answer format. This would resemble an interrogation. Time ought to be allowed for all to reveal aspects of their character and status in a rather natural, almost poetic fashion. As in any polite conversation, room must be allowed for the very articulate to go off on tangents that may reveal subtle aspects of their character and abilities.

Indeed the style with which a person presents himself or herself and interacts with others provides a very good hint as to leadership capabilities, maturity, intelligence, sophistication, and insightfulness. Almost everything that is spoken and how it is presented is relevant to leadership skills. All of this information is somewhat intuitively tied together to create a picture of the whole person, not simply what he or she does in a meeting.

INTERCULTURAL CONFLICT

How do we know if there is a full-blown conflict or just a disagreement? How do we know if the conflict is escalating or deescalating? When is it time to resolve the conflict? How do we resolve it? And, when is it beyond resolution?[1] Most of the answers to these questions we tacitly learn simply by growing up in a particular culture. They are unconsciously acquired so early in life that they are taken for granted and held to be universal or true of everyone. In fact, they are only true for those within our own specific culture. We usually first become aware that others may not share our assumptions regarding conflict and negotiation when we encounter those who are culturally different.

What could be perceived as a genuine conflict in one culture may be just a lively disagreement in another. For example, mainstream white Americans usually state their arguments in a **factual-inductive** manner.[2] Relevant facts are sequentially presented in a fairly unemotional way leading to a conclusion. The greater the number of facts at the onset, the more persuasive the argument. Black Americans tend to be more **affective-intuitive** or deductive. They begin with an emotional position followed by a variety of facts somewhat poetically or metaphorically connected to support their conclusions.

These differences in rhetorical style result in whites being viewed as insincere, impersonal, and deceptive by black Americans while blacks are perceived as irrational, too personal, and abrasive by white Americans. Arguments develop, and many times are lost, because of these differences in style, not substance or content.

As a black leader presents an affective-intuitive argument, other blacks might spontaneously join in with comments of encouragement, agreement, and support. This call-and-response pattern between speaker and audience is often a part of the traditional Black Church. Truth is communicated with emotional intensity. To whites, blacks may appear to be on the verge of a confrontation and united in a clique.

Whites sometimes reactively withdraw into a super factual-inductive mode in an effort to settle things down before they get out-of-hand. "Now let's just calm down and consider the relevant facts in this matter." This is said rather matter-of-factly, without much emotion, to encourage rationality. The white emphasis on fact, logical presentation, and lack of emotion comes off as cold, condescending, patronizing, and further evidence that whites do not really want to hear the views of blacks.

White Americans often assume that there is a short distance between an emotional, verbal expression of disagreement and a physical conflict, whereas for black Americans there is a much greater distance.[3] Stating a position with feelings is a sign of sincerity for most black Americans. However, it might be interpreted as an indication of uncontrollable anger or instability for white Americans and, even worse, an impending confrontation.

Threatening words usually indicate **intent** for whites, while they may be used for affect among blacks. A verbal "threat" to whites could be only an "attention getter" for blacks. This is true of many high-context languages and relationships.

Perhaps when you were a child and did some mischief, your mother threatened you with mild bodily harm. In the context of your relationship, you knew her words were designed to show her feelings and get your undivided attention. You did not call 911.

In most "to be" or high-context cultures, people try to "keep a lid on" disagreements to maintain harmony within the community or group. This internalization of negative feelings means that when they erupt, their expression will be very emotional. And, because everyone knows everyone else, any conflict affects the entire group.

If a Mexican offends a friend, nothing may be said. Because they know each other so well, there is an unspoken and perhaps unconscious assumption that the offender will intuitively sense the other person's hurt or anger from subtle, nonverbal cues. If the offended person must explicitly verbalize feelings, the offender was obviously too insensitive to "read" the other's feelings.

The commitment to a personal relationship is so strong that the Mexican would rather lose an argument than lose a friend.[4] The whole person is unconditionally accepted as a friend—good and bad, rational and irrational. An argument is no grounds for terminating a friendship.

Most Anglos' friendships are conditional on the rule that friends remain rational or "civil." An emotional expression of anger is equated with irrationality and consequently the termination of a relationship. Of course, when Anglos abruptly withdraw from a relationship after an outburst of genuine anger, many Mexicans begin to doubt the sincerity of the friendship in the first place.

Among Mexicans, until there is an exchange of sincere emotional words, no negotiations are taking place. They might assume they are beginning the process of negotiation with their emotional outburst while Anglos believe that the situation is beyond resolution or at "the end of the rope."[5]

CONFLICT RESOLUTION

In close-knit communities, if harm should come to another, and you could prevent it but do not, then you are held indirectly responsible for the harm. The assumption of indirect responsibility permits and even demands that a third-party intermediary step in to resolve disputes. Intermediaries must be associated with the disputants and strive to bring about compromise so that everyone wins. After all, they must continue to live and work together after everything is settled. There is a natural inclination to search for win-win solutions.

In traditional American Indian courts, the object of adjudication is to mediate a case to the satisfaction of all involved, not to establish fault or guilt and then to punish.[6] The court ensures restitution and compensation to the victim and his or her family so that harmony is restored within the community. The court plays the role of third-party intermediary.

Intermediaries might be elders or others who are held in high esteem and are personally known to everyone involved in the conflict. There is no way that the disputants can resolve their disagreements without losing face unless others assume this role of intermediary. Consequently, when others fail to intervene, they are sometimes held accountable for perpetuating the conflict.

In Western, urban societies there is no assumption of indirect responsibility and disputes are usually resolved by the parties directly involved. If a matter must be resolved by intervention, the judge or jury must appear neutral or uninvolved. Resolution is often determined by a decision of right or wrong based upon the facts or merit of the case. Compromise is seldom a desired goal. It is a win-lose proposition.

The Camp David Accords were negotiated in ways that were exceedingly culturally adept. Prime Minister Menachem Begin of Israel and President Anwar Sadat of Egypt met with President Jimmy Carter, a trusted third-party, long before they came to the U.S. Perhaps because Carter is from rural Georgia—a high-context culture—he intuitively understood the cultural dynamics of negotiation in the Middle East. In addition, he is perceived as a sincere, moral, and religious man by almost everyone. These are qualities that are highly regarded in the Middle East.

Carter spent time developing interpersonal rapport with both heads of state before they left their countries. Sadat journeyed to Jerusalem and met with former Israeli Prime Minister Golda Meier. They discussed their grandchildren and other personal matters. While this may not appear to be essential to negotiating the end of a conflict between states, it was the first step in the conflict resolution action chain.

At Camp David, Carter not only used his good offices to resolve this conflict, but he also played the traditional Middle Eastern role of *wasta* or third-party intermediary. This allowed both heads of state to avoid any loss of face or unpleasantness in direct face-to-face negotiation and yet provided for peaceful and serious resolution of differences.

ARTICLES

This section continues the discussion of international conflict from the previous section. Section V considered the role of the media and national images. Now we will consider the intercultural aspects of conflict beginning with American foreign policy.

It is almost impossible to separate local and national concerns from foreign affairs in the world today. Domestic and global issues are increasingly interrelated. Various articles in this text have dealt with the issue of diversity in America and especially the idea that the U.S. is a pluralistic nation—a melting pot. According to the lead article in this section by Benjamin Schwarz, diversity is a myth that America is exporting abroad in its foreign policy. He claims that the U.S. may be more pluralist than many other nations, but at least as much as other countries it "was formed by conquest and force, not by conciliation and compromise."[7]

Schwarz is provocative and controversial. Some may find his position to be "realistic" and others "cynical." In the post-Cold War era, the world is filled with ethnic, nationalist, and separatist conflicts ("ENS" wars), but there is little the U.S. can do. Still, Americans are motivated to be involved, not because of external threat but rather because of their own insecurities. The anxiety they feel over the fragmentation in Bosnia, Rwanda, the Baltic republics, Chechnya, Macedonia, and Georgia arises from the sense that American society is fragmenting.

The next piece ("The Clash of Civilizations?") was published in the summer of 1993 in the journal *Foreign Affairs,* and according to its editors "stirred up more discussion in three years than any other article they had published since the 1940s."[8] Contrary to Schwarz's article, Samuel P. Huntington argues that resurgent ethnicity is not the cause of all the violence in the post-Cold War era but the ancient civilizational antagonisms. He explains in his article:

> It is my hypothesis that the fundamental source of conflict in this new world will not be primarily ideological or primarily economic. The great divisions among humankind and the dominating source of conflict will be cultural. Nation states will remain the most powerful actors in world affairs, but the principal conflicts of global politics will occur between nations and groups of different civilizations. The clash of civilizations will dominate global politics. The fault lines between civilizations will be the battle lines of the future.

In Huntington's view, world affairs will be dominated by the interaction between seven or eight major civilizations, most built on religious empires of the past. But it will be primarily "the West versus the rest." He is especially concerned about a connection between Confucian and Islamic civilizations. Huntington hypothesizes that Confucian countries will sell arms to Islamic countries and they will join together to battle Western civilization.

Huntington's article has been expanded into a book titled, *The Clash of Civilizations and the Remaking of World Order*, which is reviewed by Michael Ignatieff in his article, "Fault Lines." He notes that Huntington's emphasis on tradition, culture, and religion is a welcome departure from the narrow focus on state interests among "realists" in international relations theory. However, some of the worst wars in human history have occurred within civilizations, not between them. Even today, Huntington ignores the clash of values, interests, and traditions within civilizations, such as within Europe, between Europe and the U.S., or divisions within Islam.

Huntington contends (as does Schwarz) that the West cannot and should not intervene in the affairs of other civilizations because such intervention is useless. Instead, America should strengthen itself, reassert pride in its core values, and stop the slide into multiculturalism.

These two articles raise some disturbing questions. Are Schwarz and Huntington versions of contemporary American neo-isolationism?[9] Are they simply reacting to multiculturalism and internationalism with a new kind of unilateralism? Do they reflect the psychological need Americans may have to find an "enemy" since the loss of their long-standing Soviet enemy?[10] Is this a manifestation of the xenophobia that has become popular in America today? Is it possible to withdraw from the world and its conflicts and are isolationism and unilateralism really in the interest of America?

We then turn to the area of cross-cultural communication, negotiation, and crisis resolution, beginning with journalist and Pulitzer Prize-winner Juan Williams' discussion of the work of Thomas Kochman in "Missing the Message." Kochman has devoted most of his life to the study of African-American styles of communication and demonstrates how they differ from white American styles. While many of his findings are controversial, they nevertheless lead us to consider the cross-cultural communication aspects of interracial misunderstanding, conflict and negotiation.

Glen Fisher's article "International Negotiation: Cross-Cultural Perception" offers a more international perspective. To fully understand the dynamics of international conflict and negotiation, he urges us to consider how people from different cultures perceive the world. The psychology of cross-cultural communication and conflict demands that we also consider cultural differences in logic and ways in which disputes are resolved.

Dean Pruitt also discusses international conflict and negotiation but takes a much more psychological approach in his "Achieving Integrative Agreements in Negotiation." Finding win-win solutions on the international level requires that we determine what each party needs in order to feel that they have "won."

The most interesting example of this approach is his discussion of two sisters who have an orange. One sister wants to make orange juice, while the other wants to bake an orange-flavored cake. One solution might be to simply cut the orange in half. However, a better solution is to allow the sister who wants to make juice to use all of the orange except the peel, which could then be used by the other sister to make an orange cake.

"Cross-Cultural Considerations in Hostage Negotiations" is a paper that Mitchell R. Hammer and I presented to criminologists involved in hostage negotiations. We discovered that many of the principles and practices of domestic hostage negotiation fail to consider cultural factors or the dynamics of intercultural communication.

The last three articles in this section provide case studies of difficulties in cross-cultural negotiations. Mu's discussion of intercultural business negotiations between Chinese and Westerners ("Culture and Business") and Tenhover's "American-Japanese Negotiation" provide culture-specific examples of how culture affects the way business is conducted in China and Japan. They stress the importance of understanding the underlying logic and values imbedded in Asian cultures.

Asian-American differences in negotiation would be expected, but are usually unexpected when it comes to Americans and Europeans. David Altany ("Culture Clash") describes the vast differences in negotiating styles in many different European cultures.

ENDNOTES

[1]Much of this discussion of intercultural conflict in groups is a modification and excerpt from "The Multicultural Child Care Staff," by Gary R. Weaver, *Child and Youth Care Administrator* (CYCA) (Fall 1988): 49–55.

[2]Edmund Glenn, D. Witmeyer, and K. Stevenson, "Cultural Styles of Persuasion," *International Journal of Intercultural Relations* 1, (3), 1977: 52–66.

[3]See Thomas Kochman, *Black and White Styles in Conflict* (Chicago: University of Chicago Press, 1981).

[4]R. Dias-Guerrero, *Psychology of the Mexican Culture and Personality* (Austin: University of Texas Press, 1975).

[5]See Gary Weaver, "Law Enforcement in a Culturally Diverse Society," *FBI Law Enforcement Bulletin* 61, (9) (September 1992): 1–7 and "Psychological and Cultural Dimensions of Hostage Negotiation," in *Dynamic Processes of Crisis Negotiation: Theory, Research and Practice*, Randal G. Rogan, Mitchell R. Hammer, and Clinton R. Van Zandt, eds. (Westport, CT: Praeger, 1997), 115–127.

[6]V. Deloria, Jr., and C.M. Lytle, *American Indians, American Justice* (Austin: University of Texas Press, 1983), 111. See also Carol Chiago Lujan, "American Indians, Criminal Justice and Stereotyping," in *Understanding Cultural Diversity*, Elliott Caggins, ed. (Laurel, MD: American Correctional Association, 1993), 56–71.

[7]Kenneth C. Davis, the author of *Don't Know Much About History: Everything You Need to Know About American History but Never Learned* (New York: Avon Books, 1990), describes how Benjamin Franklin once sponsored a Pennsylvania act that paid a bounty for the scalps of American Indians. President Andrew Jackson, and his successor Martin Van Buren, instituted the policy of Indian "removal" or forcible eviction which culminated in the expulsion of thousands of Indians in the deadly forced march known as the "Trail of Tears" in 1836. Kenneth C. Davis, "Ethnic Cleansing Didn't Start in Bosnia," *The New York Times*, 3 September 1995, sec. 4, 1, 6.

[8]From Preface of Samuel P. Huntingon's *The Clash of Civilizations and the Remaking of World Order* (Upper Saddle River, NJ: Simon & Schuster, 1996), 13.

[9]See Arthur M. Schlesinger, Jr., "Back to the Womb? Isolationism's Renewed Threat," *Foreign Affairs* 74 (4) (July/August 1995): 2–8. Schlesinger argues that the U.S. has traditionally been isolationist in its foreign policy, but not when it comes to commerce. Furthermore, he suggests that the version of isolationism in the late 1990s is typified by unilateralism and a distrust of international organizations.

[10]See Robert D. Kaplan, "The Coming Anarchy," *The Atlantic Monthly*, February 1994, 44–76. Kaplan's article was almost as controversial as Huntington's article although he sees the U.S. threatened by the political, social, and economic chaos and environmental degradation in the non-West, especially Africa.

61

The Diversity Myth: America's Leading Export

Benjamin Schwarz

Solipsism is a perennial American temptation. In a grotesquely comic muddle of causes and cultures, Lyndon Johnson once sought to buy off the North Vietnamese with promises of a Great Society-style project along the Mekong. Variants of the cry "Why can't they be more like us?" have long served as a staple of American tourists and foreign-policy mandarins alike. We have made ourselves at home in the world, characteristically, by regarding it as America in the making.

Thus imbued with ourselves, we often get the world wrong. Mussolini was not an impetuous New Dealer, nor Ho Chi Minh a Democratic pol. The West Bank is not the American South, nor is the cause of the Palestinian homeland an exotic version of the black struggle for civil rights. Similarly, the ethnic tumult loosed by the end of the Cold War is not to be assessed by pious invocations of our multi-ethnic, multiracial heritage of tolerance and civic comity. The bloodlettings in Bosnia, Rwanda, Chechnya, and Haiti have no parallel in the Parson Weems idea of our past which we trumpet abroad. Not that they are incommensurably worse than anything in the American experience. Rather, the history we hold up as a light to nations is a sanctimonious tissue of myth and self-infatuation. We get the world wrong because we get ourselves wrong. Taken without illusion, our history gives us no right to preach—but it should

Benjamin Schwarz is a Senior Fellow at the World Policy Institute in New York. Reprinted from *The Atlantic Monthly,* May 1995, 57–67. Copyright © 1995 by Benjamin Schwarz.

prepare us to understand the brutal realities of nation-building, at home and abroad.

Over the past few years the American foreign-policy community has discovered that the world is riddled with ethnic, nationalist, and separatist conflicts ("ENS" wars, in Pentagon-speak). Characterizing the post-Cold War world as a simmering cauldron, experts in the State Department and on the National Security Council, in the foundations and the think tanks, point not only to Bosnia and Rwanda but also to the Baltic republics and Macedonia, to Moldova and Georgia, and assert that, as the former CIA director James Woolsey put it, the world is "more dangerous" now than during the Cold War. Sometimes it seems that such a pronouncement is uttered and met with as much relief as concern, for this new phenomenon supposedly means that expert advice, and Cold War bureaucracies, remain indispensable despite the end of the Cold War. Indeed, in proliferating conferences, workshops, and interagency working groups the national-security community is greeting ENS wars with the same entrepreneurial alarm with which it met the specter of Communist insurgency in the 1960s and "low-intensity conflict" in the 1980s. "The main strategic challenge for the United States," according to Leslie Gelb, the president of the Council on Foreign Relations, is to "develop plans . . . to stem civil wars."

The foreign-policy community's anxiety springs from convictions like those expressed by Warren Zimmermann, the former ambassador to Yugoslavia, when he declared that the war in Bosnia, for instance, has "baleful implications for . . . the United States," because what is at stake there is "the values of the melting pot." America's anxiety over the fragmentation of foreign states and societies arises from our sense that American society is fragmenting, culturally and ethnically. We are desperate to repair what the foreign-policy community terms "failed states" and "divided societies," for such success would prove to us that the liberal notions of pluralism and tolerance upon which we would like to believe that American unity was founded remain vital enough to build communities abroad and, perhaps more important, at home.

The problems with this approach start with a misunderstanding of history. The foreign-policy community usually describes ENS wars as products of the post-Cold War era. They are nothing of the sort. Bosnias have, of course, been occurring with grim regularity for millennia. These wars are also described as throwbacks to more intolerant and violent eras, and the assumption is made that if only the combatants could be placed on the path to modernity, the problem would be solved. It would be comforting to believe that such struggles are merely a relapse, a bloody detour on mankind's progressive road to tolerance and pluralism. But from 1945 to 1975, Harold Isaacs has reckoned in *Idols of The Tribe* (1975), while the Cold War raged and the world reached unprecedented levels of prosperity, what are now called ENS conflicts killed some 10 million people: two million of them in India, another two million in Biafra's civil war, half a million in Bangladesh, and another half a million in Indonesia, with the remainder being casualties of tribal civil wars in Nigeria, the Congo, Chad, and Sudan, or Nagas killed by Indians, Chinese killed by Malays, Tibetans killed by Chinese, Colombians killed by Colombians, Tutsis and Hutus killed by one another in Burundi, Catholics and Protestants in Ulster, Turks and Greeks in Cyprus, and Papuans and Indonesians in New Guinea. Europe's immunity from this killing spree came at a terrible price: the superpower confrontation that divided the continent, the energies exhausted in the killing of 70 million people from 1914 to 1945, and Moscow's sanguinary efforts to subdue separatist elements in the Soviet republics during the 1920s and 1930s all contributed to Europe's postwar stability.

Even more ahistorical and naive is the paradigm that the U.S. foreign-policy community insists on applying to internal conflicts. Guided by faith in the nostrums of the liberal tradition and by the mechanistic notion, learned in civics class, that a community is built by balancing competing interests, American foreign-policy experts urge societies riven by conflict to avoid "winner takes all" politics and to guarantee that regardless of election results, the weaker groups, too, will have a voice in national political and cultural affairs. To accomplish this, coalition governments, the guaranteed division of key offices, and a system of reciprocal vetoes are recommended. These devices, so the thinking goes, will ameliorate ethnic, nationalist, and religious divisions. And the experts agree that those divisions will be less likely to erupt in violent conflict if divided societies elevate tolerance and unity above ethnic, nationalist, or religious domination as their organizing principles.

All these measures may seem reasonable enough. But they depend upon a host of faulty assumptions, perhaps the most important being that the strongest group in a divided society will be willing to make major concessions—concessions that in fact jeopardize its preponderant position. The "solutions," then, presuppose agreement and stability as much as they secure them, for they can be implemented only when there is already a strong desire for compromise.

But, as the English historian Lewis Namier wrote in his discussion of nationalism in nineteenth-century Europe, "states are not created or destroyed, and frontiers redrawn or obliterated, by argument and majority votes; nations are freed, united, or broken by blood and iron, and not by a generous application of liberty." Despite the historical failure of reason and compromise in such situations, foreign-policy experts and officials continue to place great stock in reasonable solutions. Their ideas about settling internal conflicts are fundamentally distorted by their idealized view of America's own history and development.

SWALLOWING UP PEOPLES

We are all pluralists now; everyone favors "tolerance" and "diversity." We regard these qualities as central to the American creed and central to the "democratic values" the export of which has been the avowed aim of every U.S. President since Franklin Delano Roosevelt. Democracy assures a voice to each disparate group and thus, according to prevailing notions, gives rise to the American community, for from these competing voices come compromise and unity. America, therefore, is regarded as a highly successful model of a multiethnic, multicultural, multireligious, and polyglot society. Out of many we are one. With this understanding of their country's cultural and political development, U.S. statesmen and foreign-policy observers ingenuously and smugly ask fragmented societies, Can't you all get along, just as we do over here?

For 200 years Americans have been congratulating themselves on their happy ability to live together. They have taken as the model for their self-image J. Hector St. John de Crèvecoeur's 1782 account of the United States, *Letters From an American Farmer.* Few observations on the American people have been quoted over the years with such self-satisfaction.

> Whence came all these peoples? they are a mixture of English, Scotch, Irish, French, Dutch, Germans and Swedes. From this promiscuous breed, that race now called Americans have arisen. . . . What then is the American, this new man? He is either an European, or the descendant of an European, hence that strange mixture of blood, which you will find in no other country. . . . Here individuals of all nations are melted into a new race of men. . . .

Upholders of this ideal of American pluralism, however, must quote Crèvecoeur, for it is hard to find contemporaries who shared his view. Although non-English people had flocked to America in large numbers, mixed with settlers of English blood, and thereby lost their genetic and cultural distinctiveness, most observers painted a picture of this amalgamation very different from Crèvecoeur's; they understood that America was characterized by ethnic dominance, not ethnic pluralism.

In a typical account a Swedish minister visiting what he hoped would be the settlements of his countrymen along the Delaware River in 1745 was sad to report,

> I found in this country scarcely one genuine Swede left, the most of them are either in part or in whole on one side or other descended from English or Dutch parents. . . . The English are evidently swallowing up the people and the Swedish language is so corrupted that if I did not know the English, it would be impossible to understand the language of my dear Sweden.

The minister's lament is highly revealing. By crying out that the English are "swallowing up the people" and pointing to language as evidence, he correctly defined amalgamation and pluralism in the American context.

Although in 1790 only about 60 percent of the white U.S. population was of English origin, America was culturally quite homogeneous; most of the non-English people had lost much of their cultural distinctiveness to the unsparing dominance of the English language, customs, and institutions, and had lost much of their original genetic character to English numerical superiority. The American "nationality" was not a blending of all the peoples that populated the United States, or even an amalgam of the white Europeans inhabiting the country. An "American" was a modified Englishman. To become an American was to subject oneself to a hegemony so powerful that many Americans ignored or denied existing diversities. John Jay, for instance, was oblivious of the approximately 40 percent of his fellow white citizens who were of non-English origin when he wrote in the second *Federalist* paper,

> Providence has been pleased to give this one connected country to one united people; a people descended from the same ancestors, speaking the same language, professing the same religion . . . similar in their manners and customs. . . .

A hundred and twenty-nine years later, in 1916, after wave upon wave of immigrants had inundated the United States, the liberal critic Randolph Bourne, in calling for a cosmopolitan, heterogeneous American culture, described an America that would have been quite familiar to Jay. Bourne bewailed a "melting pot" under one aegis: "English snobberies, English religion, English literary styles, English literary reverences and canons, English ethics, English superiorities." An elite composed of Americans of Anglo-Saxon descent—which, Bourne acknowledged, included himself—was "guilty of just what every dominant race is guilty of in every European country: the imposition of its own culture upon the minority peoples." A popular guide for immigrant Jews at the time put it another way: to become American, it advised, "forget your past, your customs, and your ideals."

Thus, long before the United States' founding, and until probably the 1960s, the "unity" of the American people derived not from their warm welcoming of and accommodation to nationalist, ethnic, and linguistic differences but from the ability and willingness of an Anglo elite to stamp its image on other peoples coming to this country. That elite's religious and political principles, its customs and social relations, its standards of taste and morality, were for 300 years America's, and in basic ways they still are, despite our celebration of "diversity." Whatever freedom from ethnic and nationalist conflict this country has enjoyed (and it has been considerably less than our national mythology would have us believe) has existed thanks to a cultural and ethnic predominance that would not tolerate conflict or confusion regarding the national identity.

CLEANSING ETHNICS

This cultural predominance, which amounted to the repression, not the celebration, of ethnic diversity, was expressed in the concept of the melting pot that the pluralist Bourne had so criticized. Today, through an Orwellian process, that term has acquired a meaning nearly opposite to its original. Now it is most often used as the former ambassador Warren Zimmermann uses it—to describe the ideal of what might be called the American tapestry. According to this ideal, American society is a colorful blending of different ethnic and national elements, a tapestry that can be woven only in a society tolerant of, and indeed prizing, diversity. But the melting pot, an idea that governed American attitudes toward the various national and ethnic groups coming to the United States from the nineteenth to the mid-twentieth century, was once recognized as a concept in opposition to tolerance and pluralism. Because immigrants created a dependent working class favored by industrialists, there was never a political movement in the United States powerful enough to effect the complete exclusion of foreigners; however, these groups would not be permitted to vitiate Anglo-American domination.

"Americanization" was a process of coercive conformity according to which the United States was a melting pot, not a tapestry. American society wasn't viewed as the product of a little of Russia, a little of Italy, and a little of Poland all mixed together. Instead the various nationalities were made into Americans as ore is refined into gold. Americanization purified them, eliminating the dross. The Americanization movement's "melting pot" pageants, inspired by Israel Zangwill's play, celebrated not tolerance but conformity to a narrow conception of American nationality by depicting strangely attired foreigners stepping into a huge pot and emerging as immaculate, well-dressed, accent-free "American-looking" Americans—that is, Anglo-Americans. Sinclair Lewis recognized the melting pot, in *Main Street,* as a means by which "the sound American customs absorbed without one trace of pollution another alien invasion." Americanization, then, although it did not cleanse America of its ethnic minorities, cleansed its minorities of their ethnicity.

For better or worse, the current fragmentation and directionlessness of American society is the result, above all, of a disintegrating elite's increasing inability or unwillingness to impose its hegemony on society as a whole. Nevertheless, that a single group whose proportion of the population has declined continuously throughout American history could so dominate American cultural and political life for three centuries—could in fact define what it meant to be an American—is a remarkable achievement.

The hegemony that has unified America has been at bottom not so much cultural and linguistic as physical. America didn't simply evolve, it was made by those who claimed it fiercely and rendered it in their image. Today's foreign-policy experts, among them Zbigniew Brzezinski, who characterize Russia as congenitally expansive, driven by an almost evil "imperial impulse" to dominate or absorb its bordering states, and who assert that as long as Russia does not respect the sovereignty of other states it cannot be a democracy, would arrive at a clearer perspective of such an "impulse" if they reflected on their own country's history and development. At least as much as other countries, the United States was formed by conquest and force, not by conciliation and compromise. For America, no less than for Russia, nation-building has been a ruthless undertaking. America's founders described the United States not as a country but as an empire, and for reasons of national security, economic development, and racial chauvinism (the same motivations impelling Russian "imperialism" today) they embarked on a course of imperial expansion.

This meant, of course, taking land that belonged to others and subjecting foreign peoples to American rule. Even though the North American continent was at the time inhabited by various Native American tribes and divided among Spain, Great Britain, and the United States, John Quincy Adams confidently declared in 1811 that it was "destined . . . to be peopled by one nation, speaking one language, professing one general system of religious and political principles, and accustomed to one general tenor of social usages and customs." To Adams and his contemporaries there was, of course, no doubt that America should effect this imperial union. A Kentuckian added a more mercenary gloss to Adams' prophecy, boasting that Americans were "as greedy after plunder as ever the old Romans were, Mexico glitters in our Eyes— the word is all we wait for." By 1846 America was ready to pounce. In a war of conquest—a war that Ulysses S. Grant judged "one of the most unjust waged by a stronger against a weaker nation"—a democratic United States swallowed present-day Texas, California, New Mexico, Arizona, Nevada, Utah, and parts of Colorado and Wyoming.

Moreover, building America required nearly 300 years of genocidal wars against Native Americans, a fact that impels today's historians to characterize American expansion on the continent as "invasion" rather than "settlement." These wars, one of the longest series of ethnic conflicts in modern history, were resolved not by power sharing but by obliteration. Although this record engenders much handwringing today, it is impossible to imagine the United States existing if a more reasonable course had been pursued. For from

the "American" point of view, a reasonable accommodation would have required that, in Theodore Roosevelt's blunt phrase, the vast continent be set aside "as a game preserve." America's great ethnic struggle should have taught Americans that many conflicts are simply irreconcilable. As Representative Richard Wilde, of Georgia, asked with resignation in 1830, describing the United States' destruction of Native Americans as the price of its development, "What is history but the obituary of nations?"

YANKEE LEVIATHAN

Of course, just as the United States entered the final stage of its subjugation and liquidation of Native Americans, it nearly destroyed itself in the other central episode of its nation-building—a brutal and irreconcilable nationalist-separatist conflict in which one vision of America crushed another. The Civil War—a conflict that, the historian William Appleman Williams wrote, "undercuts the popular mythology that America is unique," and he added, "Only a nation that avoided such a conflict could make a serious claim to being fundamentally different"—is an apt example of how reasonable solutions to separatist conflicts hardly ever work. When the United States was established, the North and the South accepted each other as effectively two distinct economic and ideological entities based on antagonistic systems of property: the North was industrial, liberal-bourgeois, and capitalist, while the South was agricultural, aristocratic, paternalistic, and anticapitalist. To dampen sectional conflict, the Constitution, through the three-fifths clause and other devices, guaranteed the South a disproportionate voice in national politics. Yet this guaranteed outcome, so lauded by policy analysts today as a means of forestalling internal conflict, could not work in the long run for the United States. As the North's power and ambitions grew, it was unwilling to abide by arrangements based on a previous and obsolete calculus of relative strength, while the South was not satisfied with merely a diminishing respect for its view. It wanted to determine its own future without being subordinate to or dependent on an opposing and increasingly threatening, ideology and political economy.

In the end the North's vision—of a powerful centralized state, a "Yankee Leviathan," deemed necessary for capitalist development—emerged as the nation's. This vision, despite a persistent mythology promulgated by the victors, was triumphant not because it was intellectually or morally superior but because the North won a test of physical strength. Indeed, it is difficult to imagine a better proof of the idea that might makes right—a doctrine supposedly anathema to liberals—than the outcome of our own Civil War. Eugene Genovese, a clear-eyed historian, has written,

> General Sherman, not the indomitable ideology of liberalism, marched through Georgia. The notion that America has always united on liberal principles breaks down here. . . . We should not forget that our liberal, confident, tolerant, and good-natured bourgeoisie, when for once confronted with a determined and powerful internal foe, forgot its commitment to reason together and reached for its revolver.

Our separatist conflict was followed not, as Yankees assert, by national reconciliation but by military occupation to impose a new political and economic order on the defeated land and by a century of regional hostility and estrangement.

WHITE OVER BLACK

America would have seen more conflicts between white Americans of different ethnic and religious backgrounds (and classes) if these had not been muted by whites' common hatred and fear of black Americans. There is an obvious problem with Crèvecoeur's discussion of the new American "race" in the passage quoted earlier. It excludes the very element of American society that has given America some of its most distinctive characteristics: the African. Even for Crèvecoeur, supposedly the voice of tolerance, there were severe limits on who could be included in the American mixture. The American was "either an European, or the descendant of an European"; the American could not be a black man or woman.

The struggle to make one nation of America's original two—black and white—is an enterprise that might never succeed, and that America's founders did not believe was possible. After all, Thomas Jefferson's pluralist vision, which established a standard of religious and political tolerance to which Americans still aspire, didn't extend to the black race. Jefferson's apologists are fond of quoting his statement, about black men and women, that "nothing is more certainly written in the book of fate than that these people are to be free." But they fail to quote his concluding clause: "Nor is it less certain that the two races, equally free, cannot live in the same government." Jefferson hated slavery because he knew it to be wrong, but he also hated it because it brought black people to America. Convinced that blacks were alien, inferior, and dangerous, Jefferson had a vision for America that required that they be not only emancipated but also expelled from the country. Advocating a program of ethnic cleansing, he was determined that blacks be removed "beyond the reach of mixture." Thus Jefferson's notions of democracy, upon which our ideals of pluralism are founded, depended not merely on racial supremacy but on racial homogeneity.

DEMOCRACY AS THE PROBLEM

When considering other countries' internal conflicts, Americans should keep in mind what their own Civil War and Indian wars have proved: embattled minorities—nations within nations—don't just want respect; they want not to be treated as appendages of the majority's state. Israel gives its Arab minority within its pre-1967 borders the same voting rights it accords its Jewish citizens. In the interwar period the Sudeten Germans received respect and a disproportionate political voice from a democratic Czechoslovakia. Today the Quebecois are given the same treatment in Canadian national politics. Nevertheless, significant numbers within these minorities were or are unsatisfied with these arrangements, because solutions to civil conflicts which grant special guarantees to minorities almost always ask those minorities to accept less than they want. But another oft-touted solution—transforming nation-states into civil states, in which political power is not determined by membership in the majority's ethnic, nationalist, or religious group—demands that the majority accept far less than it wants and, indeed, less than it already has. To many within the majority, such a solution means sacrificing a living, breathing national character to the abstract and bloodless notion of a political community.

It is, for example, an unspoken rule of Israeli politics, applying as much to Labor as to Likud, that no Arab or Arab-dominated party shall be invited to participate in a political coalition. No matter how much Israel might want to ameliorate internal conflict, it won't jettison its national character and dismantle that which defines its statehood. The promotion of the civil state and the weakening of the nation-state would be unacceptable not only to Israel but also to wholly secular states in the advanced industrialized community as well—to Germany and Japan, for example, which both tend to define citizens as those who belong to the dominant national group.

Divided societies face a conundrum: dissatisfied minorities want, at a minimum, a real voice in determining their future—but a real voice for the minority means real sacrifice for the majority. Canada's proposed 1992 Charlottetown Accord, for instance, was a model of reasonable techniques for forestalling internal conflict: predominantly Francophone Quebec was assured 25 percent of the seats in the House of Commons; three judges on the Supreme Court, out of nine, were to be drawn from Quebec; and bills affecting the French language and culture would have required a majority of the Senate as a whole and a majority of Francophone senators, too. These solutions, which might have assuaged the Francophone minority, were roundly rejected by Anglophone Canada, which was unwilling to relinquish the political power and the cultural dominance it maintained by virtue of being the majority. If such compromises are unworkable in a Western democracy, there is little reason to assume that they will work in the emerging and failed states that now concern the American national-security community.

The Clinton Administration, along with many Republican foreign-policy leaders, looks to a global democratic makeover to tame the seemingly intractable ethnic, nationalist, and separatist passions that have destabilized the post-Cold War world. "Democratic enlargement" has, in fact, emerged as the central tenet of the Administration's foreign policy. But for the reasons discussed above, it is, as John Stuart Mill observed, "next to impossible" to build a true democracy—as opposed to a system of majority tyranny—in a multi-ethnic society. Moreover, democracy hardly immunizes a society against internal conflict and separatism, as the 620,000 dead in America's Civil War attest. Democracy, which permits—in fact, encourages—competition for power and benefits among contesting groups, actually exacerbates internal tensions and conflicts.

Many of those policymakers who advocate democratic enlargement argue that before violence erupts in states divided by internal differences, America should urge those states to adopt democratic or, more accurately, power-sharing solutions. But in the past whenever such efforts have not been backed by U.S. force, they have failed, because those groups with power are disinclined to relinquish it voluntarily. Such blandishments amount, whatever the motivation, to crass interference in another state's internal affairs. How would Americans feel if Japan, out of a sincere desire to stabilize a dangerously divided United States, tried to pressure it to adopt the radical power-sharing solutions of Lani Guinier (the law professor whose nomination for a Justice Department post was withdrawn by the Clinton Administration) to effect a political order in which minorities were assured a more powerful voice in the U.S. political process?

Policymakers seek benign, if ineffective, democratic and power-sharing solutions to internal conflicts around the world, because historically workable solutions are unpalatable. In 1914 Prince Bernhard von Bulow, then a former German Chancellor, starkly summarized those solutions when he wrote that "in the struggle between nationalities one nation is the hammer, the other the anvil, one is the victor and one is the vanquished." Stability within divided societies is normally based on some form of domination, and once internal differences become violent, usually only the logic of force can lay them to rest.

Lamentably, the most stable and lasting solution to ethnic and nationalist conflicts has been ethnic cleansing and partition. The Czech Republic and Poland are today far more stable and more likely to remain democratic than they would otherwise be because of their ruthless decisions, following the Second World War, to expel forcibly the German minorities that had caused them so much trouble in the interwar years. Cyprus, too, became considerably more stable after the Turkish army partitioned it, forcing the relocation of 200,000 people, mostly Greek Cypriots, in 1974.

DOMESTIC INSECURITIES

More reasonable power-sharing solutions sometimes do emerge in divided societies, but usually only after the opposing sides have exhausted themselves in a bloody contest. The struggle in the 1940s and 1950s between Colombia's liberals and conservatives, for instance, finally resulted in a textbook resolution of civil differences. Both factions were assured a voice in national politics, and the presidency alternated between the two parties. But the two sides were willing to compromise only after more than a quarter of a million Colombians had been killed in civil war. For both, compromise was the second-best solution, to which they agreed only after they had done their best to eradicate their opponents. Arriving at solutions "reasonable" or not—can take centuries and will often be bloody. So, although the Pentagon, the State Department, and the Carnegie Endowment have spent enormous energy of late generating ideas and strategies for how America can prevent, tame, or end ENS conflicts, the United States really has only two options in these situations. Adopting a passive role once violence has erupted in a failed state, Washington can await the time when mutual exhaustion or the triumph of one group over another will create an opening for intervention in a purely peacekeeping ca-

pacity. Alternatively, the United States can effectively intervene, not by building civil societies or pacifying such conflicts but by helping one side impose its will on the other, as Turkey did in Cyprus. This sort of intervention, of course, can hardly be called "peacekeeping" or "peacemaking": it is, however, what great-power intervention usually amounts to, as the United States has shown in, among other places, the Philippines (1898–1913), Haiti (1915–1934), Nicaragua (1912–1925; 1926–1933), and Vietnam (1961–1973).

Such intervention, which is nothing more than the naked exercise of power, should be an option only when specific, vital U.S. interests are threatened. They are not threatened in any actual or in most potential ethnic and separatist conflicts. Because "humane" solutions are ineffective, and because effective solutions are too inhumane for the United States to consider in any but the most threatening situations, America is largely impotent in the face of ENS wars.

Why, then, has the foreign-policy community made such conflicts the focus of so much of its post-Cold War strategizing? What, for instance, does Leslie Gelb mean when he insists that foreign civil wars are "the new core problem in post-Cold War politics" and that "democracies have a large practical as well as moral stake in finding reasonable responses" to them?

The motivation behind this latest summons to a foreign-policy crusade, as with earlier summonses, lies not in external threats but in our own insecurities. These conflicts scare us because we see in them an image of ourselves. After four centuries we are nagged by the facts that we do not "all get along" and that the apparent success of our own multiethnic and multicultural experiment might have been engendered not by tolerance but by hegemony. Without the dominance that once dictated, however ethnocentrically, what it meant to be an American, we are left with only tolerance and pluralism to hold us together. Unfortunately, the evidence from Los Angeles to New York, from Miami to Milwaukee, shows that such principles are not so powerful as we had believed and hoped. Afraid to face our own problems directly, we look elsewhere, and encourage other countries to prove to us that more pluralism and more tolerance are all that are needed to reunite divided societies. Thus for the past three years *Los Angeles Times* editorials have often shifted focus from racial divisions in the city and the debate over the changing ethnic and linguistic makeup of California to warn of what they define as the broad American interest at stake in the former Yugoslavia. In urging U.S. intervention there the *Times* argues, for instance, that the United States is a "citizen-based, multi-ethnic state," and that "it is safe only in a world where, in principle, all states are comparably organized," since "if ethnicity begins to replace citizenship as the basis for statehood, chaos would ensue, a chaos that would not leave America untouched." Or, as Warren Zimmermann solipsistically claims. "What happens in Bosnia matters to Americans." Externalizing our problems, he bizarrely sees a threat to the United States from the Bosnian Serbs because if their ideas prevailed here at home, our tolerant, multi-ethnic society would be jeopardized. Zimmermann uses Arthur Schlesinger, Jr.'s critique of American "ethnic ideologues"—who, according to Schlesinger, "have set themselves against the old American ideal of assimilation"—to indict the Bosnian Serbs for the same crime. In fact, however, the Bosnian Serbs' ideas are much closer to the "old American ideal of assimilation" than we would like to think.

A crusade in support of multinational, multicultural tolerance abroad really seeks to validate it at home. But attempting to validate a myth is futile. Before we export our myth, we had best recognize that we have not yet found a "reasonable" solution here, and that perhaps such a solution cannot be found.

62

The Clash of Civilizations?

Samuel P. Huntington

THE NEXT PATTERN OF CONFLICT

World politics is entering a new phase, and intellectuals have not hesitated to proliferate visions of what it will be—the end of history, the return of traditional rivalries between nation states, and the decline of the nation state from the conflicting pulls of tribalism and globalism, among others. Each of these visions catches aspects of the emerging reality. Yet they all miss a crucial, indeed a central, aspect of what global politics is likely to be in the coming years.

It is my hypothesis that the fundamental source of conflict in this new world will not be primarily ideological or primarily economic. The great divisions among humankind and the dominating source of conflict will be cultural. Nation states will remain the most powerful actors in world affairs, but the principal conflicts of global politics will occur between nations and groups of different civilizations. The clash of civilizations will dominate global politics. The fault lines between civilizations will be the battle lines of the future.

Conflict between civilizations will be the latest phase in the evolution of conflict in the modern world. For a century and a half after the emergence of the modern international

Samuel P. Huntington, former foreign policy aide to President Jimmy Carter, is the Eaton Professor of the Science of Government and Director of the John M. Olin Institute for Strategic Studies at Harvard University. This article is the product of the Olin Institute's project on "The Changing Security Environment and American National Interests." Reprinted from *Foreign Affairs,* 72, no. 3 (Summer 1993): 22–49.

system with the Peace of Westphalia, the conflicts of the Western world were largely among princes—emperors, absolute monarchs and constitutional monarchs attempting to expand their bureaucracies, their armies, their mercantilist economic strength and, most important, the territory they ruled. In the process they created nation states, and beginning with the French Revolution the principal lines of conflict were between nations rather than princes. In 1793, as R. R. Palmer put it, "The wars of kings were over; the wars of peoples had begun." This nineteenth-century pattern lasted until the end of World War I. Then, as a result of the Russian Revolution and the reaction against it, the conflict of nations yielded to the conflict of ideologies, first among communism, fascism-Nazism and liberal democracy, and then between communism and liberal democracy. During the Cold War, this latter conflict became embodied in the struggle between the two superpowers, neither of which was a nation state in the classical European sense and each of which defined its identity in terms of its ideology.

These conflicts between princes, nation states and ideologies were primarily conflicts within Western civilization. "Western civil wars," as William Lind has labeled them. This was as true of the Cold War as it was of the world wars and the earlier wars of the seventeenth, eighteenth and nineteenth centuries. With the end of the Cold War, international politics moves out of its Western phase, and its centerpiece becomes the interaction between the West and non-Western civilizations and among non-Western civilizations. In the politics of civilizations, the peoples and governments of non-Western civilizations no longer remain the objects of history as targets of Western colonialism but join the West as movers and shapers of history.

THE NATURE OF CIVILIZATIONS

During the Cold War the world was divided into the First, Second and Third Worlds. Those divisions are no longer relevant. It is far more meaningful now to group countries not in terms of their political or economic systems or in terms of their level of economic development but rather in terms of their culture and civilization.

What do we mean when we talk of a civilization? A civilization is a cultural entity. Villages, regions, ethnic groups, nationalities, religious groups, all have distinct cultures at different levels of cultural heterogeneity. The culture of a village in southern Italy may be different from that of a village in northern Italy, but both will share in a common Italian culture that distinguishes them from German villages. European communities, in turn, will share cultural features that distinguish them from Arab or Chinese communities. Arabs, Chinese and Westerners, however, are not part of any broader cultural entity. They constitute civilizations. A civilization is thus the highest cultural grouping of people and the broadest level of cultural identity people have short of that which distinguishes humans from other species. It is defined both by common objective elements, such as language, history, religion, customs, institutions, and by the subjective self-identification of people. People have levels of identity: a resident of Rome may define himself with varying degrees of intensity as a Roman, an Italian, a Catholic, a Christian, a European, a Westerner. The civilization to which he belongs is the broadest level of identification with which he intensely identifies. People can and do redefine their identities and, as a result, the composition and boundaries of civilizations change.

Civilizations may involve a large number of people, as with China ("a civilization pretending to be a state," as Lucian Pye put it), or a very small number of people, such as the Anglophone Caribbean. A civilization may include several nation states, as is the case with Western, Latin American and Arab civilizations, or only one, as is the case with Japanese civilization. Civilizations obviously blend and overlap, and may include subcivilizations. Western civilization has two major variants, European and North American, and Islam has its Arab, Turkic and Malay subdivisions. Civilizations are nonetheless meaningful entities, and while the lines between them are seldom sharp, they are real. Civilizations are dynamic; they rise and fall; they divide and merge. And,

as any student of history knows, civilizations disappear and are buried in the sands of time.

Westerners tend to think of nation states as the principal actors in global affairs. They have been that, however, for only a few centuries. The broader reaches of human history have been the history of civilizations. In *A Study of History*, Arnold Toynbee identified 21 major civilizations; only six of them exist in the contemporary world.

WHY CIVILIZATIONS WILL CLASH

Civilization identity will be increasingly important in the future, and the world will be shaped in large measure by the interactions among seven or eight major civilizations. These include Western, Confucian, Japanese, Islamic, Hindu, Slavic-Orthodox, Latin American and possibly African civilization. The most important conflicts of the future will occur along the cultural fault lines separating these civilizations from one another.

Why will this be the case?

First, differences among civilizations are not only real; they are basic. Civilizations are differentiated from each other by history, language, culture, tradition and, most important, religion. The people of different civilizations have different views on the relations between God and man, the individual and the group, the citizen and the state, parents and children, husband and wife, as well as differing views of the relative importance of rights and responsibilities, liberty and authority, equality and hierarchy. These differences are the product of centuries. They will not soon disappear. They are far more fundamental than differences among political ideologies and political regimes. Differences do not necessarily mean conflict, and conflict does not necessarily mean violence. Over the centuries, however, differences among civilizations have generated the most prolonged and the most violent conflicts.

Second, the world is becoming a smaller place. The interactions between peoples of different civilizations are increasing; these increasing interactions intensify civilization consciousness and awareness of differences between civilizations and commonalities within civilizations. North African immigration to France generates hostility among Frenchmen and at the same time increased receptivity to immigration by "good" European Catholic Poles. Americans react far more negatively to Japanese investment than to larger investments from Canada and European countries. Similarly, as Donald Horowitz has pointed out, "An lbo may be . . . an Owerri Ibo or an Onitsha Ibo in what was the Eastern region of Nigeria. In Lagos, he is simply an Ibo. In London, he is a Nigerian. In New York, he is an African." The interactions among peoples of different civilizations enhance the civilization-consciousness of people that, in turn, invigorates differences and animosities stretching or thought to stretch back deep into history.

Third, the processes of economic modernization and social change throughout the world are separating people from long-standing local identities. They also weaken the nation state as a source of identity. In much of the world religion has moved in to fill this gap, often in the form of movements that are labeled "fundamentalist." Such movements are found in Western Christianity, Judaism, Buddhism and Hinduism, as well as in Islam. In most countries and most religions the people active in fundamentalist movements are young, college-educated, middle-class technicians, professionals and business persons. The "unsecularization of the world," George Weigel has remarked, "is one of the dominant social facts of life in the late twentieth century." The revival of religion, "la revanche de Dieu," as Gilles Kepel labeled it, provides a basis for identity and commitment that transcends national boundaries and unites civilizations.

Fourth, the growth of civilization-consciousness is enhanced by the dual role of the West. On the one hand, the West is at a peak of power. At the same time, however, and perhaps as a result, a return to the roots phenomenon is occurring among non-Western civilizations. Increasingly one hears references to trends toward a turning inward and "Asianization" in Japan, the end of the Nehru legacy and the "Hinduization" of India, the failure of Western ideas of socialism and nationalism and hence "re-Islamization" of the Middle East, and now a debate over Westernization versus Russianization in Boris Yeltsin's country. A West at the peak of its power confronts non-Wests that increasingly have the desire, the will and the resources to shape the world in non-Western ways.

In the past, the elites of non-Western societies were usually the people who were most involved with the West, had been educated at Oxford, the Sorbonne or Sandhurst, and had absorbed Western attitudes and values. At the same time, the populace in non-Western countries often remained deeply imbued with the indigenous culture. Now, however, these relationships are being reversed. A de-Westernization and indigenization of elites is occurring in many non-Western countries at the same time that Western, usually American, cultures, styles and habits become more popular among the mass of the people.

Fifth, cultural characteristics and differences are less mutable and hence less easily compromised and resolved than political and economic ones. In the former Soviet Union, communists can become democrats, the rich can become poor and the poor rich, but Russians cannot become Estonians and Azeris cannot become Armenians. In class and ideological conflicts, the key question was "Which side are you on?" and people could and did choose sides and change sides. In conflicts between civilizations, the question is "What are you?" That is a given that cannot be changed. And as we know, from Bosnia to the Caucasus to the Sudan, the wrong answer to that question can mean a bullet in the head. Even more than ethnicity religion discriminates sharply and exclusively among people. A person can be half-French and half-Arab and simultaneously even a citizen of two countries. It is more difficult to be half-Catholic and half-Muslim.

Finally, economic regionalism is increasing. The proportions of total trade that were intraregional rose between 1980 and 1989 from 51 percent to 59 percent in Europe, 33 percent to 37 percent in East Asia, and 32 percent to 36 percent in North America. The importance of regional economic blocs is likely to continue to increase in the future. On the one hand, successful economic regionalism will reinforce civilization-consciousness. On the other hand, economic regionalism may succeed only when it is rooted in a common civilization. The European Community rests on the shared foundation of European culture and Western Christianity. The success of the North American Free Trade Area depends on the convergence now underway of Mexican, Canadian and American cultures. Japan, in contrast, faces difficulties in creating a comparable economic entity in East Asia because Japan is a society and civilization unique to itself. However strong the trade and investment links Japan may develop with other East Asian countries, its cultural differences with those countries inhibit and perhaps preclude its promoting regional economic integration like that in Europe and North America.

Common culture, "in contrast, is clearly facilitating the rapid expansion of the economic relations between the People's Republic of China and Hong Kong, Taiwan, Singapore and the overseas Chinese communities in other Asian countries. With the Cold War over, cultural commonalities increasingly overcome ideological differences, and mainland China and Taiwan move closer together. If cultural commonality is a prerequisite for economic integration, the principal East Asian economic bloc of the future is likely to be centered on China. This bloc is, in fact, already coming into existence. As Murray Weidenbaum has observed,

> Despite the current Japanese dominance of the region, the Chinese-based economy of Asia is rapidly emerging as a new epicenter for industry, commerce and finance. This strategic area contains substantial amounts of technology and manufacturing capability (Taiwan), outstanding entrepreneurial, marketing and services acumen (Hong Kong), a fine communications network (Singapore), a tremendous pool of financial capital (all three), and very large endowments of land, resources and labor (mainland China). . . . From Guangzhou to Singapore, from Kuala Lumpur to Manila this influential network—often based on extensions of the traditional clans—has been described as the backbone of the East Asian economy.[1]

Culture and religion also form the basis of the Economic Cooperation Organization, which brings together ten non-Arab Muslim countries: Iran, Pakistan, Turkey, Azerbaijan, Kazakhstan, Kyrgyzstan, Turkmenistan, Tadjikistan, Uzbekistan and Afghanistan. One impetus to the revival and expansion of this organization, founded originally in the 1960s by Turkey, Pakistan and Iran, is the realization by the leaders of several of these countries that they had no chance of admission to the European Community. Similarly, Caricom, the Central American Common Market and Mercosur rest on common cultural foundations. Efforts to build a broader Caribbean-Central American economic entity bridging the Anglo-Latin divide, however, have to date failed.

As people define their identity in ethnic and religious terms, they are likely to see an "us" versus "them" relation existing between themselves and people of different ethnicity or religion. The end of ideologically defined states in Eastern Europe and the former Soviet Union permits traditional ethnic identities and animosities to come to the fore. Differences in culture and religion create differences over policy issues, ranging from human rights to immigration to trade and commerce to the environment. Geographical propinquity gives rise to conflicting territorial claims from Bosnia to Mindanao. Most important, the efforts of the West to promote its values of democracy and liberalism as universal values, to maintain its military predominance and to advance its economic interests engender countering responses from other civilizations. Decreasingly able to mobilize support and form coalitions on the basis of ideology, governments and groups will increasingly attempt to mobilize support by appealing to common religion and civilization identity.

The clash of civilizations thus occurs at two levels. At the micro-level, adjacent groups along the fault lines between civilizations struggle, often violently, over the control of territory and each other. At the macro-level, states from different civilizations compete for relative military and economic power, struggle over the control of international institutions and third parties, and competitively promote their particular political and religious values.

THE FAULT LINES
BETWEEN CIVILIZATIONS

The fault lines between civilizations are replacing the political and ideological boundaries of the Cold War as the flash points for crisis and bloodshed. The Cold War began when the Iron Curtain divided Europe politically and ideologically. The Cold War ended with the end of the Iron Curtain. As the ideological division of Europe has disappeared, the cultural division of Europe between Western Christianity, on the one hand, and Orthodox Christianity and Islam, on the other, has re-emerged. The most significant dividing line in Europe, as William Wallace has suggested, may well be the eastern boundary of Western Christianity in the year 1500. This line runs along what are now the boundaries between Finland and Russia and between the Baltic states and Russia, cuts through Belarus and Ukraine separating the more Catholic western Ukraine from Orthodox eastern Ukraine, swings westward separating Transylvania from the rest of Romania, and then goes through Yugoslavia almost exactly along the line now separating Croatia and Slovenia from the rest of Yugoslavia. In the Balkans this line, of course, coincides with the historic boundary between the Hapsburg and Ottoman empires. The peoples to the north and west of this line are Protestant or Catholic; they shared the common experiences of European history—feudalism, the Renaissance, the Reformation, the Enlightenment, the French Revolution, the Industrial Revolution; they are generally economically better off than the peoples to the east; and they may now look forward to increasing involvement in a common European economy and to the consolidation of democratic political systems. The peoples to the east and south of this line are Orthodox or Muslim; they historically belonged to the Ottoman or Tsarist empires and were only lightly touched by the shaping events in the rest of Europe; they are generally less advanced economically; they seem much less likely to develop stable democratic political systems. The Velvet Curtain of culture has replaced the Iron Curtain of ideology as the most significant dividing line in Europe. As the events in Yugoslavia show, it is not only a line of difference; it is also at times a line of bloody conflict.

Conflict along the fault line between Western and Islamic civilizations has been going on for 1,300 years. After the founding of Islam, the Arab and Moorish surge west and north only ended at Tours in 732. From the eleventh to the thirteenth century the Crusaders attempted with temporary success to bring Christianity and Christian rule to the Holy Land. From the fourteenth to the seventeenth century, the Ottoman Turks reversed the balance, extended their sway over the Middle East and the Balkans, captured Constantinople, and twice laid siege to Vienna. In the nineteenth and early twentieth centuries as Ottoman power declined Britain, France, and Italy established Western control over most of North Africa and the Middle East.

After World War II, the West, in turn, began to retreat; the colonial empires disappeared; first Arab nationalism and then Islamic fundamentalism manifested themselves; the West became heavily dependent on the Persian Gulf countries for its energy; the oil-rich Muslim countries became money-rich and, when they wished to, weapons-rich. Several wars occurred between Arabs and Israel (created by the West). France fought a bloody and ruthless war in Algeria for most of the 1950s; British and French forces invaded Egypt in 1956; American forces went into Lebanon in 1958; subsequently American forces returned to Lebanon, attacked Libya, and engaged in various military encounters with Iran; Arab and Islamic terrorists, supported by at least three Middle Eastern governments, employed the weapon of the weak and bombed Western planes and installations and seized Western hostages. This warfare between Arabs and the West culminated in 1990, when the United States sent a massive army to the Persian Gulf to defend some Arab countries against aggression by another. In its aftermath NATO planning is increasingly directed to potential threats and instability along its "southern tier."

This centuries-old military interaction between the West and Islam is unlikely to decline. It could become more virulent. The Gulf War left some Arabs feeling proud that Saddam Hussein had attacked Israel and stood up to

Western Christianity circa 1500

Orthodox Christianity and Islam

RUSSIA

FINLAND

SWEDEN

ESTONIA

LATVIA

LITHUANIA

BELA-RUSSIA

POLAND

CZECH REP.

UKRAINE

SLOVAKIA

SLOVENIA

HUNG.

MOLD.

CROATIA

ROMANIA

SERBIA

BULGARIA

MONTE-NEGRO

MACEDONIA

ALB.

ITALY

GREECE

TURKEY

Black Sea

N

0 ⊢——⊣ 200
MILES

Source: W. Wallace, *The Transformation of Western Europe* (London: Pinter, 1990). Map by Ib Ohlsson for *Foreign Affairs*.

the West. It also left many feeling humiliated and resentful of the West's military presence in the Persian Gulf, the West's overwhelming military dominance, and their apparent inability to shape their own destiny. Many Arab countries, in addition to the oil exporters, are reaching levels of economic and social development where autocratic forms of government become inappropriate and efforts to introduce democracy become stronger. Some openings in Arab political systems have already occurred. The principal beneficiaries of these openings have been Islamist movements. In the Arab world, in short, Western democracy strengthens anti-Western political forces. This may be a passing phenomenon, but it surely complicates relations between Islamic countries and the West.

Those relations are also complicated by demography. The spectacular population growth in Arab countries, particularly in North Africa, has led to increased migration to Western Europe. The movement within Western Europe toward minimizing internal boundaries has sharpened political sensitivities with respect to this development. In Italy, France and Germany, racism is increasingly open, and political reactions and violence against Arab and Turkish migrants have become more intense and more widespread since 1990.

On both sides the interaction between Islam and the West is seen as a clash of civilizations. The West's "next confrontation," observes M. J. Akbar, an Indian Muslim author, "is definitely going to come from the Muslim world. It is in the sweep of the Islamic nations from the Maghreb to Pakistan that the struggle for a new world order will begin." Bernard Lewis comes to a similar conclusion:

> We are facing a mood and a movement far transcending the level of issues and policies and the governments that pursue them. This is no less than a clash of civilizations—the perhaps irrational but surely historic reaction of an ancient rival against our Judeo-Christian heritage, our secular present, and the world-wide expansion of both.[2]

Historically, the other great antagonistic interaction of Arab Islamic civilization has been with the pagan, animist, and now increasingly

Christian black peoples to the south. In the past, this antagonism was epitomized in the image of Arab slave dealers and black slaves. It has been reflected in the on-going civil war in the Sudan between Arabs and blacks, the fighting in Chad between Libyan-supported insurgents and the government, the tensions between Orthodox Christians and Muslims in the Horn of Africa, and the political conflicts, recurring riots and communal violence between Muslims and Christians in Nigeria. The modernization of Africa and the spread of Christianity are likely to enhance the probability of violence along this fault line. Symptomatic of the intensification of this conflict was the Pope John Paul II's speech in Khartoum in February 1993 attacking the actions of the Sudan's Islamist government against the Christian minority there.

On the northern border of Islam, conflict has increasingly erupted between Orthodox and Muslim peoples, including the carnage of Bosnia and Sarajevo, the simmering violence between Serb and Albanian, the tenuous relations between Bulgarians and their Turkish minority, the violence between Ossetians and Ingush, the unremitting slaughter of each other by Armenians and Azeris, the tense relations between Russians and Muslims in Central Asia, and the deployment of Russian troops to protect Russian interests in the Caucasus and Central Asia. Religion reinforces the revival of ethnic identities and restimulates Russian fears about the security of their southern borders. This concern is well captured by Archie Roosevelt:

> Much of Russian history concerns the struggle between the Slavs and the Turkic peoples on their borders, which dates back to the foundation of the Russian state more than a thousand years ago. In the Slavs' millennium-long confrontation with their eastern neighbors lies the key to an understanding not only of Russian history, but Russian character. To understand Russian realities today one has to have a concept of the great Turkic ethnic group that has preoccupied Russians through the centuries.[3]

The conflict of civilizations is deeply rooted elsewhere in Asia. The historic clash between Muslim and Hindu in the subcontinent manifests itself now not only in the rivalry between Pakistan and India but also in intensifying religious strife within India between increasingly militant Hindu groups and India's substantial Muslim minority. The destruction of the Ayodhya mosque in December 1992 brought to the fore the issue of whether India will remain a secular democratic state or become a Hindu one. In East Asia, China has outstanding territorial disputes with most of its neighbors. It has pursued a ruthless policy toward the Buddhist people of Tibet, and it is pursuing an increasingly ruthless policy toward its Turkic-Muslim minority. With the Cold War over, the underlying differences between China and the United States have reasserted themselves in areas such as human rights, trade and weapons proliferation. These differences are unlikely to moderate. A "new cold war," Deng Xiaoping reportedly asserted in 1991, is underway between China and America.

The same phrase has been applied to the increasingly difficult relations between Japan and the United States. Here cultural difference exacerbates economic conflict. People on each side allege racism on the other, but at least on the American side the antipathies are not racial but cultural. The basic values, attitudes, behavioral patterns of the two societies could hardly be more different. The economic issues between the United States and Europe are no less serious than those between the United States and Japan, but they do not have the same political salience and emotional intensity because the differences between American culture and European culture are so much less than those between American civilization and Japanese civilization.

The interactions between civilizations vary greatly in the extent to which they are likely to be characterized by violence. Economic competition clearly predominates between the American and European subcivilizations of the West and between both of them and Japan. On the Eurasian continent, however, the proliferation of ethnic conflict, epitomized at the extreme in "ethnic cleansing," has not been totally random. It has been most frequent and most violent between groups belonging to different civilizations. In Eurasia the great historic fault lines between civilizations are once more aflame. This is particularly true along the boundaries of the crescent-shaped Islamic bloc of nations from the bulge of Africa to central Asia. Violence also occurs between Muslims, on the one hand, and Orthodox Serbs in the Balkans, Jews in Israel, Hindus in India, Buddhists in Burma and Catholics in the Philippines. Islam has bloody borders.

CIVILIZATION RALLYING: THE KIN-COUNTRY SYNDROME

Groups or states belonging to one civilization that become involved in war with people from a different civilization naturally try to rally support from other members of their own civilization. As the post-Cold War world evolves, civilization commonality, what H. D. S. Greenway has termed the "kin-country" syndrome, is replacing political ideology and traditional balance of power considerations as the principal basis for cooperation and coalitions. It can be seen gradually emerging in the post-Cold War conflicts in the Persian Gulf, the Caucasus and Bosnia. None of these was a full-scale war between civilizations, but each involved some elements of civilizational rallying, which seemed to become more important as the conflict continued and which may provide a foretaste of the future.

First, in the Gulf War one Arab state invaded another and then fought a coalition of Arab, Western and other states. While only a few Muslim governments overtly supported Saddam Hussein, many Arab elites privately cheered him on, and he was highly popular among large sections of the Arab publics. Islamic fundamentalist movements universally supported Iraq rather than the Western-backed governments of Kuwait and Saudi Arabia. Forswearing Arab nationalism, Saddam Hussein explicitly invoked an Islamic appeal. He and his supporters attempted to define the war as a war between civilizations. "It is not the world against Iraq," as Safar Al-Hawali, dean of Islamic Studies at the Umm Al-Qura University in Mecca, put it in a widely circulated tape. "It is the West against Islam." Ignoring the rivalry between Iran and Iraq, the chief Iranian religious leader, Ayatollah Ali Khamenei, called for a holy war against the West: "The struggle against American aggression, greed, plans and policies will be counted as a jihad, and anybody who is killed on that path is a martyr." "This is a war," King Hussein of Jordan argued, "against all Arabs and all Muslims and not against Iraq alone."

The rallying of substantial sections of Arab elites and publics behind Saddam Hussein caused those Arab governments in the anti-Iraq coalition to moderate their activities and temper their public statements. Arab governments opposed or distanced themselves from subsequent Western efforts to apply pressure on Iraq, including enforcement of a no-fly zone in the summer of 1992 and the bombing of Iraq in January 1993. The Western-Soviet-Turkish-Arab anti-Iraq coalition of 1990 had by 1993 become a coalition of almost only the West and Kuwait against Iraq.

Muslims contrasted Western actions against Iraq with the West's failure to protect Bosnians against Serbs and to impose sanctions on Israel for violating U.N. resolutions. The West, they alleged, was using a double standard. A world of clashing civilizations, however, is inevitably a world of double standards: people apply one standard to their kin-countries and a different standard to others.

Second, the kin-country syndrome also appeared in conflicts in the former Soviet Union. Armenian military successes in 1992 and 1993 stimulated Turkey to become increasingly supportive of its religious, ethnic and linguistic brethren in Azerbaijan. "We have a Turkish nation feeling the same sentiments as the Azerbaijanis," said one Turkish official in 1992. "We are under pressure. Our newspapers are full of the photos of atrocities and are asking us if we are still serious about pursuing our neutral policy. Maybe we should show Armenia that there's a big Turkey in the region." President Turgut Özal agreed, remarking that Turkey should at least "scare the Armenians a little bit." Turkey, Özal threatened again in 1993, would "show its fangs." Turkish Air Force jets flew reconnaissance flights along the Armenian border; Turkey suspended food shipments and air flights to Armenia; and Turkey and Iran announced they would not accept dismemberment of Azerbaijan. In the last years of its existence the Soviet government supported Azerbaijan because its government was dominated by former communists. With the end of the Soviet Union, however, political considerations gave way to religious ones. Russian troops fought on the side of the Armenians, and Azerbaijan accused the "Russian government of turning 180 degrees" toward support for Christian Armenia.

Third, with respect to the fighting in the former Yugoslavia, Western publics manifested sympathy and support for the Bosnian Muslims and the horrors they suffered at the hands of the Serbs. Relatively little concern was expressed, however, over Croatian attacks on Muslims, and participation in the dismemberment of Bosnia-Herzegovina. In the early stages of the Yugoslav breakup, Germany, in an unusual display of diplomatic initiative and muscle, induced the other 11 members of the European Community to follow its lead in recognizing Slovenia and Croatia. As a result of the Pope's determination to provide strong backing to the two Catholic countries, the Vatican extended recognition even before the Community did. The United States followed the European lead. Thus the leading actors in Western civilization rallied behind their coreligionists. Subsequently Croatia was reported to be receiving substantial quantities of arms from Central European and other Western countries. Boris Yeltsin's government, on the other hand, attempted to pursue a middle course that would be sympathetic to the Orthodox Serbs but not alienate Russia from the West. Russian conservative and nationalist groups, however, including many legislators, attacked the government for not being more forthcoming in its support for the Serbs. By early 1993 several hundred Russians apparently were serving with the Serbian forces, and reports circulated of Russian arms being supplied to Serbia.

Islamic governments and groups, on the other hand, castigated the West for not coming to the defense of the Bosnians. Iranian leaders urged Muslims from all countries to provide help to Bosnia; in violation of the U.N. arms embargo, Iran supplied weapons and men for the Bosnians; Iranian-supported Lebanese groups

sent guerrillas to train and organize the Bosnian forces. In 1993 up to 4,000 Muslims from over two dozen Islamic countries were reported to be fighting in Bosnia. The governments of Saudi Arabia and other countries felt under increasing pressure from fundamentalist groups in their own societies to provide more vigorous support for the Bosnians. By the end of 1992, Saudi Arabia had reportedly supplied substantial funding for weapons and supplies for the Bosnians, which significantly increased their military capabilities vis-à-vis the Serbs.

In the 1930s the Spanish Civil War provoked intervention from countries that politically were fascist, communist and democratic. In the 1990s the Yugoslav conflict is provoking intervention from countries that are Muslim, Orthodox and Western Christian. The parallel has not gone unnoticed. "The war in Bosnia-Herzegovina has become the emotional equivalent of the fight against fascism in the Spanish Civil War," one Saudi editor observed. "Those who died there are regarded as martyrs who tried to save their fellow Muslims."

Conflicts and violence will also occur between states and groups within the same civilization. Such conflicts, however, are likely to be less intense and less likely to expand than conflicts between civilizations. Common membership in a civilization reduces the probability of violence in situations where it might otherwise occur. In 1991 and 1992, many people were alarmed by the possibility of violent conflict between Russia and Ukraine over territory, particularly Crimea, the Black Sea fleet, nuclear weapons and economic issues. If civilization is what counts, however, the likelihood of violence between Ukrainians and Russians should be low. They are two Slavic, primarily Orthodox peoples who have had close relationships with each other for centuries. As of early 1993, despite all the reasons for conflict, the leaders of the two countries were effectively negotiating and defusing the issues between the two countries. While there has been serious fighting between Muslims and Christians elsewhere in the former Soviet Union and much tension and some fighting between Western and Orthodox Christians in the Baltic states, there has been virtually no violence between Russians and Ukrainians.

Civilization rallying to date has been limited, but it has been growing, and it clearly has the potential to spread much further. As the conflicts in the Persian Gulf, the Caucasus and Bosnia continued, the positions of nations and the cleavages between them increasingly were along civilizational lines. Populist politicians, religious leaders and the media have found it a potent means of arousing mass support and of pressuring hesitant governments. In the coming years, the local conflicts most likely to escalate into major wars will be those, as in Bosnia and the Caucasus, along the fault lines between civilizations. The next world war, if there is one, will be a war between civilizations.

THE WEST VERSUS THE REST

The West is now at an extraordinary peak of power in relation to other civilizations. Its superpower opponent has disappeared from the map. Military conflict among Western states is unthinkable, and Western military power is unrivaled. Apart from Japan, the West faces no economic challenge. It dominates international political and security institutions and with Japan international economic institutions. Global political and security issues are effectively settled by a directorate of the United States, Britain and France, world economic issues by a directorate of the United States, Germany and Japan, all of which maintain extraordinarily close relations with each other to the exclusion of lesser and largely non-Western countries. Decisions made at the U.N. Security Council or in the International Monetary Fund that reflect the interests of the West are presented to the world as reflecting the desires of the world community. The very phrase "the world community" has become the euphemistic collective noun (replacing "the Free World") to give global legitimacy to actions reflecting the interests of the United States and other Western powers.[4] Through the IMF and other international economic institutions, the West promotes its economic interests and imposes on other nations the economic policies it thinks appropriate. In any poll of non-Western peoples, the IMF undoubtedly would win the support of finance ministers and a few others, but get an overwhelmingly unfavorable rating from just about everyone else, who would agree with George Arbatov's characterization of IMF officials as "neo-Bolsheviks who love expropriating other people's money, imposing undemocratic and alien rules of economic and political conduct and stifling economic freedom."

Western domination of the U.N. Security Council and its decisions, tempered only by occasional abstention by China, produced U.N. legitimation of the West's use of force to drive Iraq out of Kuwait and its elimination of Iraq's sophisticated weapons and capacity to produce such weapons. It also produced the quite unprecedented action by the United States, Britain and France in getting the Security Council to demand that Libya hand over the Pan Am 103 bombing suspects and then to impose sanctions when Libya refused. After defeating the largest Arab army, the West did not hesitate to throw its weight around in the Arab world. The West in effect is using international institutions, military power and economic resources to run the world in ways that will maintain Western predominance, protect Western interests and promote Western political and economic values.

That at least is the way in which non-Westerners see the new world, and there is a significant element of truth in their view. Differences in power and struggles for military, economic and institutional power are thus one source of conflict between the West and other civilizations. Differences in culture, that is basic values and beliefs, are a second source of conflict. V. S. Naipaul has argued that Western civilization is the "universal civilization" that "fits all men." At a superficial level much of Western culture has indeed permeated the rest of the world. At a more basic level, however, Western concepts differ fundamentally from those prevalent in other civilizations. Western ideas of individualism, liberalism, constitutionalism, human rights, equality, liberty, the rule of law, democracy, free markets, the separation of church and state, often have little resonance in Islamic, Confucian, Japanese, Hindu, Buddhist or Orthodox cultures. Western efforts to propagate such ideas produce instead a reaction against "human rights imperialism" and a reaffirmation of indigenous values, as can be seen in the support for religious fundamentalism by the younger generation in non-Western cultures. The very notion that there could be a "universal civilization" is a Western idea, directly at odds with the particularism of most Asian societies and their emphasis on what distinguishes one people from another. Indeed, the author of a review of 100 comparative studies of values in different societies concluded that "the values that are most important in the West are least important worldwide."[5] In the political realm, of course, these differences are most manifest in the efforts of the United States and other Western powers to induce other peoples to adopt Western ideas concerning democracy and human rights. Modern democratic government originated in the West. When it has developed in non-Western societies it has usually been the product of Western colonialism or imposition.

The central axis of world politics in the future is likely to be, in Kishore Mahbubani's phrase, the conflict between "the West and the Rest" and the responses of non-Western civilizations to Western power and values.[6] Those responses generally take one or a combination of three forms. At one extreme, non-Western states can, like Burma and North Korea, attempt to pursue a course of isolation, to insulate their societies from penetration or "corruption" by the West, and, in effect, to opt out of participation in the Western-dominated global community. The costs of this course, however, are high, and few states have pursued it exclusively. A second alternative, the equivalent of "band-wagoning" in international relations theory, is to attempt to join the West and accept its values and institutions. The third alternative is to attempt to "balance" the West by developing economic and military power and cooperating with other non-Western societies against the West, while preserving indigenous values and institutions; in short, to modernize but not to Westernize.

THE TORN COUNTRIES

In the future, as people differentiate themselves by civilization, countries with large numbers of peoples of different civilizations, such as the Soviet Union and Yugoslavia, are candidates for dismemberment. Some other countries have a fair degree of cultural homogeneity but are divided over whether their society belongs to one civilization or another. These are torn countries. Their leaders typically wish to pursue a bandwagoning strategy and to make their countries members of the West, but the history, culture and traditions of their countries are non-Western. The most obvious and prototypical torn country is Turkey. The late twentieth-century leaders of Turkey have followed in the Attatürk tradition and defined Turkey as a modern, secular, Western nation state. They allied Turkey with the West in NATO and in the Gulf War; they applied for membership in the European Community. At the same time, however, elements in Turkish society have supported an Islamic revival and have argued that Turkey is basically a Middle Eastern Muslim society. In addition, while the elite of Turkey has defined Turkey as a Western society, the elite of the West refuses to accept Turkey as such. Turkey will not become a member of the European Community, and the real reason, as President Özal said, "is that we are Muslim and they are Christian and they don't say that." Having rejected Mecca, and then being rejected by Brussels, where does Turkey look? Tashkent may be the answer. The end of the Soviet Union gives Turkey the opportunity to become the leader of a revived Turkic civilization involving seven countries from the borders of Greece to those of China. Encouraged by the West, Turkey is making strenuous efforts to carve out this new identity for itself.

During the past decade Mexico has assumed a position somewhat similar to that of Turkey. Just as Turkey abandoned its historic opposition to Europe and attempted to join Europe, Mexico has stopped defining itself by its opposition to the United States and is instead attempting to imitate the United States and to join it in the North American Free Trade Area. Mexican leaders are engaged in the great task of redefining Mexican identity and have introduced fundamental economic reforms that eventually will lead to fundamental political change. In 1991 a top adviser to President Carlos Salinas de Gortari described at length to me all the changes the Salinas government was making. When he finished, I remarked: "That's most impressive. It seems to me that basically you want to change Mexico from a Latin American country into a North American country." He looked at me with surprise and exclaimed: "Exactly! That's precisely what we are trying to do, but of course we could never say so publicly." As his remark indicates, in Mexico as in Turkey, significant elements in society resist the redefinition of their country's identity. In Turkey, European-oriented leaders have to make gestures to Islam (Özal's pilgrimage to Mecca); so also Mexico's North American-oriented leaders have to make gestures to those who hold Mexico to be a Latin American country (Salinas' Ibero-American Guadalajara summit).

Historically Turkey has been the most profoundly torn country. For the United States, Mexico is the most immediate torn country. Globally the most important torn country is Russia. The question of whether Russia is part of the West or the leader of a distinct Slavic-Orthodox civilization has been a recurring one in Russian history. That issue was obscured by the communist victory in Russia, which imported a Western ideology, adapted it to Russian conditions and then challenged the West in the name of that ideology. The dominance of communism shut off the historic debate over Westernization versus Russification. With communism discredited Russians once again face that question.

President Yeltsin is adopting Western principles and goals and seeking to make Russia a "normal" country and a part of the West. Yet both the Russian elite and the Russian public are divided on this issue. Among the more moderate dissenters, Sergei Stankevich argues that Russia should reject the "Atlanticist" course, which would lead it "to become European, to become a part of the world economy in rapid and organized fashion, to become the eighth member of the Seven, and to put particular emphasis on Germany and the United States as the two dominant members of the Atlantic alliance." While also rejecting an exclusively Eurasian policy, Stankevich nonetheless argues that Russia should give priority to the protection of Russians in other countries, emphasize its Turkic and Muslim connections, and promote "an appreciable redistribution of our resources, our options, our

ties, and our interests in favor of Asia, of the eastern direction." People of this persuasion criticize Yeltsin for subordinating Russia's interests to those of the West, for reducing Russian military strength, for failing to support traditional friends such as Serbia, and for pushing economic and political reform in ways injurious to the Russian people. Indicative of this trend is the new popularity of the ideas of Petr Savitsky, who in the 1920s argued that Russia was a unique Eurasian civilization.[7] More extreme dissidents voice much more blatantly nationalist, anti-Western and anti-Semitic views, and urge Russia to redevelop its military strength and to establish closer ties with China and Muslim countries. The people of Russia are as divided as the elite. An opinion survey in European Russia in the spring of 1992 revealed that 40 percent of the public had positive attitudes toward the West and 36 percent had negative attitudes. As it has been for much of its history, Russia in the early 1990s is truly a torn country.

To redefine its civilization identity, a torn country must meet three requirements. First, its political and economic elite has to be generally supportive of and enthusiastic about this move. Second, its public has to be willing to acquiesce in the redefinition. Third, the dominant groups in the recipient civilization have to be willing to embrace the convert. All three requirements in large part exist with respect to Mexico. The first two in large part exist with respect to Turkey. It is not clear that any of them exist with respect to Russia's joining the West. The conflict between liberal democracy and Marxism-Leninism was between ideologies which, despite their major differences, ostensibly shared ultimate goals of freedom, equality and prosperity. A traditional, authoritarian, nationalist Russia could have quite different goals. A Western democrat could carry on an intellectual debate with a Soviet Marxist. It would be virtually impossible for him to do that with a Russian traditionalist. If, as the Russians stop behaving like Marxists, they reject liberal democracy and begin behaving like Russians but not like Westerners, the relations between Russia and the West could again become distant and conflictual.[8]

THE CONFUCIAN-ISLAMIC CONNECTION

The obstacles to non-Western countries joining the West vary considerably. They are least for Latin American and East European countries. They are greater for the Orthodox countries of the former Soviet Union. They are still greater for Muslim, Confucian, Hindu and Buddhist societies. Japan has established a unique position for itself as an associate member of the West: it is in the West in some respects but clearly not of the West in important dimensions. Those countries that for reason of culture and power do not wish to, or cannot, join the West compete with the West by developing their own economic, military and political power. They do this by promoting their internal development and by cooperating with other non-Western countries. The most prominent form of this cooperation is the Confucian-Islamic connection that has emerged to challenge Western interests, values and power.

Almost without exception, Western countries are reducing their military power; under Yeltsin's leadership so also is Russia. China, North Korea and several Middle Eastern states, however, are significantly expanding their military capabilities. They are doing this by the import of arms from Western and non-Western sources and by the development of indigenous arms industries. One result is the emergence of what Charles Krauthammer has called "Weapon States," and the Weapon States are not Western states. Another result is the redefinition of arms control, which is a Western concept and a Western goal. During the Cold War the primary purpose of arms control was to establish a stable military balance between the United States and its allies and the Soviet Union and its allies. In the post-Cold War world the primary objective of arms control is to prevent the development by non-Western societies of military capabilities that could threaten Western interests. The West attempts to do this through international agreements, economic pressure and controls on the transfer of arms and weapons technologies.

The conflict between the West and the Confucian-Islamic states focuses largely, although not exclusively, on nuclear, chemical and biological weapons, ballistic missiles and other sophisticated means for delivering them, and the guidance, intelligence and other electronic capabilities for achieving that goal. The West promotes nonproliferation as a universal norm and nonproliferation treaties and inspections as means of realizing that norm. It also threatens a variety of sanctions against those who promote the spread of sophisticated weapons and proposes some benefits for those who do not. The attention of the West focuses, naturally, on nations that are actually or potentially hostile to the West.

The non-Western nations, on the other hand, assert their right to acquire and to deploy whatever weapons they think necessary for their security. They also have absorbed, to the full, the truth of the response of the Indian defense minister when asked what lesson he learned from the Gulf War: "Don't fight the United States unless you have nuclear weapons." Nuclear weapons, chemical weapons and missiles are viewed, probably erroneously, as the potential equalizer of superior Western conventional power. China, of course, already has nuclear weapons; Pakistan and India have the capability to deploy them. North Korea, Iran, Iraq, Libya and Algeria appear to be attempting to acquire them. A top Iranian official has declared that all Muslim states should acquire nuclear weapons, and in 1988 the president of Iran reportedly issued a directive calling for development of "offensive and defensive chemical, biological and radiological weapons."

Centrally important to the development of counter-West military capabilities is the sustained expansion of China's military power and its means to create military power. Buoyed by spectacular economic development, China is rapidly increasing its military spending and vigorously moving forward with the modernization of its armed forces. It is purchasing weapons from the former Soviet states; it is developing long-range missiles; in 1992 it tested a one-megaton nuclear device. It is developing power-projection capabilities, acquiring aerial refueling technology, and trying to purchase an aircraft carrier. Its military buildup and assertion of sovereignty over the South

China Sea are provoking a multilateral regional arms race in East Asia. China is also a major exporter of arms and weapons technology. It has exported materials to Libya and Iraq that could be used to manufacture nuclear weapons and nerve gas. It has helped Algeria build a reactor suitable for nuclear weapons research and production. China has sold to Iran nuclear technology that American officials believe could only be used to create weapons and apparently has shipped components of 300-mile-range missiles to Pakistan. North Korea has had a nuclear weapons program underway for some while and has sold advanced missiles and missile technology to Syria and Iran. The flow of weapons and weapons technology is generally from East Asia to the Middle East. There is, however, some movement in the reverse direction; China has received Stinger missiles from Pakistan.

A Confucian-Islamic military connection has thus come into being, designed to promote acquisition by its members of the weapons and weapons technologies needed to counter the military power of the West. It may or may not last. At present, however, it is, as Dave McCurdy has said, "a renegades' mutual support pact, run by the proliferators and their backers." A new form of arms competition is thus occurring between Islamic-Confucian states and the West. In an old-fashioned arms race, each side developed its own arms to balance or to achieve superiority against the other side. In this new form of arms competition, one side is developing its arms and the other side is attempting not to balance but to limit and prevent that arms build-up while at the same time reducing its own military capabilities.

IMPLICATIONS FOR THE WEST

This article does not argue that civilization identities will replace all other identities, that nation states will disappear, that each civilization will become a single coherent political entity, that groups within a civilization will not conflict with and even fight each other. This paper does set forth the hypotheses that differences between civilizations are real and important; civilization-consciousness is in-creasing; conflict between civilizations will supplant ideological and other forms of conflict as the dominant global form of conflict; international relations, historically a game played out within Western civilization, will increasingly be de-Westernized and become a game in which non-Western civilizations are actors and not simply objects; successful political, security and economic international institutions are more likely to develop within civilizations than across civilizations; conflicts between groups in different civilizations will be more frequent, more sustained and more violent than conflicts between groups in the same civilization; violent conflicts between groups in different civilizations are the most likely and most dangerous source of escalation that could lead to global wars; the paramount axis of world politics will be the relations between "the West and the Rest"; the elites in some torn non-Western countries will try to make their countries part of the West, but in most cases face major obstacles to accomplishing this; a central focus of conflict for the immediate future will be between the West and several Islamic-Confucian states.

This is not to advocate the desirability of conflicts between civilizations. It is to set forth descriptive hypotheses as to what the future may be like. If these are plausible hypotheses, however, it is necessary to consider their implications for Western policy. These implications should be divided between short-term advantage and long-term accommodation. In the short term it is clearly in the interest of the West to promote greater cooperation and unity within its own civilization, particularly between its European and North American components; to incorporate into the West societies in Eastern Europe and Latin America whose cultures are close to those of the West; to promote and maintain cooperative relations with Russia and Japan; to prevent escalation of local inter-civilization conflicts into major inter-civilization wars; to limit the expansion of the military strength of Confucian and Islamic states; to moderate the reduction of Western military capabilities and maintain military superiority in East and Southwest Asia; to exploit differences and conflicts among Confucian and Islamic states; to support in other civilizations groups sympathetic to Western values and interests; to strengthen international institutions that reflect and legitimate Western interests and values and to promote the involvement of non-Western states in those institutions.

In the longer term other measures would be called for. Western civilization is both Western and modern. Non-Western civilizations have attempted to become modern without becoming Western. To date only Japan has fully succeeded in this quest. Non-Western civilizations will continue to attempt to acquire the wealth, technology, skills, machines and weapons that are part of being modern. They will also attempt to reconcile this modernity with their traditional culture and values. Their economic and military strength relative to the West will increase. Hence the West will increasingly have to accommodate these non-Western modern civilizations whose power approaches that of the West but whose values and interests differ significantly from those of the West. This will require the West to maintain the economic and military power necessary to protect its interests in relation to these civilizations. It will also, however, require the West to develop a more profound understanding of the basic religious and philosophical assumptions underlying other civilizations and the ways in which people in those civilizations see their interests. It will require an effort to identify elements of commonality between Western and other civilizations. For the relevant future, there will be no universal civilization, but instead a world of different civilizations, each of which will have to learn to coexist with the others.

ENDNOTES

[1] Murray Weidenbaum, *Greater China: The Next Economic Superpower?* St. Louis: Washington University Center for the Study of American Business, Contemporary Issues, Series 57, February 1993, 2–3.

[2] Bernard Lewis, "The Roots of Muslim Rage," *The Atlantic Monthly*, vol. 266, September 1990, 60; *Time*, June 15, 1992, 24–28.

[3] Archie Roosevelt, *For Lust of Knowing* (Boston; Little, Brown and Company, 1988), 332–333.

[4] Almost invariably Western leaders claim they are acting on behalf of "the world community." One minor lapse occurred during the run-up to the Gulf War. In an interview on "Good Morning America," Dec. 21, 1990, British Prime Minister John Major referred to the actions "the West" was taking against Saddam Hussein. He quickly corrected himself and subsequently referred to "the world community." He was, however, right when he erred.

[5] Harry C. Triandis, *The New York Times*, Dec. 25, 1990, 41, and "Cross-Cultural Studies of Individualism and Collectivism," Nebraska Symposium on Motivation, vol. 37, 1989, 41–133.

[6] Kishore Mahbubani, "The West and the Rest," *The National Interest*, Summer 1992, 3–13.

[7] Sergei Stankevich, "Russia in Search of Itself," *The National Interest,* Summer 1992, 47–51; Daniel Schneider, "A Russian Movement Rejects Western Tilt," *Christian Science Monitor,* 5 February 1993, 5–7.

[8] Owen Harries has pointed out that Australia is trying (unwisely in his view) to become a torn country in reverse. Although it has been a full member not only of the West but also of the ABCA military and intelligence core of the West, its current leaders are in effect proposing that it defect from the West, redefine itself as an Asian country and cultivate close ties with its neighbors. Australia's future, they argue, is with the dynamic economies of East Asia. But, as I have suggested, close economic cooperation normally requires a common cultural base. In addition, none of the three conditions necessary for a torn country to join another civilization is likely to exist in Australia's case.

63

Fault Lines

Michael Ignatieff

A few years ago in an influential article in *Foreign Affairs,* Samuel P. Huntington, the Harvard political scientist and foreign policy aide to President Jimmy Carter, and before that reputedly one of the architects of the "strategic hamlets" policy in Vietnam, proposed that the war of political systems, ideologies and interests was over and the war of cultures had begun. The tectonic states of the emerging world order were seven or eight civilizations—Western, Eastern Orthodox, Latin American, Islamic, Japanese, Chinese, Hindu and ("possibly") African.

Africa was listed as only a possible civilization because it was divided into Islamic and non-Islamic components, as well as Saharan and sub-Saharan. Jewish civilization was another possibility. Although in the end Mr. Huntington lined the Jews up with the so-called Judeo-Christian heritage of the West. Given the interpenetration of civilizations, these boxes were bound to be a little fuzzy at the edges, But this problem aside, the Huntington thesis did make the insightful claim that the real actors to watch on the international stage were no longer states or even resurgent ethnicities but the civilizational identities built on the religious empires of the past.

"Realistic" analysts of international affairs had neglected these deeply buried religious allegiances during the cold war. Now they were returning with a vengeance, and Mr. Huntington was among the first to argue that it was not at all the violence in the post-cold war world but the ancient civilizational antagonisms.

Thus, American policy makers should not have been surprised by the savagery and longevity of Russia's difficulty in Chechnya; it was never just a secessionist conflict but a battle to the death between Orthodoxy and Islam on the fault line between the two civilizations. Similarly, the Yugoslav conflict was a civilizational war among Orthodoxy and Islam. Had the Bush Administration understood this, it might have tried to arrange a peaceful divorce instead of trying to keep the federation together.

However welcome the Huntington emphasis on tradition, culture and religion after the grindingly narrow emphasis among "realists" on state interests, there are problems with the idea that most modern conflict is civilizational. Some of the worst wars in human history have occurred not between civilizations but within them. Common civilizational ties did not prevent Europeans from slaughtering one another between 1914 and 1945. Moreover, in a place like the former Yugoslavia, civilizational differences over religion were more a pretext for war than a cause. Religious quarrels were fading away until nationalist elites fanned them into flames.

In expanding the *Foreign Affairs* article into "The Clash of Civilizations and the Remaking of World Order," Mr. Huntington has thickened out his argument, but it remains controversial. If there are seven or eight world civilizations, he says, the West had better shed the hubristic notion that its civilization is destined to spread its values across the globe. The West is "unique"—but its values are not universal. Universalism, Mr. Huntington maintains, is just a leftover from imperialism. Western aid workers have no business telling the Afghan Taliban to allow their women to go to school. Washington has no business tying human rights conditions to its trade with China. It is a significant change of heart for a former architect of American policy in Vietnam to assert that "Western intervention in the affairs of other civilizations is probably the single most dangerous source of instability and potential global conflict in a multi-civilizational world."

Michael Ignatieff's most recent book is *Blood and Belonging: Journeys into the New Nationalism.*

This was a review of Samuel P. Huntington's *The Clash of Civilization and the Remaking of World Order* published in *The New York Times Book Review,* 1 December 1996, 13.

But Western intervention is not just dangerous, Mr. Huntington argues, it is also useless. Civilizational wars, like that between Islam and Orthodoxy on Russia's southern frontier, aren't susceptible to Western mediation: they've smoldered for centuries and are likely to keep on doing so. "The first requirement of peace in a multicivilizational, multi-polar world," Mr. Huntington writes, is the "abstention rule": that "core states abstain from intervention in conflicts in other civilizations." The West should stay out of any conflict between China and Japan; Islam should stay out of conflicts in Europe, even on behalf of Islamic minorities there.

While the West should pursue "commonalities"—shared values and interests—with other civilizations, it should discard the chief moral fiction of post-1945 liberal internationalism: the belief that cultural difference is secondary and common human interests are primary. An allied liberal delusion, in Mr. Huntington's view, is the promotion of multicultural policies both at home and abroad. American liberals were self-deluded to think a multi-ethnic Bosnia was defensible; in reality there could never be peace between the region's Christians and Muslims. The underlying problem is not "fundamentalism," Mr. Huntington baldly asserts. The core values of even moderate Islam are antithetical to the rights-based individualism of the West.

Instead of intervening in the civilizational wars of others or believing that its values and products are exportable around the globe, Mr. Huntington argues that the West should come home to its own moral disarray and begin setting its own house in order. Its relative decline vis-à-vis the rising civilizations of China and Japan is bound to increase, he warns, unless we reassert pride in our core values, teach them to our children and halt the slide into crime, hedonism and the queasy moral relativism that accompanies the spread of multiculturalism. Instead of diluting our values further by accommodating the traditions of Hispanic and Asian immigrants, the United States—as the core state of the West—must reassert its essential European and Judeo-Christian heritage.

Mr. Huntington seems to be arguing that the resurgence of civilizational identities may be all right for foreigners, but if it begins to spread among Mexican-, Chinese-, Japanese-, Cuban-, or Haitian-Americans it had better be stopped. But if every other multi-ethnic, multicultural state is doomed to fracture into its component ethnic parts, why should the United States miraculously hold the Jeffersonian line?

And the question is not only whether it can, but whether it should. Mr. Huntington never clearly specifies when the right to cultural difference—which is what the United States is surely all about—shades into moral decline. He is deeply unclear about what conditions of cultural coherence and consensus are actually compatible with the convulsive changes that accompany modern life. His ruling assumptions are profoundly conservative and static. His civilizations are unified, self-contained compartments, not the promiscuously interacting, heterogeneous and constantly changing amoebas we know them to be.

Mr. Huntington neglects the clash of values, interests and traditions within civilizations—clashes, for example, that divide Europe and the United States. From the Suez crisis of 1956 through the Allies' disarray over Bosnia, civilizational commonalities across the North Atlantic have not been able to trump sharp differences of national interest and national tradition. Likewise, he drastically understates the divisions within Islam. The war in Afghanistan began as a battle between Russian and Islamic civilization: it has turned into a war within Islam, between Sunnis and Shiites, city Muslims and rural ones, with at least four regional Islamic powers—Pakistan, Iran, Tajikistan, Uzbekistan—fighting for hegemony there. Mr. Huntington's brush is too broad for these subtler shades in the mottled map of world conflict.

This said, the Huntington argument that the West should stop intervening in civilizational conflicts it doesn't understand makes a powerful claim internationalists cannot easily ignore. The question is whether there remain certain human interests that all civilizations had better endorse for our common survival. Genocide is genocide, famine is famine, and a world where civilizations no longer intervene to save strangers from these universal threats is one that not even Samuel P. Huntington would feel safe in.

64

Missing the Message

Juan Williams

Black comedian Eddie Murphy once powdered his face white and set out to discover how the other half—the white half—really lives. In a hilarious "Saturday Night Live" sketch, a white shopkeeper insists on giving the powder-white Eddie a free newspaper when they are alone, and a party breaks out among whites on a commuter bus when the last black person gets off.

The gap between black and white has been the stuff of comedy for years, bringing fame to performers from Dick Gregory to Murphy and Richard Pryor. But to Thomas Kochman, an anthropologist at the University of Illinois at Chicago, differences between blacks and whites are a subject of serious study—and he thinks they are no laughing matter.

The German-born Kochman, a 49-year-old linguist, sociologist and former welfare case-worker, is fascinated by the differences. He believes blacks and whites have sharply contrasting approaches to important issues from politics to power to sex and often fail to recognize it—which leads to misunderstandings between individuals and to what he sees as a growing divergence between the black and white communities.

A Kochman example:

Jesse Jackson is speaking at a political rally and starts out chanting, "I AM SOMEBODY!" Kochman sees whites in the audience frown. He feels himself pull back.

Reprinted from *The Washington Post*, 9 February 1985, 1, 8 (B). Copyright © 1985, The Washington Post.

"I can't believe that academics, black colleagues of mine, can stand up and start shouting, clapping," Kochman says. "In my gut I'm shocked. I'm not used to being brought into a scene that way."

He suggests that a white audience equates emotional involvement with loss of control; such scenes raise the specter of demagoguery to whites—they suspect a highly charged speaker is trying to manipulate them.

From the black perspective, he says, the impact is very different.

"The sister who faints at the Baptist revival never seems to lose her glasses, so how much control is lost?" he says, adding that blacks are accustomed to dealing with high-energy speakers and are able to look beyond the style to the substance of the message.

"Whether spirited speaking can be manipulated beyond blacks' ability to control it doesn't concern blacks—it concerns whites who make the ethnocentric judgment that to be emotionally involved with a speaker is to be manipulated," he says.

He points out that posters of Martin Luther King Jr., Malcolm X, Louis Farrakhan and Jackson most often show them with their mouths open, hands extended, emphasizing some point in a speech.

"To blacks that says the man in the picture is powerful, strong, seeking truth by emotionally engaging ideas, taking them on," says Kochman. "Whites have a different perspective . . . they see themselves being harangued."

Chicago Mayor Harold Washington, who feels he has been misunderstood by his city's whites, especially the press, distributed copies of Kochman's book "Black and White Styles in Conflict" to the city hall press corps.

"A careful study of the news coverage of the mayoral campaign and of this administration over the past two years demonstrates the need for all reporters to read this book," the mayor told the journalists, according to Chicago newspapers.

Detroit Mayor Coleman Young sent Kochman a letter telling him he felt his book explained a lot of Young's problems with whites in Detroit.

Kochman's theory is that blacks have a "high offense, high defense" culture, in which aggressive language, cocky behavior and florid clothing are not only accepted but enjoyed as a source of power that "feeds" life. Blacks are able to handle the brashness of such language or behavior in others without losing control or being overwhelmed.

White Americans, in Kochman's view, generally contain differences and anger as well as styles of speech and dress so as not to impose on each other. As a result whites feel threatened or disturbed by displays of anger or ostentatious dress.

For example, he says, blacks make a distinction between arguing and fighting that whites do not. For blacks, verbal confrontation can go a long way before physical confrontation is threatened. "The extreme of arguing is 'woofing,' like Ali and Fraser, like the Black Panthers and Louis Farrakhan," Kochman says.

"Whites hear the same words from the same people and think; Fight, danger. Blacks understand woofing is going on. Whites think fight before blacks think fight."

He says, however, that in this case his definition of "white" really applies most to the white Protestant tradition. Ethnic whites, particularly Jews, Irish and Italians, often "love to argue, love to boast and joke," he says. "It is the difference between self-contained cultures and expressive cultures as much as black and white."

The differences apply to private matters as well as to public ones.

Kochman cites the case of a young black woman who complained that a white coworker had put his hand on her thigh after lunch one day without first broaching the subject of his sexual interest.

"Why did he have to be so damn sneaky?" Kochman says she asked.

Yet, he says, from the white perspective there was nothing sneaky about it. The man had offered her rides home, had discussed business projects with her, talked about TV shows and current events, taken her to lunch and often paid the bill. Then came the touching.

"If she had been white the sexual interest would have been implied by his actions," says Kochman, adding that an open discussion of sex would have been considered offensive and

pushy. For the black woman, however, an honest discussion would have been preferable to the approach the man took. "To a black woman it is not offensive to have her sexuality acknowledged," he says.

According to Kochman's schematic a black male's more aggressive, verbal approach would have been easier for the black woman to deal with because she would have recognized it as sexual interest and been able to accept or reject appropriately. The more subtle white approach slipped under her radar.

Kochman, a lanky, loose-jointed man with a casual manner, grew up in upper Manhattan. He has never lived in a black neighborhood.

Yet he finds himself teaching blacks and whites about black cultural signals and concedes it makes for tense situations when blacks find themselves being lectured about themselves by a white.

"At one point," he says, "there was a strong sense that I was an interloper in this field. Now I'm accepted as an anomaly. . . ."

While teaching at the Northeastern Illinois University's Center for Inner City Studies, he remembers facing a class of 39 black men and women earning their master's degrees in urban education, wondering what this "white boy" was going to tell them about their language.

Two years later, feeling growing tension from black students, he gave up that professorship, handing a course in black English to a black teacher. He began his work as a communications professor at the University of Illinois in 1970. His classes are generally 70 percent white.

He came to this career after working for a year for the New York City welfare department investigating clients' eligibility, a job that took him into black neighborhoods. In 1966 he got a summer job collecting black idiomatic expressions in the Bronx for a study on the "Idiom of the Negro Ghetto."

Fascinated by the work, he went to the Center for Inner City Studies for more work on black American life. That led to his doctorate from New York University in linguistics and sociology. He moved into anthropology as he began to compile and dissect the cultural differences between blacks and whites.

Kochman said he works by observing life in black neighborhoods, among black students and colleagues, and by building networks for interviews and field work among his black contacts.

He acknowledges his ideas have been slow to be accepted in academic circles. The orthodox view, he says, is that blacks have no separate culture, and that differences between black and white behavior are due to the effects of discrimination and poverty on black families.

That approach, he argues, has led not only whites but blacks to assume that discussing differences between them would lead to the conclusion that black behavior is inferior.

"It's the politeness conspiracy," says Kochman, "and it leaves many prejudices in place."

Kochman says his worst moments come when middle-class blacks, interpreting his work as an attempt to show them inferior to whites because they are different, react by saying, "I've never seen blacks act like that."

"That makes whites wonder if I know what the hell I'm talking about," says Kochman. "At that point I have to rely on other black people, even some whites, to say they know the reality I'm referring to but they've never put it into thoughts and words: Black people and white people act differently."

Kochman is now studying how black-white differences affect politics, as part of a broader look at "mainstreaming," or bringing different ethnic and cultural styles together in the American melting pot.

Cultural differences, he says, culminate in the growing divide between black and white political perspectives. The split was highlighted by the last presidential election, when about 90 percent of blacks voting opposed President Reagan while roughly 65 percent of whites voting cast ballots for him, according to an ABC news exit poll.

The heart of the difference in selecting national leaders, according to Kochman, is that blacks treasure boldness and audacity as signs of leadership ability, while in "mainstream American politics," boldness and audacity are taken to mean an individual is not stable, not a team player.

Similar differences in approach extend to black and white professional situations, according to Kochman, and as a result, good workers with the best of intentions often end up at odds when one is black and one is white.

Blacks value confrontation in an office setting as well as at home, Kochman says, as a way of "truth-seeking." To blacks a colleague who will not confront another colleague about a problem is not concerned—they feel he does not attach importance to either the problem or the other person involved.

But whites, Kochman said, find confrontations and arguments a sign of disunity or conflict in the office. Whites interpret black desire to dispute differences as a troublesome habit even as blacks see it as evidence of caring about producing the best work.

One of Kochman's examples of conflict in the office occurs when two white managers are talking as a black colleague approaches. The two whites finish their conversation before greeting the colleague. The black person considers this behavior to be rude and is angered before he says anything. This creates distance and tension between the black and the whites. Kochman believes a group of blacks would typically interrupt their conversation to acknowledge a person approaching the group.

This tension results from the practice of whites emphasizing subject matter over personal relationships versus blacks' favoring personal relationship over subject matter.

"That's a cultural clash, a difference in styles," says Kochman. "And it leaves both people offended, and puzzled because they don't appreciate the other cultural perspective."

Kochman argues that cultural differences often confuse attempts to deal with racism on both sides. In his book he cites the example of blacks condemning racist whites before a racially mixed group. Some whites in the group feel uncomfortable and begin to defend themselves as not racists.

"To blacks that itself is evidence that they are racists," says Kochman, "because in black culture a person may speak generally without directing his remarks against the people who are listening. But if those people start to react as if it's about them—the old saying is 'if the shoe fits, wear it.'"

Recognizing cultural differences may improve understanding, but Kochman acknowledges that this isn't always enough to overcome prejudice. "If a person doesn't know the difference in cultures, that's ignorance," he says. "But if a person knows the difference and still says that the mainstream culture is best, that 'white is right,' then you've got racism."

65

International Negotiation: Cross-Cultural Perception

Glen Fisher

The process of negotiating internationally is assuming ever greater importance for all of us, whether treating large or small matters. As our real world becomes a more and more interdependent one, a larger range of problems that heretofore might have been resolved domestically now have to be negotiated internationally. Therefore, the questions for the concerned citizen include: what difference does it make when negotiators and their general publics reflect contrasting national experiences, cultures, and patterns of thinking, and how well are we addressing this special dimension in conducting world affairs?

Too often, if we follow the international negotiation process at all, we focus primarily on substance, tactics, strategy, the obvious interests to be served. But after all, negotiation is a study in social psychology—but in the international case, a study that must also include the psychology of cross-cultural communication. As people turn to dealing across national boundaries, it becomes less likely that even the most cosmopolitan negotiators will reason from the same starting assumptions, the same images of the world, or even the same patterns of logic. Ultimately, in understanding any negotiation process, one needs to anticipate how the issue will in fact be per-

Reprinted from *The Humanist* 43 (November/ December 1983): 14–18. Reprinted by permission of Glen Fisher, Monterey Institute of International Studies.

ceived. The new challenge is to enter the cross-cultural factor into the equation.

One might recall certain essentials of perceiving and responding. We know that people do not react to events and issues on the basis of some empirical reality but on the basis of their *images* of it—which almost always will be something a bit different. We like to think in our scientific age that our enlightened images of what is going on will coincide with reality. But psychologists insist that our perceptual habits are locked in much more than we usually realize and that, as our mental computers are programmed to add context and meaning to that which our senses receive, we tend to perceive the world and its events as we expect it to appear.

A brief classroom-type example of physical perception illustrates the points. A group is asked to describe the shape of a table top located in the corner of the room. All agree that it is rectangular. Yet there would be no rectangle on the retina of any eye in the room— no one would be so positioned to actually see a rectangle. But everyone there has had a lot of experience with table tops and with right angles. So the mind of each supplies what the retina cannot, and the table top is perceived as a rectangle. In fact, this perceptual habit is so locked in that it becomes almost impossible to perceive anything else if in fact the top were not rectangular. This, of course, is the basis for the fun and games that psychologists pursue in optical illusions.

This ability to add to the picture is handy; it would be awkward to have to position oneself so that a full rectangle could be perceived each time the object came to one's attention. When events and issues are more abstract, when they include ideas, beliefs, plans, and institutions, the need to add meaning from the data and experience banks of the mind is all the greater. And effective meaning is all the more subject to experiential differences such as those that are supplied by being socialized in varying cultures and circumstances. Because it is normal to take much of this programming for granted when it is learned largely out of awareness, it is also normal to project this same "common sense" onto others with whom one is interacting. When the interaction is cross-national, the chances for error, for misperceptions, or for misattributing motives increase enormously. All this strikes at the very heart of international negotiation. Yet it is the subject of relatively little studied analysis.

CULTURAL PREDISPOSITION

Do cultural predispositions really count? Actually, it is difference in cultural traditions or belief systems such as religion that often is the issue, as in the Middle East. But the international observer who is tuned to look for it can often find enough havoc played by less obvious cultural conflict to cause concern for our competence in bridging it. For example, cultural conditioning enters into American-Japanese business negotiation. Americans feel comfortable with lawyers, precise contractual arrangements, and legal remedies; Japanese consider the need for lawyers an unfortunate fallback solution when trust and sincerity fail to sustain a business relationship. Thus, even when a contract is signed, the subjective meaning and the assumptions regarding performance can be at least a few degrees out of synchronization.

I recall the prolonged debate that took place regarding the fall session agenda as the United Nations General Assembly organized one September when I was a junior member of the U.S. delegation. The General Assembly had to decide what issues to include, what they would be titled, and to what committee they would be assigned. The American delegation had a hard time getting very interested in prolonged detailed negotiation on all these matters after the basic decision was reached to include a given item at all. Once that was decided, they did not care very much what the issue was called; they were pragmatic on assignment to committees. Not so the Latin Americans, the French, the Russians, or the Indians. They would argue endlessly, to the great frustration of the Americans, as to precisely how an issue would be labeled and by what principle it would be assigned to committee. To them, it made a real difference; for by stating the principle and by defending the issue at the start, the logic by which the matter would substantially be treated would have been set—the deductive approach.

The Americans were more inclined to see this as a waste of time, preferring the inductive approach: what difference does it make what you call it? We will look at the facts and details when the time comes.

Thoughtful translators and interpreters find that culturally based inclinations toward the deductive pattern on the one hand or the inductive on the other will affect their efforts to transmit equivalent meaning and nuance. Does the statement "The subject of the meeting is aggression" mean the same as "Aggression is the subject of the meeting"? In one, the immediate, less abstract item is placed first—the meeting—while in the other the principle to be decided gets first place. Perhaps this is too fine a distinction to count, but such style preferences have been studied, and specialists find that, when you put a full range of all such differences in patterns of thinking together, negotiators may be talking past each other to a serious degree. I have talked with colleagues who have participated in disarmament talks with the Soviets. They report that months have been wasted in a standoff between the Soviets' insistence on debating general principles first, only then letting the facts fall into place as convenient to the agreed principles, while the Americans start with emphasis on details and numbers and a need to agree on the facts that in final agreement will lead up to the guiding principles.

CULTURE AND LANGUAGE

We could gain much appreciation of the cultural gaps which have to be closed by paying closer attention to the relationship between culture and language, including the varicolored meanings that words and expressions take on in translation. In negotiation practice, the degree to which languages are taken to be equitable is alarming. The naïve negotiator uses interpreters like mechanical devices. You put an idea in here and it comes out there. They may even report that the interpretation process provides an advantage—it gives them more time to think. Better yet, if the counterpart speaks English, however imperfectly, communication is assumed to be assured! Such an approach represents a disgracefully superficial understanding of language and culture in an age when so much depends on it and when English itself is used extensively as a second language in so many differing cultural settings.

I recall the reflections of one of our outstanding official interpreters who had been the other person in the room with three different American presidents as they conferred privately with heads of other states. The languages involved were English, French, Polish, and Russian. He felt, as he reflected on the linguistic and cultural factors, that, while he was self-assured in knowing that he was one of the most competent interpreters in the business, frequently the principals for whom he was trying to bridge the language gap were not even talking about the same issues and that there was nothing that he could do about it short of taking over with extended explanatory lectures to each party and, even then, leaving much to fall between the cracks. "It loses something in translation" can be equivalent to international misunderstanding.

Examples come quickly to mind. Consider the subjective feeling that goes with the word *compromise* as translated into the cultural contexts of differing countries. To Americans, it is a positive matter; an agreement gains moral sanction by having resulted from compromising. To Spanish speakers, it is more probable that by compromising something is lost, honor is not upheld, principle is diluted. Or consider the idea patterns which go with the English "fair play"—try translating that into any other language. If it can be done at all, what happens to the idea patterns that go with it? Do they survive intact? I understand that the French get along on *le fer plé*. Latin Americans play soccer in possibly more decorous fashion with *juego limpio*. But one is forced to the conclusion that "fair play" cannot translate in full depth of meaning when there is no equivalence in the thoughts and assumptions that go with the expression. At least, this makes it a bit difficult to assume "fair play" in a negotiation process!

Language, culture, and communication style mix together to complicate understanding. It is difficult to politely say "no" in Japanese, and in practice a direct "no" is avoided in a number of languages. Even what the outsider would assume to be "yes" in Japanese is better taken as "I hear you—go on. I am listening." Such differences in style can inject serious confusion in anticipating intentions or judging agreement in a negotiation process or even in conducting routine business. In fact, when Masaki Imai, a Japanese Internationalist from the corporate world, wrote a book for the benefit of English-speaking managers to help them in their dealings with the Japanese, the title of his book was *Never Take "Yes" for an Answer*.

All this forces us to consider how profound the consequences of national character can be when it comes to conducting all the international dialogue by which our ever increasing elbow-bumping is managed. We can only be suggestive here. However, a sampling of contrasting value orientations that might significantly affect the way that issues are confronted is well worth pursuing.

LONG TERM, SHORT TERM

When Americans are involved, consider the value placed on time. Some observers think that in international negotiations Americans tend especially to look toward quick answers and short-range solutions. Americans want to get on with the matter at hand directly, put a solution in place, and proceed to the next matter of business. In policy decisions, they pay less real attention to consequences that are five years down the line and much less to those that are several generations away. Even the French, who in world perspective are in many ways culturally very close to Americans, tend to think in longer range, to attack problems for the enduring future, to seek solutions that will evolve over a more extended period. Consequently, in debate the two nations may well have conceptualized negotiating problems in differing ways—including how to deal with the communists or the volatilities of the Third World.

It may be recalled that in the Vietnam conflict the time element was taken into account in totally different ways. Americans wanted to do their thing quickly, resolve in short order the issue of who would govern and by what principles, and get out. The Viet Cong saw the conflict in much longer range. They talked of outlasting the Americans, of seeing their objectives enduring over generations. After the Americans departed, the thought, even expressed explicitly by President Ford, was to "get Vietnam behind us," to go on forthrightly to new problems without brooding over that which had passed behind.

So much for learning from history. This kind of thinking is a world apart from Argentine conceptions of the past as reality, by which they were so highly motivated as to try to regain the Malvinas Islands despite the decades over which the British had seen them established in all practicality as the Falklands. The Soviets also base strategy on a special time perspective that goes with their ideology— their analysis of the course of history makes ultimate change in their favor "inevitable."

In world affairs, it is not surprising that Americans are the activists; an optimistic, activist outlook is central to our achievement-motivated culture. We once joked around the State Department that there is one option in international relations that Americans simply never have: that is, to do nothing. This is not a possible choice in our strategy, despite the probability that in many cases doing nothing, or waiting for someone else to address a problem, would be the best solution. Such is not the American way. Foreign Service officers routinely suffer in the estimation of activistically oriented presidents when they want diplomacy to take a longer course or urge that other than quick direct action be taken to address an international crisis of the moment.

Americans like to be problem solvers, to slay problems as knights slay dragons. This outlook contrasts with that of many other national characters. Americans see world events as arenas in which one should intervene and in which actions have results, in which they are the cause of effects, where fatalism has little place, where "God helps those who help themselves." This world view makes failure exceptionally painful. American "credibility" is seen to be established in success and achievement, in steadfastness in achieving the objective. If, in fact, all the effort turns out not to be successful, it seems more natural to look for the person who "goofed" than to think that

the task could not have been done or that some combination of larger forces prevailed over the direct action assumptions by which Americans made their plans and conducted their operations. Obviously, this world view has many advantages and will serve the interests of a world in which problem-addressing leadership is a crucial asset. The post-World War II Marshal Plan was so achieved, as was the very creation of the United Nations. The U.S. AID program rests on this pattern of thinking. Yet some would argue that this outlook can be counterproductive. It lends itself to the short-range strategy noted above or to a tendency to try to resolve problems too superficially by seeking technological fixes or by throwing money at international matters that need repair on the assumption that, if enough resources are expended, a favorable solution is assured.

THE VALUE OF LIFE

Examples of fundamental differences in values and in ways of thinking extend to the most basic assumptions about life and death. In World War II, the Japanese pursued a policy of suicide bombing that would not have been thinkable in American strategy. In effect, in this most dramatic of cross-culture encounters, it confirmed American readiness to perceive the Japanese as subhuman. Yet Japanese culture and expectations did supply a value and attitude pattern to support the kind of sacrifices involved, and this had to be understood to make sense out of Japanese behavior.

After the 1973 Israeli-Egyptian war, something of the same kind of contrast was suggested by a group of American psychiatrists of both Israeli and Arabic ethnic background, who had been in the area at the time. They were brought together to compare notes by the Institute of Psychiatry and Foreign Affairs—a small organization dedicated to exploring the psychological dimension of international interaction, which then sponsored their informal reporting to the State Department. One factor that seemed to stand out was the differing ways in which the fact or prospect of battlefield casualties were taken into account in military strategy and in reaction by the two publics. The Israelis reflected far more emphasis on strategy that avoided loss of life; they were more shaken by battlefield death, more ready to calculate strategy to minimize the death tally. The Egyptians, on the other hand, while clearly feeling a sense of human loss, nevertheless were more stoic and fatalistic in the event. Martyrdom in the cause was more religiously sanctioned; strategy calculation proceeded with a readiness to accept substantial casualties.

In hindsight, it is apparent that American strategists made errors in Vietnam war calculations in assuming that the North Vietnamese would hold similar views of casualties as American tacticians would. At one stage, Secretary Rusk pointed out that the North Vietnamese loss of seven hundred thousand would be the equivalent to an American loss of ten million. It was judged that the enemy simply could not go on much longer. This reasoning went astray, as we know. Americans projected their "common sense" in these matters onto their counterparts; their expectations were not borne out.

Another subtle but highly important difference in assumptions is that regarding the worth and importance of the individual. Contrasts here lead to substantial variance in reasoning about human rights and even the objectives of government itself. In the Anglo-American tradition, fundamental value is placed on the individual, on the individual's "pursuit of happiness," on self-reliance and achievement, personal political independence, and right to private ownership. From a differing perspective, the value might be placed first on the group and on its well-being—from which the individual's well-being and identity will be enhanced. This is more congenial to the thinking of traditional societies. In that view, an individual cannot be given too much license to do his or her own thing; the group comes first. It becomes more comfortable in such societies to think in terms of socialistic solutions to national problems; government is implicitly charged with protecting the collective interests of the larger group and with keeping individual excesses from prejudicing the collectivity. In that case, single-minded protection of individual freedom and a set of

laws to ensure the maximum of individual maneuverability tend to defy conventional wisdom. This makes a considerable difference in reasoning about human rights.

It might be recalled that when the Declaration of Universal Human Rights was debated in the early days of the United Nations, a standoff took place between Eleanor Roosevelt, the American negotiator, and her Russian counterpart. To the Americans, human rights were few, essentially political, and person-oriented. To the Soviets, they were many, more economic, directed toward the integrity and prosperity of the group. The Soviets were outvoted, if unconverted.

Assumptions and values are part of the social milieu into which people are socialized. Thus they define what is sanctioned and what is not, what "ought" to be, what feels right and wrong. All this becomes sustained by emotional charge, which adds even more rigidity to thinking as international dialogue is conducted. Take, for instance, the American value on contracts in business affairs noted above. Honoring the letter of a contract can become a moral matter sustained by American ideas of what defines good people and bad people. The legal system sustains it; religion adds its support. These feelings make the system work, for by far the largest part of commercial transactions and related conduct of business rests on a pattern of normal expectations rather than enforcement by the threat of formal legal reprisal. As previously noted, this traditionally has not been the basic Japanese feeling about contracts—more dependence typically was placed on feelings of trust and cooperation between the parties, which would endure as changes needed to be made in arrangements toward obtaining their mutual objectives. In this perspective, a contract would be a counterproductive straight-jacket, even immoral. Hence, when Americans and Japanese differ on the desirability of complying with exact contractual wording, it is easy to see that their respective sense of righteous indignation will soon come into play, and emotions will soon further estrange the relationship. The Japanese then are seen as devious in the first place; the Americans, as insincere and overbearing.

MEANING OF THE MESSAGE

This calls attention to a final point I wish to offer. It is normal, as established in communication psychology, for motives to be attributed, consciously or not, in understanding the meaning of a message. This is especially true in negotiation. It is recalled, probably apocryphally, that, during an international negotiation many years ago, the head of one national negotiation team died. Immediately, the other delegation assembled to try to calculate darkly what strategic motive was behind that! In any case, perhaps nothing so complicates effective international negotiation as inaccurate attribution of motive. The complication is the greater as it becomes unlikely that the full degree of misattribution will ever be fully realized.

It can be argued that completely accurate perception of the other side's intention might not bring a peaceful and happy solution. It might make the situation worse as a real conflict is made starker and the impossibility of accommodation made clearer. Still, the prospects for problem solving are clearly enhanced when the counterproductive effects of misperception and misattribution of motive are held to a minimum.

Thus we all have a vested interest in international negotiators achieving the ability to understand other cultures and their accompanying inner logic. We also have an interest in their cultivating that capacity to recognize that much of what they and their own group take as common sense and "normal" human logic constitutes, in fact, a special cultural lens, and that understanding the uniqueness of one's own basis for perception, however valid, is an essential part of managing negotiation communication. It is not an easy task to know one's self in a cross-cultural sense, as so much of one's conventional wisdom is learned out of awareness and reinforced through a lifetime of sharing the conventionalities of one's own society. Perhaps one of the greatest rewards of international exposure is that, by seeking to understand other cultures in depth, a cultural mirror is provided by which one can come to recognize more clearly the values and inner assumptions by which one's own system works.

66

Achieving Integrative Agreements in Negotiation

Dean G. Pruitt

Integrative agreements in negotiations are those that reconcile (i.e., integrate) the parties' interests and hence yield high joint benefit. They can be contrasted with compromises, which are reached when the parties concede along an obvious dimension to some middle ground and which usually produce lower joint benefit.[1] Consider, for example, the story of two sisters who quarreled over an orange.[2] A compromise agreement was reached to split the fruit in half, whereupon one sister squeezed her potion for juice while the other used the peel from her portion in a cake. For whatever reason, they overlooked the integrative agreement of giving the first sister all the juice and the second all the peel.

Integrative agreements sometimes make use of known alternatives, whose joint value becomes apparent during the controversy. But more often they involve the development of novel alternatives. Hence, it is proper to say that they usually emerge from creative problem solving. Integrative alterations (those that

Dr. Pruitt is a professor at SUNY Buffalo.

Portions of this chapter were previously published in Dean G. Pruitt, "Achieving Integrative Agreements in Negotiation," pp. 35–50, in Negotiating in Organizations, edited by M.H. Bazerham and R. J. Lewicki. Copyright © 1983 by Sage Publications, Inc. Reprinted by permission of Sage Publications, Inc. The chapter was prepared with support from National Science Foundation Grant BN583-09167.

form the basis for integrative agreements) can be devised by either party acting separately, by the two of them in joint session, or by a third party such as a mediator.

In the story of the sisters, the situation had unusually high *integrative potential* in the sense of allowing the development of an agreement that totally satisfied both parties' aspirations. Not all situations are so hopeful. For example, in negotiating the price of a car, both dealer and customer usually must reduce their aspirations in order to reach agreement.

However, most situations have more integrative potential than is commonly assumed. For example, car dealers can often sweeten the deal by throwing in a radio or other accessory that costs them little but benefits their customers a lot. Hence, problem solving is often richly rewarded.

There are four main reasons for bargainers (or the mediators assisting them) to seek integrative agreements rather than compromises:[3]

1. If aspirations are high and both sides are resistant to conceding, it may be impossible to resolve the conflict unless a way can be found to join the two parties' interests.

2. Integrative agreements are likely to be more stable. Compromises are often unsatisfactory to one or both parties, causing the issue to come up again at a later time.

3. Because they are mutually rewarding, integrative agreements tend to strengthen the relationship between the parties. This has a number of benefits, including facilitating problem solving in later conflicts.

4. Integrative agreements ordinarily contribute to the welfare of the broader community of which the two parties are members. For example, a firm will usually reap benefit as a whole if its departments are able to reconcile their differences creatively.

METHODS FOR ACHIEVING INTEGRATIVE AGREEMENTS

Five methods for achieving integrative agreements can be described. These are means by which the parties' initially opposing demands can be transformed into alternatives that reconcile their interests. They can be used by a single party, both parties working together, or a third party such as a mediator. Each method involves a different way of refocusing the issues under dispute. Hence, potentially useful refocusing questions will be provided under each heading. Information that is useful for implementing each method will also be mentioned, and the methods will be listed in order of increasing difficulty of getting this information.

The methods will be illustrated by a running example concerning a husband and wife who are trying to decide where to go on a two-week vacation. The husband wants to go to the mountains, his wife to the seashore. They have considered the compromise of spending one week in each location but are hoping for something better. What approach should they take?

Expanding the Pie

Some conflicts hinge on a resource shortage. Time, money, land, automobiles, or what-have-you are in short supply but in long demand. In such circumstances, integrative agreements can be devised by increasing the available resources. This is called expanding the pie. For example, our married couple might solve their problem by persuading their employers to give them four weeks of vacation so that they can take two in the mountains and two at the seashore. Another example is that of two milk companies who were vying to be first to unload cans on a platform.[4] The controversy was resolved when somebody thought of widening the platform.

Expanding the pie is a useful formula when the parties do not find each other's demands inherently aversive but reject them only because they seem to block the attainment of their own demands; for example, when the husband rejects the seashore because it keeps him away from the mountains and the wife rejects the mountains because they deny her the pleasures of the seashore. But it is by no means a universal remedy. Expanding the pie may yield strikingly poor benefits if there are inherent costs in the other's proposal (e.g., the husband cannot stand the seashore or the wife the mountains). Other methods are better in such cases.

Expanding the pie requires no analysis of the interests underlying the parties' demands. Hence, its information requirements are slim. However, this does not mean that a solution by this method is always easy to find. There may be no resource shortage, or the shortage may not be easy to see or to remedy.

Refocusing questions that can be useful in seeking a solution by pie expansion include: How can both parties get what they want? Does the conflict hinge on a resource shortage? How can the critical resource be expanded?

Nonspecific Compensation

In nonspecific compensation one party gets what he or she wants, and the other is repaid in some unrelated coin. Compensation is nonspecific if it does not deal with the precise costs incurred by the other party. For example, the wife in our example might agree to go to the mountains, even though she finds them boring, if her husband promises her a fur coat. Another example would be giving an employee a bonus for working during the Christmas holidays.

Compensation usually comes from the party whose demands are granted. But it can also originate with a third party or even with the party who is compensated. An example of the latter would be an employee who pampers himself or herself by finding a nice office to work in during the Christmas holidays.

Two kinds of information are useful for devising a solution by nonspecific compensation: (1) information about what is valuable to the other party (e.g., knowledge that he or she values love, attention, or money); and (2) information about how badly the other party is hurting by making concessions. This is useful for devising adequate compensation for these concessions. If such information is not available, it may be possible to conduct an "auction" for the other party's acquiescence, changing the sort of benefit offered or raising one's offer, in trial-and-error fashion, until an acceptable formula is found.

Refocusing questions that can help locate a means of compensation include: How much is the other party hurting in conceding to me? What does the other party value that I can supply? How valuable is this to the other party?

Logrolling

Logrolling is possible in complex agendas where several issues are under consideration and the parties have differing priorities among these issues. Each party concedes on low-priority issues in exchange for concessions on issues of higher priority to itself. Each gets that part of its demands that it finds most important. For example, suppose that in addition to disagreeing about where to go on vacation, the wife in our example wants to go to a first-class hotel while the husbands prefers an inn. If accommodations are a high-priority issue for the wife and location for the husband, both can reach a fairly integrative solution by agreeing to go to a first-class hotel in the mountains. Logrolling can be viewed as a variant of nonspecific compensation in which both parties instead of one are compensated for making concessions desired by the other.

To develop solutions by logrolling, it is useful to have information about the two parties' priorities so that exchangeable concessions can be identified. But it is not necessary to have information about the interests (e.g., the aspirations, values) underlying these priorities. Solutions by logrolling can also be developed by a process of trial and error in which one party moves systematically through a series of possible packages, keeping his or her own outcomes as high as possible, until an alternative is found that is acceptable to the other party.[5]

Refocusing questions that can be useful for developing solutions by logrolling include: Which issues are of higher and lower priority to myself? Which issues are of higher and lower priority to the other party? Are some of my high-priority issues of low priority to the other party and vice versa?

Cost Cutting

In solutions by cost cutting, one party gets what he or she wants and the other's costs are reduced or eliminated. The result is high joint benefit, not because the first party has changed his or her demands, but because the second party suffers less. For instance, suppose that the husband in our example dislikes the beach because of the hustle and bustle. He may be quite willing to go there on vacation if his costs are cut by renting a house with a quiet inner courtyard where he can read while his wife goes out among the crowds.

Cost cutting often takes the form of *specific compensation,* in which the party who concedes receives something in return that satisfies the precise values frustrated. For example, the employee who must work through the holidays can be specifically compensated by the award of a vacation immediately after New Year's Day. Specific compensation differs from non-specific compensation in dealing with the precise costs incurred rather than providing repayment in an unrelated coin. The costs are actually canceled out rather than being overbalanced by benefits experienced in some other realm.

Information about the nature of one of the parties' costs is, of course, helpful for developing solutions by cost cutting. This is a deeper kind of information than knowledge of that party's priorities. It involves knowing something about the interests—the values, aspirations, and standards—underlying that party's overt position.

Refocusing questions for developing solutions by cost cutting include: What costs are posed for the other party by our proposal? How can these costs be mitigated or eliminated?

Bridging

In bridging, neither party achieves its initial demands, but a new option is devised that satisfies the most important interests underlying those demands. For example, suppose that the husband in our vacation example is mainly interested in fishing and hunting and the wife in swimming and sunbathing. Their interests might be bridged by finding an inland resort with a lake and a beach that is close to woods and streams. Follett gives another homely example of two women reading in a library room.[6] One wanted to open the window for ventilation; the other wanted to keep it closed so as not to catch a cold. The ultimate solution involved opening a window in the next room, which satisfied both the need for fresh air and the need to avoid a draft. Bridging entails a creative synthesis of the parties' most important interests.

Bridging typically involves a reformation of the issue(s), based on an analysis of the underlying interests on both sides. For example, a critical turning point in our vacation example is likely to come when the initial formulation, "Shall we go to the mountains or the seashore?" is replaced by, "Where can we find fishing, hunting, swimming, and sunbathing?" This new formulation becomes the basis for constructing a search model that is designed to help locate a novel alternative.[7] The process of reformulation can be done by either or both parties or by a third party who is trying to help.

People who seek to develop solutions by bridging need information about the nature of the two parties' interests and their priorities among these interests. Priority information is useful because it is rare to find a solution, like opening the window in the next room of the library, that bridges all the two parties' interests. In the final agreement, higher-priority interests are served and lower-priority interests are discarded. For example, the wife who agrees to go to an inland lake may have forgone the lesser value of smelling the sea air and the husband may have forgone his preference for spectacular mountain vistas.

In the initial phase of search for a solution by bridging, the search model can include all the interests on both sides. But if this does not generate a mutually acceptable alternative, some of the lower-priority interests must be discarded from the model and the search begun anew. The result will not be an ideal solution but hopefully one that is mutually acceptable. Dropping low-priority interests in the development of a solution by bridging is similar to dropping low-priority demands in the search for a solution by logrolling. But the

latter is in the realm of concrete proposals, while the former is in the realm of the interests underlying these proposals.

Refocusing questions that can be raised in search of a solution by bridging include: What are the two parties' basic interests? What are their priorities among these interests? How can the two sets of high-priority interests be reconciled?

THE ANALYSIS OF INTERESTS

Two of the methods for achieving integrative agreements that were just described almost always necessitate an analysis of interests. These are cost cutting, which usually requires that somebody (one of the parties or a mediator) understand the interests of the party whose costs are cut, and bridging, which usually requires that somebody understand both parties' interests. Useful discussions of how to gain insight into interests can be found in Fisher, Ury and Pruitt,[8] and the points made in this section are supplementary to these discussions.

Interests are commonly organized into hierarchical trees, with more basic interests underpinning more superficial ones. Hence, it is often useful to go deeper than the interests immediately underlying a party's proposals to the interests underlying these interests, or even to the interests underlying the interests underlying the interests. If one goes far enough down the street, an interest may be located that can be easily reconciled with the opposing party's interests.

An example of an interest tree can be seen on the left in Figure 1. It belongs to a hypothetical boy who is trying to persuade his father to let him buy a motorcycle. At the right are listed those of the father's interests that conflict with the son's. At the top of the tree is the boy's initial proposal (buy a motorcycle), which is hopelessly opposed to his father's proposal (no motorcycle). Analysis of the boy's proposal yields a first-level underlying interest, to make noise in the neighborhood. But this is opposed to his dad's interest of maintaining peace and quiet. Further analysis of the boy's position reveals a second-level interest underlying the first level, to gain attention from the neighbors. But again this conflicts

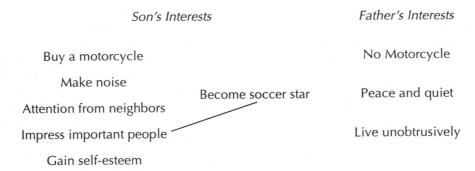

FIGURE 1
Son's Interest Tree in a Controversy with Father

with one of his father's basic interests, to live unobtrusively. The controversy is resolved only when someone (e.g., the father, the boy, the boy's mother) discovers an even more basic interest—the boy's desire to impress important people. This discovery is helpful because there are ways of impressing important people that do not contradict the father's interests (e.g., going out for the high school soccer team). At the bottom of the boy's tree is a fourth-level interest, self-esteem. But it is unnecessary to go down this far, because the controversy can be resolved at the third level.

Analysis of the interests underlying divergent positions often reveals that the initial area of disagreement had different meanings to the two parties. While there appeared to be disagreement, there was no fundamental opposition in what they were really asking. For example, one party may be more concerned with substance, while the other cares more for appearances; one may be seeking a long-term solution; and so on. Fisher and Ury list nine other dimensions of this kind.[9]

Golan gives an example of a controversy that was resolved when a mediator discovered that one party was seeking substance while the other was seeking appearance.[10] A cease-fire in the Yom Kippur War found the Egyptian Third Army surrounded by Israeli forces. A dispute arose about the control of the only road available for bringing food and medicine to this army, and the two parties appeared to be at loggerheads. After a careful analysis, the mediator, Henry Kissinger, concluded that Israel wanted actual control of the road while Egypt

wanted only the appearance that Israel did not control it for the sake of public relations. A bridging solution was found that involved continued Israeli control but the stationing of United Nations soldiers at checkpoints on the road so that they seemed to control it.

THE NATURE OF PROBLEM SOLVING

Bargainers are sometimes able to "luck into" a highly integrative agreement, as for example when a good precedent has been set in a prior negotiation. But more often they must engage in problem solving, that is, seek a new option that better satisfies both parties' interests than those currently available. The more vigorous is this problem solving, the more integrative is the final agreement likely to be, up to the limits imposed by the integrative potential.

At its best, problem solving involves a joint effort to find a mutually acceptable solution. The parties or their representatives talk freely to one another. They exchange information about their interests and priorities, work together to identify the true issues dividing them, brainstorm in search of alternatives that bridge their opposing interests, and collectively evaluate these alternatives from the viewpoint of their mutual welfare.

However, a full problem-solving discussion of this kind is not always practical because of the realities of divergent interests. One or both parties may fear that such openness will deny them an opportunity for competitive gain, or give the other party such an opportunity. When these fears exist, individual problem solving is a practical alternative. A single person or small group on one side can perform all of the functions just described: seeking insight into the other party's interests, identifying the true issues, devising mutually beneficial alternatives, and evaluating these alternatives from a joint perspective. Alternatively, a third party can do the problem solving.

Steps in Creative Problem Solving

The following sequence of steps makes most sense for a bargainer who is seeking a creative solution to a controversy.

Step 1. Ask whether there really is a conflict of interest.

Perceived conflict of interest, which is what gets people into negotiation, may be *illusory*— based on a misunderstanding about the other's aspirations or a misconstrual of the meaning of the alternatives that are readily available. If so, there is no point in continuing negotiation. Hence, the logical first step is to ask whether there really is a conflict of interest.

An example of illusory conflict can be seen in the case of a carpenter who came to look at a job in the home of the author and said that the estimate would cost fifty dollars. When asked why he expected a fee, he indicated that he feared that the author would file for an insurance payment on the basis of his estimate and then do home repairs. When assured that the homeowner was all thumbs with tools, he withdrew the request for a fee.

Step 2. Set reasonably high aspirations, based on one's basic interests, and be ready to stick to them.

Aspirations are the goals that underlie a party's demands. They are based on that party's interests, as he or she sees them; but they are not the same as interests, because they also reflect the party's assessment of the legitimacy and practicality of the various interests that might become involved in the controversy. By recommending high aspirations, we are urging bargainers to take their own interests very seriously. Bargainers who do not do so are likely to yield ground too rapidly. If one bargainer takes this approach, he or she will be exploited. If both bargainers do so, they are likely to reach agreement so fast that they overlook the integrative potential in the situation and achieve only a low-level compromise.

By urging bargainers to stick to their aspirations, we are saying that protracted conflict is often necessary for the development of truly integrative solutions.[11] The party must maintain high aspirations even though they may at first seem incompatible with the other's aspirations. This seems paradoxical, but we hasten to add that we are not talking about heavily competitive conflict. Creative conflicts are in the category of vigorous discussions or mild arguments. Each party seeks to understand and foster its own basic interests while remaining flexible about the means for achieving these interests.

We are also not endorsing bullheadedness. Aspirations should start and remain high but not so high as to outrun any reasonable integrative potential. If they start or stay too high, time will be lost, and the other may withdraw because the conflict seems hopeless.

Step 3. Seek a way to reconcile both parties aspirations.

Having set high aspirations, the party should seek a way to reconcile these aspirations with those held by the other. The various refocusing questions discussed earlier should be posed, and one or more search models developed in an effort to achieve the interests that both parties find most central. The success of Step 3 often depends on whether the party was in touch with his or her basic interests at Step 2, that is, whether the party's aspirations reflect the root interests that lie at the base of the interest tree underpinning his or her demands.

Step 4. Lower aspirations and search some more.

If agreement is not reached at Step 3, a choice should be made between two further options. Either party can reduce his or her own aspirations to some degree—that is, concede on or discard low-priority interests—and try again. Or, if the party's search model includes the other's aspirations as well as his or her own, the party can lower these aspirations and then, if a solution is found, try to persuade the other that such a reduction is desirable.

Step 4 should be repeated over and over again until an agreement is reached or a breakoff becomes inevitable.

Being Firm but Conciliatory

The strategy described in Steps 2 and 3 of the sequence just given can be described as *firm but conciliatory*. The party is advised to be firm about his or her own basic interests—yielding only when it is clear that they cannot be attained—but conciliatory toward the other in the sense of being also responsive to the other's basic interests. An important aspect of being conciliatory is to be flexible with regard to how one's own interests are achieved so as to be open to new ideas about how to reconcile them with the other's interests. Hence, this strategy can also be described as one of *firm flexibility*—the party should be firm with regard to ends but flexible with regard to the means to these ends. A quotation from Fisher and Ury captures the essence of firm flexibility: "It may not be wise to commit yourself to your position, but it is wise to commit yourself to your interests. This is the place . . . to spend your aggressive energies."[12]

An example of a firm but conciliatory strategy can be seen in actions taken by President John F. Kennedy in 1961 during the Second Berlin Crisis. The Russians, led by Premier Nikita Khrushchev, had been trying to end American occupation of West Berlin by threatening to sign a separate peace treaty with East Germany and buzzing planes in the Berlin Corridor. Recognizing that some concessions had to be made, Kennedy "decided to be firm on essentials but negotiate on nonessentials."[13] In a speech on July 25, he announced three fundamental principles that ensured the integrity and continued American occupation of West Berlin. The firmness of these principles was underscored by a pledge to defend them by force and a concomitant military buildup.[14] Yet Kennedy also indicated flexibility and a concern about Russian priorities by calling for negotiations to remove "actual irritants" to the Soviet Union and its allies. Two results were achieved: the building

of the Berlin Wall, which can be viewed as a bridging solution that solved the problem of population loss from East Germany without disturbing American rights in or the independence of West Berlin, and eventual negotiations that put these principles in writing.

Searching for a Formula

When complex issues are under consideration, a two-step approach is often essential. The early stages of problem solving must be devoted to devising an overarching formula—a brief statement of common objectives that can serve as a road map to the eventual agreement. Only then is it possible to devise an efficient agenda for working out the details of the agreement.[15] If a formula is not developed, the proceedings are likely to get so mired down in detail that momentum will be lost and the parties will draw or turn to a contentious approach.

An example of a formula would be the basic agreement in the Camp David talks between Israel and Egypt. In essence, Israel agreed to withdraw from the Sinai and to begin talks about Palestinian autonomy in exchange for a peace treaty with Egypt. This formula, somewhat augmented in the Camp David Accords, became the basis for many years of further negotiation to fill in the details.

THE ROLE OF CONTENTIOUS BEHAVIOR

Contentious behavior consists of all those actions that are designed to elicit concessions from the other party. Examples include persuasive arguments, threats, and positional commitments.

Contentious behavior has traditionally been assumed to militate against the development of integrative agreements,[16] and there is a solid research evidence supporting this assumption.[17] There are four reasons why this should be true:

1. Contentious behavior ordinarily involves standing firm on a particular demand rather than standing firm on one's interests. Hence, it is incompat-

ible with the flexibility about means that is an important element of successful problem solving.

2. Contentious behavior encourages hostility toward the other by a principle of psychological consistency. This diminishes the party's willingness to contribute to the other's welfare and, hence, the party's willingness to devise or accept jointly beneficial alternatives.

3. Contentious behavior encourages the other to feel hostile and engage in contentious behavior in return. A conflict spiral may ensue in which both parties become increasingly rigid and progressively more reluctant to take any actions that benefit the other.

4. Contentious behavior signals to the other that the party has a win-lose orientation, calling into question the possibility of achieving a jointly beneficial agreement. This reduces the likelihood that the other will engage in problem solving.

However, the indictment against contentious behavior has clearly been overdrawn. Under some circumstances, this behavior can actually make problem solving more likely or contribute to the effectiveness of problem solving. This can occur in two ways:

1. It encourages the other to deal with the controversy. If present circumstances favor the other, it is often necessary for the party to employ threats to force the other to pay attention to the party's concerns. While such threats run the risk of eliciting contentious behavior in return and a conflict spiral, they are often successful at encouraging problem-solving behavior by the other party,[18] especially if presented tactfully and coupled with a promise of problem solving.

An example can be seen at the beginning of the Second Berlin Crisis, when Premier Khrushchev threatened to sign a separate peace treaty with East Germany if the status of West Berlin was not settled to his liking. At the same time, he proposed negotiation. Had he not made this threat, which was tantamount to a proposal to give East Germany control of the access routes to West Berlin, it is doubtful that the West would have accepted his offer of negotiation.

2. It underlies the party's areas of firmness. Threats and other contentious actions are means of communication. They can be used to emphasize the rigidity of the party's high-priority interests, making it doubly clear that certain elements of the party's position are nonnegotiable. An example would be the Kennedy speech mentioned earlier in which he threatened to use force to defend the integrity of an American access to West Berlin. Concomitant troop movements added emphasis to his message. Such a message can contribute to the development of integrative solutions in two ways:

(a) It makes the other less hopeful of trying to dislodge the party from the party's areas of firmness. Instead, the party is motivated to try to devise a way to live within these constraints (i.e., to engage in problem solving).

(b) It provides information to the other about the party's interests, facilitating the other's problem-solving efforts.

In short, because of the risks associated with contentious behavior, there is a tendency to underrate its potential contribution to the development of integrative agreements. However, we must hasten to add that, in most cases, contentious behavior can make this contribution only if one is also ready to engage in problem solving. In addition to employing occasional hard tactics in an effort to underscore firmness about one's interests, one must also dramatize a concern about the other's welfare and one's flexibility about the means for achieving these interests. Otherwise, the other's response to contentious tactics will usually be limited to adoption of the same tactics for the same purpose of defense or retaliation.

ENDNOTES

[1]M. P. Follett, "Constructive Conflict," in H. C. Metcalf and L. Urwick, eds., *Dynamic Administration: The Collected Papers of Mary Parker Follett* (New York: Harper and Row, 1940).

[2]R. Fisher and W. Ury, *Getting to YES* (Boston: Houghton Mifflin, 1981).

[3]D. G. Pruitt, *Negotiation Behavior* (New York: Academic Press, 1981).

[4]Cited by Follett, *op. cit.*

[5]H. H. Kelley and D. P. Schnitski, "Bargaining," in C. G. McClintock, ed., *Experimental Social Psychology* (New York: Holt, Rinehart and Winston); D. G. Pruitt and P. J. D. Carbevale, "The Development of Integrative Agreements," in V. J. Derlega and J. Grzelak, eds., *Cooperation and Helping Behavior* (New York: Academic Press, 1982).

[6]Follett, *op. cit.*

[7]H. A. Simon, *Models of Man: Social and Rational* (New York: Wiley, 1957).

[8]Fisher and Ury, op. cit.; D. G. Pruitt, "Indirect Communication and the Search for Agreement in Negotiation," *Journal of Applied Social Psychology, 1*, 1971: 205–239.

[9]Fisher and Ury, 77.

[10]M. Golan, *The Secret Conversations of Henry Kissinger: Step-by-Step Diplomacy in the Middle East* (New York: Quadrangle, 1976).

[11]A. C. Filley, *Interpersonal Conflict Resolution* (Glenview, IL: Scott, Foresman, 1975).

[12]Fisher and Ury, 55.

[13]G. H. Snyder and P. Diesing, *Conflict Among Nations* (Princeton: Princeton University Press, 1977).

[14]D. G. Pruitt and J. Holland, *Settlement in the Berlin Crisis, 1958–1962,* Special Study No. 18 of the Council on International Studies, State University of New York at Buffalo, 1972.

[15]I. W. Zartman, "Negotiations as a Joint Decision-Making Process." *Journal of Conflict Resolution, 21,* 1977: 619–638. Reprinted in I. W. Zartman, ed., *The Negotiation Process* (Beverly Hills, CA: Sage, 1978).

[16]R. R. Blake, and J. S. Mouton, "Intergroup Problem Solving in Organizations: From Theory to Practice," in W. C. Austin and S. Worchel, eds., *The Social Psychology of Intergroup Relations* (Monterey, CA: Brooks/Cole, 1979); M. Deutsch, *The Resolution of Conflict: Constructive and Destructive Processes* (New Haven: Yale University Press, 1973); R. E. Walton and R. B. McKersie, *A Behavioral Theory of Labor Negotiations: An Analysis of A Social Interaction System* (New York: McGraw-Hill, 1965).

[17]D. G. Pruitt, *Negotiation Behavior.*

[18]D. G. Pruitt and J. M. Gleason, "Threat Capacity and the Choice Between Independence and Interdependence," *Personality and Social Psychology Bulletin, 4,* 1978: 252–255.

67

Cultural Considerations in Hostage Negotiations

Mitchell R. Hammer and
Gary R. Weaver

INTRODUCTION

The communicative dynamics involved in hostage negotiation are characterized by relatively high levels of cognitive uncertainty and emotional anxiety coupled with increased confrontational interaction and communication resulting from police response to the situation. According to Soskis and Van Zandt, the majority of these hostage taking events arise because of hostage takers' cognitive or emotional inability to manage the various stressors in their lives.[1]

From Tactical Assault to Negotiation

A common approach used by law enforcement personnel in handling hostage taking events prior to 1972 often focused on two courses of action: permit the hostage taker to surrender, or engage the police tactical (SWAT) team in a planned assault. The highly publicized hostage taking situation that occurred during the Munich Olympics in 1972 and the resultant deaths of Israeli athlete-hostages at the hands of terrorists made law enforcement

---

Excerpted from a paper presented at the annual conference of The American Society of Criminology, Reno, Nevada, November 8–12, 1989.

professionals take a second look at these standard hostage taking police procedures.[2]

The New York City Police Department (NYPD) is generally credited with developing the first comprehensive program of hostage taking procedures which involved a radically new approach: the initiation of negotiation with the hostage taker as the preferred method of resolving hostage taking situations. Approximately one year after the Munich Olympic tragedy, this "negotiation" approach received its first test in a hostage taking barricade situation in Brooklyn in 1973 where 13 hostages were kept for 47 hours by four militant Moslem hostage takers. The hostages eventually escaped and later, the hostage takers surrendered.[3] Since then, the principles developed by Dr. Schlossberg and the methods developed by the NYPD's hostage negotiation team have been widely disseminated throughout U.S. law enforcement agencies.

Since 1973, a plethora of writings emerged concerning various aspects of hostage negotiation situations. By far the majority of this literature is written from a "psychological" point of view; whether it concerns the "Stockholm syndrome" *vis-à-vis* hostages or the psychological "profiles" of hostage takers.

While psychological contributions to understanding hostage negotiation scenarios have been substantial, little attention has been directed toward the intercultural communication aspects of hostage negotiation. For example, in a recent review of over 500 articles and books concerned with hostage negotiation, only a handful of writings were found which even mention "culture" or "intercultural communication" as important considerations in hostage negotiation.

NYPD HOSTAGE EVENT DATA

A total of 137 hostage taking incidents were recorded by the New York Police Department between the years 1972 and 1982.[4] Of these, almost half (48%) were barricade situations, 36% were kidnapping, and 4% were hijacking (the remaining 12% were not categorized). Overall, hostages were released by the hostage takers in 38% of the cases and rescued by authorities in 35% of the incidents. The majority (66%) of the hostage takers were arrested at the scene. In 91% of the cases, neither hostage taker nor hostage were killed.

The Interpersonal Dimension

Two sets of findings are particularly relevant to the focus of this paper. One set of findings concerns the fundamentally *interpersonal* nature of the hostage taking event. Over half (56%) of the hostage taking incidents involved only one hostage taker and most of the hostage takers were men (87%). While most of the hostage taking incidents (41%) occurred in the home of the hostage taker, the hostage was usually unrelated (60%) to the hostage taker. In only 39% of the cases was a trained law enforcement negotiator used while 33% involved no negotiations at all. Most (31%) of the incidents lasted two hours or less. While the hostage taking predominately involved some sort of a family dispute, the most common demand made concerned money (39%). However, 24% of the hostage takers made no demands at all. Even in those cases where specific demands were made, however, in most (57%) of the cases, none of the hostage takers' demands were met. Further, most hostage takers (61%) did *not* set any deadlines at all for demands to be met.

A typical hostage taking situation is domestic in setting and interpersonal in its communicative context. First, most hostage taking incidents take place in the home of the hostage taker, are not dominated by instrumental "demands" (e.g., give me $100,000) and are typically resolved in less than two hours without the aid of a trained negotiator. Second, the hostage takers' demands are usually *not* met— yet the lives of the hostages are not taken *and* the hostage taker is neither killed nor commits suicide; rather, he/she is arrested. Third, the hostage taker appears to be neither particularly suicidal nor violent in behavior toward the hostages. As Head comments: ". . . most hostage takers (and most hostages) will not be killed during the hostage event and indeed will probably suffer no physical harm whatsoever. This reinforces the notion that hostage takers are willing to negotiate and are not bent on self-destruction."[5] In this sense, the hostage taker behaves quite rationally, given the crisis situation in which the hostage taker is enmeshed.

These findings suggest that crisis communication between the police negotiator and the hostage taker involves substantial interpersonal relationship dynamics between hostage taker and negotiator in addition to the instrumental goal (bargaining) dynamics. While the bargaining dynamic typically involves specific goal-directed, cost-benefit orientations which are played out at relatively low levels of emotional involvement within a strategic policy perspective (i.e. "trade-off" behaviors between negotiators and hostage takers, e.g., "I'll give you X if you give me Y"), the interpersonal dynamic of hostage negotiation involves typically high levels of tension with issues of trust and respect dominating the negotiation interaction.

Demands, therefore, function not only as an expression of the possible hostage taker's instrumental goals (a bargaining objective), but also function along the lines of a relational and communicative topic designed to build trust between interactants. Demands, therefore, take on an important interpersonal meaning; not always an exact correspondence to their literal, content meaning. Thus, instrumental goals and demands (e.g., money) can often function more as a demand for attention than a specific monetary demand.[6]

For instance, in a study of the negotiation dynamic involved in the seven day Talladega Prison hostage incident in 1991[7] results indicate that during the initial phase of the negotiations, the hostage takers' use of demands and threats were mostly interpersonally contexted, suggesting the hostage takers' communicative behaviors were substantially oriented toward a relationally based, negotiated resolution of the conflict.

The Cross-Cultural Dimension

A second set of findings from the NYPD Hostage Event Data suggest that the hostage taker/ police negotiator interactions are significantly *intercultural* in composition, involving differing values, beliefs, verbal and nonverbal communication patterns and interaction rituals. According to Head, thirty-five percent of the hostage takers were white-American, 26% black-American, 10% Hispanic, 1% Asian, and 7% other (non-white).[8] (In 32% of the cases, however, the ethnic background of the hostage taker is unknown.) Most (63%) of the hostage takers were between the ages of 20–49. Over three-fourths (86%) spoke English, 2% spoke Spanish, and 6% were mixed (i.e., spoke English and another language).

These findings indicate that *a significant percent of hostage takers were non-white* (44%). In those instances when the police negotiator has a different cultural background than the hostage taker (e.g., Anglo-American negotiator, Latin-American hostage taker), a cross-cultural as well as an interpersonal dynamic may be operative during the negotiation. Yet research in the areas of interethnic communication[9] clearly indicates that cultural differences in communication do influence interethnic interactions.

Further, demographic analysis and projections point to the probability that interethnic hostage negotiation incidents may likely increase in the future. There were 29 million blacks, 17 million Hispanics and 5.1 million Asians; a total of 53 million non-white people living in the U.S. at the end of 1985. Projections suggest that in California, whites will drop from 64% to 48% of the state's population by the year 2010 and in the next century, blacks, Hispanics and Asians will outnumber whites in the U.S.[10] Further, since 1946, a total of 2.2 million refugees and 15.2 million immigrants were admitted to the U.S. Since the 1980s, the total number of immigrants admitted averaged 575,000 per year.

PSYCHOLOGICAL TYPOLOGIES

One dominant approach to classifying hostage taking situations focuses on the personality characteristics of the individual hostage taker.[11] Quite a number of typologies have been proffered in describing the personality of the hostage taker. For example, Cooper classifies hostage takers in terms of six categories: political extremists, fleeing criminals, institutionalized persons, wronged persons, religious fanatics and mentally disturbed persons.[12] Middendorf views hostage takers in terms of their basic

motivations: political motives, escape motives, and personal gain motives.[13] Perhaps the most common typology is offered by Hacker, who categorizes hostage takers as crusaders (highly motivated political terrorists), criminals (individuals caught in the act of a crime who take hostages as bargaining tools), and "crazies" (hostage takers with a history of mental disorder).[14] In a similar vein, Schlossberg also identifies three typologies: group oriented hostage takers, professional criminals, and "psycho's."[15]

These typologies appear to be influential on the perceptions and actions of hostage negotiators. As Head states:

> It is apparent that law enforcement agencies do implicitly and explicitly rely upon typologies of hostage takers in formulating responses to hostage situations. Various assumptions of hostage taker behavior are based upon these classifications of the hostage taker by the police. Conversations with various hostage negotiators (as reflected in the NYPD data) and descriptions in a variety of media accounts (contained in the HEAD data) seem to indicate a clear preference on the part of the responding agents to be able to classify a hostage taker into a predisposed category.[16]

This more psychological approach emphasizes a static trait operational philosophy as the framework for negotiator interaction with hostage takers.[17] This focus on the psychological traits of hostage takers is viewed by some researchers, however, as a significant limitation to our knowledge of crisis negotiations.[18]

PRINCIPLES OF HOSTAGE NEGOTIATION

In addition to the development and use of these typologies, a number of principles have been advanced which law enforcement negotiators generally follow in hostage taking situations. These guidelines are based on the psychiatric model and crisis intervention techniques; the idea that "an individual who is seeking help be in a controlled atmosphere. . . ."[19]

One principle is that the hostage has no intrinsic value; rather the taking of a hostage is a tool for getting attention. As Schlossberg argues:

> Imagine you are standing with a hostage. The police are called and they arrive on the scene. The police walk over to you and say "What's going on here?" You say, "I've got a hostage here, I want a million dollars, I want a trip to Europe, etc." The police then say "Gee, that's very interesting." They turn around, they get back into their police car and then they drive away, leaving you standing there. What value is that hostage to you? The hostages are taken in order to create an audience.[20]

Second, it is in the hostage taker's best interest as much as the police's to maintain the safety of the hostage. That is, the hostage taker knows that should a showdown occur, the victory will clearly go to the police.

Third, the act of hostage taking, in one sense, represents a "creative act" on the part of the hostage taker in response to a high degree of frustration.[21] The subsequent activity of *negotiation*, however, goes beyond a creative act and engages the hostage taker in an act of problem-solving. According to Schlossberg, this problem solving strategy is designed to reduce or eliminate this frustration. However, if problem-solving is ineffective:

> . . . then they [the hostage taker] move into the aggressive stage. . . . We [the negotiator], in a sense, are involved in keeping him [sic] in that problem-solving phase, creating an atmosphere conducive to keeping a person working on a problem. Why? Because as long as somebody is working on the problem, then he does not get aggressive. If he does not get aggressive, he is not going to hurt anyone.[22]

Fourth, a fundamental goal of the negotiator is to *reduce* the level of tension or anxiety in the situation. This is often accomplished by helping the hostage taker "ventilate" (to express pent up frustrations and anxieties in a supportive, "safe" communicative environment) to the hostage negotiator who assumes the role of a "significant other."[23]

Fifth, the hostage taker must be contained; to create that controlled environment in which therapeutic communication can take place.

Sixth, face-to-face negotiations should be avoided and "third parties" should not be used as negotiators. This advice is based on the premise that the risks outweigh the benefits in face-to-face interaction while the police negotiator is trained to handle hostage taking incidents and is therefore a more effective choice as negotiator.

TYPOLOGIES AND CROSS-CULTURAL NEGOTIATION

Given the findings presented earlier that hostage taking situations are largely interpersonal in orientation and often intercultural in composition, a number of modifications to the above guidelines appear warranted. The first observation that perhaps could be made is that reliance on "psychological typologies" such as the crusader, criminal and crazy do not adequately explain the behavioral differences that may exist in these tension-filled hostage taking situations. While the typologies may be useful from a clinical perspective, from a communicative and negotiation viewpoint, the labels do not adequately suggest the communicative differences between the typologies that are important to know in *negotiation* with hostage takers.

Typologies and the Interpersonal Dimension

Second, the typology of the crusader, criminal and crazy identify particular personality types that do not accurately characterize the hostage taker nor the actual situation in which most hostage taking occurs; namely, domestic settings which are interpersonal in nature and involve generally rational (i.e., problem-solving) behavior on the part of the hostage taker. Psychological typologies such as crusader, criminal and crazy do not sufficiently describe the actual hostage situation. For instance, for the criminal, the typology suggests that hostages function as bargaining chips; yet the relatively low use of "demands" and lack of "demand deadlines" would seem to indicate that the actual instrumental demands issued are not literal messages so much as they are relationship messages. Watzlawick, Beavin & Jackson clearly describe these two aspects of communication messages as follows:

> . . . any communication implies a commitment and thereby defines the relationship. This is another way of saying that a communication not only conveys information [the content function], but that at the same time it imposes behavior [the relationship function].[24]

This does not imply that these demand messages should be communicatively ignored; only, that the function of the demand message is perhaps far more relational in its meaning than literal (content based) and that the negotiators' response to these messages should include a heavy dose of relational support. In short, it would appear from the NYPD data that the "demands" made by hostage takers may be most effectively met via relational feedback rather than more "bargaining" style negotiation behavior.

Similarly, the use of the typology of "crazy" is also troublesome. While the hostage taker may be subsequently psychologically evaluated and categorized as a "paranoid schizophrenic," his/her *communicative behavior* during the hostage negotiation is, as Schlossberg suggests, problem-solving oriented; i.e., rational. Further, the negotiator's communicative behavior during the negotiations is also rational; i.e., problem-solving oriented. Therefore, *for purposes of the communicative dynamics that occur during negotiation,* the psychological label of crazy or psycho can lead to a misinterpretation of hostage taker actions by the negotiator. As long as the hostage taker is "talking," he/she is engaging in some level of rational, problem-solving behavior and is, from an interpersonal communication sense, not crazy or psycho in his/her interaction behavior. This is not to say that the content of his/her communication may be delusionary. However, the process of communication that is taking place between the negotiator and the hostage taker (even if the content of the discussions involves "spiders on the walls") is "problem-solving" and therefore, at least to some degree, is rational.

Typologies and the Cross-Cultural Dimension

The typologies also do not explain differences in perception, values and communication negotiation rules and actions that are culturally determined. In this sense, a crusader is a crusader, a criminal is a criminal and a crazy is a crazy regardless of cultural background. Yet even with individuals identified as paranoid schizophrenic, a person enacts his/her paranoia in culturally appropriate ways; ways frequently quite different to paranoid behavior in other cultures.

For example, one fundamental communication value in Cuban-American culture is that of *personalismo* (a concern for personal dignity and a personal approach to social relations). Related to this is the communicative value of individuality (the uniqueness of the individual; a quality which resides within each person) and respect (something a person deserves because of his/her personal qualities or standing in the community).

In 1987, 200 Cuban prison inmates in Oakdale, Louisiana rioted and held 28 prison employees hostage for nine days. On the final day, Bishop Augustin Roman, an Auxiliary Bishop of Miami's Roman Catholic Archdiocese, was flown into the prison (in response to repeated requests for his presence from the Cuban prisoners) where he conducted Sunday mass and urged the prisoners to give up. The Bishop had a great deal of "respect" because of his position in the community; he was somebody who the prisoners could trust. Further, his communication during and after the mass was distinctly "cultural." That is, he stressed that the individuality of the Cuban prisoners was not tarnished and he communicated throughout a strong degree of *personalismo* to the prisoners. Finally, he established a surrender ritual within which the director of the Bureau of Prisons and the Bishop himself signed a petition from the prisoners. This was a ceremonial "surrender with dignity" in which the lead negotiator was dressed in white and carried a two-foot cross.[25] In this case, a third party, communicating in themes relevant to the Cuban prisoners and structuring the situation to enable a "culturally appropriate" termination of the hostage situation to take place, played a significant "cultural" role in the hostage negotiations.

PRINCIPLES AND CROSS-CULTURAL NEGOTIATION

Ventilation, Language and Cross-Cultural Negotiation

One guideline suggests that the role of the negotiator should be to reduce tension by letting the hostage taker "ventilate." In a broad sense, this admonition would apply to almost every culture. If hostage takers are allowed to really express their feelings, tensions would likely decrease. However, negotiators must be aware that when and how people vent their feelings varies with culture. In mainstream American culture, the general pattern is to control emotional outbursts; the greater the degree of "emotionality" in a communication transaction, the closer the individual is to being "out of control."[26] Therefore, the negotiator walks a fine line in helping the hostage taker to "ventilate," while at the same time attempting to communicate that the atmosphere is secure and safe, so that the hostage taker does not lose control.

For Anglo-American negotiators, the purpose of ventilating is to not only express emotion, but to expel emotion; that is, to get rid of emotional tension so a more rational (that is, unemotional) problem-solving process can begin. In Anglo-American culture, emotion is generally viewed as dysfunctional to problem-solving and is to be either controlled or expelled. Generally, emotionality in communication is a sign of instability to many Anglo-Americans, not sincerity. This cultural view towards the role emotion plays in negotiation causes an Anglo-American negotiator to use a *lack* of emotionality in his/her verbal communication behavior as a yardstick for determining the degree to which the hostage taker is problem-solving. Generally, the closer an Anglo-American is to losing control and becoming aggressive, hostile,

or "going physical," the more emotionality is evidenced in his verbal discourse.

In Hispanic- and African-American cultures, there is a greater degree of "emotional elasticity." That is, a greater tolerance exists concerning the expression of emotion in conflict situations. Further, greater emotionality is associated with greater sincerity and concern (i.e., the more emotional one is, the more trustworthy one is). In short, the "yardstick" is different; emotionality does not communicate irrationality but sincerity, and emotional outbursts do not necessarily mean that one is close to being "out of control."

Based on personal discussions with the FBI negotiators who were at the Oakdale prison situation described earlier, these cultural patterns did, in fact, emerge and lead to misunderstandings. For instance, during the first few days of negotiation, the Cuban prisoner negotiators appeared to the Anglo-American negotiators to be highly charged, very emotional and potentially explosive. Yet the emotionality expressed during this initial phase was far more cultural in origin (as the Anglo-American negotiators later found out) and did not indicate imminent danger to the hostages.

Related to the issue of emotional expressiveness is the language in which ventilation occurs. This is a particularly important issue when negotiating cross-culturally. Again, in the Oakdale prison riot, during negotiations, the Cuban prisoners were required to negotiate in English in spite of the fact that they preferred to speak Spanish. This was done in order to deny the Cuban negotiators emotional spontaneity and to make the negotiations more "rational."[27]

Clearly, this position has some merit, particularly from the Anglo-American cultural perspective. However, ventilation involves a high degree of "emotional spontaneity." It is extremely difficult to "ventilate" in a second language. When ventilation is a primary concern during a negotiation session, the requirement that the hostage taker speak in English when his English skills are weak actually appears to contradict the purpose of ventilation and it also likely increases, rather than decreases, the level of tension.

Containment and Cross-Cultural Negotiation

A second guideline typically followed is to contain the hostage taking situation. While containment prevents escape or the unintended involvement of bystanders, it is possible for a hostage taker to perceive this tactic as encirclement—a hostile act—which might increase tension and provoke a violent reaction. In the field of international relations, containment is a reactive, protective and somewhat passive tactic. This is similar to the meaning of containment within the crisis intervention model discussed earlier (i.e., to create a controlled environment in which therapeutic communication can take place).

Within the hostage taking literature, however, there seems to be a sense that containment means isolation and maintaining a "pressure cooker" atmosphere. For instance, a number of ways have been suggested to "contain" a hostage taking situation, including turning off the telephone, electricity, gas and water. As Head comments, "containment efforts may continue to tighten the noose, the vigil taking from several hours to several days or even weeks. . . ."[28] In this sense, such terms as "impoverish the environment," "manipulate anxiety," and "proactive manipulation" really mean to exert pressure, to tighten the thumbscrews. In the hostage taking situation at the Oakdale prison discussed earlier, helicopters were flown over the prison yard periodically to constrict the "body space" of the inmates. As Van Zandt and Fuselier state:

> As part of the plan to keep controlled pressure on the inmates, negotiators recommended helicopters make frequent overflights of the detention center. Such flights were suspended during actual negotiations or when it appeared the inmates' stress level might cause them to harm the hostages.[29]

One example of this occurred Tuesday, November 24th. The inmates saw the helicopter overflights as threatening and demanded the flights end. When the helicopters continued flying near the detention center, the inmates responded to this increased sense of threat by destroying the telephone they used to communicate with the negotiators.

Constricting body space as a form of containment is not containment as it is classically viewed. Rather, constricting body space only produces anxiety, it is an aggressive act. In this sense, cutting off power, water or food is *not* containment. It is a form of punishment. Taking away such reinforcers produces exactly the same reactions as pain;[30] the most common being to disengage from problem-solving behavior and initiate irrational aggression.

Finally, when hostage takers believe they are morally right, that the pain or punishment is undeserved, tightening the noose only causes them to dig in their heels.[31] For instance, Germany's bombing of London during World War II did not produce the result of England giving up. Rather, the British only fought on more valiantly. Containment, when it is obtrusive and intrusive is not containment; it is aggression. The result most often is to increase tension and reduce problem-solving behavior; thus increasing the possibility of aggressive action to be taken by the hostage taker. Further, this can escalate tension, not reduce it. Research by Hammer, Rogan, Van Zandt and Laffon concerning the negotiation dynamics involved in the seven day Talladega Prison siege supports this contention.[32] They found that increased threats by hostage takers were made in a reactive fashion, as a response to feeling threatened by "containment" actions taken by the law enforcement negotiation/tactical teams.

Face-to-Face Interaction, Third Parties and Cross-Cultural Negotiation

Finally, a common guideline is to avoid face-to-face negotiations and to not employ third parties in the negotiation process. Given the danger of negotiators being taken hostage or losing their lives, limiting face-to-face interaction is certainly a wise precaution in most situations. If the hostage taker is Anglo-American, negotiating by telephone can be as effective as face-to-face encounters. However, because many non-Western peoples tend to rely more on nonverbal behavior and less on verbal interaction compared to Anglo-Americans,[33] it may be more difficult to establish trust in negotiations when it is conducted through the telephone.

The use of a third party or a "go-between" is not a strong cultural practice among Americans. However, it is a common method of resolving conflict and interpersonal disputes among more collectivistic societies (e.g., Asian, African, Latin American cultures).[34] The use of the Bishop as a go-between discussed earlier at the Oakdale prison was a logical "cultural strategy" for the Cuban prisoners. Similarly, during the so-called *Hanafi* siege in Washington, DC in March of 1977, the end came peacefully following face-to-face negotiations between the Muslim hostage takers and the Ambassadors of three Muslim countries: Iran, Egypt and Pakistan. All of the hostages were released and their captors arrested and charged with armed kidnapping. The cultural strategy of the "go-between" coupled with face-to-face interaction in this particular case was soundly employed to resolve this dangerous situation.

CONCLUSION

During a hostage negotiation, the outside professional most likely to be consulted by law enforcement officials is a psychologist. Many of the guidelines and procedures used in negotiations have been developed by psychologists. Also, it is the psychologist who may serve as part of the tertiary team to provide advice and counseling support to police negotiators. Psychologists are often called in as well to develop a "psychological profile" of the hostage taker.

A psychological profile is quite useful when it enables a negotiator to anticipate the *behavior* of a hostage taker and to identify those tactics that would most likely motivate the hostage taker to release the hostages and give him/herself up.

Yet a psychological profile is only of limited value when the hostage taker is from a culture different from that of the police negotiator or police psychologist. What is needed in these cases is to develop a "cultural profile" that can aid the negotiator.

Members of a culture share a similar *cultural image* of themselves and their world.

Those who share a culture also tend to share similar behavior patterns. This is particularly evidenced in communication patterns (the sending and receiving of messages). It is only through increased understanding and skill in cross-cultural communication that we can know the perceptual world of hostage takers from cultures different from our own and can explain and predict their behavior. If a male hostage taker is Cuban, we can generalize and expect that he is unlikely to give up if he loses face or is shamed in the process. We know that he tends to build trust through more personalized communication patterns and such status and role indicators as age, gender and community position of negotiators or "go-betweens" will influence his attitude and behavior toward the negotiation process. Yet we also know that these cultural patterns are not invariant.

A cultural profile provides the negotiator with one more tool with which he/she can more effectively influence the outcome of a hostage situation. To ignore this tool and assume that all hostage takers perceive, think, value and behave in the same manner can lead to major miscalculations when dealing with hostage takers from different cultural backgrounds. A cultural profile allows the negotiator to avoid these culturally based errors and maximize alternatives for negotiating positive outcomes. Incorporating the notion of intercultural communication allows greater refinement and expansion of the negotiation guidelines that are followed by many negotiators in a hostage taking incident.

ENDNOTES

[1] D. A. Soskis and C. R. Van Zandt, "Hostage Negotiation: Law Enforcement's Most Effective Nonlethal Weapon," *The FBI Management Quarterly,* no. 6, 1986: 1–8.

[2] T. Pierson, "An Approach to Barricaded Subjects," *Law and Order,* Sept. 1980: 40–42; W. B. Head, "The Hostage Response," Ph.D. dissertation, The School of Criminal Justice, The State University of New York at Albany, 1988.

[3] F. Bolz, and E. Hershey (1979). *Hostage Cop* (New York: Rawson, Wade Publishers, 1979).

[4] See Head, *op. cit.,* for full details of this analysis.

[5]*Ibid.,* 145.

[6]H. Schlossberg, "Police Response to Hostage Situations," in J. T. O'Brien and M. Marcus, eds., *Crime and Justice in America* (New York: Pergamon Press, 1979): 209–220.

[7]M. R. Hammer, R. G. Rogan, C. Van Zandt and A. Laffon, "Communication Dynamics in a Crisis Situation: Negotiating the Talladega Prison Takeover," unpublished manuscript, 1993.

[8]Head, *op. cit.*

[9]M. R. Hammer and W. B. Gudykunst, "The Influence of Ethnicity and Sex on Social Penetration in Close Friendships," *Journal of Black Studies*, no. 17, 1987: 418–437; W. B. Gudykunst and M. R. Hammer, "The Influence of Ethnicity, Gender, and Dyadic Composition on Uncertainty Reduction in Initial Interactions," *Journal of Black Studies*, no. 18, 1987: 191–214; M. R. Hammer, "The Influence of Ethnic and Attitude Similarity on Initial Social Penetration," in Y. Y. Kim, ed., *Interethnic Communication: Current Research* (Newbury Park, CA: Sage Publications, 1986): 225–237; W. B. Gudykunst and M. R. Hammer, "The Influence of Social Identity and Intimacy of Interethnic Relationships on Uncertainty Reduction Processes," *Human Communication Research,* no. 4, 1988: 569–601; G. Weaver, "American Identity Movements: A Cross-Cultural Confrontation," in G. Weaver, ed., *Readings in Cross-Cultural Communication*, 2d ed., (Needham Heights, MA: Simon & Schuster Publishing, 1987): 88–92; G. Weaver, "Multicultural Child Care Staff," *Child and Youth Care Administration*, no. 1, 1988: 49–55; T. Kochman, *Black and White Styles in Conflict* (Chicago, IL: The University of Chicago Press, 1981).

[10]Copeland & Griggs Productions, *Valuing Diversity* (a videotape), San Francisco, CA, 1987.

[11]G. D. Fuselier, "A Practical Overview of Hostage Negotiations," *FBI Law Enforcement Bulletin*, no. 55, 1986: 1–4; G. D. Fuselier, C. R. Van Zandt and F. J. Lanceley, "Hostage/Barricade Incidents," *FBI Law Enforcement Bulletin,* 1991: 6–12; M. S. Miron and A. P. Goldstein, *Hostage* (New York: Pergamon Press, 1979); T. Strentz, "Negotiating with the Hostage Taker Exhibiting Paranoid Schizophrenic Symptoms," *Journal of Police Science and Administration*, no. 14, 1986: 12–16.

[12]H. H. A. Cooper, *The Hostage-Takers* (Boulder, CO: Paladin Press, 1981).

[13]W. Middendorf, "New Developments in the Taking of Hostages and Kidnapping—A Summary," *National Criminal Justice Reference Service Translation,* Washington, D.C., 1975.

[14]F. J. Hacker, *Crusaders, Criminals, Crazies: Terror and Terrorism in Our Time* (New York: W. W. Norton, 1976).

[15]Schlossberg, *op. cit.*

[16]Head, 144.

[17]S. Duck, "How to Lose Friends Without Influencing People," in M. E. Roloff and G. R. Miller, eds., *Interpersonal Process: New Directions in Communication Research* (Newbury Park, CA: Sage Publications, 1987): 278–298; D. R. Peterson, "Conflict," in H. H. Kelley, E. Berschied, A. Christensen, J. H. Harvey, J. L. Huston, G. Levinger, E. McClintock, L. A. Paplau and D. R. Peterson, eds., *Close Relationships* (New York: W. H. Freeman, 1983): 360–396.

[18]W. A. Donohue, R. G. Rogan, C. Ramesh and C. Borchgrevink, "Tracking the Double-Bind in Hostage Negotiation," paper presented to the Interpersonal and Small Group Division of the Speech Communication Association Annual Conference, Chicago, November 1990; R. G. Rogan, "An Interaction Analysis of Negotiator and Hostage-Taker Identity-Goal, Relational-Goal, and Language Intensity Message Behavior Within Hostage Negotiations: A Descriptive Investigation of Three Negotiations," Ph.D. dissertation, Michigan State University, *Dissertation Abstracts International*, no. 51, 1990: 12A.

[19]Schlossberg, 209.

[20]*Ibid.,* 219.

[21]*Ibid.*

[22]*Ibid.,* p. 215.

[23]*Ibid.*

[24]P. Watzlawick, J. H. Beavin and D. D. Jackson, *Pragmatics of Human Communication* (New York: W. W. Norton, 1987), 51.

[25]G. D. Fuselier, C. R. Van Zandt and F. J. Lanceley, "Negotiating the Protracted Incident: The Oakdale and Atlanta Prison Sieges," *FBI Law Enforcement Bulletin,* 1991: 6–12.

[26]See Kochman, *Black and White Styles in Conflict,* for a fuller description of these patterns and the patterns discussed below.

[27]C. R. Van Zandt and G. D. Fuselier, "Nine Days of Crisis Negotiations: The Oakdale Siege," *Corrections Today*, July 1989: 16–24.

[28]Head, 66.

[29]C. R. Van Zandt and G. D. Fuselier, 18.

[30]N. Azrin, "Pain and Aggression," in G. Weaver, ed., *Readings in Cross-Cultural Communication*, 2d ed. (Needham Heights, MA: Simon & Schuster, 1987): 264–269.

[31]For a Discussion of this General Issue, see J. D. Frank, "The Face of the Enemy," in G.

Weaver, ed., *Readings in Cross-Cultural Communication,* 2d ed. (Needham Heights, MA: Simon & Schuster, 1987): 33–38.

[32]Hammer, Rogan, Van Zandt, and Laffon, *op. cit.*

[33]E. T. Hall, "How Cultures Collide," *Psychology Today,* 10 (7), 1976; W. B. Gudykunst and Y. Y. Kim, *Communicating with Strangers* (New York: Harcourt, 1992); G. Weaver, "Law Enforcement in a Culturally Diverse Society," *FBI Law Enforcement Bulletin,* September 1992: 1–7.

[34]Gundykunst and Kim, *op. cit.*

ADDITIONAL REFERENCES

Condon, John C. *Good Neighbors: Communicating with the Mexicans,* Yarmouth, ME: Intercultural Press, 1985.

Graham, K., "The Hmong and Cultural Change: Migration to a New World," unpublished paper, The International Communication, The School of International Service, The American University, Washington, D.C., 1989.

Olney, D., "Population Trends," in G. L. Hendreicks et al. *The Hmong in Transition,* New York: Center for Migration Studies, 1986: 179–184.

Shuter, R., "The Hmong of Laos: Orality, Communication, and Acculturation," in L. Samovar and R. Porter, eds., *Intercultural Communication: A Reader,* 6th ed., Belmont, CA: Wads-worth, 1991: 270–276.

68

Culture and Business: Interacting Effectively to Achieve Mutual Goals

Mu Dan Ping

Many of the efforts businesspeople from different countries make to conclude deals and establish relationships with each other do not fail because of external factors such as money, technology, the market, product, politics, economics or technical considerations. These failures are more often caused by a lack of understanding of cultural differences, involving such factors as personal values, expectations and the perceptions held by people from different cultures.

The inability to interact effectively in a cross-cultural interchange can lead to misunderstandings and have a negative effect on people and business between two countries such as China and the United States.

The following case study about how an American company pursued a contract with a Chinese paper mill for the purchase of papermaking machine illustrates the point. The later discussion of factors involved in effective cross-cultural interchanges uses examples from the case study. The story in the study is true, but the

Ms. Mu is a Chinese attorney and business consultant affiliated with the international law firm of Bryan Cave in Los Angeles.

Reprinted from *East Asian Executive Reports*, March 15, 1995, 6–17, by permission of International Executive Reports.

names of persons, companies, locations, and so forth, are fictitious to preserve confidentiality.

CASE STUDY

Because of a shortage of paper supplies in China, the Chinese Central Committee in the early 1990s had approved funds for the purchase of advanced papermaking equipment from abroad, and a paper mill in Hebei Province was looking for a supplier.

Innocents Abroad

Mr. Johnson, the president of a papermaking machinery factory in the American Midwest, learned of the opportunity through his local Chamber of Commerce and responded immediately with the relevant data and specifications. A month later, Johnson was invited to visit the paper mill, and he and his senior engineer, Mr. Smith, left for China, enthusiastic about a potential contract that could generate $15 million to $20 million in sales.

When they arrived in China, they were met by the mill's general manager himself, Mr. Wang, and other people from the mill. They were escorted to a nice hotel and told to rest up for a while; a banquet would be held for them that evening.

At the banquet, the American visitors were warmly welcomed by several officials of the Hebei provincial government and Wang, as well as others from the mill. One of the officials toasted "friendship and long-term working relationships" between the Chinese and their American guests. Both Johnson and Smith were somewhat puzzled; as far as they were concerned, their mission was to promote the sale of papermaking machines.

The food was delicious, and the Americans were overwhelmed by the many courses. They were told several times during the evening: "This is your first time to visit China. The Chinese have a saying: first time as a stranger, second time as an old friend."

In the next three days, Johnson and Smith were totally involved in a very busy schedule. They visited the paper mill, looked around the workshops, and had a full-day meeting with Wang and several engineers; they spent half a day with officials from various government departments, including those in charge of the paper mill. The Americans had expected the meetings to focus on specifications, data, price, and contract terms, but most of the time was spent on introductions and descriptions of the Chinese mill and the American company. The Chinese spent a significant amount of time explaining the importance of the purchase and the expansion of paper productions in China.

In the remaining day and a half, the Americans were escorted on sightseeing tours and treated to two full meals a day, each consisting of 10 or more courses. Mr. Wang was with them at every dinner (he said he wanted to make sure his visitors were treated well). The night before they returned to the U.S., Johnson and Smith were given a farewell dinner, with one toast after another, and one course after another. The atmosphere was full of hospitality. Finally, the hosts and guests stood together for several pictures, their arms full of presents, from Chinese silks to handicrafts.

The Americans were touched by the kindness and generosity of their host, but they were disappointed because neither could figure out whether the Chinese had any intention of buying their papermaking equipment. The talk of "friendship" and "long-term working relationships" had perplexed them; they didn't want to waste time on a relationship until they had a contract. In addition, the tight schedule had exhausted them. On the one hand, they had been well looked after, but on the other hand they had felt constrained. They had expected to have free time to look around on their own.

After their return to the U.S., Johnson and Smith sent a "thank you" note and an invitation to Mr. Wang and his colleagues to visit the American company. Two weeks later, Mr. Wang accepted, and the visit was scheduled for early fall.

The French Connection

In the meantime, the Chinese had also invited Mr. Pierre, the president of a French papermaking machinery company near Paris. He and his senior engineer arrived for a four-day stay and were treated as the Americans had been.

Three weeks after returning to Paris, Pierre sent three company representatives—an engineer, a salesperson, and the public relations director—to visit the Chinese mill. They stayed for two weeks, spending most of their time in the workshops, chatting with the engineers, workers, and Mr. Wang himself. They also spent time with authorities at different government levels. They were aware of their competitor in the U.S., who had better technology than theirs.

Through their casual conversations, the French learned the price range and the specific equipment features the Chinese were looking for. They also learned that the Chinese wanted the manufacturer to provide training and other after-sales services. They invited Wang and other senior managers and engineers to dinner several times. On Sundays, they paid visits to Wang's family and other employees' families, leaving presents from Paris. These friendly gestures made the Chinese feel quite comfortable in working with the French.

Hospitality, American Style

In the early fall, Mr. Wang, a senior engineer and an interpreter visited the American company. They arrived on a Sunday to find a taxi waiting for them at the airport. They were taken to a nice hotel and were notified that their dinner was arranged for 6:30 P.M. at the hotel. They dined alone on salad, steak, steamed vegetables and mashed potatoes, all of which tasted strange and pretty awful to them.

The next morning, a taxi picked them up and took them to the American company, where Mr. Johnson and his colleagues greeted them at the gate and escorted them to a conference room. Three piles of materials were ready and waiting for the Chinese visitors, including the U.S. company's brochure and technical information. The Americans had prepared full professional presentations with lantern slides and a projector, but the meeting went slowly because of the difficult translations. A lunch of sandwiches was served in the conference room.

The Americans felt they had done their best to impress the visitors with their technology and facilities, but they got no clue as to how their presentations were received. When Johnson sounded out the interpreter, the response was, "Not bad."

That evening, the Americans held a dinner for their guests at a French restaurant, but the beautiful tableware and elaborately prepared French food did not seem to stimulate the visitors' appetites. After dinner, the Chinese were presented with pens and leather briefcases as gifts.

On the second day, the Chinese were shown around the factory and watched a demonstration of the operational process. They were very impressed with the technology, which was considered first class worldwide. They learned that the price was reasonable, and after-sales services would be provided. However, the training would be at the Chinese firm's expense.

At the end of the day, when Johnson asked what the next step would be, Wang replied that the Chinese would report to their supervisory authorities, make a decision, and inform the American firm. Before they said goodbye, Johnson told the visitors that the next day would be "free time," in which they could do some shopping and sightseeing on their own. The Chinese were taken back to their hotel, where they again dined alone.

Wang and his colleagues spent most of the next day in the hotel. They didn't know where to go or what to do. They felt that the day was wasted and that they had been left alone because they were not respected. The Americans seemed to think that their own work and time were more important than spending time with the visitors. The Chinese were angry and disappointed. Good prices and superior technology did not make up for the perceived slight.

Hospitality, French Style

The next month, Wang, his senior engineer, and a French interpreter left China for Paris. Although they arrived on Sunday, they were met by Mr. Pierre and his assistant.

The French drove their guests to the hotel, helped them settle in, and then took them to a Chinese restaurant for dinner. During the next three days, the visitors met with Pierre, his senior engineers, and salespeople. They were shown around the workshops and watched demonstrations of the operational process. The Chinese realized that some of the specific features of the facility were not as advanced as those of the American company. Moreover, the French firm's price was higher, but it offered to provide free training an after-sales services.

During their four days in Paris, the Chinese ate mostly Chinese cuisine; Pierre took them to a French restaurant just once. On their last day, the Chinese were escorted to a sightseeing tour by their hosts.

At the farewell dinner held for the visitors, Wang told Pierre that he would send a letter of intent as soon as he got back to China, and both sides could then prepare for negotiations. He stated that the Chinese felt comfortable working with their French host. There was one toast after another to friendship and a long-term working relationship.

WHY WORRY ABOUT CULTURAL DIFFERENCES?

As this case study illustrates, the inability to interact effectively in cross-cultural interchanges generates misunderstandings and can be costly not only in terms of lost business.

- In this case, the American firm seems to be the main loser: it lost a potential opportunity to make an attractive deal.

- But the Chinese company was also a loser: it lost the potential opportunity to obtain a papermaking facility with world-class technology at a reasonable price. The Chinese government had modified its budget in order to purchase the most advanced facility, and it lost the opportunity to achieve this goal.

- While the French company won the contract, it sold non-competitive technology, and thereby may have been a loser in the long term: had it lost the business, it may have been forced to upgrade its technology to become more competitive.

The case study also illustrates the importance in cross-cultural interchanges of the perceptions held by people from different cultures. Our attitudes and behavior toward people from other cultures depend on how we perceive them; and the way we look at things depends on where we stand.

The people of the world's diverse cultures are increasingly dependent on each other, and in today's fast-paced business world, it has become critical for them to understand each other. Yet many things get in the way.

KEY FACTORS IN EFFECTIVE CROSS-CULTURAL INTERCHANGE

Lens Phenomenon

How can people from different cultures interact effectively in order to achieve mutual goals? Interaction with others depends on how we interpret or view their behavior, and on how well we understand how our own behavior is being viewed and interpreted.

People observe behavior through a "lens" in their minds. The lens is used to interpret various behaviors and thus determine their meaning. The lens is influenced by one's own cultural environment.

As the case study demonstrates, people going into another culture carry their own cultural distortions along. They may experience difficulties in the foreign country because of their own upbringing or culture, or because they lack an understanding of the foreign culture. They tend to view everything in the host culture through the unique lens of their own cultural background, reflected in their cultural values, expectations and perceptions.

Values

C. G. Burke and K. Stewart have identified six shared values necessary for the existence of human social groups: honesty, trust, courage, respect for human dignity, fairness, and love.[1] They maintain that all cultures have these values in their own combinations or mixes. These values, however, cannot be observed directly. What is observed is behavior, which is interpreted as an expression of certain values. So while all cultures share these values,

the behaviors through which they are expressed differ and are subject to interpretation.

Which specific behaviors are viewed as demonstrating such values as honest, trustworthiness and courage depends on interpretation. Thus, identical behaviors can be viewed differently depending on the unique lens through which the viewer interprets them. People from different cultures may hold shared values, but they do not necessarily attribute the same meanings to identical behaviors. We tend to judge other people on our own terms.

In the case study, for example, the Chinese arranged a busy, tight schedule for their American visitors. In the Chinese view, this was the hospitable thing to do, showing care and respect for their guests. The Americans, however, felt constrained by the tight schedule and experienced a sense of loss of freedom. They would have preferred to have some time on their own.

The Americans, in turn, based on their own value system, arranged a loose, relaxed schedule for their Chinese visitors. The Chinese, however, viewed this as showing a lack of respect for them and felt they had been insulted and mistreated.

On both sides, the initial intention was to do a favor for the other party, but because of ignorance of each other's value systems, the favor was viewed disfavorably. Both assumed the schedule they made for their guests was valid and showed respect, and they never questioned this assumption.

Why do people behave so differently and interpret behaviors so differently? To deal with this question, we need to examine attributed values.

According to I. C. Brown, some cultures demand honesty with members of one's own culture group but accept a more relaxed standard when strangers are involved.[2] What does a "more relaxed standard" mean? Most of us assume we have an underlying standard that defines what honesty is, but how do we define what behavior demonstrates this honesty? Assuming that being honest is being straightforward, how straightforward one can be depends on the people one is being straightforward to; that is, on whether they are family, friends or strangers. One may choose not to be straight-forward with a stranger based on consider-ations of diplomacy or caution, but the stranger may think one is simply not honest.

What is missing in Brown's analysis is that "honesty" is an interpretation—an attributed value. The issue here is not about being honest with one's own group and accepting a more relaxed standard with strangers. Different be-haviors are interpreted as reflecting honesty or dishonesty depending upon the viewer's per-ceptual lens. All societies value honesty; the issue is how each society interprets what con-stitutes honest behavior.

In the case study, Mr. Wang and his col-leagues interpreted their American host's failure to meet them at the airport and spend time showing them around the city as demonstrating a lack of respect. They acted on their attributed value and decided not to do business with the American firm. Mr. Johnson may well have re-spected his Chinese visitors, but he simply did not know how to express this respect in a way the Chinese would understand.

In cross-cultural interactions, people of-ten assume that their interpretation of others' behavior is the true one. They take their attrib-uted values and meanings for granted. Many are so locked into their own perceptual lenses that they often do not even realize that their interpretations are simply conjectures, and that alternative interpretations are possible.

The lesson at the core of the case study is that people cannot conduct cross-cultural in-terchange effectively unless they are willing to challenge their own conjectures. In this con-text, there is no objective or universal truth. When people with different perceptual lenses interact, they need to make efforts to suspend judging and condemning others' behaviors.

Expectations

R. M. Stogdill has defined an expectation as the readiness for reinforcement."[3] In other words, an individual's behavior is influenced by the way he or she anticipates that events will occur. People tend to do the things they expect will lead to rewards and avoid doing those they expect will lead to undesired outcomes.

Expectations can act as self-fulfilling prophecies. Expecting certain things to hap-pen shapes behavior in such a way that the probability that the expected will actually hap-pen is increased.[4] On the other hand, expecta-tions can be unrealistically high, and unful-filled expectations can make matters worse. When people's expectations are not realized, they may attribute motives to the "offender" based on their own cultural constructs.

To use the case study as an example, the expectations and behaviors of Mr. Johnson and Mr. Wang are compared in the Table 1.

This comparison suggests that expecta-tions may influence individuals in understand-ing, communicating and interacting with each other. Valid understanding and effective inter-actions are hindered when:

- we expect other people to know what we know;
- we expect other people to behave the way we do;
- we overestimate or underestimate our-selves or others and are not aware of the gap between our expectations and reality.

Johnson and Wang did not share the same expectations. Each expected his counterpart to be aware of the other's way of doing busi-ness. Johnson went to China to obtain the contract, and he assumed the Chinese side was aware of this. For Wang, the parties had to get to know each other before any business was established, and he assumed the Ameri-can side knew this.

Johnson's expectation was not fulfilled during his trip to China. He was disappointed. To fulfill his expectations about obtaining the contract, he created a "more professional" situ-ation for the Chinese visit to his company. He assumed that Mr. Wang would appreciate this. He expected Wang to respond as he, Johnson, expected. Mr. Johnson's unfulfilled expecta-tions actually made matters worse.

Similarly, Wang came to the U.S. expect-ing to be treated as he had treated the Ameri-cans. Wang expected Johnson to behave as he, Wang, expected. His unfulfilled expectations also made matters worse: he decided to give up the first-class technology and the reasonable price.

Where is reality in all this? How can people assess reality in order not to build up too-high expectations? It appears that those who are constantly aware of the gap between expectations and reality make an effort to understand where reality lies, and behave in ways that tend to reduce the gap. Different perceptions of reality, however, expand the gap.

Perceptions

In perceiving the world, people take certain cues from their environment, but there are too many cues for any person to pay attention to at the same time. Thus, individuals have many ways of reducing these cues and organizing them into meaningful pieces of information. The ways in which people take information from the environment become subconscious and habitual.

The following example is based on the author's separate conversations with a Chinese engineer and an American quality control manager, both of whom had previously worked together in a department of a Sino-American joint venture in southern China. As background, the Chinese tend to perceive supervisory roles as more authoritarian than do Americans, who prefer participatory decision-making. The example recounts verbal conversation in quotation marks, with the percep-

tions being made by the Chinese and the American in parentheses.

American: "How long will it take you to finish this report?"
(Perceptions—American: I asked him to participate. Chinese: This is strange. He is the boss. Why doesn't he tell me?)
Chinese: "I do not know. How long should it take?"
(Perceptions—American: He refuses to take responsibility. Chinese: I asked him for an order.)
American: "You are in the best position to analyze the time requirements."
(Perceptions—American: I'm pressing him to take responsibility for his own actions. Chinese: This does not make sense! I'd better give him an answer.)
Chinese: "Ten days."
(Perceptions—American: He lacks the ability to estimate time; this estimate is totally inadequate.)
American: "Take fifteen. Is it agreed you will do it in fifteen days?"
(Perceptions—American: I've offered a contract. Chinese: These are my orders, 15 days.)

The report, in fact required 20 days of regular work. So the Chinese engineer worked day and night, but at the end of the 15th day, he needed one more day. The scenario continues.

TABLE 1
Comparison of Johnson and Wang's Expectations and Behavior

	Expectations	Expected Conversations	Behavior	When Expectations Were Unfulfilled
Mr. Johnson	• To get the job done. • To obtain the contract and *close* the deal.	Specifications, price and contract terms.	Professional and technically-oriented.	Felt disappointed and confused.
Mr. Wang	• To establish a long-term relationship. • To obtain the contract and confirm that the relationship has been built in order to *begin* the future working together.	Background and introduction of the company; training and services after the purchase.	Hospitable and less technically-oriented.	Felt hurt and not respected.

American: "Where is the report?"

(Perceptions—American: I am making sure he fulfills his contract. Chinese: He is asking for the report.)

Chinese: "It will be ready tomorrow."

(Perceptions—Chinese: I am working very hard and am cooperating with my superior.)

American: "But we had agreed it would be ready today."

(Perceptions—American: I must teach him to fulfill a contract. He should learn to be more professional. Chinese: This is not fair! Not only did he give me wrong orders, but he does not even appreciate that I am doing a 20-day job in 16 days.)

Outcome: The Chinese engineer went to the general manager and asked for a transfer to a different department.

(Perceptions—The American is surprised. Chinese: I can't work for such a man; he looks down on me.)

This example illustrates the important role perceptions play in how people understand the world, and also just how wrong these perceptions can be. At almost every point in the conversation, the statement of one person is meant in a way that does not match the perception of the other person, to the detriment of the relationship.

People behave on the basis of what they perceive reality to be, and not necessarily on the basis of what really is. As they receive information, they assemble it and incorporate it into a meaningful experience unique to themselves. They paint a picture of the real world that expresses their personal view, and no two people paint exactly the same picture. All are bound by the limits of their own perceptual world, which is culturally shaped.[5]

The skill needed to work with people from another culture is the ability to correctly interpret the meaning of the other's behavior, verbal or nonverbal.

To return to the case study, from the Americans' perspective, the deal seemed to be based on common sense; the American company had first-class technology and a reasonable price, and the Chinese should have bought the machines from the U.S. firm. But human beings are not always that rational; they do not always make decisions based on economics or professional points. The Chinese realized that the equipment they purchased from the French company was not as advanced as the American machine, and that furthermore, the price was higher. But they decided to work with the French because they felt comfortable working with them. And they felt comfortable because the way in which they were treated made them feel they were understood and respected, from the Chinese perspective, of course.

Mr. Pierre won the contract because he correctly interpreted the Chinese party's needs and behavior. It can be assumed that he may have observed, or even carefully studied, Chinese etiquette. He also sent three representatives to China to learn about the firm's needs. He organized the information and perceived that the Chinese considered training and after-sale services more important than the purchase price. The Chinese were concerned that their big investment would be wasted if there were no trained workers to operate the machine or if technical problems were left unresolved. On the basis of his accurate perception and understanding, Mr. Pierre turned his company's disadvantage into an advantage.

OTHER FACTORS

Certainly there are other factors that help create misunderstandings when people of different cultures interact. The important thing is to be aware of cultural differences.

American Insurance and Chinese Luck

Last year, I took several American clients to visit a high-tech industrial development zone in China. Because of the tax benefits available in the zone, they wanted to explore the possibility of establishing a wholly owned facility there. The Chinese administrators showed them around and helped them select a site. While walking around, we saw some Chinese workers laying water pipes, and one American asked me to ask the workers about the water pressure. I asked him to be more specific. He said: "If we put up a building of several stories here, we will need to know whether the water supply is sufficient in case of fire; we'll probably have to consider the insurance issue as well."

I translated. The Chinese administrators looked at each other in confusion. Then one said: "Of course we have a sufficient water supply. They don't have to worry about that. Fire? Insurance? What bad luck to think of fire now when they haven't started anything yet. We all know it will bring them bad luck if they think this way. By the way, will you please ask him if they plan to set up a cemetery before they set up their office building." After I translated, everyone laughed.

Apparently, the American notion of "insurance" and the Chinese notion of "luck" need to be explained if the two sides are to understand each other and communicate effectively.

Two-Level and One-Level Interactions

As the examples in this article illustrate, Americans in general interact on two levels: the professional/business level, and the personal level. The Chinese mainly interact on the personal level. This is why it's often said that the the most important factors in doing business with the Chinese are relationships, relationships, and relationships.

In the American culture, individuals separate a conflict issue from the person involved in the conflict. People can argue and scream at each other over a task-oriented point and not take any of it personally; they can remain friends. People can also do business with each other on the professional/business level without being friends at all.

In the Chinese culture, however, an issue is closely tied up with the person who originally raised it, and disagreement can be taken personally. To openly disagree with or confront someone in public is considered a severe blow and an extreme insult, causing both sides to "lose face." The Chinese prefer to do business with people they trust or consider friends.

For example, suppose that an American manager has been appointed to conduct a joint venture with a Chinese state-run company and is assigned to select skilled workers to employ at the venture. American management theory is based on the premise that each person in the organization will perform his or her tasks in a way that will promote the organization. The American manager therefore, on the basis of shared American values, prefers to hire qualified people; helping or hiring friends or relatives will be subordinated to the development of organizational objectives. In the Chinese culture, however, interpersonal relationships depend to a large extent on the value of the trust, and in this regard, greater distinctions are made between outsiders and insiders. Hiring friends and relatives therefore, on the basis of shared Chinese values, is a common practice in Chinese organizations.

To minimize cultural misunderstandings, the manager can examine the different Chinese and American solutions to all management questions being considered and determine in advance when to modify a management practice to fit the situation. The manager should also know where the difference exists and be able to intervene at the point rather than in another area.

Language Differences

Anyone involved in cross-cultural activities acknowledges the importance of being skilled in the host country language, but many believe that a competent interpreter who is equipped with far more than just the knowledge of words is all that is necessary.

A competent interpreter does not simply translate words but also conveys connotations. To a great extent, the accuracy of translation depends upon the interpreter's skill in both languages and understanding of both cultures.

Culture and language can inhibit communication. They also influence our perceptions and judgments. Knowledge of the other culture and fluency in the language can help increase understanding of the intended message. It is wise to rely on competent interpreters to bridge cultural gaps.

SKILLS FOR EFFECTIVE INTERCULTURAL EXCHANGE

Developing the following skills will help improve intercultural exchange:

- *Communicate Respect.* The ability to express respect for others—to convey, verbally and nonverbally, positive regard, encouragement and sincere interest—is an important part of conducting effective relations in every country. But it is difficult to know how to communicate respect to persons in another culture. When interacting with people from another culture, consider how to demonstrate respect for them.

- *Be Nonjudgmental.* Avoid moralistic, value-laden, evaluative statements, and listen in such a way that others can fully explain themselves. Most people like to feel that what they do and say will not be judged before they have an opportunity to fully explain themselves. The ability to withhold judgment and remain objective until one has enough information requires an understanding of the other person's point of view. It is an important skill.

- *Realize that Perceptions Are Personal.* Recognize the influence of one's own values, perceptions, opinions and knowledge on human interactions, and regard them as relative, rather than absolute. Realize that your own perceptions are not necessarily valid for the rest of the world. Personalize observations, be more tentative in conclusions, and demonstrate an ability to communicate that "this is my way, what is your way?" There is no "one and only" way.

- *Show Empathy.* This is the ability to "put yourself in someone else's shoes"—to understand others from their own point of view and to understand how they feel about the matter under consideration. But empathy also means understanding how one's position looks from the other fellow's shoes.

- *Tolerate Ambiguity.* This is the ability to react to new, different and unpredictable situations—to cope with cultural differences, accept a degree of frustration, deal with changed circumstances and people—with little visible discomfort or irritation. Excessive discomfort often leads to frustration and hostility, which are not conducive to effective interpersonal relations. Learning to manage the feelings associated with ambiguity is a skill necessary for those who must adapt to a new environment and work effectively with people who have different values. This skill is particularly important when doing business in China. China is currently going through two major transitions: change from an isolated and small-scale peasant society to an open, large-scale industrialized country; and change from a rigid, centrally planned economy to a market economy. Business people going there should expect a lot of uncertainties and ambiguities.

ENDNOTES

[1] C. G. Burke and K. Stewart, "The Drivers of Organizational Behavior and Culture," Working Paper of University of Southern California, 1992.

[2] I. C. Brown, *Understanding Other Cultures* (Upper Saddle River, NJ: Prentice-Hall, 1974).

[3] R. M. Stogdill, "Personnel Factors Associated with Leadership: A Survey of the Literature," *Journal of Psychology* (January 1984).

[4] D. Hellriegel, J. W. Slocum, and R. W. Woodman, *Organizational Behavior* (St. Paul, MN: West Publishing Company, 1986).

[5] J. Heil, *Perception and Cognition* (Berkeley: University of California Press, 1983).

69

American-Japanese Negotiations

Gregory R. Tenhover

THE IMPACT OF CULTURE ON NEGOTIATION

The book *Hidden Differences: Doing Business With the Japanese,* written by Edward T. Hall and his wife Mildred Reed Hall, provides a straightforward analysis of the unstated rules of Japanese-American business relations. The three main premises of the book offer a starting point for looking at the impact culture exerts on negotiations between Japanese and Americans.

First, the Halls assert that cultural differences are of crucial importance: "Despite popular beliefs to the contrary, the single greatest barrier to business success is the one erected by culture."[1] Second, most cultural differences lie hidden beneath the surface of our awareness. Third, the greater the distance between cultures, the greater the chances of misunderstanding and conflicts between them—and it is difficult to find two cultures more different than the American and Japanese.

NEGOTIATIONS BETWEEN JAPANESE AND AMERICANS

Quite simply, Americans and Japanese view "negotiation" in very different ways. In fact, the very idea of scheduling a specific time to sit down and negotiate is a Western one. Americans who have experience negotiating with the Japanese often complain that the entire

idea of holding a formal session to specifically negotiate seems very foreign to the Japanese, who seem to treat negotiation almost as a ritualistic enactment of an agreement which has been hammered out behind the scenes. While Americans may approach negotiation as a "highly competitive game," the Japanese more often feel that they are "defending a valuable territory."

These fundamental differences in the way Americans and Japanese view negotiations are further complicated by differences in cultural values, attitudes, beliefs and thinking, which are reflected in different ways of communicating, organizing information, presenting ideas, persuading, solving conflicts and making decisions.

THE AMERICAN NEGOTIATION STYLE

Most Americans are not aware that they have any particular national negotiation style. However, many experts say that when viewed through the eyes of our foreign partners and clients we indeed have a style of bargaining all our own. John Graham and Yoshi Sanno, two experts of Japanese-American negotiations, characterize the American approach to bargaining as the "John Wayne Style," which is often characterized by a "Shoot first, ask questions later mentality."[2] To understand the American approach to bargaining, we must consider the basic aspects of our cultural background—in particular our immigrant heritage, our frontier history and, finally, much of the training that goes on in today's business and law schools.

Our history has been dramatically influenced by our immigrant ancestors who made fierce independence one of the most sacred of American values. Our frontier mentality, which glorified independence, actually lessened the need to negotiate:

> When a conflict arose we could always just move on. Moreover, the long distance people had to travel to see each other meant that a social system developed where fewer and shorter negotiations were the norm. While such independence was a necessity for taming a wide open land, our glorifications of independence can be fatal at the bargain-

Reprinted from *Unlocking the Japanese Business Mind.* Washington, DC: Japan-America Business Academy, a division of Transemantics, Inc., 1994.

ing table because negotiation is by definition a situation of interdepend-ence—a situation Americans have never handled well.[3]

The way we are educated also exerts a tremendous influence on the way we negotiate. Americans place a high value on winning, and competition is an essential component of our socialization process. The person who formulates the best arguments, assembles the best evidence and eloquently presents his or her case while tearing down an opponent's argument, wins respect and, in turn, high marks.

While such skills are indeed important, other skills which are underemphasized can be more important in the context of international negotiation. According to Graham and Sanno: "We don't teach our students how to ask questions, how to get information, how to listen, how to identify the decision makers, or how to use questioning as a powerful persuasive strategy. In fact few of us realize that in most places in the world the one who asks the questions controls the process and thereby accomplishes more in bargaining."[4]

THE JAPANESE NEGOTIATION STYLE

Graham and Sanno claim "the Japanese negotiation style is perhaps the most distinctive in the world." The typical Japanese negotiation style is characterized by intuition, indirectness, disguising or suppressing real feelings, persistence, avoidance of self praise and diligent information-gathering about the other side's needs and intentions. The historical and cultural roots of the Japanese style run much deeper than those of the American style.

The natural environment of Japan has had a pervasive impact on the national character of the Japanese, which in turn influences the process of negotiation. Three main environmental factors are important. First, because of Japan's isolation and mountainous geography, social systems and personal relationships developed in an environment which dictated that cooperation was essential. Next, Japan, as one of the most densely populated countries in the world, fostered a tightly organized society that places a premium on obedience and cooperation. Finally, the historical importance of rice

cultivation and the community effort it requires further reinforced the importance of group cooperation.

In a historically agrarian society such as Japan, the family and the village become the key, with the needs and desires of individuals sublimated to those of the group. "Because of this unique combination of environmental influences, a social system evolved in Japan that avoids conflict and promotes harmony."[5]

TATE SHAKAI— HIERARCHICAL RELATIONS

One of the most important, if not the most important, differences between Japanese negotiation style and others, particularly American, concerns status relationships. Japan is often characterized as a vertical society (*tate shakai*) because the most basic building block of human relations is hierarchy; in Japanese society equality is very rare—everyone and everything is ranked at least slightly below or above the nearest apparent equal.[6]

Within the context of negotiation, social hierarchy dictates that the role of the buyer and seller are very different in Japan. Although there are cases when Japanese sellers are more powerful—as in the case of a huge manufacturer versus a small retailer—most often Japanese buyers expect and receive deference from Japanese sellers. The following excerpt from a pamphlet provided by the Manufactured Imports Promotion Organization of Japan makes this point abundantly clear:

> In Japan, as in other countries the 'buyer is king,' only here he or she is 'kinger.' Here, the seller, beyond meeting pricing, delivery, special specifications, and other usual conditions, must do as much as possible to meet a buyer's wishes. Many companies doing business in Japan make it a practice to deliver more than is called for under the terms of their contracts.[7]

Quite simply, status relations dictate what is said, how it is said and what strategies and tactics can be used in Japanese business negotiations—the behavioral norms of the seller are different from those of the buyer. While Americans expect to, and do, influence business outcomes at the negotiation table, negotiation to the Japanese can be more of a ritual, where positions and actions are determined to be pre-specified status relations.

AMAE IN THE BUYER-SELLER RELATIONSHIP

This hierarchical relationship between buyers and sellers in Japan is very difficult for Americans to understand, because we don't see how the lower status sellers can help from being taken advantage of by higher status buyers. While it may be true that Japanese buyers have the freedom to dictate terms and get little argument from sellers, along with this freedom goes an implicit responsibility to understand the needs and take care of the seller. Japanese sellers trust Japanese buyers not to take advantage of them because inherent in the relationship is the concept of *amae*.

Amae is the noun form of *amaeru,* a verb which means "to depend and presume upon another's benevolence." The closest translation for this word in English is "dependency," and *amae* literally refers to the feelings of closeness and dependency found in the emotions an infant feels for its mother. This mother-child relationship, which both American and Japanese cultures regard as normal and necessary for the healthy mental and emotional growth of children, is a familiar one. But, whereas Americans try to escape from dependency on others as they grow older, the Japanese actually encourage and institutionalize this type of dependence into adulthood.

These deep emotions and the needs and responsibilities they engender operate throughout the Japanese life span. Quite simply, *amae* is the glue which holds Japanese society together.[8] Buyers in Japan must consider the needs of the seller before making demands, while in the United States it's usually every man for himself.

AMERICAN THINKING ABOUT NEGOTIATION

Americans often perceive negotiation as an opportunity to sit down and forge an agreement through debate and confrontation. Our attempts at persuasion take place, for the most part, at the negotiating table. We gain prestige by being articulate and persuasive, and are often called upon to be so spontaneously. Open intellectual debate and argument is acceptable and often stimulating in both formal and informal settings.

In American negotiations, individuals or small groups often have the authority to change positions; we enjoy bargaining and assume the process of give-and-take takes place at the negotiating table, not behind the scenes. Compromise and trading concessions are seen as an integral part of the adversarial process. Most of all, Americans see negotiations as problem-solving exercises.

JAPANESE THINKING ABOUT NEGOTIATION

It should be clear that Japanese thinking about negotiation is quite different from American. The Japanese consider what is good for the group—often in the long run—as the ultimate aim, while Americans may feel that profits or the good of the individual, often in the short-term, is the final goal.

In general, the Japanese are not comfortable with articulate and dynamic expression or intellectual confrontation. Open debate and disagreement often disturb and embarrass them, especially in formal situations. The surprises and open displays of power which are often integral parts of adversarial proceedings in the West are not tolerated in Japanese society. The Japanese are rarely argumentative, even when correct. They avoid confrontation and its perceived damage to personal relations.

Conversely, the American approach to business is more impersonal, allowing for freedom to be argumentative whether right or wrong. The Japanese feel it is essential to cultivate a good emotional setting for negotiation and get to know the decision makers, while Americans feel that too much personal involvement may constitute a conflict of interest.[9]

While Americans often attempt to persuade by direct confrontation at the table, the Japanese prefer to attempt persuasion behind the scenes, where neither side risks losing face. Saving face is crucial in Japan, and decisions can be made on the basis of saving a person or group embarrassment. Meanwhile, American decisions often disregard face-saving, and tend to be made more on a strict cost-benefit basis. The idea of negotiation as a process of give-and-take conflicts violently with the laborious way the Japanese arrive at the positions they bring to the table. Compromise and trading concessions are not viewed as particularly desirable or virtuous by the Japanese.

Japanese positions are arrived at by a group consensus process behind the scenes, where responsibility and authority are diffused. Consequently, the Japanese have precious little flexibility to change positions "on the fly" at the bargaining table, while Americans often pride themselves on having full authority and responsibility in bargaining to get the deal done. This limited authority on the part of Japanese negotiators often means that key decision makers are not even present, forcing them to constantly check back with superiors or the home office. Such actions cause Americans to feel they are wasting time or being obstructed in the bargaining process.

IMAGES OF JAPANESE NEGOTIATORS

In a 1983 article by John Greenwald entitled "The Negotiation Waltz,"[10] *Time* magazine asked international business professionals for their observations on negotiating with the Japanese, eliciting a variety of enlightening responses:

> "They can carry on negotiations until you're just plain tired of it."
>> —*Bernard Appel, Executive Vice President, Radio Shack*

> "Allow five times as long as usual when doing business in Japan."
>> —*Paul David, Australian Attorney*

> "The Japanese practice of asking the same question ten to twelve times, of four or five different sources, greatly extended the talks."
>> —*Joseph David, Director of International Marketing for State of Tennessee*

> "The Japanese negotiators seemed to know more about our labor and management problems than we did."
>> —*British Leyland Official*

> "German and American businessmen wish to come to the point straightaway, while Japanese want to create a personal atmosphere."
>> —*Andreas Meckel, Dusseldorf Steel*

> "The American feeling is that it is the horse buyer's fault if he fails to ask if the horse is blind. For the Japanese, however, a deal is more a discussion where mutual interests lie."
>> —*George White, Harvard Business School*

Other informal studies reveal that Americans and Japanese have different images of each other as negotiators.[11] In no particular order, Americans said that Japanese are: slow and methodic, not conscious of time, polite and formal, not logical, excessively detail-oriented, indirect, evasive, and even sneaky. Moreover, Americans feel the Japanese take too much time to establish relationships, ask for too much unnecessary information, ask the same questions over and over, keep pushing the same points, do not like to bargain or haggle, and change very slowly.

On the other hand, Japanese say that Americans are: proud and self-centered, too informal, disrespectful and pushy, shallow in their thinking (they don't think deeply about proposals before presenting them), overly concerned with the bottom line, "one-step-at-a-time" thinkers, legalistic, and poorly organized. They also feel that Americans: enjoy confrontation and argument (even among themselves), change their minds far too often, do not pay enough attention to the "big picture," and do not seem to have unified negotiating teams.

CULTURAL FLUENCY—THE KEY TO SUCCESSFUL NEGOTIATIONS

If Americans and Japanese really are fundamentally different, what is the best way to ensure successful negotiations between the two? The answer lies in developing cultural fluency, which is a function of understanding

how and, more importantly, why people behave, think and perceive the world as they do
in each culture. After we begin to develop
cultural fluency, we can then acquire the practical skills that will enable us to switch cultural styles and manage the process of negotiation to accomplish our specific goals. True
cultural fluency also depends on being able to
understand the many subtle and not so subtle
ways we are influenced by our own American
culture. This last point cannot be stressed
enough—to really understand the Japanese
we first must understand ourselves.

ENDNOTES

[1] Edward T. Hall and Mildred Reed Hall, *Hidden Differences: Doing Business With the Japanese*
(Garden City, New York: Anchor Press/Doubleday,
1987), xvii.

[2] John L. Graham and Yoshihiro Sanno, *Smart
Bargaining: Doing Business with the Japanese* (New
York: Harper Business, 1989), 8.

[3] *Ibid.*

[4] *Ibid.*, 9.

[5] *Ibid.*, 20.

[6] Jared Taylor, *Shadows of the Rising Sun: A Critical View of the Japanese Miracle* (Tokyo, Japan:
Charles E. Tuttle Company, Inc., 1983): 42.

[7] Graham and Sanno, 21.

[8] Hall and Hall, 55.

[9] Nancy J. Adler, *International Dimensions of
Organizational Behavior* (Belmont, CA: Wadsworth, Inc., 1986): 154–155.

[10] John Greenwald, "The Negotiation Waltz,"
Time Magazine, 1 August 1983: 41–42.

[11] Gregory R. Tenhover, Research done for
Clarke Consulting Group at Intel Japan, K.K.,
1990.

REFERENCE

Condon, John C. *With Respect to the Japanese.*
    Yarmouth, Marine: Intercultural Press, 1984.

70

Culture Clash

David Altany

A U.S. manufacturing executive eager to expand into the European market arrives at a potential business partner's headquarters in France. He strides into the meeting room, enthusiastically wrings his host's hand and says, "I've heard a great deal about you; please, call me Bill." Eager to show off his product, the American opens his briefcase and suggests getting right down to business.

By this point, if the French executive hasn't abandoned the meeting room with a strained look on his face, chances are he is either hiding his discomfort or is accustomed to American ill manners.

ILL MANNERS? TO THE FRENCH, YES.

Regardless of how well-intentioned the American executive's greeting was, he did not take the time to research French business customs. Had he done his homework, he would have learned that the French are very formal and deliberate in the way they warm up to strangers. The American's chummy handshake and the comment, "I've heard a great deal about you; please, call me Bill," probably embarrassed his host, who is accustomed to a more formal handshake and greeting (first names are rarely used in France, even among colleagues). The executive also didn't consider how this common American greeting might be translated or interpreted. Most people would be startled if a stranger greeted them by saying, "I know all about you."

French businesspeople similarly are uncomfortable launching directly into business

Reprinted from *Industry Week*, 2 October 1989, 4, 14–16, 20. Copyright © 1989 by Penton Publishing, Inc., Cleveland, Ohio.

matters, as the American urged. They first like to get to know prospective business partners to assess their personal compatibility and to build a mutual trust.

The cultural differences between the United States and countries in the European Community (EC) may at times appear subtle, but the need to understand them is becoming increasingly important. A wave of American businesses are rushing to gain a presence in the European market to take advantage of the benefits that the Europe 1992 trade pact is likely to give to companies within the EC.

"Americans have to adapt to their hosts' way of doing business early on in negotiations to ensure their success," says Jerry Underwood, a former Deere & Co. executive who now is a director specializing in international issues at the U.S. Dept. of Commerce.

Language differences pose obvious hurdles for negotiators, but to a large extent these can be overcome with help of a good translator. Many Americans, however, make the mistake of assuming that bridging the language gap is all that's necessary to communicate effectively with European business partners. Just as important to clear communication are the use of body language, expressions, and a knowledge of your foreign associate's cultural background.

From early adolescence we begin learning subtle ways to communicate—through our use of eye contact, hand gestures, tone of voice, and through our posture—that are very different from those learned by people in other countries.

Learning to adapt to unfamiliar body language and to accommodate a foreign businessperson's cultural patterns is important in establishing trust, says Lewis Griggs, San Francisco-based producer of the film series and book *Going International*.[1] "Two American strangers can determine fairly quickly whether they are trustworthy and likable to each other or not. That's key to doing any kind of business. This becomes much more difficult when you go outside your own culture, though. We might meet someone from another culture, and because our antennas are searching around for understandable clues to their disposition and personality but can't find any, we get anxious. In this kind of situation we usually presume that the other person is untrustworthy. At the very least, we feel that doing business with that person is uncomfortable."

Americans often resist adapting to cultural differences because they believe that the American way is logical and works well, and because it is the only system they are familiar with. "Americans have a natural inward business philosophy that leads to ethnocentric behavior, and economic conditions have played a role in maintaining that," says Mr. Underwood. "Exports make up a very small percent of total U.S. output—less than 6%. In a country like Denmark that figure is near 60%. So the mentality of trying to reach out to other markets is second nature to the European businessperson, but not to an American."

Although foreign customs initially strike some Americans as strange or backward, in most cases these have their own logic and benefits. For instance, Americans often feel that the European practice of meticulously cultivating personal relationships with business associates slows the expedient conduct of business; they argue that time is money, and the Europeans waste time. But to Southern Europeans, trust and long-term commitment—not legal contracts and short-term gains—are the heart and soul of a solid business relationship. And the European approach, slower though it is, usually leads to longer and stronger business alliances.

The development of these long-term alliances can bring rich rewards for European business partners. "A European purchaser may sacrifice a few dollars in sticking with a familiar supplier, but these executives are more interested in linking up with companies that will make concessions over the long haul—for instance, to make a design change, or to hold the line on price increases in the event of a financial crunch," says Charles Valentine, director of international advisory services at the accounting firm of Ernst & Young.

Although many European businessmen share this and several other managerial approaches, it would be a mistake to lump all European countries' business behavior together into one homogeneous "European" style. Each region has its own distinctive customs and style, which often vary a great deal from one country to the next. The use of business cards, for instance, is appreciated and expected in France and Italy, but is somewhat uncommon in Britain.

Negotiating styles also vary among European countries. The Dutch and Germans are competitive negotiators who go straight to the point. In negotiating with the Dutch, there usually is little room for conflict or debate. The French, on the other hand, love to debate issues. "An integral part of dealmaking in France is the debate," says Sondra Snowdon, president of Snowdon International, an international consulting firm. "The French like to show their intellect and challenge your intellect. Successfully selling to the French requires convincing them of the merits of your product through intellectual debate—not through flashy presentations or high-pressure techniques."

On a much more basic level, every country has its own etiquette for greeting people, dining, and entertaining. And just as anyone who ignores etiquette in America can be an embarrassment, Americans who ignore the customs of foreign countries make the formation of business relations more difficult.

"The French don't understand the way Americans eat, and consider it very ill-mannered," says Ms. Snowdon. "One of the biggest mistakes an American executive can make is to take his American table manners with him to France."

"The French get quite disturbed watching an American switch the fork and knife back and forth between hands. Although it is the norm in America, only peasants and vagrants in France eat this way. So it can be embarrassing for a Frenchman to be seen in an exclusive restaurant, even with a prominent American business executive, if that executive appears unsophisticated," Ms. Snowdon says.

This and countless other examples underscore the need to adapt and assimilate foreign cultural patterns. A sharp American executive will spend hours analyzing the marketing strategy, balance sheets, and organizational structure of a U.S. competitor or potential partner.

But few take the time to learn a few courteous foreign expressions when conducting business with unfamiliar executives in European firms.

Not only is that impolite—it's bad business.

SPAIN

"If an American businessman wants to be successful in Madrid, he has to learn to be patient," advises Robert Kohn, the U.S. commercial counselor in Spain.

A good appetite won't hurt either.

The business lunch is an integral part of conducting business in Spain, and Spanish businessmen conduct these meetings with great ceremony. In contrast to fast-paced American "power" lunches, business lunches in Madrid typically stretch from 2:30 to 5:00 p.m. (then it's back to work till 8:30 or 9:00 p.m.).

Friendship is a more important part of business relationships in Spain than in the U.S. In America, business comes first, and friendship or pleasure comes later, if at all. But in Spain, knowing and liking a business associate is a *prerequisite* for the conduct of business. Lunches in Spain as such are used to develop these personal associations.

A lunch in Spain may include three to six courses, topped off by cognac, coffee, and cigars. Mr. Kohn cautions not to discuss business before the drinks and cigars are brought out, which signals the transition from personal to business matters. "I've known American businessmen who have shocked their Spanish hosts by pulling out their portfolios and charts before dinner is even served," he says.

Although quite a few Spanish people do understand some English, it's a good idea to have an interpreter anyway, because that reduces the chances of a misunderstanding. "The Spanish are eager to attempt to speak English and establish direct communications with Americans, but problems can sometimes arise from that," says Mr. Kohn.

GREECE

Difficult though it is to comprehend, America's bumbling federal bureaucracy moves with the swiftness of Mercury compared with Greece's formidable and slothful legion of government-paid paper pushers. Greece's government plays an unusually large role in the country's economy; about 70% of the national output is generated by the government sector. Consequently, conducting business—especially on a large scale—requires working through government channels.

Because of Greece's daunting bureaucracy (as in Spain and Portugal), developing contracts within the country is crucial to establishing credibility when bidding for government contracts. "Business in Greece is very personalized—family connections, political connections, business connections, long-term relationships—these all are very important," says Jerry Mitchell, the U.S. commercial counselor in Greece. "How well-connected you are is often more important than the quality of the product you make."

As in Spain and Portugal, the quality of the personal relationship is extremely important to the success of business partnerships in Greece.

In their style of speaking, American businessmen tend to be more blunt than their Greek counterparts. Ironically, this approach is often viewed with suspicion. "When Americans are straightforward, businessmen in Greece often look behind the face value of what has been said for other meanings, when the Americans didn't intend any other such interpretations. Greeks are candid, but they take a softer, less direct approach," says Mr. Mitchell.

Contracts are also handled differently in Greece than in the U.S. When an American businessman submits his "best and final offer" for a contract, he is frequently unwilling to negotiate substantial changes in the proposal; Americans also will observe contracts to the letter regardless of changing circumstances. In Greece, however, negotiations aren't finished even after a contract has been awarded. A contract in Greece is viewed as an *evolving* document of agreement. As a result of these differences, American businessmen negotiating in Greece must adapt to the Greek way of handling a contract.

ITALY

Italian cars may not be the engineering envy of the world, but in their design and styling they have no rivals. This holds true beyond cars, as well: Appearance and style are very important to Italian businessmen.

To Italian businessmen, the appeal and polish of a presentation reflect the quality of the product or the company itself. "Polish and elegance mean a great deal in Italy, and when giving presentations, American executives should be organized, clear, and exact," says Snowdon International's Ms. Snowdon.

"Every culture has its own soft spots and preferences," says Ernst & Young's Mr. Valentine. "Americans look for price and reliability, Germans respect solid engineering, and the Italians and French the quality of design."

Italian businessmen are confident, shrewd, and competent negotiators.

"They commonly have the perception that Americans are interested only in making money," says Ms. Snowdon. So the American who is conscious of style and expresses an interest in Italian art and culture can both disarm and charm Italian executives who accept this stereotype.

Italians take great pride in their business acumen. Most Italian businessmen eschew the advice of outside consultants and even inhouse specialists, relying instead on the instincts of top executives. Italians take more pride in their individual expertise than in the reputation or size of the company to which they belong. As a result, they will judge another company by the expertise and polish of its executives and representatives, rather than by the company's size or reputation.

WEST GERMANY

If you want to hear it straight, ask a West German.

West German businessmen are technically oriented, disciplined, and orderly. In contrast to the majority of U.S. executives—who usually have financial backgrounds—most West German top executives have degrees in engi-

neering and the sciences. To appeal to West Germans' technical tastes, Americans should be direct and factual in manner. Glitzy presentations and sensational sales presentations are sure to flop. The use of hyperbole and excessive mannerisms such as backslapping are considered unbusinesslike.

Unlike businessmen in several Southern European countries, West Germans generally do not strongly emphasize the development of personal relationships with business associates. To the contrary, they value privacy and strive to keep their business and personal lives separate.

Most West Germans are very methodical and conservative in their business approach. Experts say West Germans are often repulsed by Americans' emphasis on making a fast buck through financial gimmickry and risk taking. Because of these conservative business attitudes, women, and to a lesser extent young business associates, are frequently at a disadvantage in negotiations.

BRITAIN

Whereas most Americans are hellbent on getting the job done fast, the British are enamored with conducting business matters "properly," without offense or imposition.

The British are very civil and reserved; they do not admire overt ambition and aggressiveness, and are offended by hard-sell tactics. British businessmen are highly confident, but rarely brag about their finances, or position.

This tone of understatement extends beyond self-characterizations. British executives' speaking style is more subtle and indirect than most Americans', requiring more sensitivity and inference from the listener. When a British person subtly prefaces a statement with, "It's a bit surprising that . . ." or "Are you quite certain that . . . ," his remark is probably meant to convey more of a critical or admonishing tone than most Americans will infer.

The British are good negotiators, but do not have high regard for bargaining in general. "The British do not appreciate negotiations very much—they do not view debate as a sport as the French do," says Ms. Snowdon. "Negotiations were not as prevalent in Britain's past as in other European countries' because businessmen operated within 'old-boy' networks and through gentlemen's agreements confined to the very few and well-connected. So a clear and reasonable approach to negotiations with the British is the best approach."

OTHER EC COUNTRIES

Belgium is culturally divided between the Walloons, who speak French, and the Flemands, who speak Flemish. It is impolite to discuss the cultural dichotomy of Belgium or to confuse the two groups or the cultural identity of the person you are associating with. *Netherlanders* (the Dutch) are straightforward and pragmatic. Making a reasonable proposal in negotiations is preferable to leaving room for later concessions. *Luxembourgers* are trilingual and highly accommodative to other cultures. In *Portugal,* take the time to establish a rapport with your foreign associate. Be prepared to bargain, but don't haggle. *The Republic of Ireland* should not be confused or associated with Northern Ireland or the United Kingdom; it is politically and culturally distinct from both. Similarly, *Denmark* should not be repeatedly referred to only within the context of being a Scandinavian country.

ENDNOTE

[1]Lennie Copeland and Lewis Griggs, *Going International: How to Make Friends and Deal Effectively in the Global Marketplace* (New York: Random House, 1985).

Selected Bibliography

CULTURE AND CROSS-CULTURAL COMMUNICATION

Benedict, Ruth. *Patterns of Culture*. 1934, reprint, New York: Mentor Books, 1959.

Birdwhistell, Ray L. *Kinesics and Context: Essays on Body Motion Communication*. Philadelphia: University of Pennsylvania Press, 1970.

Borden, G. *Cultural Orientation: An Approach to Understanding Intercultural Communication*. Englewood Cliffs, NJ: Prentice Hall, 1991.

Brislin, Richard. *Understanding Culture's Influence on Behavior*. New York: Harcourt Brace Jovanovich College Publishers, 1993.

Brislin, Richard. *Cross-Cultural Encounters*. Elmsford, NY: Pergamon Press, 1981.

Coupland, N., H. Giles and J. Wiemann. *"Miscommunication" and Problematic Talk*. Newbury Park: Sage, 1991.

Glenn, Edmund. *Man and Mankind: Conflict and Communication Between Cultures*. Norwood, NJ: Ablex Publishing Corporation, 1981.

Gudykunst, W. and S. Ting-Toomey. *Culture and Interpersonal Communication*. Beverly Hills: Sage, 1988.

Hall, Edward T. *The Dance of Life: The Other Dimension of Time*. Garden City, NY: Doubleday, 1983.

_____. *Beyond Culture*. Garden City, NY: Doubleday, 1976.

_____. *The Hidden Dimension*. Garden City, NY: Doubleday, 1966.

_____. *The Silent Language*. Garden City, NY: Doubleday, 1959, (in paperback, Fawcett, 1961).

Hayakawa, S.I. *The Use and Misuse of Language*. Greenwich, CT: Fawcett, 1962.

Hoijer, Harry, ed. *Language in Culture*. Chicago: University of Chicago Press, 1954.

Kluckhohn, Florence and Fred Strodtbeck. *Variations in Value Orientations*. Evanston, IL: Row, Peterson & Co., 1984.

Lustig, M.W. and J. Koester. *Intercultural Competence: Interpersonal Communication Across Cultures, Second Edition*. New York: HarperCollins College Publishers, 1996.

Martin, Judith N. and Thomas K. Nakayama. *Intercultural Communication in Contexts*. Mountain View, CA: Mayfield Publishing Company, 1997.

Matson, Floyd W. and Ashley Montagu, eds. *The Human Dialogue: Perspectives on Communication*. New York: The Free Press, 1967.

Mead, Margaret. *Culture and Commitment*. Garden City, NY: Doubleday, 1970.

Montagu, Ashley. *Touching: The Human Significance of the Skin*. New York: Columbia University Press, 1971.

Montagu, Ashley and Floyd Matson. *The Human Connection*. New York: McGraw-Hill Book Company, 1979.

Northrop, F.S.C. *The Meeting of East and West*. Collier, 1966.

Samovar, Larry A. and Richard E. Porter, eds., *Intercultural Communication, Eighth Edition,* Belmont, CA: Wadsworth, 1996.

Singer, Marshall. *Intercultural Communication: A Perceptual Approach*. Englewood Cliffs, NJ: Prentice-Hall, 1987.

Smith, Elise C. and Louise Fiber Luce, eds. *Toward Internationalism: Readings in Cross-Cultural Communication*. Rowley, MA: Newbury House Publishers, Inc., 1979.

Tannen, Deborah. *That's Not What I Meant!* New York: Ballantine, 1986.

_____. *Conversational Style: Analyzing Talk Among Friends*. Norwood, NJ: Ablex Publishing Corporation, 1984.

Tönnies, Ferdinand. *Gemeinschaft and Gesellschaft*. Tubingen: Mohr, 1937.

Weaver, Gary R. ed., *Readings in Cross-Cultural Communication, Second Edition*. Lexington, MA: Ginn Press, 1987.

_____. ed., *Culture, Communication and Conflict, Second Edition*. Needham Heights, MA: Simon & Schuster, 1997.

Articles

Kim, P.S. and J. Ofori-Dankwa. "Utilizing Cultural Theory as a Basis for Cross-Cultural Training: An Alternative Approach," *Public Administration Quarterly* 18, issue 4 (Winter 1995): 478–500.

Mehrabian, A. "Communication Without Words," *Psychology Today* 2 no. 4 (1968): 53–55.

Stewart, Edward C., Jack Danielian and Robert J. Foster. "Simulating Intercultural Communication Through Role-Playing. Washington, DC: Office, Chief of Research and Development, Dept. of the Army, and The George Washington University Human Resources Research Office, Technical Report 69-7 (May 1969).

Weaver, Gary R., "Understanding the Influence of Culture," *Japan Related* 12 (May/June 1995): 6–7.

AMERICAN CULTURAL STUDIES: THE DOMINANT CULTURE, ETHNIC GROUPS AND THE IMMIGRANT EXPERIENCE

Chermayeff, Ivan, Fred Wasserman and Mary J. Shapiro. *Ellis Island: An Illustrated History of the Immigrant Experience*. New York: Macmillan Publishing Company, 1991.

del Rio, Angel. *The Clash and Attraction of Two Cultures: The Hispanic and Anglo-Saxon Worlds in America*. Baton Rouge: Louisiana State University Press, 1965.

de Tocqueville, Alexis. *The Recollections of Alexis de Tocqueville*. London: The Harvill Press, 1948.

Glazer, Nathan and Daniel Patrick Moynihan. *Beyond the Melting Pot*. Cambridge, MA: The M.I.T. Press, 1963.

Handy, Robert T. *The Christian America: Protestant Hopes and Historical Realities: Second Edition*. Oxford: Oxford University Press, 1984.

Harrison, Lawrence R. *The Pan-American Dream: Do Latin American's Cultural Values Discourage True Partnership with the United States and Canada?* New York: Basic Books, 1997.

Ignatiev, Noel. *How the Irish Became White*. New York: Routledge, 1995.

Jones, Landon Y. *Great Expectations: America and the Baby Boom Generation*. New York: Ballantine, 1980.

Lasch, Christopher. *The Culture of Narcissism: American Life in an Age of Diminishing Expectations*. New York: W. W. Norton, 1979.

Lipset, Seymour Martin. *American Exceptionalism: A Double-Edged Sword*. New York: W. W. Norton, 1996.

McClelland, David. *The Achieving Society*. New York: Free Press, 1961.

Riesman, David. *The Lonely Crowd: A Study of the Changing American Character*. Garden City, NY: Doubleday & Company, Inc. Copyright, 1950, 1953, by Yale University Press

_____. *Selected Essays from Individualism Reconsidered*. Garden City, NY: Doubleday & Company, Inc. Copyright, 1954, by The Free Press.

Schlesinger, Jr., Arthur M. *The Cycles of American History*. Boston: Houghton Mifflin Company, 1986.

Spradley, James P. and Michael A. Rynkiewich. *The Nacirema: Readings on American Culture*. Boston: Little, Brown and Company, 1975.

Stewart, Edward C. and Milton Bennett. *American Cultural Patterns: A Cross-Cultural Perspective, Revised Editions*. Yarmouth, Maine: Intercultural Press, Inc., 1991.

Ungar, Sanford J. *Fresh Blood: The New American Immigrants*. New York: Simon & Schuster, 1995.

Yankelovich, Daniel. *New Rules: Searching for Self-Fulfillment in a World Turned Upside Down*. New York: Random House, 1981.

Articles

Davis, K.C. "Ethnic Cleansing Didn't Start in Bosnia." *New York Times,* 3 September 1995, 1, 6.

Schwarz, Benjamin. "The Diversity Myth: America's Leading Export." *The Atlantic Monthly,* May 1995, 57–67.

Weaver, Gary R. "American Identity Movements: A Cross-Cultural Confrontation." *Intellect,* March 1975, 377–380.

——, "American Cultural Values." (in Japanese) *Kokusai Bunka Kenshu (Intercultural Training)* 14, Japan Intercultural Academy of Municipalities (Winter 1977): 14–20.

RACE: COMMUNICATION, CONFLICT, DISCRIMINATION, AND THE WORKPLACE

Cobbs, P.M. and W.H. Grier. *Black Rage*. New York: Basic Books, Inc., 1968.

Dickens, F. and J.B. Dickens. *The Black Manager: Making it in the Corporate World,* ANACOM, 1982.

Kochman, Thomas. *Black and White Styles in Conflict*. Chicago: University of Chicago Press, 1981.

Pugh, R. *Psychology and the Black Experience*. CA: Books/Cole, 1972.

Takaki, Ronald, ed. *From Different Shores: Perspectives on Race and Ethnicity in America*. Oxford: Oxford University Press, 1987.

Thomas, R. Roosevelt. *Beyond Race and Gender*. New York: ANACOM, 1991.

Articles

Kochman, Thomas. "Crosscultural Communication: Contrasting Perspectives, Conflicting Sensibilities." *Florida FL Reporter* 9 (Spring/Fall 1971): 53–54.

Leinster, C. "Black Executives: How They're Doing." *Fortune,* 18 January 1988, 109–120.

Patterson, Orlando. "The Paradox of Integration." *The New Republic,* 6 November 1995, 14–27.

Rich, A.L. and D.M. Ogawa. "Intercultural and Interracial Communication: An Analytical Approach," in L.A. Samovar and R.E. Porter, eds. *Intercultural Communication: A Reader*. Belmont, CA: Wadsworth Publishing Co., 1982, 43–49.

Weaver, Gary R. "Police and the Enemy Image in Black Literature." In *The Police in Society*. Emilio C. Viano and Jeffrey H. Reiman, eds., Lexington, MA: D.C. Heath & Company, 1975, 139–47.

Wolf, Eric R., "Perilous Ideas: Race, Culture, People." *Current Anthropology* 35, no. 1 (February 1994): 1–7.

GENDER: COMMUNICATION, CONFLICT, DISCRIMINATION, AND THE WORKPLACE

Adler, Nancy J., and D. Israeli, eds. *Women In Management Worldwide*. New York: M. E. Sharpe, Inc., 1988.

Loden, M. *Feminine Leadership or How to Succeed in Business Without Being One of the Boys*. New York: Times Books, 1985.

Morrison, A.M., R.P. White and E. Van Elsor. *Breaking the Glass Ceiling: Can Women Reach the Top of America's Largest Corporations?* Reading, MA: Addison Wesley, 1987.

Tannen, Deborah. *You Just Don't Understand: Women and Men in Conversation*. New York: William Morrow, 1990.

Articles

Adler, Nancy J. "Expecting International Success: Female Managers Overseas." *Columbia Journal of World Business*. (Fall 1986): 79–84.

_____. "Women in International Management: Where are They?" *California Management Review* 16, no. 4 (Summer 1984): 78–79.

_____. "Women Do Not Want International Careers: and Other Myths About Women in International Management." *Organizational Dynamics* 13 (Autumn 1984): 66–79.

Cohen, Rosalie A. "Conceptual Styles, Culture, Conflict and Nonverbal Tests of Intelligence." *American Anthropologist* 71 (1969): 828–856.

Hymowitz, C. and T. Schellhardt. "The Glass Ceiling: Why Women Can't Seem to Break the Invisible Barrier that Blocks Them from the Top Jobs." *The Wall Street Journal*, 24 March 1986, 1D, 4D-5D.

CROSS-CULTURAL ADAPTATION AND ORIENTATION

Austin, Clyde N., ed. *Cross-Cultural Reentry: A Book of Readings*. Abilene, TX: A.B.U. Press, 1986.

Furnham, Adrian and Stephen Bochner. *Culture Shock: Psychological Reaction to Unfamiliar Environments*. New York: Methuen, 1986.

Lui, Z. *Two Years in the Melting Pot*. Los Angeles: China Books and Periodicals, Inc., 1984.

McCluskey, Karen C., ed. *Notes from a Traveling Childhood*. Washington, DC: Foreign Service Youth Foundation, 1994.

Paige, R.M., ed. *Education for the Intercultural Experience: Second Edition*. Yarmouth, Maine: Intercultural Press, Inc., 1993.

Sheehy, Gail. *Passages: Predictable Crises of Adult Life*. New York: Bantam, 1977.

Smith, Carolyn D., ed. *Strangers at Home: Essays on the Effects of Living Overseas and Coming "Home" to a Strange Land*. Bayside, NY: Aletheia, 1996.

Articles

Adler, Peter S. "Beyond Cultural Identity: Reflection on Cultural and Multicultural Man." *Topics in Culture Learning,* 2 Center for Cultural and Technical Interchange Between East and West, Inc., Honolulu (August 1974): 23–40.

_____. "The Transitional Experience: An Alternative View of Culture Shock." *Journal of Humanistic Psychology* 15 (1975): 13–23.

Brislin, Richard W. and H. Van Buren IV. "Can They Go Home Again?" *Cultural Exchange* 9 (1974): 19–24.

Gullahorn, J.R. and J.E. Gullahorn. "An Extension of the U-Curve Hypothesis." *Journal of Social Issues* 19 no. 3 (1963): 33–47.

Oberg, Kalvero. "Culture Shock: Adjustment to New Cultural Environments." *Practical Anthropologyist* 7 (1960): 177–82.

Tung, Rosalie L. "Selection and Training of Personnel for Overseas Assignment." *Columbia Journal of World Business* (Spring 1981): 68–78.

Weaver, Gary R. "Understanding and Coping With Cross-Cultural Adjustment Stress." Revised version in *Education for the Intercultural Experience, Second Edition.* R. M. Paige, ed. Yarmouth, Maine: Intercultural Press, Inc., 1993, 137–167. Originally published in *Cross-Cultural Orientation: New Conceptualizations and Applications,* R. M. Paige, ed., Lanham, MD: University Press of America, 1986, 111–145. Also found in *Culture, Communication and Conflict,* G. Weaver, ed., Needham Heights, MA: Ginn Press, 1994, 169–189.

_____. "The Process of Reentry." revised version, *The Advising Quarterly* 27 (Winter 1994): 1, 3–8. Originally published in 2 (Fall 1987): 1–7.

_____. "Reverse Culture Shock." *Aspire Newsletter,* NAFSA, 1, no. 1 (Fall 1991): 5–7 and 6, no. 3 (Spring 1996): 10–11. Shorter version published in *HARIRI-GRAM,* Hariri Foundation, 7, issue 2 (Spring 1992): 1, 7.

Weaver, Gary R., and Phil Uncapher. "The Nigerian Experience: Overseas Living and Value Change." Paper and workshop presented at Seventh Annual SIETAR Conference, Vancouver, B.C., Canada, 11 March 1981.

Weaver, Gary R. "From the New Lander to a New Land." *TransAtlantic Perspectives,* no. 29 (Winter 1994): 9–10.

CROSS-CULTURAL COUNSELING AND EDUCATION

Eldering, Lotty, and Jo Kloprogge, eds. *Different Cultures, Same School: Ethnic Minority Children in Europe.* Amsterdam: Swets & Zeitlinger B.V. Publishers, 1989.

Marsella, A. and Paul Pedersen, eds. *Cross-Cultural Counseling and Psychotherapy.* New York: Pergamon, 1981.

Pedersen, P., et al., eds. *Counseling Across Cultures.* Honolulu: The University Press of Hawaii, 1976.

Rushkoff, Douglas. *The GenX Reader.* New York: Ballantine Books, 1994.

Weaver, Gary R. and James Weaver, eds. *The University and Revolution.* Englewood Cliffs, NJ: Prentice-Hall, Inc., 1969.

Articles

Jackson, Gerald Gregory. "The Roots of the Backlash Theory in Mental Health." *The Journal of Black Psychology* 6, no.1 (August 1979): 17–45.

Lambo, Thomas Adeoye. "Psychotherapy in Africa." *Psychotherapy and Psychosomatics* 24 (1974): 311–326.

Weaver, Gary R. "Facing the Cultural Crisis in Child Care." *Journal of Child and Youth Care Work* 4 (Summer 1988): 5–27.

_____. "The Crisis of Cross-Cultural Child and Youth Care." in *Choices in Caring: Contemporary Approaches to Child and Youth Care Work*. Mark Kreuger and Norman Powell eds., Washington: Child Welfare League, 1990, 65–103.

_____. "Race and Identity in Child Care Work." *Child Care Work in Focus*. National Organization of Child Care Worker Associations, Inc., 4, no. 3 (Fall 1981): 1, 45.

_____. "Child and Youth Care Institutions: Melting Pots or Cookie Cutters?" in *Old Limitations New Challenges: Towards Unifyinq Values and Practice in Child and Youth Care Programmes*. Brian Gannon ea., Durban, South Africa: National Association of Child Care Workers, 1991, 6–11.

_____. "Communication and Conflict in the Multicultural Classroom." *Adult Learning* (May/June 1995): 23–24.

CROSS-CULTURAL MANAGEMENT

Adler, Nancy J. *International Dimensions of Organizational Behavior, Third Edition*. Cincinnati: South-Western College Publishing, 1997.

Christopher, Robert. *The Japanese Mind*. New York: Fawcett Columbine, 1983.

Doi, Takeo. *The Anatomy of Dependence: The Key Analysis of Japanese Behavior*. Tokyo: Kodansha International Ltd., 1971.

Hofstede, Geert. *Culture's Consequences: International Differences in World-Related Values*, Abridged edition, Beverly Hills: Sage, 1984.

Johnston, W., and A. Packer. *Workforce 2000: Work and Workers for the 21st Century*. Indianapolis: Hudson Institute, 1987.

Lane, H., and J. DiStefano. *International Management Behavior: Second Edition*. Boston: PWS-Kent Publishing Company, 1992.

Masakazu, Yamazaki. *Individualism and the Japanese: An Alternative Approach to Cultural Comparison*. Tokyo: Japan Echo Inc., 1994.

Moran, R.T. and P.R. Harris. *Managing Cultural Synergy*. Houston: Gulf Publishing Company, 1981.

Schein, E.H. *Organizational Culture and Leadership*. San Francisco: Jossey-Bass Publishers, 1985.

Shusta, Robert M., et. al. *Multicultural Law Enforcement: Strategies for Peacekeeping in a Diverse Society*. Englewood Cliffs, NJ: Prentice Hall, 1995.

Tenhover, Gregory R. *Unlockinq the Japanese Business Mind*. Washington: Transemantics, Inc., 1994.

Thomas, R.R. *Beyond Race and Gender*. New York: AMACOM, 1991.

Trompenaars, F. *Riding the Waves of Culture: Understanding Diversity in Global Business*. Burr Ridge, IL: Irwin Professional Publishing, 1994.

Articles

Adler, Nancy J. "Cross-Cultural Management: The Ostrich and the Trend." *Academy of Management Review* 8, no. 1 (April 1983): 226–232.

_____. "Cultural Synergy: The Management of Cross-Cultural Organizations." in *Trends and Issues in OD: Current Theory and Practice*. W. Burket and L.D. Goodstein, eds. San Diego: University Associates, 1980, 163–184.

Adler, Nancy J., and M. Jelinek. "Is Organization Culture Culture Bound?" *Human Resource Management* 25, no. 1 (Spring 1986): 73–90.

Cox, Jr., T. "The Multicultural Organization." *The Executive*. Academy of Management publication 5, no. 2 (May 1991): 34–47.

Goldstein, Jeffrey, and Marjorie Leopold. "Corporate Culture vs. Ethnic Culture." *Personnel Journal* (November 1990).

Hofstede, Geert. "Motivation, Leadership and Organization: Do American Theories Apply Abroad?" *Organizational Dynamics* (Summer 1980): 42–64.

Lieberman, Gregg. "Managing the Multicultural Meeting." Meetings & Conventions (April 1991): 42–43, 48–49.

Rhinesmith, Stephen H. *Cultural Organizational Analysis: The Interrelationship of Value Orientations and Managerial Behaviors*. Cambridge, MA: McBer Publications Series Number 5, (1970).

Schein, E.H. "What You Need to Know About Organizational Culture." *Training and Development Journal* (January 1986): 30–31.

_____. "Coming to a New Awareness of Organizational Culture." *Sloan Management Review* (Winter 1984): 3–16.

Solomon, Jolie. "As Cultural Diversity of Workers Grows, Experts Urge Appreciation of Differences." *Wall Street Journal* 12 September 1990, B1, B13.

Thomas, R. Roosevelt. "From Affirmative Action to Affirming Diversity." *Harvard Business Review* (March–April 1991): 107–117.

Watts, P. "Bias Busting: Diversity Training in the Workplace." *Management Review* (December 1987): 51–54.

Weaver, Gary R. "The Multicultural Child Care Staff: Meeting the Needs of a Diverse Client Population." *Child and Youth Care Administrator* (Fall 1988): 49–55.

_____. "Working With a Multi-Cultural Staff." In *Old Limitations New Challenges*. Brian Gannon ed., Durban, South Africa: National Association of Child Care Workers, 1991, 86–90.

_____. "Law Enforcement in a Culturally Diverse Society." *FBI Law Enforcement Bulletin* (September 1992): 1–7.

Wilkins, A.L. "The Creation of Company Cultures: The Role of Stories and Human Resource Systems." Human Resource Management 23, no. 1 (Spring 1984): 41–60.

Wolman, R. "Cultivating Cultural Awareness: The New Face of Management Training." *Training News* (February 1987): 10–14, 19.

PSYCHOLOGICAL ASPECTS OF CONFLICT, NEGOTIATION AND PERSUASION

Adorno, T.W., et al. *The Authoritarian Personality: Part I*. New York: John Wiley & Sons, Inc., Science Editions, 1964. Copyright by The American Jewish Committee, 1950.

_____. *The Authoritarian Personality: Part II.* New York: John Wiley & Sons, Inc., Science Editions, 1964. Copyright by The American Jewish Committee, 1950.

Allport, G.W. *The Nature of Prejudice.* Garden City, NY: Doubleday/Anchor Press, 1958.

Festinger, Leon. *A Theory of Cognitive Dissonance.* Stanford, CA: Stanford University Press, 1957.

Janis, I. *Groupthink, Second Edition.* Boston: Houghton Mifflin, 1982.

Maslow, Abraham. *Motivation and Personality, Second Edition.* New York: Harper and Row, 1970.

_____. *Toward a Psychology of Being.* Princeton: D. Van Nostrand Company, Inc., 1962.

McMains, Michael J., and Wayman C. Mullins. *Crisis Negotiations: Managing Critical Incidents and Hostage Situations in Law Enforcement and Corrections.* Cincinnati: Anderson Publishinc Co., 1996.

Rogan, Randall G., Mitchell R. Hammer and Clinton R. Van Zandt, eds. *Dynamic Processes of Crisis Negotiation.* Westport, CT: Praeger, 1997.

Rokeach, M. *The Nature of Human Values.* New York: Free Press, 1973.

_____. *The Open and Closed Mind: Investigations Into the Nature of Belief Systems and Personality Systems.* New York: Basic Books, 1960.

Rubin, T.I. *Reconciliations: Inner Peace in an Age of Anxiety.* New York: Viking Press, 1980.

Articles

Brislin, B., E. Casas, M. McCaulley, G. Weaver, and H. Pelikan. "Culture-Type Panel." *Psychological Type and Culture—East and West: A Multicultural Research Symposium: Proceedings,* Raymond Moody, ed., Gainesville, FL: Center for Applications of Psychological Type, 1995, 37–56.

Glenn, Edmund, D. Witmeyer and K. Stevenson. "Cultural Styles of Persuasion." *International Journal of Intercultural Relations* 1, no. 3 (1977): 52–66.

Maslow, Abraham H. "A Dynamic Theory of Human Motivation." in Charles R. Lawrence, ed. *Man, Culture and Society.* New York: Brooklyn College Press, 1962.

Pelikan, H. "Psychological Type, MBTI and Culture: An Interview with Katharine D. Myers and Gary R. Weaver." Bethesda, MD: unpublished paper, copyright, Pelikan Associates, 25 August 1992.

Weaver, Gary R. "Psychological and Cultural Dimensions of Hostage Negotiation." *Dynamic Processes of Crisis Negotiation.* R.G. Rogan, M.R. Hammer and C.R. Van Zandt, eds. Westport, CT: Praeger, 1997, 115–127.

CULTURAL AND PSYCHOLOGICAL ASPECTS OF NATIONAL IMAGES AND INTERNATIONAL CONFLICT

Barnet, Richard J. *The Rocket's Red Glare.* New York: Simon & Schuster, 1990.

Boulding, Kenneth. *The Image.* Ann Arbor: The University of Michigan Press, 1956.

Fisher, Glen. *American Commmunication in a Global Society.* Norwood, NJ: Ablex Publishing Corporation, 1979.

Fromm, Erich. *May Man Prevail?* Garden City, NY: Anchor, Doubleday & Company, Inc., 1961.

Huntington, Samuel P. *The Clash of Civilizations and the Remaking of World Order.* New York: Simon & Schuster, 1996.

Jervis, Robert. *Perception and Misperception in International Politics.* Princeton: Princeton University Press, 1976.

Khuri, Fuad I. *Tents and Pyramids: Games and Ideology in Arab Culture from Backgammon to Autocratic Rule.* London: Saqi Books, 1990.

Mowlana, Hamid, George Gerbner and Herbert I. Schiller, eds. *Triumph of the Image: The Media's War in the Persian Gulf—A Global Perspective.* Boulder: Westview Press, 1992.

Shaheen, Jack G. *The TV Arab.* Bowling Green, OH: Bowling Green State University Popular Press, 1984.

White, Ralph R. *Nobody Wanted War: Misperception in Vietnam and Other Wars.* Garden City, NY: Anchor Books, Doubleday & Company, Inc., 1970.

Articles

Bronfenbrenner, Urie. "The Mirror-Image in Soviet-American Relations." *Social Issues* 17, no. 3 (1961): 45–56.

Kaplan, Robert D. "The Coming Anarchy," *The Atlantic Monthly,* February, 1994, 44–76.

Schlesinger, Jr., Arthur. "Back to the Womb? Isolationism's Renewed Threat." *Foreign Affairs* (July–August, 1995): 2–8.

Ungar, Sanford J. "Pressing for a Free Press." *Foreign Policy* 77 (Winter 1989–90): 132–153.

White, Ralph K. "Misperception in the Arab-Israeli Conflict." *Journal of Social Issues* 33, no. 1 (1977): 190–220.

Names Index

M

Mahbubani, Kishore, 492, 496
Maher, Brendan A., 177, 205–211
Major, John, 496
Malcolm X, 10, 285, 499
Malsberg, B., 337
Malson, Lucien, 368
Mann, Horace, 364
Manson, Charles, 270, 276–277
Mao Zedong, 447
Marcos, Ferdinand, 79
Marshall, Samuel Lyman Atwood, 420
Martin, Joanne, 147
Martin, R. P., 203
Martin, S., 134–135, 335
Maslow, Abraham H., 44, 53, 155, 157, 203, 218, 254, 265, 285, 288
Massie, Joseph L., 146
Matson, Floyd W., 77
Matthews, B., 336
May, Rollo, 262, 265
Mbiti, John S., 324, 335
McAdoo, H., 334
McCain, Mark, 146
McCann, E., 134
McCarthy, J. D., 337
McCarthy, Joseph, 10, 61
McCarthy, Sarah J., 270, 276–281
McClelland, David C., 5, 76–77, 155, 157, 368
McClelland, L., 338
McCurdy, Dave, 495
McGrew, J., 329, 336
McKersie, Robert B., 517
McLaughlin, Clara J., 334
McMahon, Jim, 297–298
McNamara, Robert, 445
McNeill, D., 265
Mead, Margaret, 368
Mehrabian, Albert, 5, 23–27, 203–204, 390–391
Meier, Golda, 469
Mendenhall, M., 184
Mercil, M. C., 391
Merrill, Dave, 91
Milgram, Stanley, 277–281
Milhomme, Janet, 297, 307
Miller, G., 265
Miller, W. E., 264
Milloy, Courtland, 274
Mindel, C., 335
Mirvis, Philip H., 146
Mitchell, T., 229
Mizio, E., 329, 336, 338
Monohan, T., 339
Montagu, Ashley, 77
Moran, Robert T., 94, 134, 183–184
Morin, Richard, 403

Morland, J. K., 337
Morse, William C., 391
Mouton, Jane Srygley, 517
Mowlana, Hamid, 404
Moynahan, Daniel P., 65
Mu Dan Ping, 471, 528–536
Mumford, E., 157
Murdock, G., 265
Murphy, Eddie, 499
Murrow, Edward, R., 425
Myrdal, Gunnar, 360, 368

N

Nader, Ralph, 427
Naipaul, V. S., 491
Namier, Lewis, 474
Neisser, Ulric, 335
Nelson, S., 327, 336
Nelson, W., 336
Newcomb, Theodore Mead, 391
Newfield, Jack, 284, 288
Newman, Ruth G., 391
Newman, William H., 139, 146
Nichols, E., 325, 335
Nietzche, Friedrich, 77
Nigro, F. A., 121, 134
Nigro, Lloyd G., 121, 134
Nisbett, Richard, 438
Nitze, Paul, 437
Nixon, Richard, 11, 57, 442
Nobles, W. W., 330, 337
Novak, Michael, 134, 257, 265
Nystron, Paul C., 146

O

Oberg, Kalvero, 176, 185–186, 187–188, 193, 202
Oedipus, 354
Ogawa, Dennis M., 3, 54–59, 94, 368
Ogungbesan, Kolawale, 336
Olney, Douglas P., 527
Ong, Walter J., 289, 292, 308
Ornstein, Robert E., 324, 334–335
Osgood, Charles Egerton, 434, 445
Ouchi, William G., 146, 159
Owens, S., 337
Ozal, Turgut, 489

P

Paige, R. Michael, 187, 238
Parsons, Talcott, 141, 146
Pasamanick, B., 337
Pascale, Richard Tanner, 146
Pasteur, A., 325–326, 335
Patterson, Orlando, 92, 95–100
Paul, Benjamin D., 133
Paul, L., 339

Paul, S., 264
Perlmutter, Howard V., 147
Perls, Frederick, 220
Peters, Thomas J., 147
Petrov, V., 445
Philips, Susan Umston, 391
Piaget, Jean, 77
Pierson, T., 525
Pinderhughes, C., 340
Pines, M., 334
Pool, Ithiel de Sola, 6
Poortinga, Ype H., 147, 157
Porter, Richard E., 52, 54, 368, 527
Posner, Barry Z., 146
Poussaint, Alvin F., 334, 339
Powell, Colin, 95
Price–Williams, D., 37, 52
Pruitt, Dean G., 471, 509–517
Pryor, Richard, 499
Pryzwanski, W., 338

Q

Quaddafi, Moammar, 418

R

Rabinowitch, Eugene, 415, 417
Rafky, D., 339
Rapoport, A., 323, 334, 463
Raspberry, William, 270, 309–310, 390
Reagan, Ronald, 79, 285–286, 364, 418, 435–436
Redding, S. G., 147
Reich, Charles A., 368
Reisman, David, 288
Reissman, F., 339
Rensberger, B., 391
Reza Palavi, Shah of Iran, 440
Rhinesmith, Stephen H., 127, 134, 137, 146
Rich, Andrea L., 3, 54–59, 94
Rich, S., 368, 391
Richardson, Lewis F., 454, 463–464
Richmond, B., 335
Rickford, John R., 311
Rivers, L., 339
Roberts, Karlene, 147
Rodin, J., 391
Rogan, Randall G., 472, 524, 526
Rohrlich, Paul E., 6, 84–87
Rokeach, Milton, 33, 46–48, 52–53, 59, 76
Roland, Alan, 354
Roman, Augustin, 522
Roosevelt, Archie, 488, 496
Roosevelt, Eleanor, 507
Roosevelt, Franklin Delano, 47, 474
Roosevelt, Theodore, 293–294, 307

Subject Index

Loss of cues: and culture shock, 189–190; and reentry, 230

M

Managing diversity, 89–94, 114–119, 120–135
Masculine: contrast with feminine, 151–152, 155–156
Mass psychology, 269–276
Mean world syndrome, 410–411
Me decade, 268–269; *See also* culture of narcissism, 285
Media, mass: portrayal of Arabs, 421–428; and violence, 400–401, 403–404, 405–407, 409–413
Melodramatic/escapist: contrast with tragic/realistic perception, 399–400, 407–408; violence, 399–400
Melting pot myth, 4, 60–61, 89, 123, 293–294, 309–310, 360–363, 383–384. *See also* deficit model; liberal; cookie-cutter model
Mexican culture, 14, 446, 468
Middle East, *see* Arab cultures
Mind/body dichotomy, 343–344, 348–352
Minorities: in childcare, 355–369, 370–391; in U.S. workforce, 104–105, 108–109
Mirror image, 401, 429–434, 435–445, 446–451, 458–459
Misperception, 48–52. *See also* perceptions.
Monochronic: contrast with polychronic, 3, 12–14, 324
Mote-beam phenomenon, 450
Multicultural: individuals, 175, 242–249, 250–266; organization culture, 144–145; workforce, 89–91; third-culture kids (TCKs), 239–241
Multiculturalism, 89–94

N

National Image, 398–399, 354–364
Nation-state, 470, 473–481, 482–496
Native American (American Indian), 13, 60, 62, 101, 274, 293, 307, 371–373, 472
Need for Achievement: contrast with Need for Affiliation, 65, 75
Need for Power, 29, 397–398

Negotiation: cross-cultural aspects of, 465–472, 503–508, 518–527, 528–536, 537–541; integrative agreements, 509–517; and language, 503–508. *See also* hostage negotiation; intermediary
Nigerian: adaptation, 230, 234; mental health, 269, 341–347; students in U.S. 196
Nganga (African healer), 344, 346
Nonverbal communication, 2–3, 6, 9, 12, 15–16, 23–27, 102, 226–227, 232, 380, 542; body language (kinesics), 3, 6, 12, 15–16, 25, 380; cues, 468; gender differences, 24; space (proxemics), 3, 12, 15–16; status, 25–26; time (chronemics), 3, 12, 15
Nuclear weapons, 414–417, 435, 436–437, 442–444

O

Obedience, 276–281
Organization culture, 92–93, 136–147, 295; multicultural, 144–145

P

Palestinians, 424–426
Paranoia, paranoid, 213; world view, 398–399, 404, 418
Parochialism, 124–126
Perception, 28–53, 398–399. *See also* misperception.
Personalismo, 523
Personality, 36–48
Persian Gulf War, 421–428
Pluralism, 89, 123, 293–294, 473–476, 478, 480–481
Police (law enforcement), 525; and negotiation, 518–520. *See also* hostage negotiation
Polychronic: contrast with monochronic time, 3, 12–14, 324
Portuguese culture, 544, 546
Positive disintegration, 212, 263
Possibilistic vs. probabilistic thought, 379, 398
Poverty, 97, 398
Power distance, 75, 77, 149–151, 153–155
Prejudice, 197, 389–390
Premature return, 175
Pro-us illusion, 443
Psychic numbing, 401, 414–417

Psychotherapy: in Africa, 269, 272, 341–347; in India, 348–354; with children in U.S. 370–391
Puerto Rico, 382–383

Q

Quality circles, 159

R

Race relations, 89–92, 95–100
Racism, 60–61, 98–99, 356, 366
Realism, 460–470, 497
Realistic humanism, 367. *See also* diunitality; synergy
Reentry stress (reverse culture shock), 173–174, 194, 222–229, 230–238, 244; "Been-Tos," 234–235, 388; of children in institutions, 383–384; coping strategies, 235–236; phases, 237; symptoms, 234–235; training, 224–229; Uncle Charlie syndrome, 222, 233. *See also* culture shock; decompression
Relational: contrast with analytic thought, 62–63, 76, 199, 309–310, 376–377; concept of self, 351–352
Russian culture, 429–434, 507
Russian, contrast with American culture, 429–434

S

Sapir-Whorf hypothesis, 29, 187, 230
Scandinavian culture, 12, 546
Schizoid, 64
Schizophrenia, 177, 195, 205–211, 212–216; in Asia, 353; and black Americans, 333; and body language, 26; language of, 205–211; treatment, 346
Self-actualization, 285
Self-concept: Chinese, 351–352; Indian, 348–351; Japanese, 351–352; mind/body, 351–352, 343–344, 348–354; and relational model, 350–352
Self-fulfilling prophecy, 383, 450
Shame: contrast with guilt, 348–351. *See also* face and honor.
SIETAR (Society for International Education, Training and Research, 78–79, 84
Social class, 57, 332–333, 366
Soviet Union (USSR), 398, 401–402,